# BREAK CLAUSES

This is the only book to deal exclusively with the important topic of break clauses, which affect a significant proportion of all landlord and tenant relationships.

The book provides a comprehensive and authoritative survey of the law relating to the drafting and operation of break clauses. It covers over 500 cases relevant to the topic. The book also considers the areas of the law that interrelate with break clauses, including contractual construction, assignment, estoppel, mistake and professional negligence.

Previous editions of Break Clauses have been referred to as "scholarly and practical" (Sir Kim Lewison) and "excellent and much needed" (Lord Neuberger).

This new edition includes the most recent and relevant judgments that have had an important impact on the law affecting break clauses. There are two new chapters: one on the interrelationship between break clauses and compulsory purchase (of particular relevance in light of large-scale projects such as HS2 and Crossrail) and one on the interrelationship between break clauses and rent review.

The third edition covers new legal developments, including the new Electronic Communications Code and its impact on break clauses.

# Break Clauses

## *Third Edition*

Mark Warwick QC
and
Nicholas Trompeter QC

•HART•
OXFORD • LONDON • NEW YORK • NEW DELHI • SYDNEY

HART PUBLISHING

Bloomsbury Publishing Plc

Kemp House, Chawley Park, Cumnor Hill, Oxford, OX2 9PH, UK

1385 Broadway, New York, NY 10018, USA

29 Earlsfort Terrace, Dublin 2, Ireland

HART PUBLISHING, the Hart/Stag logo, BLOOMSBURY and the Diana logo are trademarks of Bloomsbury Publishing Plc

First published in Great Britain 2022



A catalogue record for this book is available from the British Library.

Library of Congress Cataloging-in-Publication data

Names: Warwick, Mark, author. | Trompeter, Nicholas, author.

Title: Break clauses / Mark Warwick and Nicholas Trompeter.

Description: Third edition. | Oxford ; New York : Hart, 2022. | Includes bibliographical references and index.

Identifiers: LCCN 2021044659 (print) | LCCN 2021044660 (ebook) | ISBN 9781509942039 (hardback) | ISBN 9781509942053 (pdf) | ISBN 9781509942046 (Epub)

Subjects: LCSH: Leases—England. | Landlord and tenant—England.

Classification: LCC KD899 .W37 2022 (print) | LCC KD899 (ebook) | DDC 346.4204/34—dc23/eng/20211029

LC record available at https://lccn.loc.gov/2021044659

LC ebook record available at https://lccn.loc.gov/2021044660

ISBN: HB: 978-1-50994-203-9
ePDF: 978-1-50994-205-3
ePub: 978-1-50994-204-6

Typeset by Compuscript Ltd, Shannon
Printed and bound in Great Britain by CPI Group (UK) Ltd, Croydon CR0 4YY

MIX
Paper from responsible sources
FSC® C013604

To find out more about our authors and books visit www.hartpublishing.co.uk. Here you will find extracts, author information, details of forthcoming events and the option to sign up for our newsletters.

# *Foreword to the Second Edition*

IT IS STRIKING, and to the uninitiated it may be surprising, that an apparently relatively niche topic such as break clauses in leases can provide enough in the way of legal problems and issues to justify a book running to over 300 pages and over 500 reported cases. Many non-lawyers may wonder whether this is a tribute to the ingenuity of lawyers or the ineptitude of those involved in drafting and operating the clauses. However, as any reader of this excellent book will quickly realise, break clauses have thrown up many practical and legal problems, which fully justify the full and careful treatment which this book gives the topic.

It is in fact unsurprising that break clauses in leases have given rise to so much difficulty. Experience shows that there is something about the landlord and tenant relationship generally that has a tendency to produce uncertainties, conflicts and disputes, which require legal advice and often end up in court, in arbitration or in mediation. I suspect that it is due partly to the human condition (which the whole panoply of the law inevitably reflects), partly to the fact that both landlord and tenant feel that they 'own' the demised premises, and partly because of the difficult relationship between property law and contract law, which inevitably arises in the field of leases.

And break clauses in particular have specific features which notoriously produce difficult and contentious points of law – contractual interpretation, time limits, form and service of notices, preconditions, and interrelationship between contract law and statute law. On top of that, the exercise of a break clause is inherently quite likely to produce conflict. While it will, of course, sometimes suit both landlord and tenant if the lease determines early, in many cases the very market forces which impel one party to operate the break clause will cause the other party to want the lease to continue. Economic influences will therefore often encourage the recipient of a break notice to try and find grounds for invalidating it – so the break notice is served and the seeds of conflict are sown.

It is not only the existence of over 500 cases relevant to the topic which is worthy of comment: what is also striking from a quick perusal of those 500 cases is how many of them were decided in the past 30 years. Indeed, there have been sufficient new judicial decisions over the past four years to justify a second edition of this book since the publication of the first edition in late 2011. The large number of recent cases on the topic not only illustrates how productive of litigation break clauses still are; it also emphasises how many difficult problems can frequently arise from break clauses, and therefore how essential it is to have an up-to-date book on the topic. Legal academics and students; developers, owners, occupiers and managers of property; and lawyers and others who advise and represent those people all need an authoritative and comprehensive book on break clauses. Mark Warwick QC and Nicholas Trompeter deserve gratitude and praise for having taken time out of their busy practices to produce a second edition of this book.

The book is well and clearly structured, so that any reader can easily identify and find the passage or passages which deal with the problem in hand. The authors have succeeded in producing a book on break clauses which is both scholarly and practical, and both full and concise. The authors express themselves clearly and readably, and, quite rightly, they have an eye both on the academic reader and on the practitioner, and they cover all legal aspects of what one might call the full life of a break clause – from what a break clause actually is to the effect of exercising a break clause. But, very sensibly, the authors have not stopped there. Apart from referring to break clauses in different types of lease (and the consequential statutory impact), they have included chapters on drafting break clauses, exercising break clauses and professional negligence in connection with break clauses.

It is interesting and gratifying to note that, as with all the best and full legal treatments of a specific topic, reading this book shines a light on much wider areas of law than one might at first sight expect. Insolvency, assignment, estoppel, mistake, side agreements, unjust enrichment are just some of the areas which have come into play in cases involving break clause cases, and all those areas are relevantly covered in this book.

From a selfish perspective, it has been interesting to remind myself of cases which I argued when at the Bar or subsequently decided when a judge – from *Adams v Green* in 1978 (frighteningly, over 35 years ago), to *Marks and Spencer Plc v BNP Paribas Securities* at the end of last year. The latter case was decided just in time for the authors to cover it in this book. It illustrates rather well three of the points made above. First, it shows that new points keep on coming in relation to break clauses; secondly, it shows that break clauses often produce difficult points; thirdly, it shows how break clause cases can involve wider points of law – in that case the law of implied terms.

In summary, this is an excellent and much needed book which treats a difficult and significant topic very well both academically and practically.

David Neuberger
*UK Supreme Court*
*March 2016*

# *Foreword to the First Edition*

In recent years break clauses have been one of the most litigated areas of the law of landlord and tenant. Most of the cases have concerned attempts to exercise tenants' rights to break.

The inclusion of a tenant's right to break in a commercial lease in some ways gives the tenant the best of both worlds. He can terminate the lease if he chooses to exercise the break; or stay for the remainder of the term if he chooses not to. Why would the landlord agree to the inclusion of a clause which gave the tenant the best of both worlds? The answer, I suspect, is that in most cases the quid pro quo for the break clause is the tenant's agreement to an upward-only rent review clause. If the tenant took a shorter term without the break, and had the right to renew the lease under the Landlord and Tenant Act 1954, then the rent could go down on renewal. So from the landlord's perspective a longer term with a break clause is a limited form of guaranteeing the income stream.

At the drafting stage the landlord will try to make the break difficult to exercise. He will try to hedge it about with conditions to be fulfilled. The tenant, for his part, will try to excise or dilute the conditions. Many of the cases concern both the interpretation of such conditions, and also the factual question whether they have been fulfilled.

If the tenant tries to exercise the break, the chances are that he does so because the market had changed. He is paying more than the rental value of the leased property and wants cheaper accommodation elsewhere. The consequence of failure will be expensive. But the change in economic conditions will be precisely the reason why the landlord will fiercely resist the tenant's attempt to break the lease. He will pick over the tenant's notice exercising the break looking for any possible error; and he will examine minutely whether the tenant has fulfilled any conditions on which the validity of the break notice depends. Does it specify the right date? Was it served by the right person? Was it given to the right person? Was it given in accordance with any stipulated timetable? Did the tenant comply sufficiently with his obligations under the lease? Has the tenant given vacant possession? If any one of these questions elicits even a plausible negative answer, the stage is set for a full-scale battle.[1]

Landlords' break clauses are products of different economic circumstances. The most common form of landlord's break clause is a redevelopment break clause. Naturally enough, when the market is slow break clauses of this kind are less common. Here the principal battleground has been lease renewals under the Landlord and Tenant Act 1954. Ever since Mr David Neuberger (unadorned as he then was) won the unwinnable appeal in *Adams v Green* the courts have been trying to repair the damage. The story is told in Chapter 9 of this book.[2]

[1] This passage was cited by Lewison LJ in *Siemens Hearing Instruments Ltd v Friends Life Ltd* [2014] EWCA Civ 382, [2014] 2 P&CR 5 [3].

[2] Now to be found at Chapter 18.

Mark Warwick and Nicholas Trompeter have produced a comprehensive guide to the many questions that arise when drafting, exercising and litigating break clauses. It is both scholarly and practical. It will be invaluable to all those involved in the property industry. A guide through the complexities and pitfalls on the path to breaking a lease is a necessity; because as WC Fields memorably said: 'Never give a sucker an even break'.

Kim Lewison
*Royal Courts of Justice*
*London WC2A 2LL*

# *Preface*

'THIS IS YET another case about the exercise of a break option in a lease.' So remarked Fancourt J in *GKN Aerospace Services Ltd v Duncan Investments Ltd*.[1] Indeed, in the three years or so since the previous edition of this work was published, the number of cases relating to the exercise of break options has continued unabated. These cases have concerned a wide range of issues relevant to the topic of break clauses, including the assignability of a break option (*Sackville UK Property Select II (GP) No 1 v Robertson Taylor Insurance Brokers Ltd*[2]), service of a break notice by a limited partnership (*Vanquish Properties (UK) LP v Brook Street (UK) Ltd*[3]) or by an equitable landlord (*Sandhar & Kang Ltd v Ijaz*[4]), the time for exercising a break option (*GKN Aerospace Services Ltd v Duncan Investments Ltd*[5]), service of a break notice at the recipient's place of abode or business (*Levett-Dunn v NHS Property Services Ltd*[6]), indirect service of a break notice (*UKI (Kingsway) Ltd v Westminster City Council*[7]), the requirement to yield up vacant possession as a condition for the successful exercise of a break option (*Capitol Park Leeds Plc v Global Radio Services Ltd*[8]) and the insertion of break clauses into a renewal tenancy under the Landlord and Tenant Act 1954 (*Dukeminster Ltd v West End Investments (Cowell) Ltd*[9]). In the circumstances, we considered that the time was right for a new edition of this work. The law is as stated on 6 October 2021.

Mark Warwick QC
Nicholas Trompeter QC
Selborne Chambers

[1] [2020] EWHC 3719 (Ch), at [1].
[2] [2018] L&TR 22.
[3] [2016] L&TR 33.
[4] [2018] EWHC 3071 (Ch).
[5] [2020] EWHC 3719 (Ch).
[6] [2016] Ch 637.
[7] [2019] 1 WLR 104.
[8] [2021] EWCA Civ 995.
[9] [2019] L&TR 4.

# *Acknowledgements*

GRATEFUL ACKNOWLEDGEMENT IS made to the ICLR for the use of extracts from *Brown & Root Technology Ltd v Sun Alliance and London Assurance Co* Ltd [2001] Ch 733, *Mannai Investment Co Ltd v Eagle Star Life Assurance Co Ltd* [1997] AC 749, *Merton London Borough Council v Jones* [2009] 1 WLR 1269 and *Dickinson v St Aubyn* [1944] KB 454.

While every care has been taken to establish and acknowledge copyright, and to contact the copyright owners, the publishers apologise for any accidental infringement and would be pleased to come to a suitable agreement with the rightful copyright owners in each case.

# Contents

*Foreword to the Second Edition* ........ *v*
*Foreword to the First Edition* ........ *vii*
*Preface* ........ *ix*
*Acknowledgements* ........ *xi*
*Table of Cases* ........ *xix*
*Table of Statutes* ........ *xxxvii*
*Table of Statutory Instruments* ........ *xlix*

1. **The Nature of a Break Clause** ........ 1
   A Definition ........ 1
   A Break Notice is not a Notice to Quit ........ 1
   The Right to Terminate is Unilateral ........ 2
   Forfeiture and Acceptance of Repudiatory Breach Distinguished ........ 2
   A Break Clause is a Type of Option ........ 3
   The Applicability of *Braganza* Restrictions on the Exercise of a Break Clause ........ 4
   Break Clauses can Appear in All Types of Tenancies and in Many Different Forms ........ 6

2. **Formalities and Registration** ........ 7
   Formalities ........ 7
   Registration ........ 7

3. **Assignment** ........ 9
   The Historical Position ........ 9
   Tenancies Granted before 1 January 1996 ........ 10
   Tenancies Granted on or after 1 January 1996 ........ 13
   Formalities for Assignment ........ 15
   Restrictions on Assignability ........ 17
   Severance of the Reversion ........ 20
   Assignment of Part of the Demise ........ 22
   The Position of Equitable Assignees ........ 23
   The Position where the Break Clause is not Contained in a Lease ........ 30

4. **Who May Exercise the Break Clause** ........ 32
   Introduction ........ 32
   Where the Lease is Silent or Unclear ........ 32
   Joint Lessees ........ 33
   Joint Lessors ........ 34
   The Survivor(s) of Joint Lessors/Lessees ........ 34
   Where the Landlord is also One of the Tenants ........ 34
   Concurrent Lessees ........ 36

The Position with Leases Taking Effect in Equity ........ 36
Equitable Assignees of the Term or Reversion ........ 37
Upon Reassignment of a Lease Containing a Personal Break Clause ........ 38
Former or Non-landlords/Tenants ........ 42
Agents ........ 42
Partnerships ........ 47
Insolvency ........ 49
Receivers and Managers ........ 50
Personal Representatives ........ 50

**5. The Form and Content of the Break Notice** ........ 53
Introduction ........ 53
Compliance with Indispensable Conditions ........ 54
Mistakes in the Break Notice: The General Approach ........ 55
The Objective Approach to the Construction of Notices ........ 59
The 'Relevant Objective Contextual Scene' ........ 62
Mistakes as to the Break Date ........ 65
Mistakes as to the Identity of the Serving Party ........ 69
Mistakes as to the Identity of the Intended Recipient ........ 75
Mistakes as to the Identity of the Demised Premises ........ 77
Break Notices Marked 'Without Prejudice' ........ 78
Break Notices Marked 'Subject to Contract' ........ 79

**6. The Time for Exercise of the Break Clause and Service of the Break Notice** ........ 81
Introduction ........ 81
References to the 'Commencement of the Term' ........ 82
The Time for Exercise of the Break Clause ........ 84
The Specified Period of Notice ........ 91
The 'Corresponding Date' Rule ........ 94
Other Fractions of Time ........ 96
The Effect of Late Service ........ 98
Acceptance of Short Service of a Break Notice ........ 100

**7. The Method of Service of a Break Notice** ........ 101
Introduction ........ 101
Compliance with the Prescribed Contractual Method for Service ........ 101
Particular Contractual Methods for Service ........ 106
'Indirect' Service ........ 111
Section 196 of the Law of Property Act 1925 ........ 114
Section 7 of the Interpretation Act 1978 ........ 121
Service at Common Law ........ 122

**8. On Whom the Break Notice Should be Served** ........ 124
Introduction ........ 124
Joint Lessees/Lessors ........ 124
Multiple Parties ........ 124

Concurrent Lessees ....... 125
The Position with Leases Taking Effect in Equity ....... 126
Equitable Assignees of the Term or Reversion ....... 126
Former Landlords/Tenants ....... 126
Agents ....... 127
Partnerships ....... 128
Insolvency ....... 128
Receivers and Managers ....... 129
Where the Intended Recipient has Deceased ....... 129
Personal Representatives ....... 129

**9. Conditions in a Break Clause: General Principles ....... 132**
Introduction ....... 132
Identification of the Conditions ....... 132
The Principle of Strict Compliance ....... 135
De Minimis Failures to Comply with Conditions ....... 139
The Time for Compliance ....... 139
Spent Breaches ....... 144
Words of Qualification ....... 146
Settlements/Side Agreements ....... 151
Service of a Break Notice without Fulfilling Conditions ....... 156

**10. Particular Conditions in a Tenant's Break Clause ....... 157**
Introduction ....... 157
Vacant Possession ....... 157
Payment of Rent and Other Sums ....... 171
Repairing Obligations ....... 184
Reinstatement Obligations ....... 185

**11. The Recovery of 'Overpaid' Rent and Other Sums ....... 187**
Introduction ....... 187
Implication of a Term in the Lease ....... 187
Implied Agreement ....... 193
Restitution for Unjust Enrichment ....... 195

**12. Redevelopment Break Clauses ....... 200**
Conditions in a Landlord's Break Clause ....... 200
Intention, Desire and Other Linguistic Formulations ....... 200
The Scope of the Break Clause ....... 204
Redevelopment Break Clauses under the 1954 Act ....... 206
Redevelopment Break Clauses under the 1993 Act ....... 206
The Electronic Communications Code ....... 209

**13. Invalid Break Notices: Waiver, Estoppel and Withdrawal ....... 214**
Introduction ....... 214
Waiver and Estoppel: General Principles ....... 214

The Operation of Waiver and Estoppel in the Break Clause Context.................218
Unilateral Waiver in Respect of Performance of Conditions.............................231
The Server of a Notice Cannot Rely upon his Own Wrong ..............................231
Silence...............................................................................................233
Withdrawal of a Break Notice...................................................................236
Countermanding a Break Notice................................................................238
Sequential Break Notices ........................................................................238

**14. The Effect of Exercising a Break Clause ..........................................241**
As between Landlord and Tenant...............................................................241
As Regards an Underlessee.......................................................................243

**15. Break Clauses and Compulsory Purchase ........................................246**
Introduction.........................................................................................246
Compensation: General Principles .............................................................247
Compensation for an Interest Subject to a Break Clause .................................249

**16. Break Clauses and Rent Review .......................................................252**
Introduction.........................................................................................252
Procedural Relevance.............................................................................252
Substantive Relevance............................................................................260

**17. Professional Liability .......................................................................264**
Introduction.........................................................................................264
Failure to Advise During a Transaction .......................................................265
Failure to Remind of an Approaching Break Date...........................................268
Failure to Draw Attention to Preconditions ..................................................269
Failure to Give Proper Notice...................................................................271
Contributory Negligence .........................................................................271

**18. Business Tenancies...........................................................................273**
Introduction.........................................................................................273
Termination of Business Tenancies by the Landlord .......................................273
Termination of Business Tenancies by the Tenant...........................................275
The Position of Sub-tenants.....................................................................275
The Extent of the 'Broken' Demise.............................................................276
The Insertion of Break Clauses into New Leases under the 1954 Act..................277

**19. Residential Tenancies .......................................................................288**
Introduction.........................................................................................288
Termination of Rent Act Tenancies............................................................288
Termination of Assured Tenancies .............................................................290
Termination of Assured Shorthold Tenancies.................................................292
Termination of Contractual Tenancies without Any Security of Tenure ............300

20. **Agricultural Tenancies** 302
Introduction 302
Termination of Tenancies of Agricultural Holdings 302
Termination of Farm Business Tenancies 309
Allotments 312

21. **Drafting Break Clauses** 313
General Remarks 313
Matters to be Addressed when Drafting a Break Clause 314

22. **Practical Advice when Exercising a Break Clause** 316
Advice for the Party Seeking to Exercise the Break Clause 316
Advice for the Recipient of a Break Notice 318
Litigation Tactics for the Tenant 318
Litigation Tactics for the Landlord 319

*Appendix 1: Break Clause for the Landlord – On One or More Specified Dates* 321
*Appendix 2: Break Clause for the Landlord – Incorporating a Rolling Break* 322
*Appendix 3: Break Clause for the Tenant – On One or More Specified Dates* 323
*Appendix 4: Break Clause for the Tenant – Incorporating a Rolling Break* 324
*Appendix 5: Particulars of Claim – Landlord's Claim for Declaration etc* 325
*Appendix 6: Defence and Counterclaim – In Response to Landlord's Claim for Declaration etc* 327
*Index* 329

# *Table of Cases*

REFERENCES ARE TO PARAGRAPH NUMBERS


120 Packington Street, Islington, Re (1960) 110 SJ 672 .......... 3.38
2 Speedwell Estates Ltd v Dalziel [2002] HLR 43 .......... 5.1
3M United Kingdom Plc v Linklaters & Paines [2006] PNLR 30 .......... 17.10, 17.11, 17.11
88, Berkeley Road, NW9, Re [1971] Ch 648 .......... 7.69
A Company (No 0005945 of 2006), Re [2007] BPIR 1 .......... 10.50, 10.51, 11.11
A Debtor, Re [1939] Ch 251 .......... 7.22
Aberdeen Steak Houses Ltd v Crown Estate Commissioners [1997] 2 EGLR 107 .......... 12.8
Achieving Perfection Ltd v Gray (unreported, 18 May 2015) .......... 5.1
Adams and Kensington Vestry, Re (1884) 27 Ch D 394 .......... 3.46
Adams v Green [1978] 2 EGLR 46 .......... 18.20, 18.25, 18.26, 18.27, 18.28, 18.32, 18.42
Agbaje v Agbaje [2010] 1 AC 628 .......... 9.67
Ageas (UK) Ltd v Kwik-Fit (GB) Ltd [2013] EWHC 3261 (QB) .......... 6.3, 22.3
Al Saloom v Shirley James Travel Service Ltd (1981) 42 P&CR 181 .......... 16.9, 16.13, 16.14, 16.18
Aldford House Freehold Ltd v Grosvenor (Mayfair) Estate [2018] EWHC 3430 (Ch), unaffected by the appeal at [2020] Ch 270 .......... 4.54
Alfred Street Properties Ltd v National Asset Management Agency [2020] EWHC 397 (Comm) .......... 13.2
Alghussein Establishment v Eton College [1988] 1 WLR 587 .......... 13.43
Allam & Co v Europa Poster Services [1968] 1 All ER 826 .......... 5.62
Amika Motors Ltd v Colebrook Holdings Ltd [1981] 2 EGLR 62 .......... 18.29, 18.30, 18.32, 18.42
Arlington Business Parks GP Ltd v Scottish & Newcastle Ltd [2014] CSOH 77 .......... 9.44
Armstrong v Sheppard & Short Ltd [1959] 2 QB 384 .......... 13.10
Arundel Corp v Khokher [2003] EWCA Civ 1784 .......... 7.34
Assethold Ltd v 110 Boulevard RTM Co Ltd [2017] 4 WLR 181 .......... 5.1
Attorney General's Reference (No 3 of 1999) [2001] 2 AC 91 .......... 7.18
Attorney-General of Belize v Belize Telecom Ltd [2009] 1 WLR 1988 .......... 4.17, 11.7, 11.7, 11.8, 11.10, 11.14, 11.16
Avocet Industrial Estates LLP v Merol Ltd [2012] L&TR 13 .......... 9.25, 10.40, 10.41, 10.42, 10.43, 10.44, 10.77, 10.78, 10.79, 10.80, 10.81, 10.82, 13.11, 13.50, 13.51, 13.53, 13.54
AWD Chase De Vere Wealth Management Ltd v Melville Street Properties Ltd [2009] CSOH 150 .......... 5.53
Bairstow Eves (Securities) Ltd v Ripley (1993) 65 P&CR 220 .......... 9.21, 9.22, 9.23, 9.25
Baker Tilly Management Ltd v Computer Associates UK Ltd [2009] EWHC 911 (Ch) .......... 5.52

Baker v Baxendale Walker Solicitors [2016] EWHC 664 (Ch) ....17.7
Bank of New York Mellon (International) Ltd v Cine-UK Ltd [2021] EWHC 1013 (QB) ....11.45
Banning v Wright [1972] 1 WLR 972 ....13.2
Barclays Bank of Swaziland Ltd v Hahn [1989] 1 WLR 506 ....7.23
Barclays Bank Plc v Bee [2002] 1 WLR 332 ....5.19, 5.29, 5.32
Barnard, Re [1932] 1 Ch 269 ....4.57
Barnes v City of London Real Property Co [1918] 2 Ch 18 ....3.1
Barrett v Morgan [2000] 2 AC 264 ....1.6, 1.7, 14.9, 18.12
Bass Holdings Ltd v Morton Music Ltd [1988] 1 Ch 493 ....9.16, 9.25, 9.42, 9.48, 9.49, 9.50, 10.80, 10.82
Bassett v Whiteley (1983) 45 P&CR 87 ....9.54, 9.55, 9.56, 9.57
Bastin v Bidwell (1881) 18 Ch D 238 ....9.32, 9.33, 9.34, 9.41, 13.38
Batt Cables Plc v Spencer Business Parks Ltd 2010 SLT 860 ....7.39, 7.40, 7.42
BDW Trading Ltd (T/A Barratt North London) v JM Rowe (Investments) Ltd [2010] EWHC 1987 (Ch), upheld on appeal [2011] EWCA Civ 548 ....1.10, 6.36, 13.3, 13.38, 13.43
Beanby Estates Ltd v Egg Stores (Stamford Hill) Ltd [2003] 1 WLR 2064 ....7.79
Bebington v Wildman. See Bebington's Tenancy, Re
Bebington's Tenancy, Re; Bebington v Wildman [1921] 1 Ch 559 ....3.55, 13.67
Beevers v Mason (1978) 37 P&CR 452 ....10.40, 10.41
Ben Cleuch Estates Ltd v Scottish Enterprise [2008] CSIH 1, 2008 SC 252 ....7.40, 7.42, 13.27
Bennett v Fowler (1840) 2 Beav 302 ....13.40
Betty's Cafés Ltd v Phillips Furniture Stores Ltd [1959] AC 20 ....12.7
Biondi v Kirklington & Piccadilly Estates Ltd [1947] 2 All ER 591 ....6.4, 6.5, 6.24, 6.25, 6.27
Bird v Baker (1858) 1 E&E 12 ....6.7, 6.11
Bishopsgate Parking (No 2) Ltd v The Welsh Ministers [2012] UKUT 22 (LC) ....15.17
Bishopsgate Space Management Ltd v London Underground Ltd [2004] 2 EGLR 175 ....15.14, 15.15, 15.16, 15.18
Blindley Heath Investment Ltd v Bass [2017] Ch 289 ....13.8
Blore v Giuliani [1903] 1 KB 356 ....14.3
Blunden v Frogmore Investment Ltd [2003] 2 P&CR 6, [2002] 2 EGLR 29 ....7.28, 7.46, 7.63, 7.79, 18.10
Borough of Morecambe and Heysham v Warwick (1958) 9 P&CR 307 ....7.42
Bottin (International) Investments Ltd v Venson Group Plc [2004] EWCA Civ 1368 ....7.25
Boufoy-Bastick v The University of the West Indies [2015] UKPC 27 ....6.64
Boyce v Rendalls (1983) 268 EG 268 ....17.3
BP Oil UK Ltd & Ors v Lloyds Bank Plc [2004] EWCA Civ 1710, affirming [2004] EWHC 496 (Ch) ....4.36
Bradshaw v Pawley [1980] 1 WLR 10 ....6.8, 6.11
Braganza v BP Shipping Ltd [2015] 1 WLR 1661 ....1.16, 1.17, 1.18
Bremer Handels GmbH v C Mackprang Jr [1979] 1 Lloyd's Rep 221 ....13.3
Bridgers v Stanford [1991] 2 EGLR 265 ....5.58, 5.61

Bridgewater Canal Co Ltd v Geo Networks Ltd [2010] 1 WLR 2576, overturned on appeal [2011] 1 WLR 1487 ............ 12.35, 12.36
British Rail Pension Trustee Co Ltd v Cardshops Ltd [1987] 1 EGLR 127 ............ 5.66
British Telecommunications Plc v Sun Life Assurance Society Plc [1996] Ch 69 ............ 10.83
Broadway Investments Hackney Ltd v Grant [2007] HLR 23 ............ 19.5
Brown & Root Technology Ltd v Sun Alliance and London Assurance Co Ltd [2001] Ch 733 ............ 3.60, 3.61, 3.71
Brown's Operating System Services Ltd v Southwark Roman Catholic Diocesan Corp [2007] L&TR 375 ............ 11.16
Buckland v Papillon (1866) LR Ch App 67 ............ 6.36
Burman v Mount Cook Land Ltd [2002] Ch 256 ............ 5.1, 5.2
Business Environment Bow Lane Ltd v Deanwater Estates Ltd [2007] L&TR 26 ............ 2.2
C Richards & Son Ltd v Karenita Ltd (1972) 221 EG 25 ............ 16.6
CA Webber (Transport) Ltd v Railtrack Plc [2004] 1 WLR 320 ............ 7.18
Canas Property Co v KL Television Services [1970] 2 QB 433 ............ 10.55
Cannon Brewery Co v Signal Press Ltd (1929) 139 LT 384 ............ 7.64
Canonical UK Ltd v TST Millbank LLC [2013] L&TR 15 ............ 10.61, 10.62, 10.63, 10.64, 10.65, 10.66, 10.68, 17.12
Capital and City Holdings Ltd v Dean Warburg Ltd [1989] EGLR 90 ............ 10.47, 10.48, 10.49, 10.51, 10.55, 10.65
Capitol Park Leeds Plc v Global Radio Services Ltd [2020] EWHC 2750 (Ch), overturned on appeal [2021] EWCA Civ 995 ............ 9.2, 9.13, 10.12, 10.17, 10.19, 13.37
Carapanayoti & Co Ltd v Comptoir Commercial Andre & Cie SA [1972] 1 Lloyd's Rep 139 ............ 6.51, 6.52, 6.53, 6.54
Carradine Properties Ltd v Aslam [1976] 1 WLR 442 ............ 5.14, 5.16, 5.17, 5.18, 5.38
Carradine Properties Ltd v D J Freeman & Co [1955–95] PNLR 219 ............ 17.6, 17.20
Cartledge v E Jopling & Sons Ltd [1963] AC 758 ............ 9.26
Cartwright v MacCormack [1963] 1 WLR 18 ............ 6.28, 6.73
Cathay Pacific Airways Ltd v Lufthansa Technik AG [2020] EWHC 1789 (Ch) ............ 1.18
CBS United Kingdom Ltd v London Scottish Properties Ltd [1985] 2 EGLR 125 ............ 18.43
Central Estates Ltd v Secretary of State for the Environment [1996] 72 P&CR 482 ............ 16.6, 16.19, 16.20
Charles Follett Ltd v Cabtell Investment Ltd [1986] 2 EGLR 76 ............ 18.43
Charles v Judicial and Legal Service Commission [2002] UKPC 34 ............ 7.18
Charman v Dorset CC (1986) 52 P&CR 88 ............ 12.7
Chartered Trust Plc v Davies (1998) 76 P&CR 396 ............ 1.9
Cheall v Association of Professional Executive Clerical and Computer Staff [1983] 2 AC 180 ............ 13.43
Chetty v Chetty [1916] 1 AC 603 ............ 4.66, 8.27
Chiswell Estates v Griffon Land & Estates Ltd [1975] 1 WLR 1181 ............ 7.28, 7.73
City of London Corp v Fell [1994] 1 AC 458 ............ 3.1, 3.2
City Offices (Regent Street) Ltd v Europa Acceptance Group Plc [1990] 05 EG 71 ............ 12.15
Coastplace Ltd v Hartley [1987] QB 948 ............ 3.33
Coates v Diment [1951] 1 All ER 890 ............ 12.13, 12.14, 20.15
Cobbe v Yeoman's Row Management Ltd [2008] 1 WLR 1752 ............ 13.5, 13.9

Collier v Williams [2006] 1 WLR 1945 ....... 7.35
Commercial Union Life Assurance Co Ltd v Label Ink Ltd [2001] L&TR 29 ....... 9.63
Consensus Business Group (Ground Rents) Ltd v Palgrave Gardens Freehold Co Ltd [2020] 2 P&CR 13 ....... 5.19
Cook v Taylor [1942] 2 All ER 85 ....... 10.9
Cooke v Scotfield Ltd (unreported, 4 April 2000) ....... 9.84
Cordon Bleu Freezer Food Centres Ltd v Marbleace Ltd [1987] 2 EGLR 143 ....... 13.68, 13.69
Cornerstone Telecommunications Infrastructure Ltd v Compton Beauchamp Estates Ltd [2020] 1 P&CR 15, upheld on appeal at [2021] EWCA Civ 90 ....... 12.31, 12.33, 12.34, 12.45, 12.47
Country Personnel Ltd v Alan Pulver & Co [1987] 1 WLR 916 ....... 17.7
Coventry CC v J Hepworth & Sons [1983] 46 P&CR 170 ....... 16.10, 16.21
Cowan v Wrayford [1953] 1 WLR 1340 ....... 20.14
Cowen v Phillips (1863) 33 Beav 18 ....... 4.21
Cowthorpe Road 1-1A Freehold Ltd v Wahedally [2017] L&TR 4 ....... 5.1
Craddock v Secretary of State for Transport [2021] UKUT 2 (LC) ....... 12.7
Cranfield v Bridgegrove [2003] 1 WLR 2441 ....... 7.35
Credit Lyonnais SA v Russell Jones & Walker [2003] PNLR 2 ....... 17.25, 17.26, 17.27
Criterion Buildings Ltd v McKinsey & Company Inc (United Kingdom) [2021] EWHC 216 (Ch) ....... 1.18
Crossco No 4 Unlimited v Jolan Ltd [2011] EWHC 803 (Ch), upheld on appeal [2012] 1 P&CR 16 ....... 12.7, 13.14, 13.15, 13.16
Cumberland Consolidated Holdings Ltd v Ireland [1956] 1 KB 264 ....... 10.3, 10.4, 10.5, 10.6, 10.7, 10.8, 10.11, 10.12, 10.17, 10.18, 10.19, 10.21, 10.27, 10.28, 10.29, 10.31
Cunliffe v Goodman [1950] KB 237 ....... 12.4, 12.9
Dann v Spurrier (1803) 3 B&P 399 ....... 4.2, 4.3
Datnow v Jones [1985] 2 EGLR 1 ....... 13.12
Davy's of London (Wine Merchants) Ltd v City of London Corp [2004] 3 EGLR 39 ....... 18.20, 18.40, 18.42
Day v Coltrane [2003] 1 WLR 1379 ....... 10.41
De Bussche v Alt (1878) 8 Ch D 286 ....... 13.10
Delta Vale Properties Ltd v Mills [1990] 1 WLR 445 ....... 5.14, 5.17, 5.18
Denham Bros Ltd v W Freestone Leasing Pty Ltd [2003] QCA 376 ....... 3.23, 3.32
Deutsche Morgan Grenfell Group Plc v IRC [2007] 1 AC 558 ....... 11.37, 11.38, 11.39
Dickinson v St Aubyn [1944] KB 454 ....... 14.2
Dies v British and International Mining and Finance Corp [1939] 1 KB 724 ....... 10.55
Director of Buildings and Lands v Shun Fung Ironworks Ltd [1995] 2 AC 111 ....... 15.5
Disraeli Agreement, Re [1939] 1 Ch 382 ....... 20.15
Divall v Harrison & Anr [1992] 2 EGLR 64 ....... 4.42
Dodds v Walker [1981] 1 WLR 1027 ....... 6.28, 6.57, 6.58, 6.59, 6.61
Dodika Ltd v United Luck Group Holdings Ltd [2021] EWCA Civ 638 ....... 5.29, 5.60
Dodson Bull Carpet Co Ltd v City of London Corp [1975] 1 WLR 781 ....... 18.15
Doe d. Bryan v Bancks (1821) 4 B&Ald 401 ....... 13.43
Doe d. Clarke v Smaridge (1845) 7 QB 957 ....... 20.24

Doe d. Cox v Roe (1803) 4 Esp 184 ....................5.60
Doe d. Neville v Dunbar (1826) Moo & M 9 ....................7.76
Doe d. Mann, Clerk v Walters (1830) 10 B & C 626 ....................4.54
Doe, on the demise of Green v Baker (1818) 8 Taunt 241 ....................4.56
Doe, on the several demises of Marsack v Read (1810) 12 East 57 ....................4.65
Donmez v Barnes & Partners [1996] EGCS 129 ....................17.8
Dowding v Matchmove [2017] 1 WLR 749 ....................13.42
Dreams Ltd v Pavilion Property Trustees Ltd [2020] L&TR 22 .................... 9.2, 10.16
Duchess of Argyll v Beuselinck [1972] 2 Lloyd's Rep 172 ....................17.2
Dukeminster Ltd v West End Investments (Cowell Group) Ltd [2019] L&TR 4 ....................18.43, 18.45
Dun & Bradstreet Software Services (England) Ltd v Provident Mutual Life Assurance Association [1998] 2 EGLR 175 ....................4.49, 9.25, 11.24, 13.22, 13.23, 13.24
Earl of Cadogan v Guinness [1936] Ch 515 .................... 6.8
Earl of Harrowby v Snelson [1951] 1 All ER 14 ....................8.28
Eason & Son (NI) Ltd v Central Craigavon Ltd (Lands Tribunal of Northern Ireland, Case No BT/80/2001) ....................18.20, 18.47
East Lindsey DC v Thompson (2001) 82 P&CR 33 ....................3.59
East v Pantiles (Plant Hire) Ltd [1982] 2 EGLR 111 .................... 6.65, 6.69
Ebrahim Dawood Ltd v Heath (Est 1927) Ltd [1961] 2 Lloyd's Rep 512 ....................11.43
Edell v Dulieu [1924] AC 38 ....................19.44
Edwards v Strong, The Times, 9 November 1994 ....................8.28
Edwin Woodhouse Trustee Co Ltd v Sheffield Brick Co Plc [1984] 1 EGLR 130 ......16.25
EE Ltd v Islington LBC [2019] 2 P&CR 13 ....................12.42, 12.45
EE Ltd v Sir James H E Chichester [2019] UKUT 164 (LC) ....................12.45
Egerton v Rutter [1951] 1 KB 472 ....................8.28
Elitestone Ltd v Morris [1997] 1 WLR 687 ....................10.16
Ellis v Rowbotham [1900] 1 QB 740 .................... 10.46, 10.55, 11.11, 11.14, 17.12
Elsden v Pick [1980] 1 WLR 898 .................... 6.79, 13.29, 20.6
Ener-G Holdings Plc v Hormell [2012] EWCA Civ 1059 ....................6.3, 7.13, 7.14, 7.15, 7.16, 7.17, 7.19, 7.36, 7.42
Enfield London BC v Devonish (1997) 29 HLR 691 ....................7.46, 7.46, 7.47
Engell v Fitch (1869) LR 4 QB 659 ....................10.9
E.ON UK Plc v Gilesports Ltd [2013] 1 P&CR 4 .................... 5.1
Epping Forest DC v Essex Rendering Ltd [1983] 1 WLR 15 .................... 5.1
Equinox Industrial (GP2) Ltd v Sketchley Ltd [2003] EWHC 2 (Ch) ....................3.39, 4.29, 4.30, 4.31, 4.35, 4.36
Esson Properties Ltd v Dresser UK Ltd 1997 SC 304 .................... 6.48, 6.49
Extra MSA Services Cobham Ltd v Accor UK Economy Holdings Ltd [2011] EWHC 775 (Ch) ....................13.43, 13.44, 13.45
Fagan v Knowsley Metropolitan BC (1985) 50 P&CR 363 ....................7.39
Farrow v Orttewell [1933] 1 Ch 480 ....................3.56
Fawaz v Aylward (1997) 29 HLR 408 ....................19.23, 19.26
Fernandez v McDonald [2004] 1 WLR 1027 ....................5.19, 19.18
Fibrosa Spolka Akeyjna v Fairbairn Lawson Combe Barbour Ltd [1943] AC 32 ......11.41
Fifield v W&R Jack Ltd [2001] L&TR 4 ....................13.33, 13.34, 13.35

Finch v Underwood (1876) 2 Ch 310 ........................... 9.19, 9.20, 9.25, 9.30, 9.31, 10.84
Fish & Fish Ltd v Sea Shepherd UK [2015] AC 1229 ........................... 9.26
Fisher v Taylors Furnishings Stores Ltd [1956] 2 QB 78 ........................... 12.4
Fitzhugh v Fitzhugh [2012] 2 P&CR 14 ........................... 4.14, 4.15, 4.16, 4.17
Fitzroy House Epworth Street (No 1) Ltd v Financial Times Ltd [2006] 1 WLR 2207 ........................... 9.61, 9.62, 9.64, 9.66, 9.67, 22.8
Flather v Hood (1928) 44 TLR 698 ........................... 20.4
Fleet Electrics v Jacey Investments [1956] 1 WLR 1027 ........................... 12.4
Fletcher Estates (Harlescott) Ltd v Secretary of State for the Environment [2000] 2 AC 307 ........................... 15.9
Foster v Robinson [1951] 1 KB 149 ........................... 19.5
Frankland v Capstick [1959] 1 WLR 204 ........................... 5.20
Fred Long & Sons Ltd v Burgess [1950] 1 KB 115 ........................... 4.68, 8.28
Freeman v Evans [1922] 1 Ch 36 ........................... 13.61, 13.62, 13.63
Freeman v Hambrook [1947] VLR 70 ........................... 3.56, 3.66, 3.68
Freeman v Read (1863) 4 B& S 174 ........................... 6.59
Freetown Ltd v Assethold Ltd [2013] 1 WLR 701 ........................... 7.79
Friary Holroyd and Healey's Breweries Ltd v Singleton [1899] 2 Ch 261 ........................... 3.46, 13.20
Gajapatiraju v The Revenue District Officer, Vizagaptam [1939] AC 302 ........................... 15.8
Galinski v McHugh (1989 21 HLR 47, (1989) 57 P&CR 359 ........................... 7.18, 7.28, 8.20
Ganton House Investments Ltd v Corbin [1988] 2 EGLR 69 ........................... 13.40
Ganton House Investments v Crossman Investments [1995] 1 EGLR 1995 ........................... 18.43
Gardner v Blaxill [1960] 1 WLR 752 ........................... 9.52, 9.53
Gardner v McCusker (unreported), Birmingham CC ........................... 19.31
Garston v Scottish Widows' Fund and Life Assurance Society [1998] 1 WLR 1583 ........................... 5.36, 18.11
Gate Gourmet Luxembourg IV SARL v Morby [2016] Bus LR 218 ........................... 7.24, 7.26
Gateway Housing Association v Personal Representatives of Ali [2021] 1 WLR 289 ........................... 8.28, 8.30
Gemini Press Ltd v Parsons [2012] EWHC 1608 (QB) ........................... 3.35, 3.36, 3.37
Gentle v Faulkner [1990] 2 QB 267 ........................... 3.61
Germax Securities Ltd v Spiegal (1979) 37 P&CR 204 ........................... 5.31
Gidden v Chief Constable of Humberside [2010] RTR 9 ........................... 20.7
Giedo Van Der Garde BV v Force India Formula One Team Ltd [2010] EWHC 2373 (QB) ........................... 11.41
GKN Aerospace Services Ltd v Duncan Investments Ltd [2020] EWHC 3719 (Ch) ........................... 6.18, 6.21
Gladstone v Bower [1960] 1 QB 170 ........................... 19.44, 20.3, 20.4
Glencore Grain Ltd v Flacker Shipping Ltd (The Happy Day) [2003] 1 CLC 537 ........................... 13.2
Gold v Brighton Corporation [1956] 1 WLR 1291 ........................... 18.27
Goldman Sachs International v Procession House Trustee Ltd [2018] L&TR 28 ........................... 9.9, 9.10, 9.11, 9.13, 9.14, 10.12, 10.16
Goldsmith's Company v West Metropolitan Railway Co [1904] 1 KB 1 ........................... 6.28
Gorbachev v Guriev [2019] EWHC 2684 (Comm) ........................... 7.26
Goulandris v Knight [2018] 1 WLR 3345 ........................... 5.1
Gouldandris v Knight [2018] 1 WLR 3345 ........................... 7.79

GR Property Management Ltd v Safdar [2020] EWCA Civ 1441..............................7.18
Grange v Quinn [2013] 1 P&CR 18 ...................................................................... 1.9
Grant v Edmondson [1931] 1 Ch 1...................................................................... 3.4
Gray v Bompas 142 ER 899 ........................................................................10.35, 10.37
Greenclose Ltd v National Westminster Bank Plc [2014] EWHC 1156 (Ch)...... 7.16, 7.17
Gregson v Cyril Lord Ltd [1963] 1 WLR 41..........................................................12.6
Grey v Friar (1854) 4 HL Cas 565...................................................9.16, 9.17, 9.18, 9.47
Griffith v Pelton [1958] Ch 205 ..............................................3.30, 3.31, 3.32, 3.33, 3.46
Griffiths v Evans [1953] 1 WLR 1424 ..................................................................17.2
Grimes v Trustees of the Essex Farmers and Union Hunt [2017] L&TR 28...............7.31
Gulf Agencies Ltd v Ahmed [2016] EWCA Civ 44...................................................12.4
Hackney LBC v Snowden (2001) 33 HLR 49 .............................................6.79, 13.29
Hall v Meyrick [1957] 2 QB 455 ........................................................................17.2
Hall v Richardson (1789) 3 Term Reports 462......................................................6.43
Hamiltonhill Estates Ltd v Central Regional Council 1996 GWD 21-1564 ................6.48
Hammersmith and Fulham LBC v Monk [1992] AC 478 ............................... 1.2, 4.10
Hammonds v Danilunas [2009] EWHC 216 (Ch), affirmed on appeal at [2009] EWCA Civ 1400..........................................................................................4.55
Hankey v Clavering [1942] 2 KB 326.................................................5.8, 5.9, 5.57, 14.1
Hannaford v Smallacombe [1994] 1 EGLR 9.........................................................10.41
Harbour Estates Ltd v HSBC Bank Plc [2005] Ch 194 ...................3.11, 3.12, 3.27, 3.28, 3.33, 3.40, 3.44
Hare v Gocher [1962] 2 QB 641 .........................................................................6.40
Harmond Properties Ltd v Gajdzis [1968] 1 WLR 1858 ...........................................4.46
Hart v Emelkirk [1983] 1 WLR 1289.....................................................................4.65
Hartshorne v Watson 132 ER 1183 ......................................................................14.3
Hastie & Jenkinson v McMahon [1990] 1 WLR 1575 ............................................ 5.1
Havant International Holdings Ltd v Lionsgate (H) Investment Ltd [2000] L&TR 297 .....................................................................5.29, 5.41, 5.50, 5.51
Hawtrey v Beaufort Ltd [1946] 1 KB 280...................................................... 5.57, 8.20
Haywood v Newcastle upon Tyne NHS Trust [2018] 1 WLR 2073.....7.76, 7.77, 7.78, 7.79
Heron Garage Properties Ltd v Moss [1974] 1 WLR 148 .......................................13.40
Herrmann v Withers LLP [2012] PNLR 28..............................................................17.7
Hersey v Giblett (1854) 18 Beav 174....................................................................6.36
Hexstone Holdings Ltd v AHC Westlink Ltd [2010] L&TR 22 ....................................................4.50, 4.52, 4.54, 6.19, 6.20
HFI Farnborough LLP v Park Garage Group Plc [2012] EWHC 3577 (Ch)..........9.3, 9.7
Hicks v 89 Holland Park (Management) Ltd [2019] EWHC 1301 (Ch), reversed on appeal [2020] EWCA Civ 758 .........................................................1.18
Higgins v ERC Accountants & Business [2017] EWHC 2190 (Ch) .........................13.58
Hiscox v Outhwaite [1992] 1 AC 562 ...................................................................13.8
HMRC v Benchdollar Ltd [2009] EWHC 1310 (Ch) ...............................................13.8
Hoare v National Trust (1998) 77 P&CR 366........................................................15.10
Hogg Bullimore & Co v Co-Operative Insurance Society Ltd (1985) 50 P&CR 105 ........................................................................................6.48
Hogg v Brooks (1885) 15 QBD 256 ......................................................................7.75

Holwell Securities Ltd v Hughes [1974] 1 WLR 155 .......... 7.79, 13.65
Homes v Smith [2000] Lloyd's Rep Bank 139 .......... 10.41
Horn v Sunderland Corp [1941] 2 KB 25 .......... 15.4, 15.6
Hotgroup Plc v The Royal Bank of Scotland Plc (As Trustee of Schroder Exempt Property Unit Trust) [2010] EWHC 1241 (Ch) .......... 8.3, 8.4
Hough v Greathall Ltd [2015] EWCA Civ 23 .......... 12.7
Hounslow London BC v Pilling [1993] 1 WLR 1242 .......... 4.9, 4.10
HPUT Trustee No 1 Ltd v Boots UK Ltd (unreported, 24 May 2021) .......... 18.50
Hudson Bay Apparel Brands LLC v Umbro International Ltd [2010] ETMR 62 .......... 13.3
Hughes v Metropolitan Railway Company (1877) 2 App Cas 439 .......... 13.2
Humber Oil Terminals Trustee Ltd v Associated British Ports [2012] EWCA Civ 596, [2012] L&TR 27 .......... 6.28, 12.4
Hussain v Bradford Community Housing Trust Ltd [2010] HLR 16 .......... 19.18
Hussein v Mehlman [1992] 2 EGLR 87 .......... 1.9
ING Bank NV v Ros Roca SA [2012] 1 WLR 472 .......... 13.49, 22.8
Ingall v Moran [1944] KB 160 .......... 4.67, 4.68, 8.28
Intergraph (UK) Ltd v Wolfson Microelectronics Plc [2012] EWHC 528 (Ch) .......... 9.77, 9.78, 9.79, 9.80, 9.81, 9.82, 9.83
IRC v Hobhouse [1956] 1 WLR 1393 .......... 6.64
IRC v John Lewis Properties Plc [2002] 1 WLR 35 .......... 3.9
IRC v Southend-on-Sea Estates Co Ltd [1915] AC 428 .......... 12.6
Isteed v Stoneley (1580) 1 And 82 .......... 3.11
Italica Holdings SA v Bayadea [1985] 1 EGLR 70 .......... 7.29
J A Pye (Oxford) Ltd v Graham [2003] 1 AC 419 .......... 10.7
James v Heim Gallery (London) Ltd (1981) 41 P&CR 269 .......... 13.7
Jelley v Buckman [1975] QB 488 .......... 3.52
Jervis v Pillar Denton Ltd [2015] Ch 87 .......... 10.45
JH Edwards & Sons Ltd v Central London Commercial Estates Ltd [1984] 2 EGLR 103 .......... 18.31, 18.32, 18.38, 18.42
John Laing Construction Ltd v Amber Pass Ltd [2004] 2 EGLR 128 .......... 10.32, 10.33, 10.34, 10.35, 10.36, 10.37
John v George (1996) 71 P&CR 375 .......... 13.13
Jones & Ors v Phipps (1868) LR 3 QB 567 .......... 4.44, 4.51
Jones d. Griffiths v Marsh (1791) 4 TR 464 .......... 7.76
Jones v Gates [1954] 1 WLR 222 .......... 12.11
JSC BTA Bank v Ablyazov [2012] EWHC 648 (Comm) .......... 4.65
JW Spear & Sons Ltd v Zynga Inc [2012] EWHC 1374 (Ch) .......... 22.13
Kaiser Engineers & Constructors Inc v E R Squibb & Sons Ltd (unreported, 12 November 1971) .......... 3.54
Kammins Ballrooms Co Ltd v Zenith Investments (Torquay) Ltd [1971] AC 850 .......... 1.10, 13.2
Keith Bayley Rogers & Co v Cubes Ltd (1976) 31 P&CR 412 .......... 5.62, 18.13
Kelly v Rogers [1892] 1 QB 910 .......... 14.14
Kenneth Allison Ltd v A E Limehouse & Co [1992] 2 AC 105 .......... 7.21
Kinane v Mackie-Conteh [2005] EWCA Civ 45 .......... 13.42
Kinch v Bullard [1999] 1 WLR 423 .......... 7.60, 7.61, 7.62, 13.65

Klein v London Underground Ltd [1996] 1 EGLR 249 ............ 15.18
Kleinwort Benson Ltd v Lincoln CC [1999] 2 AC 349 ............ 11.35, 11.38
Knight and Hubbard's Underlease, Re [1923] 1 Ch 130 ............ 4.45
Korogluyan v Matthew (1975) 30 P&CR 309 ............ 10.9
Kosmar Villa Holidays Plc v Trustees of Syndicate 1243 [2008] Bus LR 931 ............ 13.4
Kushner v Law Society [1952] 1 KB 264 ............ 2.3
Kutchukian v Keepers and Governors of John Lyon School [2013] 1 WLR 2842 ............ 12.24
Kwik Lets Ltd v Khaira [2020] EWHC 616 (QB) ............ 1.18
L R Wingfield Ltd v Clapton Construction and Investment Co Ltd (1967) 201 EG 769 ............ 4.4
Ladyman v Wirral Estates Ltd [1968] 2 All ER 197 ............ 6.28, 6.32
Laine v Cadwallader (2001) 33 HLR 36 ............ 13.20
Lancashire Insurance Co Ltd v MS Frontier Reinsurance Ltd [2012] UKPC 42 ............ 13.17, 13.18
Lancecrest Ltd v Asiwaju [2005] L&TR 22 ............ 5.21, 5.22, 5.23, 5.24, 5.25, 5.26, 5.27
Land Settlement Association v Carr [1944] KB 657 ............ 20.26
Land v Sykes [1992] 1 EGLR 1 ............ 5.20
Lantic Sugar Ltd v Baffin Investments Ltd [2009] EWHC 3325 (Comm) ............ 7.36, 7.42
Lay v Ackerman [2004] HLR 40 ............ 5.20, 5.41
Lazarus Estates Ltd v Beasley [1956] 1 QB 702 ............ 5.20
Leeds CC v Barclays Bank Plc [2021] EWHC 363 (Comm) ............ 13.3
Leek and Moorland Building Society v Clark [1952] 2 QB 788 ............ 4.6
Legal & General Assurance (Pension Management) v Cheshire CC [1984] 269 EG 40 ............ 16.11, 16.12, 16.18
Legal & General Assurance Society Ltd v Expeditors International (UK) Ltd [2006] L&TR 368, upheld on appeal [2007] 2 P&CR 10 ............ 9.69, 9.70, 9.71, 9.72, 9.73, 9.74, 9.75, 9.76, 10.3, 10.6, 10.13, 10.14, 10.17,10.21, 10.32
Lemmerbell Ltd & Anr v Britannia LAS Direct Ltd (formerly LAS Direct Ltd) [1999] L&TR 102 ............ 4.43, 4.61, 5.43, 5.44, 5.45, 5.50
Lemon v Lardeur [1946] 1 KB 613 ............ 4.42
Leonard Becker v Hill Street Properties Ltd [1990] 2 EGLR 78 ............ 18.37, 18.38, 18.41, 18.42
Leslie & Godwin Investments Ltd v Prudential Assurance Co Ltd [1987] 2 EGLR 95 ............ 18.20
Lester v Garland (1808) 15 Ves Jun 248 ............ 6.28, 6.30, 6.35, 6.51, 6.72
Levett Dunn v NHS Property Services Ltd [2016] Ch 637 ............ 7.29, 7.30, 7.35, 8.14, 8.17, 8.18
Linpac Mouldings Ltd v Aviva Life and Pensions UK Ltd [2010] 1 P&CR 11, upheld on appeal [2010] EWCA Civ 395, [2010] L&TR 10 ............ 3.3, 3.39, 4.30, 4.32, 4.33, 4.34, 4.35, 4.37, 4.39, 4.40, 4.41, 17.9
Liverpool CC v Irwin [1977] AC 239 ............ 11.10
Livewest Homes Ltd v Bamber [2019] 1 WLR 6389 ............ 19.17, 19.23
Lloyd v Nowell [1895] 2 Ch 744 ............ 13.40
Lomas v JFB Firth Rixon [2012] EWCA Civ 419, [2012] 2 All ER (Comm) 1076 ............ 1.18, 11.40
London & Clydeside Estates Ltd v Aberdeen DC [1980] 1 WLR 182 ............ 7.18

London Borough of Southwark v Akhtar. See Southwark LB v Akhtar
London Kendal Street No 3 Ltd v Daejan Investments Ltd [2019] L&TR 22 ............12.5
Lord Inchiquin v Lyons (1887) 20 LR Ir 474 ............13.61
Lowenthal v Vanhoute [1947] 1 KB 342............13.62
Lower Street Properties Ltd v Jones (1996) 28 HLR 877............19.18
Lower v Sorrell [1963] 1 QB 959 ............13.63, 13.64
Luttenberger v North Thoresby Farms Ltd [1992] 1 EGLR 261, [1993] 1 EGLR 3 ............10.41
M&P Enterprises (London) Ltd v Norfolk Square Hotels Ltd [1994] 1 EGLR 129............5.31
Macara (James) Ltd v Barclay [1945] KB 148 ............10.9
Mackley v Nutting [1949] 2 KB 55............8.28
Majorstake v Curtis [2008] 1 AC 787 ............9.67, 12.28, 12.29, 12.30
Malkinson v Trim [2003] 1 WLR 463............4.55
Manchester and Milford Railway Company (1880) 14 Ch D 645............4.64
Manchester Diocesan Council for Education v Commercial & General Investments Ltd [1970] 1 WLR 241 ............7.20
Mancini v Coventry CC (1985) 49 P&CR 127 ............12.7
Mannai Investment Co Ltd v Eagle Star Life Assurance Co Ltd [1997] AC 749 ............ 1.14, 4.59, 5.1, 5.2, 5.7, 5.8, 5.10, 5.11, 5.14, 5.15, 5.16, 5.17, 5.19, 5.20, 5.26, 5.28, 5.29, 5.33, 5.34, 5.38, 5.41, 5.42, 5.54, 9.25
Manorlike Ltd v Le Vitas Travel Agency and Consultancy Services Ltd [1986] 1 All ER 574 ............6.13, 6.14, 6.15, 6.16, 6.17
Manotarn Ltd v Rose & Birn (a firm) (unreported, 20 July 1995)............17.13, 17.30
Margaronis Navigation Agency Ltd v Henry W Peabody & Co of London Ltd [1965] 2 QB 430............9.26
Marine Trade SA v Pioneer Freight Futures Co Ltd BVI [2010] Lloyd's Rep 631.......11.40
Marks & Spencer Plc v BNP Paribas Securities Services Trust Co (Jersey) Ltd [2013] L&TR 31, reversed on appeal [2014] L&TR 36, further appeal dismissed [2015] UKSC 72 ............10.45, 10.46, 10.67, 10.68, 10.69, 10.72, 11.4, 11.5, 11.6, 11.7, 11.8, 11.10, 11.11, 11.12, 11.13, 11.14, 11.15, 11.16, 11.18, 11.45, 17.12
Marren v Dawson Bentley & Co Ltd [1961] 2 QB 135............6.28
Maskell v Horner [1915] 3 KB 106............11.30, 11.32
Matthey v Curling [1922] 2 AC 180............10.86, 10.87
Maurice Investments Ltd v Lincoln Insurance Services Ltd [2007] 1 P&CR 14 ..........5.66
Max Factor Ltd v Wesleyan Assurance Society [1996] 2 EGLR 210, upheld on appeal (1997) 74 P&CR 8 ............ 3.39, 4.26, 4.27, 4.28, 4.29, 4.30, 4.35, 4.36, 17.11
May v Borup [1915] 1 KB 830............13.59
Mayor and Burgesses of the London Borough of Hackney v The Hackney African Organisation [1999] L&TR 117 ............5.31
McGann v Bisping [2017] EWHC 2951 (Comm) ............7.12
Meadfield Properties Ltd v Secretary of State for the Environment [1995] 1 EGLR 39............ 6.33, 6.35

Mediterranean Salvage and Towage Ltd v Seamar Trading and Commerce Inc (The Reborn) [2009] EWCA Civ 531....11.10
Menelaou v Bank of Cyprus UK Ltd [2016] AC 176....11.28
Merton London BC v Jones [2009] 1 WLR 1269....10.7, 10.32
Metrolands Investments Ltd v Dewhurst Ltd [1986] 52 P&CR 232.....16.22, 16.23, 16.24
Metropolitan Properties v Cordery (1980) 39 P&CR 10....7.34
Micrografix v Woking 8 Ltd (1996) 71 P&CR 43....5.35
Mid Essex Hospital Services NHS Trust v Compass Group UK and Ireland Ltd [2013] BLR 265....1.18
Mid Essex Hospital Services NHS Trust v Compass Group UK and Ireland Ltd [2013] EWCA Civ 200....9.67
Midland Bank Trust Co Ltd v Hett, Stubbs & Kemp [1979] Ch 384....17.2
Millburn-Snell v Evans [2012] 1 WLR 41....4.67
Minister of Transport v Pettitt (1969) 20 P&CR 344....15.14
Minkin v Landsberg [2015] EWCA Civ 1152....17.6
Mitchell v Watkinson [2014] EWCA Civ 1472....8.28
Moncure v Cahusac [2006] UKPC 54....6.27, 13.39
Monk v Largo Foods Ltd [2016] EWHC 1837 (Ch)....1.18
Moodie v Hosegood [1952] AC 61....8.28
Morby v Gate Gourmet Luxembourg IV SARL [2016] EWHC 74 (Ch)....7.22
Morecambe and Heysham Corp v Warwick (1958) 9 P&CR 307....7.29
Morley v Royal Bank of Scotland [2020] EWHC 88 (Ch)....1.18
Morris v The London Rent Assessment Committee [2002] HLR 48.... 5.55, 5.56
Mortgage Express Ltd v Bowerman & Partners [1996] 1 All ER 836....17.3
Moss v Barton (1866) LR 1 Eq 474....6.36
Moss v Mobil Oil Co Ltd [1988] 1 EGLR 71....18.16
Motor Oil Hellas (Corinth) Refineries SA v Shipping Corp of India (The Kanchenjunga) [1990] 1 Lloyd's Rep 391.... 13.2, 13.5
Mourant Property Trust Ltd v Fusion Electronic (UK) Ltd [2009] EWHC 3659 (Ch)....9.65
MPS2 Ltd v The Department for Housing, Communities and Local Government (unreported, 11 June 2019)....18.46
Muller v Trafford [1901] 1 Ch 54....3.11
Multon v Cordell [1986] 1 EGLR 44.... 6.25, 6.26, 6.27
MW Trustees Ltd v Tellular Corp [2011] L&TR 19....5.59, 13.28
MWB Business Exchange Centres Ltd v Rock Advertising Ltd [2019] AC 119....13.42
National Car Parks Ltd v The Paternoster Consortium Ltd [1990] 1 EGLR 99....18.34, 18.35, 18.36, 18.42
National Oilwell (UK) Ltd v Davy Offshore Ltd [1993] 2 Lloyd's Rep 582....4.53
National Westminster Bank Ltd v Betchworth Investments Ltd [1975] 1 EGLR 57....7.33
Natt v Osman [2015] 1 WLR 1536....7.18
New Zealand Government Property Corp v HM&S Ltd [1982] 1 WLR 1145....10.16
New Zealand Shipping Co Ltd v Societe des Ateliers et Chantiers de France [1919] AC 1....13.43
Newbold v Coal Authority [2014] 1 WLR 1288.... 1.14, 5.1
Newborough (Lord) v Jones [1975] Ch 90.... 7.54, 7.59

Newham LBC v Benjamin [1968] 1 WLR 964 ............ 15.7
Newman v Keedwell (1978) 35 P&CR 393 ............ 4.6
Newtown Management Pty Ltd v Owners of Strata Plan 67219 [2009] NSWSC 19 ............ 9.27
Norman v Ricketts (1886) 3 TLR 182 ............ 10.40
Norwegian American Cruises A/S v Paul Mundy Ltd (the 'Vistafjord') [1988] 2 Lloyd's Rep 343 ............ 13.8
Norwich Union Life & Pensions v Linpac Mouldings Ltd [2010] 1 P&CR 11 .... 1.1, 3.15
Norwich Union Life Insurance Society v Tony Waller Ltd [1984] 1 EGLR 126 ............ 5.64
Notting Hill Housing Trust v Roomus [2006] 1 WLR 1375 ............ 19.18
Nottingham Building Society v Peter Bennett & Co (a firm) (1997) The Times 26 February ............ 7.66
Nurdin & Peacock Plc v DB Ramsden & Co Ltd [1999] 1 WLR 1249 ............ 11.20, 11.21, 11.24, 11.32, 11.33, 11.36
NYK Logistics (UK) Ltd v Ibrend Estates BV [2011] 4 All ER 539 ............ 10.8, 10.11, 10.22, 10.23, 10.24, 10.29, 10.32, 10.87
Nynehead Developments Ltd v RH Fibreboard Containers Ltd [1999] 1 EGLR 7 ....... 1.9
O'May v City of London Real Property Co Ltd [1983] 2 AC 726 ........ 18.20, 18.21, 18.47
Official Solicitor v Thomas [1986] 2 EGLR 1 ............ 10.41
Oliver Ashworth (Holdings) Ltd v Ballard (Kent) Ltd [2000] Ch 12 ............ 14.7
Olympia & York Canary Wharf Ltd v Oil Property Investment Ltd (1995) 69 P&CR 43 ............ 4.30, 4.37
OOO Abbott v Econowall UK Ltd [2016] EWHC 660 (IPEC) ............ 13.58
Orakpo v Manson Investments [1978] AC 95 ............ 11.26
Orchard (Developments) Holdings Plc v Reuters Ltd [2009] EWCA Civ 6 ............ 7.9, 7.10, 22.2
P Phipps & Co Ltd v Rogers [1925] 1 KB 14 ............ 6.69
Pacitti Jones v O'Brian 2006 SC 616 ............ 6.61, 6.62
Pacol Ltd v Trade Lines Ltd (The Henrik Sif) [1982] 1 Lloyd's Rep 456 ............ 13.52
Paddock Investments Ltd v Lory [1975] 2 EGLR 5 ............ 12.11, 20.5
Papillon v Brunton (1860) 5 H&N 518 ............ 7.76, 8.20
Parker v Camden London BC [1986] 1 Ch 162 ............ 4.65
Parker v Taswell (1858) 2 De G&J 559 ............ 4.21
Parkinson v Barclays Bank Ltd [1951] 1 KB 368 ............ 12.17
Parry v Million Pigs Ltd [1980] 260 EG 281 ............ 20.15
Patel v Earlspring Properties Ltd [1991] 2 EGLR 131 ............ 5.26
Patel v Keles [2010] Ch 332 ............ 12.8
Patel v Peel Investments (South) Ltd [1992] 2 EGLR 116 ............ 13.4, 13.30, 13.31, 13.32, 13.70
PCE Investors Ltd v Cancer Research UK [2012] 2 P&CR 5 ............ 10.56, 10.57, 10.58, 10.59, 10.65, 10.66, 10.68, 11.9, 11.44, 13.54, 13.56, 13.57, 13.58
Peaceform Ltd v Cussens [2006] 3 EGLR 67 ............ 5.34
Pease v Carter [2020] 1 WLR 1459 ............ 5.19, 5.31
Peel Developments (South) Ltd v Siemens Plc [1992] 2 EGLR 85 ............ 4.48
Peeling v Guidice (1963) 186 EG 113 ............ 6.77

Peer Freeholds Ltd v Clean Wash International Ltd [2005] 1 EGLR 47 ............ 5.34, 5.39
Pennell v Payne [1995] QB 192.........................................14.8, 14.9, 14.10, 14.11, 18.12
Pennington v Crossley & Sons Ltd (1897) 13 TLR 513 ..........................................10.40
Persimmon Homes (South Coast) Ltd v Hall Aggregates (South Coast) Ltd [2009] EWCA Civ 1108.....................................................................................................13.3
Petroplus Marketing AG v Shell Trading International Ltd [2009] 2 Lloyd's Rep 611 .......................................................................................................13.43
Peyman v Lanjani [1985] 1 Ch 457.......................................................................13.3
Pickard v Sears (1837) 6 Ad & El 439......................................................................13.9
Pickersgill v Riley [2004] PNLR 31 ..........................................................................17.5
PNC Telecom plc v Thomas [2003] BCC 202 ............................................................ 5.1
Pointe Gourde Quarrying and Transport Co Ltd v Sub-Intendent of Crown Lands [1947] AC 565...........................................................................15.9, 15.17
Polglass v Oliver (1831) 2 Cr&J 15 ........................................................................10.41
Porter v Shephard (1796) 6 TR 665 ..........................................................................9.17
Poyser and Mills' Arbitration, Re [1964] 2 QB 467 ..................................................20.7
Practice Direction (Probate: Notice to Quit) [1995] 1 WLR 1120 ..............................8.29
Presentaciones Musicales SA v Secunda [1994] Ch 271 .............................................4.54
Price v West London Investment Building Society Ltd [1964] 1 WLR 616 ......... 7.29, 7.32
Procter & Gamble Technical Centres Ltd v Brixton Plc [2003] 2 EGLR 24.............................................................................5.2, 5.7, 5.45, 5.46
Procter v Procter [2021] EWCA Civ 167...................................................................4.13
Prudential Assurance Co Ltd v Exel UK Ltd [2010] 1 P&CR 7 ...... 5.29, 5.41, 5.47, 13.25
Pugh v Duke of Leeds (1777) 2 Cowp 714 ...............................................................6.71
PW & Co v Milton Gate Investments Ltd [2004] Ch 142 ....................... 1.8, 14.10, 14.11
Pye v Stodday Land Ltd [2016] 4 WLR 168 .....................3.56, 3.59, 3.67, 3.68, 3.75, 3.76
Quartermaine v Selby (1889) 5 TLR 223 ................................................................ 8.2
Queen Elizabeth's Grammar School Blackburn Ltd v Banks Wilson [2002] PNLR 14 ..............................................................................................................17.7
Quesnel Forks Gold Mining Co Ltd v Ward [1920] AC 222...................................13.43
QuirkCo Investments Ltd v Aspray Transport Ltd [2012] L&TR 19 ..... 9.25, 9.27, 10.52, 10.53, 10.54, 10.55, 10.73, 10.74, 10.75, 10.76, 11.9, 11.45
R v Inhabitants of Horsley (1807) 8 East 405 ..........................................................4.68
R v Soneji [2006] 1 AC 340 .......................................................................................7.18
R (Bottomley) v The General Commissioners of Income Tax Pontefract Division [2009] EWHC 1708 (Admin) .............................................................13.3
R (Zaporozhchenko) v City of Westminster Magistrates' Court [2011] 1 WLR 994 ................................................................................................. 6.61, 6.62
R & A Millett (Shops) Ltd v Legal & General Assurance Society Ltd [1985] 1 EGLR 103...................... 16.30, 16.31, 16.32, 16.33, 16.34, 16.35
Rahman v Kenshire [1981] 2 EGLR 102 ......................................................... 16.7, 16.8
Reardon Smith Line Ltd v Yngvar Hansen-Tangen (trading as HE Hansen-Tangen) [1976] 1 WLR 989 ...................................................................................... 5.14, 5.29
Reda v Flag Ltd [2002] UKPC 38 ..............................................................................1.18
Rede v Farr (1817) 6 M&S 121 ................................................................................13.43
Reed Personnel Services Plc v American Express Ltd [1997] 1 EGLR 229 ......... 9.58, 9.59

Rees v Windsor-Clive [2021] 1 P&CR 12 ........ 12.12
Reichman v Beveridge [2007] Bus LR 412 ........ 1.9
Relvok v Dixon (1973) 25 P&CR 1 ........ 10.35
Rennie v Westbury Homes (Holdings) Ltd [2007] EWCA Civ 1401 ........ 5.2, 5.20, 5.30
Renshaw v Magnet Properties South East LLP [2008] 1 EGLR 42 ........ 3.59
Republic of India v India Steamship Co Ltd (No 2) [1998] AC 878 ........ 13.8
Republic of India v India Steamship Co Ltd (The Indian Endurance) [1996] 3 All ER 641 ........ 13.52
Rex v Braithwaite [1918] 2 KB 319 ........ 7.29
Richo International Ltd v Alfred C Toepfer International GmbH (The Bonde) [1991] 1 Lloyd's Rep 136 ........ 13.43
Rider v Ford [1923] 1 Ch 541 ........ 6.36
Right v Cuthell (1804) 5 East 491 ........ 4.54
Rightside Properties Ltd v Gray [1975] 1 Ch 72 ........ 6.55
Riverside Park Ltd v NHS Property Services Ltd [2017] L&TR 12 ........ 10.13, 10.15, 10.16, 10.27, 10.28
Roberts v JW Ward & Son (1981) 125 SJ 120 ........ 17.28
Robinson v Thames Mead Park Estate Ltd [1947] 1 Ch 334 ........ 9.40, 9.41
Roe d. Bamford v Hayley (1810) 12 East 464 ........ 3.9
Ropemaker Properties Ltd v Bella Italia Restaurants Ltd [2018] L&TR 32 ........ 5.2, 8.3, 9.25, 13.3, 13.21, 13.40, 13.66
Rose, [1949] Ch 78 ........ 3.61
Rose, [1952] Ch 499 ........ 3.61
Rothwell v Chemical & Insulating Co Ltd [2008] AC 281 ........ 9.26
Royal Bank of Canada v Secretary of State for Defence [2004] 1 P&CR 28 ........ 5.63, 10.11, 10.30, 10.31
Royal Life Insurance v Phillips (1991) 61 P&CR 182 ........ 5.20, 5.66
RP Howard Ltd v Woodman Matthews & Co [1983] BCLC 117 ........ 17.17, 17.18, 17.19, 17.20
Rugby Joint Water Board v Footitt [1973] AC 202 ........ 15.9, 15.14, 15.16
Ryan v Villarosa [2019] 1 WLR 515 ........ 3.46
S Franses Ltd v Cavendish Hotels (London) Ltd [2019] AC 249 ........ 12.4, 12.5, 12.6
Sackville UK Property Select II (GP) No 1 v Robertson Taylor Insurance Brokers Ltd [2018] L&TR 22 ........ 3.21, 3.46, 3.70, 3.71, 3.75, 4.53, 5.48, 5.49
Samarenko v Dawn Hill House Ltd [2013] Ch 36 ........ 6.75
Samuel Properties (Developments) Ltd v Hayek [1972] 1 WLR 1296 ........ 6.78, 16.3
Sandhar & Kang Ltd v Ijaz [2018] EWHC 3071 (Ch) ........ 4.21
Scandinavian Trading Tanker Co AB v Flota Petrolera Ecuatoriana (The Scaptrade) [1983] 2 AC 694 ........ 6.75
Schalit v Nadler [1933] 2 KB 79 ........ 3.56, 3.64
Schnabel v Allard [1967] 1 QB 627 ........ 6.45, 6.46, 6.47
Scholl Manufacturing Ltd v Clifton (Slim-Line) Ltd [1967] Ch 41 ........ 1.4, 18.5, 18.6, 18.7, 18.8, 18.9, 18.10
Scottish Mutual Assurance Society Ltd v British Telecommunications Plc (unreported, 18 March 1994) ........ 10.86
Scribes West Ltd v Relsa Anstalt (No 3) [2005] 1 WLR 1847 ........ 3.64, 3.68, 3.69

Secretary of State for Communities and Local Government v South Essex College of Further and Higher Education [2016] 7 WLUK 780 ................................10.25, 10.26
Secretary of State for Environment, Transport and Regions v Baylis (Gloucester) Ltd (Costs) (2000) 80 P&CR 324 ..........................................................................10.9
Secretary of State for Environment, Transport and Regions v Unicorn Consultancy Services Ltd & [2000] NPC 108................................17.21, 17.22, 17.23, 17.24, 17.29
Seward v Drew (1898) 67 LJ QB 322 ................................................................ 3.15, 3.56
Sheridan v Blaircourt Investments Ltd [1984] 1 EGLR 139.........................................5.66
Shiloh Spinners Ltd v Harding [1973] AC 691 ............................................................6.75
Shirlcar Properties Ltd v Heinitz (1983) 268 EG 362..................................................5.66
Shurbanova v Forex Capital Markets Ltd [2017] EWHC 2133 (QB) ..........................1.18
Shuter v Hersh [1922] 1 KB 438 ...............................................................................19.5
Sidebotham v Holland [1895] 1 QB 378 ......................................................... 6.41, 6.42
Sidney Bolsom Investment Trust Ltd v E Karmios & Co (London) Ltd [1956] 1 QB 529.......................................................................................................5.20
Siemens Hearing Instruments Ltd v Friends Life Ltd [2014] EWCA Civ 382, [2014] 2 P&CR 5 ................................ 1.12, 1.15, 5.2, 5.3, 5.5, 5.6, 9.25, 18.10, 22.1
Simons v Associated Furnishers Ltd [1931] 1 Ch 379.............................. 9.35, 9.36, 9.47
Sims v Dacorum DC [2014] UKSC 63 ......................................................................... 1.2
Sirhowy Investments Ltd v Henderson [2014] EWHC 3562 (Ch)........... 9.24, 9.50, 13.43
Siu Yin Kwan v Easter Insurance Co Ltd [1994] 2 AC 199 ........................................4.53
Smith v Express Dairy Ltd [1954] JPL 45 ...................................................................3.59
Smith v Kinsey [1936] 3 All ER 73 ........................................................ 3.48, 3.49, 3.50
Smith v Mather [1948] 2 KB 212...............................................................................8.28
Somerfield Stores Ltd v Spring (Sutton Coldfield) Ltd [2010] EWHC 2084 (Ch) ........12.7
Sopwith v Stutchberry (1985) 17 HLR 50 ................................................................10.41
Southport Old Links Ltd v Naylor [1985] 1 EGLR 66.................................18.15, 18.16
Southwark LB v Akhtar [2017] L&TR 36 ...................................................... 7.73, 7.74
Spectra Pty Ltd v Pindari Pty Ltd [1974] 2 NSWLR 617................................7.4, 7.5, 7.7
Speedwell Estates Ltd v Dalziel [2002] HLR 43 ......................................................... 5.2
Spencer v Taylor [2014] HLR 9...................................................................................19.18
Spencer's Case (1583) 5 Co Rep 16a .............................................................. 3.1, 3.11
Sprio v Glencrown Properties Ltd [1991] Ch 537.......................................................1.11
St Martin's Property Investments Ltd v CIB Properties Ltd [1999] L&TR 1 .......................................................16.36, 16.37, 16.38, 16.39, 16.40, 17.9
St Marylebone Property Co Ltd v Fairweather [1963] AC 510..................................14.8
Stait v Fenner [1912] 2 Ch 504 ........................................................... 3.15, 3.56, 3.57
Standard Life Investments Property Holdings Ltd v W & J Linney Ltd [2010] EWHC 480 (Ch), [2011] L&TR 9................... 1.14, 3.21, 5.56, 8.6, 8.7, 8.8, 8.9, 22.3
Stena Line Ltd v Merchant Navy Ratings Pension Fund Trustees [2010] EWHC 1805 (Ch), upheld on appeal [2011] EWCA Civ 543 ..............................13.8
Stephenson & Son v Orca Properties Ltd [1989] 2 EGLR 129 .....7.72, 16.16, 16.18, 16.20
Stevens, Re [1897] 1 Ch 422 .....................................................................................4.66
Stewart v Chapman [1951] 2 KB 792.........................................................................6.28
Stidolph v American School in London Educational Trust Ltd (1969) 20 P&CR 802 .........................................................................................................5.31

Stobart Group Ltd v Stobart [2019] EWCA Civ 1376 ....5.20
Stoczina Gdanska v Latvian Shipping Company [1998] 1 WLR 574....11.42
Stolt Loyalty, The [1993] 2 Lloyd's Rep 281 ....13.52
Stylo Shoes Ltd v Prices Tailors Ltd [1960] Ch 396.... 7.18, 7.29
Sugarman v Porter [2006] 2 P&CR 14 ....3.27
Sun Alliance and London Assurance Co Ltd v Hayman [1975] 1 WLR 177 .... 7.27, 7.41
Sunrose Ltd v Gould [1962] 1 WLR 20....5.14
Superstrike v Rodrigues [2013] 1 WLR 3848....19.31
Sutton v Norwich CC [2020] UKUT 90 (LC); appeal dismissed [2021]
1 WLR 1691 .... 5.1
Svenson v Payne (1945) 71 CLR 531....13.10
Swift (P&A) Investments v Combined English Stores Group Plc
[1989] AC 632.... 3.4, 3.15
Sykes v Midland Bank Executor Co [1971] 1 QB 113....17.7
System Floors Ltd v Ruralpride Ltd [1995] 1 EGLR 48 ....2.1, 3.77, 3.78, 3.79, 3.80
Taita Hotel Ltd v Spelman [1963] NZLR 206....4.38
Tanham v Nicholson (1872) LR 5 HL 561 .... 7.76, 7.77
TAQA Bratani Ltd v JZ Nippon Exploration and Production (UK) Ltd
[2020] EWHC 58 (Comm)....1.18
Tayleur v Wildin (1868) LR 3 Exch 303 ....13.60, 13.61, 13.62
Taylor Fashions Ltd v Liverpool Trustees Co Ltd [1982] 1 QB 133....13.10, 13.49, 22.8
Taylor v Diamond [2012] EWHC 2900 (Ch)....10.8
Taylor v Neate (1888) 39 ChD 538....4.64
TBAC Investments Ltd v Valmar Works Ltd [2015] EWHC 1213 (Ch) ....5.40
TCG Pubs Ltd v Master and Wardens or Governors of the Art or Mystery
of the Girdlers of London [2017] EWHC 772 (Ch) .... 13.2, 13.3
Teathers Ltd, Re [2013] 1 P&CR 11....10.87
Teoco UK Ltd v Aircom Jersey 4 Ltd [2018] EWCA Civ 23.... 6.3
Thompson v McCullough [1947] KB 447 ....3.58
Tillmanns Butcheries Pty Ltd v Australasian Meat Industry Employees'
Union (1979) 42 FLR 331 ....9.67
Tinkler v HMRC [2021] UKSC 39 ....13.8
Tinn v Hoffmann & Co (1873) 29 LT 217....7.20
Topfell Ltd v Galley Properties Ltd [1979] 1 WLR 446 ....10.9, 10.10
Torminster Properties Ltd v Green [1983] 1 WLR 676 ....11.16
Total Oil Great Britain Ltd v Thompson Garages (Biggin Hill) Ltd
[1972] 1 QB 318.... 1.9
Townsends Carriers Ltd v Pfizer Ltd (1977) 33
P&CR 361.... 4.47, 5.59, 7.37, 7.38, 7.39, 7.40, 7.41
Tradax Export SA v Dorada Compania Naviera SA (The Lutetian)
[1982] 2 Lloyd's Rep 140....13.52, 13.53
Trafford Housing Trust v Rubenstein [2013] UKUT 0581 (LC) ....7.73
Trafford MBC v Total Fitness (UK) Ltd [2003] 2 P&CR 2 .... 5.2, 5.37
Trane (UK) Ltd v Provident Mutual Life Assurance [1995] 1 EGLR 33.... 6.9, 6.10, 6.11
Triumph Controls – UK Ltd v Primus International Holding Co [2019]
EWHC 565 (TCC).... 6.3

Trocette Property Co Ltd v Greater London Council (1974) 28 P&CR 408 ............15.10
Trollope & Colls Ltd v North West Metropolitan Regional Hospital Board [1973] 1 WLR 601 ............11.7
Trow v Ind Coope (West Midlands) Ltd [1967] 2 QB 899............6.29, 6.30, 6.31, 6.40
Truegold International Ltd v Questrock Ltd [2010] EWHC 966 (Ch)............7.11, 7.12
Trustees of Henry Smith's Charity v Kyriakou (1990) 22 HLR 66............7.56, 7.58
Trustees of the Magdalen and Lasher Charity v Shelower (1968) 19 P&CR 389............12.10
Tseitline v Mikhelson [2015] EWHC 3065 (Comm)............7.22, 7.23, 7.24, 7.67
TSG Building Services Plc v South Anglia Housing Ltd [2013] EWHC 1151 (TCC)............1.18
Tulk v Moxhay (1848) 2 Ph 774............3.1
Turner v Walsh [1909] 2 KB 484............3.64
Turner v Wandsworth LBC (1995) 69 P&CR 433............12.6
UBS AG v Rose Capital Ventures Ltd [2018] EWHC 3137 (Ch)............1.18
UKI (Kingsway) Ltd v Westminster CC [2019] 1 WLR 104............5.1, 7.41, 7.42
Union Eagle Ltd v Golden Achievements Ltd [1997] AC 514............6.75, 6.76
United Dominions Trust (Commercial) Ltd v Eagle Aircraft Services Ltd [1968] 1 WLR 74............1.13, 5.6
United Scientific Holdings Ltd v Burnley BC [1978] AC 904............1.13, 6.4, 6.74, 6.78, 9.25, 16.2, 16.3, 16.8, 16.10, 16.13, 16.20
Valentines Properties Ltd v Huntco Corp Ltd [2001] UKPC 14............6.2
Van Haarlam v Kasner Charitable Trust (1992) 64 P&CR 214............7.55
Vanquish Properties (UK) LP v Brook Street (UK) Ltd [2016] L&TR 33............4.58, 4.59
Vaughan v Von Essen Hotels 5 Ltd [2006] EWHC 3586 (Ch)............7.7, 7.8, 7.19
Victory Place Management Co Ltd v Kuehn [2018] HLR 26............1.18
Viola's Indenture of Lease [1909] 1 Ch 244............4.7, 4.8, 4.9
Vodafone Ltd v Hanover Capital Ltd [2020] EW Misc 18 (CC)............18.20, 18.48
W J Alan & Co Ltd v El Nasr Export & Import Co Ltd [1972] 2 QB 189............13.4
Waaler v Hounslow LBC [2017] 1 WLR 2817............1.18
Walker v Hatton (1842) 10 M&W 249............13.62
Walsh v Lonsdale (1882) 21 Ch D 9............4.21
Walters v Whitelock (unreported) 19 August 1994............7.22
Wandsworth London BC v Attwell (1995) 27 HLR 536............7.45
Wang v IRC [1994] 1 WLR 1286............7.18
Warborough Investment Ltd v Central Midlands Estates Ltd [2007] L&TR 10............7.65
Weg Motors Ltd v Hales [1962] Ch 49............3.12, 3.13, 3.14, 3.79
Weinbergs Weatherproofs Ltd v Radcliffe Paper Mills Co Ltd [1958] Ch 437............18.4
West Country Cleaners (Falmouth) Ltd v Saly [1966] 1 WLR 1485............9.37, 9.38, 9.39, 9.43, 13.36
West Middlesex Golf Club Ltd v Ealing LBC (1994) 68 P&CR 461............10.83
Westway Homes Ltd v Moores (1992) 63 P&CR 480............5.66
Whelton Sinclair v Hyland [1992] 2 EGLR 158............6.32
Wigan BC v Scullindale Global Ltd [2021] EWHC 779 (Ch)............1.18, 6.36, 6.39, 9.84, 13.19, 13.46, 13.47
Wilbraham v Colclough [1952] 1 All ER 979............8.28

Wilkinson v Colley (1777) 5 Burrow 2694 ....................4.65
William Hill (Southern) Ltd v Govier [1984] 1 EGLR 121 ....................16.15
Willmott v Barber (1880) 15 Ch D 95 ....................13.9, 13.10
Wirrall BC v Smith (1982) 43 P&CR 312 ....................8.28
Wombwell Urban DC v Burke [1966] 2 QB 149 ....................20.32
Woolley v Clark (1822) 5 B&A 744 ....................4.66, 4.67, 8.27, 8.28
Woolwich Equitable Building Society v IRC [1993]
AC 70 ....................11.19, 11.21, 11.22, 11.23, 11.27, 11.30, 11.32
Wordsley Brewery v Halford (1903) 90 LT 89 ....................3.3, 4.20
WX Investments Ltd v Begg [2002] 1 WLR 2849 ....................7.70, 7.71
Yager v Fishman & Co [1944] 1 All ER 552 ....................17.14, 17.15, 17.16, 17.17
Yates Building Co Ltd v R J Pulleyn & Sons (York) Ltd [1976]
1 EGLR 157 (CA) ....................7.6, 7.7, 7.9
York v Casey [1998] 2 EGLR 25, (1999) 31 HLR 209 ....................5.31, 10.68
Young v Higgon (1840) 6 M&W 49 ....................6.28
Youngmin v Heath [1974]1 WLR 135 ....................4.68
Yukos Finance BV v Lynch [2017] EWHC 1812 (Comm) ....................7.24
Zarvos v Pradhan [2003] EWCA Civ 208 ....................12.6
Zoan v Rouamba [2000] 1 WLR 1509 ....................6.28, 6.40

# *Table of Statutes*

REFERENCES ARE TO PARAGRAPH NUMBERS


Acquisition of Land Act 1919 ........ 15.1
s 2 ........ 15.7
Acquisition of Land Act 1981 ........ 15.1
s 4(2) ........ 15.11
Acquisition of Land (Authorisation Procedure) Act 1946 ........ 15.1
Administration of Estates Act 1925
s 1 ........ 4.66, 8.27
s 3 ........ 4.66, 8.27
s 9 ........ 4.67, 4.68, 8.28
s 9(3) ........ 8.28
s 21 ........ 4.67
Agricultural Holdings Act 1923 ........ 20.26
s 25(1) ........ 19.44, 20.3, 20.4
s 50 ........ 20.15
Agricultural Holdings Act 1948 ........ 3.67, 20.5
s 23(1) ........ 6.79, 13.29, 20.6
s 24(1), (2) ........ 20.14
s 92 ........ 7.54
s 92(1) ........ 20.7
Agricultural Holdings Act 1986 ........ 3.67, 20.1, 20.2, 20.16, 20.31, 20.32
s 1(1), (2), (4) ........ 20.2
s 2(1) ........ 20.2
s 3(1) ........ 20.2
s 4 ........ 20.2
s 12 ........ 20.5
Pt III (ss 25–33) ........ 20.3
s 25(1) ........ 20.3, 20.4, 20.5, 20.6
s 25(2)(a)–(d) ........ 20.5
s 25(3) ........ 20.5
s 25(4) ........ 20.5
s 26 ........ 20.12, 20.13
s 26(1) ........ 20.10, 20.14
s 26(2) ........ 20.10
s 27(1), (2) ........ 20.13
s 27(3) ........ 20.12, 20.13
s 27(3)(a)–(f) ........ 20.12
s 27(4)–(6) ........ 20.13
Pt V (ss 60–78) ........ 20.15

s 60(1) ........ 20.15
s 78(1) ........ 20.15
s 84A ........ 20.5
s 93 ........ 20.7, 20.27
s 93(1) ........ 20.7, 20.27
s 93(2), (3) ........ 20.8
s 93(4) ........ 20.7
s 93(5) ........ 20.9
s 96(1) ........ 20.5, 20.15
s 96(2) ........ 20.5
s 98(1) ........ 20.2
s 98(2) ........ 20.5
Sch 3
Pt I ........ 20.14
Case A ........ 20.10
Case B ........ 12.11, 12.12, 20.10
Case C ........ 20.10
Case D ........ 20.10
Case E ........ 20.10
Case F ........ 20.10
Case G ........ 20.10
Case H ........ 20.10
Pt II
para 9 ........ 20.5
Sch 12
para 4 ........ 20.5
Agricultural Tenancies Act 1995 ........ 20.1, 20.16, 20.17
s 1(1)–(6) ........ 20.17
s 2 ........ 20.17
s 4 ........ 20.17
s 4(1) ........ 20.2
s 5 ........ 20.22
s 5(1) ........ 20.18, 20.23
s 5(2), (4) ........ 20.18
s 6 ........ 20.23
s 6(1) ........ 20.24, 20.25
s 6(2) ........ 20.25
s 6(3) ........ 20.24
s 7 ........ 20.20, 20.22
s 7(1) ........ 20.20
s 7(3) ........ 20.21
s 16(1) ........ 20.28
s 36 ........ 20.27
s 36(1) ........ 20.27
s 36(2)(c) ........ 20.27

s 36(3) ........ 20.27
s 38(1) ........ 20.28
Agriculture Act 1920
s 28........ 19.44
Agriculture Act 1947
s 109(1)........ 20.2
Allotments Act 1922........ 20.29, 20.31
s 1(1)(a) ........ 20.30
s 22(1) ........ 20.29
Allotments Act 1950........ 20.29
Apportionment Act 1870........ 10.46, 10.55
Commonhold and Leasehold Reform Act 2002
s 79(8) ........ 5.1
Communications Act 2003
s 106........ 12.32
s 106(1)........ 12.32
s 106(3)(a) ........ 12.35
Sch 3A........ 12.31
Companies Act 1985 ........ 3.1, 4.60
s 368........ 5.1
s 654(1)........ 8.24
Companies Act 2006 ........ 3.1, 4.60
s 44........ 4.21
s 1012(1) ........ 8.24
Compulsory Purchase Act 1965 ........ 15.1
s 1(3) ........ 15.3
s 7 ........ 15.6, 15.7
s 10........ 15.6
s 20........ 15.7, 15.14
Compulsory Purchase (Vesting Declarations) Act 1981........ 15.1, 15.12
Conveyancing Act 1881 ........ 3.1
s 10........ 3.64
s 11........ 3.1
Coronavirus Act 2020
s 81........ 19.1
Sch 29........ 19.1
para 1(1) ........ 19.1
County Courts Act 1984
s 38(1) ........ 4.65
Deregulation Act 2015
s 32........ 19.31
s 33........ 19.32, 19.38
s 33(1) ........ 19.33, 19.38
s 33(2) ........ 19.34, 19.37, 19.38
s 33(2)(a), (b) ........ 19.36

s 33(3) .......... 19.34
s 33(5) .......... 19.36
s 33(6) .......... 19.37
s 33(10) .......... 19.35
s 33(11) .......... 19.35
s 33(13) .......... 19.33, 19.35
s 34 .......... 19.32
s 34(1) .......... 19.38
s 34(2) .......... 19.38
s 34(4) .......... 19.38
s 34(5) .......... 19.38
s 34(6) .......... 19.38
s 34(7) .......... 19.38
s 34(8) .......... 19.38
s 35 .......... 19.18
s 38 .......... 19.39
s 39 .......... 19.39
s 40(7) .......... 19.33
s 41(1)–(3) .......... 19.32, 19.39
Digital Economy Act 2017
s 4 .......... 12.31
s 4(10) .......... 12.34
Sch 1 .......... 12.31
Sch 2 .......... 12.34
Sch 3
Pt 2 .......... 12.47
Distress for Rent Act 1737 .......... 14.7
s 18 .......... 14.5, 14.7
Grantees of Reversions Act 1540 .......... 3.1
Housing Act 1961
s 19 .......... 10.9
Housing Act 1988 .......... 19.2, 19.15
Pt I (ss 1–45) .......... 19.10
s 1(1) .......... 19.10
s 1(2) .......... 19.10
s 1(6) .......... 19.10
s 5 .......... 19.16
s 5(1) .......... 19.11, 19.18
s 5(1)(a), (b) .......... 19.12
s 5(1A) .......... 19.14
s 5(2) .......... 19.12, 19.20
s 5(3) .......... 19.13
s 5(4) .......... 19.12
s 6A .......... 19.11
s 7 .......... 19.11, 19.12
s 7(1), (3), (4), (6A), (7) .......... 19.14

s 18(1), (2) ........ 14.13
s 19A ........ 19.16, 19.22
s 21...... 11.3, 19.11, 19.17, 19.23, 19.27, 19.31, 19.32, 19.33, 19.34, 19.36, 19.37, 19.38
s 21(1) ........ 19.17, 19.19, 19.20, 19.21, 19.22, 19.23, 19.25, 19.39
s 21(1)(b) ........ 19.17, 19.26, 19.29
s 21(1A), (1B) ........ 19.17
s 21(2) ........ 19.17
s 21(4) ........ 19.18, 19.19, 19.20, 19.21, 19.22, 19.39
s 21(4)(a) ........ 19.18, 19.29
s 21(4)(b) ........ 19.21
s 21(4B) ........ 19.20
s 21(4C) ........ 19.20
s 21(4D) ........ 19.21
s 21(4E) ........ 19.21
s 21(4ZA) ........ 19.18
s 21(5) ........ 19.22
s 21(6) ........ 19.20
s 21(7) ........ 19.20, 19.41
s 21(8) ........ 19.19
s 21A ........ 19.39, 19.40
s 21A(1), (2) ........ 19.39
s 21B ........ 19.39, 19.41
s 21B(1) ........ 19.39
s 21B(3) ........ 19.39
s 21C(1) ........ 11.3
s 45(1) ........ 19.11
Sch 1 ........ 19.10
para 2(1)(b) ........ 19.10
Sch 2 ........ 19.14
ground 1–16 ........ 19.14
Sch 2A ........ 19.16

Housing Act 1996
s 178 ........ 19.38

Housing Act 2004
s 11 ........ 19.33
s 12 ........ 19.33
s 33(13) ........ 19.33
s 40(7) ........ 19.33
Pt VI Ch 4 (ss 212–215C) ........ 19.28
s 212(2) ........ 19.28
s 212(8) ........ 19.28
s 213 ........ 19.29
s 213(1) ........ 19.28
s 213(3) ........ 19.28, 19.29, 19.31
s 213(4) ........ 19.28
s 213(5) ........ 19.28, 19.31

s 213(6) ........ 19.28, 19.29, 19.31
s 213(6)(a) ........ 19.29, 19.31
s 213(7) ........ 19.28, 19.30
s 213(10) ........ 19.28
s 214 ........ 19.31
s 214(1) ........ 19.29
s 215(1) ........ 19.29
s 215(2) ........ 19.29
s 215(2A) ........ 19.29
s 215(3) ........ 19.30
s 215(5) ........ 19.29
s 215A ........ 19.31
s 215A(4) ........ 19.31
s 215B ........ 19.31
s 215C ........ 19.31
Sch 13A ........ 5.1
Human Rights Act 1998 ........ 1.2
s 3 ........ 15.1
Increase of Rent and Mortgage Interest (Restrictions) Act 1920 ........ 19.5
Insolvency Act 1986
s 144(1) ........ 4.63
s 145 ........ 4.63, 8.24
s 181(2) ........ 4.30
s 283(1) ........ 4.61
s 283(5) ........ 8.22
s 306(1) ........ 4.61, 8.22
s 436 ........ 4.61
Sch B1
para 43(6) ........ 8.23
para 52 ........ 4.62
para 67 ........ 4.62
para 68(1) ........ 4.62
Sch 4
para 7 ........ 4.63
Interpretation Act 1978
s 7 ........ 7.73, 7.74, 20.7
Land Charges Act 1972
s 2 ........ 2.4
Land Clauses Consolidation Act 1845 ........ 15.1
Land Compensation Act 1973 ........ 15.1
s 1 ........ 15.1
s 37 ........ 15.7, 15.17
s 47 ........ 15.14
Land Compensation Act 1961 ........ 15.1
s 1 ........ 15.3
s 5(2) ........ 15.6, 15.7

s 5(3) .......... 15.9
s 5(4) .......... 15.11
s 5(6) .......... 15.6
s 5A(3), (4) .......... 15.12
s 6A .......... 15.9
s 6B .......... 15.11
s 14 .......... 15.11
s 39(1) .......... 15.3
Land Registration Act 1925
s 19(2)(a) .......... 4.22
Land Registration Act 2002 .......... 3.72, 4.22
s 4(1)(c) .......... 2.5, 4.22, 4.23
s 4(1)(d) .......... 4.22, 4.23
s 4(1)(g) .......... 4.23
s 4(2) .......... 4.22
s 6(1) .......... 4.23
s 6(3) .......... 4.23
s 6(4) .......... 4.23
s 7(1) .......... 4.23
s 7(2)(b) .......... 4.23
s 23(1) .......... 3.74, 3.75
s 24 .......... 3.73, 3.75
s 24(b) .......... 3.75
s 27(1) .......... 3.72
s 27(2)(a) .......... 3.72
Landlord and Tenant Act 1730 .......... 14.7
s 1 .......... 14.5
Landlord and Tenant Act 1927
s 23 .......... 7.18, 7.73, 8.15
s 23(1) .......... 8.16, 8.17
s 23(2) .......... 8.15, 8.16, 8.17, 8.18
Landlord and Tenant Act 1954 .......... 4.40, 5.31, 12.6, 18.17, 18.42
Pt I (ss 1–22) .......... 5.55
Pt II (ss 23–46) .......... 6.57, 12.18, 12.42, 12.47, 15.16, 17.17, 17.19, 18.1, 18.4, 18.11, 18.12, 18.35, 18.40, 20.3
s 24 .......... 12.47, 18.4
s 24(1) .......... 18.3, 18.12
s 24(2) .......... 1.4, 5.3, 5.4, 5.5, 5.6, 9.25
s 25 .......... 5.32, 5.58, 5.61, 5.62, 18.4, 18.5, 18.7, 18.8, 18.10, 18.12, 18.13, 18.14, 18.15, 18.16, 18.29, 21.6
s 25(6) .......... 5.32
s 26 .......... 5.20, 18.11
s 26(2) .......... 1.4
s 29(3) .......... 6.57
s 30(1) .......... 12.10
s 30(1)(f) .......... 12.3, 12.4, 12.5, 12.7, 12.45, 18.36

s 30(1)(g) .......... 12.3, 12.7, 12.8
s 31(1)(f) .......... 12.26
s 32 .......... 18.17
s 33 .......... 18.17, 18.18, 18.20, 18.21, 18.22, 18.43
s 34 .......... 15.8, 18.17, 18.48
s 35 .......... 18.17, 18.20, 18.21, 18.22
s 35(1) .......... 18.19
s 37 .......... 21.6
s 38A .......... 12.42, 12.47
s 42 .......... 4.33
s 43(4) .......... 12.47
s 44 .......... 18.13
s 44(1) .......... 18.12
s 69 .......... 1.4
s 69(1) .......... 18.2, 20.3
Sch 6
para 1 .......... 18.12
Landlord and Tenant Act 1985
s 20 .......... 7.73
s 20B .......... 7.74
Landlord and Tenant Act 1988 .......... 4.40
s 1(3) .......... 5.1
Landlord and Tenant (Covenants) Act 1995 .......... 3.5, 3.16, 3.17, 3.21, 3.70, 3.71, 4.19, 5.45
s 3 .......... 3.21, 3.23
s 3(1) .......... 3.18
s 3(1)(a), (b) .......... 3.19
s 3(2) .......... 3.18
s 3(3) .......... 3.18
s 3(6) .......... 3.18, 3.19
ss 3–16 .......... 3.16
s 4(b) .......... 4.19
s 15(1) .......... 4.19
ss 17–20 .......... 3.16
s 28(1) .......... 3.20, 3.70, 3.80
s 28(5) .......... 4.19
Law of Property Act 1925 .......... 3.1, 3.22, 3.50
s 34(2) .......... 4.55
s 52 .......... 4.21
s 54(2) .......... 4.21
s 61 .......... 6.70
s 63 .......... 3.27, 3.28, 3.29, 3.44
s 63(1)–(3) .......... 3.26
s 84 .......... 6.8
s 101 .......... 19.38

s 139 .... 14.8
s 140 .... 3.49, 3.52
s 140(1) .... 3.47, 3.52
s 140(2) .... 3.47, 3.51, 3.52, 20.21, 20.24
s 141 .... 3.7, 3.8, 3.9
s 141(1) .... 3.63
s 141(2) .... 3.63, 3.64, 3.65, 3.66, 3.67, 3.68, 3.69
s 142 .... 3.7, 3.10, 3.11, 3.13, 3.14, 3.15, 3.23
s 142(1) .... 3.11, 3.79
s 149(6) .... 20.5, 20.21
s 196 .... 7.29, 7.30, 7.43, 7.44, 7.45, 7.48, 7.49, 7.50, 7.51, 7.55, 7.56, 7.58, 7.61, 7.62, 7.73, 7.74, 7.75
s 196(3) .... 7.49, 7.51, 7.53, 7.54, 7.55, 7.59, 7.60, 7.61, 7.63, 13.65
s 196(4) .... 7.49, 7.51, 7.68, 7.69, 7.70, 7.71, 7.72
s 196(5) .... 7.44, 7.45, 7.46, 7.47, 7.48
s 205(1)(ii) .... 3.27
s 205(1)(xiii) .... 4.21
Law of Property (Miscellaneous Provisions) Act 1989
s 1 .... 4.21
s 1(3) .... 4.21
s 2 .... 2.2, 13.42
Law of Property (Miscellaneous Provisions) Act 1994
s 17(1) .... 8.26
s 18(1) .... 8.30
Leasehold Reform Act 1967
s 14 .... 12.10
s 17(1) .... 12.10
Leasehold Reform, Housing and Urban Development Act 1993 .... 3.59, 12.19, 12.20
s 13 .... 5.1
s 40 .... 12.24
s 42 .... 12.19, 12.28
s 45 .... 12.28
s 47(1) .... 12.28
s 47(2) .... 12.28
s 47(2)(b) .... 12.29
s 56 .... 12.24
s 56(1) .... 12.19, 12.20
s 57(1) .... 12.20
s 57(6) .... 12.20
s 57(7)(b) .... 12.21, 12.23
s 61 .... 12.21, 12.22, 12.23, 12.26
s 61(1) .... 12.22, 12.26, 12.27, 12.28
s 61(2) .... 12.22, 12.25, 12.26
s 90(1) .... 12.24
Sch 14 .... 12.23, 12.27

Limited Partnerships Act 1907 .......... 4.57
s 4(2) .......... 4.57
s 6(1) .......... 4.57
s 7 .......... 4.57
s 8B(2) .......... 4.57
Limited Partnerships Act 2000 .......... 4.57
s 1(1), (2), (5) .......... 4.60
Local Government Finance Act 1988
Sch 4A .......... 5.1, 7.41
Local Government (Miscellaneous Provisions) Act 1976 .......... 15.1
Local Government, Planning and Land Act 1980 .......... 15.1
Partnership Act 1890 .......... 4.57
s 1(1) .......... 4.55
s 5 .......... 4.57
s 24(5) .......... 4.57
Party Wall etc Act 1996
s 15 .......... 5.1
Planning and Compensation Act 1991 .......... 15.1
Protection from Eviction Act 1977 .......... 19.2, 19.6
s 5 .......... 19.42, 19.44
s 5(1) .......... 6.79, 13.29, 19.43
s 5(1)(a), (b) .......... 19.44
Rent Act 1957 .......... 6.46, 6.47
s 16 .......... 6.45
Rent Act 1977 .......... 6.46, 6.47, 19.2, 19.4, 19.5
s 1 .......... 19.3
s 2(1) .......... 19.3
s 3(1) .......... 19.5
ss 4–16 .......... 19.3
s 24(3) .......... 19.3
s 98(1) .......... 19.7
s 98(2) .......... 19.8
s 137(3) .......... 14.13
Sch 15
Pt I (cases 1–10) .......... 19.9
Pt II (cases 11–20) .......... 19.9
case 19 .......... 7.57
Sale of goods Act 1893
s 30(3) .......... 11.43
Senior Courts Act 1981
s 37(1) .......... 4.65
s 113 .......... 4.69
Telecommunications Act 1984
Sch 2 .......... 12.32

Telecommunications Infrastructure (Leasehold Property) Act 2021
s 1 ........ 12.31
Town and Country Planning Act 1947
s 105 ........ 7.42
Town and Country Planning Act 1959 ........ 15.1
Town and Country Planning Act 1971
s 194(2)(b) ........ 12.7
Town and Country Planning Act 1990
s 151 ........ 12.7
Trustee Act 1925
s 34(2) ........ 4.55

# *Table of Statutory Instruments*

REFERENCES ARE TO PARAGRAPH NUMBERS


Agricultural Holdings (Arbitration on Notices) Order 1987, SI 1987/710
art 7 ....................................................................................................20.5
art 14 ....................................................................................................20.5
Assured Shorthold Tenancy Notices and Prescribed Requirements (England) Regulations 2015, SI 2015/1646..........................................................................
reg 2(1), (2) ....................................................................................................19.40
reg 3(2)–(6) ....................................................................................................19.41
Assured Tenancies (Amendment) (England) Order 2010, SI 2010/908
art 3 ....................................................................................................19.10
Assured Tenancies and Agricultural Occupancies (Forms) (England) Regulations 2015, SI 2015/620
reg 3(fa) ....................................................................................................19.19
Civil Procedure Rules 1998, SI 1998/3132
Pt 6....................................................................................................7.35
r 6.9(3) ....................................................................................................7.35
Pt 15
r 15.9 ....................................................................................................22.12
Electronic Communications Code (Jurisdiction) Regulations 2017, SI 2017/1284
reg 3 ....................................................................................................12.45
Electronic Communications Code (Transitional Provisions) Regulations 2017, SI 2017/1008 ....................................................................................................12.34
Energy Performance of Buildings (England and Wales) Regulations 2012
reg 6(5) ....................................................................................................19.40
Gas Safety (Installation and Use) Regulations 1998
reg 36(6), (7) ....................................................................................................19.40
Housing (Tenancy Deposits) (Prescribed Information) Order 2007 (SI 2007/797)
art 2 ....................................................................................................19.28
Insolvent Partnerships (Amendment) Order 2005, SI 2005/1516 ...............................4.62
Land Registration Rules 2003, SI 2003/1417
r 163....................................................................................................4.66
Limited Liability Partnerships (Amendment) Regulations 2005, SI 2005/1989............4.62
Limited Liability Partnerships (Application of Companies Act 2006) Regulations 2009, SI 2009/1804....................................................................................................4.60
Notices to Quit (Prescribed Information) Regulations 1988, SI 1988/2201.................19.6
Schedule ....................................................................................................19.43
Tribunal Procedure (First-tier Tribunal) (Property Chamber) Rules 2013, SI 2013/1169
r 6(3)(a) ....................................................................................................20.11
r 27(4)(b) ....................................................................................................20.11

# 1

# *The Nature of a Break Clause*

## A DEFINITION

1.1 A 'break clause' is a type of option entitling a landlord or tenant unilaterally to determine a fixed-term lease before the fixed term expires by effluxion of time. It has been described judicially as 'a right by written notice to terminate a lease on a date, usually called "the break date", where, in the absence of such notice, it would endure beyond the break date'.[1]

## A BREAK NOTICE IS NOT A NOTICE TO QUIT

1.2 A notice served pursuant to a break clause is sometimes referred to, in cases and elsewhere, as a notice to quit. However, it is not a notice to quit. Although a notice to quit is one form of unilateral mechanism for bringing a tenancy to an end, its use only applies where there is a periodic tenancy. A periodic tenancy involves a succession of 'periods' or 'terms', and only continues for so long as all the parties to it agree that it shall continue. It only takes one person (eg one of the landlords or one of the tenants) to object to the continuance to a periodic tenancy, to enable that tenancy to be brought to an end. Thus a notice to quit is valid even if served by only one of two or more joint tenants.[2]

1.3 In contrast to a notice to quit, a break notice seeks to determine the existing fixed term of a lease. Therefore a break notice has to be served by, or on behalf of, all of the parties in whom the interest is vested. Thus if the interest of the tenant is vested in more than one party all those parties must join in serving a break notice.

1.4 In this book we intend to refer to a notice served pursuant to a break clause as a break notice, and not a notice to quit.[3]

[1] *Norwich Union Life & Pensions v Linpac Mouldings Ltd* [2010] 1 P&CR 11, at [43], per Lewison J.

[2] *Hammersmith and Fulham London Borough Council v Monk* [1992] AC 478. The coming into force of the Human Rights Act 1998 has not altered the position: *Sims v Dacorum District Council* [2014] UKSC 63.

[3] However, it is worth noting that the expression 'notice to quit', which features both in ss 24(2) and 26(2) of the Landlord and Tenant Act 1954, is defined by s 69 of that Act as meaning 'a notice to terminate a tenancy (whether a periodical tenancy or a tenancy for a term of years certain) given in accordance with the provisions (whether express or implied) of that tenancy'. This statutory definition is apt to encompass a break notice. See *Scholl Mfg Co Ltd v Clifton (Slim-Line) Ltd* [1967] 1 Ch 41. Business tenancies are addressed in more detail in Chapter 18.

## THE RIGHT TO TERMINATE IS UNILATERAL

**1.5** Provided that the exercise of a break clause satisfies any and all contractually agreed pre-conditions, its effect will be to determine the fixed term of a lease. Thus whether the break notice is served by a landlord or a tenant, the recipient's consent is not needed in order for the break to be effective. Indeed, the recipient is often unwilling for a lease to be broken, hence the plethora of case law dealing with disputes over the exercise of break clauses.

**1.6** Even if the recipient of a break notice is happy to see a lease ended, and cooperates in a break, this does not constitute the surrender of the lease. Surrenders are consensual and do not involve the operation of an existing provision within a lease. This distinction was emphasised by Lord Millett in *Barrett v Morgan*.[4]

**1.7** One consequence of there being a surrender of a lease is that any sublease granted out of that lease survives the surrender. This is because 'it is a general and salutary principle of law that a person cannot be adversely affected by an agreement or arrangement to which he is not a party'.[5] However, the ending of the term of a lease by the operation of a break clause will automatically put an end to the term of any sublease created out of that lease. This position is deemed fair because the parties to the sublease could, by looking at the lease, have made themselves aware of any break clause within it.

**1.8** Since a valid break notice automatically ends the term of the sublease carved out of it, any attempt to preserve the sublease upon the exercise of a break clause will fail, irrespective of the language used.[6]

## FORFEITURE AND ACCEPTANCE OF REPUDIATORY BREACH DISTINGUISHED

**1.9** Where a landlord or tenant has committed a breach of a significant term of the lease amounting to a repudiation, the innocent party is faced with a choice between accepting that repudiation and thereby terminating the lease, or affirming the lease and thereby waiving the breach.[7] So, for example, a tenant was found to have accepted a repudiatory breach of the lease by the landlord in *Hussein v Mehlman*.[8] Similarly, in the case of a lease where the tenant commits a breach of covenant entitling the landlord to forfeit, the landlord must decide whether to forfeit the lease (whether by action or otherwise) or, for example, to accept rent and thereby waive the right to forfeit the lease for that breach.

[4] *Barrett v Morgan* [2000] 2 AC 264.

[5] *Barrett v Morgan* [2000] 2 AC 264, at 271D.

[6] *PW & Co v Milton Gate Investments Limited* [2004] Ch 142.

[7] In the past, doubts have been expressed as to whether the doctrine of repudiation is capable of applying to a lease. See eg *Total Oil Great Britain Ltd v Thompson Garages (Biggin Hill) Ltd* [1972] 1 QB 318, at 324, per Lord Denning MR. Notable also is the debate between Lord Millett and Neuberger J in the Blundell Lecture, 26 June 2000, where Lord Millett spoke for the proposition that the contractual doctrine of repudiatory breach of contract forms no part of the law of landlord and tenant. The position appears to have moved on since then, such that, in *Grange v Quinn* [2013] 1 P&CR 18, at [70], Jackson LJ was able to say: 'Although there were earlier indications to the contrary, it is now clear that a lease may be brought to an end by repudiation and acceptance …' See further *Chartered Trust Plc v Davies* (1998) 76 P&CR 396, *Nynehead Developments Ltd v RH Fibreboard Containers Ltd* [1999] 1 EGLR 7 and *Reichman v Beveridge* [2007] Bus LR 412.

[8] *Hussein v Mehlman* [1992] 2 EGLR 87.

1.10 The acceptance of a repudiatory breach of contract and the act of forfeiture are two methods by which a lease may be terminated unilaterally. They are distinct from the exercise of a break clause because the right to accept a repudiatory breach of contract and the right to forfeit have the effect of putting the innocent party to an election of the sort described by Lord Diplock in *Kammins Ballrooms Co Ltd v Zenith Investments (Torquay) Ltd*.[9] The right to terminate a lease by the exercise of a break clause is different. This was emphasised by Patten LJ in *BDW Trading Ltd (T/A Barratt North London) v JM Rowe (Investments) Ltd*, where he said:[10]

> The lease with a break clause entitling the landlord or tenant to terminate the lease after the end of part of the term does not have to be exercised immediately unless the lease so provides. In most cases it will remain exercisable at any time after the right has arisen. The continued acceptance of rent by the landlord will not, without more, operate as a waiver of his rights under the break clause because there is nothing inconsistent between the continuation of the landlord and tenant relationship and the reservation of the right to break. If it is exercisable at any time during the remainder of the term the landlord is not put to an election and does not make an election by continuing to perform the contract until he chooses to exercise his right to break.

## A BREAK CLAUSE IS A TYPE OF OPTION

1.11 In *Spiro v Glencrown Properties Ltd*, Hoffmann J (as he then was) described an option as follows:[11]

> An option is not strictly speaking either an offer or a conditional contract. It does not have all the incidents of the standard form of either of these concepts. To that extent it is a relationship sui generis. But there are ways in which it resembles each of them.

1.12 More recently, in *Siemens Hearing Instruments Ltd v Friends Life Ltd*, Lewison LJ explained:[12]

> In its classic form an option is a unilateral (or 'if') contract. The promisor agrees to do something (typically to sell something) if the promisee does or refrains from doing something. The promisee himself does not make any promise: it is up to him whether he does or refrains from doing whatever it is that triggers the promisor's obligation. That is why it is called an option.

1.13 Many of the detailed points discussed in this book arise as a consequence of a break clause being a type of option. This key point was explained by Lord Salmon in *United Scientific Holdings Limited v Burnley Borough Council*, where he said as follows:[13]

> Options to determine or to renew are not agreements to determine or renew. They are no more that irrevocable offers (kept open for good consideration) to do so providing the tenant complies with certain conditions usually before a certain date. If the tenant complies with the conditions in time, he thereby accepts the offer. The offer plus the acceptance constitutes a fresh agreement determining or renewing the lease as the case may be (see the *United Dominion Trust*

[9] *Kammins Ballrooms Co Ltd v Zenith Investments (Torquay) Ltd* [1971] AC 850, at 882.

[10] *BDW Trading Ltd (T/A Barratt North London) v JM Rowe (Investments) Ltd* [2011] EWCA Civ 548, at [78].

[11] *Sprio v Glencrown Properties Ltd* [1991] Ch 537, at 544.

[12] *Siemens Hearing Instruments Ltd v Friends Life Ltd* [2014] EWCA Civ 382, [2014] 2 P&CR 5, at [24].

[13] *United Scientific Holdings Limited v Burnley Borough Council* [1978] AC 904, at 951A.

case [1968] 1 WLR 74, Lord Denning MR at page 81). The same is true, *mutatis mutandis*, of an option to acquire the reversion. Neither equity nor the common law would ever intervene to make a contract for the parties. Anything which falls short of a complete acceptance of the offer is of no effect except sometimes as a counteroffer.

**1.14** There are two vital consequences of the above reasoning:

(1) *The rule of strict compliance.* All the indispensable requirements of a break clause must be strictly complied with. This is illustrated by Lord Hoffmann's well-known example in *Mannai Investment Co Ltd v Eagle Star Life Assurance Co Ltd*, where he said: 'If the clause had said that the notice had to be on blue paper, it would have been no good serving a notice on pink paper, however clear it might have been that the tenant wanted to terminate the lease'.[14] Thus, the court may be expected to enforce strict compliance with the provisions of a break clause and not to be deflected by submissions that to do so is unfair. As Lewison J has explained:[15]

> ... one part of fairness is that contractual stipulations are complied with. The exercise of a break clause has important consequences for both landlord and tenant and there are powerful policy considerations for certainty in this area of the law.

(2) *The rule of inflexibility.* Just as the courts will not make a contract for the parties, they will not unmake it. Therefore if all the requirements of a break clause have been satisfied, the courts will determine that the lease is 'broken'. There is no scope for equity to intervene or grant 'relief' against the loss of a lease (unlike the law of relief against forfeiture of a lease).

**1.15** The fact that a break clause is a type of option was emphasised by Lewison LJ in *Siemens Hearing Instruments Ltd v Friends Life Ltd*.[16] That case contains a detailed and scholarly analysis of the authorities concerned with options and option notices, the 'clear moral' of which is encapsulated in the following concluding remarks:[17]

> if you want to avoid expensive litigation, and the possible loss of a valuable right to break, you must pay close attention to all the requirements of the clause, including the formal requirements, and follow them precisely.

## THE APPLICABILITY OF *BRAGANZA* RESTRICTIONS ON THE EXERCISE OF A BREAK CLAUSE

**1.16** Where a contract confers a decision-making power on one party, the law imposes certain restrictions on the manner in which the power may be exercised. In *Braganza v BP Shipping Ltd*,[18] Baroness Hale explained:

> [18] Contractual terms in which one party to the contract is given the power to exercise a discretion ... are extremely common. It is not for the courts to rewrite the parties' bargain for them,

[14] *Mannai Investment Co Ltd v Eagle Star Life Assurance Co Ltd* [1997] AC 749, at 776B. This example was cited by Sir Stanley Burnton in *Newbold v Coal Authority* [2014] 1 WLR 1288, at [70].

[15] *Standard Life Investments Property Holdings Limited v W & J Linney Limited* [2010] EWHC 480 (Ch), [2011] L&TR 9, at [25].

[16] *Siemens Hearing Instruments Ltd v Friends Life Ltd* [2014] EWCA Civ 382, [2014] 2 P&CR 5.

[17] *Siemens Hearing Instruments Ltd v Friends Life Ltd* [2014] EWCA Civ 382, [2014] 2 P&CR 5, at [66].

[18] *Braganza v BP Shipping Ltd* [2015] 1 WLR 1661.

still less to substitute themselves for the contractually agreed decision-maker. Nevertheless, the party who is charged with making decisions which affect the rights of both parties to the contract has a clear conflict of interest. That conflict is heightened where there is a significant imbalance of power between the contracting parties as there often will be in an employment contract. The courts have therefore sought to ensure that such contractual powers are not abused. They have done so by implying a term as to the manner in which such powers may be exercised, a term which may vary according to the terms of the contract and the context in which the decision-making power is given.

**1.17** Depending upon the terms and the context of the contract involved, the implied term identified by Baroness Hale requires the decision-making process to be 'lawful and rational in the public law sense, that the decision is made rationally (as well as in good faith) and consistently with its contractual purpose'.[19] The content of this implied term engages not only the decision-making process (ie whether the right matters have been taken into account) but also the outcome of that process (ie where, even though the right things have been taken into account, the result is so outrageous that no reasonable decision-maker could have reached it).

**1.18** Importantly, however, there is a distinction to be drawn between contractual discretionary powers (which are subject to a *Braganza* duty)[20] and 'a simple decision whether or not to exercise an absolute contractual right'[21] (which is not).[22] The exercise of an option falls into the latter category.[23] In consequence, it is inappropriate to imply a *Braganza* duty so as to fetter the right of a landlord or tenant to exercise a break right. Indeed, in a series of cases going back a number of years, the courts have consistently held that unqualified termination provisions take effect in accordance with their terms and are not subject to any kind of implied restraint.[24]

[19] *Braganza v BP Shipping Ltd* [2015] 1 WLR 1661, at [30].

[20] In the landlord and tenant context, see eg *Waaler v Hounslow LBC* [2017] 1 WLR 2817, at [23], per Lewison LJ (decision to carry out improvements); *Victory Place Management Co Ltd v Kuehn* [2018] HLR 26, at [33], per Vos C (decision to refuse consent to keep a pet in the property); *Hicks v 89 Holland Park (Management) Ltd* [2019] EWHC 1301 (Ch), at [53]–[56], per HHJ Pelling QC (decision to refuse consent to plans, drawings or specifications) (reversed on appeal at [2020] EWCA Civ 758, but not on this point); *Criterion Buildings Ltd v McKinsey & Company Inc (United Kingdom)* [2021] EWHC 216 (Ch), at [45], per HHJ Paul Matthews (sitting as a judge of the High Court) (decision to apportion service charges between tenants).

[21] *Mid Essex Hospital Services NHS Trust v Compass Group UK and Ireland Ltd* [2013] BLR 265, at [83], per Jackson LJ.

[22] See eg *Shurbanova v Forex Capital Markets Ltd* [2017] EWHC 2133 (QB), at [93], per HHJ Waksman QC (sitting as a judge of the High Court) (contractual power to revoke trades by a customer on an online foreign exchange and commodities facility); *UBS AG v Rose Capital Ventures Ltd* [2018] EWHC 3137 (Ch), at [56], per Chief Master Marsh (lender's power to call in a loan secured by a mortgage); *Morley v Royal Bank of Scotland* [2020] EWHC 88 (Ch), at [160], per Kerr J (also concerning a lender's power to call in a loan); *Kwik Lets Ltd v Khaira* [2020] EWHC 616 (QB), at [66], per Tipples J DBE (contractual power entitling one party to a settlement agreement to suspend payments to the other).

[23] As illustrated by *Cathay Pacific Airways Ltd v Lufthansa Technik AG* [2020] EWHC 1789 (Ch), at [150]–[183], per Mr John Kimbell QC (sitting as a deputy judge of the High Court) (concerning the exercise of an option contained in a long-term aircraft engine maintenance contract to remove engines from a fleet of aircraft). See also *Wigan Borough Council v Scullindale Global Ltd* [2021] EWHC 779 (Ch), at [74], per HHJ Hodge QC (sitting as a judge of the High Court) ('… The right to serve a Break Notice conferred by clause 9.2 of the Lease does not depend upon the Council having any particular intention or justification beyond Scullindale's failure to achieve the second Milestone. If that is established, then prima facie the right to terminate the Lease is exercisable without more …').

[24] *Reda v Flag Ltd* [2002] UKPC 38, at [42], per Lord Millett (contractual right to terminate a contract of employment); *Lomas v IFB Firth Rixon* [2012] EWCA Civ 419, at [46], per Longmore LJ (right to terminate an

## BREAK CLAUSES CAN APPEAR IN ALL TYPES OF TENANCIES AND IN MANY DIFFERENT FORMS

**1.19** A break clause will comprise part of the bargain between the parties. Therefore, in principle, it can take any form that the parties choose. Also break clauses can feature in all types of lease: commercial, residential, agricultural or anything other.

**1.20** Although the parties are the arbiters of the language used in any lease, standard clauses (appearing in practitioners' textbooks, or in solicitors' standard precedents) mean that there are various concepts or phrases which are commonly encountered in practice. This book seeks to consider various forms of break clause, and how they should be approached.

ISDA Master Agreement); *TSG Building Services Plc v South Anglia Housing Ltd* [2013] EWHC 1151 (TCC), at [51], per Akenhead J (contract for the provision of gas servicing works terminable by either party for no, good or bad reason); *Monk v Largo Foods Ltd* [2016] EWHC 1837 (Ch), at [54], per Mr David Foxton QC (sitting as a deputy judge of the High Court) (termination of consultancy agreement); *TAQA Bratani Ltd v JZ Nippon Exploration and Production (UK) Ltd* [2020] EWHC 58 (Comm), at [49], per HHJ Pelling QC (sitting as a judge of the High Court) (concerning a right of termination in a joint venture agreement).

# 2

# *Formalities and Registration*

## FORMALITIES

2.1 A break clause typically appears in a lease. However there is nothing, in principle, from preventing a break clause from existing in a separate document, either entered into at the same time as the lease (as a side letter or agreement) or subsequently (as a variation of the lease). Provided that the side letter, agreement or variation is supported by consideration then it should be valid. So, for example, there was a break clause (expressed as a landlord's agreement to accept a surrender) in a side letter in *System Floors Limited v Ruralpride Limited.*[1] Although the letter was a not in the form of a deed, there was no challenge to its validity.

2.2 However the courts may approach alleged side or collateral agreements with circumspection. Thus, in *Business Environment Bow Lane Limited v Deanwater Estates Limited*, the Chancellor stated:[2]

> In a normal conveyancing transaction in a commercial context with both parties represented by experienced solicitors the usual course of dealing is to ensure that all agreed terms are put into the contract and conveyance, transfer or lease. Accordingly those who assert a collateral contract in relation to a term not so contained must show that it was intended to have contractual effect separate from the normal conveyancing document. Otherwise it will be invalidated by Section 2 Law of Property (Miscellaneous Provisions) Act 1989 even if evidence as to its existence is admitted.

In other words, the more formally the break clause is documented the better.

2.3 If the contractual term of the lease is for longer than a three-year period then the existence of a clause permitting termination prior to the expiry of three years will not obviate the obligation for the lease to be by deed.[3]

## REGISTRATION

2.4 A break clause is not a land charge and does not have to be protected by registration in order to bind successors in title.[4]

[1] *System Floors Limited v Ruralpride Limited* [1995] 1 EGLR 48.
[2] *Business Environment Bow Lane Ltd v Deanwater Estates Ltd* [2007] L&TR 26, at 43.
[3] *Kushner v Law Society* [1952] 1 KB 264.
[4] Section 2 of the Land Charges Act 1972.

**2.5** The grant of a lease 'for a term of years absolute of more than seven years from the date of the grant' must be registered at the Land Registry.[5] The Land Registry will normally record the existence of a break clause that appears in a lease on the register. Transfers of unregistered leases, with more than seven years unexpired at the date of the disposition, must also be registered.

**2.6** Assuming that a registered lease has been successfully 'broken' it will be appropriate to close the leasehold title. Any record of the 'broken' lease should also be removed from a superior registered title.

[5] Section 4(1)(c) of the Land Registration Act 2002.

# 3

# *Assignment*

## THE HISTORICAL POSITION

3.1 Prior to the sixteenth century, a lease of land was regarded in law as no more than a personal contract, giving rise to no proprietary rights or obligations. However, in the sixteenth century, it was established that on the transfer of the reversion or of the leasehold interest, the benefit and burden of those covenants in the lease which 'touched and concerned' the land demised by the lease passed to, and were enforceable by and against, successors in title of the original parties. So far as transfers of the reversion were concerned, this change in the law was first brought about by the Grantees of Reversions Act 1540 (the salient provisions of which were later carried forward into the Conveyancing Act 1881 and the Law of Property Act 1925).[1] As regards transfers of the leasehold interest, the change was effected at common law by *Spencer's Case*.[2] As Lord Templeman explained in *City of London Corporation v Fell*:[3]

> At common law, after an assignment, the benefit of a covenant by the original landlord which touches and concerns the land runs with the term granted by the lease. The burden of a covenant by the original tenant which touches and concerns the land also runs with the term: see *Spencer's Case* (1583) 5 Co Rep 16a.

Lord Templeman went on:

> The principle that the benefit and burden of covenants in a lease which touch and concern the land run with the term and with the reversion is necessary for the effective operation of the law of landlord and tenant. Common law, and statute following the common law, recognise two forms of legal estate in land, a fee simple absolute in possession and a term of years absolute ... Common law, and statute following the common law, were faced with the problem of rendering effective the obligations under a lease which might endure for a period of 999 years or more beyond the control of any covenantor. The solution was to annex to the term and the reversion the benefit and burden of covenants which touch and concern the land. The covenants having been annexed, every legal owner of the term granted by the lease and every legal owner of the

[1] In those Acts, the equivalent expression to 'touch and concern' is 'has reference to the subject matter of the lease'. However, the expressions in substance and effect mean the same thing. In *Barnes v City of London Real Property Co* [1918] 2 Ch 18, at 33, Sargant J explained (in relation to s 11 of the Conveyancing Act 1881): '[That provision] enacts that the obligation of a covenant entered into by a lessor with reference to "the subject-matter of the lease" shall bind the reversionary interest. Was this an obligation with reference to the subject-matter of the lease? I do not think the law was intended to be altered at all by that enactment as regards the character of the obligation. I think the words of the statute expressed the same idea as that conveyed by the old phrase "touching the land" ...'.

[2] *Spencer's Case* (1583) 5 Co Rep 16a.

[3] *City of London Corporation v Fell* [1994] 1 AC 458, at 464–65.

reversion from time to time holds his estate with the benefit of and subject to the covenants which touch and concern the land. The system of leasehold tenure requires that the obligations in the lease shall be enforceable throughout the term, whether those obligations are affirmative or negative. The owner of a reversion must be able to enforce the positive covenants to pay rent and keep in repair against an assignee who in turn must be able to enforce any positive covenants entered into by the original landlord. Common law retained the ancient rule that the burden of a covenant does not run with the land of the covenantor except in the case of a lease, but even that rule was radically modified by equity so far as negative covenants were concerned: see *Tulk v Moxhay* (1848) 2 Ph 774.

3.2 Thus, the effect of common law on a lease is to create proprietary rights and obligations which are independent of the rights and obligations personal to the original covenantor. Common law achieves that effect by annexing the personal rights and obligations so far as they touch and concern the land to the term and to the reversion. Nourse LJ summarised the position in *City of London Corporation v Fell*, when he said[4] 'The contractual obligations which touch and concern the land having become imprinted on the estate, the tenancy is capable of existence as a species of property independently of the contract'.

3.3 The right of a landlord or a tenant to bring a tenancy to an end by notice is an incident of the relationship of landlord and tenant. This is the common law position in relation to notices to quit in respect of a periodic tenancy: see for example *Wordsley Brewery v Halford* (notice to quit invalid when served by the original lessor who had, prior to the service of the notice, granted a concurrent lease).[5] In the same way, the benefit and burden of a break clause in a lease will, on an assignment, ordinarily pass with the reversion or the term, as 'touching and concerning' the respective estates of the landlord and the tenant and as conditions of the enjoyment of those estates.[6]

3.4 Over time, there has been criticism of the 'touch and concern' test, the rules of which have long been said to be arbitrary.[7] Be that as it may, the common law position relating to the passing of the benefit and burden of landlord and tenant covenants on an assignment has now been substantially modified by various statutory provisions, as shall be detailed in the following paragraphs.

## TENANCIES GRANTED BEFORE 1 JANUARY 1996

3.5 A detailed discussion of the law on the enforceability of landlord and tenant covenants is outside the scope of this work.[8] However, there is a fundamental distinction between leases granted before 1 January 1996 and those granted on or after 1 January 1996. For leases granted on or after 1 January 1996, the principles applicable

[4] *City of London Corporation v Fell* [1993] QB 589, at 604.

[5] *Wordsley Brewery v Halford* (1903) 90 LT 89.

[6] *Linpac Mouldings Ltd v Aviva Life and Pensions UK Ltd* [2010] EWCA Civ 395, at [44], per Etherton LJ.

[7] See for example: *Grant v Edmondson* [1931] 1 Ch 1, at 28, per Romer LJ; and *Swift (P&A) Investments v Combined English Stores Group Plc* [1989] AC 632, at 640, per Lord Oliver.

[8] For a comprehensive review of the law, the reader may refer to TM Fancourt QC *Enforceability of Landlord and Tenant Covenants* (Sweet & Maxwell, 3rd edn).

to the transmissibility of leasehold covenants are governed by the Landlord and Tenant (Covenants) Act 1995 (on which see **3.16** below). For leases granted before 1 January 1996, the principles are governed by a mix of common law rules and statute.

3.6 This section considers the transmissibility of the benefit and burden of break options in pre-1996 leases.

### (a) Where the Landlord Transfers the Reversion

3.7 In relation to tenancies granted before 1 January 1996, the position on a transfer of the reversion is governed by ss 141 and 142 of the Law of Property Act 1925 (the '1925 Act').

3.8 As regards the benefit of a break clause, s 141 of the 1925 Act provides:

> (1) Rent reserved by a lease, and the benefit of every covenant or provision therein contained, having reference to the subject-matter thereof, and on the lessee's part to be observed or performed, and every condition of re-entry and other condition therein contained, shall be annexed and incident to and shall go with the reversionary estate in the land, or in any part thereof, immediately expectant on the term granted by the lease, notwithstanding severance of that reversionary estate, and without prejudice to any liability affecting a covenantor or his estate.

3.9 The language of s 141 plainly applies to the benefit of a break clause (unless the break clause is expressed to be purely personal in nature), since such a clause is a covenant or provision which has 'reference to the subject-matter' of the lease[9] or is otherwise a 'condition of re-entry'. In other words, subject to any term to the contrary effect in the deed of transfer,[10] the benefit of a break clause shall be 'annexed and incident to, and shall go with the reversionary estate in the land, or in any part thereof, immediately expectant on the term granted by the lease'.

3.10 As regards the burden of a break clause, s 142 of the 1925 Act provides as follows:

> (1) The obligation under a condition or of a covenant entered into by a lessor with reference to the subject-matter of the lease shall, if and as far as the lessor has power to bind the reversionary estate immediately expectant on the term granted by the lease, be annexed and incident to and shall go with that reversionary estate, or the several parts thereof, notwithstanding severance of that reversionary estate, and may be taken advantage of and enforced by the person in whom the term is from time to time vested by conveyance, devolution in law, or otherwise …

3.11 As may be apparent, s 142 is concerned with (inter alia) an 'obligation under a condition … entered into by a lessor with reference to the subject matter of a lease'.

[9] In this regard, it is to be noted that a break clause is a right annexed to the reversion (and the term) at common law. See *Roe d. Bamford v Hayley* (1810) 12 East 464, at 469, per Lord Ellenborough CJ. ('A covenant by a lessor that he would renew at the end of his term has been adjudged to run with the land and to bind the grantee of the reversion; and there is no substantial difference, in point of construction, between a stipulation for extending the term, and a stipulation for shortening it.').

[10] *Inland Revenue Commissioners v John Lewis Properties Plc* [2002] 1 WLR 35, at [12], per Lightman J (upheld on appeal at [2003] Ch 513).

In *Harbour Estates Ltd v HSBC Bank Plc*, it appears to have been assumed (without argument) that the burden of a break clause constituted just such an 'obligation under a condition' so that it would pass on an assignment of the reversion without an express transfer.[11] It is respectfully submitted that such an assumption is correct. It has been established law since *Spencer's Case*[12] that the burden of an option to renew a tenancy runs with the reversion.[13] There is no reason in principle why the burden of a break option should be treated any differently.

3.12 Indeed, the view expressed in *Harbour Estates* may be seen as consistent with the decision in *Weg Motors Limited v Hales*.[14] The facts of that case were relatively complicated. However, in essence the freeholder, GR Investments Ltd, on 26 July 1938, demised certain premises in St John's Wood, London, to Weg Motors Ltd for a term of 21 years; and, by a separate document, conferred on Weg Motors Ltd the option of taking a further lease of 21 years upon giving notice in writing at any time before 25 December 1959 and subject to certain other conditions being satisfied. In those circumstances, the grantor of the option was obliged 'to grant … a further lease of the said premises …' GR Investments Ltd was subsequently dissolved and the freehold title devolved on the trustees of the Royal Liver Friendly Society (who were the first three named defendants). By notice dated 30 April 1959, Weg Motors Ltd sought to exercise its option for renewal of the lease. The defendants were not prepared to agree to the grant of a new lease. Therefore, Weg Motors Ltd issued a writ claiming specific performance of the option. Its case succeeded both before Danckwerts J and the Court of Appeal.

3.13 At trial Danckwerts J found that the lease and the option agreement were part of a single transaction. On this finding, he proceeded to hold that GR Investments Ltd had been under an obligation or had covenanted to grant a new lease on the exercise of the option by Weg Motors Ltd; and that, if necessary so to decide, such an obligation or covenant ran with the reversion expectant on the lease within the meaning of s 142 of the 1925 Act. The Court of Appeal agreed. As Donovan LJ said:[15] 'If it be necessary that the agreement should qualify as a covenant within section 142, I think it does so, notwithstanding that it is contained in a separate document.'

3.14 Of course, *Weg Motors* concerned an option to renew, as opposed to an option to determine, a lease. Given the language used in the instrument in question, it is perhaps unsurprising that the judge at first instance and the Court of Appeal considered that the option agreement contained an obligation or covenant within the scope of s 142.

### (b) Where the Tenant Assigns the Term

3.15 As mentioned at 3.3 above, the right to terminate a lease is incident to the lease. Therefore, just as under s 142 of the 1925 Act the burden of a break clause will pass to the

[11] *Harbour Estates Ltd v HSBC Bank Plc* [2005] Ch 194, at 202G, 212E.
[12] *Spencer's Case* (1583) 5 Co Rep 16a.
[13] *Isteed v Stoneley* (1580) 1 And 82. See also *Muller v Trafford* [1901] 1 Ch 54, at 60, per Farwell J.
[14] *Weg Motors Ltd v Hales* [1962] Ch 49.
[15] *Weg Motors Ltd v Hales* [1962] Ch 49, at 76–77.

transferee of the reversion, the benefit of a break clause will also pass to the assignee of the term. The converse is also true.[16] However, this is not the case where the break option is purely personal to a specific tenant.[17]

## TENANCIES GRANTED ON OR AFTER 1 JANUARY 1996

**3.16** The Landlord and Tenant (Covenants) Act 1995 ('the 1995 Act') came into force on 1 January 1996. It created two classes of tenancy for the purposes of the law of enforceability of landlord and tenant covenants as between the original parties to a lease and/or their successors in title. Subject to certain limited exceptions, the classes of tenancy comprise: (i) 'new tenancies' (ie those granted on or after 1 January 1996); and (ii) 'other tenancies' (ie those granted before 1 January 1996). 'New tenancies' are governed by the statutory code for the enforceability of landlord and tenant covenants contained in ss 3–16 and 21 of the 1995 Act. Sections 17–20 of the 1995 Act apply to 'new' and to 'other' tenancies.

### (a) 'New' Tenancies

**3.17** As mentioned in **3.16** above, the 1995 Act came into force on 1 January 1996 and, with certain limited exceptions, applies in relation to leases granted on or after that date.

**3.18** Insofar as is relevant, s 3 of the 1995 Act provides as follows:

> (1) The benefit and burden of all landlord and tenant covenants of a tenancy –
>
> (a) shall be annexed and incident to the whole, and to each and every part, of the premises demised by the tenancy and of the reversion in them, and
>
> (b) shall in accordance with this section pass on an assignment of the whole or any part of those premises or of the reversion in them.
>
> (2) Where the assignment is by the tenant under the tenancy, then as from the assignment the assignee –
>
> (a) becomes bound by the tenant covenants of the tenancy …
>
> (b) becomes entitled to the benefit of the landlord covenants of the tenancy except to the extent that they fall to be complied with in relation to any such premises.
>
> (3) Where the assignment is by the landlord under the tenancy, then as from the assignment the assignee –
>
> (a) becomes bound by the landlord covenants of the tenancy …

[16] See *Seward v Drew* (1898) 67 LJ QB 322 and *Stait v Fenner* [1912] 2 Ch 504. The position was expressed clearly in *Norwich Union Life and Pensions Ltd v Linpac Mouldings Ltd* [2010] 1 P&CR 11, at [43], where Lewison J said: 'The break clause is an expression used to describe a right by written notice to terminate a lease on a date (usually called the break date) where in the absence of such a notice, it would endure beyond the break date. Such a right is a right that is incident to the lease or reversion, as the case may be, and in the ordinary way, passes to an assignee. In the ordinary way, the purpose of a tenant's break clause is to enable the tenant in possession to bring the relationship of landlord and tenant to an end. Again, in the ordinary way, the person entitled to exercise the right is the person in whom the legal estate is vested.'

[17] *Swift (P&A) Investments v Combined English Stores Group Plc* [1989] AC 632, at 642, per Lord Oliver.

(b) becomes entitled to the benefit of the tenant covenants of the tenancy except to the extent that they fall to be complied with in relation to any such premises.

…

(6) Nothing in this section shall operate –

(a) in the case of a covenant which (in whatever terms) is expressed to be personal to any person, to make the covenant enforceable by or (as the case may be) against any other person …

**3.19** The broad effect of this provision is that the benefit of all 'landlord covenants' and the burden of all 'tenant covenants' are annexed and incident to the whole, and each and every part of the demised premises. Likewise, the benefit of all 'tenant covenants' and the burden of all 'landlord covenants' are annexed and incident to the reversion, and each and every part thereof.[18] The benefit and burden of all landlord and tenant covenants pass on an assignment of the whole or any part of the demised premises or the reversion.[19] The exception to this general rule is in the case of a covenant which is expressed to be personal to any person.[20]

**3.20** The 1995 Act defines 'landlord covenant' as, in relation to a tenancy, a covenant falling to be complied with by the landlord of premises demised by the tenancy. A 'tenant covenant' means, in relation to a tenancy, a covenant falling to be complied with by the tenant of premises demised by the tenancy. A 'covenant' is itself defined as including a term, condition and obligation.[21]

**3.21** In the previous edition of this work, it was pointed out that, because a break clause confers merely a unilateral right to determine the lease, it was questionable whether such a clause could properly be described as a 'covenant' (as defined) 'falling to be complied with' by either the landlord or the tenant for the purposes of the 1995 Act.[22] However, the position has now been clarified in *Sackville UK Property Select II (GP) No 1 v Robertson Taylor Insurance Brokers Ltd*,[23] where Fancourt J explained that: 'The obligation of the Landlord, which is a "landlord covenant" for the purposes of the Act, is the obligation to treat the lease as terminated with effect from the specified date *if* a valid notice is served' (emphasis in original).[24] In other words, for the purposes of the 1995 Act, a tenant's break option is or includes a 'landlord covenant' and (conversely) a landlord's break option is or includes a 'tenant covenant' capable of transmission in accordance with the provisions of the 1995 Act.

[18] Section 3(1)(a).
[19] Section 3(1)(b).
[20] Section 3(6).
[21] Section 28(1).
[22] Indeed, there was then no reported authority of which the authors were aware which addressed the question whether a break clause is apt to be described as a 'landlord covenant' or a 'tenant covenant' (as defined), such that the benefit or burden of the same passes under s 3 of 1995 Act (subject to the exception referred to above); although Lewison J appears to have proceeded on this assumption in *Standard Life Investments Property Holdings Ltd v W&J Linney Ltd* [2011] L&TR 9, at [21].
[23] *Sackville UK Property Select II (GP) No 1 v Robertson Taylor Insurance Brokers Ltd* [2018] L&TR 22, at [33], per Fancourt J.
[24] Although, on this analysis, the 'covenant' does not 'fall to be complied with' unless and until the break option is validly exercised. Therefore, it might be said that, pending that contingency arising, the break option is not a 'covenant' at all.

### (b) 'Other' Tenancies

**3.22** The enforceability of obligations in 'other tenancies', as between the original parties and/or their successors in title, remains governed by the mix of common law principles and the provisions contained in the 1925 Act as described in **3.5** above.

## FORMALITIES FOR ASSIGNMENT

**3.23** As already explained,[25] by operation of s 142 of the 1925 Act or s 3 of the 1995 Act, the benefit of a break option will pass automatically upon an assignment of a lease or a transfer of the reversion. Thus, there is no need for a separate assignment of the break option.[26]

**3.24** It should be recalled that the assignor of the term or the reversion is not obliged to assign the benefit of a break clause upon the assignment. He may, if he so wishes, retain (or purport to retain) the benefit for himself; although it is highly doubtful that the break clause could ever then be exercised.[27]

**3.25** The purpose of this section is to consider other modes of assignment.

### (a) Section 63 of the Law of Property Act 1925

**3.26** Section 63 of the 1925 Act provides as follows:

> (1) Every conveyance is effectual to pass all the estate, right, title, interest, claim, and demand which the conveying parties respectively have, in, to, or on the property conveyed, or expressed or intended so to be, or which they respectively have power to convey in, to, or on the same.
> (2) This section applies only if and as far as a contrary intention is not expressed in the conveyance, and has effect subject to the terms of the conveyance and to the provisions therein contained.
> (3) This section applies to conveyances made after the thirty-first day of December, eighteen hundred and eighty-one.

**3.27** This provision is a statutory 'all estate' clause the effect of which is that, unless a contrary intention appears, a conveyance will automatically pass the whole estate, title and interest which the vendor has in to, or on the property conveyed, without the need for express mention. Under s 205(1)(ii) of the 1925 Act, a 'conveyance' includes a mortgage, charge, lease, assent, vesting declaration, vesting instrument, disclaimer, release and every

[25] See **3.10**.

[26] That said, as a matter of best practice a practitioner acting for an assignee of the term or the reversion who wishes to take the benefit of a break clause (assuming the benefit is assignable) should include appropriate express provision in the contract of assignment. In the absence of any express mention of the option to determine in the assignment of the lease, it may be necessary to decide whether the language of the documentation can be construed as extending to the option. See for example *Denham Bros Ltd v W Freestone Leasing Pty Ltd* [2003] QCA 376 (concerning whether the words 'all the rights title and interest of the lessor under the said lease including the option' were sufficient to transfer the benefit of an option to renew).

[27] See the discussion at **4.40–4.41** below.

other assurance of property or of an interest therein by any instrument, except a will. As was said by Lindsay J in *Harbour Estates Ltd v HSBC Bank Plc*:[28]

> [The object of Section 63] was to avoid the litany of express mentions of ancillaries and sweepings up which, in order to ensure that everything passed that could pass with the conveyance, had become the standard language of conveyancers. That standard language was, by statute, instead to be read into every conveyance (including a written assignment of a lease) unless a contrary intention was expressed in the conveyance … [Focusing] … on the words 'the property conveyed', one looks to see what, in terms of estates and interests, was the main corpus intended to be transferred, and then, in the absence of an express contrary intention, one may give full literal effect to the words of the section.

**3.28** There are, of course, limits to the effect of s 63. As Lindsay J went on to say:[29] 'But there has to be the required nexus between "the property conveyed" and the right, claim or demand in issue; an entirely personal right would not pass as it would not be "in, to or on" the property conveyed.'

**3.29** Thus, save where a contrary intention appears (eg where the break clause is expressed to be purely personal to a specified tenant), upon an assignment, the effect of s 63 of the 1925 Act will be for the benefit of an option to determine the lease to pass automatically upon assignment of the term or the reversion.

### (b) The Principle in Griffith v Pelton

**3.30** *Griffith v Pelton*[30] concerned a lease containing an option for the lessee to purchase the fee simple of the demised premises. The lessee was described in the lease as including 'her executors, administrators and assigns'. By an assignment dated 3 August 1948, the original tenant (Miss Blaker) assigned to the plaintiff the residue of the term. The assignment contained no reference to the option. The question arose whether an assignment of the term had carried with it the benefit of the option. The Court of Appeal held that it had. Jenkins LJ, giving the judgment of the court, said:[31]

> The first of the two questions stated above therefore seems to us to come down to the narrow issue whether the assignment of August 3, 1948, being on the face of it a mere assignment of the term, without any reference to the benefit of the option, operated, in view of the terms of the proviso, or, in other words, the contract, creating the option, as an assignment of the benefit of the option; or whether an express reference to the benefit of the option in the assignment of the term was necessary to produce that result. We think that upon the true construction of the proviso, including the definition to be read into it of the term lessee as including the lessee's assigns, the original parties to the lease must be taken to have agreed that the option should be exercisable by Miss Blaker herself or by any assignee of the term to whom she might assign the benefit of the option, and that a mere assignment of the term should operate as an assignment of the benefit of the option to the assignee of the term.

[28] *Harbour Estates Ltd v HSBC Bank Plc* [2005] Ch 194, at 208D (cited with approval by Peter Smith J in *Sugarman v Porter* [2006] 2P&CR 14, at [40]).

[29] *Harbour Estates Ltd v HSBC Bank Plc* [2005] Ch 194, at 208G.

[30] *Griffith v Pelton* [1958] Ch 205.

[31] *Griffith v Pelton* [1958] Ch 205, at 227–28.

3.31 Therefore, the Court of Appeal held that the benefit of an option passed with the term granted by a lease notwithstanding the fact that it was not mentioned in the assignment.

3.32 In *Denham Bros Ltd v W Freestone Leasing P/L*,[32] McMurdo P considered that *Griffith v Pelton* presented some 'particular conceptual difficulties'. This was because: 'It is one thing to say that the parties to the original lease could reach agreement as to the assignability of the benefit of a particular covenant, but quite another to say that they could also agree to effect the assignment on the happening of a specified event, the assignment of the term'. Indeed, rather than looking first to the terms of the lease to determine assignability, and then to the terms in which the lease was assigned in order to determine whether the benefit of the option had passed with it, in *Griffith v Pelton* 'the court managed to deduce assignability and assignment from the original lease'. To put it another way, the decision in *Griffith v Pelton* appears to elide the question whether the benefit of an option is *assignable* with the question whether it was *assigned*.

3.33 Nonetheless, *Griffith v Pelton* remains good law in this jurisdiction and has since been followed.[33] Therefore, depending on the 'true construction of the proviso' (to adopt the language of Jenkins LJ), it is likely to be the case that the benefit of a break option will be assigned together with a transfer of the reversion or the term.[34]

## RESTRICTIONS ON ASSIGNABILITY

3.34 On a true construction of the instrument in question, it may be that the break clause is expressed to be purely personal to a specified landlord or tenant, or assignable only to a limited class of people. Thus, the break clause may refer to 'the tenant, here meaning X only' or it may only be assignable to 'the tenant, or a permitted assignee, being a group company in the X group of companies'. This section considers wording which might restrict the assignability of the benefit of a break option.

### (a) Purely Personal Break Clauses

3.35 An example of a purely personal break clause is to be found in *Gemini Press Limited v Parsons*.[35] In that case, the landlord (a Miss Parsons) had demised premises in

[32] *Denham Bros Ltd v W Freestone Leasing P/L* [2003] QCA 376, at [75].

[33] See eg *Coastplace Ltd v Hartley* [1987] QB 948. In that case, the defendants as sureties had covenanted with the lessors and their successors that the lessees would pay the rents under a lease. The lessors assigned the reversion to the plaintiffs without expressly assigning the benefit of the surety covenant. French J decided that what he identified as the principle in *Griffith v Pelton* applied and concluded, at 961: '... the original parties to the covenant must be taken to have agreed that the covenant of surety should be enforceable by the landlord or by the persons for the time being entitled to the reversion immediately expectant upon the determination of the term; and that the mere transfer of the reversion should operate as an assignment of the benefit of the covenant'.

[34] *Cf Harbour Estates Ltd v HSBC Bank Plc* [2005] Ch 194, at 202F, where Lindsay J considered that *Griffith v Pelton* was of no assistance in determining whether there had been an assignment of the benefit of a break clause because it was contemplated by the parties that the benefit of the break clause might not pass with the lease.

[35] *Gemini Press Limited v Parsons* [2012] EWHC 1608 (QB).

Horsham to Sussex Press Limited for a term of 20 years from a date in September 1995. By a deed dated 8 February 2002, licence was given to Sussex Press Limited to assign the lease to Ashdown Company UK Limited ('Ashdown'). The deed also effected a variation of the lease by the insertion of a break clause worded as follows:

> If Ashdown Co UK Limited shall be desirous of terminating the term herby granted and shall give to the landlord notice in accordance with sub-clause 6.6(b), then providing that the rent hereby reserved has been paid and Ashdown Co UK Limited has substantially observed and performed the covenants on the lessee's part herein contained, then at the expiration of such notice this lease shall absolutely cease and determine.

**3.36** In 2005, Ashdown assigned the lease to Gemini Press Limited ('Gemini'). By two notices in February and March 2009, Gemini purported to terminate the lease on the September quarter day under the terms of the break clause. Miss Parsons challenged the validity of the notice on the basis that the break clause was personal to Ashdown. Miss Parsons succeeded at trial. Gemini appealed.

**3.37** Dismissing the appeal, Cooke J said:[36]

> [11] ... the language of the parties in relation to the break clause is deliberately different from that which appears elsewhere in the deed of variation. Elsewhere the expressions 'tenant' and 'assignee' have been used, but in relation to this particular clause there is reference only to the Ashdown Company. In my judgment, it is clear, as it was to the Judge, that the language used was designed to express the intention that the right was to be limited to the entity concerned and was not to be a right which was capable of assignment with the lease to further assignees.
>
> [12] In those circumstances, in my judgment, this appeal cannot succeed. The break provision expressly referred to Ashdown and, on a proper construction of the original lease, the deed of variation and the licences to assign, there is only one possible conclusion, which is that the break clause was personal only and did not give rise to the possibility of assignment, allowing the appellant to exercise the right as it purported to do in due course.

**3.38** Generally speaking, however, the court may be slow to infer that the benefit of a break clause is purely personal in the absence of clear words. See, for example, *Re 120 Packington Street, Islington* (assignee of the reversion entitled to exercise break clause even though 'lessee' was defined to include persons claiming under him and there was no corresponding definition of 'lessor').[37]

**3.39** As stated above, the benefit of a purely personal break clause (ie one in favour of a specific landlord or tenant only) will not pass on an assignment of the reversion or the term, either at common law or under statute. In this scenario difficult questions arise as to what happens if the lease is then re-assigned back to the original landlord or tenant.[38] These questions are considered in Chapter 4.

[36] *Gemini Press Limited v Parsons* [2012] EWHC 1608 (QB), at [11]–[12].

[37] *Re 120 Packington Street, Islington* (1960) 110 SJ 672.

[38] *Max Factor Limited v Wesleyan Assurance Society* (1997) 74 P&CR 8; *Equinox Industrial (GP2) Limited v Sketchley Limited* [2003] EWHC 2 (Ch); *Linpac Mouldings Limited v Aviva Life and Pensions UK Limited* [2010] L&TR 10.

### (b) 'Hybrid' Break Clauses

**3.40** In the case of a break clause which is assignable only to a limited class of people, it may be that the break clause is, nonetheless, sufficiently impersonal that it will pass under the statutory provisions referred to above. An interesting example of this is to be found in *Harbour Estates Ltd v HSBC Bank Plc*.[39] That case concerned a lease (technically, an underlease) dated 13 January 1994, made between Midland Bank Plc ('Midland') as landlord and Stafford Properties Ltd (a subsidiary of Midland) as tenant. The lease contained what was described as a 'hybrid' break clause, ie one which was neither wholly personal nor such as invariably passed with the term. It was worded as follows:

> 6. The tenant may determine this lease on 23 June 1999, 23 June 2004 or 23 June 2009 by serving on the landlord not less than six months written notice of its desire to terminate the term on such date ...
>
> ...
>
> 6.5 The benefit of this clause 6 is personal to Stafford Properties Ltd and shall not be capable of assignment to or be exercise [sic] by any other person provided that the benefit of this clause 6 may be assigned to an assignee of this lease pursuant to paragraph 11 of the sixth schedule ("a permitted assignee") where the permitted assignee is a group company ...

**3.41** On 8 December 1999, the reversion immediately expectant upon the determination of the lease became vested in Royal Bank of Canada Trust Co (Jersey) Limited ('RBC'). On the same date, RBC gave licence to Stafford Properties Limited licence to assign the lease to Midland, which by then, had been re-named HSBC Bank Plc ('HSBC'). Clause 3 of the assignment simply provided as follows: 'In consideration of the performance and observance of the covenants by the buyer contained in this assignment the seller assigns to the buyer the property to hold to the buyer for the unexpired residue of the term subject to the performance of the covenants.'

**3.42** On 14 November 2003, HSBC sent to its then landlord, Harbour Estates Limited, a notice of determination purporting to terminate the lease on 23 June 2004. The landlord indicated that the validity of the break notice was not accepted. Therefore, on 8 March 2004, the landlord commenced proceedings for (inter alia) a declaration that HSBC was not entitled to bring the lease to an end as at 23 June 2004.

**3.43** At trial, there was no dispute that HSBC was a 'group company' as defined in the sixth schedule to the lease, and that, as such, in accordance with clause 6.5, the benefit of the break clause was capable of being assigned to it. However, the landlord contended that, whilst the benefit of the break clause was capable of being assigned, it was not in fact assigned prior to the last date upon which six months' notice could have been given so as to have exercised the break clause as at 23 June 2004. The landlord's argument was premised on the basis that the break clause did not 'touch and concern' the land; and that, there being no automatic transfer of the benefit under the 'touches and concerns' doctrine, there was no express or implied mention in the assignment of the benefit of the

[39] *Harbour Estates Ltd v HSBC Bank Plc* [2005] Ch 194.

break clause being included. Thus (the argument ran) the tenant did not have the benefit of the break clause when it served the break notice.

**3.44** Lindsay J rejected the landlord's arguments and held that the tenant was entitled to terminate the lease by operation of the break clause. Having referred to, and considered the limitations of the scope of, s 63 of the 1925 Act (see above), he said as follows (with emphasis in the original):[40]

> It is the unusual hybridity of the break clause which gives rise to difficulty in assigning it to one category or another; it is plainly not wholly personal and the arguments I have just described, on balance, enable me, in my judgment, to regard it as 'touching and concerning', or as having reference to the subject matter of, the lease. Its benefit, even if I am correct in limiting section 63's apparently broad language as I have done, thus passed with the term on the assignment, even though it was not mentioned, as it was a right 'in, to or on the property conveyed' *and* touched and concerned the land.

### (c) Definition of 'Landlord' and 'Tenant'

**3.45** A lease commonly defines 'landlord' and 'tenant' so as to include 'executors, administrators and assigns' or 'successors in title' or 'persons deriving title under him'. Sometimes, a question arises as to whether the person serving a break notice falls within the scope of the definition in question.

**3.46** Although each case will turn on the proper construction of the particular lease in question, it is thought that, in this context, the reference to an 'assign' or 'successor in title' or 'person deriving title' is not apt to include an equitable assignee or someone other than person in whom the legal interest in reversion (in the case of a landlord transferee) or legal term of years (in the case of a tenant assignee) is vested.[41] The position of equitable assignees is discussed further at **3.56** below.

## SEVERANCE OF THE REVERSION

**3.47** Insofar as is relevant, s 140 of the 1925 Act provides as follows:

> (1) Notwithstanding the severance by conveyance, surrender, or otherwise of the reversionary estate in any land comprised in a lease, and notwithstanding the avoidance or cesser in any other manner of the term granted by a lease as to part only of the land comprised therein, every condition or right of re-entry, and every other condition contained in the lease, shall be apportioned, and shall remain annexed to the severed parts of the reversionary estate as severed, and

[40] *Harbour Estates Ltd v HSBC Bank Plc* [2005] Ch 194, at 213G–213H.

[41] *Re Adams and Kensington Vestry* (1884) 27 Ch D 394, at 402, per Cotton LJ; *Friary Holroyd and Healey's Breweries Ltd v Singleton* [1899] 1 Ch 86, at 90, per Romer J (unaffected by the reversal of the decision on the facts at [1899] 2 Ch 261); *Griffith v Pelton* [1958] Ch 205, at 227, per Jenkins LJ; *Sackville UK Property Select II (GP) No 1 Ltd v Robertson* [2018] L&TR 22, at [34], per Fancourt J; *Ryan v Villarosa* [2019] 1 WLR 515, at [62], per Morgan J.

> shall be in force with respect to the term whereon each severed part is reversionary, or the term in the part of the land as to which the term has not been surrendered, or has not been avoided or has not otherwise ceased, in like manner as if the land comprised in each severed part, or the land as to which the term remains subsisting, as the case may be, had alone originally been comprised in the lease.
>
> (2) In this section 'right of re-entry' includes a right to determine the lease by notice to quit or otherwise; but where the notice is served by a person entitled to a severed part of the reversion so that it extends to part only of the land demised, the lessee may within one month determine the lease in regard to the rest of the land by giving to the owner of the reversionary estate therein a counter notice expiring at the same time as the original notice.

**3.48** The effect of this provision is that, where a landlord grants part of his reversion to an assignee, all covenants, all conditions and rights of re-entry are apportioned on the severance of the reversion and are annexed to the severed parts thereof. This means that, so far as the benefit of a landlord's break clause is concerned, both reversioners will be able to determine the lease of the part of the reversion with which they are interested. This is well-illustrated by *Smith v Kinsey*.[42] In that case, a Mr White owned five cottages with their gardens. On his death, his executors sold the five cottages and gardens together, except for one garden plot, which was sold separately to the plaintiff. The defendant was at the time of the sale the tenant of one of the cottages and of this plot. On 27 September 1933, the plaintiff served a notice to quit on the defendant seeking to terminate her tenancy of the plot on 25 March 1934 'or at the end of your tenancy, which will expire next after the end of 6 months after the date of the service of this notice'. The defendant did not comply with the notice. The plaintiff brought proceedings for possession. The plaintiff was unsuccessful at trial on the basis that the owner of one part of a severed reversion could not give a valid notice of re-entry. The plaintiff appealed.

**3.49** The Court of Appeal unanimously allowed the appeal. Giving the lead judgment, Lord Wright MR referred to s 140 of the 1925 Act and said:[43]

> I think that the effect of that section is in the present case to render this a good notice. There has been a severance by conveyance; every condition or right of re-entry appertaining to the land was apportioned; and the right of re-entry, which included the right to determine the tenancy by notice to quit, has remained, annexed to the severed part of the reversionary estate – that is to say, in this case to the small garden plot. In those circumstances I see no ground for holding that the plaintiff was not within his rights in claiming to recover possession of this piece of land.

**3.50** Romer LJ agreed, saying as follows:[44] '… since the coming into operation of the Law of Property Act, 1925, the assignee of part of a reversion can serve a proper notice to quit in respect of the part of the land assigned to him'.

**3.51** It will be observed that s 140(2) of the 1925 Act gives the tenant of a split reversion the statutory right, within one month of the service of a reversioner's notice to quit,

[42] *Smith v Kinsey* [1936] 3 All ER 73.
[43] *Smith v Kinsey* [1936] 3 All ER 73, at 76.
[44] *Smith v Kinsey* [1936] 3 All ER 73, at 77.

to elect to end the lease of the rest of the land by giving to the owner of that other part a counter-notice expiring at the same time as the first notice.

**3.52** In *Jelley v Buckman*, it was emphasised by the Court of Appeal that severance of the reversion does not operate to replace the existing lease by two separate leases.[45] In this regard, Stamp LJ said:[46]

> Now it is no doubt correct that the effect of the legislation is that each reversioner has rights and remedies similar to those which he would have had if he had granted a separate tenancy of the land in respect of which he is owner. But it is one thing to say that each reversioner has rights and remedies similar to or even indistinguishable from the rights and remedies which he would have had if there had been two separate tenancies and quite another thing to say that this operates against the tenant and that he therefore has two tenancies; and we cannot read section 140 as producing the latter result. We can find nothing in the section to suggest for a moment that the legislature intended that following a severance to which the lessee was not a party he should find himself holding part of his land under one tenancy and part under another. In relation to a lease for years as opposed to a weekly tenancy the change in the law would be dramatic and had the legislature intended to create that result one would expect to find some clear expression of that intention. Not only is there an absence of such an expression of intention but we find in this section positive indications that what was assumed or contemplated was the continued existence of the pre-existing lease. We refer in this connection first to subsection (1) speaking as it does of 'the term' – not 'the respective terms' – 'whereon each severed part is reversionary' and subsection (2) speaking of the right to determine 'the lease', emphasising the definite article preceding 'lease'.

**3.53** Therefore, where the landlord has severed the reversion, and the tenant has the benefit of a break clause, the break notice should be served on both reversioners. This is because the burden of the tenant's break clause will be apportioned, and shall remain annexed to the severed parts of the reversionary estate as severed.

## ASSIGNMENT OF PART OF THE DEMISE

**3.54** In *Kaiser Engineers & Constructors Inc v E R Squibb & Sons Ltd.*[47] Russell LJ (as he then was) said: 'It is common ground that for [a break notice to be effective] it must on its true construction be a determination of the whole relationship of landlord and tenant under [the] lease.'

**3.55** This reflects the common law position that a notice to quit referring to part only of the demise is invalid and ineffective.[48] Thus, where a break clause refers to the whole of the demised premises, and the tenant assigns part of those premises, neither the original tenant nor the assignee will be able to exercise the option to determine (unless, perhaps, they can jointly exercise the break).

[45] *Jelley v Buckman* [1975] QB 488.
[46] *Jelley v Buckman* [1975] QB 488, at 497–98.
[47] *Kaiser Engineers & Constructors Inc v E R Squibb & Sons Ltd* (unreported, 12 November 1971).
[48] *Re Bebington's Tenancy* [1921] 1 Ch 559.

THE POSITION OF EQUITABLE ASSIGNEES

## (a) The Position at Common Law

3.56 At common law, it is only the legal assignee of the term or the reversion who can exercise a break clause.[49] This common law rule is illustrated by a number of cases as follows.

3.57 *Stait v Fenner*[50] concerned a lease which contained a tenant's break option. In 1899, the tenant (Dr Fenner) with the written licence of the landlord, by deed assigned the term of the lease to Miss Court. In 1902, Miss Court (also with the landlord's licence) assigned the lease to Mrs Irvine. Mrs Irvine fell into arrears. In due course, Mrs Irvine 'handed over' to Dr Fenner the lease and the two assignments but did not re-assign the term back to him. In turn, Dr Fenner (with the licence of the landlord) by deed 'assigned' the premises to Mr Macnab. Mr Macnab gave notice to the landlord to determine the lease. The landlord contended that the notice was ineffectual to terminate the lease because it was not given by the person in whom the leasehold estate was vested. Neville J agreed. He said:[51]

> As a matter of fact, no assignment from Mrs Irvine was ever obtained, and beyond question the term is now legally vested in her ... The question, therefore, as to whether this notice was effectual I answer in the negative. In my opinion, the legal estate in the term being outstanding, it was not competent for the lessee or any assignee of the lessee who had not the legal estate vested in him to give a notice.

3.58 In *Thompson v McCullough*,[52] Mr McCullough was the tenant of a house. The freehold was owned by Mr Kirkbride. Mr McCullough sub-let the house to Mr Thompson. On 1 April 1946, Mr Thompson agreed with Mr Kirkbride to buy the house and paid a deposit. On 10 April, he made a further payment of £29. On 12 April, he gave a notice to quit to Mr McCullough. On 21 June, he paid the balance of the purchase price. At first instance, the county court judge found that the deed conveying the freehold of the house from Mr Kirkbride to Mr Thompson was delivered as an escrow, and that it could not, on completion of the payment of the purchase price on 21 June, validate the

[49] *Seaward v Drew* (1898) 67 LJ QB 322 (concerning the purported exercise of a break clause by an equitable chargee of the term); *Stait v Fenner* [1912] 2 Ch 504, at 512, per Neville J ('... the legal estate in the term being outstanding, it was not competent for the lessee or any assignee of the lessee who had not the legal estate vested in him to give a notice [to quit] ...'); *Farrow v Orttewell* [1933] 1 Ch 480, at 491, per Lord Hanworth ('... Inasmuch as Mr Orttewell had not, by October 9, completed the purchase of these farms he was then only the owner in equity and not the legal owner of the farm, and the learned judge has held that he had no right at that time to issue a notice to quit to the tenant. From that decision there is no appeal to this Court ...'); *Freeman v Hambrook* [1947] VLR 70, at 75, per O'Bryan J ('... in the absence of a relationship of landlord and tenant by estoppel, or of agency ... it is for the legal owner of the lease (or I should think for the like reason, the legal owner of the reversion) to give a notice to quit ...'); *Pye v Stodday Land Ltd* [2016] 4 WLR 168, at [9], per Norris J ('... To be valid at common law the notice to quit must be given by the person entitled to the landlord's reversionary estate ...'). *Cf Schalit v Nadler* [1933] 2 KB 79 (beneficial owner of a lease has no legal right to distrain from rent against sub-tenant).

[50] *Stait v Fenner* [1912] 2 Ch 504.

[51] *Stait v Fenner* [1912] 2 Ch 504, at 511–12.

[52] *Thompson v McCullough* [1947] KB 447.

notice to quit given on 12 April which was invalid because the legal estate in the house had not then passed. In dismissing Mr Thompson's appeal, the Court of Appeal proceeded on the basis that the notice given on 12 April was an invalidity; and that the satisfaction of the condition of escrow could not retrospectively make it valid. Morton LJ said:[53]

> The second contention for the landlord is that … the delivery of the conveyance relates back so as to make his notice to quit of April 12 effective. Apart from authority, that would seem to me a very startling proposition. It involves that a man can effectively as landlord give a notice to a tenant at a time when it is quite uncertain whether he, the giver of the notice, will ever be the landlord in fact. On April 12 it was quite uncertain whether the present landlord would ever pay the balance of the purchase money. In fact, he did not pay it until long after the notice to quit had expired. For relation back to have such an effect as that would render the position of a tenant quite intolerable.

**3.59** In *Smith v Express Dairy*,[54] the defendant company let a shop to the plaintiff which subsequently assigned the reversion to a subsidiary. There came a point where the subsidiary company served a notice to quit on the plaintiff at a time when the transfer of the reversion had not been registered. The tenant took the point that the notice to quit was bad because it was not served by his landlord. This point was upheld by Harman J, who held that, as the transfer of the property had not been registered, the legal estate remained in the defendant. Therefore, unless the subsidiary company had given the notice to quit as the agent of the defendant, or could be inferred to have given it as agent, the notice to quit was bad. In view of the evidence that the subsidiary company had dealt with the property as owners in the description of the property in the notice to quit, there was no room for an inference of agency and the notice accordingly was invalid.

**3.60** The opposite outcome was arrived at in *Brown & Root Technology Ltd v Sun Alliance and London Assurance Co Ltd*.[55] There, Sun Alliance and London Assurance Co Ltd ('Sun Alliance') granted to Brown & Root Technology Ltd ('Technology') a lease which entitled Technology to give notice to terminate the same by serving not less than 12 months' notice expiring at the end of the seventh year of the term. In 1993, Technology became a wholly-owned subsidiary of Brown & Root Ltd ('B&R') and, at the end of May 1993, it was decided that B&R would take a transfer from Technology of its business and assets, including the lease. Sun Alliance granted a licence to assign. The necessary conveyancing documents were duly executed, but the transfer of the lease, which was registrable, was never registered at HM Land Registry in the name of B&R. On 10 September 1994, Technology served a break notice on Sun Alliance. Sun Alliance refused to accept that the break notice was valid. The question was whether there was an assignment of the lease by Technology. If there had been, then Technology was not entitled to serve the break notice; if there had not been, then it was. At trial, Sun Alliance persuaded the judge that the break notice was invalid. Technology appealed.

[53] *Thompson v McCullough* [1947] KB 447, at 454.

[54] *Smith v Express Dairy Ltd* [1954] JPL 45. Although the report is extremely short, the decision was followed by HHJ Collins CBE in *Renshaw v Magnet Properties South East LLP* [2008] 1 EGLR 42, at [10] (which concerned the validity of a counter-notice served under the Leasehold Reform, Housing and Urban Development Act 1993); and has been cited with apparent approval by Keene LJ in *East Lindsey District Council v Thompson* (2001) 82 P&CR 33, at [23] and Norris J in *Pye v Stodday Land Ltd* [2016] 4 WLR 168, at [12].

[55] *Brown & Root Technology Ltd v Sun Alliance and London Assurance Co Ltd* [2001] Ch 733.

3.61 Allowing the appeal, Mummery LJ said, at 741–42:

> It is common ground that there has been no transfer (and therefore no assignment) of the legal title to the lease; that, as between Technology and B&R, the equitable title to the lease was capable of passing by virtue of a specifically enforceable contract to assign the lease; that, if this were unregistered land, the assignment would occur on the execution of the deed of assignment and the conveyance of the legal estate thereby, and not on the conclusion of the contract to assign; and that, depending on the context, the passing of the equitable or beneficial interest may amount to a transfer or assignment of the property in question, even though there has been no registration of the transfer, as required by statute, to perfect the legal title. The judge referred to the cases of *In re Rose* [1949] Ch 78 and *In re Rose* [1952] Ch 499 as instances of a bequest of shares and an inter vivos gift of shares which took effect as between donor and donee and in accordance with donative intent before the registration of the transfers of the shares pursuant to the provisions of the Companies Act. Until registration there was no transfer so far as the company was concerned, but that did not prevent the gift from being effective as between others.
>
> … This case is not a matter of beneficial ownership between parties to the transfer of the lease: the issue of assignment or no assignment affects the legal position of a third party, the lessors, who have given their licence to assign but are not a party to the transfer. As was observed by Jenkins LJ in *In re Rose* [1952] Ch 499, 518 it is necessary to keep clear and distinct the position between the transferor and the transferee and the position of a third party. Transfer of the beneficial title is not, in this context, relevant to the legal relationship between the lessees and the lessors. The issue is not what rights Technology and B&R have against each other, but what rights Technology and Sun Alliance have against each other. That is a question of legal, not equitable, rights.
>
> … As between lessors and lessees, there is binding Court of Appeal authority in *Gentle v Faulkner* [1990] 2 QB 267 for the proposition that assignment means, in the absence of a context showing an extended meaning, an assignment of the legal estate, and not of the beneficial interest, eg by declaration of trust of the lease. It is not a matter of intention to assign, a point highly relevant to the passing of beneficial title, but of whether a defined event has occurred. That event is not completion, as [Counsel for Sun Alliance] contended; it is the transfer of the legal title to the lease, so as to create the legal relationship of lessor and lessee between B & R and Sun Alliance.

3.62 Thus, the Court of Appeal had no hesitation in finding that the original lessee's notice to terminate was valid. There had been no transfer of legal title to the lease, and so the original tenant retained the right to exercise the break clause.

### (b) The Effect of s 141(2) of the Law of Property Act 1925

3.63 As already explained at 3.8 above, in the case of a tenancy granted before 1 January 1996, the effect of s 141(1) of the 1925 Act is that 'the benefit of every covenant or provision therein contained, having reference to the subject-matter thereof, and on the lessee's part to be observed or performed, and every condition of re-entry and other condition therein contained, shall be annexed and incident to and shall go with the reversionary estate in the land'. Section 141(2) then adds as follows: 'Any such rent, covenant or provision shall be capable of being recovered, received, enforced, and taken advantage of, by the person from time to time entitled, subject to the term, to the income of the whole or any part, as the case may require, of the land leased.'

**3.64** This provision confers on 'the person … entitled … to the income of the whole or any part … of the land leased' (including an equitable assignee) the right to enforce and take advantage of the benefit of every covenant or provision contained in the lease.[56]

**3.65** The question, then, is whether this provision modifies the common law rule above, so that an equitable assignee who brings himself within the terms of s 141(2) (ie as being the person entitled to the income of the land) has the right concurrently with the legal owner of the reversionary interest to serve a break notice on the tenant.

**3.66** In *Freeman v Hambrook*,[57] the landlords (Mr and Mrs Freeman) brought an action against the tenants to recover possession of a house of which the tenants had become weekly tenants on 27 October 1945. On that date, the owner of the house was Mr Ellis. On 30 October 1945, Mr and Mrs Freeman entered into a contract with Mr Ellis for the purchase of the house, subject to the consent of the Treasurer of the Commonwealth of Australia. This consent was obtained on 3 December; and on 21 December, the transfer was signed by Mr Ellis. The transfer was not lodged with the Titles Office until 11 February 1946. In the meantime, on 9 January, Mr and Mrs Freeman gave to the tenants a notice to quit, requiring them to deliver up possession on or before 14 March. The tenants contended that Mr and Mrs Freeman, not being on 9 January 1946 the legal owners of the reversion, were not entitled to give notice to quit. The landlords relied upon s 141(2) of the 1925 Act as entitling them to give the notice. As to this, O'Bryan J said:[58]

> the section is not concerned with the right at common law, or by custom or by statute … by notice to terminate a lease by year to year or month to month or from week to week, or such other periodical tenancy which otherwise continues from period to period. Such a termination of a lease is not brought about by the exercise of a condition of forfeiture or re-entry with which this section is concerned. The principal provisions of this section have been the law in England since 1881, but, so far as I know, there is no authority, by decision, judicial *dictum* or text-book, for saying that it goes the length for which [Counsel for the landlords] contended. This action is not, to use the words of section 141(2), an action to enforce or to take advantage of a covenant or provision contained in the lease. Therefore, in my opinion, that section has nothing to do with the problem I have to decide.

**3.67** A similar view was expressed by Norris J in *Pye v Stodday Land Ltd*.[59] That case concerned the validity of a notice to quit served on an annual periodic tenant under the Agricultural Holdings Act 1986. The notice was given by Ripway Properties Limited before it was registered as proprietor of the reversion (ie when it was an equitable assignee). Relying on the authorities referred to at **3.57–3.59** above, Norris J concluded

[56] On the purpose and scope of s 141(2), see: *Turner v Walsh* [1909] 2 KB 484, at 493–95, per Farwell LJ (decided under s 10 of the Conveyancing Act 1881) ('… The tenth section makes no alteration in the rights of anyone, but merely alters procedure, so as to give the right of action to the person entitled to the proceeds of such action …'); *Schalit v Joseph Nadler Ltd* [1933] 2 KB 79; and *Scribes West Ltd v Relsa Anstalt (No 3)* [2005] 1 WLR 1847.

[57] *Freeman v Hambrook* [1947] VLR 70.

[58] *Freeman v Hambrook* [1947] VLR 70, at 77.

[59] *Pye v Stodday Land Ltd* [2016] 4 WLR 168.

that the notice was invalid at common law. He went on to reject the argument that Ripway was entitled to serve the notice by operation of s 141(2) of the 1925 Act. He said:[60]

> The case under appeal does not concern the contractual arrangements made between Mr Pye and his landlord. The notice to quit in this case was not served in the right of any contractual provision in the tenancy agreement. Mr Pye had an annual periodic tenancy. 'The right to determine a tenancy from year to year by a notice to quit is a necessary incident to such tenancy': Woodfall (cited above) at para 17.198. The right to serve the notice to quit arose from the nature of the estate granted and held: and the relevant relationship is 'privity of estate' not 'privity of contract'. The notice to quit could only be served by the legal owner of the reversion, not the equitable owner. The legal owner of the reversion was Stodday: not Ripway. So I reject the second argument.

**3.68** As in *Freeman v Hambrook*, the notice to quit in *Stodday* was not served 'in the right of any contractual provision in the tenancy agreement' (per Norris J). Of course, a break notice is different since it *is* served in accordance with a such a right. The significance of this distinction is illustrated by *Scribes West Ltd v Relsa Anstalt (No 3)*.[61] In that case, the tenant occupied premises in Kensington. RA was registered as freehold proprietor of the premises on 10 November 1993. On 28 February 2001, RA transferred the reversion to RB and notice of the assignment was given to the tenant. However, the transfer was not registered until 3 January 2002. On 16 July 2001, RB peaceably re-entered the premises on the grounds of rent. The sole issue before the Court of Appeal was whether, for the purposes of a valid forfeiture by RB, it was sufficient that the transfer of the reversion had been executed and notice given to the lessee, notwithstanding that the transfer had not been registered. At first instance, the judge held that it was, applying s 141(2) of the 1925 Act. The Court of Appeal agreed. Chadwick LJ (with whom Rix and Mummery LJJ agreed) said:

> [10] RB's case, which the judge accepted, was that on 16 July 2001, the date of forfeiture, although it was not the registered freehold proprietor of the premises, it had taken a valid equitable assignment of the rents, and notice had been given to the lessee. It was therefore entitled (albeit only in equity) to receive the rents of the property, which was sufficient to bring it within the emphasised words of section 141(2).
>
> [12] … The word 'entitled' [in s 141(2)] does not of itself import a distinction between legal and equitable interests. It connotes simply an enforceable right to the relevant income. An equitable assignee of the right to rent has such an enforceable right as against the assignor and, at least following notice, against the lessee … Thus, in the present case, RB is for the time being 'the person … entitled to the income … of the land leased'. Nor does it seem to me to matter if this in theory results in RB having that right concurrently with RA, as legal owner. The section is designed to extend rights to enforce, without taking away existing rights; and in any event anything done by RA could only be done as trustee for RB.

**3.69** Following the reasoning in *Scribes*, in the case of a lease granted prior to 1 January 1996, it might be said that an equitable assignee of the reversion could (in principle) rely on s 141(2) in order to validate a break notice which would otherwise

[60] *Pye v Stodday Land Ltd* [2016] 4 WLR 168, at [32].
[61] *Scribes West Ltd v Relsa Anstalt (No 3)* [2005] 1 WLR 1847.

be invalid at common law. However, it is important to recall that nothing in s 141(2) has an effect on or varies the language of the lease itself. If, in order to be valid, a break notice has to be given by 'the landlord' – here meaning the person in whom the legal interest in the reversion is vested – then it is submitted that s 141(2) will be of no assistance if the notice is given by any other person.

## (c) The Effect of the Landlord and Tenant (Covenants) Act 1995

**3.70** As described at 3.17 above, under the 1995 Act, as from an assignment of a 'new tenancy', the assignee becomes bound by the landlord covenants and entitled to the benefit of the tenant covenants or (as the case may be) bound by the tenant covenants and entitled to the benefit of the landlord covenants. For these purposes, a 'tenancy' includes 'an agreement for a tenancy' (so includes an equitable lease) and an 'assignment' includes an 'equitable assignment'.[62] Referring to these provisions, in *Sackville UK Property Select II (GP) No 1 v Robertson Taylor Insurance Brokers Ltd*,[63] Fancourt J said:

> The Act of 1995 does not distinguish between the effect of an assignment and an 'equitable assignment'. Both have the effect of releasing an assignor tenant from the tenant covenants and transferring the benefit of the landlord covenants to the assignee as from the assignment. Since 'tenancy' is defined as including an agreement for a tenancy, the definition of 'assignment' as including an 'equitable assignment' must extend the Act's reach to an assignment that is not yet effective at law, eg a specifically enforceable agreement to assign or an unregistered or formally defective assignment.

**3.71** It follows from this analysis that, in the case of a lease granted on or after 1 January 1996, an equitable assignee of the term or the reversion takes the benefit of (respectively) a tenant's or landlord's break notice. However, this does not mean automatically that an equitable assignee of such a lease can validly exercise a break option contained therein.[64] In *Sackville* itself, the lease was granted on 14 March 2013. It contained a break option exercisable by 'the Tenant' defined as including 'successors in title' and 'any person in whom this Lease may from time to time be vested by whatever means'. On 29 March 2017, the tenant (Robertson) assigned the lease to an assignee (Integro). Integro was not registered as proprietor of the term until 7 July 2017. Prior to

[62] Section 28(1).

[63] *Sackville UK Property Select II (GP) No 1 v Robertson Taylor Insurance Brokers Ltd* [2018] L&TR 22, at [32].

[64] The uncertainty regarding the position is noted by the Law Commission in its Consultation Paper 'Updating the Land Registration Act 2002' (Law Com 227), at §5.71, where it is said: 'The implication from Brown & Root Technology Ltd v Sun Alliance & London Assurance Co Ltd is that only registered proprietors can serve valid break notices, at least in the case of "old" leases, meaning leases granted before the Landlord and Tenants (Covenants) Act 1995 came into force on 1 January 1996. Although it is not clear, it could be that this is not a problem for "new" leases. Assignments of leases granted after 1995 or of the reversion to such leases are governed by the Landlord and Tenant (Covenants) Act 1995, which enables both a legal and equitable assignment to pass the benefit and burden of covenants. This may cover break clauses. Therefore, for leases granted after 1995, a landlord or tenant whose assignment was not yet registered might be able to validly serve or be served a break notice.'

that date, on 2 May 2017, Integro gave notice purportedly exercising the break option. Fancourt J held that the notice was invalid. He explained (with emphasis in the original):

> [33] … a break option confers a unilateral right on the grantee and only a contingent obligation on the grantor. The obligation of the Landlord, which is a 'landlord covenant' for the purposes of the Act, is the obligation to treat the Lease as terminated with effect from the specified date *if* a valid break notice is served. But the obligation is only triggered if the condition is satisfied. In my judgment, Integro obtained the benefit of the Landlord's obligation in cl.6.10 [ie the break clause] on the date of the Assignment and Robertson was released from the tenant covenants with effect from the same date, but the Landlord's obligation to treat the Lease as ending on 14 March 2018 [ie the break date] depends on 'the Tenant' giving appropriate notice. So the relevant question is whether the definition of 'the Tenant' includes a person who as equitable assignee is entitled to the benefit of the landlord covenants.
>
> [34] In my judgment, although the Lease created a new tenancy to which the provisions of the Act of 1995 apply, the Act does not vary the meaning of the condition in the break option. Integro was not on 2 May 2017 the 'successor in title' of Robertson within the meaning of cl.1.2.1 of the Lease. Title to the legal term of years remained with Robertson. Nor was the Lease 'vested' in Integro, even though Integro by statute had the benefit of the landlord covenants of the Lease. On the contrary, the Lease remained vested in Robertson but Robertson held the Lease on trust for Integro.

### (d) 'Owner's Powers' Under the Land Registration Act 2002

**3.72** Under the Land Registration Act 2002 (the '2002 Act') certain types of 'dispositions' of registered estates or registered charges are 'required to be completed by registration' and do not operate at law 'until the relevant registration requirements are met'.[65] For these purposes, in the case of a registered estate, 'dispositions which are required to be completed by registration' include a 'transfer'.[66] The period between the date of the disposition and the date of registration is known colloquially as the 'registration gap'.

**3.73** Section 24 of the 2002 Act provides that a person is 'entitled to exercise owner's powers in relation to a registered estate or charge' if he is (a) the registered proprietor or (b) 'entitled to be registered as the proprietor'. A disponee of a registered estate falls within category (b) during the period of the registration gap.

**3.74** The expression 'owner's powers' in relation to a registered estate is defined in s 23(1) as consisting of (inter alia) 'power to make a disposition of any kind permitted by the general law in relation to an interest of that description'.

**3.75** It is important to appreciate that a person's right to exercise owner's powers by virtue of being entitled to be registered as the proprietor (s 24(b)) is limited to his powers of disposition 'under the general law' (s 23(1)). In other words, s 24 does not give an equitable transferee power to do what only a legal proprietor can do. As already described

[65] Section 27(1).
[66] Section 27(2)(a).

at 3.56, under the general law, the giving of a notice to quit is one of the instances in which the ownership of the equitable title to the term or the reversion does not suffice for the service of an effective notice.[67] The same is also true of a break option.[68]

**3.76** It follows that, during the registration gap, an equitable assignee cannot rely upon owner's powers in order to validate the giving of a break notice. From a practical perspective, upon a transfer of the reversion or the term of a lease, the relevant legal documentation should constitute the transferee as agent of the transferor in respect of all matters concerning the estate pending registration.[69] This will enable the transferee to exercise a break option during the registration gap should it wish to do so.

## THE POSITION WHERE THE BREAK CLAUSE IS NOT CONTAINED IN A LEASE

**3.77** An option to determine a lease may be conferred by an instrument other than a lease, for example, by a side letter. This does not present any particular conceptual problems so far as assignments are concerned. Thus, in *System Floors Ltd v Ruralpride Ltd*,[70] Midland Oak Properties Ltd ('Midland Oak'), granted to System Floors Ltd ('System Floors') under its then name three leases for terms of 21 years from 24 June 1977 of respectively units 20, 22, 23 and 24 Marlissa Drive, Coventry. On the same day Midland Oak wrote on its headed paper to System Floors a letter headed 'Re: Units 20, 22, 23 and 24 Marlissa Drive, Coventry', one copy of which was countersigned by System Floors by way of acknowledgment and agreement. The letter was in the following terms:

> In consideration of your today taking from us Leases respectively of Units 20, 22 and 23 and 24 Marlissa Drive, Coventry WE HEREBY AGREE with you in relation to the Leases as follows … If within three months after any of the dates for review of rent contained in any of the Leases or (if later) the date upon which the rent payable from any such review date shall be agreed or determined in accordance with the Lease you shall desire to surrender any of the Leases (as a whole but not in part) and if you shall within three months after such review date or such alternative date as aforesaid (as to which period of time is of the essence) give to us notice in writing of your intention so to do, then … we will upon the date occurring three months after such notice accept a surrender of the demised premises from you.

**3.78** Although drafted in terms of a surrender, this side letter amounted to the grant to System Floors of an option to determine the leases. The question was whether this side letter bound Ruralpride Ltd ('Ruralpride'), Midland's Oak successor in title to the reversion of the leases.

**3.79** Answering this question in the affirmative, Morritt LJ said as follows:[71]

> It is contended that the obligations undertaken in the letter … come within [Section 142(1) of the 1925 Act] with the consequence that they may be enforced against Ruralpride, as the person now entitled to the reversionary estate. That is disputed by Ruralpride.

[67] *Pye v Stodday Land Ltd* [2016] 4 WLR 168, at [37].
[68] *Sackville UK Property Select II (GP) No 1 v Robertson Taylor Insurance Brokers Ltd* [2018] L&TR 22, at [37]–[38].
[69] *Pye v Stodday Land Ltd* [2016] 4 WLR 168, at [41].
[70] *System Floors Ltd v Ruralpride Ltd* [1995] 1 EGLR 48.
[71] *System Floors Ltd v Ruralpride Ltd* [1995] 1 EGLR 48, at 50.

> It was established by the decision of this court in *Weg Motors Ltd v Hales* [1962] Ch 49, that [Section 142(1) of the 1925 Act] applies to promises contained in an independent document not under seal. In its written submissions Ruralpride sought to distinguish the case on the basis that in that case the independent document defined the parties as including their successors in title. But in the view I take of the construction of the letter in this case, that is not a distinction which can be drawn. Thus, the subsection may apply notwithstanding that the obligations are undertaken in a letter. The question is whether the obligations 'were entered into by a lessor with reference to the subject-matter of the lease'.

3.80 Thus, System Floors was entitled to rely on the side letter as against the assignee of the reversion.[72]

[72] The position is more straightforward in the case of a lease granted on or after 1 January 1996, since the definition of 'covenant' in the 1995 Act includes a covenant contained in a 'collateral agreement,' meaning 'in relation to a tenancy … any agreement collateral to the tenancy, whether made before or after its creation' (s 28(1)).

# 4

# *Who May Exercise the Break Clause*

## INTRODUCTION

**4.1** Depending on the drafting of the lease (or other instrument) in question, a break clause may be exercisable by the landlord, or the tenant or both. However, from this simple proposition a variety of possible scenarios arise. These are considered below.

## WHERE THE LEASE IS SILENT OR UNCLEAR

**4.2** Where the lease (or other instrument) is silent or unclear as to who is entitled to exercise a break clause, the option will usually be interpreted as being confined to the benefit of the tenant alone. Thus, in *Dann v Spurrier*,[1] the defendant (Mr John Spurrier), as landlord, entered into an agreement with Mr William Atkinson, as tenant, worded as follows:

> I William Atkinson of Saint Olaves, Southwark, have this day agreed to take on lease of John Spurrier the dwelling-house and premises now occupied by him in Old Broad-street ... to hold for 7, 14, or 21 years, at the yearly rent of one hundred and fifty pounds, payable half yearly, including all taxes which are to be paid by the said John Spurrier, the term and rent to commence from Christmas next.

**4.3** Mr Atkinson subsequently disposed of his interest to the plaintiff (Mr Richard Dann). Mr Spurrier gave notice to Mr Dann to quit the premises at Christmas 1798, which he refused to do, alleging that Mr Spurrier had no right to determine the agreement at the expiration of the first seven years; but that the agreement conferred such a right on the tenant only. Considering this question, Lord Alvanley CJ said the following:[2]

> It remains therefore for us to consider, notwithstanding the opinions thrown out in these cases, whether, according to the construction which deeds between lessor and lessee have received, the power of determining the lease in this case must not be confined to the lessee? ... The lease agreed for in the present case was seven, 14, or 21 years. An option, therefore, was certainly intended. If then the principle be just, that a lease is to be construed most favourably for the lessee, why are we to determine in this instance that the option is in the lessor? If indeed a provision had been inserted that the lease should be determinable at the option of either party, the lessor would have been entitled to take advantage of it; but where no such proviso is inserted, the true construction seems to be that the lessee is entitled, at his option, to take that term which is most beneficial to himself.

[1] *Dann v Spurrier* (1803) 3 B&P 399.
[2] *Dann v Spurrier* (1803) 3 B&P 399, at 403–404.

**4.4** Similarly, in *L R Wingfield Ltd v Clapton Construction and Investment Co Ltd*,[3] a lease contained a clause in these terms:

> In case either the lessor or the lessee shall desire to determine the term hereby granted at the end of the seventh ... year ... and shall give to the lessor not less than six months' previous notice in writing ... the present demise ... shall cease and be void.

**4.5** The lessor served a notice purporting to terminate the lease. Stamp J held that the words 'either the lessor or' were inconsistent with the rest of the clause and, having regard to the general principle that a lease was to be construed against a landlord, and the fact that the burden was on the landlord to satisfy the court that the clause conferred on him a right to determine, the notice to quit would be declared invalid.

## JOINT LESSEES

**4.6** Absent an express term to the contrary, a break notice must be given by all joint lessees in order to be valid.[4] A notice given by one of two joint lessees on behalf of both could only be good if the court was able to infer, or there were facts which otherwise proved, the existence of an agency (on which see **4.42–4.52** below).

**4.7** *Re Viola's Indenture of Lease*[5] concerned an indenture of lease dated 2 February 1906, made between O F Viola (the lessor) of the first part and Mr and Mrs Humphrey (the lessees) of the second part. The lease contained a proviso that if 'the lessees' should be desirous of terminating the lease at the end of the first three years of the term, and of such desire should give to the lessor six months' previous notice in writing, then at the end of such three years the term would come to an end. On 3 October 1907, Mr Humphrey, the husband, alone gave notice in writing to the lessor to determine the lease at the end of the first three years of the term. The lessor did not accept the notice. The lessees sought a declaration that a valid notice to determine the lease had been given.

**4.8** At trial, Warrington J declared that, upon a true construction of the lease, no effective notice to determine the term had been given. He said:[6]

> The terms of the proviso are express; both lessees must be desirous and express their desire to determine the term. A notice therefore by one of them cannot be a notice by both to determine the lease.

**4.9** In *Hounslow London Borough Council v Pilling*,[7] Nourse LJ approved of *Re Viola's Indenture of Lease* and held that a break notice cannot be given by one only

[3] *L R Wingfield Ltd v Clapton Construction and Investment Co Ltd* (1967) 201 EG 769.

[4] *Leek and Moorland Building Society v Clark* [1952] 2 QB 788, at 793, per Somervell LJ ('... If one considers a lease to joint lessees for a term certain with a right of renewal, it would be obvious, we think, that both must join in requiring a renewal ...'); *Newman v Keedwell* (1978) 35 P&CR 393, at 398, per Fox J ('... if a lease is granted for a fixed term of years with power to the tenant to determine after a period I should have thought that normally it would not be competent to a single joint tenant in the case of a beneficial joint tenancy to exercise the power without the authority of his co-tenant ...').

[5] *Re Viola's Indenture of Lease* [1909] 1 Ch 244.

[6] *Re Viola's Indenture of Lease* [1909] 1 Ch 244, at 247.

[7] *Hounslow London Borough Council v Pilling* [1993] 1 WLR 1242, at 1247A.

of two (or more) joint tenants. In *Pilling*, the council had granted, and Mr Pilling and Miss Doubtfire had taken, a joint weekly tenancy of a dwelling house. In the agreement, Mr Pilling and Miss Doubtfire were together defined as 'the tenant'. By clause 14, 'the tenant' was obliged 'to give the council four weeks' written notice or such lesser period as the council may accept when the tenant wishes to end the tenancy and give possession of the premises'. On 6 December 1991, having left the demised premises following incidents of domestic violence, Miss Doubtfire wrote to the council giving notice that she wished to terminate the tenancy. Mr Pilling refused to give up possession. The council commenced possession proceedings and obtained a possession order. Mr Pilling successfully appealed on the basis that Miss Doubtfire's 6 December 1991 letter was an invalid break notice.

**4.10** The position in relation to the service of a break notice by one of two (or more) joint lessees may be contrasted with the service of a notice to quit terminating a periodic tenancy. In *Hammersmith and Fulham London Borough Council v Monk*,[8] the House of Lords held that a contractual periodic tenancy held by two or more joint tenants continued only so long as they all agreed to its continuation, so that, in the absence of any contrary term in the agreement, the tenancy was determinable by a notice to quit given by one joint tenant without the concurrence of the other or others. In *Pilling*, Nourse LJ distinguished *Monk* on the basis that *Monk* decided only that the continuation of a periodic joint tenancy beyond the end of each period of it depends on the joint will of the tenants, so that if one of them gives notice determining it at the end of a period it does not continue.

## JOINT LESSORS

**4.11** The above principle applies equally to break notices given by joint lessors. All of the joint lessors must join in the giving of a notice to exercise a landlord's break clause.

## THE SURVIVOR(S) OF JOINT LESSORS/LESSEES

**4.12** As far as the authors are aware, there is no reported authority concerning the question whether an option to determine a lease in favour of A and B is exercisable by A only after the death of B. However, it is thought that a break clause exercisable by 'the lessee' or the 'the lessor' can be exercised by the survivor of joint lessees/joint lessors.

## WHERE THE LANDLORD IS ALSO ONE OF THE TENANTS

**4.13** Suppose A and B grant a lease to B and C which contains a break clause.[9] Can the break (depending on whether it benefits the landlord or the tenant), be validly exercised

[8] *Hammersmith and Fulham London Borough Council v Monk* [1992] 1 AC 478.

[9] As to the legal possibility of A and B granting a lease to B and C, see the illuminating discussion in *Procter v Procter* [2021] EWCA Civ 167.

by A or C alone in circumstances where B refuses to join in service? The answer seems to be that the break could not be validly exercised.

**4.14** So, for example, in *Fitzhugh v Fitzhugh*,[10] three brothers (Geoffrey, Harry and Anthony) granted a licence to one of the brothers (Anthony) and his wife (Karen) to use certain farm outbuildings and various fields. Geoffrey, Harry and Anthony were described in the licence as 'the Licensor'; and Anthony and Karen as 'the Licensee'. The licence was expressed to terminate automatically on the happening of various events, including the following at clause 4(b):

> The Licensee commits any … persistent breaches of this Licence and the Licensor having given written notice to the Licensee of such breach or breaches the Licensee fails within such period as the Licensor may specify to rectify such breaches if capable of rectification.

**4.15** Anthony and Karen did not pay the annual licence fee under the licence. On 16 February 2006 (by which time Geoff had passed away), solicitors purportedly writing on behalf of 'all the family members' made various requests of Anthony and Karen, including that they pay the licence fee arrears. They did not do so. Over three years later, Harry commenced proceedings against Anthony seeking various heads of relief, including possession of the land the subject of the licence.

**4.16** There was no dispute that Anthony and Karen had been guilty of 'persistent breaches' of the licence. Therefore, the only issue was whether the solicitors' letter of 16 February 2006 was a valid notice for the purposes of clause 4(b). In turn, that depended on whether, as a matter of interpretation, 'the Licensor' in clause 4(b) meant both Harry and Anthony, or whether it meant, or could be read as meaning, a reference just to Harry. At trial, Morgan J decided the question in favour of Harry. Anthony appealed.

**4.17** The Court of Appeal unanimously allowed the appeal. Giving the lead judgment, Rimer LJ explained as follows:[11]

> [19] … Anthony is expressly described as one of the individuals making up 'the Licensor' in the opening words of the licence. The phrase 'the Licensor' in cl.1 plainly includes him. So must it in cll.2 and 3. The critical question, however, is as to the meaning that the same defined phrase in cl.4(b) would convey to a reasonable person having all the background knowledge which would reasonably be available to the audience to whom the licence is addressed (see the *Belize Telecom* case, at [16], per Lord Hoffmann).
>
> [20] In my view, such a person would regard it as improbable that in this short, simple, professionally drawn document the defined phrase 'the Licensor' was intended to mean one thing in the opening words of the document, the same thing in cll.1 to 3 but something else in cl.4(b). There is, on the face of the document, nothing to suggest that there should in cl.4(b) be any such change of meaning, or that something has gone wrong with its drafting so as to support the conclusion that 'the Licensor' does not there mean the same as it means elsewhere. If, as is the ordinary inference, it does mean the same, the reasonable person might well also foresee the potential for practical difficulty in the event (as happened) that Harry wanted to serve a cl.4(b) notice on Anthony: in particular, he might foresee the possibility that Anthony would refuse to join in its service.

[10] *Fitzhugh v Fitzhugh* [2012] 2 P&CR 14.
[11] *Fitzhugh v Fitzhugh* [2012] 2 P&CR 14, at [19]–[20].

**4.18** Thus, absent express wording permitting A to terminate the licence in circumstances where B refused to join in service of a notice of termination, B was able to frustrate the efforts of party A in bringing the agreement to an end.

## CONCURRENT LESSEES

**4.19** A concurrent or overriding lease is one granted subject to and with the benefit of a lease which is already in existence.[12] It entitles the concurrent lessee to the rent reserved in the previous lease, and to the benefit of the covenants contained in it during the then residue of the term granted by the first lease, and the continuance of the concurrent lease. As from the date of the grant of the concurrent lease, the concurrent term operates as an assignment of the reversion during such time as the two terms run concurrently.[13]

**4.20** Given that a concurrent lessee is entitled to the benefit of the covenants contained in the previous lease, the concurrent lessee is the proper person to serve notice to quit on the original lessee.[14] By parity of reasoning, it is suggested that a concurrent lessee would be similarly entitled to exercise a break clause under the original lease (unless the break clause was expressed to be exercisable only by the original lessor).

## THE POSITION WITH LEASES TAKING EFFECT IN EQUITY

**4.21** There are certain formalities which apply for the creation of a lease.[15] A lease which is void at law for want of compliance with these formalities may still operate as an agreement for lease which takes effect in equity.[16] A party to such an agreement is considered to hold the lease under the same terms in equity as if a lease had been granted.[17]

[12] Woodfall, *Landlord and Tenant*, Vol 1, 6.018.

[13] However, in the case of a 'new tenancy' within the meaning of the Landlord and Tenant (Covenants) Act 1995, the effect of s 15(1) appears to make tenant covenants under the original 'new tenancy' enforceable both by the original lessor and the concurrent lessee. Similarly, the combined effect of ss 4(b) and 28(5) of the 1995 Act makes clear that the statutory transmission of the benefit of the landlord's right of re-entry under the tenancy only occurs where the landlord assigns the whole of his interest in the reversion in the whole or part of the demised premises, as the case may be. Thus, on the grant of a concurrent lease a right of re-entry contained in the original 'new tenancy' will be exercisable by both the original landlord and the concurrent lessee.

[14] *Wordsley Brewery Co v Halford* (1903) 90 LT 89.

[15] It is provided by s 52 of the Law of Property Act 1925 that, except in the case of leases or tenancies not required by law to be made in writing (as to which, see below) leases will be void for the purpose of creating a legal estate unless made by deed. Section 54(2) enables legal leases to be created by parol provided that they (i) take effect in possession, (ii) do so for a term not exceeding three years and (iii) do so at the best rent which can reasonably be obtained without taking a fine (as defined in s 2015(1)(xiii)). The formal requirements for a deed are contained in s 1 of the Law of Property (Miscellaneous Provisions) Act 1989 and (where a company is involved) s 44 of the Companies Act 2006.

[16] *Parker v Taswell* (1858) 2 De G&J 559, at 570–71, per Lord Chelmsford LC ('… I think it would be too strong to say that because it is void at law as a lease, it cannot be used as an agreement enforceable in equity, the intention of the parties having been that there should be a lease, and the aid of equity being only invoked to carry that intention into effect …'); *Cowen v Phillips* (1863) 33 Beav 18, at [21], per Sir John Romilly MR ('… It is not under seal, and therefore, under the Act, it is not a lease; but, although it is void as a lease, the question is, whether it is not valid as an agreement. I have no doubt that it is a valid contract, and that this Court would specifically enforce it …').

[17] *Walsh v Lonsdale* (1882) 21 Ch D 9, at 14–15, per Jessell MR.

It follows that a break right in a lease taking effect in equity only is capable of being exercised by the equitable landlord or tenant (as the case may be).[18]

**4.22** It is submitted that the same principles will apply if there has been a failure to comply with the 'requirement for registration' under the Land Registration Act 2002.[19] The requirement for registration applies on the occurrence of certain specified events, including:

(a) The grant out of a qualifying estate[20] in land (i) for a term of years absolute of more than seven years from the date of the grant, and (ii) for valuable or other consideration, by way of gift or in pursuance of an order of any court;[21] and
(b) The grant out of a qualifying estate of an estate in land for a term of years absolute to take effect in possession after the end of the period of three months beginning with the date of the grant.[22]

**4.23** Where the requirement of registration applies, the responsible estate owner[23] must, before the end of the period for registration, apply to the registrar to be registered as the proprietor of the registrable estate.[24] The period for registration is two months beginning with the date on which the relevant event occurs, or such longer period as the registrar may provide.[25] If the requirement of registration is not complied with, the transfer, grant or creation becomes void as regards the transfer, grant or creation of a legal estate.[26] In a case falling within s 4(1)(c) or s 4(1)(d), this means that the grant 'has effect as a contract made for valuable consideration to grant … the legal estate concerned'.[27]

## EQUITABLE ASSIGNEES OF THE TERM OR REVERSION

**4.24** The position of regarding equitable assignees is addressed in more detail in Chapter 3.[28] Generally speaking, a break clause will only be exercisable by the party in whom the legal interest in the reversion or the term is vested.

[18] *Sandhar & Kang Ltd v Ijaz* [2018] EWHC 3071 (Ch), at [196]–[198], per Mr Edwin Johnson QC (sitting as a Deputy Judge of the High Court). That case concerned a lease containing a landlord's break right. The lease was validly executed as a deed on behalf of the landlord company. However, the signature of the tenant individual had not been witnessed as required by s 1(3) of the Law of Property (Miscellaneous Provisions) Act 1989. Therefore, the lease did not take effect as a valid lease operating at law: it qualified as an agreement for lease, taking effect as a lease in equity. Nonetheless, the break notice given by the landlord was effective to terminate the lease.

[19] The Land Registration Act 2002 came into force on 13 October 2003. For the position prior to 13 October 2003, see s 19(2)(a) of the Land Registration Act 1925 (not authorising 'the registration of a lease granted for a term not exceeding twenty-one years …').

[20] Defined in s 4(2) as 'a freehold estate in land' or 'a leasehold estate in land for a term which, at the time of the transfer, grant or creation, has more than seven years to run'.

[21] Section 4(1)(c).

[22] Section 4(1)(d).

[23] If the requirement of registration applies otherwise than because of s 4(1)(g), then the 'responsible estate owner' is the transferee or grantee of the registrable estate which his transferred or granted: s 6(3).

[24] Section 6(1).

[25] Section 6(4).

[26] Section 7(1).

[27] Section 7(2)(b).

[28] See **3.56–3.76**.

UPON REASSIGNMENT OF A LEASE CONTAINING A PERSONAL BREAK CLAUSE

**4.25** As described in Chapter 3,[29] it is not uncommon for a break clause to be expressed to be personal to a specific tenant (eg 'the tenant, here meaning X only'). In this scenario, difficult questions arise as to what happens to the option upon assignment, and re-assignment, of the lease.

**4.26** It has been held that, where a break clause is personal to the original tenant, then, once the lease is assigned, an option to determine ceases to have any contractual life. So, in *Max Factor Ltd v Wesleyan Assurance Society*, Auld LJ said, in relation to a personal break clause:[30]

> Once [the tenant] assigned the [lease] to [the assignee] I do not see what continuing contractual life there was in the break clause. It did not pass to [the assignee] with the term, and [the tenant] retained nothing to which it could relate. It was dead. [The assignee] could not, by re-assignment of the [lease], bring it to life again.

**4.27** In agreement, Aldous LJ said:[31]

> There can be no commercial sense in the tenant bargaining for, or the landlord conceding, that once the tenant had chosen to assign the lease and realised any value it had, the right to determine the lease should revive if the tenancy should be reassigned to the original tenant.

**4.28** There was, however, a powerful dissent from Staughton LJ who remarked as follows:[32]

> In this court it was argued (without a respondent's notice), and I understand that my colleagues accept, that the right conferred by clause 5.09 on the Lessee [i.e. the right to determine the lease] 'disappeared' when there was an assignment to [the assignee] because it was a personal right; and it could not be created once more on a reassignment. I do not agree that the right disappeared. In my view it was assigned like all the other rights of the original Lessee; it was merely of no value while it belonged to [the assignee]; but it became once more a right of some value when there had been a reassignment.

**4.29** Nonetheless, the majority view in *Max Factor* has been followed subsequently. So, for example, in *Equinox Industrial (GP2) Ltd & Anr v Sketchley Ltd*,[33] a lease was granted to a company called Sketchley Plc. Clause 8 of the lease contained a break clause exercisable by 'the Tenant'. However, the clause also included the following wording: 'For the purposes of this clause 8 … the Tenant shall mean Sketchley plc only and not its successors in title or its assigns'. On 8 September 1999, Sketchley Plc assigned the lease to a third party. On 15 January 2002, the lease was then reassigned into the name of the original tenant (save that, by this time, Sketchley Plc had changed its name to Sketchley Ltd). On 19 June 2002, Sketchley Ltd served a notice under clause 8 of the lease purporting to determine the lease at the end of the tenth year of the term. The landlord sought a declaration that the notice was invalid. So, the issue before the court was whether Sketchley Ltd

[29] See **3.34**.
[30] *Max Factor Ltd v Wesleyan Assurance Society* (1997) 74 P&CR 8, at 13.
[31] *Max Factor Ltd v Wesleyan Assurance Society* (1997) 74 P&CR 8, at 18.
[32] *Max Factor Ltd v Wesleyan Assurance Society* (1997) 74 P&CR 8, at 18.
[33] *Equinox Industrial (GP2) Ltd & Anr v Sketchley Ltd* [2003] EWHC 2 (Ch).

was entitled to serve a notice to determine the lease having regard to the fact that the break clause was made personal to Sketchley Plc and did not pass to its successors in title or assigns.

4.30 Lawrence Collins J granted judgment in favour of the landlord. He said:[34]

> [31] I ... accept the contention of the Claimants that there is commercial sense in an arrangement under which a right, such as a right to determine a lease, is available to the original lessee but which ends should that lessee choose to assign the lease. The original lessee then has two options. It can retain the benefit of the lease and enjoy the special personal right conferred on it or it can realise the value of the lease by assigning it but recognising that the special personal right is then no longer operable so that any price for the assignment will not reflect this right. What is less commercially intelligible is an arrangement under which the original lessee can assign the lease but then hope or expect that it can still exercise the special right if at some appropriate date in the future it re-acquires the lease. If the right can be revived there is inevitably a measure of continuing uncertainty involved. Such a position would be obviously unattractive to a landlord especially if it intends to transfer the reversion, and the same uncertainty would affect any purchaser of the reversion.
>
> [32] The construction contended for by Sketchley Ltd would be of very doubtful commercial benefit to a tenant. If Sketchley Ltd is correct the right to determine the lease can be revived by an assignee re-assigning the lease to the original tenants (as it says has occurred in this case). Yet the landlord could prevent the revival of the right by refusing consent to the proposed re-assignment, and in doing so would be acting reasonably: *Olympia & York*. Both Auld LJ and Aldous LJ in *Max Factor* [1996] 2 EGLR 10 at pp 212 and 214 relied on this point in concluding that re-assignment did not revive the right. Nor do I consider that it makes a difference to this conclusion (as Mr Morgan QC contended for Sketchley Ltd) that the court has a power to make a vesting order in favour of the original tenant under section 181(2) of the Insolvency Act 1986. The court has a discretion, and the landlord could object to an order unless the original tenant gave an undertaking not to operate the break clause.[35]

4.31 Thus, Lawrence Collins J held[36] that the wording of the break clause had the effect of:

> making it clear ... that it is only the original lessee, as original lessee, which can exercise the break clause. For the purposes of the break clause, Sketchley Ltd falls within the category of those who are excluded from the benefit of the clause.

4.32 *Max Factor* was also followed in *Linpac Mouldings Ltd & Ors v Aviva Life and Pensions UK Ltd*.[37] That case concerned two leases dated 4 February 1972, and a third lease dated 18 February 2005. Linpac Mouldings Limited ('Linpac') had become the tenant under the 1972 leases following the grant in 1986 of a licence to assign, which contained a break clause worded as follows:

> The Landlord and the Assignee hereby agree that if the Assignee (here meaning Linpac Mouldings Ltd only) shall desire to determine the Lease on the First day of December Two thousand and ten and shall give to the Landlord not less than eighteen months previous notice

[34] *Equinox Industrial (GP2) Ltd & Anr v Sketchley Ltd* [2003] EWHC 2 (Ch), at [31]–[32].

[35] In *Linpac Mouldings Ltd & Ors v Aviva Life and Pensions UK Ltd* [2010] 1 P&CR 11, at [63], Lewison J described this reasoning as 'compelling'.

[36] *Equinox Industrial (GP2) Ltd & Anr v Sketchley Ltd* [2003] EWHC 2 (Ch), at [33].

[37] *Linpac Mouldings Ltd & Ors v Aviva Life and Pensions UK Ltd* [2010] 1 P&CR 11; upheld on appeal at [2010] L&TR 10.

> in writing of such desire … then immediately on the expiration of such notice everything in the Lease shall cease and be void.

**4.33** The 2005 lease also contained a break clause in favour of 'the Tenant' which was defined for those purposes as meaning:

> Linpac Mouldings Limited as original tenant or any company forming part of the same group of companies (within the meaning of S 42 of the Landlord and Tenant Act 1954).

**4.34** On 22 February 2005, Linpac assigned the three leases (with the consent of its landlord) to Linpac Automotive Limited ('Automotive'). Linpac and Automotive were then associated companies. Later on in time, Automotive ceased to be a member of the same group as Linpac and changed its name to Ecomold Limited ('Ecomold'). On 11 March 2009, Ecomold sought the landlord's consent to the re-assignment of the three leases to Linpac. The landlord refused consent to the assignment of the 1972 leases (but granted consent in relation to the 2005 lease) on the ground that an assignment of the 1972 leases would create a risk that Linpac would seek to terminate those leases to its (the landlord's) disadvantage. Notwithstanding the refusal of consent, on 3 April 2009, Ecomold executed a transfer of the three leases to Linpac. Thereupon, Ecomold and Linpac (in its capacity as beneficial owner) purported to exercise the break clauses under the three leases. On 15 April 2009, the landlord commenced proceedings seeking, inter alia, a declaration that the break notices served were of no effect.

**4.35** The trial was heard by Lewison J, who granted the declaratory relief sought by the landlord. Giving reasons for so doing, he said:[38]

> In the present case, there is no commercial sense in attributing to the parties an intention that the right should revive if Linpac should re-acquire the lease. If Linpac wish to retain the right to break, the remedy was in its own hands. It could have sublet the property instead of assigning the lease. That was the conclusion Lightman J reached in the *Max Factor* case and his reasoning was expressly approved by Auld and Aldous LJJ on appeal. For the reasons I have given, I consider that I ought to follow *Max Factor* and *Equinox* despite the small differences in wording between members of the same family of personal break clauses. I hold, therefore, that Linpac is not entitled to exercise the break clauses even if and when it re-acquires the leases.

**4.36** From the above authorities it follows that, absent wording to the contrary, where a break clause is expressed to be personal to the original tenant, it is only the original tenant, in that capacity, who can exercise the break clause. However, the wording of the lease (or other instrument in question) may provide otherwise. This is evident from *BP Oil UK Ltd & Ors v Lloyds Bank Plc*,[39] in which Mr Michael Brindle QC (sitting as a Deputy Judge of the High Court) accepted the submission on behalf of the claimants that no clear principle arises from the *Max Factor* and *Equinox* cases which is not dependent on the particular wording of the document in question.[40] His decision was upheld on appeal,[41] where Arden LJ, reiterated the point that those cases turned

[38] *Linpac Mouldings Ltd & Ors v Aviva Life and Pensions UK Ltd* [2010] 1 P&CR 11, at [63].
[39] *BP Oil UK Ltd & Ors v Lloyds Bank Plc* [2004] EWHC 496 (Ch).
[40] *BP Oil UK Ltd & Ors v Lloyds Bank Plc* [2004] EWHC 496 (Ch), at [14].
[41] *BP Oil UK Ltd & Ors v Lloyds Bank Plc* [2004] EWCA Civ 1710.

on 'the construction of the leases in question'.[42] In *BP Oil* itself, it was held that a 'put' option requiring Lloyds to take a lease, was capable of being revived on, and exercisable following, re-assignment of that lease to the tenants.

**4.37** The foregoing accords with the decision of the Court of Appeal in *Olympia & York Canary Wharf Ltd v Oil Property Investment Ltd*.[43] In that case, E granted a lease to N for a term of 25 years from 8 March 1985. The lease contained a common form provision prohibiting assignment without the lessor's previous consent, such consent not to be unreasonably withheld. The lease also contained a tenant's break clause which enabled the lease to be determined at the end of the tenth year of the term. The right conferred by the break clause was exercisable only by N, the original lessee. In October 1987, N assigned the lease to O. However, N remained liable on its covenant to pay rent for the whole of the term of the lease. In March 1991, the freehold reversion of the property was acquired by L. Subsequently, in May 1992, O became insolvent and an administration order was made. O did not wish to retain the lease and desired to re-assign it to N. N was willing to accept a re-assignment because this would enable it to exercise the break clause and thereby put an end to its continuing rental liability as original lessee. So it came about that the administrators of O sought L's consent for assignment of the lease to N. L refused. O then sought various declarations, including a declaration that L was unreasonably withholding its consent to the assignment. The case was argued on the assumption that, if N re-acquired the lease, it would be able to exercise the break clause. As Lewison J later noted in *Linpac*:[44]

> The case was argued on the basis that (1) unless the lease was vested in it, [the tenant] could not operate the break clause and (2) if it re-acquired the lease, it would be able to exercise that right. Although Sir Donald Nicholls V-C, questioned the latter assumption, he did not question the former. Leggatt and Henry LJJ appeared to accept both assumptions as correct.

**4.38** Also of note is the decision of the Supreme Court of New Zealand in *Taita Hotel Ltd v Spelman*.[45] In that case, the lease provided that the lessee could renew the lease on notice 'if the lessee shall still be the lessee'. The original lessee assigned the lease, and when the landlord challenged the right of the assignee to give notice of renewal the assignee sought the landlord's consent to re-assign the lease to the original lessee. It was held by McGregor J that the original tenant would be entitled to the benefit of the right to renew if the lease was re-assigned to him. It was held that the fact that there had been an assignment would not prevent the original lessee from 'still' being the lessee.

**4.39** The possibility of a tenant losing the right to break a lease upon reassignment represents fertile ground for professional liability. As Etherton LJ warned in *Linpac*:[46]

> it would be reasonable to expect, both before and after the cases just mentioned, that competent property advisers would take particular care to make unambiguously clear, if intended, that a person will be entitled to break a lease not only when they are the tenant, but even after they have assigned the lease.

[42] *BP Oil UK Ltd & Ors v Lloyds Bank Plc* [2004] EWHC 496, at [15].
[43] *Olympia & York Canary Wharf Ltd v Oil Property Investment Ltd* (1995) 69 P&CR 43.
[44] *Linpac Mouldings Ltd & Ors v Aviva Life and Pensions UK Ltd* [2010] 1 P&CR 11, at [30].
[45] *Taita Hotel Ltd v Spelman* [1963] NZLR 206.
[46] *Linpac Mouldings Ltd & Ors v Aviva Life and Pensions UK Ltd* [2010] L&TR 10, at [47].

## FORMER OR NON-LANDLORDS/TENANTS

**4.40** Absent something extraordinary, only the party in whom the interest of the landlord or tenant is vested can exercise the break clause. This point was considered on appeal in *Linpac*,[47] where Linpac's argument was limited to the question whether it was entitled to exercise the break clauses in the 1972 leases and the 2005 leases (see **4.32** above) at any time *after* it had assigned them to Automotive/Ecomold, but *before* it re-acquired them. Dismissing any such suggestion, Etherton LJ said:[48]

> provision for a former tenant to bring a lease to an end at a time when the lease is not vested in them would be extraordinary, even if technically possible. It would be extraordinary ... because of the difficulties of obtaining vacant possession from the business tenant entitled to the benefit of the security of tenure conferred by the 1954 Act, the improbability of the landlord or any assignee from the tenant being content to accept such a provision, and the availability of a more obvious and straightforward route to achieve the same practical end by the tenant subletting rather than assigning. It is not surprising, in the light of such considerations as these, that Lightman J and the Court of Appeal in Max Factor gave very short shrift to the argument of [the tenant] that it could exercise the right to determine even at a time when the lease was not vested in them.

**4.41** Similar comments were made by Lewison J at first instance,[49] where he said:[50] 'Although it would, I accept, be theoretically possible to create a fixed term lease capable of termination by someone who was neither the landlord nor the tenant, it would be an extraordinary, if not a unique creation.'

## AGENTS

### (a) The General Rule

**4.42** Since a break notice must be given by the lessee/lessor (save for a quite exceptional case), a notice given by someone who is not the lessee/lessor is invalid. However, unless the wording of the lease expressly or impliedly forbids it, a notice may be validly given by an agent acting on behalf of the lessee/lessor if: (i) the notice states that it is given by the agent on behalf of the lessee/lessor; and (ii) the agent is duly authorised so to give it. So, for example, in *Lemon v Lardeur*,[51] a notice to quit, purportedly given by the husband of the tenant, was held to be ineffective. Similarly, in *Divall v Harrison & Anr*,[52] the Court of Appeal held that a notice to quit, served by a firm of solicitors, but not expressed to be given in the name of the landlord, was invalid.

[47] *Linpac Mouldings Ltd & Ors v Aviva Life and Pensions UK Ltd* [2010] L&TR 10.
[48] *Linpac Mouldings Ltd & Ors v Aviva Life and Pensions UK Ltd* [2010] L&TR 10, at [45].
[49] *Linpac Mouldings Ltd & Ors v Aviva Life and Pensions UK Ltd* [2010] 1 P&CR 11.
[50] *Linpac Mouldings Ltd & Ors v Aviva Life and Pensions UK Ltd* [2010] 1 P&CR 11, at [49].
[51] *Lemon v Lardeur* [1946] 1 KB 613.
[52] *Divall v Harrison & Anr* [1992] 2 EGLR 64.

### (b) General Agency

**4.43** There is an important exception to the general rule identified in **4.42** above. So, in an appropriate case, a break notice may be given effectively *in the name of* a person other than the lessee/lessor if that person has general authority from the lessee/lessor in relation to dealings in respect of the lease. It should be noted, however, that a general agency is an 'unusual commercial relationship' since the agent will have authority to do anything in relation to the subject matter of the agency, 'even to the extent of destroying that subject matter without reference to the principal'. Thus, the inference of a general agency, in the absence of express authority creating the agency, 'requires clear evidence to support it'.[53]

**4.44** There are a number of 'general agency' cases concerning notices to quit/break notices, starting with *Jones & Ors v Phipps*.[54] In that case, the issue was whether Sir Maxwell Graves had authority from the trustees of a marriage settlement, in whom the legal estate of a farm vested, to give notice to quit, so as to determine the defendant's tenancy. Lush J said:[55]

> The decision in this case must depend on the answers to be given to two questions, one of fact, the other of law. The question of fact is, whether Sir Maxwell Graves had authority from the trustees ... to give notice to quit ... The question of law is whether, assuming that he had such authority, a notice to quit given, in his own name, not purporting to be given as agent of the trustees is valid.
>
> On the first point, we are of the opinion that the facts stated lead to the conclusion that Sir Maxwell Graves had the authority of the trustees to give a notice to quit. He had assumed the entire control over the farm from the time it was purchased in 1863 ... We therefore infer that it was with the sanction of the trustees that he ... dealt with it as his own ... It was incidental to such an authority that he should determine the tenancy by notice to quit at such time as he should think proper. As regards the defendant, he could have been under no doubt whether the notice was binding, inasmuch as he was not aware that the estate vested in trustees, but always treated with and considered Sir Maxwell as the legal, as he was in fact the equitable, owner of the farm.
>
> On the second point, we are of the opinion that it is not essential to the validity of a notice to quit by such an agent, that his agency should appear on the face of the document itself.

**4.45** In *Re Knight and Hubbard's Underlease*,[56] it was argued that a notice seeking to terminate an underlease, given by the solicitors acting on behalf of a friendly society, was invalid because the friendly society was the beneficial or equitable owner only of the leasehold interest which it sought to determine. The tenant contended that the notice ought to have been given by or on behalf of the legal owners of the leasehold interest, that

[53] *Lemmerbell Ltd & Anr v Britannia LAS Direct Ltd (formerly LAS Direct Ltd)* [1999] L&TR 102, at 110, per Peter Gibson LJ.

[54] *Jones & Ors v Phipps* (1868) LR 3 QB 567.

[55] *Jones & Ors v Phipps* (1868) LR 3 QB 567, at 571–72.

[56] *Re Knight and Hubbard's Underlease* [1923] 1 Ch 130.

is, the trustees of the friendly society. Rejecting this argument, Sargant J held[57] that, not only were the trustees the mere nominees of the friendly society, and bound to act under the direction of the committee of management, but also, the trustees did, in fact, leave the management of the various interests in the subject property in the hands of the friendly society and the friendly society's agent. On the evidence, it was clear that the trustees, as the legal owners of the property, allowed the friendly society, as the absolute beneficial owners, to have the full management of it, and to deal directly with the tenant.

**4.46** In *Harmond Properties Ltd v Gajdzis*,[58] a notice to quit was served on a tenant by a firm of solicitors stating that they were acting '[on] behalf of your landlord Mr R P Harvey'. In fact, the landlord was Harmond Properties Ltd, and Mr Harvey was its director. At trial, the evidence was that Mr Harvey had acted as if he was the landlord in every way and it was clear that the tenant had always thought of him as the landlord. Thus, the county court judge decided that he was acting as a general agent and could give a valid notice to quit. This decision was upheld on appeal (although it may be observed that Willmer LJ said[59] that the case was 'rather peculiar' and turned 'on [its] particular facts').

**4.47** In *Townsends Carriers Ltd v Pfizer Ltd*,[60] a break notice had been served, not by the tenant company, but by an associated company, not on the landlord company, but on an associated company. The tenant and the landlord had consigned the whole conduct and management of the tenancy and of the tenancy itself to agents on their behalf, allowing their respective associated companies to deal with the property as if they were landlord and tenant respectively in respect of matters such as an increase in rent and variations of the lease. In the circumstances, Sir Robert Megarry V-C held that the break notice had been validly served, saying:[61]

> It has long been settled that if a landlord leaves the general control of the property in the hands of an agent, a notice to quit may be perfectly valid even if it is given by the agent in his own name, as if he were the landlord, and does not disclose any agency or purport to be given as agent for the landlord.

**4.48** In *Peel Developments (South) Ltd v Siemens Plc*,[62] a break notice was served by the tenants on a subsidiary of the landlord company. That subsidiary was found to have acted as managing agent of the property. Judge Paul Baker QC (sitting as a Deputy Judge of the High Court), on the evidence that the management of the property was carried out by the subsidiary, held that the subsidiary was the general agent of the landlord and the notice was validly served on the subsidiary.

**4.49** By contrast, in *Dun & Bradstreet Software Services (England) Ltd & Anr v Provident Mutual Life Assurance Association & Anr*,[63] the Court of Appeal reversed a

[57] *Re Knight and Hubbard's Underlease* [1923] 1 Ch 130, at 141.
[58] *Harmond Properties Ltd v Gajdzis* [1968] 1 WLR 1858.
[59] *Harmond Properties Ltd v Gajdzis* [1968] 1 WLR 1858, at 1864–65.
[60] *Townsends Carriers Ltd v Pfizer Ltd* (1977) 33 P&CR 361.
[61] *Townsends Carriers Ltd v Pfizer Ltd* (1977) 33 P&CR 361, at 365.
[62] *Peel Developments (South) Ltd v Siemens Plc* [1992] 2 EGLR 85.
[63] *Dun & Bradstreet Software Services (England) Ltd & Anr v Provident Mutual Life Assurance Association & Anr* [1998] 2 EGLR 175.

decision that the subsidiary of the tenant was the general agent of the tenant, in circumstances where the tenant held the lease on bare trust for the subsidiary, and the subsidiary was in occupation and paid the rent on the tenant company's behalf. Peter Gibson LJ said:[64]

> both sides were fully alert to the fact that [the subsidiary] was not the tenant ... The payment of the rent and other sums due under the leases by [the subsidiary] was an act associated with occupation of the demised premises ... The payment and the occupation were not to my mind indicative of agency, still less of general agency ... What [the subsidiary] did in relation to the demised premises seems to me to fall some way short of demonstrating that it was the general agent of [the tenant]. All that it did ... was consistent with the beneficial occupation of the premises. The termination of the leases was an act of a different nature, aimed at destroying the assets in question.

**4.50** In *Hexstone Holdings Ltd v AHC Westlink Ltd*,[65] the primary issue was whether the term created by an underlease entered into between Hexstone Holdings Limited ('Hexstone') and AHC Westlink Limited ('AHC') on 7 January 2008 was determined on 31 October 2009 through the exercise by the tenant of a break provision. Importantly, AHC was part of the Stobart Group of companies, one of which was Eddie Stobart Limited ('ESL'). On or about 19 August 2008, Hexstone received a letter on ESL's notepaper informing it that, with effect from 1 July 2008, AHC would change its name and be known as ESL. In reliance on this letter, Hexstone directed all future rent invoices to the accounts department of ESL. In fact, the change of name never occurred, and the true name of the original tenant under the underlease remained AHC (with AHC and ESL remaining entirely separate companies). In April 2009, it was desired to exercise the break provision contained in the underlease. To that end, ESL served a break notice on Hexstone. Hexstone subsequently challenged the validity of this notice, claiming that it had not been served by the tenant under the underlease. Edward Bartley Jones QC (sitting as a Deputy Judge of the High Court) rejected the contention that ESL was acting as AHC's general agent because he did not have any material before him to enable him to find that a general agency was created.

**4.51** It should be emphasised that, if a break notice is given by a general agent without stating that that person is acting as an agent, it is not sufficient for the person relying upon the notice to show merely that the giver was in fact duly authorised to give it. *In addition*, it must be shown that the circumstances of the case are such that the recipient can act upon the notice safely in the knowledge that it will be binding on the principal of the giver.[66] Such circumstances will include where: (i) the recipient knows that the giver was authorised to give the notice; (ii) the principal has held out the giver of the notice as authorised to give the notice; or (iii) the recipient has been led to believe that the giver of the notice is the principal.

[64] *Dun & Bradstreet Software Services (England) Ltd & Anr v Provident Mutual Life Assurance Association & Anr* [1998] 2 EGLR 175, at 178.

[65] *Hexstone Holdings Ltd v AHC Westlink Ltd* [2010] L&TR 22.

[66] *Jones & Ors v Phipps* (1868) LR 3 QB 567, at 572; *Lemmerbell Ltd & Anr v Britannia LAS Direct Ltd (formerly LAS Direct Ltd)* [1999] L&TR 102, at 111.

**4.52** This is well illustrated by *Hexstone*, where Edward Bartley Jones QC said:[67]

> even if [ESL] … had been duly authorised by AHC to give the Notice still, because of the absence of reference to agency on the face of the Notice, the same could not possibly have been valid … unless the circumstances were such that Hexstone, as recipient, could act on the Notice safely in the knowledge that it would be binding on the principal (AHC) …
>
> I find it impossible to see how Hexstone could safely have acted on the Notice in the knowledge that it would be binding on AHC. There is no question of Hexstone knowing that [ESL] had been authorised to give the Notice … Nor is there any question of AHC having held out [ESL] as authorised to give the Notice … What in fact had happened [by the 19 August 2008 announcement] is not a case of 'holding out' but, rather, an assertion that AHC would, henceforth, be known as [ESL].

### (c) Further Complication with Unidentified/Undisclosed Principals

**4.53** There is a further complication in a case where a break notice is served by an agent on behalf of an undisclosed or unidentified principal. Before an undisclosed or unidentified principal can take the benefit of an agent's act as his own, it must be established that the agent intended to bind the principal, ie to do the act on behalf of the principal.[68] This proved fatal to the valid exercise of a break option in *Sackville UK Property Select II (GP) No 1 Ltd v Robertson Taylor Insurance Brokers Ltd*.[69] In that case, the lease contained a tenant's break option. The lease was granted to Robertson. On 29 March 2017, Robertson assigned the lease to Integro. Integro was not registered as proprietor of the lease until 7 July 2017. On 2 May 2017, Integro's solicitor (Mr White) purported to serve a break notice terminating the lease. The solicitor gave evidence as follows: 'John Owens [the principal of Integro] did not instruct me to serve the break notice on behalf of either [Integro] or [Robertson]. All John Owens wanted was for the break notice to be served by whichever company was entitled to serve the break notice'. Mr Owens' evidence added: '… our instructions were to effect a termination of the Lease by the service of a break notice'. Referring to this evidence, Fancourt J said:[70]

> for Integro to claim that the break notice was served on behalf of Robertson as well as on behalf of Integro, the Defendants must be able to show that either Mr White or Integro itself intended the notice to be given in that behalf. Mr White plainly did not. Mr Owens' evidence is that he intended the Lease to be terminated and that he instructed Mr White to serve a valid notice. In my judgment, Mr Owens' understandable desire to break the Lease by serving a valid notice is not to be equated with an intention that the notice be served on behalf of Robertson (or Robertson and Integro). He delegated the question of what notice was needed (and who was to give it) to Mr White. In those circumstances, there is no arguable case on the evidence before me that either Integro or Mr White intended the break notice to be served on behalf of Robertson. That is fatal to any argument that the notice can be deemed to have been given on behalf of Robertson.

[67] *Hexstone Holdings Ltd v AHC Westlink Ltd* [2010] L&TR 22, at [42]–[43].
[68] *National Oilwell (UK) Ltd v Davy Offshore Ltd* [1993] 2 Lloyd's Rep 582; *Siu Yin Kwan v Easter Insurance Co Ltd* [1994] 2 AC 199.
[69] *Sackville UK Property Select II (GP) No 1 Ltd v Robertson Taylor Insurance Brokers Ltd* [2018] L&TR 22.
[70] *Sackville UK Property Select II (GP) No 1 Ltd v Robertson Taylor Insurance Brokers Ltd* [2018] L&TR 22, at [49].

### (d) Ratification

**4.54** It should be noted that, where an agent without authority serves a break notice, it cannot be saved by subsequent ratification on the part of the principal.[71] This is because subsequent ratification is not apt unilaterally to turn a notice which was bad when it was given into a good one.

## PARTNERSHIPS

### (a) Private Partnerships

**4.55** Section 1(1) of the Partnership Act 1890 provides that a partnership is 'the relation which subsists between persons carrying on a business in common with a view of profit.' As a matter of law, a partnership has no distinct legal entity.[72] This means that a partnership as such cannot be a landlord or a tenant. Since a legal estate in land can only be held by a legal person or persons,[73] the landlord or the tenant will be the partners who are the parties to the lease. Where there are more than four partners in the partnership, the named partners will hold the property on trust for the partnership.

**4.56** Consequently, where a partnership seeks to exercise a break option, the break notice should be given by those partners in whom the legal interest in the reversion or the term (as the case may be) is vested.[74]

### (b) Limited Partnerships

**4.57** On 1 January 1908, the Limited Partnerships Act 1907 (the '1907 Act') came into force. The 1907 Act introduced a new kind of partnership known as a 'limited partnership.'[75] Although the 1907 Act amends the general law of partnership in certain

[71] *Right v Cuthell* (1804) 5 East 491, at 499, per Lawrence J; *Doe d. Mann v Walters* (1830) 10 B & C 626, at 632–33, per Littledale J; *Presentaciones Musicales SA v Secunda* [1994] Ch 271, at 278–79, per Dillon LJ; *Hexstone Holdings Ltd v AHS Westlink Ltd* [2010] L&TR 22, at [32], per Edward Bartley Jones QC (sitting as Deputy Judge of the Chancery Division); *Aldford House Freehold Ltd v Grosvenor (Mayfair) Estate* [2018] EWHC 3430 (Ch), at [91]–[99], per Fancourt J (this point unaffected by the appeal at [2020] Ch 270).

[72] *Malkinson v Trim* [2003] 1 WLR 463, at [23], per Chadwick LJ; *Hammonds v Danilunas* [2009] EWHC 216 (Ch), at [106], per Warren J (affirmed on appeal at [2009] EWCA Civ 1400).

[73] See s 34(2) of the Trustee Act 1925 and s 34(2) of the Law of Property Act 1925.

[74] See *Doe v Baker* (1818) 8 Taunt 241. In that case, Green was in partnership with two others. Baker was the tenant of a house under a lease granted by Green alone. Green served a notice to quit. Baker argued that the notice was a nullity. Gibbs CJ rejected the argument. He said, at [242]: 'The agreement stipulated for the determination of the tenancy, upon certain terms agreed upon between the parties at the time of its execution, viz. the one party giving the other three months' notice to quit. Upon the expiration of the three months after the notice to quit had been served, the tenancy expired, and Green became entitled to maintain this action'.

[75] The 1907 Act prescribes that a limited partnership must consist of 'one or more persons called general partners, who shall be liable for all debts and obligations of the firm, and one or more persons to be called limited partners' (s 4(2)). Unlike a general partner, a limited partner 'shall not take part in the management of the partnership business, and shall not have power to bind the firm' (s 6(1)). *Cf* the position under s 5 and s 24(5) of the Partnership Act 1890.

respects, 'the Partnership Act 1890 and the rules of equity and common law applicable to partnerships' still apply to limited partnerships except so far as those rules are inconsistent with the express provisions of the 1907 Act.[76] Hence, as with a partnership under the Partnership Act 1890, a limited partnership has no legal personality of its own and is 'merely a combination of persons for the purposes of carrying on a particular trade or trades';[77] although, the name of a limited partnership must end with the words 'limited partnership' or the abbreviation LP.[78] Therefore, the principles at **4.55–4.56** apply with equal force to a limited partnership.

**4.58** The potential significance of this is clear from the result in *Vanquish Properties (UK) LP v Brook Street (UK) Ltd.*[79] In that case, the claimant was a limited partnership which (at the material time) comprised four limited partners and one general partner named Vanquish Properties GP Ltd ('Vanquish GP'). The defendant was the tenant of certain premises under a lease granted by The Mayor and Commonalty and Citizens of the City of London ('City Corp'). The lease contained a break option exercisable by 'the Lessors' meaning 'the estate owner or estate owners for the time being of the reversion of the premises granted by the Lease'. On 22 March 2016, City Corp granted an overriding lease of the premises to the 'Vanquish Properties (UK) Limited Partnership acting by its general partner Vanquish Properties GP Limited'. On the same day that the overriding lease was granted, solicitors acting for the claimant served on the defendant a purported break notice as 'agents for Vanquish Properties (UK) Limited Partnership'.

**4.59** The claimant argued that the notice was valid on the basis that the limited partnership was the 'Lessor' for the purposes of the lease. Chief Master Marsh rejected this argument as being 'legally impossible' because a 'legal estate in land can only be held by a legal person or persons'.[80] He concluded that, since the overriding lease described the lessee as the claimant 'acting by its general partner', the 'Lessor' was Vanquish GP, i.e. the general partner. In consequence, the break notice was invalid because the claimant (the limited partnership) was not in a position to give the notice in the first place.[81]

### (c) Limited Liability Partnerships

**4.60** By virtue of s 1(1) of the Limited Liability Partnerships Act 2000, there is 'a new form of legal entity to be known as a limited liability partnership'. A limited liability partnership 'is a body corporate (with legal personality separate from that of its members)'.[82] Accordingly, 'the law relating to partnerships does not apply to a limited

[76] Section 7.
[77] *Re Barnard* [1932] 1 Ch 269, at 272, per Farwell J.
[78] Section 8B(2).
[79] *Vanquish Properties (UK) LP v Brook Street (UK) Ltd* [2016] L&TR 33.
[80] *Vanquish Properties (UK) LP v Brook Street (UK) Ltd* [2016] L&TR 33, at [22].
[81] Chief Master Marsh also went on to reject an argument that the notice could be 'saved' applying the decision in *Mannai Investment Co Ltd v Eagle Star Life Assurance Co Ltd* [1997] AC 749. This is the subject of further discussion in Ch 5. Mann J subsequently granted permission to appeal the Chief Master's decision, but the appeal was not heard, there being a confidential settlement.
[82] Section 1(2) of the Limited Liability Partnerships Act 2000.

liability partnership'.[83] Many of the provisions of the Companies Act 2006 apply to a limited liability partnership, albeit in an amended form.[84] Therefore, as with a company registered under the Companies Act 2006, where a limited liability partnership wishes to exercise a break option, it may do so in its own name.

## INSOLVENCY

### (a) Trustees in Bankruptcy

**4.61** Once a bankruptcy order is made, the bankrupt's estate vests in the Official Receiver, until a trustee in bankruptcy is appointed, at which point the property vests in the trustee.[85] The bankrupt's estate comprises, inter alia, all property belonging to or vested in the bankrupt at the commencement of the bankruptcy.[86] Given the wide definition of the word 'property' in s 436 of the Insolvency Act 1986, this is apt to include leases and options in gross. The trustee is thus entitled to exercise a break clause (subject to its terms).

### (b) Administrators

**4.62** The administration of companies is governed by Sch B1 to the Insolvency Act 1986, with effect from 15 September 2003. The administration regime was applied to partnerships from 1 July 2005 (by the Insolvent Partnerships (Amendment) Order 2005) and from 1 October 2005 to limited liability partnerships (by the Limited Liability Partnerships (Amendment) Regulations 2005). After the appointment of an administrator, he takes 'custody or control of all property to which he thinks the company is entitled'[87] and is under a duty to manage the company's affairs, business and property in accordance with any creditors' proposals approved under para 52 and any revisions to those proposals.[88] So, although, during the period of administration, the company's property remains vested in the company, the decision whether or not to exercise an option must be taken by the administrators, acting as agents of the company. A break notice should be given by the administrators in this capacity.

### (c) Liquidators

**4.63** Liquidation is the corporate equivalent to bankruptcy. When a winding-up order has been made, or where a provisional liquidator has been appointed, the liquidator or the provisional liquidator (as the case may be) is required to take into his custody or under

[83] Section 1(5).
[84] See eg the Limited Liability Partnerships (Application of Companies Act 2006) Regulations 2009/1804.
[85] Section 306(1) of the Insolvency Act 1986.
[86] Section 283(1) of the Insolvency Act 1986.
[87] Paragraph 67, Sch B1 to the Insolvency Act 1986.
[88] Paragraph 68(1), Sch B1 to the Insolvency Act 1986.

his control all the property and things in action to which the company is or appears to be entitled.[89] So, in contrast to the position of a trustee in bankruptcy, the company's property does not vest automatically in the liquidator (although an application for a vesting order may be made under s 145). A liquidator has the power 'to do all acts and execute, in the name of and on behalf of the company, all deeds, receipts and other documents'.[90] This means that, unless the company's property is vested in the liquidator, if the company wishes to exercise a break clause, notice should be given by the liquidator on behalf of the company.

## RECEIVERS AND MANAGERS

**4.64** In broad terms, a 'receiver' is a person 'who receives rents or other income paying ascertained outgoings' in respect of the property which is subject to his authority; but who 'does not ... manage the property in the sense of buying or selling or anything of that kin'.[91] A receiver has no power or authority to carry on a business. By contrast, a 'manager' has such power.[92] Thus, if it is desired that trading should not cease, a receiver and manager should be appointed.

**4.65** A receiver/receiver and manager may be appointed by the High Court 'in all cases in which it appears to the court to be just and convenient to do so'.[93] In most cases, however, a receiver/receiver and manager is appointed out of court, under the authority of some statute or a contractual power. Generally speaking, a receiver/receiver and manager is only authorised to do such things as covered by the terms of the appointing instrument. Depending on the scope of the court order, statute or contract under which the receiver/receiver and manager is appointed, this may (or may not) include the ability to serve a break notice on behalf of a landlord or tenant.[94]

## PERSONAL REPRESENTATIVES

**4.66** Where an executor is appointed by a will (as opposed to a statutory appointment or an appointment by the court), he derives title from the will;[95] and the property of the deceased vests in the executor from the moment of the testator's death.[96] In this respect,

[89] Section 144(1) of the Insolvency Act 1986.

[90] Paragraph 7, Sch 4 to the Insolvency Act 1986.

[91] *In re Manchester and Milford Railway Company* (1880) 14 ChD 645, at 653, per Jessell MR.

[92] *Taylor v Neate* (1888) 39 ChD 538, at 544, per Chitty J.

[93] Section 37(1) of the, Senior Courts Act 1981; and see s 38(1) of the County Courts Act 1984 which confers a similar power on the county court. Although s 37(1) does not make express reference to the appointment of a manager, it has long been recognised that the power to make such an appointment derives from that provision: see *Hart v Emelkirk* [1983] 1 WLR 1289; *Parker v Camden London Borough Council* [1986] 1 Ch 162; *JSC BTA Bank v Ablyazov* [2012] EWHC 648 (Comm).

[94] For cases where a receiver has validly given a notice to quit, see eg *Wilkinson v Colley* (1777) 5 Burrow 2694; *Doe v Read* (1810) 12 East 57.

[95] *Woolley v Clark* (1822) 5 B&A 744, at 745–46, per Abbott CJ; *Chetty v Chetty* [1916] 1 AC 603, at 608, per Lord Parker.

[96] Sections 1 and 3 of the Administration of Estates Act 1925.

the subsequent grant of probate acts only as authenticated evidence of the executor's title. It is for this reason that an executor will not be registered at HM Land Registry as the proprietor of registered land without a grant of probate.[97] However, because an executor's title is derived from the will he may, before he proves the will, do almost all the acts which are incident to his office (subject to certain exceptions relating to the commencement and maintenance of litigation).[98] Presumably, this will include the ability to exercise a break clause.

4.67 The position is different on intestacy. As described above, an executor may carry out most of the acts relating to his office before probate. By contrast, for an administrator, the general rule is that a party entitled to a grant of administration can do nothing as administrator before obtaining a grant.[99] Until then, the deceased's property vests in the Public Trustee pursuant to s 9 of the Administration of Estates Act 1925.[100] After his appointment, an administrator has the same rights and liabilities and be accountable in like manner as if he were the executor of the deceased.[101]

4.68 Interesting questions arise where an intended administrator wishes to exercise a break clause prior to the grant of administration. As mentioned already, a party entitled to the grant can do nothing as administrator before the grant itself. Therefore, it may be expected that a break notice served by that party prior to the grant is a nullity. However, it is also to be observed that 'when a grant of administration is made, the intestate's estate ... vests in the person to whom the grant is made, and the title thereto relates back to the date of the intestate's death'.[102] Although there is no directly relevant authority of which the authors are aware, it is suggested that the principle of 'relation back' would not operate to validate an otherwise invalid break notice. Here, reference may be made to *Fred Long & Sons Ltd v Burgess*.[103] In that case, a contractual tenant died and her sons continued to live in the house. The landlords served a notice to quit on the President of the Probate, Divorce and Admiralty Division of the High Court,[104] and started an action for possession against the sons. When the case reached the county court, the sons' solicitors asked for and were granted an adjournment in order that one of the sons might take

[97] Land Registration Rules 2003 (SI 2003/1417), r 163.

[98] *In Re Stevens* [1897] 1 Ch 422, 429, per North J.

[99] *Woolley v Clark* (1822) 5 B&A 744, at 745–46, per Abbott CJ; *Ingall v Moran* [1944] KB 160, 168, per Luxmoor LJ; *Millburn-Snell v Evans* [2012] 1 WLR 41.

[100] Presumably, therefore, where property has vested in the Public Trustee, the Public Trustee would be entitled to take action in relation to such property (including exercising a break clause) relying on his statutory title.

[101] Section 21 of the Administration of Estates Act 1925.

[102] *Ingall v Moran* [1944] KB 160, at 168, per Luxmoore LJ; and see also *R v The Inhabitants of Horsley* (1807) 8 East 405, at 410, per Lord Ellenborough CJ ('... The grant of letters of administration, though it may have the effect of vesting the leasehold property in the administratrix by relation, so as to enable her to bring actions in respect of that property for all matters affecting the same subsequent to the death of the intestate ...') and *Youngmin v Heath* [1974]1 WLR 135, at 136H, per Lord Denning MR ('... When Mr Heath in 1972 became the attorney administrator for the sister, he became entitled to the tenancy as administrator, and his title related back to the time when Miss Reni died in October 1970 ...').

[103] *Fred Long & Sons Ltd v Burgess* [1950] 1 KB 115.

[104] Because at that time s 9 of the Administration of Estates Act 1925 provided: 'Where a person dies intestate, his real and personal estate, until administration is granted in respect thereof, shall vest in the Probate Judge in the same manner and to the same extent as formerly in the case of personal estate it vested in the ordinary'. Since 1 July 1995, the Public Trustee has taken the place of the Probate Judge.

out letters of administration. The grant was obtained, and at the adjourned hearing the county court judge held that, by reason of the doctrine of relation back, the deceased's tenancy from the date of her death vested in the administrator who was entitled to hold over as statutory tenant. The Court of Appeal reversed the decision and held that the doctrine of relation back did not apply. Bucknill LJ said:[105]

> I think that, on principle, and, historically, the vesting of the estate in the President is a positive act with some legal substance. Normally the court, formerly composed of the Probate Judge, appoints a person or persons to deal with the property of the intestate through a grant of administration, but I see no reason why in a case of necessity the President should not have legal power to give directions about the property. If he cannot do so, no one can. That is why the property is vested in him. If the President's position is such as I have indicated, I think he must have the legal capacity to receive a valid notice to quit, and such notice, after the proper lapse of time, has full legal effect. If no grant of administration has been made, there is no other person but the President to whom the notice to quit can validly be given. At any date subsequent to the death of the intestate, a grant of administration may be made. There is no time limit in this matter. If a grant made years after the death is to make invalid the notice to quit validly given to the President, confusion and uncertainty will prevail and injustice may be done to those who have acted on the assumption that the notice to quit given to the President had full legal effect.

**4.69** If an intended administrator is desirous of exercising a break clause prior to the grant of administration, the safest route would be to make an application to court (on an urgent basis, if necessary) pursuant to s 113 of the Senior Courts Act 1981 for a limited grant, ie limited to the deceased's real estate or to a part thereof.

[105] *Fred Long & Sons Ltd v Burgess* [1950] 1 KB 115, at 119–20.

# 5

# *The Form and Content of the Break Notice*

## INTRODUCTION

**5.1** A break clause is almost invariably exercised by giving notice in writing.[1] Sometimes, the notice, although otherwise given in accordance with the terms of the lease, will be in the incorrect form or contain a mistake or ambiguity on its face. In all cases of this sort, the 'correct approach'[2] is to look at the particular contractual provisions pursuant to which the notice is given and identify what its requirements are. Having done so, it should then be possible to arrive at a conclusion as to whether or not the notice served under it adequately complies with those requirements. If anything in the notice contains what appears to be a mistake or ambiguity on its face, then it may be (depending on the particular contractual provisions in question) that there will be scope for the application of the test laid down in the seminal decision of the House of Lords in *Mannai Investment Co Ltd v Eagle Star Life Assurance Co Ltd*[3] ('*Mannai*').

[1] Under the general law, 'writing' includes electronic modes of communication. So, it has been held that: (i) service of a list of documents by fax under the terms of a consent order was permissible (*Hastie & Jenkinson v McMahon* [1990] 1 WLR 1575); (ii) a letter sent by fax constitutes a validly deposited notice to convene an extraordinary general meeting under s 368 of the Companies Act 1985 (*PNC Telecom plc v Thomas* [2003] BCC 202); (iii) a 'written application' under s.1(3) of the Landlord and Tenant Act 1988 can be made via email (*E.ON UK Plc v Gilesports Ltd* [2013] 1 P&CR 4, at [51], per Arnold J); (iv) an email satisfies the requirement for a notice 'in writing' under s. 13 of the Leasehold Reform (Housing and Urban Development) Act 1993 (*Achieving Perfection Ltd v Gray* (unreported, 18 May 2015), per HHJ Coltart (sitting in the county court at Brighton); albeit a contrary view was arrived at by HHJ Dight (sitting in the county court at London) in *Cowthorpe Road 1-1A Freehold Ltd v Wahedally* [2017] L&TR 4 (a decision referred to as 'more legalistic than principled' in *Emmett & Farrand on Title*, Vol. 2, §28.300)); (v) service of a copy notice under s 79(8) of the Commonhold and Leasehold Reform Act 2002 can be effected by way of attachment to email (*Assethold Ltd v 110 Boulevard RTM Co Ltd* [2017] 4 WLR 181, at [13], per Judge John Behrens); (vi) reference to a 'document' in s 15 of the Party Wall etc Act 1996 can include a document in electronic form (*Goulandris v Knight* [2018] 1 WLR 3345, at [18]); (vii) a completion notice served under Sch 4A to the Local Government Finance Act 1988 can be served via email (*UKI (Kingsway) Ltd v Westminster City Council* [2019] 1 WLR 104); and (viii) notice of intent under Sch 13A of the Housing Act 2004 can be validly served by email (*Sutton v Norwich City Council* [2020] UKUT 90 (LC); appeal dismissed at [2021] 1 WLR 1691). Failure to comply with a requirement for notice to be in 'writing' can be expected to invalidate the notice: see eg *Epping Forest District Council v Essex Rendering Ltd* [1983] 1 WLR 158, at 162, per Lord Templeman.

[2] *Speedwell Estates Ltd v Dalziel* [2002] HLR 43, at [22], per Rimer J (cited with approval in *Burman v Mount Cook Land Ltd* [2002] Ch 256, at [26], per Chadwick LJ); *Newbold v The Coal Authority* [2014] 1 WLR 1288, [70], per Sir Stanley Burnton.

[3] *Mannai Investment Co Ltd v Eagle Star Life Assurance Co Ltd* [1997] AC 749.

## COMPLIANCE WITH INDISPENSABLE CONDITIONS

5.2 As shall be described in more detail below, the test articulated in *Mannai* is concerned with how a contractual notice would be interpreted by the 'reasonable recipient'. Critically, however, that test has no application where a party fails to satisfy an indispensable condition in the lease as to the form or content of the break notice: such conditions must be strictly complied with.[4] Failure to comply will render the notice invalid.[5] As Lord Hoffmann memorably said in *Mannai* itself:[6] 'If the clause had said that the notice had to be on blue paper, it would have been no good serving a notice on pink paper, however clear it might have been that the tenant wanted to terminate the lease.'

5.3 The principle of strict compliance is vividly illustrated by the decision of the Court of Appeal in *Siemens Hearing Instruments Ltd v Friends Life Ltd*.[7] In that case the tenant's break clause was worded as follows:

> 19.2 … the Tenant may determine the Term on the Termination Date by giving the Landlord not more than 12 months' and not less than six month's written notice, which notice must be expressed to be given under section 24(2) of the Landlord and Tenant Act 1954. The term will then determine on the Termination Date.

5.4 The draftsman of the lease made a technical error in the drafting of clause 19.2, since s 24(2) of the Landlord and Tenant Act 1954 does not envisage a notice being given thereunder. Rather, s 24(2) simply preserves the ability of a tenant to serve a contractual break notice or common law notice to quit, just as it preserves the landlord's ability to forfeit the lease for breach of covenant.

5.5 The tenant duly served a break notice which complied with the provisions of the lease in all respects save that it was not 'expressed to be given under s 24(2) of the Landlord and Tenant Act 1954'. Indeed the notice made no reference to the 1954 Act at all. At trial, Mr Nicholas Strauss QC (sitting as a Deputy Judge of the High Court) decided that the

[4] It has been observed that the concept of an 'indispensable' condition is puzzling, because if a requirement of an option is a condition, it is by definition indispensable: see K Lewison *The Interpretation of Contracts* (Sweet & Maxwell, 7th edn, 2020), §16.112, fn 230.

[5] *Speedwell Estates Ltd v Dalziel* [2002] HLR 43, at [17], per Rimer J ('It is … important to emphasise that the House of Lords was not saying that anything less than proper compliance with the terms of a contractual break clause would be sufficient to effect the break'); *Burman v Mount Cook Land Ltd* [2002] Ch 256, at [26], per Chadwick LJ; *Procter & Gamble Technical Centres Ltd v Brixton Plc* [2003] 2 EGLR 24, at [21], per Neuberger J (referring to the 'difference between the strict compliance that is required where there is a specific stipulation, and the question of how the notice would be interpreted by a reasonable recipient …'); *Trafford MBC v Total Fitness (UK) Ltd* [2003] 2 P&CR 2, at [49], per Jonathan Parker LJ ('… there is no basis in … *Mannai* for, in effect, rectifying any defects or omissions in the notice so as to bring it into line with the relevant requirements …'); *Rennie v Westbury Homes (Holdings) Ltd* [2007] EWCA Civ 1401, at [14], per Dyson LJ ('… where the case is one where it is an indispensable condition that the notice should contain 'specific information', the omission of that information invalidates the notice …'); *Siemens Hearing Instruments Ltd v Friends Life Ltd* [2014] 2 P&CR 5, at [38], per Lewison LJ ('The majority of speeches in that case [*Mannai*] give no support to the notion that there is a species of permitted non-compliance with the formal requirements of a clause prescribing the method of exercise of an option …').

[6] *Mannai Investment Co Ltd v Eagle Star Life Assurance Co Ltd* [1997] AC 749, at 776B.

[7] *Siemens Hearing Investments Ltd v Friends Life Ltd* [2014] 2 P&CR 5. See also *Ropemaker Properties Ltd v Bella Italia Restaurants Ltd* [2018] L&TR 32, at [34] (unilateral right to terminate an agreement for lease conditional upon notice being given by the tenant to the landlord *and* the tenant's guarantor (a company within the same group of companies); failure to give notice to the guarantor was fatal to the exercise of the right).

notice was valid, forming the view that the missing words 'made no difference at all' and were a 'meaningless formula'.[8] The landlord appealed.

5.6 The Court of Appeal unanimously held that the break notice was invalid. The only reasoned judgment was given by Lewison LJ. After a thorough and careful analysis of the law of options, he said:[9]

> [55] … in the case of a unilateral (or 'if') contract such as an option, the terms of exercise must be fully complied with … Notices given under statutes and some kinds of notices given under contracts (eg rent review notices) even if labelled 'options' do not fall into that special class of case. If the judge's approach were correct I do not see how it could be restricted to compliance with conditions about the form of notices. It would surely also apply to trivial failures to comply with other conditions (eg a notice served a few minutes late or trivial breaches of repairing obligations). In all such cases the court would be invited to answer the question: did the parties really mean that such trivial non-compliance would defeat a valuable right? But in the case of a unilateral (or 'if') contract that has never been a relevant question …
>
> [64] … Here there was no compliance with the formal requirement of clause 19.2 that the notice be 'expressed' in a particular way. There was quite simply no reference in the notice to section 24(2) at all.
>
> [65] I do not accept that in the field of unilateral (or 'if' contracts) there is any room for the notion of substantial compliance. As Diplock LJ said in *United Dominions Trust [United Dominions Trust (Commercial) Ltd v Eagle Aircraft Services Ltd* [1968] 1 WLR 74, 83] the question is whether the relevant event has occurred. That question is to be answered 'Yes' or 'No'. It cannot be answered 'Almost'. Either a purported exercise of an option satisfies both the formal and substantive provisions of the clause, or it does not. If it does not, then it is ineffective. In my judgment ours is such a case. I appreciate that that is a harsh result, but hard cases make bad law.[10]

5.7 In other words, *Mannai* cannot be used in an attempt to obviate the need to comply with the formal requirements of a break clause. Or, to put it another way: it does not 'give a green light to inaccurate and sloppily drafted notices'.[11]

## MISTAKES IN THE BREAK NOTICE: THE GENERAL APPROACH

5.8 Prior to the decision in *Mannai*, the courts tended to adopt an extremely rigid and inflexible approach to mistakes in the drafting of contractual notices. This is exemplified by *Hankey v Clavering*.[12] In that case, the lease in question was for a term of 21 years from 25 December 1934. The break clause conferred on either party the right to determine the lease at the expiration of the first seven years, by six calendar months' notice. The landlord gave notice to the tenant's solicitors in the following terms:

> As I may have to be away for some time in the near future, I will be obliged if you would accept the six months' notice to terminate your client's lease which I am allowed to give on 21 June 1941. This would mean that he would have to give up the cottage on 21 December 1941.

[8] *Siemens Hearing Investments Ltd v Friends Life Ltd* [2014] L&TR 8, at [40].
[9] *Siemens Hearing Investments Ltd v Friends Life Ltd* [2014] 2 P&CR 5, at [55], [64]–[65].
[10] Permission to appeal was refused by the Supreme Court.
[11] *Procter & Gamble Technical Centres Ltd v Brixton Plc* [2003] 2 EGLR 24, at [35], per Neuberger J.
[12] *Hankey v Clavering* [1942] 2 KB 326.

5.9 This was obviously a mistake on the part of the landlord, because the six months' notice should have expired on 25, not 21, December. At first instance, Asquith J held that the notice could be saved on the basis that it had been accepted as a good notice by the tenant's solicitors; but that solution was rejected by the Court of Appeal on the facts. The Court of Appeal (Lord Greene MR and Lord Clauson), held that the notice was ineffective. They regarded the point as so clear that they gave judgment *ex tempore*. Lord Greene MR said:[13]

> Notices of this kind are documents of a technical nature, technical because they are not consensual documents, but, if they are in proper form, they have of their own force without any assent by the recipient the effect of bringing the demise to an end. They must on their face and on a fair and reasonable construction do what the lease provides that they are to do. It is perfectly true that in construing such a document, as in construing all documents, the court in a case of ambiguity will lean in favour of reading the document in such a way as to give it validity, but I dissent entirely from the proposition that, where a document is clear and specific, but inaccurate on some matter, such as that of date, it is possible to ignore the inaccuracy and substitute the correct date or other particular because it appears that the error was inserted by a slip. By the clear wording of this notice the plaintiff purported to bring the lease to an end on 21 December 1941. In so doing he was attempting to do something which he had no power to do, and, however much the recipient might guess, or however certain he might be, that it was a mere slip, that would not cure the defect because the document was never capable on its face of producing the necessary legal consequence.

5.10 This kind of strict approach was disapproved of in *Mannai* as being 'highly artificial and capable of producing results which offend against common sense'.[14]

5.11 *Mannai* concerned two leases in identical terms, both dated 11 March 1992. The two leases were for a term of '10 years subject to the provisions of clause 7(13) … from and including 13 January 1992'. Clause 7(13) of each lease provided:

> The tenant may by serving not less than six months' notice in writing on the landlord or its solicitors such notice to expire on the third anniversary of the term commencement date determine this lease and upon expiry of such notice this lease shall cease and determine and have no further effect.

5.12 The 'third anniversary of the term commencement date' was 13 January 1995. However, by two letters dated 24 June 1994 (served on the landlord more than six months before 13 January 1995) the tenant gave notice to the landlord in respect of each lease as follows:

> Pursuant to Clause 7(13) of the lease we as tenant hereby give notice to you to determine the lease on 12 January 1995.

The tenant contended that the leases were determined by the notices. At trial, the tenant succeeded. On appeal to the Court of Appeal, the landlord was successful. The tenant appealed to the House of Lords.

5.13 By a majority (Lord Goff of Chieveley and Lord Jauncey of Tullichettle dissenting), the House of Lords allowed the tenant's appeal.

[13] *Hankey v Clavering* [1942] 2 KB 326, at 329–30.
[14] *Mannai Investment Co Ltd v Eagle Star Life Assurance Co Ltd* [1997] AC 749, at 778A.

5.14 The first speech of the majority was given by Lord Steyn. He based his decision on a number of propositions, as follows:[15]

(1) This is not a case of a contractual right to determine which prescribes as an indispensable condition for its effective exercise that the notice must contain specific information. After providing for the form of the notice ('in writing'), its duration ('not less than six months') and service ('on the landlord or its solicitors'), the only words in clause 7(13) relevant to the content of the notice are the words 'notice to expire on the third anniversary of the term commencement date determine this lease'. Those words do not have any customary meaning in a technical sense. No terms of art are involved. And neither side has suggested that anything should be implied into the language. That is not surprising since the tests governing the implication of terms could not conceivably be satisfied. The language of clause 7(13) must be given its ordinary meaning. A notice simply expressed to determine the lease on the third anniversary of the commencement date would therefore have been effective. The principle is that that is certain which the context renders certain: *Sunrose Ltd v Gould* [1962] 1 WLR 20.

(2) The question is not how the landlord understood the notices. The construction of the notices must be approached objectively. The issue is how a reasonable recipient would have understood the notices. And in considering this question the notices must be construed taking into account the relevant objective contextual scene. The approach in *Reardon Smith Line Ltd v Yngvar Hansen-Tangen (trading as HE Hansen-Tangen)* [1976] 1 WLR 989, which deals with the construction of commercial contracts, is by analogy of assistance in respect of unilateral notices such as those under consideration in the present case. Relying on the reasoning in Lord Wilberforce's speech in the *Reardon Smith* case, at pp 996D–997D, three propositions can be formulated. First, in respect of contracts and contractual notices the contextual scene is always relevant. Secondly, what is *admissible* as a matter of the rules of evidence under this heading is what is arguably relevant. But admissibility is not the decisive matter. The real question is what evidence of surrounding circumstances may ultimately be allowed to influence the question of interpretation. That depends on what meanings the language read against the objective contextual scene will let in. Thirdly, the inquiry is objective: the question is what reasonable persons, circumstanced as the actual parties were, would have had in mind. It follows that one cannot ignore that a reasonable recipient of the notices would have had in the forefront of his mind the terms of the leases. Given that the reasonable recipient must be credited with knowledge of the critical date and the terms of clause 7(13) the question is simply how the reasonable recipient would have understood such a notice. This proposition may in other cases require qualification ...

(3) It is important not to lose sight of the purpose of a notice under the break clause. It serves one purpose only: to inform the landlord that the tenant has decided to determine the lease in accordance with the right reserved. That purpose must be relevant to the construction and validity of the notice. Prima facie one would expect that if a notice unambiguously conveys a decision to determine a court may nowadays ignore immaterial errors which would not have misled a reasonable recipient.

(4) There is no justification for placing notices under a break clause in leases in a unique category. Making due allowance for contextual differences, such notices belong to the general class of unilateral notices served under contractual rights reserved, eg notices to quit, notices to determine licences and notices to complete: *Delta Vale Properties Ltd v Mills* [1990] 1 WLR 445, 454E–G. To those examples may be added notices under charter

[15] *Mannai Investment Co Ltd v Eagle Star Life Assurance Co Ltd* [1997] AC 749, at 767C–68G.

> parties, contracts of affreightment, and so forth. Even if such notices under contractual rights reserved contain errors they may be valid if they are 'sufficiently clear and unambiguous to leave a reasonable recipient in no reasonable doubt as to how and when they are intended to operate:' the *Delta* case, at p 454E–G, per Slade LJ and adopted by Stocker and Bingham LJJ; see *also Carradine Properties Ltd v Aslam* [1976] 1 WLR 442, 444. That test postulates that the reasonable recipient is left in no doubt that the right reserved is being exercised. It acknowledges the importance of such notices. The application of that test is principled and cannot cause any injustice to a recipient of the notice. I would gratefully adopt it.

5.15 Lord Hoffmann delivered the second speech in the majority. He began by noting that 'it is remembered that such notices, operating as they do, unilaterally to alter the rights of the parties, must comply strictly with the terms of the lease'.[16] However, he observed[17] that the case was not straightforward because the break clause in question did not 'require the tenant to use any particular form of words'. Rather, the tenant had to use words which 'unambiguously [conveyed] a particular meaning, namely an intention to terminate the lease on 13 January'. At the end of his speech, he said:[18]

> in *Carradine Properties Ltd v Aslam* [1976] 1 WLR 442, 444, Goulding J said that the test for the validity of a notice was: 'Is the notice quite clear to a reasonable tenant reading it? Is it plain that he cannot be misled by it?' … In my view … the House should state unequivocally that the test stated by Goulding J in *Carradine Properties Ltd v Aslam* [1976] 1 WLR 442 was right … The notice should be construed against the background of the terms of the lease. Interpreted in this way, the notice in the present case was valid.

5.16 The third judge in the majority was Lord Clyde. He observed:[19]

> Where a notice of termination complies precisely and unambiguously with the provision which empowers the sending of the notice then its validity should be unquestioned. Where the terms of the notice do not altogether accord with the provisions of the contract that may or may not render the notice unenforceable. The problem then may come to be one of finding a fair and reasonable construction of the notice. But there can be cases where the validity of the notice cannot be saved by any construction and will have to be regarded as bad.

5.17 Considering how a break notice should be construed, he said:[20]

> The formulation propounded by Goulding J in the *Carradine* case, at p 444, was 'Is the notice quite clear to a reasonable tenant reading it? Is it plain that he cannot be misled by it?' *Delta Vale Properties Ltd v Mills* [1990] 1 WLR 445 concerned a vendor's notice to complete which was in condition 23 of the conditions of sale, but I see no reason why any different principle of construction should apply. Slade LJ observed, at p 454:
>
> > 'In my judgment, notices to complete served under condition 23, if they are to be valid must be sufficiently clear and unambiguous to leave a reasonable recipient in no reasonable doubt as to how and when they are intended to operate.'
>
> The standard of reference is that of the reasonable man exercising his common sense in the context and in the circumstances of the particular case. It is not an absolute clarity or an absolute absence of any possible ambiguity which is desiderated.

[16] *Mannai Investment Co Ltd v Eagle Star Life Assurance Co Ltd* [1997] AC 749, at 773G.
[17] *Mannai Investment Co Ltd v Eagle Star Life Assurance Co Ltd* [1997] AC 749, at 774A.
[18] *Mannai Investment Co Ltd v Eagle Star Life Assurance Co Ltd* [1997] AC 749, at 780D–80G.
[19] *Mannai Investment Co Ltd v Eagle Star Life Assurance Co Ltd* [1997] AC 749, at 781D–81E.
[20] *Mannai Investment Co Ltd v Eagle Star Life Assurance Co Ltd* [1997] AC 749, at 782A–82D.

5.18 Thus, all three of the majority expressly approved the test laid down by Goulding J in *Carradine Properties Ltd v Aslam*;[21] and two of the three (Lord Steyn and Lord Clyde) also expressly approved the test formulated by Slade LJ in *Delta Vale Properties Ltd v Mills*.[22]

5.19 It will be noted that Lord Clyde (at 782C) appeared to suggest that the test for the validity of a notice was not one which depended upon 'absolute clarity or an absolute absence of any possible ambiguity'. However, it has since been stated that Lord Steyn's insistence for the reasonable recipient to be left 'in no doubt' that the break option is being exercised is to be preferred.[23] In other words, when faced with a break notice which contains an error or an ambiguity on its face, the court will ask: Is the notice quite clear to the reasonable recipient reading it? Is it plain that he cannot be misled by it? If these questions can be answered in the affirmative, then the notice will be valid.

## THE OBJECTIVE APPROACH TO THE CONSTRUCTION OF NOTICES

5.20 As is clear from *Mannai*, the construction of a break notice must be approached objectively, ie how the reasonable recipient would have understood the notice. It necessarily follows, therefore, that the subjective understandings and intentions of the serving party or of the recipient are irrelevant.[24] Indeed, it is inherent in the objective nature of the *Mannai* test that even 'a document which was never intended by its sender to be a valid notice may nevertheless operate as one, and vice versa'.[25] Likewise,

[21] *Carradine Properties Ltd v Aslam* [1976] 1 WLR 442. The point was confirmed by Arnold LJ (with whom Floyd and Underhill LJJ agreed) in *Pease v Carter* [2020] 1 WLR 1459, at [15].

[22] *Delta Vale Properties Ltd v Mills* [1990] 1 WLR 445.

[23] *Barclays Bank Plc v Bee* [2002] 1 WLR 332, at [35], per Aldous LJ ('[Counsel for the tenants] went on to suggest that the fact that there was doubt would not in certain circumstances settle the matter. I listened to that submission, but I believe it to be misguided. Every statement in the *Mannai* case is to the contrary …'), and at [49], per Arden LJ ('… if there is doubt about it a notice is bad …'); *Fernandez v McDonald* [2004] 1 WLR 1027, at 1031F, per Hale LJ ('Lord Steyn made it clear that the reasonable recipient should be left in no doubt as to what was intended by the notice …'). In *Pease v Carter* [2020] 1 WLR 1459, at [57], Underhill LJ referred to a test of 'reasonable doubt' (rather than 'no doubt'), saying: '… there must be no reasonable doubt as to what the notice was intended to say: that is the formula endorsed by Lord Steyn …' However, it is respectfully suggested that Underhill LJ was not laying down any different test to that in *Mannai*. See, further, the discussion in *Consensus Business Group (Ground Rents) Ltd v Palgrave Gardens Freehold Co Ltd* [2020] 2 P&CR 13, at [39]–[45], where Falk J rejected the suggestion that the test is a simple one of 'no reasonable doubt'. Although Lord Steyn in *Mannai* referred to notices containing errors being valid if they are 'sufficiently clear and unambiguous to leave a reasonable recipient in no reasonable doubt as to how and when they are intended to operate', Falk J said: '… it is important to note the reference in this passage to "sufficiently" clear and unambiguous, and the fact that the reference to "no reasonable doubt" relates to what was intended, rather than to an absence of any possible doubt about the text of the Notice.'

[24] *Rennie v Westbury Homes (Holdings) Ltd* [2007] 2 P&CR 12, at [38], per Henderson J ('… the whole point of an objective analysis of how a notional reasonable recipient would have understood the letter is that the subjective intentions and understandings of *Westbury* are irrelevant …'); *Stobart Group Ltd v Stobart* [2019] EWCA Civ 1376, at [34], per Simon LJ (rejecting the submission that an objective approach to the construction of a notice 'should not be adopted where a common subjective intent can clearly be demonstrated …').

[25] *Rennie v Westbury Homes (Holdings) Ltd* [2007] 2 P&CR 12, at [39], per Henderson J; and see also eg *Sidney Bolsom Investment Trust Ltd v E Karmios & Co (London) Ltd* [1956] 1 QB 529 (concerning a tenant's request for a new tenancy pursuant to s 26 of the Landlord and Tenant Act 1954), at 539, per Denning LJ ('Once a tenant, whatever his inmost state of mind, has to all outward appearances made a valid request in the prescribed form setting out his proposals, he cannot thereafter rely on his own mistake to say that it was a nullity or invalid … The validity of the request must be judged by the true interpretation of it without regard to

the fact that the actual recipient was not misled cannot (of itself) validate an otherwise invalid notice.[26]

**5.21** Previously, it has been suggested that the reaction of the actual recipient of a notice may be of some probative value when assessing how the reasonable recipient in his position would have understood it.[27] However, that approach must now be considered wrong in the light of *Lancecrest v Asiwaju*.[28] There, the landlord had let to the tenant certain premises in East London. The lease was for a term of 12 years from 5 February 1997, at a rent of £6,500 per annum subject to review. The relevant rent review provisions in clause 5.1 of the lease were as follows:

> (a) If the Landlords so require the basic rent shall be reviewed with effect from the end of every fourth year of the lease period (in each case 'review date').
> (b) To exercise the option to review the basic rent the Landlord shall give notice ('review notice') to the Tenant no more than 12 months before the review date stating what annual amount the Landlords propose as the basis rent from the review date ('new basic rent').
> (c) If the Tenant [does] not give Notice (Counter-Notice) to the Landlords within two months after the review notice is given (in respect of which counter-notice time is of the essence) informing the Landlords that the Tenant [does] not accept the annual amount proposed by the Landlords the new basic rent shall apply from the review date and the remaining sub clauses of this clause 5.1 shall not apply in respect of that review date.

**5.22** On 19 February 2002, the landlord's agent gave a review notice to the tenant, proposing a new rent of £30,000 with effect from the review date of 5 February 2001. Thus, the landlord's trigger notice was served well after the final date specified in clause 5.1(b). The tenant replied on 5 March 2002 by saying:

> Your notice or demand is invalid. The terms of the lease is [sic] very clear. It requires one year notice of any rent review. Until you serve me with a valid one-year notice about future rent review. I will not enter into any arbitration.

what happened behind the scenes …'), at 545, per Harman J ('The person who receives [the notice] must read it according to its true construction and is entitled to receive it as such. I cannot think it could be right to go behind a document of this sort and say: Well, as in the inmost heart of the writer he intended something else, he must not be taken to have meant what he wrote …').

[26] Consequently, previous dicta to the opposite effect must be taken to be incorrect. See eg *Lazarus Estates Ltd v Beasley* [1956] 1 QB 702, at 710, per Denning LJ ('… The misnomer was an obvious mistake which does not affect the validity of the documents. The documents were addressed to "the tenant", Mrs Beasley knew that she was the tenant, and she was not misled in any way …'); *Frankland v Capstick* [1959] 1 WLR 204, at 208, per Sellers LJ ('… But this case, I think, leaves it clear that the notice is one given on behalf of the landlord, and there is no indication in the case … that the widow was in any way deceived by this, or was under any misapprehension as to who the landlord was …'); *Land v Sykes* [1992] 1 EGLR 1, at 4D, per Sellers LJ ('… if objective construed in the light of the facts known to both landlord and tenant the meaning of the notice is clear, that is an end of the matter. But if, in fact, the tenant was not confused, I for my part think that that would suffice …').

[27] See eg *Royal Life Insurance v Phillips* (1991) 61 P&CR 182, at 192, per Nolan J ('But adopting as the cases all have as the test, the question whether a reasonably minded recipient of the letter would appreciate that it was a notice activating the rent review, it seems to me that the reaction of the tenant here is material as an indication of what at any rate this business woman did regard it as saying. I have of course no evidence as to the tenant's business experience, but it is plain from the content of her letter of June 25 that she is an articulate and intelligent woman who well knew what it was that she was responding to …'); *Lay v Ackerman* [2004] HLR 40, at [91], per Arden LJ ('… it is plain that the respondents were not in fact misled into thinking that the notice came from someone other than their landlord. That supports the conclusion that I have reached that, applying the standard of reference of a reasonable recipient in the context of the circumstances of this case, including the prior unsuccessful enfranchisement proceedings, the meaning of the notice would have been plain and the error would not have misled a reasonable recipient …').

[28] *Lancecrest Ltd v Asiwaju* [2005] L&TR 22.

5.23 In the face of the tenant's refusal to accept that the landlord was entitled to implement the rent review out of time, the landlord applied for the appointment of an independent surveyor for the purposes of determining the new rent. The independent surveyor determined the new rent to be £28,000.

5.24 One of the issues for the Court of Appeal was whether the tenant's letter of 5 March 2002 constituted a valid counter-notice under clause 5.1(c). By a majority (Neuberger and Brooke LJJ, Clarke LJ dissenting), it was held that the letter was not a valid counter-notice. As Brooke LJ trenchantly observed:[29]

> Like the judge, I find it impossible to interpret this as a notice informing the landlords that [the tenant] did not accept the annual rent they proposed as the new basic rent. He simply did not regard their notice as having any legal validity at all, and he told them so. It is hardly surprising that he also told them that he would not have anything to do with any arbitration: his notice simply was not drafted with a view to participating in the Cl.5(1) scheme at all.

5.25 In his dissenting judgment, Clarke LJ looked to the reaction of the landlord upon receiving the tenant's letter. He said:[30]

> [67] … I can see no reason why the court should not have regard to the actual reaction of the landlord in deciding what the reaction of the reasonable landlord in the position of this landlord would be.
>
> [72] If one asks whether, in the light of the letter of March 5, there was a dispute about the amount of the rent, say for the purposes of an arbitration clause, there can I think be no doubt that the answer is yes. If one asks whether the tenant was accepting the amount of the rent in the letter of March 5, the answer can in my opinion only be no. It seems to me to follow that in the letter the tenant was indeed informing the landlord that he did not accept the amount of the rent. If one asks the question … whether a reasonable landlord receiving the letter would understand that the tenant was not accepting the amount of the rent, the answer is yes. The tenant was plainly not accepting the rent; otherwise he would have said so.
>
> [74] I should add that I have reached that conclusion without regard to the fact that the landlord operated the contractual machinery to fix the new basic rent. However, the fact that it did so seems to me to give support to the view that a reasonable landlord would have understood the letter as saying that the tenant did not accept the annual amount of the rent.

5.26 Neuberger LJ recorded that he had seen the 'draft judgment of Clarke LJ' before having arrived at his ultimate conclusion.[31] He disagreed with Clarke LJ on the question whether, when deciding if a particular notice is valid, it is permissible to place some weight on the reaction of the actual recipient. He explained:[32]

> [38] … As Steyn LJ [sic] emphasised in *Mannai*, the question is not how the actual recipient landlord understood the letter, but how a reasonable person in his position would have understood it. I see the attraction of the argument that the reaction of the actual landlord may, in some circumstances, have evidential value as to how a reasonable recipient would react and that that can be said to be consistent with what was said in *Patel* [*Patel v Earlspring Properties Ltd* [1991] 2 EGLR 131] and not inconsistent with the analysis of Steyn LJ.

[29] *Lancecrest Ltd v Asiwaju* [2005] L&TR 22, at [86].
[30] *Lancecrest Ltd v Asiwaju* [2005] L&TR 22, at [67], [72], [74].
[31] *Lancecrest Ltd v Asiwaju* [2005] L&TR 22, at [36].
[32] *Lancecrest Ltd v Asiwaju* [2005] L&TR 22, at [38]–[41].

> [39] However, it appears to me, when deciding on the validity of a notice, to rely in any way on the reaction of the actual recipient is unsound in principle, and could well lead to inconsistency and unfairness. It is well established that, when interpreting a contract, it is not permissible to rely on the subsequent conduct of the parties as an aid to construction. The proper approach to the interpretation of notices is the same as that of contracts see per Hoffmann LJ [sic] in *Mannai* at 779H. Accordingly, it appears to me that the same principle must apply to interpretation of notices.
>
> [40] The question whether a particular document is a valid notice must, of course, depend on the contractual provisions under which it is said to have been served, and the precise terms of the document and the matrix of facts in which it is received. However, it is obviously desirable that the courts adopt a consistent approach to the construction of alleged notices as a matter of principle. If the reaction of the recipient of an alleged notice is to impinge on its validity, then this would almost inevitably lead to additional uncertainty in an area which (judging by the number of cases on the topic) is already bedevilled by uncertainty, and where certainty is highly desirable.
>
> [41] Further, if the fact that the recipient treats the document as a valid notice is a factor in favour of it being a valid notice, then the corollary must be that the recipient who treats the document as ineffective is entitled to rely upon that fact in order to support his contention that it is not a valid notice. In my view, that would be unfair on the sender of the document. Furthermore, it appears to me that to take into account the reaction of the recipient would actually benefit an ill-advised recipient as opposed to one who is well advised. A well-advised recipient of a document which is almost certainly not a valid counter-notice might protect himself by treating the document as a valid counter-notice, in case he turns out to be mistaken, would thereby be improving the chances of the document being held to be a valid counter-notice.

**5.27** On this point, Brooke LJ expressed his agreement with Neuberger LJ that 'the landlord's actual reaction plays no part in the legal test that has to be applied'.[33]

## THE 'RELEVANT OBJECTIVE CONTEXTUAL SCENE'

### (a) General Observations

**5.28** In considering how the reasonable recipient would have understood a break notice, the court is enjoined to take into account 'the relevant objective contextual scene'.[34] In *Mannai* itself, Lord Hoffmann said:[35]

> In practice, the only relevant background will be, as in this case, the terms of the lease itself, which may show beyond any reasonable doubt what was the intention of the person who gave the notice. There will be no question of the parties not being privy to the same background – both of them will have the lease – and no room for dispute over what the relevant background is.

**5.29** However, as a matter of law, the relevant objective contextual scene is not limited to the terms of the lease.[36] Indeed, 'the whole of the background available to the parties

[33] *Lancecrest Ltd v Asiwaju* [2005] L&TR 22, at [88].

[34] *Mannai Investment Co Ltd v Eagle Star Life Assurance Co Ltd* [1997] AC 749, at 779E–79F.

[35] *Mannai Investment Co Ltd v Eagle Star Life Assurance Co Ltd* [1997] AC 749, at 780D–780G.

[36] *Prudential Assurance Co Ltd v Exel UK Ltd* [2010] 1 P&CR 7, at [160], per Mr Jeremy Cousins QC (sitting as a Deputy Judge of the High Court) ('… the relevant contextual scene is not confined to the Lease and the terms of the Notice itself. In many cases such limited material will be all that is relevant, as Lord Hoffmann said

can be taken into account',[37] even matters 'in which one or both may take no particular interest, their minds being addressed to or concentrated on other facts'.[38] So, for example, it is entirely permissible to have regard to 'publicly available information' (such as company searches in a case where there is doubt as to the identity of the serving party or the intended recipient).[39] It seems even the existing knowledge of the recipient is, in principle, capable of being relevant to the question of construing a break notice.[40]

5.30 The broad scope of the 'contextual scene' is well-illustrated by *Rennie v Westbury Homes (Holdings) Ltd*.[41] In that case, by an agreement dated 17 September 1992, Mr and Mrs Rennie granted to Westbury an option to purchase certain land for development. The option period was for 10 years (expiring on 16 September 2002). However, Westbury also had the right to extend the option period for a further five years by the service of a notice during the last year of the option period and the payment of £20,000. Westbury duly served such a notice on 12 September 2002, ie a few days before the expiry of the option period. In evidence, Westbury gave details of steps which it had taken in relation to the land and the ultimate realisation of its development potential between September 1992 and August 2002. By the latter date, the position was that part of the land had been allocated for housing development in the Forest of Dean Local Plan Review, and preparations were being made for a forthcoming Public Inquiry. Of this, Henderson J said:[42]

> In the light of the forthcoming Public Inquiry, and the efforts that Westbury had made over the past 10 years to realise the planning potential of the land, no reasonable landowner in Mr Rennie's position could have been surprised that Westbury wished to exercise its right to extend the option. Indeed, failure to do so would, on the face of it, have been inexplicable. Accordingly, the letter of September 12, 2002 was in no sense a bolt from the blue, and the message that it conveyed was, in my judgment, the message that any reasonable landowner in Mr Rennie's position would have been expecting to receive.

## (b) Covering Letters

5.31 Importantly, it is now well-established that a covering letter is part of the relevant contextual scene against which a break notice may fall to be interpreted.[43] Thus, an error

in *Mannai* at 779E–79F. However, that will be because in many cases there will have been no correspondence or other communication between the parties in the run-up to the exercise of the break provision. To take Lord Hoffmann as indicating that only the lease and the notice were relevant would run entirely counter to the thrust of his speech *Mannai* where especially at 779F–79G cited above he clearly favoured the approach of admitting all the relevant background available to the parties to be considered to ascertain intention …').

[37] *Barclays Bank Plc v Bee* [2002] 1 WLR 332, at [51], per Arden LJ.

[38] *Reardon Smith Line Ltd v Yngvar Hansen-Tangen (trading as HE Hansen-Tangen)* [1976] 1 WLR 989, at 997, per Lord Wilberforce.

[39] *Havant International Holdings Ltd v Lionsgate (H) Investment Ltd* [2000] L&TR 297, at 304, per Hart J; *Prudential Assurance Co Ltd v Exel UK Ltd* [2010] 1 P&CR 7, at [161], per Mr Jeremy Cousins QC (sitting as a Deputy Judge of the High Court).

[40] *Dodika Ltd v United Luck Group Holdings Ltd* [2021] EWCA Civ 638, at [34], per Nugee LJ ('*Mannai* shows that the information conveyed by a unilateral notice to the reasonable recipient is in principle capable of being affected by the background context, and that includes the knowledge that the actual recipient has …').

[41] *Rennie v Westbury Homes (Holdings) Ltd* [2007] 2 P&CR 12 (upheld on appeal at [2007] EWCA Civ 1401).

[42] *Rennie v Westbury Homes (Holdings) Ltd* [2007] 2 P&CR 12, at [36].

[43] *Stidolph v American School in London Educational Trust Ltd* (1969) 20 P&CR 802, at 807, per Cross LJ ('Assuming, without deciding, that the notice alone would not be a good notice, it is conceded that any defects

or ambiguity in a break notice can be cured (or indeed compounded) by reference to a statement in a covering letter. For example, in *Germax Securities Ltd v Spiegal*,[44] the tenant held business premises under the terms of a lease dated 19 March 1971, for a term of seven years terminating on 24 June 1997. The landlords wished to bring the tenancy to an end at the termination of the term; and, on 25 November 1976, they served a notice in the form prescribed by the regulations under the Landlord and Tenant Act 1954 seeking to determine the lease on 24 June 1977. However, by error, the notice was dated 25 March 1977, instead of 25 November 1976. However, the covering letter (itself properly dated 25 November 1976), stated that the enclosed notice terminated the tenancy on 24 June 1977. The tenant contended that the notice was invalid. Buckley LJ rejected the argument. He explained:[45]

> reading the notice with the covering letter, I do not think it can be said that any reasonable tenant would have been misled here. The mistake in this case was not in the operative part of the notice; it is merely a mistake in relation to the date at which the notice purports to have been given by the landlord. That that was a mistake is clear from association of the notice with the covering letter.

5.32 To a similar effect, in *Barclays v Bee*,[46] the solicitors for the claimant landlords, who wished to redevelop business premises which were let to the defendant tenants, wrote to the tenants saying that they were enclosing a notice terminating the lease under s 25 of the Landlord and Tenant Act 1954, with a copy which they asked to be returned. In fact, by mistake they enclosed two different notices, one (referred to as document A) stating that the landlords would oppose the grant of a new lease but omitting to state the grounds on which such an application would be opposed, and the other (document B) stating that the landlords would not oppose such an application. The tenants sought clarification of the landlords' intentions. The landlords' solicitors wrote back apologising for having sent incorrect notices, stating that it was the landlords' intention to oppose the grant of a new tenancy and enclosing a third notice (document C) which stated the grounds of opposition. The tenant applied for the grant of a new tenancy, and the issue as to the validity of the notices was tried as a preliminary issue. The district judge held that document B was a valid notice, and that the landlords were accordingly precluded from

in it would be cured by the letter and the stamped, addressed envelope sent with it …'); *M&P Enterprises (London) Ltd v Norfolk Square Hotels Ltd* [1994] 1 EGLR 129, at 130L, per Judge Rich QC (sitting as a judge of the High Court) ('… In order to discover the way in which these particular notices should be construed, I think, I am entitled to look at the letter under cover of which they were in fact served upon the tenant …'); *The Mayor and Burgesses of the London Borough of Hackney v The Hackney African Organisation* [1999] L&TR 117, at 125, per Simon Brown LJ ('… by his own covering letter enclosing the counter-notice Dr Seray-Wurie [a trustee of the Hackney African Organisation] made it as plain as could be that the notice was in fact being served by the HAO and for their benefit, not his own. Read in its full context, the counter-notice here should be construed as one given by Dr Seray-Wurie on behalf of the Organisation and thus on behalf of his fellow trustees as well as himself.'); *York v Casey* (1999) 31 HLR 209, at 216, per Peter Gibson LJ ('… I do not accept for one moment that any reasonable recipient of the letter and notice would believe that the clear offer of a six months tenancy would … be extended to an offer of a term of six months plus a few days to the end of March. To my mind the letter makes clear beyond doubt that what was contemplated was a tenancy for six months certain …'); *Pease v Carter* [2020] 1 WLR 1459, at [45], per Arnold LJ ('… covering letters may be taken into account in determining how the reasonable recipient would interpret a statutory notice …').

[44] *Germax Securities Ltd v Spiegal* (1979) 37 P&CR 204.

[45] *Germax Securities Ltd v Spiegal* (1979) 37 P&CR 204, at 206.

[46] *Barclays Bank Plc v Bee* [2002] 1 WLR 332.

opposing the grant of a new tenancy. The landlords appealed successfully to the judge, whose decision was upheld in the Court of Appeal. The ratio of the Court of Appeal's decision was that although document B, standing alone, was a valid notice, the effect of documents A and B and the covering letter, when taken together, was to leave a reasonable recipient in doubt as to the landlords' intentions. Hence document B was not a valid notice. As Wilson LJ succinctly explained:[47]

> The fact that document A would in any event have been invalid under section 25(6) of the 1954 Act, in that it failed to state any ground for opposition to the grant of a new tenancy, does not disentitle it from being part of the context necessary to the construction of document B. The covering letter dated 18 December 1997 enclosed the two documents and alleged that the one was a copy of the other. Of course, as was immediately apparent to the tenant's agent, neither was a copy of the other. On the contrary, the kernel of the two documents was entirely inconsistent and the central message to the tenant was hopelessly and instantaneously confused.

## MISTAKES AS TO THE BREAK DATE

5.33 The insertion of the wrong date in a break notice is, probably, the most common type of mistake (as in *Mannai* itself). Where the lease provides for a 'once and for all' opportunity to exercise the break clause, a mistake of this sort is unlikely to be fatal. However, the position becomes more problematic from the serving party's perspective if the lease provides for more than one possible date to terminate. This is demonstrated by the following examples.

### (a) Where a Mistake as to the Date has Invalidated the Notice

5.34 In *Peaceform Ltd v Cussens*,[48] the claimant was the tenant of certain premises in Middlesex under the terms of a 25-year lease dated 14 April 1999. By clause 11.1 of the lease, the tenant was given the option to buy the freehold reversion of the premises upon giving to the landlords 'not less than 3 months' notice of [its wish to do so] expiring not later than the 6th day of February 2004'. By a letter dated 27 August 2003, the tenant's solicitor gave a notice to the landlords purportedly in compliance with clause 11.1. The tenant's solicitor wrote: 'Under the terms of the option you are entitled to not less than 3 months' notice and accordingly I confirm that this notice may be deemed to expire on 7 November 2003'. The notice erroneously gave less than three months' notice of the tenant's wish to exercise the option: the date of 7 November 2003 was (it was later said) intended to have been a reference to 7 December 2003. Nonetheless, on 20 October 2003, the tenant's solicitor sent a further letter to the defendants, repeating the error, stating that the notice would expire on 7 November 2003. The landlords accepted that the reasonable recipient of the notice, had it addressed its mind to it, would have understood that the tenant intended to specify a different expiry date from that of 7 November 2003.

[47] *Barclays Bank Plc v Bee* [2002] 1 WLR 332, at [56].
[48] *Peaceform Ltd v Cussens* [2006] 3 EGLR 67.

However, there was a range of dates between 28 November 2003 and 6 February 2004 when the notice could have expired, so that the reasonable recipient was left in reasonable doubt as to how and when the notice was intended to operate. Mr Stuart Isaacs QC (sitting as a Deputy Judge of the High Court) accepted these submissions and held the notice was invalid. He explained:[49]

> the question is whether the notice was sufficiently clear and unambiguous to have left a reasonable recipient, with knowledge of the terms of the lease and, in particular, clause 11, in no doubt as to the terms of the notice. In both *Mannai* and *Peer Freeholds*,[50] the expiry date of the notice period was clearly defined. In *Mannai*, the notice was to expire on the third anniversary of the term commencement date. In *Peer Freeholds*, the break option was exercisable at the end of the third year of the term … In contrast, in the present case, the notice period is of not less than three months expiring not later than 6 February 2004. It is not referable to a particular date or occurrence and the expiry date of the notice period is not clearly defined, nor is it clear from the context. There is, for example, no reason why the expiry date should evidently be read as 7 December 2003 or as any other date in the period when the notice could have expired … In my judgment, the notice was not sufficiently clear and unambiguous as to have left a reasonable recipient, with the requisite knowledge, in no doubt as to its terms.

### (b) Where a Mistake as to the Date has not Invalidated the Notice

5.35 In *Micrografix v Woking 8 Ltd*,[51] the tenant had a break clause entitling it to determine its lease at the expiry of the fifth anniversary of the term upon giving to the landlord not less than 12 months' previous written notice of its desire to do so. On 21 January 1994, the tenant sent a letter to the landlord enclosing a break notice. The letter said: 'We enclose by way of service upon you notice determining our lease on 23rd March 1995 pursuant to clause 8 of the lease'. The notice said: 'We … hereby give you notice that that the tenants intended to quit and deliver up possession … on 23rd March 1994'. There was an obvious discrepancy between the letter and the notice (in that the letter referred to March 1995 and the notice to March 1994). However, both dates were inappropriate, since the only date for determination of the lease was 23 June 1995. Holding that the notice was valid, Jacob J said as follows:[52]

> I turn to consider, as indicated in Carradine, what a reasonable tenant, reading the letter and the notice, would make of it and, in particular, to consider whether he would be misled by it: In so doing, I assume that the reader, the landlord, is well aware that the only date which could be given is in fact June 23, 1994 [sic – this should be 1995]. It must always be the case when construing the document that one must take into account the background knowledge of the particular reader concerned.
>
> So the landlord knows that the date of determination can be, and can only be, June 23, 1995. He sees the letter and he sees the notice. He sees that there is a mistake on the dates. He also knows that there is no requirement to specify any date, and he sees as plain as anything that the tenant wants to leave. He understands the tenant's desire because we are in a time of recession.

[49] *Peaceform Ltd v Cussens* [2006] 3 EGLR 67, at 69B–69D.
[50] See **5.39** below.
[51] *Micrografix v Woking 8 Ltd* (1996) 71 P&CR 43.
[52] *Micrografix v Woking 8 Ltd* (1996) 71 P&CR 43, at 45.

> I think he sees as plainly as anything that the tenant has made a mistake as to the date, that in any event the tenant need not have specified a date at all and that the tenant is intending to go when he can. I think he sees that because both the letter and the notice expressly refer to clause 8, thereby inviting the landlord specifically to read the letter in conjunction with clause 8.

5.36 *Garston v Scottish Widows' Fund and Life Assurance Society*[53] concerned a lease dated 10 July 1985 of office premises in Holborn. The lease was for a term of 20 years 'from the 24th day of June 1985' at a yearly rent of £47,000 subject to upwards only rent reviews at the end of every five years of the term. The lease contained a break clause entitling the tenant 'to determine the term at the expiration of the tenth year of the term' upon giving to the landlord 'at least six months' previous notice in writing'. The tenth year of the term expired on 23 June 1995. On 19 September 1994, the tenant gave notice to the landlord 'pursuant to clause 7 of the lease [ie the break clause]' of its desire to determine the lease. The notice was expressed to expire on 9 July 1995. This was followed up by a letter dated 4 October 1994 in materially identical terms. Thus, the writer of the notice and the letter made the mistake of thinking that the time for determining the lease was the expiration of the tenth year from the date of the lease (9 July 1995) instead of the expiration of the tenth year of the term (23 June 1995). The landlord claimed that the break notice was invalid. The Court of Appeal disagreed. Giving the only reasoned judgment, Nourse LJ said the following:[54]

> The notices were expressed to be served pursuant to clause 7 of the lease, which empowered the plaintiffs to determine the term thereby granted at the expiration of the tenth year, that is to say on 23 June 1995. A reasonable recipient of the letters with knowledge of the terms of the lease would have known that that was the date, and the only date, on which it could be determined. He would also have known that the date of the lease was 10 July 1985 and that the dates specified for the expiration of the notices, 9 July 1995, was the expiration of the tenth year from that date. In that state of knowledge, the reasonable recipient would have been left in no doubt that the plaintiffs wished to determine the lease on 23 June but had wrongly described the date for determination as 9 July ... While I gladly credit the reasonable recipient, this paragon of the law, with the eyesight, omniscience and diligence that they demand of him, in the end he could only reasonably have concluded that the plaintiffs, in specifying 10 July, had intended to specify the day following the day on which they wished to determine the lease by the notices under clause 7. In other words, the reasonable recipient would have been left in no doubt that the plaintiffs wished to specify 24 June as the date for the commencement of the new tenancy but had wrongly described it as 10 July.

5.37 In *Trafford MBC v Total Fitness (UK) Ltd*,[55] the lease of a car park contained a landlord's redevelopment break clause, entitling the landlord to determine the lease 'by giving the Tenant as much notice as possible but with a minimum of two weeks' notice'. On 8 October 2001, the landlord's solicitor served a break notice worded as follows:

> In accordance with the terms of the Car Park Lease (as varied by the Agreement) and for and on behalf of [the landlord] I hereby give you 17 days' notice of determination of the same and would further confirm for the avoidance of all doubt that the Car Park, the subject of the Lease, will be closed as at and from midnight on the 24th October 2001.

[53] *Garston v Scottish Widows' Fund and Life Assurance Society* [1998] 1 WLR 1583.
[54] *Garston v Scottish Widows' Fund and Life Assurance Society* [1998] 1 WLR 1583, at 1588A–88F.
[55] *Trafford MBC v Total Fitness (UK) Ltd* [2003] 2 P&CR 2.

5.38 The tenant contended that there was a fatal inconsistency or ambiguity in the notice between, on the one hand, the date on which the stipulated period expired (ie the period of 17 days) and, on the other hand, the date which was expressed, 'for the avoidance of all doubt', to be the expiry date of the notice. The Court of Appeal disagreed. Giving the only reasoned judgment, Jonathan Parker LJ said:

> [49] The process of determining whether a notice complies with the requirements of the provision pursuant to which it is given (be that provision statutory or contractual) involves, as a first step, a consideration of what, on its true construction, the notice says. The contents of the notice then have to be matched against the relevant requirements in order to determine whether it meets them …
>
> [50] In the instant case, however, we are at the first stage; that is to say, the stage of seeing what, on its true construction, the notice dated October 8, 2001 says. If, on its true construction, it gives two different expiry dates (albeit that each one falls after the expiry of the minimum period of two weeks …), then a question will arise whether one or other of those dates is to be taken as the operative date, or whether the notice is altogether invalid. But the first step is to construe the notice – and in that context *Carradine* and *Mannai* are, in my judgment, of direct relevance. The approach to construction of the notice in issue in *Mannai* adopted by the majority of the House of Lords is, in my judgment, plainly one which applies equally in the instant case. The fact that in *Mannai* recourse to surrounding circumstances yielded the important fact that there was only one date on which notice could validly expire (a state of affairs which does not arise in the instant case) does not in my judgment impact in any way on the applicability of the general principles stated by the majority of the House of Lords in that case.
>
> [53] … in my judgment the statement that 'for the avoidance of all doubt … the Car Park … will be closed as at and from midnight on the 24th October 2001' can only mean that the day on which the notice was given was to be included in reckoning the stipulated 17-day period and that the notice indeed was to expire on October 24, 2001.
>
> [55] For my part, in answer to the question posed in *Carradine*, I have no doubt at all that it would have been quite clear to a reasonable tenant reading the notice (that is to say, reading the whole of the notice) that it expired at midnight on October 24, 2001.

5.39 *Peer Freeholds Ltd v Clean Wash International Ltd*[56] concerned a lease of business premises granted on 8 November 2001. The term was for six-years less three days. The underlease provided for annual rent reviews from 22 August 2004. In addition, it contained a tenant's break option, exercisable at the end of the third year of the term by six months' previous notice in writing. On 5 January 2004, the tenant gave notice to exercise the break option 'at the end of this lease on 22nd August 2004'. In fact, the end of the third year of the term was 7 November 2004. The landlord contended that the reasonable recipient of the notice would not know whether the tenant wanted to exercise the break on 22 August or 7 November 2004. It was suggested that the reasonable recipient might think: (i) that the tenant wanted to exercise the break in accordance with the terms of the lease; or (ii) that the tenant was trying to determine the lease on 22 August 2004 and only that date because it did not want to pay the reviewed rent. Evans-Lombe J rejected these submissions and held the notice was valid. He said:[57]

> The suggestions made by [Counsel for the landlord] … as to how the landlord might have interpreted the letter of 5 January were, in my view, 'unrealistic'. It is clear that a reasonable

[56] *Peer Freeholds Ltd v Clean Wash International Ltd* [2005] 1 EGLR 47.
[57] *Peer Freeholds Ltd v Clean Wash International Ltd* [2005] 1 EGLR 47, at 50H.

> landlord, with knowledge of the provisions of clause 6.8 of the underlease, would have understood that the letter of 5 January was intended to operate the provisions of that clause in order to break the sublease at the date for which clause 6.8 provided, namely 7 November 2004, and that the 22 August 2004 date, contained in the letter as being the date for the breaking of the lease, was a mistake on the tenant's part.

5.40 It is also worthwhile noting the decision in *TBAC Investments Ltd v Valmar Works Ltd*.[58] That case concerned a contract for the sale of land, incorporating the Standard Commercial Property Conditions of Sale (2nd edn), clause 8.8.2 of which provides: 'The parties are to complete the contract within 10 working days of giving a notice to complete, excluding the day on which the notice is given'. On 18 March 2013, the vendor served on the purchaser a notice to complete by 'close of business on 1st April 2012 [sic] being 10 clear working days after the giving of this notice (exclusive of the day on which it is given)'. The purchaser pointed out that the date was erroneous in two respects. First, '2012' was wrong (since it should have referred to '2013'); and secondly, '1st April' was wrong (because 10 working days after 18 March 2013 was 3 April 2013). Thus, it was contended that the notice was invalid. Mr Kevin Prosser QC (sitting as a Deputy Judge of the High Court) disagreed. He said:[59]

> a reasonable recipient would certainly understand that: (i) the maker of the Notice intended the date for completion to be a date in 2013, not in 2012: after all, the Notice was given on 18th March 2013, and the Notice was itself wrongly dated '2012'; but (ii) the maker of the Notice did not mean that unless he could specify 1st April 2013 as the completion date he did not want to give an effective notice to complete at all; (iii) therefore the maker of the Notice was intending to specify a date which was 10 clear working days after the giving of the Notice, in accordance with Standard Condition 8.8, and as stated in paragraph 4 itself; (iv) that date, as a reasonable recipient of the Notice could easily determine for himself by consulting a diary, was 3rd April 2013.

## MISTAKES AS TO THE IDENTITY OF THE SERVING PARTY

5.41 As previously discussed,[60] absent some exceptional circumstances, a break notice can only be given by: (i) the party in whom the term or reversion is vested; or (ii) a duly appointed agent acting within the scope of his authority. However, sometimes, there may be a mistake or ambiguity on the face of the notice as to who is purporting to give it. This type of mistake or ambiguity is not of a category outside the scope of *Mannai*.[61]

[58] *TBAC Investments Ltd v Valmar Works Ltd* [2015] EWHC 1213 (Ch). As appears from the judgment of Vos LJ at [2016] EWCA Civ 1056, Lewison LJ gave permission to appeal to the purchaser on the ground that the Deputy Judge was wrong to hold that the principles in *Mannai* saved the validity of the notice to complete. However, so far as can be ascertained, the appeal never occurred.

[59] *TBAC Investments Ltd v Valmar Works Ltd* [2015] EWHC 1213 (Ch), at [69].

[60] Chapter 4.

[61] *Havant International Holdings Ltd v Lionsgate (H) Investment Ltd* [2000] L&TR 297, at 306, per Hart J ('I do not consider that the mere fact that the ambiguity in the notice goes to the question of who is purporting to give it puts it into some special category. The question in every case is whether, on a fair construction of the notice, it is quite plain that the reasonable recipient cannot be misled by it …'); *Prudential Assurance Co Ltd v Exel UK Ltd* [2010] 1 P&CR 7, at [158], per Mr Jeremy Cousins QC (sitting as a Deputy Judge of the High Court) ('… A mistake in the notice, even as to the identity of the person giving it, will not necessarily invalidate it, provided that in all the circumstances its meaning is clear, the mistake is obvious, and the recipient can safely rely upon it …').

Indeed, as Neuberger LJ explained in *Lay v Ackerman*[62] (referring specifically to a tenant's break notice):

> the purpose of the break notice [is] not to identify the tenant to the landlord, but to communicate to the landlord an intention on behalf of the tenant, and no-one other than the tenant, an unequivocal desire to determine the lease in accordance with its terms. Once a person other than the actual tenant [is] identified in the notice as the person on whose behalf the notice was served, the notice could only be valid if it could be shown that, despite the mis-identification, a reasonable person in the position of the landlord could have been in no doubt but that the notice was served on behalf of the person who was the tenant.

**5.42** This proposition is illustrated by a number of authorities, as follows.

### (a) Where a Mistake as to the Identity of the Serving Party has Invalidated the Notice

**5.43** In *Lemmerbell Ltd v Britannia LAS Direct Ltd*,[63] two commercial units had been let to the tenant, LAS Direct Ltd ('Direct'), under two different (but similarly worded) leases. In August 1992, solicitors acting for Direct and an associated group company called the Life Association of Scotland Ltd ('Life') gave notice to the landlords of the commercial units that the demised premises would be used by employees of Life, as well as by employees of Direct. In October 1994, the same solicitors sent purported break notices in respect of both commercial units, saying: 'We act on behalf of [Life], successors in title to … [the tenant] … We therefore give notice of our Client's intention … to determine this lease'. Life was not, as it so happened, the successor in title to the tenant at all. At trial, the judge found that the notices were valid. The Court of Appeal allowed the landlords' appeal and found that the break notices were ineffective to operate the break. Peter Gibson LJ delivered the leading judgment. He said:[64]

> I cannot see how the [landlords] could act upon the notices safely as being notices which were in fact, or which they had reason to believe were, binding on Direct. They would have been aware that no consent had been given to any assignment by Direct, but that was not inconsistent with there having been an effective assignment. Without the production to them of an assignment, they could not know if Life was the right person to be giving the notices.
>
> …
>
> The present case seems to me to bear little resemblance to the type of error addressed in *Mannai*. There, words containing a mere slip, obvious to the reader of the notice when read in context, were construed as meaning what they were plainly intended to mean. In the present case there is no equivalent error: the break notice is not merely given on behalf of Life rather than Direct, but it contains the explanation why it was so given, viz. Life was the successor in title to Direct. I find it impossible to see how in these circumstances it is permissible to construe the break notice as given on behalf of Direct.'

[62] *Lay v Ackerman*, at [62].
[63] *Lemmerbell Ltd v Britannia LAS Direct Ltd* [1999] L&TR 102.
[64] *Lemmerbell Ltd v Britannia LAS Direct Ltd* [1999] L&TR 102, at 114–15.

5.44 He added:[65]

> On the face of each notice, Life was said to be the tenant as successor in title to Direct and that, if true, could only have come about as a result of an assignment without consent. But such an assignment would be effective to make the assignee the lessee for the purposes of clause 7(x). The reasonable recipient could not know in the absence of proof of the assignment whether Life was the lessee. It might have been. If Life was not in fact the lessee but Direct was, the reasonable recipient could not know whether Amery-Parkes [the solicitors who served the notice] were authorised by Direct to act for it and to serve the break notice, contrary to the express terms of the notice. To my mind, because it is not obvious from each notice that there was an error in the name of the lessee nor is it obvious who the actual current lessee was nor whether Amery-Parkes were duly authorised by anyone other than Life, it is impossible as a matter of construction to cure what we now know to be the defect by substituting Direct for Life as the person on whose behalf Amery-Parkes were giving each notice.

5.45 In *Procter & Gamble Technical Centres Ltd v Brixton Plc*,[66] a lease granted in 1995 to Procter & Gamble Health & Beauty Care Ltd ('H&B') contained a break clause in favour of the tenant. Following a series of assignments, in 1998, the lease was vested in another Procter & Gamble company, namely, Procter & Gamble Technical Centres Ltd ('TC'). In 2000, a rent review memorandum was said to be executed by the landlord and the tenant, but the identity of each was wrongly stated; with H&B incorrectly identified as the tenant. In 2002, a solicitor for Procter & Gamble Group, relying on the memorandum, purported to serve a break notice, but did so in the name of H&B. Neuberger J held that the notice was invalid. He said:[67]

> [40] In the present case ... the facts show it to be at least as strong from the landlord's point of view as *Lemmerbell* ... I accept that, in *Lemmerbell*, there was reference in the notice to the fact that Life was successor in title to the original tenant. However, the fact remains that the notice was served on behalf of somebody who the recipient of the notice could reasonably have assumed was the person in whom the lease was vested, and that it was therefore the person entitled to serve the notice. That conclusion appears to me to apply equally if one looks at the first paragraph of the notice, but it does not stop there.
>
> [41] There had been a rather complex series of transactions in 1998–1999 ... It is by no means inconceivable that, after those transactions, there had been one or more other transactions relating to the property which had accidentally not been communicated to the landlord ...
>
> [43] Additionally, in this case, unlike in *Lemmerbell*, the person on whose behalf the notice was stated to be served, was the original tenant. There is therefore ... the additional possibility that a reasonable person in the [landlord's] position could not have ruled out, that the Notice was being served on behalf of someone who had good reason for wishing to put an end to the lease, but in fact had no right to do so. That is not a fanciful idea, because ... the lease was not subject to the Landlord and Tenant (Covenants) Act 1995 and therefore H&B, as the original tenant, remained liable on the tenant's contracts, despite the subsequent assignments.

5.46 Importantly, Neuberger J emphasised that break notices 'particularly if served near the last minute ... have to be clear and unambiguous because the recipient is entitled,

[65] *Lemmerbell Ltd v Britannia LAS Direct Ltd* [1999] L&TR 102, at 115–16.
[66] *Procter & Gamble Technical Centres Ltd v Brixton Plc* [2003] 2 EGLR 24.
[67] *Procter & Gamble Technical Centres Ltd v Brixton Plc* [2003] 2 EGLR 24, at [40]–[41], [43].

and may need, to make dispositions in the faith of such notices, ie on the basis that such notices can be confidently relied on'.[68] A mistake which could reasonably mislead a reasonable recipient cannot be overridden.

**5.47** In *Prudential Assurance Co Ltd v Exel UK Ltd*,[69] Prudential Assurance Co Ltd ('Prudential') had granted a lease to Tibbett & Britten Ltd ('T&B') and Tibbett & Britten Consumer Group Ltd ('Consumer'). At all material times, Consumer was a wholly-owned subsidiary of T&B, and a dormant company. The lease contained a break clause entitling 'the Tenant' to determine the lease on 24 March 2007 by giving to the landlord not less than nine months' prior written notice. In August 2004, the Exel Group of companies acquired the Tibbett & Britten group of companies, including T&B and Consumer. On 29 December 2004, T&B's name was changed to Exel UK Ltd ('Exel'). Consumer's name was not changed. On 13 June 2006, solicitors purporting to act solely for Exel (and not for Consumer) served a break notice on Prudential. The court found that, although the solicitors were authorised to serve the break notice on behalf of Exel and Consumer, the break notice would not unambiguously have been understood to be an effective notice by a reasonable recipient. Mr Jeremy Cousins QC (sitting as a Deputy Judge of the High Court) said of the notice:[70]

> [162] In my judgment the Notice, against the background described, would not unambiguously have been understood to be an effective notice by a reasonable recipient. Its own terms would generate real doubt as to whether it was served on behalf of Consumer, because they suggested that although Consumer was known to have been a lessee, the Notice was not being served on its behalf. The background described does not eliminate the doubt manifest from the Notice; it multiplies it …
>
> [163] … In the present case there was material both in the Notice, and extraneous to it, to suggest that the omission of reference to Consumer in the body of the Notice was not accidental.

**5.48** In *Sackville UK Property Select II (GP) No 1 Ltd v Robertson Taylor Insurance Brokers Ltd*,[71] the lease had been granted to Robertson. The lease contained a tenant's break option. On 23 March 2017, the landlord gave licence to Robertson to assign the lease to Integro. The licence contained a covenant on the part of Integro to apply to register the assignment of the lease at HM Land Registry within 10 days of completion of the assignment. On 29 March, Robertson assigned the lease to Integro. On 20 April, Integro gave notice of the assignment to the landlord and indicated that all future rent demands should be sent to Integro. On 2 May, EC3 Legal, solicitors acting for both Robertson and Integro, sent a notice to the landlord purporting to exercise the break option. However, the notice was expressed to be from Integro only, which was named in the notice as the 'Tenant.' Integro did not comply with its covenant to apply for registration within 10 days business days of completion of the assignment. It was not until 7 July that Integro was registered as proprietor of the lease on that date.

[68] *Procter & Gamble Technical Centres Ltd v Brixton Plc* [2003] 2 EGLR 24, at [46].
[69] *Prudential Assurance Co Ltd v Exel UK Ltd* [2010] 1 P&CR 7.
[70] *Prudential Assurance Co Ltd v Exel UK Ltd* [2010] 1 P&CR 7, at [162]–[163].
[71] *Sackville UK Property Select II (GP) No 1 Ltd v Robertson Taylor Insurance Brokers Ltd* [2018] L&TR 22.

5.49 Integro argued that the reasonable recipient of the break notice would have realised that, when the break notice stated it was served on behalf of Integro, it was referring to Robertson. Fancourt J rejected this contention. He said:[72]

> The reasonable recipient would … have been aware that Integro had covenanted in the Licence to apply to register the Assignment at the Land Registry within ten business days of the date of completion of the Assignment. It would have assumed that Integro had complied with that obligation, sending whatever further documents were necessary and appropriate, and that Integro would therefore be registered as proprietor as from the date on which the application was received by the Land Registry. That would have made Integro the right person to give the break notice. Further, in the notice of assignment, Integro's solicitors had instructed the claimants to send all future rent demands to Integro. The Landlord would therefore have been treating Integro for all purposes as the Tenant under the Lease. In my judgment, the reasonable recipient in those circumstances would be most unlikely to understand that the notice was meant to have been served by Robertson and that the name of Integro was a mistake.

### (b) Where a Mistake as to the Identity of the Serving Party has not Invalidated the Notice

5.50 In *Havant International Holdings Ltd v Lionsgate (H) Investment Ltd*,[73] a company called Havant International Holdings Ltd ('HIHL') held certain premises under the terms of a lease which contained a personal break clause. In the event, however, a break notice was given in the name of a company called Havant International Ltd ('HIL'), a wholly-owned subsidiary of HIHL, and the main operating company in the group of which HIHL was the ultimate holding company. The break notices were signed by a director of HIL, who was not a director of HIHL. On the evidence before him, Hart J found that the break notice was valid. He distinguished *Lemmerbell* as follows:[74]

> Life, rather than Direct, might have been the lessee with the right to serve the break notice; and this was precisely what was asserted by the terms of the purported notice … [But] for that fact, the Court of Appeal might have been disposed to accept the submission made on behalf of Direct that it was obvious that the solicitors were in error in stating that the notice was served on behalf of Life rather than Direct. In the present case, while HIL could conceivably have been the lessee, there were no conceivable legal circumstances in which it could have asserted a right to serve either of the break notices.

5.51 He then concluded:[75]

> The question therefore resolves to this. Would the reasonable recipient assume that there had been a mistake in the description of the company giving the notice? Or would he entertain, as a matter giving rise at least to a reasonable doubt, the possibility that HIL had taken an unlawful assignment and had done so in the mistaken belief that it had thereby become entitled to the benefit of HIHL's personal right? Without claiming to find the answer altogether easy, I have

[72] *Sackville UK Property Select II (GP) No 1 Ltd v Robertson Taylor Insurance Brokers Ltd* [2018] L&TR 22, at [54].

[73] *Havant International Holdings Ltd v Lionsgate (H) Investment Ltd* [2000] L&TR 297.

[74] *Havant International Holdings Ltd v Lionsgate (H) Investment Ltd* [2000] L&TR 297, at 305–306.

[75] *Havant International Holdings Ltd v Lionsgate (H) Investment Ltd* [2000] L&TR 297, at 306.

> concluded that the latter construction of the notice is not one which would have been seriously entertained by a reasonable recipient. The reasonable recipient would, rather, conclude that a mistake had been made in not naming HIHL as the giver of the notice. The personal nature of HIHL's right ... makes that the only explanation of the notice which carries conviction. If that is correct, the reasonable recipient would also have concluded that the notices had been signed by Mr Nahajski, a director of HIL, because he had been authorised by HIHL to do so.

5.52 In *Baker Tilly Management Ltd v Computer Associates UK Ltd*,[76] the landlord had underlet premises to a firm of accountants who, at that time, went by the name Baker Tilly Services Ltd ('BTS'), but subsequently changed its name to Baker Tilly Management Ltd ('BTM'). The underlease included a tenant's break clause. The break notice was served on the landlord by BTM, using its old name of BTS. Mr Peter Prescott QC (sitting as a judge of the High Court) held that when BTM served the notice, it was still the same legal person as BTS. The landlord had to be taken as knowing that and, accordingly, the notice to quit, despite the disparity in the names used by the tenant, was valid.

5.53 In *AWD Chase De Vere Wealth Management Ltd v Melville Street Properties Ltd*,[77] the named tenant under the lease was AWD Chase De Vere Wealth Management Ltd. The lease contained a tenant's break clause. However, the tenant (through solicitors) served a break notice purporting to be given by 'the current tenants', AWD Group Services Limited. That was a company within the same group of companies as the actual tenant. It was not and never had been the tenant under the lease. In the opinion of Lord Glennie, the notice was valid. He said:[78]

> I do not consider that the terms of the letter, unfortunate though the description of AWD Group Services Limited as 'the current tenants' was, would have caused a reasonable landlord in the position of the defenders to doubt that notice was being served on behalf of the actual tenants. It is clear from the letter that the solicitors sending it were aware of the terms of the lease ... In the first paragraph they confirm that they act on behalf of the current tenants of the property under the lease, albeit that they misname them as AWD Group Services Limited. In the second paragraph they give notice on behalf of 'our clients' that they are exercising their right to bring the lease to an end pursuant to clause 2, which, they say, requires 'the Tenant' to serve six months' notice on the landlord. It is, therefore, clear from the terms of the notice that the solicitors are aware that the notice has to be served by the tenant. That being the case, the only possibilities to explain the reference to AWD Group Services Limited are: (a) that there has been an assignation from the actual tenants, AWD Chase De Vere Wealth Management Limited to AWD Group Services Limited: or (b) that the solicitors had simply made an error in identifying the tenants under the lease. In my opinion, a reasonable landlord who knew the terms of the lease, knew that his consent was necessary before there could any assignation, knew that he had not given consent and knew further that he had not even been asked for consent, would discount the possibility that the notice was given on behalf of an assignee of the tenant. Rather, he would assume that the solicitors probably acted for all the companies within the group and that in serving the notice they had simply got the wrong company. As [Counsel for the tenant] put it, he would assume cock up rather than conspiracy.

[76] *Baker Tilly Management Ltd v Computer Associates UK Ltd* [2009] EWHC 911 (Ch).
[77] *AWD Chase De Vere Wealth Management Ltd v Melville Street Properties Ltd* [2009] CSOH 150.
[78] *AWD Chase De Vere Wealth Management Ltd v Melville Street Properties Ltd* [2009] CSOH 150, at [10].

MISTAKES AS TO THE IDENTITY OF THE INTENDED RECIPIENT

5.54 As is described in Chapter 8, the server of a break notice should ensure that the notice is served on the intended recipient(s) as specified in the lease. Sometimes, however, even though a break notice is given to the correct party, it may misidentify the intended recipient. Unless it is an indispensable condition for the validity of the break notice for it to be addressed to a particular named person, this type of mistake may not be fatal on *Mannai* principles.

### (a) Where a Mistake as to the Identity of the Intended Recipient has Invalidated the Notice

5.55 In *Morris v The London Rent Assessment Committee*[79] a notice under Part I of the Landlord and Tenant Act 1954 (terminating a tenancy) was required to be given to the tenant of a flat. The tenant in possession at the date of the notice was a Mr Fry. However, the notice was addressed to Mr Barnby, who was the original tenant. He had assigned the lease of the flat to Mr Fry some 15 years earlier. In his judgment, Mummery LJ said:[80]

> The notice was not addressed to the tenant, Mr Fry, either expressly by name or implicitly by status as tenant. It was expressly and unambiguously addressed by name to an altogether different person, Mr HG Barnby. That was not a minor error or slip. Mr Barnby was not Mr Fry, and he was not, and had long ceased to be, tenant of the flat. The reaction of the reasonable tenant receiving the notice addressed to Mr HG Barnby (or receiving an envelope so addressed) would be to think that the notice or the envelope and its contents were meant for Mr Barnby. The notice cannot be construed as a notice given to Mr Fry.

5.56 *Morris* was followed in *Standard Life Investments Property Holdings Ltd v W&J Linney Ltd.*[81] There, Mansfield District Council demised certain premises to Sun Alliance Trust Company Ltd for a term beginning on 4 April 1997 and expiring on 29 September 2116. On 6 June 1997, the lease was assigned to Capita Trust Company Limited ('Capita'). On 4 February 2004, Capita granted a sub-lease of part of the commercial premises to W&J Linney Ltd ('Linney'). On 26 November 2004, Capita granted a concurrent or overriding lease of the whole premises to Standard Life Investments Property Holdings Ltd. The lease granted by Capita to Linney contained a break clause, entitling the tenant to determine the lease on the fifth anniversary of the date of the lease upon giving to 'the Landlord' not less than six months' prior notice in writing of its desire to do so. The tenant wished to exercise the break. However, the tenant's break notice was mistakenly addressed to Capita, when it ought to have been addressed to Standard Life. To make matters worse: (i) the notice was served under cover of letter which stated expressly that the notice was given to Capita; and further (ii) the rubric at the bottom of the break notice itself contained the wording: 'Received' – and then there was a blank space – 'Capita Trust Company Ltd'. In considering whether the break notice was valid,

[79] *Morris v The London Rent Assessment Committee* [2002] HLR 48.
[80] *Morris v The London Rent Assessment Committee* [2002] HLR 48, at [11].
[81] *Standard Life Investments Property Holdings Ltd v W&J Linney Ltd* [2011] L&TR 9.

the tenant accepted that it was necessary that the recipient 'would have realised that the name Capita in the notice was an obvious mistake'.[82] On this point, after referring to the judgment of Mummery LJ in the *Morris* case, Lewison J said:[83]

> In my judgment, the same applies in the present case. There is also the additional factor that if the reasonable recipient had looked at the lease on receipt of the notice, he might have formed the view, as Linney's own solicitors did, that Capita was the right person on whom to serve the notice. In the light of the unambiguous wording of the notice and of the covering letter sent to James Lang LaSalle [the agents appointed by Standard Life], I cannot conclude that the reasonable recipient of the letter and the notice would have understood that it was meant to be addressed to Standard Life.

### (b) Where a Mistake as to the Identity of the Intended Recipient has not Invalidated the Notice

5.57 In *Hawtrey v Beaufront Ltd*,[84] a house in Somerset was demised to a limited company by a lease granted in 1939. The term was 'for the period of the national emergency or European war or threatened European war ... until such national emergency or war shall have been terminated by the signing of terms of peace'. The European war ended on 9 May 1945. On 15 June 1945, the landlords addressed a month's notice to quit to the directors of the tenant company. Croom-Johnson J said:[85]

> The point the defendants take is that the notice is a bad notice for the reason that the addressees are the directors of Beaufront Ltd, and not Beaufront Ltd. The question which I have to determine is: Is a notice in that form a good notice or not? ... I think that within the rule referred to by Lord Greene MR [in *Hankey v Clavering* [1942] 2 KB 326] that in a case of ambiguity the court will favour the reading of the document in such a way as to give it validity, I ought to construe this notice as a notice to terminate the tenancy of the limited company ... It was obviously so treated by the defendants' solicitors. They knew all about it ... [It] seems to me that any solicitor looking at this document would see that, whilst it is addressed to the directors, it is addressed to them, not in their capacity as tenants or as parties to the agreement ... but as being the persons acting on behalf of the limited company.

5.58 In *Bridgers v Stanford*,[86] the tenant company was named Bridgers. Bridgers and another company called Hamptons were both subsidiaries of Abaco Investments Plc. Bridgers was dormant. Bridgers had never actually formally assigned the tenancy agreement to Hamptons. However, Hamptons clearly operated Bridgers' business. It appeared from correspondence that one of Bridgers' directors sometimes used Bridgers' name and sometimes the name of Hamptons. The landlord served a notice under s 25 of the Landlord and Tenant Act 1954 to determine Bridgers' tenancy. However, the notice was addressed to Hamptons. Bridgers contended that the notice was invalid. The Court of Appeal disagreed. Giving the lead judgment, Lloyd LJ did not accept, 'for one moment',

[82] *Standard Life Investments Property Holdings Ltd v W&J Linney Ltd* [2011] L&TR 9, at [23].
[83] *Standard Life Investments Property Holdings Ltd v W&J Linney Ltd* [2011] L&TR 9, at [24].
[84] *Hawtrey v Beaufort Ltd* [1946] 1 KB 280.
[85] *Hawtrey v Beaufort Ltd* [1946] 1 KB 280.
[86] *Bridgers v Stanford* [1991] 2 EGLR 265.

that Bridgers (as a reasonable tenant) was confused; and said that, the misstatement of the tenant's name could not have had any serious consequences such as to invalidate the notice.[87]

5.59 *MW Trustees Ltd v Tellular Corporation*[88] concerned a lease of business premises in Reading. The lease contained a tenant's break clause, entitling the tenant to terminate the lease on 1 March 2010 upon giving to the landlord not less than six months' notice in writing to do so. The tenant addressed the break notice, not to the landlord, but to the landlord's predecessor in title. As to this, Peter Smith J said (with emphasis in the original):[89]

> Had the issue as to the form of the Notice been vital (ie it being addressed to the predecessor landlord) I would have decided that applying the Mannai principles and following an earlier decision of Megarry VC in *Townsend Carriers Ltd v Pfizer Ltd* [1977] 33 P&CR 361 that a reasonable recipient would not have been misled as to the intentions of the defendant to terminate the Lease because the Notice was addressed to the wrong person. On the construction of the Lease I do not accept that the form of the Notice requires it to be addressed to the Landlord as opposed to being sent to them. The Notice has to be given to them but it does not specify that the *contents* of the Notice require them to be referred to in it. There can be no question of the claimants being misled as to the intent by the service of the Notice.

## MISTAKES AS TO THE IDENTITY OF THE DEMISED PREMISES

5.60 Where a break notice misidentifies the premises to which it relates, the notice should not be invalidated provided that it is clear to which premises reference was intended to be made.[90] An early example of this proposition can be found in *Doe d Cox v Roe*.[91] In that case, the landlord of a public house in Limehouse gave notice to quit 'the premises which you hold of me … commonly called … the Watermans Arms'. The evidence showed that the tenant held no premises called the Watermans Arms; indeed, there were no such premises in the parish of Limehouse. But the tenant did hold premises of the landlord called the Bricklayers Arms. By reference to the background, the notice was construed as referring to the Bricklayers Arms. The meaning was objectively clear to a reasonable recipient, even though the landlord had used the wrong name.

5.61 Similarly, in *Bridgers v Stanford*,[92] the tenant occupied premises on the ground-floor and first-floor of an office building in Epsom. One of the two landlords occupied the second floor of the same building. The landlords served a notice under s 25 of the Landlord and Tenant Act 1954 to determine the tenancy. The notice was expressed to relate to the whole of the office building, not just the ground and first floors. Lloyd LJ dismissed any suggestion that this invalidated the notice. He said the tenant 'must have

[87] *Bridgers v Stanford* [1991] 2 EGLR 265, at 268E–68F.
[88] *MW Trustees Ltd v Tellular Corporation* [2011] L&TR 19.
[89] *MW Trustees Ltd v Tellular Corporation* [2011] L&TR 19, at [43].
[90] See *Dodika Ltd v United Luck Group Holdings Ltd* [2021] EWCA Civ 638, at [33], per Nugee LJ.
[91] *Doe d Cox v Roe* (1803) 4 Esp 184.
[92] *Bridgers v Stanford* [1991] 2 EGLR 265.

known that the landlord was himself occupying the second floor, so he must have known that the notice could apply only to the ground floor and the first floor'.[93] Thus, there was minimal if any scope for the tenant to be misled.

## BREAK NOTICES MARKED 'WITHOUT PREJUDICE'

### (a) 'Without Prejudice' to the Validity of an Earlier Break Notice

**5.62** A break notice can properly be served 'without prejudice' to the validity of an earlier notice.[94] So, for example, in *Keith Bayley Rogers & Co v Cubes Limited*,[95] the landlord served on the tenant a notice pursuant to s 25 of the Landlord and Tenant Act 1954 without prejudice to the validity of an earlier notice. The tenant contended that this was impermissible. Templeman J disagreed. He said:[96]

> Mr Blum [Counsel for the tenant] attacks that second notice and says that the landlord cannot have two notices and contend that they are both valid or that one of them is valid: he must make up his mind between them; but in my judgment the landlord may contend that the first notice is good, but if it is not, he may rely on the second notice. If that were not the case, a tenant could very easily threaten a landlord. The landlord serves a notice; the tenant waits for a month and then writes with some of the ingenious arguments which Mr Blum has put forward, and perhaps other ingenious arguments which Mr Blum in another case might advise thus casting doubt on the efficacy of the first notice. The trembling landlord picks up the letter and, blinded with science, plays safe, withdraws the first notice and serves a second notice. The tenant obtains a very useful reprieve during which time he will go quietly on paying a miserable rent.
>
> Mr Blum attempted to tell me that all sorts of horrors would happen if there were two notices extant at one and the same time. With great respect to him, it is sufficient for me to say I am not convinced that there is anything shocking in there being two notices extant on the same day.

**5.63** A similar situation arose *Royal Bank of Canada v Secretary of State and Defence*.[97] There, Lewison J was concerned to assess the validity of break notices served on 21 June 2002 and 29 July 2002. The second notice included the statement: 'This is without prejudice to our previous notice of 21 June 2002'. Lewison J remarked:[98]

> It is common ground that the test is whether the notice was clear to a reasonable recipient of it. In my judgment it was. The notice followed cl.8 exactly. The meaning of the quoted sentence

[93] *Bridgers v Stanford* [1991] 2 EGLR 265, at 268.

[94] *Allam & Co v Europa Poster Services* [1968] 1 All ER 826, at 839D–39E, per Buckley J ('... It is then said that because at the end of the notice there are the words "without prejudice to the validity of the notice or notices previously served on you ...", that raises a complexity for the recipient, because he has to scratch his head and say, "I have now received two notices which suggest that my agreement ... may determine on one or other of two dates according to whether notice A or notice B is to be treated as valid or effective". It is well established that where a landlord, having given notice to quit, feels it desirable to give a second notice, that that notice does not amount to a waiver of the earlier notice and is in fact without prejudice to the validity of the earlier notice, and to put into a second notice of that kind which expressly states that the second notice is without prejudice to the validity of the earlier notice is merely to state a fact ...').

[95] *Keith Bayley Rogers & Co v Cubes Ltd* (1976) 31 P&CR 412.

[96] *Keith Bayley Rogers & Co v Cubes Ltd* (1976) 31 P&CR 412, at 416.

[97] *Royal Bank of Canada v Secretary of State for Defence* [2004] 1 P&CR 28.

[98] *Royal Bank of Canada v Secretary of State for Defence* [2004] 1 P&CR 28, at [46].

was that the giver of the notice was not to be taken to have withdrawn the earlier notice and was to remain free to argue that it had validly terminated the lease ... In my judgment the second notice was also valid.

### (b) 'Without Prejudice' with no Further Words of Qualification

**5.64** The phrase 'without prejudice' (without any further qualification) is properly to be used only in the context of 'negotiations entered into between [two or more] parties with a view to settling ... litigation'.[99] However, in practice, the same formula may appear on a break notice or a covering letter. This may be so where the person responsible for serving the break notice is a non-lawyer. It is suggested that the inclusion of such words is unlikely of itself to invalidate a break notice. So, for example, in *Norwich Union Life Insurance Society v Tony Waller Ltd*,[100] the landlord's agent served a notice on the tenant with a view to triggering a rent review. The notice was headed 'without prejudice' and provided: 'We have been instructed by your landlords ... to negotiate with you in connection with the rent review contained in your lease ... It is our client's proposal to increase the rental to £11,500 per annum'. Bearing in mind the proper circumstances in which the phrase 'without prejudice' should be used, Harman J considered that the use of that formula was 'meaningless'[101] (but nonetheless concluded that the notice was ineffective to act as a trigger notice).

## BREAK NOTICES MARKED 'SUBJECT TO CONTRACT'

**5.65** Where negotiations or discussions are expressly or impliedly made 'subject to contract', then the parties remain in a state of negotiation unless and until a formal contract is drawn up and signed. However, it is not uncommon for a serving party to include the 'subject to contract' formula on the face of a notice served pursuant to the provisions of a lease.

**5.66** There are a number of rent review cases where the inclusion of such words has had the effect of invalidating either a landlord's trigger notice or a tenant's counter-notice.[102]

[99] *Ofulue v Bossert* [2009] 1 AC 990, [85], per Lord Neuberger.

[100] *Norwich Union Life Insurance Society v Tony Waller Ltd* [1984] 1 EGLR 126.

[101] *Norwich Union Life Insurance Society v Tony Waller Ltd* [1984] 1 EGLR 126, at 127M.

[102] *Shirlcar Properties Ltd v Heinitz* (1983) 268 EG 362 (landlord's purported trigger notice provided that the 'rent required as from the review date is £6,000 per annum exclusive, and we look forward to receiving your agreement'; the notice was marked 'subject to contract'; Kerr LJ said: '... I think any recipient might ask himself whether the words "Subject to contract" have the effect that the landlord is indeed bound by the figure of £6,000 put forward in the letter. Similarly, if the tenant is minded to accept that figure, and is therefore minded to write back and agree to it, he would be left in doubt, and that doubt would remain if he consulted his solicitor, as to whether any such agreement would be binding. In my view therefore this is not a sufficiently clear specification of the required rent under the rent review clause to fulfil the requirements of it ...'); *Sheridan v Blaircourt Investments Ltd* [1984] 1 EGLR 139 (tenant's purported counter-notice provided 'In view of the obvious disagreement between us, I suggest it would be appropriate to make Application to the RICS for an Independent Valuer'; the notice was marked 'without prejudice and subject to contract'; Nicholls J said: '... Were it necessary for me to consider this further point, I would, in the context of the correspondence in this particular case and having regard to the heading of the letter, have come to the conclusion that, for this reason also, it would

However, those authorities are likely to be of limited relevance when considering the validity of a break notice. Of more relevance is *Westway Homes Limited v Moores.*[103] That case concerned an option to purchase a piece of land. On 18 February 1988, agents acting on behalf of Westway gave notice to exercise the option. The notice was headed 'subject to contract'. Of this, Dillon LJ said:[104]

> I have no doubt that the words 'subject to contract' in the heading in that letter were meaningless and can have had no effect at all. This was virtually the last date for the exercise of the option. The conditions of the contract which would result from exercise of the option had been prescribed by the option agreement itself, and there was no reason whatsoever why the words 'subject to contract' should have been put in that letter … It seems to me that any solicitor reading the letter of February 18 would necessarily and reasonably have inferred that the words 'subject to contract' in the heading were in the context meaningless.

not be possible to construe the wording in this letter as an unequivocal intimation to the landlords' advisers that the tenant was requiring the ascertainment of the substituted rent to be referred to a referee …'); *Maurice Investments Ltd v Lincoln Insurance Services Ltd* [2007] 1 P&CR 14 (the landlord purported to initiate the rent review by sending to the tenant a letter marked 'subject to contract' and 'without prejudice' and proposing a rent of £360,000 in order to 'avoid the usual protracted negotiations'; HHJ Weeks (sitting as a Judge of the High Court) said: '… if [the] reasonable recipient was … asked if he was sure [that the landlord was initiating the rent review by giving notice under the lease], I think he would have said: "No". There is a possible alternative explanation, namely that the landlord is putting forward a sum in the hope of quick agreement and not specifying a sum to bring into operation the full formalities under the lease, and that he is reserving the right to notify us later of a higher figure …'). *Cf British Rail Pension Trustee Co Ltd v Cardshops Ltd* [1987] 1 EGLR 127 (tenant's counter-notice was marked 'subject to contract' and stated the rent which the tenant was prepared to agree; Vinelott J considered that these words did not deprive the notice of validity, saying: 'The words would be taken, I think, by a sensible businessman, as either a mistake (by no means an unfamiliar mistake – the words "subject to contract" are frequently used in quite inappropriate circumstances) or … as designed to ensure that the letter was not taken by the landlord as an offer capable of acceptance – a construction which is wholly consistent with the operation of the letter as a counternotice'); *Royal Life Insurance v Phillips* (1991) 61 P&CR 182 (otherwise perfectly valid landlord's trigger notice marked 'subject to contract' and 'without prejudice'; Nolan J accepted the submission made by Counsel for the tenant (Mr Lewison) that 'the combination of the words "subject to contract" and "without prejudice" would normally reflect an intention that the document could produce no legal effect' but concluded: 'That letter, as I read it, clearly was intended to have a legal effect. It is, as I have mentioned, expressly written in accordance with the terms of the lease and it does, in the terms of the lease, notify the tenant of the rent from the review date').

[103] *Westway Homes Limited v Moores* (1992) 63 P&CR 480.

[104] *Westway Homes Limited v Moores* (1992) 63 P&CR 480, at 484.

# 6

# *The Time for Exercise of the Break Clause and Service of the Break Notice*

## INTRODUCTION

**6.1** Break clauses may be exercisable on a specified date or specified dates (eg exercisable upon the expiry of the seventh year of the term); or they may be exercisable on the happening of a certain event (eg exercisable upon the landlord forming an intention to redevelop the premises). The most usual tenant's break clause typically incorporates one or more pre-determined break dates. This mechanism enables the landlord to organise cash flow. A lease that might end whenever the tenant chooses (ie a 'rolling break') is unpopular with landlords for obvious reasons.

**6.2** Well-drafted leases will almost certainly contain provisions specifying: (i) a maximum time period for the exercise of the break clause; and/or (ii) a minimum period of notice of intention to exercise the break. In all cases, time limits should be strictly complied with. Indeed, as Lord Nicholls observed in *Valentines Properties Limited v Huntco Corporation Limited*:[1]

> Inherent in a time limit is the notion that the parties are drawing a line. Once the line is crossed, a miss is as good as a mile …

**6.3** The rationale for such a strict approach is certainty: it enables the parties 'to know where they stand to take commercial decisions in the light of such knowledge'.[2] The point was made clear by Gross LJ in *Ener-G Holdings Plc v Hormell*, where he said:[3]

> [58] … strict time bars as are an aspect of certainty: there is certainly nothing uncommercial about them and they are not infrequently encountered in commercial contracts … [60] … pleas of hardship in this area are untenable.

**6.4** Because a failure to serve the break notice within the applicable time limit will almost certainly result in the loss of the ability to terminate the lease,[4] care must be taken to ensure that the lease terms are followed. In practice, this may be difficult,

[1] *Valentines Properties Limited v Huntco Corporation Limited* [2001] UKPC 14, at [20].

[2] *Ageas (UK) Ltd v Kwik-Fit (GB) Ltd* [2013] EWHC 3261 (QB), at [38], per Green J.

[3] *Ener-G Holdings Plc v Hormell* [2012] EWCA Civ 1059, at [58], [60]. Similar judicial expressions are to be found in *Teoco UK Ltd v Aircom Jersey 4 Ltd* [2018] EWCA Civ 23, at [22], per Newey LJ and *Triumph Controls – UK Ltd v Primus International Holding Co* [2019] EWHC 565 (TCC), at [98], per O'Farrell J.

[4] *United Scientific Holdings Ltd v Burnley BC* [1978] AC 904, at 962, Lord Fraser.

as is demonstrated by *Biondi v Kirklington & Piccadilly Estates Ltd.*[5] In that case (which concerned an option to renew a lease), the lease, granted for a period of 35 years from 8 February 1911, contained the following covenant:

> The lessor hereby covenants with the lessees that the lessor will on the written request of the lessees made 6 calendar months before the expiration of the terms hereby granted … grant to them a lease of the demised premises for the further term of 14 years from the expiration of the said term at the same rent and containing the like covenants and provisos as are herein contained with the exception of the present covenant for renewal, the lessees on the execution of such renewal lease to execute a counterpart thereof.

**6.5** Roxburgh J noted[6] that the phrase 'On the written request of the lessees made six calendar months before the expiration of the term hereby granted' was capable of at least four different meanings: (i) made on 8 August 1945; (ii) made at any time before 8 August 1945; (iii) made on or a reasonable time before 8 August 1945; and (iv) given so as to take effect on 8 August 1945. The judge did not say which construction was correct, only that the second construction was incorrect.

## REFERENCES TO THE 'COMMENCEMENT OF THE TERM'

**6.6** A break clause is often expressed in terms entitling the beneficiary of the clause to terminate the lease on the expiry of (say) 10 years from the 'commencement of the term'. The question then arises: should this be construed as a reference to the date on which the lease is executed (the execution date) or the starting date of the contractual term (the term date)? This is a question which has been addressed in a number of authorities.

**6.7** In *Bird v Baker*,[7] the plaintiff, by an indenture dated 19 July 1851, leased to the defendant certain premises, for a term of 14 years commencing on 25 December 1849, subject to the proviso that it should be lawful for either the landlord or the tenant to determine the demise at the expiration of the first seven years thereof, by six months' notice. Of this, Lord Campbell CJ said it was 'clear' that the intention of both parties was that the lease should be determinable at the end of seven years from Christmas 1849. Wightman J agreed, observing:[8]

> … the determination was to be at the end of seven years from the time from which the term was to run; in fact, at the end of half the term named.

**6.8** *Earl of Cadogan v Guinness*[9] was a case on s 84 of the Law of Property Act 1925. The issue was whether a particular lease was one in respect of which 50 years of the

[5] *Biondi v Kirklington & Piccadilly Estates Ltd* [1947] 2 All ER 59.
[6] *Biondi v Kirklington & Piccadilly Estates Ltd* [1947] 2 All ER 59, at 60.
[7] *Bird v Baker* (1858) 1 E&E 12.
[8] *Bird v Baker* (1858) 1 E&E 12, at 15.
[9] *Earl of Cadogan v Guinness* [1936] Ch 515.

term had expired, thus giving jurisdiction to discharge or modify restrictive covenants. However, in some obiter remarks, Clauson J said:[10]

> It is a very common experience that in the creation of leasehold interests the term which is created is expressed to run as from a date anterior to the date of the document which creates the term. It is very common indeed to find a lease in the year 1936 creating a term of 21 years as from December 25, 1935. If in such a lease there is a reference to, let us say, the first seven years of the term, or 'of the said term', then for the purpose of calculating which are the first seven years, no doubt, on the true construction of the document, the seven years should be treated as beginning from December 25, 1935, and not from the date, let us say, in March, 1936, when the document was actually executed …
>
> … [If] in a document a term which, as created is of less than twenty-one years, is spoken of as a term of twenty-one years, beginning as from a date prior to its creation, and there is a clause providing for determination at the end of the seventh or fourteenth year of the term it is perfectly easy as a matter of construction of such a document to say that the seven years according to the obvious intention of the parties is not to run as from the date of the execution of the lease but from the moment spoken of, though inaccurately, as the beginning of the term in the document.

**6.9** More recently, in *Trane (UK) Ltd v Provident Mutual Life Assurance*,[11] Judge Cooke (sitting as a judge of the High Court) had to consider a break clause worded as follows:

> If the lessee … shall desire to determine the term hereby created at the expiration of the tenth year thereof … and of such desire shall give to the lessor not less than six months' previous notice in writing in that behalf, expiring at the end of the said tenth year … then … the said term shall upon the expiration of such notice duly determine …

**6.10** There, the lease itself had been granted on 6 January 1982 (the execution date), for a term of 25 years expressed to run from 28 August 1981 (the term date). The tenant gave six months' notice to determine the lease at midnight on 5 January 1992, ie the tenth anniversary of the date on which the lease was created. One of the issues for determination was whether the break notice was served out of time. The tenant contended that the break date had to be calculated by reference to the date of execution. Judge Cooke disagreed. He remarked first:[12]

> It has to be remembered, where a lease is constituted as this one is, that although of course the estate in land cannot be created until the ink is dry on the lease the contractual provisions can by agreement be related to any of the date of execution, the date of commencement ('the term date'), if different, or some arbitrary date. There is nothing as a matter of general principle that requires any particular provision to be framed in any particular way.

**6.11** Then, after referring to *Bird v Baker* and *Bradshaw v Pawley* (amongst other authorities), Judge Cooke went on to set out the following principles of general application:[13]

> (a) Where what is in point, either because of some provision in the lease or the requirements of an Act of Parliament, is the length of the estate actually granted or enjoyed, it

[10] *Earl of Cadogan v Guinness* [1936] Ch 515, at 517–18 (cited with approval by Sir Robert Megarry V-C in *Bradshaw v Pawley* [1980] 1 WLR 10, at 15C).

[11] *Trane (UK) Ltd v Provident Mutual Life Assurance* [1995] 1 EGLR 33.

[12] *Trane (UK) Ltd v Provident Mutual Life Assurance* [1995] 1 EGLR 33, at 34K.

[13] *Trane (UK) Ltd v Provident Mutual Life Assurance* [1995] 1 EGLR 33, at 35F–35G.

is to that which the court must look and that can only be ascertained by reference to the execution date.

(b) If the provision in the lease is one which on its true construction relates to the measurement of time or the fixing of a date or an obligation, not being one tied in with the actual continuing existence of the estate at the relevant date, it is generally proper, subject to the construction of the particular instrument, to look at the term date.

(c) The parties to a lease may fix on obligations by relation to whatever they choose, whether inside or outside the period of duration of the estate.

## THE TIME FOR EXERCISE OF THE BREAK CLAUSE

### (a) 'Within' a Specified Period

**6.12** Where a person has the benefit of a break clause exercisable 'within' a specified period of time, the general rule is that he has up to and including the final moment of the period in which to exercise the right to determine the lease.[14]

**6.13** In *Manorlike Ltd v Le Vitas Travel Agency and Consultancy Services Ltd*, there was a lease for a period of three years from 9 May 1984, which contained a break clause (clause 7) in the following terms:

> If the Landlord requires possession of the demised premises at any time during the said term the Landlord shall have the right to determine this Lease by giving to the Tenant not less than 3 months' previous notice in writing expiring at any time so as to determine the same …

**6.14** On 22 May 1985 the landlords gave notice to the tenant as follows:

> WE … hereby give you notice that we require possession of the above-demised premises … we require you to vacate the said premises within a period of three months from the date of service of this notice.

**6.15** Effectively the issue was whether a requirement to vacate the premises 'within a period of three months' was a shorter period than the period of notice for which the tenant was entitled under clause 7, which was a period of 'not less than 3 months' previous notice'. In that connection it is common ground that the notice given on 22 May 1985 expired at midnight on 22/23 August 1985.

**6.16** Determining the issue in favour of the landlords, Kerr LJ said:[15]

> To my mind the word 'within', used in the context of a period of time, is capable of meaning 'before or at the expiry of' that period, as Mr Oliver [Counsel for the landlords] submits; it is not necessarily shorter than the period itself. Mr Oliver derives some assistance for that submission from one of the definitions of the word 'within' in the Oxford English Dictionary, where under No 6 the word 'within' is defined as follows: 'In the limits of a period of time; (most usually) before the end of, after not more than'. It is difficult to think of examples where the word 'within' would be used synonymously with the much more complex expression 'after not more than'. However, what emerged from the illustration of the meaning of the word 'within'

[14] *Manorlike Ltd v Le Vitas Travel Agency and Consultancy Services Ltd* [1986] 1 All ER 574.
[15] *Manorlike Ltd v Le Vitas Travel Agency and Consultancy Services Ltd* [1986] 1 All ER 574, at 575D–75G.

by the expression 'after not more than' is that in common parlance 'within' is capable of including the final moment of a period of time. If a person is required to do something within a week, or in a week, he has the full week to do it, as it seems to me, including the last moment of that week, and he is not required to complete the task in less than a week. To construe this wording of this notice so that it connotes a period of less than three months, because permission must be given 'within' three months with a consequent failure to allow a full period of three months, appears to me to strain the language in a hair-splitting and wholly artificial manner.

**6.17** Nourse LJ agreed, saying as follows:[16]

> The precise meaning of a preposition such as 'within' depends on the context in which it is used. Here it is used in a legal document and it is applied to a period of three months' notice. In such a context I see no difference between the meanings of 'within' and 'during'. In my view if someone is required to vacate premises within or during a specified period, he will comply with the requirement by walking out of the door either before, or on, the stroke of midnight on the last day of that period. So much for language pure and simple.

### (b) A Specified Period 'Before' a Specified Date

**6.18** A break clause may be worded in such a way that it appears as though notice must be given at a specified point in time before a specified date. For example, a lease may provide that a break notice must be given 'six months before the expiration of five years from the commencement of the term'. Where this is the case, the court is unlikely to construe the provision as meaning that the notice can be given only on the day falling precisely six months before the event. Indeed, a 'strict requirement for notice to be given on a single day is, if not unheard of, then at least exceptionally rare in practice'.[17]

**6.19** The point is illustrated by *Hexstone Holdings Ltd v AHC Westlink Ltd*.[18] That case concerned a break clause (clause 7.1) entitling the tenant to determine the lease: 'on October 31, 2009 (the "Option Date") (time being of the essence for such date) by giving to the landlord six months' prior written notice (time being of the essence for such notice)'.

**6.20** Mr Edward Bartley Jones QC (sitting as a Deputy Judge of the High Court) dismissed the suggestion that the wording of the break clause meant that a break notice could be served only on 30 April 2009 (ie six months prior to 31 October 2009). He said (with emphasis in the original):[19]

> On any objective analysis of the words used in clause 7.1 of the Underlease it seems to me to be a commercial absurdity to suggest the parties intended that the break notice had to be given on April 30, 2009 and *only* on that date (or if given earlier had to be drafted in such a way that whatever the date of receipt the same was expressed to take effect *only* on April 30, 2009). If this were the true construction of cl. 7.1 it is, at the very least, highly surprising that the parties did not expressly state this to be the case. Rather it seems to me that by the use of the words in parenthesis 'time to be of the essence of such notice' all that was being emphasised was that time was of the essence of the period of six months.

[16] *Manorlike Ltd v Le Vitas Travel Agency and Consultancy Services Ltd* [1986] 1 All ER 574, at 576C–67D.
[17] *GKN Aerospace Services Ltd v Duncan Investments Ltd* [2020] EWHC 3719 (Ch), at [35], per Fancourt J.
[18] *Hexstone Holdings Ltd v AHC Westlink Ltd* [2010] L&TR 22.
[19] *Hexstone Holdings Ltd v AHC Westlink Ltd* [2010] L&TR 22, at [49].

**6.21** A similar result was arrived at in *GKN Aerospace Services Ltd v Duncan Investments Ltd*.[20] That case concerned an 'Addendum' which had the effect of extending a tenancy agreement for a term expiring on 23 October 2019. Clause 2 of the Addendum contained a break option in the following terms: 'The parties agree that the Tenant may, for this Addendum only, service [sic] notice at one point, being three months prior to the anniversary of the first year …'

**6.22** At trial, the judge agreed with the landlord and interpreted this clause as meaning that, for the break option to be exercisable, the break notice had to be given within the 24-hour period exactly 'three months prior to the anniversary of the first year'. In other words, the break notice had to be served on a specified date only, and not on any other date.

**6.23** Fancourt J allowed the tenant's appeal and considered that the provision should be construed as meaning not less than three months' notice was required. He held:

> [32] The commercial purpose of a tenant break option is, broadly speaking, to give the tenant the right to terminate the lease early, if it no longer needs the demised property, subject to a reasonable period of notice to the landlord so that it can plan and arrange its affairs accordingly, and with clarity for both parties as to whether the exercise of a break option is valid. The landlord's interpretation of clause 2 tends to conflict with these commercial needs by putting the tenant at risk of not validly exercising the option and creating uncertainty on both sides as to whether the lease will end early. The tenant's interpretation, on the other hand, is in accordance with the general commercial purpose of a break option.
>
> [33] I am unable to accept that there is any true commercial purpose served by requiring notice to be given on a single day only other than, from the landlord's point of view, the prospect of the tenant tripping itself up and failing to comply …
>
> [34] Although it may not be disadvantageous to a landlord to have only three months' notice, it can only be of advantage to a landlord to have more … Although a tenant tripwire might be of benefit to a landlord, it does not objectively make commercial sense to both parties to the lease.

**6.24** However, this is not to say that a break notice to be given not less than a specified period of time before a specified date permits service of the break notice at *any* point in time prior to that date. Such a submission was rejected in the *Biondi* case: see **6.4–6.5** above.

**6.25** *Biondi* was followed in *Multon v Cordell*,[21] in which a lease of a shop and flat for a term of 35 years until 25 March 1984 gave the tenant an option to take a further 21-year term 'on written request of the tenant made three months before the expiration of the term hereby created'. The last date for such a written request to be made was therefore 25 December 1983. In 1980 the tenant's solicitors suggested in correspondence to the landlords that the words 'made three months before' meant 'made at any time before the date three months before'. The tenant's solicitors subsequently gave written notice in January 1981. In March 1981, the landlords intimated that they rejected the tenant's construction of the option. The tenant issued proceedings for specific performance.

[20] *GKN Aerospace Services Ltd v Duncan Investments Ltd* [2020] EWHC 3719 (Ch).
[21] *Multon v Cordell* [1986] 1 EGLR 44.

**6.26** HHJ Thomas (sitting as a Deputy Judge of the High Court) dismissed the tenant's claim. He held[22] that, upon the true construction of the option the written request had to be given a reasonably short time before 25 December 1983; and that, on the facts, January 1981 was not such a reasonably short time. In other words, the request was invalid because it was made before the appointed time.

**6.27** It may be noted that in both *Biondi* and *Multon*, the right to renew the lease was subject to the condition that, at the time of the request for renewal, there were no existing breaches of covenant on the part of the lessee. The position may be different where the option is expressed to be subject to a condition that the lessee's covenants have been performed and observed up to the expiration of the contractual term.[23]

### (c) A Specified Period 'From' or 'After' a Specified Date

**6.28** In *Humber Oil Terminals Trustees Ltd v Associated British Ports*,[24] Sales J observed that, where in a demise of property the term is expressed as a period 'from' a particular date, it established that 'it is usually construed as meaning the period which commences after that date'. To the same effect, in *Ladyman v Wirral Estates Ltd*,[25] Fisher J said that 'in the absence of any indication to the contrary, a term limited to commence from a certain date commences on the first moment of the day following'. This general rule has been applied consistently by the courts since *Lester v Garland*.[26] By parity of reasoning, it might be expected that, subject to the lease providing otherwise, where a break clause is exercisable within a specified period 'from' a specified date, the specified date is excluded from the time calculation.

**6.29** Controversially, in *Trow v Ind Coope (West Midlands) Ltd*,[27] Lord Denning MR was disposed to say that no distinction should be drawn between periods commencing 'on' or 'with' a date and periods commencing 'from' a date. After referring to various authorities on the topic, he said:[28]

> I acknowledge that those cases warrant this distinction between the prepositions 'with' and 'from'. But it is far too subtle for my liking. It is one of those nice distinctions in which lawyers delight. They are out of touch with the common man. If a man contracts to build a house in 12 months beginning *with* the date when the sod is first turned, it is just the same as if he said 12 months beginning *on* or *from* that date. You may well say that that date is to be *included* in either case: but you cannot say that it is *included* in one case and *excluded* in the other. (emphasis in the original)

[22] *Multon v Cordell* [1986] 1 EGLR 44, at 45B–45C.
[23] *Moncure v Cahusac* [2006] UKPC 54, at [22], per Lord Scott.
[24] *Humber Oil Terminals Trustee Ltd v Associated British Ports* [2012] EWCA Civ 596, [2012] L&TR 27, at [212].
[25] *Ladyman v Wirral Estates Ltd* [1968] 2 All ER 197, at 199C.
[26] *Lester v Garland* (1808) 15 Ves Jun 248; *Young v Higgon* (1840) 6 M&W 49; *Goldsmith's Company v West Metropolitan Railway Co* [1904] 1 KB 1; *Stewart v Chapman* [1951] 2 KB 792; *Marren v Dawson Bentley & Co Ltd* [1961] 2 QB 135; *Cartwright v MacCormack* [1963] 1 WLR 18; *Dodds v Walker* [1981] 1 WLR 1027; *Zoan v Rouamba* [2000] 1 WLR 1509.
[27] *Trow v Ind Coope (West Midlands) Ltd* [1967] 2 QB 899.
[28] *Trow v Ind Coope (West Midlands) Ltd* [1967] 2 QB 899, at 915.

**6.30** However, neither of the other two members of the Court of Appeal was prepared to take the same view. Thus, Harman LJ said:[29]

> Lord Denning MR considers that this is to draw too fine a distinction and does not accord with common sense ideas, but I cannot agree that to regard 'with' and 'from' as opposite one to the other is a fine distinction or one which the ordinary man would not understand, and I do not think this is a lawyer's quibble ... At least since the decision of Sir William Grant MR [in *Lester v Garland*], the rule, if there be a rule, is the other way and it follows that 'beginning with' and 'beginning from' mean two opposite things. In any event, the ordinary meaning of the language of the rule should be followed unless there is something to show that it should not.

**6.31** Salmon LJ agreed, saying:[30]

> It is no doubt a pity that this inconvenience should arise from the use in the rule of the word 'with' instead of the word 'from'. But even the shortest single word can affect the whole meaning of any enactment. I do not think that the proposition that a period stated 'as beginning with' a certain date does begin on that date depends upon any fine distinction, legal subtlety or empty formality. In my view it depends upon the plain and natural meaning of ordinary English words. This court has no power to rectify the rule, it cannot change the words in which it is expressed – however convenient it might be to do so.

**6.32** Of course, the wording of the lease or other instrument in question may displace the usual rule. So, in *Ladyman v Wirral Estates Ltd*,[31] the lease was for a term of three years 'from' 1 May 1963 at a rent payable quarterly in advance on 1 May. Since it was inconceivable that rent was to be paid before the commencement of the term, the usual rule of interpretation was displaced. Similarly, in *Whelton Sinclair v Hyland*,[32] the lease created a tenancy for 10 years 'from' 27 June 1976. However, that lease was granted on the expiry of an earlier lease which (as was common ground) had terminated at the last moment of 26 June 1976. It was clear that the new lease was intended to commence, and did commence, at the very moment when the old lease terminated. This was sufficient to displace the usual rule.

**6.33** Another example is *Meadfield Properties Ltd v Secretary of State for the Environment*.[33] The lease in that case was dated 15 February 1985. It contained a habendum worded as follows:

> TO HOLD the same unto the Tenant from the twenty fourth day of June One thousand nine hundred and eighty-four until 24th December Two-thousand and three (hereinafter called 'the Term' ...)

**6.34** The lease also contained a break clause entitling the tenant to determine the term 'at the expiration of the first ten years thereof' upon giving to the landlord 'six months' previous notice in writing'.

**6.35** A dispute arose because, on 21 December 1993, the tenant gave notice to the landlord to terminate the lease on 23 June 1994. The landlord contended that the notice

[29] *Trow v Ind Coope (West Midlands) Ltd* [1967] 2 QB 899, at 922.
[30] *Trow v Ind Coope (West Midlands) Ltd* [1967] 2 QB 899, at 929.
[31] *Ladyman v Wirral Estates Ltd* [1968] 2 All ER 197.
[32] *Whelton Sinclair v Hyland* [1992] 2 EGLR 158.
[33] *Meadfield Properties Ltd v Secretary of State for the Environment* [1995] 1 EGLR 39.

was invalid because, relying on the principle established in *Lester v Garland* – viz when a lease defines a term as being 'from' a certain date, it creates a term which starts on the following day – the first 10 years of the term expired on 24 June 1994. Warner J disagreed, holding that the expiration of the first 10 years of the lease occurred at midnight on 23 June 1994. In arriving at this conclusion, he accepted (albeit with 'some hesitation') the following argument advanced on behalf of the tenant:[34]

> 'Mr Barnes' [Counsel for the tenant] first argument in support of the view that the term of the lease in question here began on June 24, 1984, and that the first 10 years of it therefore expired on June 23, 1994, was a simple one. He said that the authorities [relied upon by the landlord] were all cases where a lease created a term of so many years from a specified date. In such a case it is necessary, Mr Barnes pointed out, to determine whether the first day of the term is the following day. Another way of posing the question is to ask whether the last day of the term will be the anniversary of the specified day or the day preceding that anniversary. The rule that has been established by the decisions of the courts is one for resolving that question: the presumption is that the specified day is not included in the term, but that presumption may be rebutted by indications that it was intended to be. Here, in contrast, the lease does not demise the property for a period of years from a specified date, it demises the property for a term expressed to be 'from 24th day of June one thousand nine hundred and eighty four until 24th December two thousand and three', and that, Mr Barnes, submits, is a form of words to which the rule relied upon by [the landlord] does not apply.

**6.36** Where a break option is exercisable 'from' or 'after' a specified date then, generally speaking, it remains exercisable 'at any time after the right has arisen.'[35] However, this is not invariably the position, as demonstrated by *Wigan Borough Council v Scullindale Global Ltd*.[36] In that case, the lease (granted for a term of 199 years) contained a landlord's break clause worded as follows: 'Following an Event of Default the Lessor may terminate this Lease at any time by serving on the Lessee a Break Notice.'

**6.37** The relevant 'Event of Default' was 'the Lessee not achieving any or all of the Milestones …' The 'Milestones' to be achieved by the tenant included the following: 'Prior to 23 May 2018 … to complete the Development in accordance with the Planning Permissions.'

**6.38** One of the issues before the court was whether any temporal limitation was to be placed upon the service a break notice served pursuant to this clause. The issue arose because the landlord did not exercise the break option until 16 September 2019, ie about 16 months after the Event of Default. On this point, HHJ Hodge QC (sitting as a judge of the High Court) said (with italics and underlining in the original):

> [53] As a matter of the pure construction of the Lease, I fail to see how it can be possible to read any qualifying words into the clear language of clause 9.2 because to do so would contradict the express language which the parties have chosen to use in the Lease and to which they have subscribed. By no process of construction, however vigorous or benign, can the words

[34] *Meadfield Properties Ltd v Secretary of State for the Environment* [1995] 1 EGLR 39, at 41B–41D.

[35] *BDW Trading Ltd v JM Rowe (Investments) Ltd* [2011] EWCA Civ 548, at [78], per Patten LJ. Similar observations have been made in the context of options to renew a lease: see *Hersey v Giblett* (1854) 18 Beav 174; *Moss v Barton* (1866) LR 1 Eq 474; *Buckland v Papillon* (1866) LR Ch App 67; and *Rider v Ford* [1923] 1 Ch 541.

[36] *Wigan Borough Council v Sculllindale Global Ltd* [2021] EWHC 779 (Ch).

'*at any time*' be construed as meaning '*at any reasonable time*' or '*at any time whilst an Event of Default persists*' or '*at any time between 23 May 2018 and subsequent completion of the Development in accordance with the Planning Permissions*'... The real question is whether any such temporal limitation is to be implied into the words.

**6.39** However, HHJ Hodge QC recognised (with respect, rightly) that 'any reasonable reader of the Lease would instinctively shy away from any suggestion that the [landlord's] ability to terminate the Lease on the grounds of [the tenant's] failure to achieve the second Milestone should endure throughout the remaining 197 years of the contractual term, thereby enabling the Council to bring the Lease to an end many years in the future at only two months' notice'.[37] With this in mind, the court considered that the question posed at the end of the passage above should be answered in the affirmative. HHJ Hodge QC explained (with italics in the original):

> [62] In my judgment, it is so obvious as to go without saying that both parties to the Lease proceeded on the footing that a Break Notice could only validly be served at any time whilst an Event of Default still persists. The purpose of the break clause was to enable the Council to take back the premises if either the Works were not commenced, or alternatively the Development was not completed, by 23 November 2016 and 23 May 2018 respectively. However, there is no reason to think that either party ever contemplated that the Council might be able to do so once the Works had been commenced, or the Development had been duly completed, albeit later than they should have been. In the context of a 199 year lease, particularly one containing a qualified obligation on the lessee to keep the premises open, there is every reason to conclude that the parties would never have contemplated this. I am therefore satisfied that all the parties to the Lease proceeded on the footing that a valid Break Notice could only be served '*at any time whilst an Event of Default persists*'; and that a term should be implied into clause 9.3 to this effect.

### (d) A Specified Period 'Commencing on' or 'Beginning with' a Specified Date

**6.40** Where a person has the benefit of a break clause exercisable within a specified period of time 'commencing on' or 'beginning with' a specified date, the general rule is that the period of time includes the specified date.[38] As Chadwick LJ said in *Zoan v Rouamba*:[39]

> Where ... the period within which the act is to be done is expressed to be a period beginning with a specified day, then it has been held, with equal consistency over the past 40 years or thereabouts, that the legislature (or the relevant rule making body, as the case may be) has shown a clear intention that the specified day must be included in the period.

**6.41** This is well-illustrated by *Sidebotham v Holland*.[40] In that case, the plaintiff agreed to let a house to the defendant as a yearly tenant 'commencing on May 19, 1890'.

[37] *Wigan Borough Council v Sculllindale Global Ltd* [2021] EWHC 779 (Ch), at [55].

[38] *Trow v Ind Coope (West Midlands) Ltd* [1967] 2 QB 899, at 925, 926 per Salmon LJ ('... Any period of time to be calculated as commencing or beginning with a certain day must include that day ...' and '... when a period of time is required to be calculated as beginning on or with a certain date, that date must be included in the calculation ...'); *Hare v Gocher* [1962] 2 QB 641.

[39] *Zoan v Rouamba* [2000] 1 WLR 1509, at 1516H.

[40] *Sidebotham v Holland* [1895] 1 QB 378.

The question was whether a six months' notice to quit expiring on 19 May was a good notice. The point taken on behalf of the defendant was that the notice expired one day too late, since the year expired at midnight on 18 May. Lindley LJ, with whom Lord Halsbury agreed, held:[41]

> The notice is said to be bad because it expires one day too late. The contention is that, as the tenancy commenced 'on' the 19th and not 'from' the 19th, the notice should have been to quit on the 18th and not on the 19th. Having regard to the decision in *Clayton's Case*, I think that, although the agreement was signed on the 19th, and the tenant can hardly in fact have been in possession the whole of that day, yet, in point of law, that day must be treated as the first day of the tenancy and as part of the term for which the house was agreed to be let. The tenancy cannot, therefore, be treated as commencing on the 20th to the exclusion of the 19th. One year from that day, but including that day, would expire at midnight of the 18th of the next May.

**6.42** AL Smith LJ gave a concurring judgment, in which he said:[42]

> I cannot doubt that under the agreement by its express terms the tenancy commenced on May 19, 1890. I cannot bring myself to hold, as I was invited to do by the plaintiff, that when a written agreement states that a person shall become a yearly tenant 'commencing on the 19th of May', that it means that he shall become such tenant 'commencing on the day after the 19th of May', or, in other words, as the plaintiff contends, 'commencing from the 19th of May'.

## THE SPECIFIED PERIOD OF NOTICE

### (a) Where the Lease is Silent

**6.43** Where no minimum break period is specified, notice of a reasonable period should be given. This is a question of fact dependent upon the circumstances of each individual case. So, for example, in *Goodright on the demise of Hall v Richardson*,[43] a lease granted in 1785 was expressed to be determinable in the years 1788, 1791 and 1794. Lord Kenyon CJ said:[44]

> Now in this case it is impossible to form any doubt respecting the intenting of these parties. It was intended that this lease should take effect for three years, at all events; and that it should be in the election of either of the parties to put an end to it at that time, or at the end of six years, giving reasonable notice to the other.

### (b) 'Not Less than' a Specified Period of Notice

**6.44** If the recipient of the notice is to be given 'not less than' a specified period of notice, it is suggested the date of service falls to be excluded from, whereas the date of the event falls to be included in, the time calculation.

[41] *Sidebotham v Holland* [1895] 1 QB 378, at 382–83.
[42] *Sidebotham v Holland* [1895] 1 QB 378, at 386–87.
[43] *Hall v Richardson* (1789) 3 Term Reports 462.
[44] *Hall v Richardson* (1789) 3 Term Reports 462, at 463.

**6.45** *Schnabel v Allard*[45] concerned a weekly tenancy of residential premises which attracted the protection of the Rent Act 1957, s 16 of which provided that:

> No notice by a landlord or a tenant to quit any premises let … as a dwelling shall be valid unless it is given not less than four weeks before the date on which it is to take effect.

**6.46** The landlord gave a notice to quit on Friday, 4 March 1966, to expire on Friday, 1 April 1966. Holding that the notice was valid, Lord Denning MR said:[46]

> What is the effect of the words 'not less than four weeks'? … The general rule as to notices, at any rate as between landlord and tenant, is that you exclude only one of the days and not both of them. Take the everyday periodic tenancies. In a weekly Saturday tenancy a notice to quit is good if given on one Saturday to expire on the following Saturday: or if it is given on a Friday to expire on the following Friday. I think that in this Rent Act 1957, we should apply the ordinary landlord and tenant reckoning of periodic notices. A period of 'not less than four weeks' is satisfied by being given on one day to expire that day four weeks, eg, on a Friday to expire on Friday four weeks.

**6.47** Although *Schnabel* concerned a particular provision of the Rent Act 1957, it can be seen that Lord Denning's reasoning is of general application to the law of landlord and tenant. Indeed, Lord Denning's 'general rule' was cited with approval by Whitford J in *Hogg Bullimore & Co v Co-Operative Insurance Society Limited*.[47]

**6.48** The above authorities may be contrasted with *Esson Properties Limited v Dresser UK Limited*.[48] That was an opinion of Lord Penrose sitting in the Outer House of Session in Scotland. It concerned a lease of commercial premises which contained a tenant's break clause. The break clause was exercisable subject to the tenant giving 'not less than nine months written notice' of its desire to do so. The tenant served a break notice on 31 October 1995, giving notice to break the lease on 31 July 1996. The landlord claimed that the notice was of no effect on the basis that, where the expression 'not less than' was used, it was established by authority that both the date of service and the final date of the period were excluded. Lord Penrose agreed with the landlord's argument. His reasoning is contained the following passage:[49]

> the present case has some similarity to *Hamiltonhill Estates Ltd [Hamiltonhill Estates Ltd v Central Regional Council* 1996 GWD 21-1564], though the contract in question in that case was considerably more complex and the formulation of the provisions and the use of language raised difficulties which do not arise in the present instance. I consider that this case raises a straightforward question of construction of the language involved, that the rule as set out in Greens Encyclopaedia on p 449 is applicable, and that the pursuers are entitled to succeed in this action at this stage.

**6.49** It is respectfully suggested that the decision in *Esson* should be treated with some caution. Aside from the fact that it is not binding in England and Wales, the reasoning of Lord Penrose is short. Furthermore, Lord Penrose did not have cited to him the decisions referred to above.

[45] *Schnabel v Allard* [1967] 1 QB 627.
[46] *Schnabel v Allard* [1967] 1 QB 627, at 631E–32B.
[47] *Hogg Bullimore & Co v Co-Operative Insurance Society Limited* (1985) 50 P&CR 105, at 106.
[48] *Esson Properties Limited v Dresser UK Limited* 1997 SC 304.
[49] *Esson Properties Limited v Dresser UK Limited* 1997 SC 304, at 308.

### (c) 'At Least' a Specified Period of Notice

**6.50** If the lease requires 'at least' a specified period of time for notice of the serving party's intention to exercise the right to break, it is suggested that (as with giving 'not less than' a specified period of notice) the date of service falls to be excluded from, whereas the date of the event falls to be included in, the time calculation.

**6.51** In this regard, reference may be made to the decision of the Court of Appeal in *Carapanayoti & Co Limited v Comptoir Commercial Andre & Cie SA*,[50] which concerned an option in a contract for the sale of ground-nuts. In that case, Lord Denning MR identified two groups of contractual time provision. He said (with emphasis in the original):[51]

> One group deals with cases when the instrument prescribes a period *within* which a person must act or take consequences. As, for instance, where a man must give notice or do some other thing *within* a certain number of days *from or after* some date or event. In this group you do not count the beginning day of the period, but do you count the last? That was settled in 1808 in *Lester v Garland* (1808) 65 Ves Jr. 248; and has been repeatedly followed since.

**6.52** He went on:[52]

> The other group deals with cases where the instrument prescribes that a certain time must elapse between some event and other, such as between the doing of a thing and some other date or event. In this group you do not count the day on which the act is done, nor do you count the day of the date or event. You exclude both, so as to give so many clear days. Often the instrument makes this clear by saying that he must do the act 'at least' so many days before, or 'not less' than so many weeks.

**6.53** However, he then added:[53]

> There are exceptions to this second group. For instance, in landlord and tenant cases, when a period tenancy is determinable by notice, it is always sufficient to give a notice to quit expiring on the periodic day, eg a week's notice given on one Saturday to expire on the next Saturday and so forth.

**6.54** In other words, in the landlord and tenant context, Lord Denning MR appears to equate 'at least' and 'not less than' formulations, so that in both cases the date of the event falls to be included in the time calculation.

**6.55** It may be observed that a different conclusion was arrived at in *Rightside Properties Ltd v Gray*.[54] That case concerned a contract for the sale and purchase of a property in West London. Condition 9 of the Conditions of Sale included a provision that, if the purchaser neglected or failed to perform his part of the contract, the vendor could give to the purchaser 'at least 21 days' notice in writing specifying the breach and requiring the purchaser to make good the default'. In the event, the vendor gave to the purchaser notice requiring something to be done 'within 21 days'. Walton J held[55] that

[50] *Carapanayoti & Co Limited v Comptoir Commercial Andre & Cie SA* [1972] 1 Lloyd's Rep 139.
[51] *Carapanayoti & Co Limited v Comptoir Commercial Andre & Cie SA* [1972] 1 Lloyd's Rep 139, at 142.
[52] *Carapanayoti & Co Limited v Comptoir Commercial Andre & Cie SA* [1972] 1 Lloyd's Rep 139, at 143.
[53] *Carapanayoti & Co Limited v Comptoir Commercial Andre & Cie SA* [1972] 1 Lloyd's Rep 139, at 143.
[54] *Rightside Properties Ltd v Gray* [1975] 1 Ch 72.
[55] *Rightside Properties Ltd v Gray* [1975] 1 Ch 72, at 80C.

the notice was invalid because: 'the formula "at least" indicated that the period allowed must be exclusive of both the day of service and the day of expiry of the notice'.

## THE 'CORRESPONDING DATE' RULE

**6.56** It is often the case that the specified notice period mentioned above is expressed to be calculated by reference to a number of months, or quarters or some other fraction of time. So, for example, the tenant may be required to give to the landlord 'not less than three months' notice' of his desire to exercise the break clause. In such a scenario, the 'corresponding date' rule is applied.

**6.57** This rule was discussed in *Dodds v Walker*.[56] That case was concerned with Part II of the Landlord and Tenant Act 1954, which entitles a tenant of business premises, whose tenancy has been terminated by notice given to him by his landlord, to apply to the court for a new tenancy. However, by s 29(3) of that Act (as then in force), the application to court had to be made 'not less than two nor more than four months after the giving of the landlord's notice'. The landlord had given its notice on 30 September 1978. The tenant made its application to court on 31 January 1979. Was that one day too late?

**6.58** The House of Lords was unanimous in holding that the application was out of time. In his speech, Lord Diplock stated:[57]

> that when the relevant period is a month or specified number of months after the giving of a notice, the general rule is that the month ends upon the corresponding date in the appropriate subsequent month, ie the date of that month that bears the same number as the day of the earlier month on which the notice was given.
>
> The corresponding date rule is simple. It is of easy application. Except in a small minority of cases, of which the instant case is not an example, all that the calculator has to do is mark in his diary the corresponding date in the appropriate subsequent month. Because the number of days in five months of the year is less than in the seven others the inevitable consequence of the corresponding date rule is that one month's notice given in a 30 day month is one day shorter than one month's notice given in a 31 day month and is three days shorter if it is given in February. Corresponding variations in the length of notice reckoned in days occur where the required notice is a plurality of months.

**6.59** To this, he added the following:[58]

> This simple general rule which Cockburn CJ in *Freeman v Read* (1863) 4 B& S 174, 184 described as being 'in accordance with common usage ... and with the sense of mankind,' works perfectly well without need for any modification so long as there is in the month in which the notice expires a day which bears the same number as the day of the month on which the notice was given. Such was the instant case and such will be every other case except for notices given on the 31st of a 31 day month and expiring in a 30 day month or in February, and notices

[56] *Dodds v Walker* [1981] 1 WLR 1027.
[57] *Dodds v Walker* [1981] 1 WLR 1027, at 1029B–1029D.
[58] *Dodds v Walker* [1981] 1 WLR 1027, at 1029E.

expiring in February and given on the 30th or the 29th (except in leap year) of any other month of the year. In these exceptional cases, the modification of the corresponding date rule that is called for is also well established: the period given by the notice ends upon the last day of the month in which the notice expires.

**6.60** Lord Russell illustrated the application of the rule in the case of months of different lengths by saying:[59]

> the application of the corresponding date principle inevitably produces variation in the number of days involved, depending upon the date upon which a four month notice is served and the irregular allotment of days in different months. Sometimes it is not possible to apply directly the principle, for instance if a four month notice is served on October 30 (the time beginning to run at midnight October 30/31), there being in February but 28 (or 29) days, it is not possible to find a corresponding date in February and plainly a corresponding date cannot be sought in March: The application of the corresponding date principle in such a case can only lead to termination of the four month period at midnight February 28/March 1 (or midnight February 29/March 1 in a leap year), that is an inevitable outcome.

**6.61** It is important to appreciate that the corresponding date rule 'depends for its application upon the exclusion of the day of the occurrence of the specified event'.[60] This accords with the reasoning of the Inner House of the Court of Session in *Pacitti Jones v O'Brien*.[61] The issue there concerned whether the period beginning with 8 April 2002 and ending with 7 April 2003 was a period of less than one year, each of those dates being included in the period under consideration. In giving the opinion of the court Lord Reed dealt with the argument advanced by reference to *Dodds v Walker* in this way:[62]

> [13] What Lord Diplock described as the corresponding date rule applies, in his Lordship's words, 'when the relevant period is a month or specified number of months after the giving of a notice'. The rule has the effect of excluding from the computation the day on which the notice was given …
>
> [14] The dependence of the decision in *Dodds v Walker* upon the exclusion of the terminus a quo is equally apparent from the speech of Lord Russell of Killowen (p 1030): 'My Lords, it is common ground that in this case the period of four months did not begin to run until the end of the date of the relevant service on 30 September – ie at midnight 30 September/1 October. It is common ground that ordinarily the calculation of a period of a calendar month or calendar months ends upon what has been conveniently referred to as the corresponding date. For example in a four-month period, when service of the relevant notice was on 28 September, time would begin to run at midnight 28/29 September and would end at midnight 28/29 January, a period embracing four calendar months.' This approach cannot be applied if, by statute, the court is required to count the date on which the relevant event occurred … as part of the relevant period.

[59] *Dodds v Walker* [1981] 1 WLR 1027, at 1030E.

[60] *R (Zaporozhchenko) v City of Westminster Magistrates' Court* [2011] 1 WLR 994, at [15], per Burnett J (giving the judgment of the Court).

[61] *Pacitti Jones v O'Brian* 2006 SC 616.

[62] *Pacitti Jones v O'Brian* 2006 SC 616, at [13]–[14].

**6.62** Although *O'Brien* was a Scottish case, it was cited with approval by Barnett J (giving the judgment of the Court) in *R (Zaporozhchencko) v City of Westminster Magistrates' Court*,[63] who also observed:[64]

> Lord Diplock noted that 'the corresponding date rule is simple' in its application. In cases where it does not apply, because the day of the occurrence is included in the reckoning, it is no less simple. The time limit expires on the eve of the corresponding date. All that the person concerned has to do having determined from the statutory language that the day of the occurrence is included is mark in his diary the eve of the corresponding date.

**6.63** A break clause might require notice to be served by a stated number of months (or other period) *before* a specified date or event. In that scenario, it is thought that the corresponding date rule would operate in reverse.

## OTHER FRACTIONS OF TIME

### (a) 'Year'

**6.64** If a break clause requires notice of one or more 'years' to be given, it will be a question of construction as to whether this means a calendar year, a period of 12 months reckoned from some date other than 1 January, or some other period of time.[65]

### (b) 'Quarter'

**6.65** If a break clause requires notice of one or more 'quarters' to be given, then it will be a question of construction as to whether this should be calculated by reference to the 'usual' quarter days (ie 25 March, 24 June, 29 September and 25 December) or by reference to some other specified dates. A good example of this is to be found in *East v Pantiles (Plant Hire) Limited*.[66] The lease in that case was executed on 2 October 1972. It demised the premises from 1 August 1972 for the term of 21 years. Clause 1(1) specified the amount of the rent and the manner of payment. It read as follows:

> For the first seven years of the said Lease the sum of £4500 per annum by equal quarterly payments in advance on the 14th day of August the 1st day of November the first day of February and the first day of May in each year the first payment to be made on the 1st day of August 1972.

**6.66** The effect of this provision was that the annual rent was to be paid by equal quarterly payments, so each quarterly payment is to be £1,125. Each payment was to be made in advance on the first day of every November, February and May but, in the case of every August, on the 14th of that month instead of the first.

[63] *R (Zaporozhchenko) v City of Westminster Magistrates' Court* [2011] 1 WLR 994, at [19].
[64] *R (Zaporozhchenko) v City of Westminster Magistrates' Court* [2011] 1 WLR 994, at [17].
[65] *Inland Revenue Commissioners v Hobhouse* [1956] 1 WLR 1393; *Boufoy-Bastick v The University of the West Indies* [2015] UKPC 27.
[66] *East v Pantiles (Plant Hire) Limited* [1982] 2 EGLR 111.

**6.67** The issue before the Court of Appeal was whether the landlord had served a rent review notice in time. The salient rent review clause provided that the open market rental for the property in question was to be determined as:

> such annual sum as shall be (a) specified in a notice in writing signed by or on behalf of the lessor and posted by recorded delivery post in a prepaid envelope addressed to the tenant at the demised premises at any time before the beginning of a clear period of two quarters of a year (commencing on one of the usual quarter days hereinbefore mentioned) immediately preceding the review date (and such notice shall be conclusively deemed to have been received by the tenant in due course of post).

**6.68** The review date was 1 August 1979. The landlord served a notice pursuant to the rent review clause on 26 January 1979. The tenant argued that 1 August 1979 was not the commencement date of the first quarter of the 1979/1980 year. Rather, by reference to the language of clause 1(1), the tenant contended that the first quarter of the 1979/1980 year commenced on 14 August 1979. Consequently, it was said that the landlord had failed to give notice of 'a clear period of two quarters of a year' since the review date (1 August 1979) fell within a quarter which ran from 1 May to 13 August 1979 (ie just before the August rent became payable). Therefore, on the tenant's analysis, the two complete quarters prior to the review date were the quarters 1 November 1978 to 31 January 1979 and 1 February to 30 April 1979.

**6.69** Whilst acknowledging the eccentricities of the language used in the lease in question, the Court of Appeal unanimously rejected the tenant's arguments. Giving the lead judgment, Brightman LJ said:[67]

> In order to identify the two quarters of the year to which the rent review clause refers, one has to divide the year of the lease into quarters. The term of the lease started on 1st August 1972. It therefore follows that the first quarter of the lease started on that day. It could not possibly start on any other day in the absence of some express provision in the lease. The next quarter, therefore, started on 1st November 1972, the third quarter on 1st February 1973 and the final quarter of the first year on 1st May 1973. And so it went on. Each quarter of each subsequent year must have started on the first day of each of these months. The 14th August is not indicative of the date upon which a quarter commences. It is indicative of the date upon which rent has to be paid for the quarter commencing on 1st August and ending on 31st October. In the result the rent review notice was properly served because it was posted before the beginning of a clear period of two quarters of a year immediately preceding the review date.

### (c) 'Month'

**6.70** At common law, a 'month' means a lunar month.[68] However, the common law rule was altered by s 61 of the Law of Property Act 1925.[69] Thus, unless the context

[67] *East v Pantiles (Plant Hire) Limited* [1982] 2 EGLR 111, at 112L–112M.

[68] *P Phipps & Co Ltd v Rogers* [1925] 1 KB 14, at 26, per Atkin LJ.

[69] Section 61, Law of Property Act 1925 ('… in all deeds, contracts, … and other instruments executed, made or coming into operation after [1 January 1926], unless the context otherwise requires – (a) "Month" means calendar month …').

requires otherwise, where a break clause requires notice of one or more 'months' to be given, then this is understood to be a reference to a calendar month or calendar months.

### (d) 'Day'

**6.71** In *Pugh v Duke of Leeds*,[70] Lord Mansfield said (with emphasis in the original): 'Date does not mean the *hour* or the *minute*, but the *day* of delivery: and in law there is no fraction of a day.'

**6.72** The same principle was followed by Sir William Grant MR in *Lester v Garland*,[71] where he said: 'The effect is to render the day a sort of indivisible point; so that any act, done in the compass of it, is no more referable to any one, than to any other, portion of it; but the act and the day are co-extensive.'

**6.73** It follows that, if (somewhat unusually) a break clause requires notice of one or more 'days' to be given, then unless the context requires otherwise the time period will be calculated from midnight on the commencing day, even if the notice is served at some point during that day.[72]

## THE EFFECT OF LATE SERVICE

**6.74** Time is of the essence of stipulations in break clauses. Accordingly, when dealing with options to determine, a time stipulation must be strictly complied with. Thus, in *United Scientific Holdings Ltd v Burnley BC*,[73] Lord Fraser said:

> There is a good reason why time limits should be strictly enforced in relation to an option to purchase or renew a lease, because so long as it remains open the grantor is not free to dispose of his property elsewhere, although the grantee is under no obligation to him. Similarly where a tenant has an option to break his lease, he can break it or not as he chooses, but the landlord is not free to let his property to anyone else until the time for exercising the tenant's option has expired. It is fair and reasonable, and in accordance with what I would take to be the intention of the parties, that the time limit of the restriction on the grantor should be strictly enforced.

**6.75** It follows that 'equity will not interfere' where there has been late service of a break notice.[74] In other words, equitable relief is not available to a party who gives a late break notice. An extreme example of this principle is to be found in the decision of the *Privy Council in Union Eagle Ltd v Golden Achievements Ltd*.[75] In that case, time for

[70] *Pugh v Duke of Leeds* (1777) 2 Cowp 714, at 720.
[71] *Lester v Garland* (1808) 15 Ves Jun 248, at 257.
[72] *Cartwright v MacCormack* [1963] 1 WLR 18.
[73] *United Scientific Holdings Ltd v Burnley BC* [1978] AC 904, at 962.
[74] *Samarenko v Dawn Hill House Ltd* [2013] Ch 36, at [11], per Lewison LJ; and see also the remarks of Rix LJ, at [63] ('... clause 2 was a condition which rebutted any presumption that time was not of the essence. It follows that there was no further room for the interference of equity ...').
[75] *Union Eagle Ltd v Golden Achievements Ltd* [1997] AC 514.

the completion of the sale of a flat was of the essence and was to take place at 5pm on a specified date. The purchase price was tendered at 5:10pm. The vendor refused to accept the money tendered and successfully forfeited the purchaser's deposit. Lord Hoffmann explained:[76]

> The only unusual feature was that the purchaser tendered payment of the purchase price 10 minutes after the time for completion had passed. The purchaser refused to accept that so venial a lapse should result in the loss of the contract and commenced proceedings for specific performance …
>
> The chief question in the case is whether the court has, and should have exercised, an equitable power to absolve the purchaser from the contractual consequences of having been late and to decree specific performance.
>
> … The notion that the court's jurisdiction to grant relief is 'unlimited and unfettered' (per Lord Simon of Glaisdale in *Shiloh Spinners Ltd v Harding* [1973] AC 691, 726) was rejected as a 'beguiling heresy' by the House of Lords in *Scandinavian Trading Tanker Co AB v Flota Petrolera Ecuatoriana (The Scaptrade)* [1983] 2 AC 694, 700. It is worth pausing to notice why it continues to beguile and why it is a heresy. It has the obvious merit of allowing the court to impose what it considers to be a fair solution in the individual case. The principle that equity will restrain the enforcement of legal rights when it would be unconscionable to insist upon them has an attractive breadth. But the reasons why the courts have rejected such generalisations are founded not merely upon authority … but also upon practical considerations of business. These are, in summary, that in many forms of transaction it is of great importance that if something happens for which the contract has made express provision, the parties should know with certainty that the terms of the contract will be enforced. The existence of an undefined discretion to refuse to enforce the contract on the ground that this would be 'unconscionable' is sufficient to create uncertainty. Even if it is most unlikely that a discretion to grant relief will be exercised, its mere existence enables litigation to be employed as a negotiating tactic. The realities of commercial life are that this may cause injustice which cannot be fully compensated by the ultimate decision in the case.

**6.76** He concluded:[77]

> The present case seems to their Lordships to be one to which the full force of the general rule applies. The fact is that the purchaser was late. Any suggestion that relief can be obtained on the ground that he was only slightly late is bound to lead to arguments over how late is too late, which can be resolved only by litigation. For five years the vendor has not known whether he is entitled to resell the flat or not. It has been sterilised by a caution pending a final decision in this case. In his dissenting judgment, Godfrey JA [in the Hong Long Court of Appeal] said that the case 'cries out for the intervention of equity'. Their Lordships think that, on the contrary, it shows the need for a firm restatement of the principle that in cases of rescission of an ordinary contract of sale of land for failure to comply with an essential condition as to time, equity will not intervene.

**6.77** Another example is *Peeling v Guidice*.[78] In that case, Mr Guidice was the tenant of premises under a lease which conferred an option to renew which was to be exercised 3 months before the expiration of the term. On the date for exercise of the option

[76] *Union Eagle Ltd v Golden Achievements Ltd* [1997] AC 514, at 518–19.
[77] *Union Eagle Ltd v Golden Achievements Ltd* [1997] AC 514, at 522.
[78] *Peeling v Guidice* (1963) 186 EG 113.

Mr Guidice was in prison; and he gave no notice pursuant to the terms of the option. Judge Lane gave judgment for possession for the plaintiff landlord. The Court of Appeal, dismissing Mr Guidice's appeal, held that there was no ground in equity for giving Mr Guidice relief against his failure to give notice to renew.

**6.78** Nonetheless, there may be cases where the recipient of a late break notice is prevented by his own unconscionable conduct from insisting on strict compliance with the terms of a lease.[79] This matter is dealt with in more detail in Chapter 13.

## ACCEPTANCE OF SHORT SERVICE OF A BREAK NOTICE

**6.79** Where one party has given short notice which does not comply with the requirements of the break clause, it is open for the recipient to accept the notice, thereby waiving the requirement in relation to the appropriate length of notice or the time for service. So, for example, in *Elsden v Pick*,[80] the defendant was the tenant of a farm under an agreement which was determinable on one year's notice in writing expiring on April 6 in any year. On 4 April 1977, the tenant discussed with the landlords' agent the possibility of his having to give up the farm, and on 7 April he delivered to the agent a notice of his intention to quit the farm in April 1978 together with a letter requesting the agent to accept the notice. The agent agreed to treat the notice as valid notwithstanding that the length of the notice was short. When, later, the tenant contended that the notice was ineffective to determine his tenancy, the landlords brought an action for a declaration that they were entitled to possession of the farm in April 1978. The judge held that the tenant's notice was invalid as it contravened s 23(1) of the Agricultural Holdings Act 1948, and he dismissed the landlords' action. On appeal by the landlords, the Court of Appeal held that the landlord was entitled to waive the requirement for 12 months' notice and, having done so, the tenant was not entitled to insist upon compliance with the statute.

[79] *Samuel Properties (Developments) Ltd v Hayek* [1972] 1 WLR 1296, at 1307–08 (a decision subsequently overruled by the House of Lords in *United Scientific Holdings Ltd v Burnley BC* [1978] AC 904, albeit not on this point).

[80] *Elsden v Pick* [1980] 1 WLR 898; and see also *Hackney LBC v Snowden* (2001) 33 HLR 49 (landlord waived the requirement under s 5(1) of the Protection from Eviction Act 1977 providing that no notice to quit shall be valid unless given not less than four weeks before the date on which it is to take effect).

# 7

# *The Method of Service of a Break Notice*

## INTRODUCTION

7.1 This chapter considers the method by which a break notice should be transmitted from the serving party to the intended recipient.

## COMPLIANCE WITH THE PRESCRIBED CONTRACTUAL METHOD FOR SERVICE

7.2 A well-drafted lease will contain express provisions which govern how a break notice is to be served, for example, by registered post. Generally speaking, the server should give the notice in the manner prescribed by the terms of the lease (or other instrument in question). Failure to do so may be fatal to the successful exercise of the break.

7.3 However, not all failures to comply with a prescribed method of service will have such a consequence. This is so if – as it is sometimes put – on a true construction of the break clause, the method of service is permissive or directory, rather than mandatory or obligatory. This distinction is illustrated by a large number of cases, which are addressed chronologically below.

7.4 In *Spectra Pty Ltd v Pindari Pty Ltd*[1] (an Australian case), a clause containing an option to renew a lease concluded as follows:

> Should the Lessee decide to exercise this option it shall give to the Lessor notice in writing to be sent by prepaid registered mail to the Lessor's last known place of residence of its desire so to do not later than [blank] calendar months prior to the expiration of the term hereby granted.

7.5 The option was exercised by ordinary post instead of registered post, and it was contended that this was a fatal defect. In fact, it appeared that the notice of exercise of the option had been sent by the plaintiff to the defendant prior to the expiration of the term and was received by the defendant in the normal course of post. The judge, Wootten J, said that the question in the case was whether the clause should be construed as a stipulation that prepaid registered mail is to be not merely a sufficient method of giving notice, but the sole and essential method of doing so. His conclusion was:[2]

> in the absence of a very clear indication of a contrary intention, it would not be reasonable to construe a provision for service by registered mail as excluding the giving of notice by other equally expeditious means which do in fact result in the actual receipt of the notice by the

[1] *Spectra Pty Ltd v Pindari Pty Ltd* [1974] 2 NSWLR 617.
[2] *Spectra Pty Ltd v Pindari Pty Ltd* [1974] 2 NSWLR 617, at 623.

offeror, eg personal delivery or unregistered mail, although of course in the latter event the offeree will run the risk of non-delivery.

**7.6** In *Yates Building Co Ltd v R J Pulleyn & Sons (York) Ltd*,[3] an option to purchase a certain plot of land was expressed to be exercisable by notice in writing 'such notice to be sent by registered or recorded delivery post'. In the event, the option was sent from the intending purchaser's solicitors to the intending vendor's solicitors by ordinary post. The Court of Appeal held that the prescribed form of posting was directory and not mandatory and, accordingly, the option had been validly exercised. Lord Denning said:[4]

> the question is whether the words 'such notice to be sent by registered or recorded delivery post' are mandatory or directory … The distinction is this: a mandatory provision must be fulfilled exactly according to the letter, whereas a directory provision is satisfied if it is in substance according to the general intent … In applying the rule of construction, you must look to the subject-matter, consider the object to be fulfilled, and then see whether the provision must be fulfilled strictly to the letter or whether the substance of it is enough … Looking at the object of this provision, it seems to be this. It is inserted for the benefit of the buyer so that he can be sure of his position. So long as he sends the letter by registered or recorded delivery post, he has clear proof of postage and the time of posting. But if the buyer sends it by ordinary post, he will have no sufficient proof of posting, or of the time of posting.

**7.7** *Pindari* and *Yates* may be contrasted with *Vaughan v Von Essen Hotels 5 Ltd*.[5] That case concerned a notice served pursuant to a share purchase agreement containing the following clause 11.9.1:

> Any notice or other document to be served under this Agreement may be delivered or sent by first class delivery post process to the party to be served as follows: to the Vendors at [address given] with a copy to the Vendor's solicitors marked for the attention of [name given].

**7.8** The serving party had served a copy of the relevant notice, not on the 'Vendor's solicitors' (as defined in the agreement), but on a different firm of solicitors instructed by the vendors (called PDT). The issue for the court was whether the requirement in clause 11.9.1, that a copy of the relevant notice also be given 'to the Vendors' solicitors' marked for the attention of the named solicitor, was permissive rather than mandatory. Holding that the provision was mandatory in effect, Etherton J explained as follows:[6]

> [67] … in every case, including a unilateral contract or a notice having unilateral effect, the question of what are the contractual requirements, and which of them are mandatory and which are permissive in the sense intended by Lord Denning MR in *Yates Building Company Ltd*, is itself a question to be answered applying the usual principles of contractual interpretation.
>
> [70] I have reached the conclusion that on the proper interpretation of clause 11.9.1 it was not sufficient for a copy warranty notice to be sent to solicitors who were neither [the 'Vendor's solicitors' as defined in the agreement], nor solicitors retained and authorised for the purpose of receiving any such copy notice. Tempting as it certainly is to dispose of the claimants' claim by saying that the process used by the defendant (giving a copy of the [the relevant notice] to

[3] *Yates Building Co Ltd v R J Pulleyn & Sons (York) Ltd* [1976] 1 EGLR 157 (CA).
[4] *Yates Building Co Ltd v R J Pulleyn & Sons (York) Ltd* [1976] 1 EGLR 157 (CA), at 157K.
[5] *Vaughan v Von Essen Hotels 5 Ltd* [2006] EWHC 3586 (Ch).
[6] *Vaughan v Von Essen Hotels 5 Ltd* [2006] EWHC 3586 (Ch), at [67], [70].

> PDT for the attention of Mr Davidson) had absolutely no practical prejudice for the claimants, highlighted by the fact that PDT did indeed refer the copy [of the relevant notice] to the claimants … I consider that would be an impermissible approach to contractual interpretation. It would fall on the wrong side of the line between legitimate interpretation of the Agreement in its commercial setting and having regard to its commercial objects, on the one hand, and, on the other hand, rewriting the Agreement with the benefit of hindsight in order to achieve an outcome which might be considered to be reasonable.

7.9 The decision in *Yates* was further considered by the Court of Appeal in *Orchard (Developments) Holdings Plc v Reuters Ltd.*[7] There Rix LJ said[8] that, in *Yates*, the reference to 'such notice to be sent by registered or recorded delivery post' was evidential only, and not as a requirement of the validity or effectiveness of the notice. In other words, those words could be read: 'and for the purpose of evidencing the timely receipt of the notice, it will be of assistance to the buyer to use registered or recorded delivery post but he may use other methods of delivery.'

7.10 *Orchard* itself concerned the service of a break notice under the terms of a lease which provided: 'Unless the receiving party or its authorised agent acknowledges receipt a notice is valid only if it is given by hand sent by registered post or recorded delivery'. Of this formulation, Rix LJ said[9] that:

> What is remarkable about the present case … is the introduction of the words 'is valid only' … That, in my judgment, is a provision which goes to essential validity, not evidence.

Thus, service by hand, by registered post or recorded delivery was mandatory or obligatory.

7.11 A different conclusion was arrived at in *Truegold International Ltd v Questrock Ltd.*[10] That case concerned an option to purchase certain freehold property in Essex. The option agreement contained a notice provision at clause 16 worded as follows:

> any notice given under the terms of this Agreement shall be deemed to be effectively served if delivered to or left at or sent by registered or recorded delivery post or facsimile transmission addressed to the Vendor's Solicitors and the Purchaser's Solicitors (as the case may be).

7.12 Referring to this provision, Mr Jeremy Cousins QC (sitting as a Deputy Judge of the High Court) said:[11]

> It seems to me also that the option agreement was capable of being exercised by a letter sent to the registered office of the Claimant … Clause 16 of the option agreement, in my judgment, was simply permissive. It created another means by which service of a notice could be affected upon the Claimant. Ordinarily a solicitor does not have authority to deal with an option agreement, receipt of notice thereunder, on behalf of his client. What clause 16 did was to introduce

[7] *Orchard (Developments) Holdings Plc v Reuters Ltd* [2009] EWCA Civ 6.
[8] *Orchard (Developments) Holdings Plc v Reuters Ltd* [2009] EWCA Civ 6, at [34].
[9] *Orchard (Developments) Holdings Plc v Reuters Ltd* [2009] EWCA Civ 6, at [35].
[10] *Truegold International Ltd v Questrock Ltd* [2010] EWHC 966 (Ch).
[11] *Truegold International Ltd v Questrock Ltd* [2010] EWHC 966 (Ch), at [40]. A similarly worded provision for giving notice to terminate a management agreement was considered to have 'permissive' effect in *McGann v Bisping* [2017] EWHC 2951 (Comm), at [251], per Mr Richard Salter QC (sitting as a Deputy Judge of the High Court).

> an additional method of effecting service. But it seems to me that a fairly good indication that it was not intended to be an exhaustive method of service, that is to say by serving upon a solicitor, is that it would, of course, have been possible that by the time that a notice came to be served the relevant party could have no solicitor acting for it, but the original solicitors might have gone out of business and no other solicitors might have been appointed pursuant to clauses 1.11 or 1.12.

**7.13** Also of relevance is the decision of the Court of Appeal in *Ener-G Holdings Plc v Hornell*.[12] That case concerned a notice clause in a share purchase agreement which had a number of subsections. Subsection (i) provided that 'any notice … under this Agreement shall be in writing and signed by or on behalf of the party giving it'. Subsection (ii) stated that 'any such notice may be served by delivering it personally or by sending it by pre-paid recorded delivery post …'. Subsection (iii) contained deeming provisions relating to the service of notices in accordance with the subsection (ii).

**7.14** By a majority (Longmore LJ giving a powerful dissent), the Court of Appeal agreed with the judge that the word 'may' in the context of the second subsection was permissive. Thus, notice of a warranty claim which had been delivered to the recipient's home address whilst he was out, and then picked up by the recipient later that afternoon, was validly served. Giving the lead judgment, Lord Neuberger MR said as follows:[13]

> [32] In my view, clear words would normally be required before one could ascribe to the parties an intention that a recipient who actually receives a notice in time should nonetheless be treated as not having received the notice at all. In this case, the point is rather reinforced by the point … that, if a notice is sent by recorded delivery to the prescribed address, it is deemed to have been served, even if it is not actually received. If that is right, it would seem a little curious to ascribe to the parties an intention that a notice sent or delivered in another way was, in the absence of clear words, deemed not to have been served, even though it was clear that, as a matter of fact, it had been received and read by the intended recipient.
>
> [33] Accordingly, there is a strong commercial argument, as well as a strong argument based on the language of the Agreement, for saying that the first Notice was delivered when [the recipient] saw it.

**7.15** Gross LJ agreed, also stating that 'clear words' were normally required before a notice clause could be construed as providing exclusive methods for service. He said:[14]

> there is, for my part, the yet more persuasive argument that exclusivity requires clear wording because of the consequences which can follow. Exclusivity entails that, regardless of the actual knowledge of the intended recipient, any mode of service other than those specified in clause 13.2 will not suffice. The Court will of course give effect to exclusivity – notwithstanding the consequences – if indeed that is the bargain the parties have made; however, as already foreshadowed, there is no such clear wording here.

**7.16** The decision in *Ener-G* was distinguished in *Greenclose Ltd v National Westminster Bank Plc*.[15] In that case, Mrs Justice Andrews DBE was invited to construe

[12] *Ener-G Holdings Plc v Hornell* [2012] EWCA Civ 1059.
[13] *Ener-G Holdings Plc v Hornell* [2012] EWCA Civ 1059, at [32]–[33].
[14] *Ener-G Holdings Plc v Hornell* [2012] EWCA Civ 1059, at [65].
[15] *Greenclose Ltd v National Westminster Bank Plc* [2014] EWHC 1156 (Ch).

the provisions of clause 12 of the 1992 ISDA Master Agreement (Multi Currency-Cross Border Form), the salient part of which read as follows (with added emphasis):

> Any notice or other communication in respect of this Agreement may be given in any manner set forth ... to the address or number or in accordance with the electronic messaging system details provided (see the Schedule) and will be deemed *effective* as indicated:
>
> (i) if in writing and delivered in person or by courier, on the date it is delivered;
> (ii) if sent by telex, on the date the recipient's answerback is received;
> (iii) if sent by facsimile transmission, on the date that transmission is received by a responsible employee of the recipient in legible form (it being agreed that the burden of proving receipt will be on the sender and will not be met by a transmission report generated by the sender's facsimile machine);
> (iv) if sent by certified or registered mail (airmail, if overseas) or the equivalent (return receipt requested) on the date that mail is delivered or its delivery is attempted; or
> (v) if sent by electronic messaging system, on the date that electronic message is received.

7.17 After referring to *Ener-G*, the judge said of the clause in question:[16]

> [103] In my judgment, the arguments in favour of a mandatory construction in this case are far more compelling than they were in *Ener-G Holdings v Hormell*. By contrast with the sub-clause in that case, section 12(a) of the Master Agreement is not about risk allocation, it is about validity. It is not concerned with deemed receipt, but with deemed effectiveness ... In most cases section 12(a) requires delivery or receipt to be proved by the person who seeks to rely upon the notice; in the case of a fax there are additional evidential requirements. Thus the function of section 12(a) cannot be to shift the risk of non-delivery or non-receipt to the intended recipient if any of the stipulated forms of notice are adopted.
>
> [104] In any event, section 12(a) does not say that 'notice given by any of the following methods shall be deemed effective as indicated'. It says that 'notice may be given in any manner set forth' (it then refers to the Schedule) '*and* will be deemed effective as indicated'. The 'and' is important. It signifies that the section is not exclusively about when a notice is deemed effective; the first part of the section deals with the permitted means of giving notice, and the second deals with the date on which any notice given by each of those permitted methods will be deemed to be effective. All the indications are that it is intended to be comprehensive.

7.18 The above authorities all draw a distinction between 'mandatory' or 'obligatory' and 'permissive' or 'directory' methods of service.[17] However, this dichotomy may be viewed as unsatisfactory given that the characterisation of a contractual provision as either 'permissive' or 'directory' does no more than state a conclusion as to the consequence of non-compliance rather than assist in determining what consequence the parties to the contract intended.[18] Indeed, in *R v Soneji*,[19] Lord Steyn (with whom

[16] *Greenclose Ltd v National Westminster Bank Plc* [2014] EWHC 1156 (Ch), at [103]–[104].

[17] A similar approach is to be found in the authorities on s 23 of the Landlord and Tenant Act 1927: see *Stylo Shoes Ltd v Prices Tailors Ltd* [1960] Ch 396, at 405–406, per Wynn-Parry J; *Galinski v McHugh* (1988) 57 P&CR 359, at 365, per Slade LJ; and *CA Webber (Transport) Ltd v Railtrack Plc* [2004] 1 WLR 320, at [26], per Peter Gibson LJ.

[18] *Cf* by analogy *London & Clydeside Estates Ltd v Aberdeen District Council* [1980] 1 WLR 182, at 189–90, per Lord Hailsham LC; *Wang v Inland Revenue Commissioner* [1994] 1 WLR 1286, at 1296, per Lord Slynn; Attorney General's Reference (No 3 of 1999) [2001] 2 AC 91, at 117–18, per Lord Steyn; *Charles v Judicial and Legal Service Commission* [2002] UKPC 34, at [12], per Tipping J.

[19] *R v Soneji* [2006] 1 AC 340, at [23].

Lord Carswell and Lord Brown agreed) went so far as to say that 'the rigid mandatory and directory distinction, and its many artificial refinements, have outlived their usefulness'. It is submitted that the better 'modern approach' is described in *Natt v Osman*.[20] There, the Court of Appeal considered the position where a statutory process or procedure for the exercise or acquisition by a person of some right conferred by the statute does not expressly state the consequences of the failure to comply with that process or procedure. The Chancellor (Sir Terence Etherton) expressed the view that it was unsatisfactory to distinguish between mandatory and directory requirements prescribed by the process or procedure in question. He said,[21] in a passage which (mutatis mutandis) may apply equally to a notice provision in a contract:

> the characterisation of the statutory provisions as either mandatory or directory really does no more than state a conclusion as to the consequence of non-compliance rather than assist in determining what consequence the legislature intended. The modern approach is to determine the consequence of non-compliance as an ordinary issue of statutory interpretation, applying all the usual principles of statutory interpretation. It invariably involves, therefore, among other things according to the context, an assessment of the purpose and importance of the requirement in the context of the statutory scheme as a whole.

**7.19** Ultimately, as Etherton J emphasised in *Von Essen*, the conclusion as to the consequences of non-compliance with any prescribed form of machinery in a lease for the service of a break notice is to be determined by reference to the usual principles of contractual interpretation. It follows that care needs to be taken when relying on any particular authority as an aid to construction of a lease or other instrument (although a party who is looking to advance a 'permissive' construction of the clause may take some comfort from the 'clear words' dicta in the *Ener-G* case).

**7.20** Where a particular method of service of a break notice is prescribed in a lease, but not in terms insisting that only service in that method shall be binding, service on the recipient by any other mode which is no less advantageous to him will normally be effective.[22]

## PARTICULAR CONTRACTUAL METHODS FOR SERVICE

### (a) Personal Service

**7.21** A lease may prescribe that a break notice is to be served personally on the recipient. In this regard, the concept of 'personal service' is well understood to mean service on the recipient personally; as opposed to service by the server (or anyone else)

[20] *Natt v Osman* [2015] 1 WLR 1536. See also *GR Property Management Ltd v Safdar* [2020] EWCA Civ 1441, at [46], per Lewison LJ.

[21] *Natt v Osman* [2015] 1 WLR 1536, at 1542A–42B.

[22] *Tinn v Hoffmann & Co* (1873) 29 LT 217, at 274, per Honeyman J; *Manchester Diocesan Council for Education v Commercial & General Investments Ltd* [1970] 1 WLR 241, at 246C, per Buckley J (a case concerning acceptance of an offer to purchase a property).

personally. So, in *Kenneth Allison Ltd v A E Limehouse & Co*,[23] Lord Bridge and Lord Goff explained (respectively):[24]

> personal service requires that the document be handed to the person to be served or, if he will not accept it, that he be told what the document contains and the document be left with or near him.
>
> Personal service means what it says. Prima facie, the process server must hand the relevant document to the person upon whom it has to be served. The only concession to practicality is that, if that person will not accept the document, the process server may tell him what the document contains and leave it with him or near him.

7.22 Lord Goff's test recognises a distinction between where a document is accepted by the recipient (ie the document is 'handed to' him) and where it is not accepted (ie the recipient is 'told' what the document contains).[25] In *Tseitline v Mikhelson*,[26] it was emphasised that the reference in the first limb of the test to a document being 'handed to' a recipient is 'to the handing over of a document itself, in a situation where its nature is immediately and readily apparent on its face'. Thus, where the intended recipient is simply handed a notice in an unmarked envelope, without any explanation or other basis for knowing what the envelope contained, personal service would not have been effected.[27] The question of what amounts to 'telling' in the context of the second limb of the test was considered by Hoffmann LJ in *Walters v Whitelock*,[28] where he said:

> The question in this case is whether the process server can be said to have told the appellant what the documents contained. The evidence, as we have seen, is that he said: 'I have documents for you:' It is accepted that the appellant was familiar with the process server from all the previous occasions on which he had been served, and that he must therefore have known that the documents related to this litigation in which he was involved.
>
> With what degree of particularity does the rule require that the person served be told what the documents contain? In my judgment, one must look at this in a practical way. I think it is sufficient if it is brought to his attention that it is a legal document which requires his attention in connection with proceedings. The purpose of the requirement that he be told is that he should not be able to say that he ignored the document on the grounds that it was simply junk mail or something which did not necessarily require his attention at all.

7.23 Referring to this authority, in *Tseitline*, Phillips J said:[29]

> the process of leaving a document with the intended recipient must result in them acquiring knowledge that it is a legal document … Whilst this is expressed as requiring that the intended

[23] *Kenneth Allison Ltd v A E Limehouse & Co* [1992] 2 AC 105.

[24] *Kenneth Allison Ltd v A E Limehouse & Co* [1992] 2 AC 105, at 113, 124.

[25] In *Morby v Gate Gourmet Luxembourg IV SARL* [2016] EWHC 74 (Ch), at [31], Mr Recorder Edward Murray (sitting as a Deputy Judge of the Chancery Division) said of the second limb of the test: 'It is a sensible, common sense test that resolves an important practical difficulty of effecting personal service arising in many cases, namely, the refusal of an astute potential recipient of personal service to accept the proffered document …'.

[26] *Tseitline v Mikhelson* [2015] EWHC 3065 (Comm), at [24], per Phillips J.

[27] *Re A Debtor* [1939] Ch 251, at 256, per Sir Wilfred Greene MR; *Walters v Whitelock* (unreported, 19 August 1994), per Hoffmann LJ ('… The purpose of the requirement that he be told is that he should not be able to say that he ignored the document on the grounds that it was simply junk mail or something which did not necessarily require his attention at all …').

[28] *Walters v Whitelock* (unreported) 19 August 1994.

[29] *Tseitline v Mikhelson* [2015] EWHC 3065 (Comm), at [34].

recipient be 'told' the nature of the document, the focus is on the knowledge of the recipient, not the process by which it is acquired. Whilst in most cases knowledge of the nature of the document will be found to have been imparted by a simple explanation, it is clear that it can be also readily be inferred from pre-existing knowledge, prior dealings or from conduct at the time of or after service, including conduct in evading service: see *Barclays Bank of Swaziland Ltd v Hahn* [1989] 1 WLR 506 at 512A.

**7.24** So, for example, personal service of documents has been effected by: (i) leaving a black bag containing documents immediately in front of the recipient on an airport check-in counter, which the recipient 'leafed through' before leaving without the documents;[30] (ii) handing documents to the recipient's friend, in the presence of the recipient, who (after some discussion regarding alleged errors in the documents) put them in a rubbish bin;[31] and (iii) attempting to hand documents to the recipient who was entering an art gallery, but who refused to take them, notwithstanding that he fully appreciated to what the documents related.[32]

**7.25** As regards personal service of a notice on a corporate entity, useful reference may be made to *Bottin (International) Investments Ltd v Venson Group Plc*.[33] That case concerned a notice served pursuant to a share purchase agreement. Personal service of the notice was sought to be effected by the notice being left with the receptionist at the defendant company's office. Of this, Peter Gibson LJ said[34] as follows:

> I agree with Mr Glick when he says that personal delivery of a notice to a company is effected by delivering the notice to somebody authorised to receive it. I disagree with him when he says that the only person to have such authority is somebody in a senior position in the company. The function of a receptionist ordinarily is to receive people visiting, and letters or parcels being delivered to, the employer of the receptionist. In the present case there was in evidence the witness statement of the process server, Mr Greenman, who delivered the December notice to the receptionist; that was accepted on the receptionist's express assurance that it would come to the attention of a director.

**7.26** Personal service of a notice cannot be effected by serving an agent, in the absence of his principal.[35]

### (b) Service by Post/Facsimile/Email

**7.27** Leases frequently provide that a notice can be served by being 'sent' to the intended recipient by post, or by facsimile or email. In *Sun Alliance and London Assurance Co Ltd v Hayman*,[36] Lord Salmon said the following:[37]

[30] *Yukos Finance BV v Lynch* [2017] EWHC 1812 (Comm).
[31] *Gate Gourmet Luxembourg IV SARL v Morby* [2016] Bus LR 218.
[32] *Tseitline v Mikhelson* [2015] EWHC 3065 (Comm).
[33] *Bottin (International) Investments Ltd v Venson Group Plc* [2004] EWCA Civ 1368.
[34] *Bottin (International) Investments Ltd v Venson Group Plc* [2004] EWCA Civ 1368, at [48].
[35] *Gate Gourmet Luxembourg IV SARL v Morby* [2016] Bus LR 218, at [45], per Mr Recorder Edward Murray (sitting as a Deputy High Court Judge); cited with apparent approval in *Gorbachev v Guriev* [2019] EWHC 2684 (Comm), at [27], per HHJ Pearce.
[36] *Sun Alliance and London Assurance Co Ltd v Hayman* [1975] 1 WLR 177.
[37] *Sun Alliance and London Assurance Co Ltd v Hayman* [1975] 1 WLR 177, at 185D.

> According to the ordinary and natural use of English words, giving a notice means causing a notice to be received. Therefore, any requirement in a statute or a contract for the giving of a notice can be complied with only by causing the notice to be actually received – unless the context or some statutory or contractual provision otherwise provides …
>
> Statutes and contracts often contain a provision that notice may be served upon a person by leaving it at his last known place of abode or by sending it to him there through the post. The effect of such a provision is that if notice is served by any of the prescribed methods of service, it is, in law, treated as having been given and received.

7.28 In other words, if a lease or other instrument provides that a notice can be served by being 'sent' to the recipient by post or (by extension) by facsimile or email, the provision will have the effect that a notice served or given or sent by one of the prescribed methods will be deemed to be received, even if it is not actually received, by the intended recipient.[38]

### (c) Service at the Recipient's 'Place of Abode' or 'Place of Business'

7.29 Commonly, a notice provision in a lease (whether expressly or by reference to s 196 of the Law of Property Act 1925) will permit service of notices at the recipient's last-known 'place of abode' or 'place of business'. Generally speaking, these expressions are capable of a wide construction. So, for example, depending on the context, 'place of abode' may include a place where the recipient of the notice works and has his business.[39]

7.30 It is important to note that the recipient's place of abode or place of business can be an address described as such in a lease, even if the recipient in fact resides or carries on business elsewhere. So, for example, in *Levett-Dunn v NHS Property Services Ltd*[40] the landlord comprised four persons 'all of 75 Tyburn Road Erdington Birmingham'. The lease contained a tenant's break option. The clause dealing with service of notices incorporated the provisions of s 196 of the Law of Property Act 1925. Thus, a break notice would be sufficiently served if 'left at the last-known place of abode or business … of the … lessor.' The tenant served break notices at the Tyburn Road address. When the lease was granted, only one of the four persons comprising the landlord (S) had any active connection with the Tyburn Road address. However, S had transferred his interest in the reversion, and had ceased to be one of the landlords, by the time the tenant exercised the break option. Nonetheless, the break notice was validly served

[38] *Chiswell v Griffon Land & Estates Ltd* [1975] 1 WLR 1181, at 1188–89, per Megaw LJ; *Galinski v McHugh* (1988) 57 P&CR 359, at 365, per Slade LJ; *Blunden v Frogmore Investments Ltd* [2003] 2 P&CR 6, at [42]–[45], per Robert Walker LJ.

[39] See eg *Rex v Braithwaite* [1918] 2 KB 319; *Morecambe and Heysham Corporation v Warwick* (1958) 9 P&CR 307; *Stylo Shoes Ltd v Price's Tailor's Ltd* [1960] Ch 396; *Price v West London Investment Building Society Ltd* [1964] 1 WLR 616; *Italica Holdings SA v Bayadea* [1985] 1 EGLR 70. Notably, in *Levett Dunn v NHS Property Services Ltd* [2016] Ch 637, at [43], Judge David Cooke (sitting as a judge of the High Court) thought it would 'not necessarily be appropriate to draw an analogy' between cases concerning service of court documents under the CPR and 'those where the notice is served in the context of an existing contractual relationship between the parties'.

[40] *Levett Dunn v NHS Property Services Ltd* [2016] Ch 637.

on the remaining three landlords. Judge David Cooke (sitting as a judge of the High Court) said:

> [51] A person may choose to describe one place as his place of business for a particular purpose, even if he in fact carries out more business activities somewhere else. If he does so, is the person he tells required to look behind that statement and investigate the extent and nature of the business activity carried on there? I would suggest not.
>
> [56] … In this case, in my view, the address given is an 'abode or place of business' because the landlord has, on the true construction of the leases, nominated it as such, and not because in any other sense, the landlord actually abided there or carried on any business there. That being so, it remains such a place until the landlord nominates some other address or, perhaps, the tenant acquires actual knowledge that it cannot be an address at which the landlord can be reached.

**7.31** This result is consistent with *Grimes v Trustees of the Essex Farmers and Union Hunt*,[41] in which Henderson LJ remarked (in the context of a provision regulating service of a notice to quit) that: 'One evident purpose of specifying an address in the Particulars is to provide an address for service … and if the tenant moves from that address without notifying [the landlord] of his new address, he must clearly be taken to accept that risk that notices served at the specified address will not come to his attention.'[42]

### (d) Service at the Recipient's 'Last Known' Place of Abode or Business

**7.32** A contractual provision entitling service of a notice at the recipient's 'last known' place of abode or business is designed to deal with the case where the serving party is unaware of a change of address on the part of the intended recipient.[43]

**7.33** *National Westminster Bank Ltd v Betchworth Investments Ltd*[44] was a decision of the Court of Appeal on service by the landlord of notice under a break clause in a 14-year lease. The only point at issue was as to the meaning of the expression 'last known address' within the meaning of clause 4(3) of the lease. The facts were striking because the landlord's notice exercising its right under the break clause was sent to an address at 157 Victoria Street, London, SW1 which was then no longer in existence: the building had been demolished; and the envelope containing the notice was returned by the Post Office to the landlord. Nonetheless, service of the break notice was held to be valid. As explained by Lawton LJ and Mackenna J (respectively):[45]

> In my judgment, this appeal turns solely upon the construction of the words 'last known address' in clause 4(3) of the lease. Those words are words in ordinary usage in English. In

[41] *Grimes v Trustees of the Essex Farmers and Union Hunt* [2017] L&TR 28. In that case, the relevant provision regarding service of notices permitted either party to the lease to serve any notice on the other 'at the address given in the Particulars or such other address as has previously been notified in writing'. Henderson LJ (with whom Macur and Beatson LJJ agreed) considered that this ought to be read disjunctively, so that notice could be served, either at the address given in the Particulars, or (instead) at such other address as had previously been notified in writing.

[42] *Grimes v Trustees of the Essex Farmers and Union Hunt* [2017] L&TR 28, at [27].

[43] *Price v West London Investment Building Society Ltd* [1964] 1 WLR 616, at 623, per Diplock LJ.

[44] *National Westminster Bank Ltd v Betchworth Investments Ltd* [1975] 1 EGLR 57.

[45] *National Westminster Bank Ltd v Betchworth Investments Ltd* [1975] 1 EGLR 57, at 58M, 59D.

> no way are they words of art. They have no special meaning in law. They must be construed in the way ordinary people accustomed to the accurate use of the English language would construe them. In my judgment, no useful purpose is served by a detailed semantic analysis of the phrase. What would the ordinary person regard as the last known address of this company?'
>
> '… Victoria Street was an address of the [tenant] known to the [landlord], and the only address of which they ever knew, and therefore … it was that [tenant's] 'last known address,' so that the notice sent to it was properly served.

**7.34** Naturally, when considering the 'last known' address of the intended recipient, the state of knowledge on the part of the serving party is very important. This can cause difficulties for the serving party where an agent is involved, because where any fact or circumstance, material to any transaction, business or matter in respect of which an agent is employed, comes to his knowledge in the course of such employment, and is of such a nature that it is his duty to communicate it to his principal, the principal is deemed to have notice thereof as from the time when he would have received such notice if the agent had performed his duty, and taken such steps to communicate the fact or circumstance as he ought reasonably to have taken.[46] In other words, the circumstances of the case may be such that the serving party is to be treated as having the knowledge of the agent as to the 'last known' address of the intended recipient. In this scenario, if the agent fails to inform his principal of the correct address, the notice may be served at the incorrect address.

**7.35** Under the former rules for service under Part 6 of the CPR,[47] there was some authority to the effect that, when it came to identifying a defendant's 'last known residence' or 'last known place of business,' the court was concerned with the claimant's actual *or* constructive knowledge, ie knowledge which, exercising reasonable diligence, he could acquire.[48] However, it is doubtful whether this approach would apply in the context of a contractual notice provision.[49]

## 'INDIRECT' SERVICE

**7.36** It has been said that, if a party 'is required to serve X and, mistakenly purports to serve Y, the mere fact that Y informs X of the purported service so that X knows of it, cannot convert Y's receipt of the documents into good service upon X'.[50]

[46] *Metropolitan Properties v Cordery* (1980) 39 P&CR 10, at 15, per Megaw LJ; *Arundel Corporation v Khokher* [2003] EWCA Civ 1784, at [16], per Mummery LJ.

[47] Prior to 1 October 2008, the provisions regulating service of a claim form in CPR Part 6 did not contain the equivalent of (what is now) CPR 6.9(3). This makes it clear that a claimant only comes under a duty to 'take reasonable steps to ascertain the address of the defendant's current residence or place of business' where he has 'reason to believe' that the relevant address of the defendant is 'an address at which the defendant no longer resides or carries on business'.

[48] *Cranfield v Bridgegrove* [2003] 1 WLR 2441 [103], per Dyson LJ; *Collier v Williams* [2006] 1 WLR 1945, at [71], per Dyson LJ.

[49] *Levett Dunn v NHS Property Services Ltd* [2016] Ch 637, at [49] and [56].

[50] *Lantic Sugar Ltd v Baffin Investments Ltd* [2009] EWHC 3325 (Comm), at [40], per Gross J (cited with approval in *Ener-G Holdings Plc v Hornell* [2012] EWCA Civ 1059, [60], per Gross LJ).

7.37 However, in *Townsends Carriers Ltd v Pfizer Ltd*,[51] some obiter remarks of Sir Robert Megarry V-C suggest otherwise. That case concerned a lease of certain warehouse premises dated 13 August 1970, granted for a term of seven years from 1 September 1970. The lease contained a break clause (at clause 4(c)) worded as follows:

> If either the landlord or the tenant shall desire to determine the term hereby granted at any time after August 31, 1973, and shall give to the other party 12 months previous notice in writing of such desire ... then ... immediately on the expiration of such notice the present demise and everything herein contained shall cease and become void.

7.38 The break notice was served, not by the tenant company, but by an associated company, not on the landlord company, but on an associated company. The tenant and the landlord had consigned the whole conduct and management of the tenancy and of the tenancy itself to agents on their behalf, allowing their respective associated companies to deal with the property as if they were landlord and tenant respectively in respect of matters such as an increase in rent and variations of the lease. Thus, on agency principles, the break notice had been validly served. However, during the course of his judgment, Sir Robert Megarry V-C suggested:[52]

> [Counsel for the landlord] emphasised that clause 4(c) of the lease requires the tenant to 'give' notice to the landlord, and he said that although the landlord had ultimately received the notice, no notice had ever been given to the landlord as such. However, I do not think that a requirement to 'give' notice is one that excludes the indirect giving of notice. The question is whether the notice has been given, not whether it has been given directly. If the notice emanates from the giver and reaches the ultimate recipient, I do not think it matters if it has passed through more hands than one in transit.

7.39 The approach in *Townsends Carriers* was not followed in *Batt Cables Plc v Spencer Business Parks Plc*,[53] a decision of Lord Hodge, sitting in the Outer House of the Scottish Court of Session. The lease in that case contained a break clause that permitted either the landlord or the tenant to terminate the lease on the tenth, fifteenth and twentieth anniversaries of the term date. The lease also contained a clause which related to the giving of notice as follows:

> All notices which require to be given in terms of this lease shall be in writing and shall be deemed to be sufficiently given if sent by first class recorded delivery post addressed ... in the case of the Landlords, to the Landlords ... at their Registered or Head Office.

7.40 Lord Hodge considered that 'the requirement to give notice to the landlords excludes the indirect giving of notice, contrary to the view of Megarry V-C in *Townsends Carriers Ltd* in relation to the English law of landlord and tenant'.[54] In arriving at this opinion, Lord Hodge followed the approach of the Inner House of the Scottish Court of Session in *Ben Cleuch Estates Ltd v Scottish Enterprises*,[55] in which Lord Macfadyen

[51] *Townsends Carriers Ltd v Pfizer Ltd* (1977) 33 P&CR 361.
[52] *Townsends Carriers Ltd v Pfizer Ltd* (1977) 33 P&CR 361, at 366.
[53] *Batt Cables Plc v Spencer Business Parks Ltd* 2010 SLT 860. See also *Fagan v Knowsley Metropolitan Borough Council* (1985) 50 P&CR 363.
[54] *Batt Cables Plc v Spencer Business Parks Ltd* 2010 SLT 860, at 865.
[55] *Ben Cleuch Estates Ltd v Scottish Enterprise* 2008 SC 252, at 267.

said of a break clause providing for the break notice to be 'given' by the tenant to the landlord: 'a notice addressed to a party other than the landlord and sent to the registered office of that other party cannot be regarded as notice given to the landlord'.

7.41 The position has been considered further by the Supreme Court in *UKI (Kingsway) Ltd v Westminster City Council*.[56] That case concerned the service of a completion notice under the provisions of Schedule 4A to the Local Government Finance Act 1988, which provides a mechanism by which a new building (not yet occupied) may be brought into the rating list. The building in question was developed by UKI to provide office accommodation. On 5 March 2012, the council delivered a completion notice by hand to a building, addressed to the 'Owner.' The notice was given to a receptionist, employed by ECO (a managing agent). Although ECO was under contract with UKI, it had no authority to accept service of documents on its behalf. The receptionist scanned and emailed a copy of the notice to UKI. The Upper Tribunal thought that, since the notice issued by the council reached the hands of the intended recipient, it mattered not that the route was indirect. The Court of Appeal disagreed, on the basis that this approach failed to give effect to the concept (in the relevant statutory provision) of 'service on the owner by the authority'. The Supreme Court restored the order of the Upper Tribunal. Lord Carnwath (with whom Baroness Hale, Lord Kerr, Lord Lloyd-Jones and Lord Kitchin agreed) said:

> [36] … For my part I would accept that the means by which the notice arrives at its destination is not wholly immaterial … The real issue, as I see it, adopting the words of Lord Salmon in the *Sun Alliance* case [1975] 1 WLR 177, 185 is whether the authority 'caused' the notice to be received by UKI. In other words there must be a sufficient causal connection between the authority's actions and the receipt of the notice by the recipient.
>
> [39] This approach to indirect service is consistent with that of Megarry V-C in the *Townsends Carriers* case 33 P&CR 361. I would agree with Gloster LJ … that his words cannot be read as intended to embrace 'all situations' where ultimately the intended recipient 'has come to know of the contents of the notice'. There needs to be actual receipt of the notice, and a sufficient causal link with the actions of the council.

7.42 In reaching this conclusion, it is notable that the Supreme Court was not referred to any of the decisions in *Lantic Sugar*, *Ener-G*, *Ben Cleuch* or *Batt Cables*.[57] Nonetheless, those cases must now be read in light of the remarks of Lord Carnwath in *UKI Kingsway*. In other words, subject to the particular requirements of the break clause in question, it may be possible to effect service of a break notice indirectly on the intended recipient via a third party (or third parties) provided there is a 'sufficient causal link' between receipt of the notice and the actions of the serving party.[58]

[56] *UKI (Kingsway) Ltd v Westminster City Council* [2019] 1 WLR 104.

[57] Although, *Lantic Sugar* was referred to in the Court of Appeal: see [2017] EWCA Civ 430, at [40], [43], [53]. So, presumably, the Supreme Court was aware of the decision.

[58] In this context see also *Borough of Morecambe and Heysham v Warwick* (1958) 9 P&CR 307 in which the Divisional Court considered that an enforcement notice under s 105 of the Town and Country Planning Act 1947 was validly served when a housing officer employed by the Corporation visited a butcher's shop occupied by Mr Warwick and gave the notice to a lady who agreed to give it to him.

SECTION 196 OF THE LAW OF PROPERTY ACT 1925

## (a) The Applicability of s 196 to Break Notices

**7.43** Frequently, a lease will expressly apply s 196 of the Law of Property Act 1925 ('the 1925 Act') to the service of any notices thereunder, including break notices. However, what is the position where s 196 is not expressly incorporated?

**7.44** Section 196 of the 1925 Act extends to (inter alia)[59] 'notices required to be served by any instrument affecting property executed or coming into operation after the commencement of this Act unless a contrary intention appears'.

**7.45** As may be apparent, this provision extends the operation of s 196 only to notices 'required' to be served by an instrument affecting property, unless a contrary intention appears. Thus, s 196 does not apply to common law notices to quit. As was explained by Glidewell LJ in *Wandsworth London Borough Council v Attwell*:[60]

> a tenancy agreement which makes no express provision for the service of a notice to quit to determine the tenancy does not 'require' such notice to be served. Thus in that situation section 196(5) does not apply.

**7.46** Technically, a break notice is not 'required' to be served by an instrument affecting property. This is because the party with the benefit of a break clause has merely the right, on notice, to terminate the lease in certain specified circumstances, ie the server of a break notice has the choice whether or not to do so. Nonetheless, there is an argument to the effect that, absent wording to the contrary, s 196(5) will apply to a break notice to be served by an instrument affecting property. Support for this proposition can be found in some obiter remarks of Kennedy LJ in, *Enfield London Borough Council v Devonish*.[61] That case concerned a succession of two tenancy agreements, the first of which contained the following provision, at condition 3: 'The tenancy may be ended by the tenant giving to the Housing Manager not less than four weeks' written notice expiring on any Monday or by the Council giving similar notice to the tenant.'

**7.47** At trial, the parties proceeded on the basis that this provision was not incorporated into the second tenancy agreement. Nonetheless, referring to this provision, Kennedy LJ said as follows:[62]

> If the council's written Conditions of Tenancy had been incorporated into the tenancy agreement which was relevant in 1994, then those conditions could have constituted an instrument for the purposes of section 196(5), but as I have already explained we have to deal with this case on the basis that they formed no part of that tenancy agreement. Before us Mr Luba also pointed out that, even if the Conditions of Tenancy had been incorporated, condition 3 was not so worded as to 'require' the service of a notice to quit. Its wording was, he submitted, permissive. For present purposes it is unnecessary to reach a firm conclusion in relation to that

[59] Section 196(5), Law of Property Act 1925.
[60] *Wandsworth London Borough Council v Attwell* (1995) 27 HLR 536, at 541.
[61] *Enfield London Borough Council v Devonish* (1997) 29 HLR 691. See also *Blunden v Frogmore Investments Ltd* [2003] 2 P&CR 6, at [21], per Robert Walker LJ.
[62] *Enfield London Borough Council v Devonish* (1997) 29 HLR 691, at 697.

submission, but I incline to the view that in reality the wording of clause 3 was sufficiently mandatory to come within the scope of section 196(5). It provided that if a tenancy was to be ended written notice as prescribed had to be given.

7.48 Adopting the same reasoning, a break notice served pursuant to a break clause in an instrument affecting property is a notice 'required' to be served within the meaning of s 196(5) of the 1925 Act. Accordingly, if this is correct, even where it is not expressly incorporated into a lease, s 196 will apply to the service of break notices (unless a contrary intention appears).

## (b) The Effect of s 196

7.49 So far as material s 196 of the 1925 Act provides as follows:

> (3) Any notice required or authorised by this Act to be served shall be sufficiently served if it is left at the last-known place of abode or business in the United Kingdom of the lessee, lessor, mortgagee, mortgagor, or other person to be served, or, in case of a notice required or authorised to be served on a lessee or mortgagor, is affixed or left for him on the land or any house or building comprised in the lease or mortgage.
>
> (4) Any notice required or authorised by this Act to be served shall also be sufficiently served, if it is sent by post in a registered letter addressed to the lessee, lessor, mortgagee, mortgagor, or other person to be served, by name, at the aforesaid place of abode or business, office, or counting-house, and if that letter is not returned by the postal operator … undelivered; and that service shall be deemed to be made at the time at which the registered letter would in the ordinary course be delivered.

7.50 Section 196 is a 'deeming' provision which avoids disputes as to whether or not a notice has, in fact, been received by the intended recipient. In other words, if service in accordance with s 196 is proved, it does not matter that the notice may not have been received by the intended recipient. It does not matter, even if it were to be clearly established that the notice (say) had gone astray in the post.

7.51 As may be apparent from the provisions quoted above, s 196 recognises two methods of service. Thus, where it applies, any notice required or authorised by the 1925 Act to be served shall be sufficiently served if:

(1) It is left at the last-known place of abode or business in the United Kingdom of the lessee, lessor, or other person to be served, or, in case of a notice required or authorised to be served on a lessee, is affixed or left for him on the land or any house or building comprised in the lease;[63] or
(2) If it is sent by post in a registered letter addressed to the lessee, lessor, or other person to be served, by name, at the aforesaid place of abode or business, and if that letter is not returned by the postal operator (within the meaning of the Postal Services Act 2000) concerned undelivered.[64]

[63] Section 196(3), Law of Property Act 1925.
[64] Section 196(4), Law of Property Act 1925.

7.52 Each of these methods of service merit separate comment below.

### (c) 'Leaving' the Notice Pursuant to s 196(3)

7.53 As mentioned in 7.51 above, s 196(3) of the 1925 Act provides that a notice shall be sufficiently serviced if (inter alia) it is 'left at' the last-known place of abode or business in the United Kingdom of the lessee or lessor.

7.54 A vivid example of the operation of this provision is to be found in *Newborough (Lord) v Jones*.[65] In that case, a landlord gave notice to quit under s 92 of the Agricultural Holdings Act 1948 (which contains materially the same wording as s 196(3) of the 1925 Act). What in fact happened was that the landlord went to the tenant's farmhouse (which was the correct address for service) with a copy of the notice to quit in an envelope. He knocked at the house door, got no answer, and slipped the envelope under the bottom of the side or back door, which was the door which was mostly used by the tenant and his family. Unfortunately, it ended up being slipped under the linoleum behind the tenant's door and did not come to the tenant's attention. Nonetheless, the notice was valid. As Russell LJ explained:[66]

> In the present case it is quite impossible to say that the action of the landlord in putting the notice under the door was other than leaving it at the proper address in a manner which a reasonable person, minded to bring the document to the attention of the tenant, would adopt. Consequently, it appears to me that … the landlord must win.

7.55 Another example is to be found in *Van Haarlam v Kasner Charitable Trust*.[67] In that case, Harman J held that service of a forfeiture notice was validly affected by putting it through the letterbox at the demised premises, when the tenant was in prison, to the landlord's knowledge, and when the tenant's solicitors had requested the landlord to correspond directly with them. After describing how service had been affected, and quoting the relevant parts of s 196(3), Harman J said:[68]

> [The landlord's] service seems to me quite undoubtedly good service within the terms of section 196(3). It fulfils the requirements exactly. It was attacked on the ground that it was not a proper or reasonable thing to do when it was well known, at that date in 1989, that [the tenant] was locked up in prison, when it was well known that solicitors were acting for him and were asking to receive all documents, to serve it by delivering it in accordance with section 196. In my judgement that is unarguably not correct. It is perfectly lawful, it may not be very attractive, but it is perfectly lawful according to the letter of the law, which is sufficiently complied with, to serve this notice by serving it through the doorway. It did in fact come to nobody's notice.

7.56 Also of note is *The Trustees of Henry Smith's Charity v Kyriakou*.[69] There, the landlords had granted the tenant a protected shorthold tenancy of a room for the period of two years from 1 May 1986. The room was situated in a five-storey building. On the

[65] *Newborough (Lord) v Jones* [1975] Ch 90.
[66] *Newborough (Lord) v Jones* [1975] Ch 90, at 94.
[67] *Van Haarlam v Kasner Charitable Trust* (1992) 64 P&CR 214.
[68] *Van Haarlam v Kasner Charitable Trust* (1992) 64 P&CR 214, at 221.
[69] *The Trustees of Henry Smith's Charity v Kyriakou* (1990) 22 HLR 66.

ground floor were shop premises, on the first and second floor were flats and the third and fourth floors were taken up by a maisonette, divided into bed-sitting rooms including that occupied by the tenant. The two flats and the maisonette were entered from the street by a communal front entrance door giving access to a hallway and stairs leading to landings, off which the front doors to the respective flats and the maisonette were to be found. There were letter boxes in the front door and in the entrance door to the maisonette. By clause 8(3) of the tenancy agreement, any notice to be served thereunder or in connection therewith was deemed to be properly served if it complied with the provisions of s 196 of the Law of Property Act 1925.

7.57 On 24 February 1988, the landlord served an appropriate notice to quit pursuant to Case 19 of Sch 15 to the Rent Act 1977. The evidence as to service called before the judge was that a notice in proper form, accompanied by a covering letter from the landlords' solicitor was placed in an envelope properly addressed to the tenant, and was placed through the letterbox in the front of the house. The tenant contended that his place of abode was the self-contained flat and that unless somehow or other the server of the notice found his way to the self-contained flat, he could not effect service in accordance with the statutory provision. The judge and the Court of Appeal disagreed.

7.58 Giving the only reasoned judgment, Glidewell LJ expressly approved of the observations of the judge that s 196 of the 1925 Act requires leaving a notice *at* the last known place of abode, not *in* it. Thus, it is sufficient if the notice is left at a place that is the furthest that a member of the public or postman could go to communicate to tenants residing there. He went on to say:[70]

> A postman could have done no more, had he been delivering something addressed by post to [the tenant], than put it into the letterbox through which [the landlord] posted the document. Accordingly, I take the view that the judge was entirely right to conclude as a matter of law that the service was validly effected.

7.59 It is worth noting that s 196(3) imposes no requirement as to how a notice is to be 'left at' the premises in question, provided that it is left in a proper way, that is to say, in a manner which a reasonable person, minded to bring the document to the attention of the person to whom the notice is addressed, would adopt.[71]

7.60 This is clear from *Kinch v Bullard*.[72] That was not a landlord and tenant case but a case about severance of a joint tenancy between husband and wife. The husband and wife were living together, but the wife (who was terminally ill) was considering seeking a divorce. She was advised by her solicitors to give notice severing the beneficial joint tenancy of the matrimonial home, in order that her husband should not come into the whole interest on her death; and her solicitors, on her instructions, posted such a notice to her husband at the house where they were both living. On 3 August 1994, which was a Thursday, the solicitors posted the letter. On 5 or 6 August, the husband suffered a serious heart attack and was admitted to hospital on Monday, 7 August. Either on the Saturday

[70] *The Trustees of Henry Smith's Charity v Kyriakou* (1990) 22 HLR 66, at 70.
[71] *Newborough (Lord) v Jones* [1975] Ch 90, at 94, per Russell LJ.
[72] *Kinch v Bullard* [1999] 1 WLR 423.

or on the Monday the notice was delivered through the letterbox. The wife picked it up and destroyed it, presumably because at that stage she thought her husband likely to predecease her, ill though she was. The husband died a week later and the wife died about five weeks after that. Neuberger J held that the joint tenancy had been severed, applying s 196(3), and that the notice, once served, could not be recalled. During the course of his judgment, Neuberger J explained:[73]

> As a matter of ordinary language, section 196(3) provides that service of a notice 'at the last-known place of abode or business' of the addressee is good service, and there is no suggestion that it matters how that service is effected, ie whether it is by the giver of the notice, his agent, courier service, ordinary post, recorded delivery or registered post, or some other method. Provided that it can be established that, irrespective of the identity of the person who delivered the notice to a particular address, it was delivered to that address, then the notice has been validly served at that address, provided that it is the addressee's last-known abode or place of business.

**7.61** In *Bullard*, Neuberger J acknowledged that the operation of s 196 could be open to abuse. He explained:[74]

> So far as convenience is concerned, I consider that, if section 196(3) is satisfied once it is shown that the relevant document was bona fide delivered to the last-known place of abode or business of the addressee, then, although it might lead to an unfair result in an exceptional case, the law is at least simple and clear.
>
> However, I am concerned that, if it could be said that the notice in the present case was validly served, unfair advantage could be taken of an addressee by the sender of a notice if the sender (or his agent) had some means of access to the notice after it was served in accordance with section 196 but before the addressee actually saw it, and this resulted in the notice being destroyed or hidden without the addressee ever becoming aware of it.

**7.62** However, he went on to say as follows:[75]

> it cannot be right for a sender of a notice, who had intentionally taken steps to ensure that it did not in fact come to the attention of the addressee, to contend that it was served on him. In other words, whatever section 196 provides, it could not be relied on by the sender of a notice as an engine of fraud. The very purpose of serving a notice is to convey information, with legal consequences, on the addressee: it cannot be right that the sender of a notice can take positive steps to ensure that the notice does not come to the attention of the addressee, after it has been statutorily deemed to have been served, and then fall back on the statute to allege that service has none the less been effected.

**7.63** These observations were approved by the Court of Appeal in *Blunden v Frogmore Investments Ltd*.[76] Thus, where a notice-giver demonstrably acts in bad faith, he cannot rely on the deeming provisions in s 196(3). As Robert Walker LJ commented:[77]

> If the landlord had deliberately concealed his notice under the linoleum in *Newborough v Jones*, he would not have left the notice at the tenant's house in a proper way (Russell LJ's

[73] *Kinch v Bullard* [1999] 1 WLR 423, at 426–27.
[74] *Kinch v Bullard* [1999] 1 WLR 423, at 429H, 430E–30F.
[75] *Kinch v Bullard* [1999] 1 WLR 423, at 429H, 431A–31C.
[76] *Blunden v Frogmore Investments Ltd* [2003] 2 P&CR 6.
[77] *Blunden v Frogmore Investments Ltd* [2003] 2 P&CR 6, at [52].

phrase) but in a way which was deceptive and illusory. It would not strain the language of the statute to conclude that such conduct could not achieve good service. Similarly with counsel's example of a notice which was deliberately put up for only five minutes (whether in the middle of the night or in daytime) and then taken down again. The court would have little difficulty in concluding that it had not been 'affixed' within the meaning of the statute, and that it was not good service.

**7.64** Specifically in the case of a notice required or authorised to be served on a lessee, the notice will be sufficiently served if it is (inter alia) 'left for him' on the land or any house or building comprised in the lease. In this regard, in *Cannon Brewery Co v Signal Press Ltd*,[78] Humphreys J said[79] that this expression was apt to include:

> the case of a notice which is left in the hands of some person who is in fact on the premises, and in regard to whom there is reasonable ground for supposing that she will hand it to the [intended recipient], if the [intended recipient] should be available for that purpose.

**7.65** The principles derived from the above authorities were conveniently summarised by Mr Michael Briggs QC (sitting as a Deputy Judge of the High Court) in *Warborough Investment Ltd v Central Midlands Estates Ltd*,[80] where he said:[81]

> (1) a requirement that a notice be 'left at' premises does not prescribe any particular method of leaving, (2) the method chosen must be a proper method, in the sense that the method must be one, which a reasonable person minded to bring the document to the attention of the person to whom the notice is addressed would adopt. This is a wholly objective test. (3) There is no other gloss, by way of implication, to be placed on statutory provisions as to service, which are intended to be clear, simple and practical and not productive of factual dispute. (4) In particular there is no additional gloss or implication based upon inquiry as to the subjective intention or motive of the server, unless it is shown to be such as to make his use of the service provision an engine of fraud. (5) Where the server leaves the notice with a person at the demise premises, who is neither the tenant, nor the tenant's representative it is a good leaving if there is reasonable ground for supposing that the recipient will pass it on to the tenant, if the tenant is available for that purpose. The risk of the tenant's non-availability is on the tenant not the landlord. (6) Where statute or a contract permits different modes of service, the server is not required to choose between them, and to avoid by that choice a prescribed mode, because it is less likely, or even unlikely, to bring the notice to the tenant's attention. He has a right to use any prescribed mode, but his use of that mode must satisfy the above criteria.

**7.66** Finally, it should be noted a notice can be 'left with' the intended recipient even if it is taken away by the serving party. So, in *Nottingham Building Society v Peter Bennett & Co (a firm)*,[82] a process server had handed documents to a partner of the defendant firm but, when the partner read them and objected to their form, took them back. The Court of Appeal rejected the contention that the documents had not been 'left with' the partner, Waite LJ stating:

> The Oxford English dictionary gives, as the primary meaning of the transitive verb 'to leave': 'To cause or let remain' and 'to depart without taking'.

[78] *Cannon Brewery Co v Signal Press Ltd* (1929) 139 LT 384.
[79] *Cannon Brewery Co v Signal Press Ltd* (1929) 139 LT 384, at 385.
[80] *Warborough Investment Ltd v Central Midlands Estates Ltd* [2007] L&TR 10.
[81] *Warborough Investment Ltd v Central Midlands Estates Ltd* [2007] L&TR 10, at [78].
[82] *Nottingham Building Society v Peter Bennett & Co (a firm)* (1997) *The Times* 26 February.

> There appears to be a difference between those two nuances of meaning, in that one describes the mere process of allowing to remain, and the other introduces an element of departure without removal. It is understandable, given those alternative senses of the verb, that the judge should have found it a difficult point. Was the concept of 'leaving' a document introduced by the Rule to be regarded in the former sense or the latter?
>
> Once the intended recipient (assuming him to have required knowledge of its nature) has been given a sufficient degree of possession of the document to enable him to exercise dominion over it for any period of time however brief, the document has been 'left with him' in the sense intended by the Rule.

**7.67** Self-evidently, it is difficult to see how the fact that the serving party picks up a document after the recipient has walked away from or otherwise abandoned it can have 'any effect on whether [the document] had been left with the recipient prior to that abandonment'.[83]

### (d) 'Sending' the Notice Pursuant to s 196(4)

**7.68** Section 196(4) is a separate and additional provision. As mentioned in **7.51** above, it provides, in the first place, that if a notice is served by registered post then, even if it can be shown not actually to have been delivered at the relevant premises, the notice will none the less be deemed to have been served at the premises, unless returned undelivered. Although s 196(4) refers only to the sending of 'a registered letter', it also extends to recorded delivery.[84]

**7.69** The operation of s 196(4) is well-illustrated by the decision of Plowman J in *Re 88 Berkeley Road, NW9*.[85] In that case, in 1955, the plaintiff (Mrs Rickwood) and a Miss Goodwin bought 88, Berkeley Road, NW6 at the price of £2,800. They provided the money which was required to purchase the house in equal shares and the property was transferred to them as joint tenants, both legally and beneficially. Subsequently, both Mrs Rickwood and Miss Goodwin resided at the property together. In 1968, Miss Goodwin decided to sever the joint tenancy. She went to her solicitors, who advised her about the matter and drafted a notice of severance. The notice of severance was duly sent to Mrs Rickwood at the property by recorded delivery service. At trial, Mrs Rickwood's evidence (accepted by the judge) was that she never received the notice. Inquiries made of the Post Office showed that the notice had been sent by recorded delivery; and had indeed been delivered at 88, Berkeley Road and signed for by Miss Goodwin herself (who failed to pass it on to Mrs Rickwood). Those facts notwithstanding, Plowman J held that the notice of severance was validly served.[86]

**7.70** It is important to appreciate that s 196(4) also provides that (assuming that it is not returned undelivered) a notice sent by registered post or recorded delivery is deemed

[83] *Tseitline v Mikhelson* [2015] EWHC 3065 (Comm), at [27], per Phillips J.
[84] Section 1, Recorded Delivery Service Act 1962.
[85] *Re 88, Berkeley Road, NW9* [1971] Ch 648.
[86] *Re 88, Berkeley Road, NW9* [1971] Ch 648, at 655C–55D.

to have been served at the time when it would, in the ordinary course of post, have been delivered. Referring to this provision, in *WX Investments Limited v Begg*,[87] Patten J said:[88]

> [14] Service on a lessor by either registered post or recorded delivery is 'deemed to be made at the time at which the registered letter would in the ordinary course be delivered'. 'Ordinary course' is obviously a shorthand for 'ordinary course of post' ...
>
> [15] The phrase 'deemed to be made' connotes an imaginary state of affairs which may or may not accord with the reality of what has taken place. That imaginary state of affairs is also usually conclusive having regard to the purpose of the legislation and the language of the deeming provision itself.

7.71 Thus, he added:[89]

> [16] ... The language of s 196(4) leads me to think that the sub-section cannot have been intended merely to provide for service by recorded delivery at the time at which delivery in accordance with the recorded delivery system was in the particular case in question actually effected ... The critical words are not 'in the ordinary course' but rather 'shall be deemed to be made at the time at which the registered letter would'. The use of the word 'would' rather than 'was' is in my judgment indicative of a hypothetical delivery which does not depend on when the postman actually called. The date of such delivery is governed by what the Court finds to have been the time when delivery in the ordinary course of post would take place but this is to be judged by normal practice and expectations not by the circumstances or whims of the addressee at the time. A combination of fiction and reality would lead to uncertainty as to the hypothesis to be applied and would make the provisions pointless and unworkable.

7.72 This is of potential significance in the context of the service of a break notice, where mistiming by even a few minutes can be fatal to the exercise of the break. Indeed, as the observations of Patten J make clear, the date of receipt of a notice served pursuant to s 196(4) is irrelevant; rather, in ascertaining the deemed date of delivery of the notice, the court has to determine when delivery in the ordinary course of post *would* have taken place. This might be fatal to the validity of the notice.[90]

## SECTION 7 OF THE INTERPRETATION ACT 1978

7.73 It has been held[91] that wherever s 196 of the 1925 applies to the giving of a notice, so too does s 7 of the Interpretation Act 1978 (the '1978 Act'). Section 7 permits service of a notice by means of a letter posted in the ordinary post (in contradistinction to service by registered post or recorded delivery). It provides:

> Where an Act authorises or requires any document to be served by post (whether the expression 'serve' or the expression 'give' or 'send' or any other expression is used) then, unless

[87] *WX Investments Limited v Begg* [2002] 1 WLR 2849.

[88] *WX Investments Limited v Begg* [2002] 1 WLR 2849, at [14]–[15].

[89] *WX Investments Limited v Begg* [2002] 1 WLR 2849, at [16].

[90] See, for example, *Stephenson & Son v Orca Properties Ltd* [1989] 2 EGLR 129 (concerning the deadline for giving notice of a rent review to a tenant).

[91] *London Borough of Southwark v Akhtar* [2017] L&TR 36. *Cf Chiswell Estates v Griffon Land and Estates Ltd* [1975] 1 WLR 1181 (concerning s 23 of the Landlord and Tenant Act 1927) and *Trafford Housing Trust v Rubenstein* [2013] UKUT 0581 (LC) (concerning s 20 of the Landlord and Tenant Act 1985).

> the contrary intention appears, the service is deemed to be effected by properly addressing, pre-paying and posting a letter containing the document and, unless the contrary is proved, to have been effected at the time at which the letter would be delivered in the ordinary course of post.

**7.74** The potential significance of this emerges from *London Borough of Southwark v Akhtar*.[92] In that case, a lease provided that 'Section 196 of the Law of Property Act 1925 shall apply to any notice under this lease'. The Upper Tribunal considered that this wording extended to a notice given under s 20B of the Landlord and Tenant Act 1985. The serving party did not make direct use of s 196, in the sense that it did not use registered post or recorded delivery, but used ordinary post. Nonetheless, the Upper Tribunal accepted the logic of the submission that, since s 196 of the 1925 Act authorised a notice to be served by post, s 7 of the 1978 Act applied to the notice. This was the case even though it was the lease itself which incorporated the provisions of s 196. As it was put by the Tribunal: 'Where the parties have said that a statutory provision is to apply, they are not applying it in a limited form unless they say so; in the absence of proviso they must be taken to apply it with all its consequences'.[93] Since s 7 applied, it was presumed that service of the notice had taken place in the ordinary course of posting; and the recipient's bare assertion that she did not receive the notice was insufficient to rebut the presumption.

## SERVICE AT COMMON LAW

**7.75** If or where s 196 of the 1925 Act does not apply to, and there are no other express notice provisions in, the lease,[94] then the person serving the notice will have to rely upon the common law rules relating to service.

**7.76** Perhaps surprisingly, there is still controversy over what is required to effect service of a notice at common law. In *Haywood v Newcastle upon Tyne NHS Trust*,[95] Baroness Hale (with whom Lord Wilson and Lady Black agreed) surveyed a number of historic landlord and tenant cases[96] in search of the common law rule. She concluded[97] that a 'clear and universal' rule did not emerge from these cases, saying:

> [39] … Receipt in some form or other was always required, and arguably by a person authorised to receive it. In all the cases there was, or should have been, someone at the address to receive the letter and pass it on to the addressee … There are also passages to the effect that the notice must have been communicated or come to the mind of the addressee, albeit with some exceptions.

[92] *London Borough of Southwark v Akhtar* [2017] L&TR 36.

[93] *London Borough of Southwark v Akhtar* [2017] L&TR 36, at [70].

[94] As in eg *Hogg v Brooks* (1885) 15 QBD 256.

[95] *Haywood v Newcastle upon Tyne NHS Trust* [2018] 1 WLR 2073.

[96] Including *Jones d. Griffiths v Marsh* (1791) 4 TR 464; *Doe d. Neville v Dunbar* (1826) Moo & M 9; *Papillon v Brunton* (1860) 5 H&N 518; and *Tanham v Nicholson* (1872) LR 5 HL 561.

[97] *Haywood v Newcastle upon Tyne NHS Trust* [2018] 1 WLR 2073, at [39].

7.77 In a concurring judgment, after a thorough survey of the authorities, Lady Black concluded:

> [73] In short, I do not think that it has been shown that there is a clear and long-standing common law rule that service of … an 'ordinary civil notice' occurs when the notice is delivered to the recipient's address. In so far as any clear principle emerges at all from the older cases, it seems to me, particularly in the light of *Tanham v Nicholson*, to revolve around delivery to the recipient's agent, who might be the recipient's household servant, professional agent, or … family member. In each case, the agent appears to have been someone who, as part of their role, would be expected to take in communications of the type concerned for the intended recipient.

7.78 By contrast, in a strong dissent, Lord Briggs (with whom Lord Lloyd-Jones agreed) expressed the following view:

> [81] In my judgment there has been for over two centuries a term generally implied by law into relationship contracts terminable on notice, namely that written notice of termination is given when the document containing it is duly delivered, by hand or by post, to the home (or, if appropriate, business) address of the intended recipient, rather than, if later, when it actually comes to the recipient's attention, or when the recipient, absent at the time of delivery, has returned home and has had a reasonable opportunity to read it. That term is clearly identified by the common law authorities as the correct one.

7.79 Nonetheless, given the views of the majority in the *Haywood* case, it appears to be the position at common law that notice is regarded as having been served only if it has been received by, or if it has come to the attention of, the recipient (or his duly authorised agent).[98]

[98] Past authorities ought now to be read in this light. See eg *Freetown Ltd v Assethold Ltd* [2013] 1 WLR 701, at [37], per Rix LJ ('… the common law rule … requires receipt to effect service …'); *Gouldandris v Knight* [2018] 1 WLR 3345, at [19], per Patten LJ ('At common law service requires receipt of the document …'). See also *Beanby Estates Ltd v Egg Stores (Stamford Hill) Ltd* [2003] 1 WLR 2064, at 2075, per Neuberger J (a common law notice 'is not served merely by putting it in the post'); *Holwell Securities Ltd v Hughes* [1974] 1 WLR 155, at 157–58, per Russell LJ (concerning the exercise of an option to purchase a property); and *Blunden v Frogmore Investments Ltd* [2002] 2 EGLR 29, at 32, per Robert Walker LJ.

# 8

# *On Whom the Break Notice Should be Served*

## INTRODUCTION

8.1 Plainly, when it comes to serving a break notice, the terms of the lease must be observed. Thus, the server of the break notice should ensure that the notice is served on the intended recipient(s) as specified in the lease. However, the following specific scenarios merit comment.

## JOINT LESSEES/LESSORS

8.2 Where there are joint lessors or joint lessees, in the absence of any express term to the contrary, the break notice should be given to each of them.[1] The observations made above[2] are equally applicable here.

## MULTIPLE PARTIES

8.3 Occasionally, the lease will specify that the break notice has to be served on more than one party (eg a managing agent as well as the landlord or the tenant).[3] This may well be the case where, for example, the landlord holds the lease on trust for a beneficiary, and the beneficiary has, in turn, entrusted responsibility of the management of the demised premises to a third party. Thus, in *The Hotgroup Plc v The Royal Bank of Scotland Plc (as Trustee of Schroder Exempt Property Unit Trust)*,[4] clause 14.2 of the lease in question provided: '… no notice will be deemed to be validly served on the Landlord unless a copy of the notice is also served on Schroder Property Investment Management Limited'.

8.4 The latest date for exercise of the break clause in that case was 3 October 2009, and the landlord was served with the necessary break notice on 14 September 2009.

[1] *Quartermaine v Selby* (1889) 5 TLR 223.

[2] See **4.6–4.12**.

[3] See eg *Ropemaker Properties Ltd v Bella Italia Restaurants Ltd* [2018] L&TR 32 ('… either the landlord or the tenant may … give notice to the other and the guarantor to determine this agreement …').

[4] *The Hotgroup Plc v The Royal Bank of Scotland Plc (As Trustee of Schroder Exempt Property Unit Trust)* [2010] EWHC 1241 (Ch).

However, Schroder Property Investment Management Limited was only served with a break notice on 19 November 2009. Mr Charles Hollander QC (sitting as a Deputy Judge of the High Court) held that the break clause had not been validly exercised, with the consequence that the Royal Bank of Scotland was entitled to a declaration that the break clause option had not been complied with.

## CONCURRENT LESSEES

**8.5** The nature of a concurrent lease has been described above.[5]

**8.6** In *Standard Life Investments Property Holdings Ltd v W&J Linney Ltd*,[6] the court had to consider whether the original landlord, or the concurrent lessee, was the appropriate person on whom a break notice should be served. The facts were as follows. On 4 April 1996, Mansfield District Council demised commercial premises to Sun Alliance Trust Company for a term beginning on 4 April 1997 and expiring on 29 September 2116. On 6 June 1997, the lease was assigned to Capita Trust Company. On 4 February 2004, Capita granted a sub-lease of a unit within the commercial premises to W & J Linney. The sub-lease contained a definition of 'Landlord' as follows:

> ... the party so described at the head of this Lease and where the context so admits the person for the time being entitled to the reversion immediately expectant on the determination of the term.

**8.7** Clause 9 of the sub-lease stated: 'If the Tenant wishes to determine this Lease on the 5th anniversary of the date of this Lease and shall give to the Landlord not less than six months' prior notice in writing to such effect ... then this Lease shall come to an end ...'

**8.8** On 26 November 2004, Capita demised the commercial premises to Standard Life for a term beginning on 4 April 1997 and expiring 26 September 2116. Thus, Capita's reversionary interest in the premises was limited to 3 days in 2116. In 2008, Linney wished to exercise the break clause and so, on 23 July 2008, its solicitors wrote to Capita at its registered office enclosing a break notice addressed to Capita. Capita took the view that the notice ought to have been served upon Standard Life. The court had to decide the issue.

**8.9** At trial, Linney argued first that Capita was defined in the sub-lease as 'the Landlord' and that that definition continued to apply even after Capita ceased to be the holder of the immediate reversion. Thus, the break notice was properly served on Capita. Lewison J held[7] that such a construction of the sub-lease did not make commercial common sense. For:

> It would mean that the current reversioner could have his income stream removed from him without his knowledge. Someone who was once the landlord but no longer is would have no interest in checking whether the conditions applicable to the exercise of the break clause,

[5] See **4.19**.
[6] *Standard Life Investments Property Holdings Ltd v W&J Linney Ltd* [2011] L&TR 9.
[7] *Standard Life Investments Property Holdings Ltd v W&J Linney Ltd* [2011] L&TR 9, at [21].

> whether as to timing or compliance with covenants, had been complied with and would have no interest in communicating with the current landlord. One of the conditions applicable to the exercise of the break clause is the giving of vacant possession. Vacant possession can only be given to the current landlord. It cannot, in my judgment, have been contemplated that the tenant could simply move out of the premises and return the keys to the landlord without having given him any notice of his intention to do so … In my judgment … the only person on whom a valid notice could be served was [Standard Life].

**8.10** Thus, absent express wording to the contrary, a break notice must be served by the tenant on the holder of the current reversion. The authors have yet to encounter such contrary wording in practice.

## THE POSITION WITH LEASES TAKING EFFECT IN EQUITY

**8.11** The position in relation to leases taking effect in equity has been addressed above.[8] The principles identified there apply equally in the case of the recipient of a break notice. In other words, a break right in a lease taking effect in equity only is capable of being exercised by giving notice to the equitable landlord or tenant (as the case may be).

## EQUITABLE ASSIGNEES OF THE TERM OR REVERSION

**8.12** The position in relation to equitable assignees is addressed in more detail in Chapter 3.[9] Generally speaking, a break notice must be served on the party in whom the legal interest in the reversion or the term is vested. Therefore, service of a break notice on an equitable assignee will (in general) be invalid.

## FORMER LANDLORDS/TENANTS

**8.13** As a corollary of the position stated in the previous paragraph, absent something extraordinary, a break notice served on a person who once was (but is no longer) the landlord or the tenant under a lease will be ineffective to operate the break clause.

**8.14** The contrary position was argued in *Levett-Dunn v NHS Property Services Ltd*.[10] That case concerned a lease dated 27 September 2010. There were four persons, including S, named as 'the landlord'. The lease contained a break option entitling the tenant to determine the lease on 10 July 2013 by giving not less than six months' prior written notice of its wish to do so. The provision of the lease dealing with service of notices provided that 'service on any one of the parties comprising the landlord shall be deemed to be service on all'. The tenant exercised the break option by delivering four separate notices to each of the parties named as the landlord. By the point in time

[8] See **4.21**.
[9] See **3.56–3.76**.
[10] *Levett-Dunn v NHS Property Services Ltd* [2016] Ch 637.

that the notices were delivered, S had transferred his interest in the reversion to the other three persons. No notice of the transfer had been given to the tenant, which was unaware of the fact.

**8.15** Notwithstanding that S had ceased to have an interest in the premises, the tenant argued that it was entitled to regard him still as one of the persons comprising 'the landlord' for the purposes of the lease. The tenant claimed it was entitled to do so by virtue of s 23(2) of the Landlord and Tenant Act 1927.

**8.16** So far as material, s 23 of the 1927 Act provides as follows:

> (1) Any notice … under this Act shall be in writing and may be served on the person on whom it is to be served either personally, or by leaving it for him at his last known place of abode in England or Wales, or by sending it through the post in a registered letter addressed to him there …
>
> (2) Unless or until a tenant of a holding shall have received notice that the person theretofore entitled to the rents and profits of the holding (hereinafter referred to as 'the original landlord') has ceased to be so entitled, and also notice of the name and address of the person who has become entitled to such rents and profits, any claim, notice, request, demand, or other instrument which the tenant shall serve upon or deliver to the original landlord shall be deemed to have been served upon or delivered to the landlord of such holding.

**8.17** Section 23(1) is confined to (inter alia) a 'notice … under this Act' and cannot apply to a contractual notice (save to the extent that the provision is incorporated in the contract). The question in *Levett-Dunn* was whether s 23(2) had a more general application to *any* sort of notice to be served by a tenant.

**8.18** Judge David Cooke (sitting as a High Court judge) rejected the suggestion that s 23(2) had any general effect. He said:[11]

> There would be force in the argument that a provision for the protection of tenants such as section 23(2) is needed just as much for purposes of any notice or document a tenant may wish to serve as it is for notices for the specific purposes of the 1927 Act. There is obvious potential for injustice, even frustration of the rights of tenants, if they may in good faith serve the person whom they believe to be their landlord, never having been told of any change, only to be told, possibly as in this case too late to rectify matters, that that person has transferred his interest. However, I do not consider that Parliament can have intended to make a provision of general effect in section 23(2).

**8.19** Therefore, the notice served on S was a nullity.

## AGENTS

**8.20** In *Galinski v McHugh*,[12] Slade LJ said: 'under the general law of landlord and tenant, it is possible for good service of a landlord's notice to be effected by serving it on the duly authorised agent of the tenant (and vice versa)'. So, for example, in *Hawtrey v*

[11] *Levett-Dunn v NHS Property Services Ltd* [2016] Ch 637, at [38].
[12] *Galinski v McHugh* (1989) 21 HLR 47, at 55.

*Beaufort Ltd*,[13] a notice addressed to the directors of a company and received by them was held to be effectual to determine a tenancy vested in the company. From a practical perspective, if a break notice is served on an agent, prudence suggests that it be made clear by the serving party that the notice is served on the agent in its capacity as such. Failure to do so may not necessarily be fatal if the agent has general authority from the lessee/lessor in relation to dealings in respect of the lease. In this regard, the observations made above[14] apply here.

## PARTNERSHIPS

**8.21** The legal principles applicable to private partnerships, limited partnerships and limited liability partnerships have been discussed above.[15] It follows from those principles that, subject always to the terms of the lease: (i) in the case of a private partnership or a limited partnership, a break notice should be given to the partners in whom the legal interest in the reversion or the term (as the case may be) is vested; whereas (ii) by contrast, in the case of a limited liability partnership, a break notice should be served on the limited liability partnership itself.

## INSOLVENCY

### (a) Bankrupts/Trustees in Bankruptcy

**8.22** Where the grantor of an option to determine is made bankrupt, the break clause can still be exercised because, by operation of s 283(5) of the Insolvency Act 1986, the property comprised in a bankrupt's estate is so comprised subject to the rights of any person other than the bankrupt. Invariably, once the lease/option to determine has vested in the trustee by operation of s 306(1) of the Insolvency Act 1986, a break notice will need to be served on the trustee, as the party in whom the property which is subject to the option is vested. This is analogous with the position of a concurrent lessee.

### (b) Companies in Administration

**8.23** As for the exercise of a break clause against a company in administration, the break notice can be given to the company (subject to the terms of the lease). As mentioned above,[16] during the period of administration, the company's property remains vested

[13] *Hawtrey v Beaufort Ltd* [1946] KB 280, at 288, per Croom-Johnson J ('A limited company must, of course, act through agents … [While the notice] is addressed to the directors, it is addressed to them, not in their capacity as tenants … but as being the persons acting on behalf of the limited company. I think, therefore, that on a fair construction of the document it is a good notice to the defendant company'). For another example see *Papillon v Brunton* (1860) 5 H&N 518 (notice to quit delivered to landlord's agent).

[14] See **4.43–4.53**.

[15] See **4.55–4.60**.

[16] See **4.62**.

in the company. Where proceedings are commenced, or continued, for the purpose of enforcing an option against a company in administration, either the consent of the administrator or the leave of the court will be required under para 43(6) of Sch B1 to the Insolvency Act 1986.

### (c) Companies in Liquidation

**8.24** In a similar manner to a company in administration, where a company is in liquidation, unless its property has vested in the liquidator under s 145 of the Insolvency Act 1986, a break notice can continue to be served on the company itself (of course, subject to the terms of the lease). Once a company in liquidation has been dissolved after the winding up of its affairs, any property of whatever nature or any right then vested in the company is deemed to be bona vacantia and will vest in the Crown, the Duchy of Lancaster, or the Duke of Cornwall, as appropriate.[17] This means that, once the company has been dissolved, and assuming that the liquidator has not disclaimed the lease prior to the date of dissolution, a party desirous of exercising a break clause will need to serve the break notice on the Crown (ie to the Treasury Solicitor or the Duchy offices).

## RECEIVERS AND MANAGERS

**8.25** As has been seen,[18] a receiver/receiver and manager is only authorised to do such things as covered by the terms of the appointing instrument. Depending on the scope of the court order, statute or contract under which the receiver/receiver and manager is appointed, this may (or may not) include the ability to accept the service of a break notice on behalf of a landlord or tenant.

## WHERE THE INTENDED RECIPIENT HAS DECEASED

**8.26** Service of a notice affecting land which would be effective but for the death of the intended recipient is effective despite his death if the person serving the notice has no reason to believe he has died.[19]

## PERSONAL REPRESENTATIVES

**8.27** As has been seen,[20] where an executor is appointed by a will (as opposed to a statutory appointment or an appointment by the court), he derives title from the will;[21]

[17] Section 1012(1) of the Companies Act 2006 (replacing s 654(1) of the Companies Act 1985 with effect from 1 October 2009).

[18] See **4.64–4.65**.

[19] Section 17(1), Law of Property (Miscellaneous Provisions) Act 1994.

[20] See **4.66**.

[21] *Woolley v Clark* (1822) 5 B&A 744, at 745–46, per Abbott CJ; *Chetty v Chetty* [1916] 1 AC 603, at 608, per Lord Parker.

and the property of the deceased vests in the executor from the moment of the testator's death.[22] Therefore, it is submitted that a break notice may be validly served on an executor even before he proves the will.

**8.28** The position is different on intestacy. An administrator derives his authority entirely from his appointment by the court, ie by the grant of administration.[23] Until then, the deceased's real and personal estate vests in the Public Trustee pursuant to s 9 of the Administration of Estates Act 1925, albeit that the vesting of his real or personal estate in the Public Trustee by virtue of this provision does not confer on him any beneficial interest in, or impose on him any duty, obligation or liability in respect of, the property.[24] However, this does not mean the Public Trustee's title to property is 'shorn of substance'.[25] On the contrary, the vesting is a positive act, the effect of which is to confer on the Public Trustee the capacity to receive notice to quit.[26]

**8.29** It follows that, during the period when the deceased's property is vested in the Public Trustee, a break notice served upon him is presumably effective to determine a tenancy. The address for service for the Public Trustee is: The Public Trustee Office, PO Box 3010, London, WC2B 6JS.[27] Upon the grant of administration, the break notice may be served on the administrator of the deceased's estate.

**8.30** It may be noted that statute has intervened in this area. Notice affecting land which would have been authorised or required to be served on a person but for his death shall be sufficiently served before a grant of representation has been filed if (a) it is addressed to 'The Personal Representative of' the deceased (naming him) and left at or sent by post to his last know place of residence or business in the United Kingdom, and (b) a copy of it, similarly addressed, is served on the Public Trustee.[28] Apparently, this procedure is an alternative to service of a notice as described in paragraph **8.29** above.

[22] Sections 1 and 3 of the Administration of Estates Act 1925.

[23] *Woolley v Clark* (1822) 5 B&A 744, 745–46, per Abbott CJ; *Ingall v Moran* [1944] KB 160, at 168, per Luxmoor LJ. In *Gateway Housing Association v Personal Representatives of Ali* [2021] 1 WLR 289, the Housing Association served a notice to quit on 'The Personal Representatives of Mr Nuraj Ali' (who had died intestate). The Housing Association originally argued that 'where a tenancy agreement includes an express term for service of notices a notice is properly served on the tenant pursuant to that term even if served after the tenant has died'. However, at the hearing of the appeal, the Housing Association conceded that this argument could not succeed 'as the notice to quit was addressed to the personal representatives and, letters of administration not having been granted, there were not any personal representatives in whom the tenancy had vested'. See the judgment, at [30].

[24] Section 9(3) of the Administration of Estates Act 1925.

[25] *Mitchell v Watkinson* [2014] EWCA Civ 1472, at [69].

[26] *Smith v Mather* [1948] 2 KB 212 (overruled on another point in *Moodie v Hosegood* [1952] AC 61); *Mackley v Nutting* [1949] 2 KB 55; *Fred Long & Sons v Burgess* [1950] 1 KB 115; *Earl of Harrowby v Snelson* [1951] 1 All ER 140; *Egerton v Rutter* [1951] 1 KB 472; *Wilbraham v Colclough* [1952] 1 All ER 979; *Wirrall Borough Council v Smith* (1982) 43 P&CR 312; *Edwards v Strong*, *The Times*, 9 November 1994.

[27] *Practice Direction (Probate: Notice to Quit)* [1995] 1 WLR 1120.

[28] Section 18(1), Law of Property (Miscellaneous Provisions) Act 1994. The problem sought to be addressed by this provision was explained in the Law Commission's report, *Property Law: Title on Death* (Law Com No.184) (Cm 777), at §2.27: '… even if [the person wishing to serve the notice] knows of the death, he may be unable to discover whether there is a will, whether it appoints executors and if so, who they are. In any event, the risk always exists that the will is invalid or has be superseded by a later one. In the absence of a will, he must discover whether letters of administration have been granted …'.

In *Gateway Housing Association v Personal Representatives of Ali*, the Court of Appeal explained that 'what is served on the Public Trustee is only a copy of the notice to quit. It is not an independent self-standing notice … The operative document is the notice to quit and its terms determine the date of determination of the tenancy.'[29] However, service of the copy is required prior to the expiry of the operative notice in order to ensure the validity of the latter.[30]

[29] *Gateway Housing Association v Personal Representatives of Ali* [2021] 1 WLR 289, at [40].

[30] Ibid, at [53]. In that case, the operative notice was deemed served on 17 October 2018 and expired on 18 November 2018. The copy notice was received on 30 October 2018 and expired on 2 December 2018. The Court of Appeal held that the operative notice was valid.

# 9

# *Conditions in a Break Clause: General Principles*

## INTRODUCTION

**9.1** It is frequently the case that the entitlement to exercise a break clause will depend upon the fulfilment of certain substantive conditions by either the landlord or (more usually) the tenant.

## IDENTIFICATION OF THE CONDITIONS

**9.2** In most cases, the lease will identify clearly the conditions upon which the exercise of the break clause depends. However, imperfect drafting means that this is not always so. The lease then falls to be construed so as to identify the conditions. In this respect, it has been observed that 'the fact that the conditions prescribed in a break clause must be strictly complied with … does not mean that the clause must be construed strictly or, in particular, adversely to the tenant'.[1] This is well-illustrated by the following trilogy of cases.[2]

**9.3** *HFI Farnborough LLP v Park Garage Group Plc*[3] concerned leases in materially identical terms in respect of four petrol filling stations. Each lease contained a landlord's break clause worded as follows:

> The Landlord shall be entitled at any time during the Term to serve a written notice ('the Notice') on the Tenant giving not less than three months' notice to terminate this lease whereupon at the expiry of the Notice this Lease shall be determined but without affecting any rights or remedies the Landlord may have against the Tenant in respect of any previous breach of the provisions of this Lease.

**9.4** However, the leases also contained the following further provisions:

> 8.2 The Landlord will not invoke the break clause … ('the Break Clause') unless the value of the Premises on the date the Break Clause is exercised exceeds the Price …

[1] *Capitol Park Leeds Plc v Global Radio Services Ltd* [2021] EWCA Civ 995, at [20], per Newey LJ.

[2] In a slightly different context, see also *Dreams Ltd v Pavilion Property Trustees Ltd* [2020] L&TR 22. That case concerned whether, on a proper construction, an agreement for surrender of a lease was conditional upon (i) payment by the tenant of damages in respect of terminal dilapidations (it was not) and (ii) delivery up of vacant possession of the premises by the tenant (it was).

[3] *HFI Farnborough LLP v Park Garage Group Plc* [2012] EWHC 3577 (Ch).

> 8.3 If the Landlord has exercised the Break Clause (but not otherwise) then … it shall upon completing a sale of the Premises pay overage ('Overage') to the Tenant within seven days of such disposal being completed such overage to be calculated [in accordance with a prescribed formula].

**9.5** The figure given in each of the leases as 'the Price' was the price for which the landlord had purchased the freehold of the relevant petrol filling station with vacant possession.

**9.6** On 13 April 2012, the landlord served break notices pursuant to the leases, expiring on 16 July 2012. In each case, the notice was accompanied by a letter from a valuer, purporting to confirm that the value of the relevant premises exceeded 'the Price'. The tenant's solicitors responded to the break notice by saying that the landlord was only entitled to serve a break notice where it intended to sell the properties (with an overage payment being due within seven days of completion of the sale). The landlord took issue with the suggestion that there was any such requirement; and confirmed that there was no proposed sale of the freehold interests. As a consequence, there arose between the parties a dispute as to whether the landlord was entitled to exercise the break clauses if there was not an agreed sale of the premises with vacant possession at the date of the sale.

**9.7** The resolution of this dispute fell to be determined in accordance with settled principles of contractual construction. Thus, deciding the matter in favour of the tenant, HHJ Behrens (sitting as a judge of the High Court) said:[4]

> (2) I agree with [Counsel for the tenant] that clause 8.2 … was a clause primarily for the protection of [the tenant] and was designed to be a fetter on [the landlord's] otherwise unfettered right to exercise the Break Clause. I also agree that [the tenant's] construction makes more sense from a commercial point of view. It is to my mind far more likely from a commercial point of view if clauses 8.2 and 8.3 are linked and that the Break Clause can only be exercised on a sale. As [Counsel for the tenant] pointed out, on [the landlord's] construction the overage might not be payable for many years (or not at all).

**9.8** Thus, the landlord's break clause was conditional upon the landlord having agreed a sale of the relevant premises at a price exceeding the price at which it acquired the property. Since no such sale had been agreed, the landlord was not entitled to exercise the break.

**9.9** *Goldman Sachs International v Procession House Trustee Ltd*[5] involved a lease which contained, in clause 23.1, a tenant's break option conditional upon 'the tenant being able to yield up the Premises with vacant possession as provided in clause 23.2'. In turn, clause 23.2 provided: 'On the expiration of [the break notice], the Term shall cease and determine (and the tenant shall yield up the Premises in accordance with clause 11 and with full vacant possession).'

**9.10** Clause 11 was headed 'YIELDING UP.' It contained two provisions. First, in clause 11.1: 'Unless not required by the Landlord, the tenant shall, at the end of the Term, remove any alterations or additions to the Premises … and shall reinstate the Premises to

[4] *HFI Farnborough LLP v Park Garage Group Plc* [2012] EWHC 3577 (Ch), at [65].
[5] *Goldman Sachs International v Procession House Trustee Ltd* [2018] L&TR 28.

their original layout and to no less a condition than as described in the works specification.' Secondly, in clause 11.2: 'At the end … of the Term the tenant will quietly yield up the Premises to the Landlord in such condition as is set out in the works specification.'

**9.11** The tenant accepted that the exercise of the break option depended upon satisfaction of the condition to yield up the premises with vacant possession. However, there was a dispute as to whether (as the landlord contended) it was also a precondition in clause 23.1 that the tenant complied with the *entirety* of clause 23.2, ie including the obligations in clauses 11.1 and 11.2. Nugee J preferred the tenant's construction of clause 23.1. As a matter of language, he held:

> [30] … It does seem to me that the natural and ordinary meaning of the phraseology found in cl 23.1 is to read it as imposing a single condition, that is an obligation to yield up and to yield up in a certain way, and that way is with vacant possession as provided in cl 23.2, rather than to read it as importing effectively two separate conditions, that is to yield up the premises with vacant possession and to yield up the premises in accordance with cl 11.
>
> [31] The reasons that I say that are, to some extent, not capable of being precisely articulated because the way in which language strikes a reader as having a natural and ordinary meaning is an accumulation of experience of how language is ordinarily used, but doing the best I can, I think it is this. If [Counsel for the landlord's] construction had been intended, there are a number of other ways to do it which would have been, to my mind, a much more natural way of expressing the concept which he says is intended rather than the rather awkward way in which it has been done. One way, and perhaps the simplest, would simply be to put an 'and' in between the word 'possession' and 'as' so it read 'yield up the Premises with vacant possession and as provided in cl 23.2', or if one wanted to be slightly more strictly accurate 'and otherwise as provided in cl 23.2'. Another way would be to omit the reference to vacant possession at all and simply say 'to yield up the premises as provided in cl 23.2'. As [Counsel for the landlord] accepted, that would achieve precisely the same result.

**9.12** In arriving at this construction, Nugee J found little assistance from the other terms of the lease. However, he was able to place some weight on considerations of commercial common sense. He observed:

> [56] … It is perfectly true that the sort of … slightly vague obligations which are found in cl.11 … where there is likely to be room for dispute in any particular case whether the obligations have been complied with or not, are not very suitable to have as a precondition to the valid exercise of a break notice. As [Counsel for the tenant] said in the course of a short but effective reply, the one thing which does make commercial sense for both landlord and tenant is to know without much difficulty whether a break clause has been validly exercised or not because the tenant will want to know whether it really has to leave and has no further liability for rent, and the landlord will want to know whether it will get the premises back and have to re-let them.

**9.13** In *Capitol Park Leeds Plc v Global Radio Services Ltd*,[6] the lease contained a break clause conditional upon (inter alia) the tenant giving 'vacant possession of the Premises to the Landlord on the relevant Tenant's Break Date'. It was common ground that, by the relevant break date, the tenant had stripped out from 'the Premises' a range

[6] *Capitol Park Leeds Plc v Global Radio Services Ltd* [2021] EWCA Civ 995.

of items which had been landlord's fixtures and, perhaps, elements of the building itself. The landlord contended that, on a proper construction, 'the Premises' to be returned under the break option extended to the original building and to landlord's fixtures. Since the tenant had removed parts of 'the Premises', it was said that the tenant had failed to comply with the relevant precondition upon which the successful exercise of the break clause depended. The Court of Appeal disagreed. Newey LJ (with whom Laing and Moylan LJJ agreed) explained:

> [12] … [Counsel for the tenant] submitted that clause 10.1.4 of the Lease is not concerned with the physical state of [the Premises], but whether the landlord is recovering it free of things, people and interests …
>
> [13] On balance, I agree with [Counsel for the tenant] … Of itself, an obligation to give 'vacant possession' refers to giving back the property in question free of 'people, chattels, and interests',[7] not to its physical condition.
>
> [21] In all the circumstances, it seems to me that, construing it in the context of the Lease as a whole, clause 10.1.4 requires the tenant to return the 'Premises' as they are on the break date free of the 'trilogy of people, chattels, and interests'. On that basis, [the tenant's] exercise of the break clause was effective and the Lease terminated on 12 November 2017. True it may be that the building was left in a dire state … but that will not have precluded the operation of the break clause. [The landlord's] remedy is to seek compensation for whatever loss it may have suffered.

**9.14** Ultimately, the moral of the story is that 'if the landlord wishes to impose a precondition on the tenant, he should make it quite clear in the drafting of the clause what it is that the tenant has to do rather than leave it to be argued out at the stage at which it may be too late for anything to do about it, with the prize for the landlord being the potential ability to defeat the clause.'[8]

## THE PRINCIPLE OF STRICT COMPLIANCE

**9.15** Where the successful exercise of a break clause is dependent upon the satisfaction of a condition, the condition must be strictly complied with. Failure to do so will be fatal to the exercise of the break.

**9.16** One of the earliest English cases to reach the House of Lords on the question whether conditions attached to an option had to be strictly performed was *Grey v Friar*.[9] In that case, A became tenant to B of a colliery and also of some farm land. The term created was for 42 years, but the tenant had liberty to put an end to the term on giving

[7] Quotation taken from *Goldman Sachs International v Procession House Trustee Ltd* [2018] L&TR 28, at [39].

[8] *Goldman Sachs International v Procession House Trustee Ltd* [2018] L&TR 28, at [63], per Nugee J.

[9] *Grey v Friar* (1854) 4 HL Cas 565. In *Bass Holdings Ltd v Morton Music Ltd* [1988] 1 Ch 493, at 521B, Kerr LJ described *Grey v Friar* as a 'remarkably unattractive case which occupied the courts repeatedly between July 1848 and August 1853'. He added: '… "Bleak House" was published in instalments between March 1852 and September 1853, and "Jarndyce v Jarndyce" must have appeared familiar to the parties …'.

18 months' notice before the expiration of the first eight years, or of any subsequent three years. The proviso which gave the tenant this liberty, after describing the giving of the notice, contained the following words:

> Then and in such case (all arrears of rent being paid, and all singular the covenants and agreements on the part of the said lessees having been duly observed and performed), this lease, and every clause and thing herein contained, shall … determine and be utterly void.

**9.17** The issue was whether the actual performance of all the tenant's covenants was a condition precedent to the right to determine the lease. The Court of Exchequer resolved the matter in favour of the tenant; but this decision was reversed by the Court of Exchequer Chamber, which considered that the case was governed by the decision of *Porter v Shephard*.[10] As the Lord Chancellor explained when the matter reached the House of Lords:[11]

> The lease contains an infinity of covenants of the most minute description … And inasmuch as there certainly must have been some meaning intended to be given to the power of determining the lease by notice, and inasmuch as it was morally and physically impossible, or at least practically impossible, that the tenant could literally perform all the covenants, the Court of Exchequer came to the conclusion that this could not have been intended to be a condition precedent, that if the covenants were broken the parties were liable upon them; but that the power of determining the lease could not be made to depend upon the performance of something which it was impossible the tenants should in truth perform. That was the ground upon which the Court of Exchequer came to the conclusion that the performance of all the covenants was not a condition precedent; On the other hand, the Court of Exchequer Chamber, before which it came upon a writ of error, thought that the strict terms of the lease ought to be attended to, that this was a contract made between landlord and tenant, and that the landlord ought not to be bound to let his tenant free unless under circumstances coming literally within the terms upon which he had stipulated that the tenant should be able to withdraw from his tenancy, it being one of the terms of that stipulation that the tenant should not withdraw unless all the arrears of rent had been paid, and all the covenants and agreements had been duly observed and performed. The argument was that there was no absurdity in such a contract, that parties might make their own terms, that there was no ambiguity in the language, consequently that the language must be strictly adhered to, and that, therefore, unless the tenant had literally performed every covenant, he had no power of putting an end to the lease.

**9.18** The Judicial Committee of the House of Lords then consisted only of Lord Cranworth LC and Lord Brougham. The Lord Chancellor gave the only judgment, since Lord Brougham was absent through illness. The Lord Chancellor was 'very much inclined to adhere to the opinion which was formed by the Court of Exchequer' (ie in favour of the tenant).[12] However, Lord Brougham had conveyed to the Lord Chancellor the

[10] *Porter v Shephard* (1796) 6 TR 665, at 669, per Lord Kenyon CJ ('… it is impossible to read this lease without seeing that the parties intended that the tenant should do everything required of him before he could put an end to the lease …'), at 670, per Lawrence J ('It seems to me that it would be unjust as against the landlord, if this were not considered to be a condition precedent; for if it were not, the lessee, after neglecting to pay the duties which are a charge on the estate, after suffering the house to be out of repair, and the rest of the premises to lie waste, might give them up to the landlord in that state, and the landlord would be left without any remedy …').

[11] *Grey v Friar* (1854) 4 HL Cas 565, at 618–19.

[12] *Grey v Friar* (1854) 4 HL Cas 565, at 622.

opposite view, agreeing with the Court of Exchequer Chamber. Since the House of Lords was equally divided, the decision of the Exchequer Chamber stood. Thus, the tenant was required strictly to perform all of its covenants in order to exercise the option to determine the lease.

**9.19** A similar approach was adopted in *Finch v Underwood*.[13] In that case, the landlord had covenanted with the tenant, on receipt of notice from the latter, to grant a new lease 'in case the covenants and agreements on the tenant's part shall have been duly observed and performed'. Notice was duly given by the tenant but the landlord refused to renew the lease because the interior of the property needed repairs at a cost of £13 10s. At trial, Malins V-C decided that the landlord was obliged to renew the lease because the want of repair was 'trifling'. The Court of Appeal disagreed.

**9.20** James LJ considered that the case was one of compliance with a condition precedent. He held that the tenant had lost his right to a renewal of the lease by a breach of the covenant to repair. He added:[14]

> No doubt every property must at times be somewhat out of repair, and a tenant must have a reasonable time allowed to do what is necessary: but where it is required as a condition precedent to the granting of a new lease that the lessee's covenant shall have been performed, the lessee who comes to claim the new lease must show that at that time the property is in such a state as the covenants require it to be. He can easily send in his builder, get a report of what repairs are necessary, and do them before he applies for the lease. There is no hardship in requiring this of him, and I think he is not entitled to excuse himself by saying that the want of repair is trifling. The answer to that is, 'No matter; your bargain was to leave the property in thorough repair'. If he has not fulfilled his legal bargain, which is also his bargain in equity, he cannot sustain his claim for a lease.

**9.21** Another vivid illustration of the principle of strict compliance is to be found in *Bairstow Eves (Securities) Limited v Ripley*.[15] That case concerned an option to renew a lease which was exercisable 'if the tenant shall pay the rents hereby reserved and perform and observe all the covenants and obligations herein on the Tenants' part contained until the term date'. The tenant's covenants included a provision as follows:

> In the last year of the said term [ie 25 March 1988–24 March 1989] to paint in a proper and workmanlike manner all the inside wood iron and other parts heretofore or usually painted of the demised premises … and otherwise decorate in a proper and workmanlike manner all such internal parts of the demised premises that have been or ought properly to be so treated.

**9.22** In August 1987, the tenant had the premises painted and decorated internally. In November 1987, the premises were painted externally. They were not painted or decorated thereafter. One of the issues was whether the condition precedent to the exercise of the option (ie regarding performance and observance of the tenant's covenants) had been satisfied. Scott LJ considered that this issue presented no difficulty. He explained:[16]

> The relevant facts are not in dispute. The demised premises were kept in a state of good repair throughout the six year term. The judge so held and there is no basis on which his finding can

[13] *Finch v Underwood* (1876) 2 Ch 310.
[14] *Finch v Underwood* (1876) 2 Ch 310, at 315.
[15] *Bairstow Eves (Securities) Limited v Ripley* (1993) 65 P&CR 220.
[16] *Bairstow Eves (Securities) Limited v Ripley* (1993) 65 P&CR 220, at 224.

> be challenged. So the tenant was not at the term date in breach of the covenant of clause 2(4) of the lease. But it is common ground that the demised premises were not painted and decorated in the last year of the term. Painting and decoration had been carried out in August 1987 and November 1987, but not in the period March 25, 1988, to March 24, 1989. So it is plain that at the term date, March 24, 1989, the tenant was in breach of the covenant in clause 2(5) of the lease.

**9.23** Counsel for the tenant (Mr Paul Morgan QC) submitted that the condition precedent requiring the tenant to have performed and observed the tenant's covenants in the lease until the term date should be regarded as satisfied unless at the term date there were breaches for which substantial damages would be recoverable, viz the only breaches that mattered were those for which substantial damages would be recoverable. The Court of Appeal emphatically disagreed. Scott LJ said:[17]

> There is no authority that permits the Court to re-write the condition precedent so as to exclude from account a subsisting breach on the ground that only nominal damages are recoverable ... The Court is not entitled to re-write that covenant or to presume to inform [the landlord] that breach of the covenant was only trivial and should be ignored for the purposes of the condition precedent.

**9.24** Thus, the fact that no painting/decoration had been carried out in the last year of the term, even though painting/decoration had been carried out a few months earlier, meant that the tenant became disentitled to a new lease.[18]

**9.25** Although both *Finch* and *Bairstow Eves* concerned options to renew a lease, it has never been doubted that the principles applicable to compliance with conditions upon which an option to renew depends apply equally to compliance with conditions upon which a break clause depends.[19] Thus, even trivial non-compliance with a condition on which the exercise of break clause depends will preclude its successful exercise. For example, the failure to pay £150.50 + VAT in respect of insurance rent,[20] and the failure to pay about £130 in respect of default interest,[21] in each case has been held fatal to the exercise of a break clause conditional upon there being no arrears of rents or any other

[17] *Bairstow Eves (Securities) Limited v Ripley* (1993) 65 P&CR 220, at 226.

[18] See also *Sirhowy Investments Ltd v Henderson* [2014] EWHC 3562 (Ch). In that case, the tenants of a second-hand car dealership had carried out some patch repairs to two holes in a length of fencing, with the use of metal sheeting. The break clause was conditional upon the tenants having 'observed and performed the covenants contained in the lease'. Newey J remarked, at [40]: '... the Lease required [the tenants] to effect repairs in keeping with the remainder of the fencing. It was not good enough for them to attach sheeting to holes in the fence. They had to ensure that the end product was consistent with what already existed. In the circumstances, I find that [the tenants] failed in their repairing obligations as regards the fencing'. Thus, the tenants' break notice was held to be invalid.

[19] *United Scientific Holdings Ltd v Burnley BC* [1978] AC 904, at 929E–29G (Lord Diplock), at 945H (Lord Steyn), at 951A–C (Lord Salmon), at 962 (Lord Fraser); *Bass Holdings Ltd v Morton Music Ltd* [1988] 1 Ch 493, at 519D (Kerr LJ); *Mannai Investment Co Ltd v Eagle Star Life Assurance Co Ltd* [1997] AC 749, at 753–54 (Lord Goff), at 762 (Lord Jauncey), at 776B (Lord Hoffmann); *Dun & Bradstreet Software Services (England) Ltd v Provident Mutual Life Assurance Association* [1998] 2 EGLR 175, at 180B (Peter Gibson LJ); *Siemens Hearing Instruments Ltd v Friends Life Ltd* [2014] 2 P&CR 5, at [28] (Lewison LJ).

[20] *QuirkCo Investments Ltd v Aspray Transport Ltd* [2012] L&TR 19, at [51], per HHJ Keyser QC.

[21] *Avocet Industrial Estates LLP v Merol Ltd* [2012] L&TR 13, at [127], per Morgan J.

sums payable under the lease as at the relevant break date. It makes no difference if the condition upon which the break option depends has no apparent purpose or confers no benefit on the grantor of the option.[22]

## DE MINIMIS FAILURES TO COMPLY WITH CONDITIONS

**9.26** As is well known, the law is in general not concerned with matters de minimis (ie very small things). In *Fish & Fish Ltd v Sea Shepherd UK*,[23] Lord Sumption JSC referred to this legal principle and said:

> De minimis non curat lex is a necessarily imprecise principle. Most of the judges who have discussed it have done so in terms of synonyms which are not much less imprecise. But they nevertheless convey the flavour of the concept. 'Negligible' and 'trivial' are probably the commonest: see *Cartledge v E Jopling & Sons Ltd* [1963] AC 758, 771–772, per Lord Reid, and *Rothwell v Chemical & Insulating Co Ltd* [2008] AC 281, paras 44–47, per Lord Hope of Craighead. '[Trivialities], matters of little moment, of a trifling and negligible nature' was the more expansive formulation proposed by Sellers LJ in *Margaronis Navigation Agency Ltd v Henry W Peabody & Co of London Ltd* [1965] 2 QB 430, 443–44. What all of these expressions are designed to convey is that the maxim is concerned with extremes. It refers to some fact which is in principle legally relevant but is so trivial or negligible as to be no fact at all in the eyes of the law.

**9.27** However, as explained above, it has long been established at the highest level of authority that even trivial non-compliance with conditions upon which a break clause depends will preclude its successful exercise. Does this mean that the principle 'de minimis non curat lex' does not apply in the context of break clauses? It is tentatively suggested that the position may be open to argument in an extreme and extraordinary case, eg where there are 'arrears of a few pence'.[24] That said, as far as the authors are aware, this argument has yet to be advanced successfully on behalf of a party with the benefit of a break clause.[25]

## THE TIME FOR COMPLIANCE

**9.28** A break clause will almost inevitably require a notice of some kind in order for it to be exercised. The notice will be served on day 1 and expire on some later date, day X.

[22] *Siemens Hearing Instruments Ltd v Friends Life Ltd* [2014] 2 P&CR 5 (where a break option was dependent upon the break notice being 'expressed to be given under section 24(2) of the Landlord and Tenant Act 1954' notwithstanding that this provision does not contemplate a notice being given thereunder); *Ropemaker Properties Ltd v Bella Italia Restaurants Ltd* [2018] L&TR 32 (where an option to determine an agreement for lease was dependent upon the tenant serving a notice, not only on the landlord, but also on the guarantor within the same group of companies as the tenant).

[23] *Fish & Fish Ltd v Sea Shepherd UK* [2015] AC 1229, at [50].

[24] *QuirkCo Investments Ltd v Aspray Transport Ltd* [2012] L&TR 19, at [55], per HHJ Keyser QC.

[25] However, in *Newtown Management Pty Ltd v Owners of Strata Plan 67219* [2009] NSWSC 19, Ward J considered that it might be possible to construe a condition precedent as requiring 'due' compliance with the specified conditions, in the sense of disregarding trivial or de minimis defaults.

Issues often arise as to whether any conditions on which the exercise of the break clause depends have to be satisfied:

(1) on day 1;
(2) day X; or
(3) on both day 1 and day X.

**9.29** In a well-drafted lease, the language of the break clause should make the position explicit. However, this may not be so, in which case difficult questions of construction can arise. This is evident from a number of authorities, as follows.

**9.30** In *Finch v Underwood*,[26] the landlord had covenanted that he would:

> at the expiration of the term hereby granted (in case the covenants and agreements on the said tenant's part shall have been duly observed and performed), grant unto the said tenants … a fresh lease of the hereby demised premises … provided the said tenants … shall 21 days before the expiration of the term hereby granted give unto the said landlord … a notice in writing … of the intention and desire to take such fresh lease.

**9.31** Mellish LJ and Baggallay JA appear to have been of the opinion that compliance with the covenant at the date of service was required.[27] James LJ seems to have been of the opposite view, ie compliance was to be adjudged as at the date of expiry of the notice.[28] However, the determination of the issue was irrelevant since it was agreed that, at all material times (ie on day 1 and on date X) the premises were in disrepair, thereby disentitling the tenant to a new lease.

**9.32** *Bastin v Bidwell*[29] also concerned an option to renew a lease, which was worded as follows:

> the lessees, their executors, administrators, or assigns, shall be entitled, on giving six months' notice before the expiration of the said term of seven years, to have a further lease of the said premises for a term of twenty-one years from expiration of the said term of seven years, at the annual rent of £200, upon the lessees paying the rent and performing and observing the covenants of this present lease.

**9.33** In considering the time for performance of the tenant's covenants, Kay J said:[30]

> The words are 'upon the lessees paying the rent and performing and observing the covenants', and it was argued very plausibly, and I have given all the weight possible to that argument, that that may fairly mean, they are to give notice to renew, and if there is existing any breach of covenant, at the time of the notice, it will be quite sufficient if they repair that breach of covenant within the six months.

[26] *Finch v Underwood* (1876) 2 Ch 310.

[27] *Finch v Underwood* (1876) 2 Ch 310, at 316, per Mellish LJ ('It is clear, then, that at the time of applying for the lease there was an existing breach of the covenant to repair for which an action would lie …'); at 317, per Baggallay JA ('… was the Plaintiff, on the 24th of May, 1875, in a position to give a notice requiring a renewal of the lease? To entitle him to give such notice it was necessary that the condition precedent that the covenants of the original lease should be performed should have been complied with …').

[28] *Finch v Underwood* (1876) 2 Ch 310, at 315 ('… but where it is required as a condition precedent to the granting a new lease that the lessee's covenants shall have been performed, the lessee who comes to claim the new lease must shew that at that time the property is in such a state as the covenants require it to be …').

[29] *Bastin v Bidwell* (1881) 18 Ch D 238.

[30] *Bastin v Bidwell* (1881) 18 Ch D 238, at 252–53.

There are two observations to be made upon that argument: one is this, that in truth if there was a breach of covenant at the time the notice was given, to repair that breach of covenant afterwards is not in strict language performing a covenant, it is making good a breach of the covenant. Take this very case. The premises should have been painted outside in the year 1878. They were not painted outside in the year 1878; and they were not painted outside when the notice was given. Therefore, supposing they had been painted outside after the notice was given, and before the expiration of the six months, that painting outside could hardly in strict legal language be said to be a performance of the covenant. It would be in strict legal language a reparation of the breach. In popular language, and it may possibly be that those words are to be so construed, it would be a performance of the covenant.

9.34 In the event, however, Kay J did not have to decide the issue. As he explained:[31]

I have considerable difficulty in determining which of these two constructions should be preferred, that is, whether this clause means that there should be no breach at the time the notice was given, or that there should be no breach at the time that the notice expired, but I purposely avoid determining it because in this case it is quite immaterial. At both dates there were breaches of … two covenants to paint. The covenant to paint inside had not, according to this evidence, been fully performed when the six months' notice expired, and the covenant to paint outside, which should have been done in 1878, had not even been begun to be performed. Therefore I am relieved from deciding that point, and I do not desire to say any more upon it.

9.35 This issue was, however, addressed in *Simons v Associated Furnishers Ltd*.[32] There, a lease dated 31 December 1925 contained a tenant's break clause which contained the following wording:

If the company shall desire to determine the present demise at the expiration of the first five or ten years of the said term and shall give to the lessor six calendar months previous notice in writing of such their desire and shall up to the time of such determination pay the rent and perform and observe the covenants and conditions on their part hereinbefore contained then immediately on the expiration of such five or ten years as the case may be the present demise and everything therein contained shall cease and be void.

9.36 On 17 August 1929, the tenant gave notice to the landlord to determine the lease on 28 February 1930. There was no doubt that, at the date when the notice was served, there were unremedied breaches of covenant. However, all breaches of covenant had been remedied at the end of the fifth year of the term (ie the expiry of the notice). The landlord claimed that the notice was invalid. Dismissing this argument, Clauson J said:

The answer put forward on behalf of the [landlord] is that at the moment the notice was given there were unremedied breaches in existence; and, that being so, the notice was bad. Speaking for myself I am unable to find in this clause anything which makes it a condition that the rent must have been paid and the covenants performed and observed at the date when the notice was given. I find nothing to make that a crucial date. Of course, if I had to construe the condition as providing that throughout the five years there must be no instance of an unremedied breach of covenant, then it seems to follow that the existence of an unremedied breach of covenant at the particular moment the notice was given would have been, just as the unremedied breach of covenant at any other moment of the five years would have been, an answer to the defendants'

[31] *Bastin v Bidwell* (1881) 18 Ch D 238, at 253.
[32] *Simons v Associated Furnishers Ltd* [1931] 1 Ch 379.

> claim, because the condition would not have been fulfilled. But assuming that the construction which I place upon this clause is correct, I can find nothing on the construction of the clause to suggest the requirement that the condition must have been complied with at the moment the notice is given.

**9.37** Similarly, in *West Country Cleaners (Falmouth) Limited v Saly*,[33] a lease dated 27 January 1951, granted for a term of 14 years, contained a covenant to renew which stipulated that:

> If the lessees shall be desirous of renewing this lease ... for a further term of seven years and shall give to the lessor 12 months' notice in writing before the expiry of this demise then the lessor will providing all covenants herein contained have been duly observed and performed grant to the lessees a further term of the demised premises for seven years from the expiration of this lease at the same rent and subject to similar covenants and conditions as herein expressed but excluding this option for renewal.

**9.38** The lease also included a covenant on the part of the tenants at least once in each three years of the term and in the last year of the term to paint the interior of the premises.

**9.39** On 18 September 1963, the tenants purported to exercise the option given to them to renew the lease for a further term of seven years from 28 January 1965. The landlord refused to grant a renewal of the lease on the ground that the tenants were in default as regards performance of the covenants contained in the lease. At trial, the judge held that the relevant date for determining whether the tenants were eligible to exercise the option was the date of the expiry of the original term (ie 27 January 1965) and not the date when the notice purporting to exercise the option was given (ie 18 September 1963). On appeal, Danckwerts LJ (with whom Winn and Sellers LJJ agreed) said:[34]

> On the wording of the clause in the present case it is quite plain that the date of the expiration of the lease is the material time because after the period of 12 months has been fixed for giving the notice the clause proceeds: 'then the lessor will' – and then, and not before, comes the proviso requiring the covenant to paint in the last year to be duly observed and performed.
>
> It seems to me, therefore, that the covenant to paint in the last year clearly was one of the terms of the lease which had to be performed; and it is admitted – there has been no dispute – that that has not been done. Consequently, in my opinion, the objections to the refusal of the landlord to grant a further lease in the present case are misplaced; the appeal ought to be allowed; and the landlord should succeed.

**9.40** The opposite result was arrived at in *Robinson v Thames Mead Park Estate Limited*.[35] That case concerned a memorandum of agreement, entered into between a landlord and a tenant, and by which it was agreed that the tenant should take a piece of land from 22 July 1941 until 22 April 1944. The tenant covenanted to erect, during the first 12 months of the tenancy, a dwelling on the land. Clause 19 contained a covenant by the landlord that 'subject to the tenant having faithfully performed and observed' her covenants, she should have an option to continue the tenancy under a grant of a building

[33] *West Country Cleaners (Falmouth) Ltd v Saly* [1966] 1 WLR 1485.
[34] *West Country Cleaners (Falmouth) Ltd v Saly* [1966] 1 WLR 1485, at 1490E–90G.
[35] *Robinson v Thames Mead Park Estate Limited* [1947] 1 Ch 334.

lease. As a result of delay, due to various causes, the house was not completed within the first 12 months of the agreement; but the tenant's obligations were nonetheless satisfied by 19 April 1944. The landlord refused to grant the building lease to the tenant. So, the tenant commenced an action for specific performance.

**9.41** Evershed J referred to *Bastin v Bidwell*, and said:[36]

> It is, however, to be noted, in construing this particular document (and every document must be construed on its own merits) that this is not a case where the landlord grants a lease of his own house which he (the landlord) has erected, and grants the privilege to the tenant of renewal. In such a case, as Kay J points out, the strict obligation is plainly justified because the landlord may reasonably say: 'I want to be quite sure that you are in all respects a scrupulous tenant before I grant you a new tenancy'. This is a case where the tenant was entering into obligations as to the erection of new premises, both during the first three years term and later; and, I think in those circumstances, the problem which Kay J found it unnecessary to decide in the case before him, I decide in the plaintiff's favour here, namely, that it is sufficient for the purpose of this cl 19 that the tenant, when she comes to give her notice calling on the landlord to grant the lease, has then ended any previous breaches of covenants, or failure to perform covenants.

**9.42** Likewise, in *Bass Holdings Ltd v Morton Music Ltd*,[37] a lease dated 20 September 1982 – for a term of 15 years from 1 April 1982 – contained an option to renew with the following wording:

> If the tenant shall be desirous of taking a further lease of the demised premises for a further term of 125 years from the date of the term hereby granted and shall not later than 29 September 1985 give to the lessors notice in writing of such its desire and if it shall have paid the rent hereby reserved and shall have performed and observed the several stipulations on its part herein contained and on its part to be performed and observed up to the date thereof then the lessors will on payment to them by the tenant of the sum of £300,000 let the demised premises to the tenant for a further term of 125 years from the date of the term hereby granted.

**9.43** By a letter dated 19 September 1985, the tenant purported to exercise the option. The landlord denied that the option had been effectively exercised, relying upon (inter alia) alleged breaches of repairing and decorating covenants throughout the period 20 September 1982–20 September 1985. In relation to the question of the time for compliance with the conditions upon which the option depended, Kerr LJ said:[38]

> it [was] common ground that if the [tenants] were in breach at the time when they purported to exercise the option, then it must necessarily follow that it could not have been exercised validly.

**9.44** In *Arlington Business Parks GP Ltd v Scottish and Newcastle Ltd*,[39] the lease was granted for a term of years expiring in 2023. However, it could be broken as at 7 May 2013. In order to exercise that entitlement, the tenants had to give 12 months' notice and not be 'in breach of any of their obligations … at the date of service of such notice and/or the termination date'. The tenants admitted that, as at the date of their break notice, they had not fully performed their repairing obligations. However, after the notices were

[36] *Robinson v Thames Mead Park Estate Limited* [1947] 1 Ch 334, at 337.
[37] *Bass Holdings Ltd v Morton Music Ltd* [1988] 1 Ch 493, at 516E.
[38] *West Country Cleaners (Falmouth) Ltd v Saly* [1966] 1 WLR 1485, at 1490E–90G.
[39] *Arlington Business Parks GP Ltd v Scottish & Newcastle Ltd* [2014] CSOH 77.

served, the tenants spent over £1.3 million with a view to ensuring that the premises were in a proper condition as at 7 May 2013 (the break date). As to the operative date or dates for compliance with the conditions, Lord Malcolm said:[40]

> [3] … Clause SECOND provides that the tenants must not be in breach 'at the date of service of (the) notice and/or the termination date'. For the pursuers, [the landlord] submitted that this means, in effect, no breach at either or both dates. The natural meaning of the words used is that a notice is invalid if the tenants are in breach at the date of the notice, or the date of termination, or both. [The tenant] submitted that the clause means that the tenants lose the right to break if they are in breach on both dates, or at the date of termination of the lease. Failing that, the tenants must be in breach on both dates.
>
> [4] I prefer the interpretation put forward by [the landlord]. It reflects the natural meaning of the words used. [The tenant's] primary submission renders the concept of breach at the date of the notice irrelevant. It adds nothing to the alternative of breach at the date of termination. His fall-back position gives no content to the word 'or'.
>
> [11] … when one bears in mind that under clause SECOND a breach can be operative at either or both dates, I prefer [the landlord's] submission that, in the present case, the commercial purpose was to give the landlords reassurance that, come the termination date, the property would be in a proper condition, thereby allowing marketing of the subjects during the 12 months' notice period.

**9.45** On the basis of the above authorities, there is no presumption as to the date on which compliance (or non-compliance, as the case may be) with conditions for the exercise of the break falls to be assessed. Ultimately, in any given case, the language of the break clause must be closely examined in the context of the other provisions of the lease and relevant surrounding circumstances.

## SPENT BREACHES

**9.46** It has sometimes been argued that, where a break clause is conditional upon the tenant having complied or performed or otherwise observed its covenants contained in the lease, then even a past (but remedied) breach of covenant is sufficient to render the break inoperable.

**9.47** However, since the decision in *Grey v Friar*,[41] there have been numerous judicial dicta to the effect that (absent express wording to the contrary) spent breaches of covenant will not destroy the right to exercise the option. So, for example, in *Simons v Associated Furnishers Ltd*,[42] Clauson J said of the break clause in question (see **9.35** above):

> Upon a possible construction, it may make it essential that the tenant should comply with all the covenants throughout the whole period of the five years or, in other words, that the tenant must be able to say that in no single instance during that period has rent been in arrear or a covenant broken … If the condition imports that it is unfulfilled if there has been any breach

[40] *Arlington Business Parks GP Ltd v Scottish & Newcastle Ltd* [2014] CSOH 77, at [3]–[4], [11].
[41] *Grey v Friar* (1854) 4 HL Cas 565, at 592–93 (Talfourd J), at 595 (Alderson B), 599–600 (Erle J), at 608 (Coleridge J).
[42] *Simons v Associated Furnishers Ltd* [1931] 1 Ch 379, at 386.

of covenant, even if it has been remedied, the condition may be a very hard one and such as can scarcely be supposed that parties would enter into; but here I am bound by a very heavy weight of judicial opinion to hold that the true meaning of that clause is this, that it will have been complied with, if at the end of the five years 'there should not exist any cause of action in respect of performance of covenants': or, I may put it this way, the condition must be understood as 'requiring that the account between the parties must, both as to rent and covenants, be clear; the rent need not have been always paid on the day; but all arrears, if any, must have been paid up; the covenants must have been strictly kept, or, if broken, must have been satisfied'.

**9.48** The leading authority on this issue is *Bass Holdings Ltd v Morton Music Ltd*,[43] to which reference has been made in **9.42**. In that case, the tenant had served a notice on 19 September 1985 seeking to exercise an option to renew a lease. The tenant had committed a number of past breaches of covenant, all of which were undisputed but had been remedied (ie were spent). The Court of Appeal had to consider whether such spent breaches of covenant precluded the exercise of the option. The Court of Appeal unanimously resolved this issue in favour of the tenant. As explained by Kerr LJ:[44]

(2) … it must be accepted that absolute and precise compliance by the tenant with every single covenant throughout the period of the lease prior to the operative date is virtually impossible of attainment. If this were required as a condition precedent, then the option would in practice be worthless or merely at the mercy of the landlord. Therefore the parties cannot have intended that the absence of spent breaches should be a condition precedent …

(4) … While it would of course be possible to formulate a proviso which is sufficiently explicit to cause spent breaches to preclude the exercise of the option, there appears to be no reported case in which this was so; and the wording of the proviso in the present case is in a form similar to, and effectively indistinguishable from, the formulations adopted in all the cases subsequent to Grey v Friar …

(5) … The reasoning summarised in (2) above, which has led to the generally accepted conclusion that the condition precedent imposed by provisos like the present was intended to apply only to subsisting breaches, is of course particularly cogent in relation to 'break' options. In such cases it will obviously be of great importance to the landlord that the demised land or premises should be surrendered to him free from any subsisting breaches of covenant.

**9.49** To a similar effect, Nicholls LJ said:[45]

Shortly stated, the question of general importance, which arises on this appeal is whether in these clauses a condition to the effect I have mentioned requires for its fulfilment that throughout the whole term of the lease up to the specified date there shall have been no breach of any of the tenant's covenants and agreements, or whether the condition is fulfilled if at the specified date there is no subsisting breach of any of these covenants or agreements. By the shorthand expression 'no subsisting breach' I mean that in respect of the rent, covenants and agreements there is at the specified date no outstanding cause of action. I shall call the first of these two alternatives the 'never any breach' construction, and the other alternative the 'no subsisting breach' construction.

I preface my observations by noting that, although each lease falls to be construed having regard to its own particular language and terms, the degree of similarity of language in break

[43] *Bass Holdings Ltd v Morton Music Ltd* [1988] 1 Ch 493.
[44] *Bass Holdings Ltd v Morton Music Ltd* [1988] 1 Ch 493, at 518C–18H, 519B–19C.
[45] *Bass Holdings Ltd v Morton Music Ltd* [1988] 1 Ch 493, at 518C–18H, 528F–29A.

> clauses and renewal clauses in common use is sufficiently marked in crucial respects for it to be possible and sensible to consider the matter, initially, in fairly general terms.
>
> The two alternative constructions have only to be stated for it to be apparent that the 'never any breach' construction would mean that in practice the condition would be impossible of fulfilment in almost all cases of leases of buildings containing a full range of repairing and other covenants by a tenant. However diligent or even punctilious a tenant may be in carrying out his obligations under his lease, in such cases there will in practice inevitably be occasions when there will be outstanding some dilapidations which would, strictly, constitute breaches of the repairing or re-decorating covenants. Thus the practical consequence of the 'never any breach' construction in such cases would be that the break or renewal option would seldom, if ever, be exercisable by a tenant.

**9.50** Thus, although (as per Kerr LJ in *Bass Holdings*), it is theoretically possible to formulate a proviso in sufficiently explicit terms to cause spent breaches to preclude the exercise of the option, in practice this does not happen. An illustration of this principle is to be found in *Sirhowy Investments Ltd v Henderson*.[46] In that case, the tenants were entitled to exercise a break clause provided that they 'shall have paid the rent and observed and performed the covenants contained in this Lease'. Newey J found that the tenants had historically acted in breach of the terms of the lease. However, he said:[47]

> That clause spoke of [the tenants] having 'paid the rent and observed and performed the covenants contained in this Lease'. What was required as regards rent was surely that [the tenants] were up-to-date with their payments at the relevant time (as they in fact were); it would not have mattered, as it seems to me, if [the tenants] had been late in paying rent on some past occasion. Similarly, a purely historic breach of covenant with no continuing consequences should not be considered to have precluded exercise of the break clause. The parties are unlikely, I think, to have intended that any past breach of covenant, however, insignificant, should prevent [the tenants] from ever invoking clause 4.13. Clause 4.13 is better read as focusing on the position when the Lease was to be determined.

## WORDS OF QUALIFICATION

**9.51** Given the principle of strict compliance, it is now (understandably) less and less common for leases to contain break clauses dependent upon absolute and unqualified fulfilment of substantive conditions. Rather, well-advised tenants will negotiate the terms of a lease which temper the required standard of compliance.[48] Typically, this is done by the insertion of words of qualification, such as 'reasonable', 'material' and 'substantial'. The meaning and effect of such words is considered below.

[46] *Sirhowy Investments Ltd v Henderson* [2014] EWHC 3562 (Ch).

[47] *Sirhowy Investments Ltd v Henderson* [2014] EWHC 3562 (Ch), at [25].

[48] Section B3 of the RICS 'Code for leasing business premises' (1st edn, February 2020) now advises: 'A tenant's right to break should allow the tenant to walk away from the lease at a give time after informing the landlord in writing. This should normally be conditional only on the tenant having paid the main rent due under the lease and giving up occupation of the property, leaving behind no continuing subleases or occupation by others. The tenant may have other liabilities under the leases to fulfil, such as paying service charges or handing the property back in good condition, but failure to comply with these should not be used by landlords to invalidate the right to break.'

(a) **'Reasonable'**

9.52 *Gardner v Blaxill*[49] concerned a 'home-drawn' lease of certain premises in Sydenham. One of the covenants of the lease was that the tenants 'will at all times during the said term keep the premises in good and substantial repair'. In addition, the lease contained an option for renewal worded as follows:

> Provided that the tenant has reasonably fulfilled the covenants hereinbefore mentioned he has the option of continuing for an extension of seven or fourteen years providing the premises have not been taken by the housing authorities.

9.53 In an obiter passage, Paull J considered the meaning and effect of the word 'reasonably'. He said:[50]

> The proviso is not that the tenant must have fulfilled the covenants in the lease, but that the tenant must have reasonably fulfilled the covenants in the lease. Two interpretations of the word 'reasonably' have been put before me. Mr Plume, for the landlords, says that the word governs 'fulfilled' and, therefore, one starts with the fact that the tenant must fulfil his obligations under the lease. The result is, says Mr Plume, that before the tenant can extend his lease he must show that he has done that work which would be necessary to fulfil the covenant. If he has done that work, then the word 'reasonably' comes into play and the landlords may not be able to complain if the work is not quite up to the standard necessary strictly to fulfil the covenant … Mr Hirst, on the other hand, says that that is not the right way of looking at the matter. The insertion of the word 'reasonably' means that the parties have agreed that the tenant may exercise his option provided that he has behaved as a reasonable tenant might have behaved in relation to his covenants. The difference between the two points of view may best be illustrated in this way. It may well be necessary, in order to keep the premises in good and substantial repair, to repaint the premises every three years, or, indeed, at even shorter intervals, but a reasonably minded tenant might well come to the conclusion that the premises will come to no harm if the repainting is left over for a further year. In those circumstances, could a tenant exercise his option halfway through the fourth year? Mr Hirst would say, Yes; Mr Plume would say, No. I have come to the conclusion that Mr Hirst is right, and that by inserting the word 'reasonably' the parties not only intended to mean, but must be deemed to have meant, that the tenant can exercise his option provided that he behaves during his tenancy in a way in which a reasonably minded tenant might well behave.

9.54 *Bassett v Whiteley*[51] also concerned an option to renew a lease, this time, in the following terms:

> If the tenants shall be desirous of taking a lease of the demised premises for a further term of eight years from the expiration of the term hereby granted at the rent and on the terms and conditions set out in this lease (but without the provision for renewal) and shall not more than twelve nor less than six months before the expiration of the term hereby granted give to the landlord notice in writing of such their desire and if they shall have paid the rent hereby reserved and shall have reasonably performed and observed the several stipulations herein contained and on their part to be performed and observed up to the termination of the tenancy hereby created then the landlord will let the demised premises to the tenants.

[49] *Gardner v Blaxill* [1960] 1 WLR 752.
[50] *Gardner v Blaxill* [1960] 1 WLR 752, at 759–60.
[51] *Bassett v Whiteley* (1983) 45 P&CR 87.

**9.55** On 20 February and 20 May 1981, instalments of rent fell due. The tenant withheld payment until (respectively) 12 and 24 June 1981. This was because the tenant was concerned about a serious defect in the roof, by virtue of which rain was leaking badly into the demised premises. The landlord asserted that the late payment of rent precluded the tenant from exercising the option. The Court of Appeal disagreed.

**9.56** Giving the lead judgment, Waller LJ said:[52]

> Then it is necessary to look and see whether the tenant has 'reasonably performed and observed the several stipulations herein contained', and when one comes to the stipulation to pay the rent 'hereinbefore reserved at the time and in the manner aforesaid …' that has to be considered and, when considering whether that has been complied with, one has to look at what actually happened in the earlier part of 1981.
>
> In my judgment here are tenants who have regularly paid their rent on that which was regarded as the due date for the whole of their lease until, for the early part of the year, they (being concerned about the dampness in the wall), were minded to withhold the rent to try and put some pressure upon the landlord but, after two or three months, had paid the whole of the rent, one asks oneself: Can it be said that the tenants had not reasonably performed and observed the several stipulations herein contained? The judge, who approached this matter not in precisely the same way, came to the conclusion that the tenants had complied with that covenant.
>
> I have no hesitation in saying that, when one has a tenant who has performed throughout the currency of the lease all his obligations but who on one occasion, or perhaps I should say two because there are five days in issue on the second occasion, withholds the rent because he wishes to put some pressure upon his landlord to do some repairs, that he has reasonably performed and observed 'the several stipulations herein contained.

**9.57** Griffiths LJ agreed, and added that:[53]

> In my view, it is permissible to look at the conduct of the tenants throughout the term to determine whether or not they have reasonably performed and observed the several stipulations contained in their covenants.

**9.58** The above two cases were ones where the merits favoured the tenant. A different outcome was arrived at in *Reed Personnel Services Plc v. American Express Limited*.[54] In that case, the lease (technically, an underlease) gave to the tenant a once-and-for-all opportunity to determine the lease on 24 March 1994 by the giving of a least six months' notice in writing, on the proviso that the tenant 'shall up to the time of such determination pay the rent reserved by and reasonably perform and observe the covenants contained in this lease'. The lease contained various covenants to repair and redecorate the premises, some requiring continuous compliance and others requiring compliance at the end of the term. In December 1992 and January 1993, the tenant gave notice of its intention to exercise the break clause. An architect appointed by the landlord inspected the premises in October 1993 and produced a schedule of dilapidations. The total cost of repair work was approximately £21,000. The landlord sent that document to the tenant on

[52] *Bassett v Whiteley* (1983) 45 P&CR 87, at 91.
[53] *Bassett v Whiteley* (1983) 45 P&CR 87, at 92.
[54] *Reed Personnel Services Plc v American Express Ltd* [1997] 1 EGLR 229.

20 December 1993 stating that a reasonable time for complying with the repairs necessary to remedy the breaches of covenant was eight weeks. No repairs had been carried out by 7 April 1994. As a consequence, the landlord claimed that the break had not been exercised. The tenant contended that the economic value of the non-compliance was not significant compared to the annual rent and that the breaches did not affect the validity of the exercise of the break clause.

**9.59** Resolving the matter in favour of the landlord, Jacob J said:[55]

> Of course, the word 'reasonably' does qualify the word 'perform' and there are plenty of examples one can think of here where [the tenant] might reasonably have performed the obligation without actually doing it to the letter. For example, there is a requirement that there should be two coats of paint: one coat might have been quite good enough. There is a requirement of re-carpeting at the very end of the lease and it may be that if the carpet was in perfectly good condition that it would not have been necessary to comply with that obligation. I am not concerned with that kind of case at all. I am concerned with a case of total non-compliance.

**9.60** From the above cases one can conclude that if it is a pre-condition to the exercise of a break clause that a tenant has reasonably performed its covenants then the whole history of the tenancy will be material. If a tenant, in advance of exercising a break, seeks advice regarding his compliance and then follows that advice, it is likely that a judge will find that the tenant has satisfied the precondition.

### (b) 'Material'

**9.61** The leading authority on the meaning and effect of the qualifying word 'material' is *Fitzroy House Epworth Street (No 1) Limited v Financial Times Limited.*[56] That case concerned a lease dated 31 August 1994 of an office block in London for a term of 16 years commencing 1 April 1994. By clause 3(4) of the lease, it was provided that:

> the tenant … may give not less than 13 months previous notice to the landlord of termination of this lease on 1 April 2004. If: (a) the tenant has materially complied with all its obligations under this lease down to the date for which notice of termination has been given … then the term shall cease on that date and (subject as mentioned below) no party has any further rights or obligations under this lease.

**9.62** On 5 February 2003, the tenant gave notice under clause 3(4) to terminate the lease on 1 April 2004. Between 14 January and 26 March 2004 the tenant undertook a substantial repair programme in order to comply with its various repairing obligations. The tenant offered facilities for inspection to the landlords before, during and after the works were carried out but the landlords did not take them up. On the termination of the works the tenant duly vacated the premises. Immediately after 1 April 2004 the landlords claimed that the lease was still subsisting because on that date the tenant had 'materially

[55] *Reed Personnel Services Plc v American Express Ltd* [1997] 1 EGLR 229, at 232M.
[56] *Fitzroy House Epworth Street (No 1) Ltd v Financial Times Ltd* [2006] 1 WLR 2207.

failed to comply' with its repairing and other obligations under the lease. It commenced proceedings in the Technology and Construction Court seeking declarations to that effect. The tenant contended that it had materially complied with all its obligations under the lease. The proceedings were heard by Judge Thornton QC. He declared[57] that the lease had been validly terminated. The landlords appealed.

**9.63** The Chancellor gave the only reasoned judgment. He disapproved of an earlier decision of HHJ Rich QC (sitting as a Deputy High Court Judge) in *Commercial Union Life Assurance Co Ltd v Label Ink Ltd*,[58] and went on to make the following observations:[59]

> [16] I can agree that the insertion of the word 'material' must have been in order to mitigate the requirement for absolute compliance with all covenants at the relevant time then to be found in conventional break clauses. Other variations, now common, are 'reasonable' and 'substantial'. But I cannot agree that it must have been the intention to modify the rule to the extent that it is reasonably fair to both landlord and tenant. The word 'material' is susceptible to a number of nuances but what is fair and reasonable between landlord and tenant is not one of them.
>
> [24] I did not understand counsel for the tenant to submit that the test was subjective, though he did suggest that the conduct of the parties may have some evidential value in determining the issue. It cannot, I think, be seriously disputed that the issue of 'material compliance' whatever it involves must be determined on an objective basis.
>
> [35] … Materiality must be assessed by reference to the ability of the landlord to relet or sell the property without delay or additional expenditure. Where the provision is absolute then any breach will preclude an exercise of the break clause. But I see no justification for attributing to the parties an intention that the insertion of the word 'material' was intended to permit only breaches which were trivial or trifling. Those words are of uncertain meaning also and are not the words used by the parties.

**9.64** In *Fitzroy* itself, the parties' experts agreed that the landlord was able to re-let or sell the property without delay or additional expenditure; and so, as a consequence, it was held that the tenant had 'materially complied' with its covenants (entitling it to terminate the lease).

**9.65** A different result was arrived at in *Mourant Property Trust Ltd v Fusion Electronic (UK) Ltd*.[60] In that case, the lease contained a break clause exercisable by notice given not less than three months before the first anniversary of the commencement of the lease. The break clause also contained a proviso as follows:

> It shall be a condition precedent to the customer's right to determine this lease as aforesaid that: (a) the customer should deliver up vacant possession of the premises to the service provider on

[57] *Fitzroy House Epworth Street (No 1) Ltd v Financial Times Ltd* [2005] EWHC 2391 (TCC).

[58] *Commercial Union Life Assurance Co Ltd v Label Ink Ltd* [2001] L&TR 29 (especially, at [13]: '… the breach is material if, but only if, having regard to all the circumstances, and to the proper efforts of the tenant to comply with his covenants, as well as the adverse effect on the landlord of any failure to do so, it will be fair and reasonable to refuse the tenant the privilege which the lease otherwise grants …').

[59] *Fitzroy House Epworth Street (No 1) Ltd v Financial Times Ltd* [2006] 1 WLR 2207, at [16], [24], [35].

[60] *Mourant Property Trust Ltd v Fusion Electronic (UK) Ltd* [2009] EWHC 3659 (Ch).

the determination date; (b) the customer shall pay all rent and other monies properly due hereunder at the determination date; (c) there shall be no material breach of covenant on the part of a customer subsisting at the relevant determination date.

**9.66** The tenant served a break notice proposing to determine the lease on 19 March 2008. However, as at the break date, the tenant had failed to carry out necessary repairs to the premises. At trial, Mr Bernard Livesey QC (sitting as a Deputy Judge of the High Court) found that the effect of the dilapidations was that an incoming tenant would expect a rent-free period of five months by way of compensation for the works outstanding at the determination date. This being the case, applying the decision in *Fitzroy House*, the breaches of covenant were material.

### (c) 'Substantial'

**9.67** As the Chancellor identified in *Fitzroy House*,[61] another common word of qualification is 'substantial'. This is a word which is 'not only susceptible of ambiguity: it is a word calculated to conceal a lack of precision'.[62] Although there is no known reported case which addresses the meaning and effect of this word when used in a break clause, in *Fitzroy House* itself, the Chancellor remarked 'The words 'substantial' and 'material', depending on the context, are interchangeable'.[63] Thus, depending on the context, the word 'substantial' may (or may not) be construed in the same way as 'material'.

## SETTLEMENTS/SIDE AGREEMENTS

**9.68** Sometimes, after a break notice has been served, the parties may negotiate a settlement or side agreement by which they seek to resolve ancillary issues arising in connection with the exercise or intended exercise of the break clause. So, for example, where a break clause is conditional upon the tenant materially complying with all its covenants under the lease, the tenant may wish, in advance of the break date, to crystallise its prospective liabilities so that payment of a specified sum of money (eg on account of a dilapidations liability) will be sufficient to satisfy the condition. Similarly, there may be a situation where the tenant realises that it will be unable to comply with a particular condition by or before the break date; and, thus, it may seek to negotiate an extension of time to comply with, or otherwise to vary the terms of, the condition. Typically (but not invariably) these agreements are entered into before the break date.

[61] *Fitzroy House Epworth Street (No 1) Ltd v Financial Times Ltd* [2006] 1 WLR 2207, at [16].

[62] *Tillmanns Butcheries Pty Ltd v Australasian Meat Industry Employees' Union* (1979) 42 FLR 331, at 348, per Deane J (cited with approval in *Agbaje v Agbaje* [2010] 1 AC 628, at [32], per Lord Collins); *Majorstake v Curtis* [2008] 1 AC 787, at [33], per Baroness Hale.

[63] *Fitzroy House Epworth Street (No 1) Ltd v Financial Times Ltd* [2006] 1 WLR 2207, at [36]; and see also (in a different context) *Mid Essex Hospital Services NHS Trust v Compass Group UK and Ireland Ltd* [2013] EWCA Civ 200, at [126], per Jackson LJ ('Having regard to the context of this provision, I think that 'material breach' means a breach which is substantial').

As demonstrated below, questions can then arise as to whether such a side or settlement agreement is an agreement under which the parties agree that the lease will terminate in any event.

**9.69** *Legal and General Assurance Society v Expeditors International (UK) Ltd*[64] concerned two leases of premises at the Heathrow International trading estate. The tenant had options to determine the leases in question on the giving of six months' notice subject to satisfaction of preconditions as to the payment of rent and performance and observance of the tenant's covenants and the giving up of vacant possession (of which time was of the essence). The tenant had given break notices a long way ahead of the break date specified in the leases, and the parties and their respective surveyors entered into substantial negotiations about the extent of the dilapidations to the premises and the tenant's prospective liabilities in relation to the leases.

**9.70** Some months before the break date, both sets of surveyors signed a schedule agreeing that the tenant would pay £172,000 in respect of such liabilities. The narrative to the schedule indicated that it had been 'prepared as part of the full and final settlement of the Dilapidations Claims and Lease Breaks under the terms of the Lease'. The schedule also included within the agreed sum of £172,000 an amount in respect of six weeks' rent, which was thought to be the time that the landlord would need after the termination of the lease in order to put the premises into repair before re-letting. This amount was referred to in the case as the 'notional rent'.

**9.71** The schedule was then annexed to an agreement called the 'Settlement Agreement' which was executed by landlord and tenant. It did not expressly state that the lease was to come to an end, but did contain provisions for payment of the agreed amount and terms under which the landlord released the tenant from its liabilities, covenants and obligations past and present under the lease so far as related to the state and condition of the premises, and agreed to keep the premises in no worse a condition than they had been at the date upon which the schedule had been prepared.

**9.72** The agreed payment of £172,000 was duly made by the tenant which commenced vacating the premises a month before, but failed to complete that process by, the break date. The landlord contended that the failure to give vacant possession by the break date meant that the break had not been effectively exercised and the lease had not come to an end. The tenant contended that the Settlement Agreement was unconditional and meant that the lease had terminated, so that the landlord was only entitled to damages for the tenant's failure to give vacant possession.

**9.73** At first instance Lewison J held that the parties had, by entering into the Settlement Agreement, implicitly agreed that the lease would come to an end in any event. He thought that it was obvious that the parties had intended the lease to terminate, because: (i) otherwise the Settlement Agreement would have meant that for the remaining seven years of the lease the only obligation as to the state of the premises would have been that in the Settlement Agreement relating to maintaining the premises in the

[64] *Legal and General Assurance Society Ltd v Expeditors International (UK) Ltd* [2007] 2 P&CR 10.

dilapidated state that they were in when the schedule had been prepared; and (ii) it could not have been intended that, having already been paid six weeks' notional rent under the Settlement Agreement, the landlord could also collect rent in respect of the same period under the continuing lease.

**9.74** Lewison J's decision was upheld by the majority of the Court of Appeal (Clarke MR and Sedley LJ; Lloyd LJ dissenting). Clarke MR thought that the underlying basis of the landlord's claim that led to the Settlement Agreement was that the lease would come to an end on the break date, because:[65]

> there would be no sensible basis upon which the tenant could be expected to pay a sum agreed on the footing that a significant proportion of the amount paid would include notional rent after the Lease came to an end unless it did in fact come to an end.

**9.75** Sedley LJ approached matters differently. He stated:[66]

> with deference to the contrary view of Lord Justice Lloyd, I consider the judge was right. The self-evident purpose of the Settlement Agreement was to draw a line under the parties' mutual rights and obligations at 30 December 2004 when the break notices were to take effect. To this end the agreement, anticipating the break, crystallised the tenant's outstanding liabilities and the landlord's entitlements. Its intrinsic assumption was that the right of possession was irrevocably set to expire on 30 December, so that any consequences of a failure to yield possession on that date would sound in damages for trespass but could not, as they otherwise would, constitute a breach of the condition in clause 6.10.1.2. This seems to me to have been the manifest intention of the parties – manifest in the sense that without it the principal purpose of the agreement would not be achieved.

**9.76** The effect of the settlement was thus to be: (i) first, that the agreed sum would be paid in settlement of all the claims which had been put forward, namely the claims for dilapidations and reinstatement, including the claim for notional rent; and (ii) secondly, that the leases would come to an end, ie that there would in fact be a lease break on 30 December 2004. That is what was meant by a 'settlement of the Dilapidations Claims *and* Lease Breaks'.

**9.77** The opposite result was arrived at in *Intergraph (UK) Ltd v Wolfson Microelectronics Plc*.[67] In that case, the tenant held certain office premises in Swindon under the terms of a lease dated 31 March 2006 ('the Lease'). On 30 September 2008, the parties entered into a further lease of adjacent premises (referred to respectively as 'the New Lease' and 'the New Lease Premises'). The Lease (as subsequently varied) contained a break clause worded as follows, entitling the tenant to determine the Lease on 28 February 2011:

> 22.2 Subject to the pre-conditions in clause 22.3 being satisfied on the relevant Term Date … the Tenant may determine the Term on the relevant Termination Date by giving the Landlord not less than six (6) months' written notice. The Term will then determine on the relevant Termination Date [ie 28 February 2011] …

[65] *Legal and General Assurance Society Ltd v Expeditors International (UK) Ltd* [2007] 2 P&CR 10, at [55].
[66] *Legal and General Assurance Society Ltd v Expeditors International (UK) Ltd* [2007] 2 P&CR 10, at [49].
[67] *Intergraph (UK) Ltd v Wolfson Microelectronics Plc* [2012] EWHC 528 (Ch).

> 22.3 The pre-conditions are that:
>
> 2.3.2 all rent and other sums due under this Lease and the New Lease up to the relevant Termination Date have been paid in full …
>
> 22.3.4 (unless the Tenant … has (where the Premises and the New Lease Premises are still occupied by the same person) first fully complied with Clauses 13.12.2(a) and 13.12.2(b) of this Lease) the Tenant gives vacant possession of the whole of the New Lease Premises having validly exercised the option to determine contained in clause 22 ('Tenants Option to Determine') of the New Lease and fully complied with the preconditions contained in such clause.

**9.78** Clause 13.12 of the lease (as varied) provided that the tenant would not be entitled to assign or underlet the Lease unless it had first:

> (a) created (to the Landlord's reasonable satisfaction) an independent means of access to and egress from the New Lease Premises wholly out of the Premises;
> (b) reinstated all partitioning between the Premises and the New Leases [sic] Premises (save for any partitioning across the access referred to in clause 13.12.2(a)) to the Landlord's reasonable satisfaction.

**9.79** By letter dated 19 August 2010, the tenant served a break notice to determine the lease on 28 February 2011. However, by mistake, no notice was served to determine the New Lease as well. This had the result that the tenant was unable to satisfy the main precondition to an effective break of the lease in clause 22.3.4, namely giving vacant possession of the whole of the New Lease Premises at the same time. In order to get over this difficulty, the tenant sought to carry out the works required by clauses 13.12.2(a) and 13.12.2(b) (creating an independent means of access and reinstating the partitioning) so as to meet the requirements of the exception set out at the beginning of clause 22.3.4. Unfortunately, the tenant did not have sufficient time to carry out the required works in advance of the break date. Instead, on 22 February 2011, the parties entered into a side agreement. This agreement provided as follows:

> We [ie the landlord] confirm that we will accept the effectiveness of the Break Notice upon the following conditions:
>
> 1. [The tenant] is to pay all rent, service charge and interest which has been demanded to date, being £51,330.34 …
> 2. [The tenant] is to pay on or before 28 February 2011 [ie the termination date] the sum of £37,477.64 in full and final settlement of all sums due for the carrying-out of reinstatement and access works required by the conditions to the break clause and all liability for dilapidations, disrepair or wants of decoration and ancillary costs thereto under the 2006 Lease.

**9.80** The payment of £51,330.34 was duly made. However, as a result of an administrative error in the tenant's finance department, the payment of £37,477.64 was not made on or before 28 February 2011. The landlord contended that time was of the essence of this provision of the side agreement, as it had been in relation to the original preconditions to the valid exercise of the break clause in the Lease. By contrast, the tenant contended that the side agreement was one under which the parties agreed that the Lease would terminate in any event, and that time was not of the essence of the provision for payment of the specified sum on or before 28 February 2011.

**9.81** Mr Richard Snowden QC (sitting as a Deputy Judge of the High Court) considered that the side agreement was not an unqualified agreement for the determination of the Lease. Looking at the language used by the parties, he said:[68]

> [42] … The logic of [the tenant's] contention is that there was an unqualified agreement reached on 22 February 2011 for the Lease to terminate, but that the parties chose not to fix any particular date in the Agreement for payment of the arrears of rent, service charge and interest. I think that the reasonable observer who was aware of the background would think it inherently unlikely that this was what the parties meant. Whilst [the landlord] was obviously prepared to compromise in the Agreement and not to insist upon strict adherence to the terms of clause 22.3.4 of the Lease, there was no obvious commercial reason for it simply to give up the benefits of clause 22.3.2 which provided for payment of the stated amounts by 28 February 2011 (as to which time was of the essence) for an entirely open-ended obligation of the part of Wolfson to pay precisely the same amounts but at a time entirely of its choosing (subject only to payment of interest in the meantime). Instead, I think that the underlying requirement was still that payment of amounts owing needed to be made by 28 February 2011 in accordance with precondition 22.3.2 …
>
> [46] The language of Sub-paragraph 2 is also entirely consistent with a conclusion that the parties did not intend that the Lease would terminate in any event. The clause refers to the payment 'on or before 28 February 2011' of a sum 'in full and final settlement of the sums due for the carrying out of reinstatement and access works *required by the conditions to the break clause*'. That cross-reference suggests that the parties understood that they were still operating within the framework of the conditions to the break clause in the Lease but were agreeing that [the tenant] could pay an agreed sum by the specified date instead of carrying out the works that would have been required under clause 22.3.4. I think that the reasonable observer would understand that in the same way as time was of the essence in relation to the carrying out of the works by the date upon which the Break Notice was to take effect, time was also meant to be of the essence in relation to satisfaction of the substitute obligation to make payment on or before that same date.

**9.82** Mr Richard Snowden QC distinguished *Expeditors* on the basis that the agreement in *Intergraph* contained: (i) no provision for the payment of any notional rent for the period after the break date (instead requiring only payment of arrears of rent); and (ii) no language which was comparable to the narrative to the schedule to the agreement in *Expeditors* indicating the intention to settle the 'lease breaks'. Quite the reverse: the language that was used carefully referred back to the satisfaction of the preconditions for the effectiveness of the break notice.

**9.83** Ultimately, the outcome of any case such as this will turn on the interpretation of the particular agreement in question (which exercise will be carried out in accordance with the usual legal principles applicable to the interpretation of contracts). However, the obvious lesson from the above is that if, after a break notice has been served, a tenant wishes to be sure that the lease will determine on the break date, then any side agreement should make this explicit in unqualified terms.

[68] *Intergraph (UK) Ltd v Wolfson Microelectronics Plc* [2012] EWHC 528 (Ch).

SERVICE OF A BREAK NOTICE WITHOUT FULFILLING CONDITIONS

**9.84** It is not a breach of contract (still less a repudiatory breach of contract) to seek to exercise a break option without fulfilling the conditions upon which its successful exercise depends.[69] This is for the simple reason that there is no obligation on the party with the benefit of a break option to exercise it. All that can be said is that the purported exercise of a break option at a time when any conditions precedent to its exercise have not been satisfied will render the break notice an invalidity. But, the invalid exercise of a break clause in a lease 'cannot be treated as a breach of contract because there is no relevant contractual obligation that can be breached'.[70]

[69] *Cooke v Scotfield Ltd* (unreported, 4 April 2000), at [35], per Mr Peter G Whitman QC (sitting as a Deputy Judge of the Chancery Division).

[70] *Wigan Borough Council v Scullindale Global Ltd* [2021] EWHC 779 (Ch), at [132], per HHJ Hodge QC (sitting as a Judge of the Chancery Division).

# 10

# *Particular Conditions in a Tenant's Break Clause*

## INTRODUCTION

**10.1** It is commonplace to find that a tenant's break clause is only exercisable subject to compliance with certain conditions. The most common conditions are addressed below. Given the principle of strict compliance,[1] any failure to comply with the stipulated conditions (beyond, perhaps, an extreme and extraordinary case involving a de minimis failure)[2] will be fatal to the exercise of the break.

## VACANT POSSESSION

### (a) General Principles

**10.2** One of the most common preconditions upon which the successful exercise of a break clause depends is that the tenant delivers up vacant possession of the demised premises on or by the break date.

**10.3** The 'leading case'[3] on the topic of vacant possession is *Cumberland Consolidated Holdings Limited v Ireland*.[4] In that case the plaintiffs agreed to buy from the defendant a warehouse. The property was sold with vacant possession on completion. The sale was indeed completed but it was discovered that a large part of the cellars contained hardened concrete left in bags. About two-thirds of the height of the cellars was filled with rubbish consisting mainly of bags of cement which had hardened and empty drums. It was all valueless, but its presence prevented the use of the cellars for any purpose. The buyer had the rubbish removed at a cost of £80 and brought proceedings against the seller for damages for breach of contract, the breach complained of being the failure to deliver up the warehouse with vacant possession. The claim was upheld by the Court of Appeal.

[1] See **9.15–9.25** above.
[2] See **9.26–9.27** above.
[3] *Legal & General Assurance Society Ltd v Expeditors International (UK) Ltd* [2006] L&TR 368, at [35], per Lewison J.
[4] *Cumberland Consolidated Holdings Ltd v Ireland* [1956] 1 KB 264.

**10.4** The judgment of Lord Greene MR in *Cumberland* contains two possible tests for ascertaining whether or not the obligation to deliver up vacant possession had been complied with. The first was posed as follows:[5]

> Subject to the rule de minimis a vendor who leaves property of his own on the premises on completion cannot, in our opinion, be said to give vacant possession, since by doing so he is claiming a right to use the premises for his own purposes, namely as a place of deposit for his own goods inconsistent with the right which the purchaser has on completion to undisturbed enjoyment.

**10.5** The second test treated vacant possession as the right to actual unimpeded physical enjoyment of the premises. Thus Lord Greene MR stated:[6]

> We cannot see why the existence of a physical impediment to such enjoyment to which a purchaser does not expressly or impliedly consent to submit should stand in a different position to an impediment caused by the presence of a trespasser. It is true that in each case the purchaser obtains the right to possession in law notwithstanding the presence of the impediment but it appears to us that what he bargains for is not merely the right in law but the power in fact to exercise the right. When we speak of a physical impediment we do not mean that any physical impediment will do. It must be an impediment which substantially prevents or interferes with the enjoyment of the right of possession of a substantial part of the property. Such cases will be rare and can only arise in exceptional circumstances and there would normally be (what there is not here) waiver or acceptance of the position by the purchaser.

**10.6** In *Legal & General Assurance Society v Expeditors International (UK) Ltd*,[7] the facts of which are digested in **10.21** below, Lewison J referred to the two tests and said:

> [41] It seems to me that the difference between the two tests is as follows. The first test looks at the activities of the person who is required to give vacant possession. If he is actually using the property for purposes of his own otherwise than de minimis, he will be held not to have given vacant possession …
>
> [42] The second test looks at the physical condition of the property from the perspective of the person to whom vacant possession must be given. If that physical condition is such that there is a substantial impediment to his use of the property or a substantial part of it then vacant possession will not have been given. As the Court of Appeal said in the *Cumberland* case, that is likely to be satisfied only in exceptional circumstances.

**10.7** In *Merton London Borough Council v Jones*,[8] the Court of Appeal had to consider what a tenant must do in order to establish it has ceased to have possession of demised premises. Although the Court was not referred to the decisions in *Cumberland* or *Expeditors*, the case remains important because it emphasises two distinct aspects to the concept of vacant possession. As Arden LJ explained:[9]

> [47] It is clear that to acquire possession a person must both obtain physical control of the relevant property and have formed an intention to control the use of that property to the exclusion

[5] *Cumberland Consolidated Holdings Ltd v Ireland* [1956] 1 KB 264, at 270.

[6] *Cumberland Consolidated Holdings Ltd v Ireland* [1956] 1 KB 264, at 271.

[7] *Legal & General Assurance Society Ltd v Expeditors International (UK) Ltd* [2007] 1 P&CR 5, [41]–[42] (Lewison J's decision in this case on the construction and effect a separate settlement agreement was upheld by the majority of the Court of Appeal at [2007] 2 P&CR 10).

[8] *Merton London Borough Council v Jones* [2009] 1 WLR 1269.

[9] *Merton London Borough Council v Jones* [2009] 1 WLR 1269, at 1283D–84F.

of others. Curiously, apart from the sparse authority cited to us, which Wilson LJ has cited, there is little authority on when the cessation of possession occurs in law …

[48] In my judgment, two elements are necessary for a cessation of possession by a person who is not under some contractual obligation to give notice in some way. The occupier must cease to control, or to have a legal right to control, the use of the property, and, in addition, he must have ceased to have an intention to control the use of the property to the exclusion of others.

[49] The first element does not generally cause difficulty. But what is necessary to demonstrate the second element, namely that a person has ceased to have an intention to possess? In my judgment, it is not enough that he states that it is his intention to give up possession if he has done acts that belie that intention …

[51] In any event, to cease to have possession it is not enough simply to have an intention to give up possession. The intention must be acted upon in such a way that the proper inference from those acts is that there was an intention to give up possession. A person who wishes to give up possession must make that intention manifest: see per Lord Hope of Craighead in *J A Pye (Oxford) Ltd v Graham* [2003] 1 AC 419 in the passage cited by Wilson LJ, at para 30 above. This was also the view taken by Oliver Wendell Holmes Jr, a Justice of United States Supreme Court, in *The Common Law* (1881). He illustrated his view by an example (which I set out below), which shows the difference between an unimplemented intention to possess and an intention which has been made manifest. From that example Holmes drew general conclusions about what is necessary in this context to prove intention. The example was:

> 'Suppose that a finder of a purse of gold has left it in his country house, which is lonely and slightly barred, and he is a hundred miles away, in prison. The only person within 20 miles is a thoroughly equipped burglar at his front door, who has seen the purse through a window, and who intends forthwith to enter and take it. The finder's power to reproduce his former physical relation to the gold is rather limited, yet I believe that no one would say that his possession was at an end until the burglar, by an overt act, had manifested his power and intent to exclude others from the purse. The reason for this is the same which has been put with regard to the power to exclude at the moment of gaining possession. *The law deals, for the most part, with overt acts and facts which can be known by the senses. So long as the burglar has not taken the purse, he has not manifested his intent; and until he breaks through the barrier which measures the present possessor's power of excluding him, he has not manifested his power*': Lecture VI, 'Possession'. (Emphasis added.) …'

**10.8** *Cumberland* and *Expeditors* were examined by the Court of Appeal in *NYK Logistics (UK) Ltd v Ibrend Estates BV*,[10] the facts of which are set out at **10.22** below. There, Rimer LJ considered that Lewison J in the *Expeditors* case correctly identified the essence of the two grounds on which *Cumberland* was decided.[11] However, he went on to say as follows:[12]

> The concept of 'vacant possession' in the present context is not, I consider, complicated. It means what it does in every domestic and commercial sale in which there is an obligation to give 'vacant possession' on completion. It means that at the moment that 'vacant possession' is required to be given, the property is empty of people and that the purchaser is able to assume

[10] *NYK Logistics (UK) Ltd v Ibrend Estates BV* [2011] 4 All ER 539 (cited with approval in *Taylor v Diamond* [2012] EWHC 2900 (Ch), at [97], per Norris J).

[11] *NYK Logistics (UK) Ltd v Ibrend Estates BV* [2011] 4 All ER 539, at [44].

[12] *NYK Logistics (UK) Ltd v Ibrend Estates BV* [2011] 4 All ER 539 (cited with approval in *Taylor v Diamond* [2012] EWHC 2900 (Ch), at [97], per Norris J).

> and enjoy immediate and exclusive possession, occupation and control of it. It must also be empty of chattels, although the obligation in this respect is likely only to be breached if any chattels left in the property substantially prevent or interfere with the enjoyment of the right of possession of a substantial part of the property.

**10.9** It is worthwhile noting that legal impediments to the enjoyment of land may also result in a failure to deliver up vacant possession, just as physical impediments might do.[13] This is well-illustrated by *Topfell Ltd v Galley Properties Ltd*.[14] In that case, the plaintiff company agreed to purchase a property in West Croydon. The property was a converted house. A tenant lived on the first floor; and the ground floor was unoccupied. Croydon Council had served a notice under s 19 of the Housing Act 1961, whereby the Council directed that the house should only be occupied by one household. The vendors knew about, but did not disclose the existence of, this notice to the purchaser. Importantly, the contract for the sale and purchase of the property promised vacant possession of the ground floor. The purchaser found out about the notice and then sued for an abatement of the purchase price.

**10.10** Holding that the vendors could not comply with the obligation to deliver up vacant possession, Templeman LJ said as follows:[15]

> I have come to the conclusion that the vendors were contractually bound, on completion, to hand over the ground floor in a condition which would allow the plaintiffs to occupy it. It is quite plain that at the date of the contract and at the date fixed for completion, the vendors cannot do that because, by reason of the Housing Act direction, in fact, nobody can occupy the ground floor. The vendors cannot occupy it themselves, they cannot sell it to somebody who wishes to purchase it in order to go and live there himself and they cannot let it.

**10.11** From the above authorities, the following points of principle emerge:

(1) In order to satisfy a condition requiring vacant possession to be delivered up by the break date, the tenant must cease to control, or to have a legal right to control, the use of the property.
(2) In addition, the tenant must have ceased to have an intention to control the use of the property to the exclusion of others.
(3) However, to cease to have possession it is not enough simply for the tenant to have an intention to give up possession. The intention must be acted upon in such a way that the proper inference from those acts is that there was an intention to give up possession.
(4) At the moment that vacant possession is required to be given, the landlord must be able to assume and enjoy immediate and exclusive possession, occupation and control of the property.
(5) There will be no vacant possession if, at the time vacant possession is required to be given: (i) the tenant is actually using the property for his own purposes (as in *NYK Logistics* and *Legal & General*, discussed below) except where such user is de

[13] *Engell v Fitch* (1869) LR 4 QB 659; *Macara (James) Ltd v Barclay* [1945] KB 148; *Secretary of State for the Environment, Transport and the Regions v Baylis (Gloucester) Ltd (Costs) (2000)* 80 P&CR 324.

[14] *Topfell Ltd v Galley Properties Ltd* [1979] 1 WLR 446; and see also *Cook v Taylor* [1942] 2 All ER 85; *James Macara Ltd v Barclay* [1945] KB 148; *Korogluyan v Matthew* (1975) 30 P&CR 309.

[15] *Topfell Ltd v Galley Properties Ltd* [1979] 1 WLR 446, at 449G–49H.

minimis; and/or (ii) there is a substantial physical or legal impediment to the landlord's use of the property or a substantial part of it (as in *Cumberland* and *Royal Bank of Canada*, also discussed below).

10.12 Or, as the law has been summarised by reference to a 'trilogy' of factors:[16]

> what the obligation to give vacant possession normally requires is threefold. That is to return the premises to the landlord free of, or vacant of: first, people; secondly, chattels (subject to the decision of the Court of Appeal in *Cumberland Consolidated Holdings Ltd v Ireland* [1946] KB 264, which is to the effect that a party is only in breach of the obligation to give vacant possession by leaving chattels on the property if the physical impediment substantially prevents or interferes with the enjoyment of the right of possession of a substantial part of the property); and, thirdly, legal interest. So a person does not comply with the obligation to give vacant possession if it is subject to a legal right in somebody else to take possession. That trilogy of people, chattels, and interests ... I accept accurately reflects the general law of vacant possession.

### (b) Vacant Possession of What?

10.13 In the *Legal & General* case,[17] Lewison J adverted to a 'fundamental question'[18] which arises when considering whether or not a tenant has delivered up vacant possession. He said:

> [31] The first question arising under this head is vacant possession of what? In this case vacant possession of the premises. The premises will, in my view, exclude anything that is not demised. This means first in case of Unit 15 it will exclude the yard and in the case of all the units it will exclude the grass verges. Items left in these areas may amount to a trespass for which damages are recoverable, but they do not affect compliance with the condition itself.
>
> [32] Secondly, in my judgment the premises will include anything which in law has become part of the premises by annexation. A fixture installed by the tenant for the purposes of his trade become part of the premises as soon as it is installed, although the tenant retains a right to sever the fixture on termination of the tenancy. Whether something is a fixture depends on the degree and purpose of annexation; in each case looked at objectively. If something has become part of the premises by annexation then it is part of a thing of which vacant possession has to be given. Its presence does not amount to an impediment to vacant possession itself.

10.14 In the case of a break option, as in *Legal & General*, a condition of vacant possession will usually require vacant possession of the 'demised premises' (or some other similar formulation). This can give rise to difficulties when considering whether or not a tenant has removed (i) enough of its property from the 'demised premises' in order to give vacant possession or (ii) too much of the property so that it cannot deliver up vacant possession of the 'demised premises' at all.

[16] *Goldman Sachs International v Procession House Trustee Ltd* [2018] L&TR 28, at [39], per Nugee J. In *Capitol Park Leeds Plc v Global Radio Services Ltd* [2021] EWCA Civ 995, at [13], Newey LJ cited with approval from this passage of the *Goldman Sachs* case and remarked that 'an obligation to "give vacant possession" refers to giving back the property in question free of "people, chattels, and interests", not to its physical condition'.

[17] *Legal & General Assurance Society Ltd v Expeditors International (UK) Ltd* [2007] 1 P&CR 5.

[18] *Riverside Park Ltd v NHS Property Services Ltd* [2017] L&TR 12, at [62], per HHJ Saffman.

**10.15** Normally, it can be expected that the 'demised premises' will not include chattels. Therefore, in order to comply with a vacant possession condition, the tenant must remove its chattels (at least where they amount to a physical impediment which substantially prevents or interferes with the landlord's right of possession of a substantial part of the demised premises). It is important to note that chattels are not necessarily limited to loose items. They can extend to fixed items, such as demountable partitions. This proved fatal in *Riverside Park Ltd v NHS Property Services Ltd*[19] (digested in at **10.27** below), where the presence of such partitions meant that vacant possession was not given.

**10.16** More difficult issues can arise in connection with tenant's fixtures.[20] In some cases, tenant's fixtures may form part of the 'demised premises' so that they need not be removed in order to deliver up vacant possession. In other cases, the converse may be true. Equally, the position may be unclear.[21] The matter might be complicated further if there is a covenant in the lease (or an associated licence) to remove alterations or additions to and/or to reinstate the demised premises before the end of the term. This problem arose in the *Riverside Park* case, where (in an obiter passage) HHJ Saffman took the view that, if the demountable partitions had been the tenant's fixtures and had formed part of the demised premises, then the tenant's obligation to give vacant possession included removing those fixtures.[22] However, in *Goldman Sachs International v Procession House Trustee Ltd*,[23] it was argued on behalf of the tenant that this aspect of the decision in *Riverside Park* was wrong, on the basis that it contained 'no reasoning or reference to the well-understood concept of vacant possession'.[24] Nugee J left the point open. He said:

> I do not propose to decide this question. I accept the ordinary meaning of what it is to give vacant possession in terms of the trilogy of people, chattels, or interests. I accept that one cannot find in HH Judge Saffman's judgment in Riverside any real discussion of the point as

[19] *Riverside Park Ltd v NHS Property Services Ltd* [2017] L&TR 12.

[20] In *Elitestone Ltd v Morris* [1997] 1 WLR 687, at 691, Lord Lloyd said: 'The term fixture is apt to be a source of misunderstanding owing to the existence of the category of so called "tenants' fixtures" (a term used to cover both trade fixtures and ornamental fixtures), which are fixtures in the full sense of the word (and therefore part of the realty) but which may nevertheless be removed by the tenant in the course of or at the end of his tenancy. Such fixtures are sometimes confused with chattels which have never become fixtures at all.' The difference between a landlord's fixture and a tenant's fixture is explained by Lord Denning MR in *New Zealand Government Property Corporation v HM&S Ltd* [1982] 1 WLR 1145, at 1157. As he put it: 'The term "tenant's fixtures,"… means those fixtures which the tenant himself fixed into the premises for the purpose of his trade … but which do not become part of the structure itself … All these the tenant is entitled to remove when his term comes to an end. Whereas 'landlord's fixtures'… means those fixtures which the tenant himself fixes into the premises so that they become part of the structure itself.'

[21] So, for example, in *Dreams Ltd v Pavilion Property Trustees Ltd* [2020] L&TR 22, the landlord contended that a mezzanine floor and lift installed by the tenant's predecessor in title were tenant's fixtures which ought to have been removed and whose continued presence in the premises prevented the tenant from giving vacant possession. By contrast, the tenant contended that the items, when they were installed, became part of the fabric of the premises. At the time of writing, this aspect of the dispute between the parties has not been the subject of judicial resolution.

[22] *Riverside Park Ltd v NHS Property Services Ltd* [2017] L&TR 12, at [92] ('… even if I had found that the Works and particularly the partitions were not chattels but fixtures or otherwise formed part of the Premises, I would have found that there was an obligation to remove them arising out of the fact that the licence to erect them had ceased to have effect and that their presence in the Premises on the date of purported termination of the Lease meant that vacant possession of the Premises was not given.')

[23] *Goldman Sachs International v Procession House Trustee Ltd* [2018] L&TR 28.

[24] Ibid, at [41].

to whether the conclusion that the works in question were fixtures which the tenant had to remove meant that the tenant was in breach of an obligation to give vacant possession – indeed, for all one knows from the judgment, the point may not have been argued at all and may have been conceded – but I do not regard it as necessary for the purposes of this case to resolve the question.

**10.17** The cases above are concerned with the problem where a tenant leaves behind *too much*. But the condition requiring vacant possession may also be unsatisfied if the tenant leaves behind *too little*. This issue arose in *Capitol Park Leeds Plc v Global Radio Services Ltd*.[25] That case concerned a lease containing a tenant's option to terminate on 12 November 2017, subject to (inter alia) the tenant giving 'vacant possession of the Premises to the Landlord on the relevant Tenant's Break Date'. The 'Premises' were defined as 'including all fixtures and fittings at the Premises whenever fixed, except those which are generally regarded as tenant's or trade fixtures and fittings, and all additions and improvements made to the Premises'. The tenant gave notice to exercise the break option. In advance of the break date, in an attempt to comply with its reinstatement obligation, the tenant stripped out various original features of the Premises and/or fixtures which had been demised by the landlord. Thus, the landlord argued that the tenant had not given back 'the Premises' and had not satisfied the vacant possession condition in the break option. By contrast, the tenant argued that the expression 'the Premises' ought to be interpreted in an 'always speaking' sense by reference to what was on the demised land at any particular point in time. Judge Benjamin Nolan QC preferred the landlord's argument. He held:

> [66] … By including the words 'all fixtures and fittings at the Premises whenever fixed (except Tenant's fixtures)' and 'all additions and improvements made to the Premises', the Claimant was ensuring that a Tenant exercising its Break Option could not do so by handing back an empty shell of a building which was dysfunctional and unoccupiable.
>
> [67] But in the end, this is what the Defendant did. On my findings, they stopped the work unilaterally in the hope of negotiating a settlement. Those negotiations failed, the clock ran down, and the Defendant gave back considerably less than 'the Premises' as defined in the Lease. It did not give vacant possession. In my view, this is an exceptional case and therefore the second test identified in *Cumberland* and in *Legal & General* is satisfied, namely that the physical condition of the Property was such that there is a substantial impediment to the Landlord's use of the Property, or a substantial part of it.

**10.18** The Court of Appeal unanimously allowed the tenant's appeal and held that the break had been successfully operated.[26] As already described,[27] this was because, on a proper construction, the requirement to give vacant possession of the 'Premises' meant only that the tenant was obliged to return the 'Premises' as they were on the break date free of the 'trilogy of people, chattels, and interests'.[28] To the extent that the tenant had

[25] *Capitol Park Leeds Plc v Global Radio Services Ltd* [2020] EWHC 2750 (Ch); overturned on appeal at [2021] EWCA Civ 995 (CA).

[26] At [10], Newey LJ noted that the landlord did not seek to uphold the decision of the Judge insofar as he found that the second test in *Cumberland* had been satisfied. Seemingly, this was because it had been no part of the landlord's case at trial that the physical condition of the 'Premises' as at the break date was such that there was a substantial impediment to the landlord's use of the 'Premises' or a substantial part thereof.

[27] See **9.13–9.14**.

[28] See **10.12** above.

delivered up the 'Premises' in a deficient state, the landlord had a remedy in damages. As Newey LJ explained:

> [13] Of itself … an obligation to give 'vacant possession' refers to giving back the property in question free of 'people, chattels, and interests', not to its physical condition.

**10.19** These cases demonstrate some of the pitfalls which can arise where a tenant seeks to operate a break clause dependent upon satisfaction of a vacant possession condition. Prudence dictates that a tenant in this situation should not leave matters to the last minute. Rather, well before the break date, the tenant should (if possible): (a) reach agreement with the landlord as to what should (or should not) be removed; and (b) remove items which it is obliged to remove (which will be chattels and may be tenant's fixtures). Although, following *Capitol Park*, it is unlikely that the removal of too much of 'the Premises' will (of itself) preclude delivery up of vacant possession, it might be the case if so much of 'the Premises' is removed that the second test in *Cumberland* ends up being satisfied.

### (c) Examples Where Vacant Possession Has Not Been Delivered Up

**10.20** In a number of cases concerning the exercise of break options the court has found that a tenant has failed to satisfy the condition requiring it to deliver up vacant possession of the premises on the break date. These are considered chronologically below.

**10.21** In *Legal & General Assurance Society v Expeditors International (UK) Ltd*,[29] the issue was whether the tenant had successfully terminated two leases of units situated at the Heathrow Industrial Estate. The tenant had a break option entitling it to terminate the leases on 30 December 2004 by giving to the landlord not less than six months' prior notice to that effect if 'on the expiry of the notice the Tenant delivers up to the Landlord the whole of the Premises with vacant possession'.[30] The tenant duly served the requisite notice in order to exercise the break. On the day after the break date, the landlord inspected the premises and found one of the tenant's employees sweeping inside or outside one of the units. In addition, the tenant had left various items inside the units (including pallets, dismantled racking, gas tanks and so forth). Furthermore, the tenant retained the keys into the summer of 2005. After referring to the two tests in *Cumberland* (see **10.3** above), Lewison J concluded that the tenant had not delivered up vacant possession on the break date. He said:[31]

> [43] Let me take the second test first. Suppose in the present case that the tenant had tendered the keys to the landlord on December 30, 2004, had had no personnel on site and the landlord had opened the units to find the various items in them, would the mere presence of those items have led to the conclusion that vacant possession had not been given? Once I have eliminated the gas tanks, the vehicle barriers and the debris on the yard in front of Unit 15, the debris

[29] *Legal & General Assurance Society Ltd v Expeditors International (UK) Ltd* [2007] 1 P&CR 5.

[30] In the event, Lewison J found that, by virtue of a separate settlement agreement, the landlord had waived the right to rely upon this condition (a point upheld by a majority of the Court of Appeal at [2007] 2 P&CR 10).

[31] *Legal & General Assurance Society Ltd v Expeditors International (UK) Ltd* [2007] 1 P&CR 5, at [43]–[45], [48].

on the grass verges surrounding the yard to Units 16 and 17, the remaining items in my view, consisting largely of pallets and dismantled racking or garment rails, would not have amounted to a substantial physical impediment to the use of the units or a substantial part of the units. No inconvenience or impediment has in fact been asserted by the landlord. The landlord's stance is, I infer, based simply on a desire to defeat the exercise of a break and to continue to receive a rent of £344,000 a year in a weak market.

[44] The first test presents more difficulty. In the light of my finding about the keys the tenant has not in fact delivered any keys to the landlord. But even if I had accepted the tenant's case it was not suggested that keys were tendered until some five or six days after the break date. If the condition relating to vacant possession had to be complied with at all, it had to be complied with on December 30, 2004, time being of the essence. Compliance a day or two later would not have been enough.

[45] On the day after the break date … the tenant was still expecting lorries to arrive and take away material that the tenant had left behind and wanted to remove, the photographs still show the tenant in active control of the warehouses which it was using, in part, for storage of materials that it wished to take elsewhere. The tenant's employee … was still on site for that purpose. After that time the units were still locked and the landlord was not able to get into Unit 15 with keys of its own.

[48] It may seem hard that the tenant would potentially have been liable for some £2 million worth of future rent, all for the sake of at most a few thousand pounds worth of materials. But, as [the landlord] submitted, conditions of options must be precisely complied with. Notice in the present case was given almost 18 months before the break date and the tenant had plenty of time in which to effect a removal. However, having accepted [the tenant's] submissions on the effect of the settlement agreement, the [landlord's] claim fails.

**10.22** *NYK Logistics (UK) Ltd v Ibrend Estates BV*[32] concerned a lease of warehouse premises in Rotherham. The question was whether the tenant, in its claim to have exercised a break clause, had satisfied a condition which required it to give up vacant possession of the warehouse to the landlord on the break date, ie 3 April 2009. The tenant had given a valid break notice to the landlord on 26 September 2008. In January 2009, the landlord prepared a terminal schedule of dilapidations. This was passed to the tenant on 11 March 2009. On 1 April 2009, the landlord's and the tenant's surveyors had a meeting on site to discuss the dilapidations. At that meeting, the surveyors agreed that the tenant had substantially complied with its repairing and redecorating covenants, but that there were still some outstanding items of repair. Those outstanding items could not have been dealt with by the break date (3 April 2009) but could have been completed shortly thereafter. On 6 April 2009, the tenant's contractors entered the warehouse in order to carry out the remaining repairs. They worked on the repairs over 6–9 April 2009.

**10.23** At trial, the judge concluded that the tenant had failed to deliver up vacant possession of the premises by the break date. The tenant appealed. Dismissing the appeal, Rimer LJ said as follows (with emphasis in the original):[33]

[45] In the present case [the tenant] did not give such possession to [the landlord] on April 3. It made a sensible proposal at the meeting of April 1, repeated in Mr Louch's email of April 2,

[32] *NYK Logistics (UK) Ltd v Ibrend Estates BV* [2011] 4 All ER 539.
[33] *NYK Logistics (UK) Ltd v Ibrend Estates BV* [2011] 4 All ER 539, at [45]–[47].

to the effect that [the landlord] should extend its occupation for a week in order to enable it to finish the repair works, on terms that it would pay the continued security costs, although no more rent or rates. It would also give the keys to [the landlord] by April 3, so that [the landlord] would have access to the warehouse. In substance, although [the tenant] may not have so analysed it, it was proposing that it would give possession on April 3 and then make a brief return to the warehouse after April 3 as [the landlord's] licensee. Had an arrangement along such lines been agreed, it is probable that this litigation would never have happened.

[46] [The tenant's] misfortune was, however, that by April 3 it could raise no response – neither a yes nor a no – from [the landlord]. In that respect, I have some sympathy for [the tenant], but not a lot. The terms of its own proposal show that it *knew* that, in order not to prejudice the operation of the break option, it needed to obtain [the landlord's] agreement to what it wanted to do. It ought also to have known that, when that agreement was not forthcoming by April 3, its only safe course was to move everyone out of the warehouse on Friday, including its security guard; to have emailed [the landlord's] agents on that day to explain that that was what it was doing and that it would the same day deliver the keys to the agents. It could then have contacted [the landlord] on Monday April 6 and asked it whether it would permit it to return to the warehouse as its licensee in order to complete the outstanding works. Had [the tenant] taken legal advice on April 3 as to what to do, I should be surprised if such advice would have been otherwise than that [the tenant] should act along the lines I have suggested.

[47] [The tenant] did not, however, take that course. [Counsel for the tenant] made much of [the tenant's] concern that if it walked out on Friday and removed its security guard, there was a high risk that the place would be vandalised over the weekend. That may have been so. But that risk was not [the tenant's], it was [the landlord's], which also knew, or ought to have known, that [the tenant] would be likely to leave on April 3. Any concern that [the tenant] had about the vandalism point was not one that entitled it to award itself an extension of time for the giving of possession. The other point, also of obvious concern to it, was that it wanted to complete the repairs. Whilst it is true that such works would benefit [the landlord], the reason that [the tenant] wanted to carry them out was dictated exclusively by its own interests. It did not *have* to carry out them out as a condition of the exercise of the break option. It *wanted* to do them in order to avoid the prospect of a subsequent claim for damages in excess of its own cost of doing them. Its wish in that respect was also no justification for giving itself an extension of time for the giving of possession.

**10.24** *NYK* is one of many cases where the result may have been different if the tenant had taken good legal advice in proper time. A sound lawyer would have pointed out that the break clause in that case was not conditional upon the tenant delivering up the premises in repair. Hence the tenant's occupation of the premises, post the break date, to effect repairs, was unnecessary to comply with the break clause.

**10.25** *Secretary of State for Communities and Local Government v South Essex College of Further and Higher Education*[34] concerned a lease of part of the ground floor of an office block. After the grant of the lease, the tenant had erected partitioning to divide up the space into a number of rooms. The tenant served a break notice, conditional upon it giving 'possession of the whole of the premises'. However, before and just after the break date: (i) there was no correspondence in which the tenant said to the landlord that they were in the process of giving up possession; (ii) no meeting took place at which

[34] *Secretary of State for Communities and Local Government v South Essex College of Further and Higher Education* [2016] 7 WLUK 780.

possession was given up, nor were any arrangements made to do so; (iii) no keys, door codes or alarm codes were handed over by the tenant to the landlord; (iv) a quantity of chattels were left at the premises, including a photocopier (with a sign on top of it saying 'do not move'), a box of files (which the tenant was under a statutory obligation to preserve for audit purposes), and a certain quantity of cabling, wiring, trunking and electrical sockets relating to IT equipment; and (v) the partitions already mentioned (which the court considered ought to be categorised as chattels).

**10.26** The parties were agreed that there were 'two tests' for what constituted vacant possession: 'The first is, objectively viewed, has the tenant manifested a clear intention to effect a termination, and secondly, could the landlord, if it wanted, have occupied the premises without difficulty or objection at the break date?'[35] On this basis, the landlord argued that: (i) the tenant did not give up possession because it did not manifest any objective intention to do so; (ii) vacant possession was not given up because the tenant continued to make use of the premises by storing items there; and (iii) the continued presence of those items amounted to a substantial impediment to, or interference with, a substantial part of the premises. HHJ Dight (sitting in the county court at Central London) agreed. Referring to the 'two tests,' he said:

> [55] … There was no positive step taken by the [tenant] to demonstrate to the outside world that it had given up vacant possession of the property, whether they intended to do so or not. Their subjective intention is not the key issue, it is the objective manifestation of it. Going back to the factual common ground there was no correspondence saying they were giving up possession, no hand-over meeting, no delivery of keys or codes, items were left on the premises, including items that they continue to own. It was really, in my judgment, more akin to an abandonment of the premises rather than a delivery up of them.
>
> [56] Secondly … by leaving the photocopier and the files in the room and the various pieces of cleaning equipment, which I make no findings about the particular ownership or use of, the [tenant] continued to store goods there and was therefore continuing to make use of the premises after expiry of the break notice. How did they think, one asks rhetorically, that the company which owned the photocopier and had rented it to the [tenant] was going to obtain access to collect it after the time that the lease had come to an end if they did not let them in? They were, in my judgment, still making use of the premises.
>
> [57] Lastly, could the landlord, if it wanted, occupy the premises without difficulty or objection or was there a substantial impediment to use of a substantial part of it? In my judgment, the landlord could not … At the very least the partitions would have to be removed, what appear to be the relatively substantial desks would have to be removed, the photocopier and the other chattels, the trunking and cabling.

**10.27** In *Riverside Park Ltd v NHS Property Services Ltd*,[36] the lease dated 24 September 2008 contained a break option which provided that any notice exercising the break would only be effective to determine the lease 'if the Tenant gives vacant possession of the Premises to the landlord on or before [the break date]'. Notice was given exercising the break clause and the tenant vacated the building. However, it left behind a large amount of partitioning, kitchen units, floor coverings, window blinds, an intruder

[35] Ibid, at [20].
[36] *Riverside Park Ltd v NHS Property Services Ltd* [2017] L&TR 12.

alarm and water stand pipes within a large meeting room (the 'Works') which had been installed previously under a licence for alterations. In addition, the tenant had failed to return a number of programmable key fobs which gave access to the premises and had not deactivated the intruder alarm. The landlord brought a claim for a declaration that the lease had not been determined by operation of the break clause, contending that the tenant had not satisfied the vacant possession condition. The tenant argued that the presence of the Works did not mean that vacant possession had not been given. Specifically, it was said that the Works could properly be seen as tenant's fixtures and fittings which either by operation of law and/or a proper construction of the lease and licence for works had been integrated into and formed part of the demised premises. Insofar as the Works did not comprise fixtures and fittings, the tenant argued that the presence did not substantially prevent or interfere with the landlord's enjoyment of the right to possession on the test enunciated in *Cumberland*.

**10.28** The judge, HHJ Saffman (sitting as a Deputy Judge of the High Court), rejected the landlord's claim insofar as it related to the key fobs and intruder alarm. On the evidence, he found that the alarm system did not really impede the landlord's occupation of the premises after the tenant's departure. Further any uncollected key fobs could be deactivated so as to render them useless. Thus, he said:

> [41] I have already mentioned the case of *Cumberland Consolidated Holdings*. That case enunciated two tests for vacant possession both identified and considered in *Expeditors*. The first was to ask whether the seller continues after completion to claim a right to use the premises for his own purposes. It does not strike me that the claimant asserts that this applies in this case save in so far as it alleges that the fact that some key fobs were not returned and the alarm may not have been deactivated can be seen as demonstrating a right by the defendant to use the Premises for its own purposes. Let me say that in this case I do not accept that because these key fobs are reprogrammable and access to the Premises can be terminated therefore at the press of a computer button but also because the evidence is that the fobs were not returned not because the Defendant was asserting a right to use the Premises but because it simply did not physically have in its possession all the fobs that had originally been issued. As for the alarm, I accept that if it was not deactivated that is more likely to have been an oversight than evidence of an intention to continue to exert some control over the Premises.

**10.29** As regards the Works, the judge focused on the partitioning, which he found constituted chattels. The unchallenged evidence given by the landlord's director was that the partitioning had resulted in a unique 'rabbit warren' configuration of the premises which no one else would want to adopt so that works would have to be undertaken to restore the premises to an open plan before they were marketed. On this basis, the judge was satisfied that the tenant had failed to deliver up vacant possession. He said:

> [63] I am satisfied that the partitions are, to quote Lord Greene MR in *Cumberland* 'an impediment which substantially prevents or interferes with the right of possession'. In addition, if one applies Lewison J's interpretation of that test they 'deprive the Claimant of the physical enjoyment of the Premises'. Equally I am satisfied on the test adopted by Rimer LJ in *NYK* that the existence of the partitions 'substantially prevents or interferes with the enjoyment of the right of possession.
>
> [64] I do not accept that because there is no specific evidence that the claimant cannot let the Premises to anybody else that it has failed to establish that its enjoyment of the Premises has

been compromised. In addition, I do not accept that the claimant's enjoyment of the Premises is affected by the fact that it was never their intention to occupy it themselves but rather to let it. In this context in my view the claimant's enjoyment of the Premises encompasses having it in a condition in which it feels that it is a more attractive proposition to prospective lessees. [The landlord's] unchallenged evidence on this … was clear that the configuration in which the Premises were left did not meet that criterion.

[66] In all the circumstances I am satisfied that, on the assumption that the Works do not form part of the Premises, the claimant has established that vacant possession was not given and that accordingly the break clause was ineffective.

### (d) Examples Where Vacant Possession Has Been Delivered Up

**10.30** In *Royal Bank of Canada v Secretary of State for Defence*,[37] the tenant had served a series of notices on the landlord in order to terminate the lease of certain premises in Aylesbury. The landlord contended that the tenant was in repudiatory breach of contract by failing to give vacant possession on the date of the expiry of one particular notice (which in fact required the landlord to take a surrender of part of the demise). As Lewison J recounted:[38]

[40] … in January 2003 [ie after the termination date] Mr Andrews inspected the premises. In the control room forming part of J2, he discovered various abandoned chattels. The biggest item appears to have been a fitted bench. Mr Andrews described it as fitted in the same way as a kitchen unit. It had been there since before the grant of the lease. That seems to me to be a landlord's fixture and therefore something that the defendant was obliged to yield up.

[41] In addition to the bench there was a camera tripod, two briefcases, a table covered with redundant equipment, a four drawer filing cabinet, a couple of boxes and a quantity of what appears from the photographs to be electrical cable. None of it looks unwieldy or difficult to move, although I heard no evidence about that.

**10.31** After referring to the *Cumberland* decision, Lewison J continued:[39]

The test according to this case is whether the obstruction is one that substantially prevents or impedes the enjoyment of the right to possession of a substantial part of the property. J2 is one of several buildings that were surrendered and the chattels could only be said to have impeded use of part of J2. Moreover, the ease and speed with which the chattels could have been removed is, in my judgment, relevant to this question. I consider that the quantity of chattels and their type left abandoned in the control room of J2 do not pass the test.

**10.32** Another example in which a tenant succeeded in establishing that it had delivered up vacant possession is to be found in *John Laing Construction Limited v Amber Pass Limited*.[40] In that case, the tenant sought a declaration that it had validly terminated a

[37] *Royal Bank of Canada v Secretary of State for Defence* [2004] 1 P&CR 28.

[38] *Royal Bank of Canada v Secretary of State for Defence* [2004] 1 P&CR 28, at [40]–[41].

[39] *Royal Bank of Canada v Secretary of State for Defence* [2004] 1 P&CR 28, at [43].

[40] *John Laing Construction Limited v Amber Pass Limited* [2004] 2 EGLR 128. The correctness of this decision was doubted by Lewison J in *Legal & General Assurance Society Ltd v Expeditors International (UK) Ltd* [2007] 1 P&CR 5, at [46], since none of the key authorities on the concept of vacant possession had been cited to Robert Hildyard QC. The reasoning in *Amber Pass*, insofar as it relates to the continued presence of

lease dated 17 October 1988 pursuant to the operation of a break clause. The landlord counterclaimed for a declaration that the tenant's break notice was invalid and the lease still subsisted. By the time the matter got to trial, it was common ground between the parties that the only issue to be decided was whether the tenant had 'yielded up ... the entirety of the demised premises' to the landlord. The tenant contended it had yielded up possession; whereas the landlord contended otherwise.

**10.33** The factual context in which the differences between the parties arose was as follows. In mid-2001, that is, some 13 years after the lease was granted, the tenant came to a decision that the premises no longer suited its requirements. This was not only because the premises were surplus to the tenant's needs, but also because there were ongoing problems with security there. Accordingly, the tenant began a gradual process of vacating the premises; and, indeed, on 13 November 2001, the tenant wrote to the landlord informing it that the premises had been almost completely vacated and enquiring whether the landlord would be prepared to discuss a surrender of the lease. The tenant's vacation of the premises exacerbated security problems. Consequently, the landlord suggested the provision of 24-hour security protection. The tenant agreed to this and, as a further security measure, caused additional fencing and barriers to be put in place at the premises. The landlord was kept fully informed of this and recognised the need for the fencing/barriers whilst the premises were vacant (and, in fact, approved it).

**10.34** On 13 December 2002, the tenant served a break notice expressing its desire to terminate the lease on 16 October 2003. On 17 October 2003, the landlord informed the tenant that it did not consider that the lease had been terminated because (inter alia) the tenant had not yielded up vacant possession. The landlord wrote: 'There are security personnel at the premises and fencing and concrete structures are still present. The keys to the premises have not been offered up'.

**10.35** Robert Hildyard QC (sitting as a Deputy Judge of the Chancery Division) first set out a number of legal principles, including the following:[41]

> (2) ... in adjudicating upon a claim of unilateral termination, unless any special form or process is prescribed, the task of the Court is to look objectively at what has occurred and determine whether a clear intention has been manifested by the person whose acts are said to have brought about a termination to effect such termination, and whether the landlord could, if it wanted to, occupy the premises without difficulty or objection.
>
> (3) Where the termination is asserted to have been brought about by the exercise of a contractual right the validity or effectiveness of which is denied a stand-off such has arisen is not surprising. Each side is likely to be wary of doing something which adds credence to the other's case. Equally, each may wish to take reasonable steps to ensure that if the Court finds against it at the end of the day it has not worsened its exposure. In such circumstances it is necessary to assess whether there is to be extrapolated from such matters as the retention of keys or the continued presence of security staff a conclusion that the tenant has not yielded up the

security guards, also appears inconsistent with the judgment of Rimer LJ in *NYK Logistics (UK) Ltd v Ibrend Estates BV* [2011] 4 All ER 539. However, in *Merton London Borough Council v Jones* [2009] 1 WLR 1269, at 1280B–80D, Wilson LJ expressly approved the observations of the learned deputy judge concerning a party's retention of keys.

[41] *John Laing Construction Limited v Amber Pass Limited* [2004] 2 EGLR 128, at [45].

premises; or whether, alternatively, such facts are explicable, and indeed (as seems to me plain in this case) explained, by reference not to any desire to retain the premises, but to a desire to avoid further financial exposure or to keep the premises safe and a recognition on the part of the tenant that the landlord will continue to assert the lease's continuance in any event.

(5) Retention of keys is an example. The fact of retention of keys (or the failure to return them) may be significant; but equally it may not be. All it may signify is (as in *Gray v Bompas*) an oversight or a desire to protect the premises both for the benefit of the defendant and in case the claimant might be found still to be liable, without in any way signifying any assertion of rights in respect of the property or being inconsistent with an effective termination of such rights (as in *Relvok v Dixon*).

10.36 With these principles in mind, Robert Hildyard QC found that the lease had been properly terminated. He said:[42]

(7) In this case, as it seems to me, it is plain that the continued possession of the keys to the Premises did not signify any intention on the part of the Claimant to assert any rights in respect of the Premises. There is no doubt, to my mind, that had the Defendant wanted the keys it would have been given them: the Claimant's desire to be shot of the Premises could scarcely be clearer and must have been well understood by the Defendant. Although in his Supplemental Witness Statement Mr Simon Pass of the Defendant states that had the keys been offered he would have accepted them, the Defendants' Solicitors' letter of 17th October 2003 makes plain that the Defendant would have continued to insist that the Claimant had not validly exercised the break option. I am in no real doubt that even had the keys been proffered the Defendant would have stuck to its line that the break clause had not been implemented, and that such a gesture on the part of the Claimant would have been futile (except, of course, in removing the main plank to which, in the event, the Defendant eventually resorted).

10.37 Then, he added the following:[43]

Whilst I do consider it would have been a wise precaution (as Willes J said it would also have been in *Gray v Bompas*) at least symbolically to have tendered the keys and required the defendant to elect whether or not to provide for security of the premises, I do not consider the fact that this was not done can have caused the defendant any confusion at all or for any other reason signified any intention on the part of the claimant to retain rather than terminate the lease. There was and is nothing to prevent the defendant occupying the premises: it simply has not wished to do so, and has resorted instead to a variety of strained arguments to seek to justify a stance which is unrealistic and untenable.

## PAYMENT OF RENT AND OTHER SUMS

### (a) The Meaning of 'Payment'

10.38 Another extremely common condition for the exercise of a break clause is that the rent and other sums due under the lease up to the termination date have been 'paid' in full (or words to similar effect).

[42] *John Laing Construction Limited v Amber Pass Limited* [2004] 2 EGLR 128, at [45].
[43] *John Laing Construction Limited v Amber Pass Limited* [2004] 2 EGLR 128, at [47].

**10.39** Frequently, the lease will contain a definition of what is meant by 'paid' in this context, eg in cleared funds by way of bank transfer. Equally, however, there may be no definition of 'paid' at all. In these circumstances, it is necessary to consider the general law as to what is required of a creditor obliged to 'pay' a sum of money to a debtor. This is because, if there has been no 'payment' until (say) the day after the specified termination date, then the right to break the lease will have been lost.

**10.40** On general principles, 'the landlord should have the rent in cash in his hands by the due date'.[44] This reflects the common law rule that 'a creditor must pay his debt by a tender of legal currency and a cheque is not legal currency'.[45] This is well-illustrated by *Pennington v Crossley & Sons Ltd*.[46] In that case, a cheque sent by post as payment for the price of goods was purloined in the course of post and cashed by a thief. The seller, having received nothing, sued for the price. Lord Esher MR said in his judgment:[47]

> the action was for goods sold and delivered to the defendants. The only defence was payment. The defendants had not in fact paid the plaintiff anything. It was said that having posted a cheque properly addressed to the plaintiff, and the cheque having been honoured, the defendants had paid the plaintiff. That was a strong proposition. In *Norman v Ricketts* (1886) 3 TLR 182 there was what amounted to a request to send a cheque by post and the court held that the posting of the cheque was payment. There was no such request here. It was said that the proper inference from the course of business between the plaintiff and the defendants was that there was a request to the defendants to send a cheque by post, and that the plaintiff would run the risk of the cheque miscarrying in the transit. What was that course of business? Independently of any arrangement, the defendants sent to the plaintiff cheques by post on the various sales, together with a form of receipt to be signed by him. Did not that mean that the plaintiff was to send back the receipt when the cheque was received by him? Was there any course of business which showed that putting the cheque in the post was to be taken as a delivery of the cheque to the plantiff? The only facts were that the defendants always sent cheques by post, and that when the plaintiff received them he sent back the receipt duly signed. It would be most monstrous to infer from those circumstances a request to send a cheque by post and that the plaintiff would consider that he had received it as soon as it was posted.

**10.41** However, the general common law rule will not apply where there is 'an express or implied agreement to the contrary'.[48] As Shaw LJ said in *Beevers v Mason*:[49]

> This requirement [ie that the landlord should have the rent in cash in his hands by the due date] may, however, be waived by express arrangement, or by necessary implication where the facts are sufficiently strong to establish that the landlord has shown that he is content to accept payment by cheque posted by the due date of payment. Inferences of this nature are not to be too readily drawn, but, where the facts support them clearly and emphatically, they are not to be dismissed.

[44] *Beevers v Mason* (1978) 37 P&CR 452, at 458, per Shaw LJ.

[45] *Avocet Industrial Estates LLP v Merol Ltd* [2012] L&TR 13, at [49], per Morgan J.

[46] *Pennington v Crossley & Sons Ltd* (1897) 13 TLR 513.

[47] *Pennington v Crossley & Sons Ltd* (1897) 13 TLR 513, at 514.

[48] *Avocet Industrial Estates LLP v Merol Ltd* [2012] L&TR 13, at [50].

[49] *Beevers v Mason* (1978) 37 P&CR 452, at 458–59; and see also *Polglass v Oliver* (1831) 2 Cr&J 15; *Sopwith v Stutchberry* (1985) 17 HLR 50; *Official Solicitor v Thomas* [1986] 2 EGLR 1; *Luttenberger v North Thoresby Farms Ltd* [1992] 1 EGLR 261 (Court of Appeal) and [1993] 1 EGLR 3 (Ferris J); *Hannaford v Smallacombe* [1994] 1 EGLR 9; *Homes v Smith* [2000] Lloyd's Rep Bank 139; and *Day v Coltrane* [2003] 1 WLR 1379.

**10.42** In *Avocet Industrial Estates LLP v Merol Ltd*,[50] Morgan J explained that an agreement to depart from the common law rule may be inferred from conduct. He gave the following example:

> A common course of conduct which is considered in the cases is where there has been a practice of a party making periodical payments by cheque and where the cheques have been accepted.

**10.43** However, the learned judge also warned (with added emphasis).[51]

> it will normally be easier to show that a particular course of dealing justifies that finding [viz. that the course of dealing between the parties has displaced the common law rule requiring tender of currency] than it will be to show that a particular course of dealing justifies the *further* finding that, *not only* is tender by cheque acceptable, *but that* the date of the posting of the cheque is the date of payment and that the risk of loss in the post is on the creditor and not the debtor.

**10.44** In *Avocet* itself, the break clause provided that the break notice was to be of no effect if 'at the Break Date the Tenant [had] not paid to the Landlord a sum equal to 6 months annual rent'. On 11 August 2009, the tenant served on the landlord a break notice seeking to determine the lease on 17 March 2010. On 16 March 2010, the tenant delivered by hand to the landlord a cheque drawn in the amount of the break premium. One of the questions for the court was whether the course of dealing between the parties up to 16 March 2010 displaced the common law rule requiring a tender of currency and permitted a tender by cheque. On the facts, Morgan J found that, at all times up to and including 16 March 2010, there was an implied agreement that the landlord would accept payment by cheque of sums due under the lease; and that, as a consequence, the landlord was not entitled to reject the tender of the tenant's cheque on 16 March 2010.

### (b) The Amount of Rent Required to be Paid

**10.45** There are now a significant number of authorities in which the court has had to consider whether, in circumstances where a break notice expires, or a break date falls, part-way through a rental period, the tenant nonetheless has to pay the full period's rent in order to make the break effective. Although each of those cases turned on the particular wording of the lease in question, the general trend of authority clearly demonstrates that, in such circumstances, the full period's rent is payable.[52] However, this is subject to an important exception which emerges from the decision of the Supreme Court in *Marks and Spencer Plc v BNP Paribas Securities Trust Company (Jersey) Ltd*.[53]

**10.46** The first authority (although not strictly about a break clause) is *Ellis v Rowbotham*.[54] In that case, premises were let for one year from 10 June 1898 at a

[50] *Avocet Industrial Estates LLP v Merol Ltd* [2012] L&TR 13, at [50].

[51] *Avocet Industrial Estates LLP v Merol Ltd* [2012] L&TR 13, at [55].

[52] *Jervis v Pillar Denton Ltd* [2015] Ch 87, at [7], per Lewison LJ.

[53] *Marks and Spencer Plc v BNP Paribas Securities Trust Company (Jersey) Ltd* [2015] UKSC 72 (discussed at **10.67–10.71** below).

[54] *Ellis v Rowbotham* [1900] 1 QB 740 (cited with approval in *Canas Property Co Ltd v K L Television Ltd* [1970] 2 QB 433, at 442D, per Lord Denning MR; and in *Marks and Spencer Plc v BNP Paribas Securities Trust Company (Jersey) Ltd* [2015] UKSC 72, at [44], per Lord Neuberger).

total rent of £357. The agreement provided that the tenant was to pay, before taking possession, a sum which was a little over 50 per cent of the total rent and was to pay the remainder of the rent by three equal instalments on 10 September 1898, 10 December 1898 and 10 March 1899. The tenant paid the initial sum and the instalment due on 10 September 1898. He did not pay the instalment due on 10 December 1898. The landlord forfeited the tenancy on 2 March 1899. The landlord sued for the full amount of the instalment due on 10 December 1898. The tenant contended that he was only liable to pay an amount calculated by apportioning the sum of £357 on a daily basis for the period 10 June 1898 to 2 March 1899 and taking credit for the payments made. The tenant contended that this result was produced by the Apportionment Act 1870. The Court of Appeal dismissed this argument, holding that the 1870 Act only applied to sums payable in arrears.

**10.47** In *Capital and City Holdings Ltd v Dean Warburg Ltd*,[55] the issue was whether the reddendum to a lease meant that the tenant had to pay the entire quarter's rent, irrespective of whether there was a forfeiture terminating the lease during the quarter. It was held by the Court of Appeal that it did.

**10.48** The reddendum in question provided as follows:

> yielding and paying therefor during the term … yearly (and proportionately for any part of a year) the rent which shall be payable by equal quarterly payments in advance on the quarter days, the first of such payments or a proportionate part thereof to be due on the date specified in the particulars and to be in respect of the period therein mentioned.

**10.49** Ralph Gibson LJ (with whom Nicholls LJ agreed) said this:[56]

> The term was from July 7, 1987 to June 23, 1991. The quarter days were stated to be March 25, June 24, September 29, and December 25, in each year. The tenant covenanted to pay the rent at the times and in the manner provided. [Counsel for the respondents] argued that, despite the clear obligation to pay a quarter's rent on December 25, 1987, the words 'proportionately for any part of a year' and 'or a proportionate part thereof' caused that liability to be reduced by the serving of the writ. I do not agree. It seems to me that the references to the proportionate part of a year were included to deal with the fact that the term commenced on July 7, and called for a proportionate payment down to the first following quarter day. The presence of those words does not, in my judgment, modify in any way the obligation imposed by the lease on the tenant to pay a full quarter's rent on December 25, 1987.

**10.50** The next case is *Re a Company (No 0005945 of 2006)*,[57] which concerned an application to restrain the presentation of a winding-up petition for unpaid rent. The issue was whether or not rent was payable for periods after the relevant lease had been terminated under a break clause, which provided:

> If the tenant wishes to determine this lease and gives to the landlord not less than nine months' written notice within five working days of either the third or sixth anniversary of this lease and that with and up to the time of the determination pays the lease rents and substantially performs and observes the covenants contained in this lease, then on expiry of the notice

[55] *Capital and City Holdings Ltd v Dean Warburg Ltd* [1989] EGLR 90.
[56] *Capital and City Holdings Ltd v Dean Warburg Ltd* [1989] EGLR 90, at 92D–92F.
[57] *Re a Company (No 0005945 of 2006)* [2007] BPIR 1.

[and there is a redundant word 'of' at least in one copy of the clause] the term is to cease and determine immediately but without prejudice to any rights or remedies that may have accrued.

10.51 Pumfrey J held[58] that he was:

> constrained for the reasons given by Ralph Gibson LJ [in *Dean Warburg*] to hold that it is not possible to apportion the rent to a lesser period than a quarter on expiry of the term whenever that term expires in any quarter following a quarter day on which payment of the rent has been made.

10.52 In *Quirkco Investments Ltd v Aspray Transport Ltd*,[59] HHJ Keyser QC (sitting as Judge of the High Court, Chancery Division) had to consider (inter alia) whether or not, on the assumption that a lease had been validly terminated on 18 December 2010 by operation of a break clause, the tenant could claim for the repayment of rent attributable to the remainder of the December quarter.

10.53 The reddendum of the lease in *Quirkco* provided as follows:

> [YIELDING AND PAYING therefor ...]
>
> 2.2 From and including 18 December 2000 the yearly rent of eighty-five thousand two hundred and twenty-two pounds (£85,222) ... and so in proportion for any period less than a year such yearly rent to be payable by four equal quarterly payments in advance on the usual quarter days in every year without any deduction whatsoever.

10.54 The break clause provided:

> 6.11.1 The Lessee or the Lessor may determine this Lease on 18 December 2010 by serving on the other not less than 9 months prior written notice expiring on that day
>
> 6.11.2 This Lease shall only determine as a result of notice served by the Lessee under this sub-clause if at the time of expiring of such notice:
>
> 6.11.2.1 there are no arrears of any rents reserved or any other sums payable under this Lease.

10.55 HHJ Keyser QC followed the Court of Appeal in *Dean Warburg*, regarding the case as decisive. He held that the words of apportionment in the reddendum dealt merely with the liability of the tenant at the beginning of the term. He said:[60]

> [61] The claim at point (3) rests on the contention that, upon the determination of the lease on 18th December 2010 pursuant to the valid exercise of the option under the break clause, the lessee became entitled to restitution of that part of the rent paid in advance on the previous quarter day which was attributable to the few days of the quarter that post-dated the determination of the lease. That entitlement is said to arise either as a matter of the true construction of clause 2.2 of the lease or under the general law of unjust enrichment – presumably on the ground of failure of consideration.
>
> [62] No authority was cited in direct support of the defendant's contention. The reason for that, in my judgment, is that the contention is unsound.
>
> [63] The common law does not permit apportionment of rent in respect of time. The Apportionment Act 1870 does not affect the date on which rent is payable and does not authorise

[58] *Re a Company (No 0005945 of 2006)* [2007] BPIR 1, at [16].
[59] *Quirkco Investments Ltd v Aspray Transport Ltd* [2012] L&TR 19.
[60] *Quirkco Investments Ltd v Aspray Transport Ltd* [2012] L&TR 19, at [61]–[64].

apportionment in respect of time of rent payable in advance. The general principle is that rent payable in advance is payable in full on the due date, notwithstanding that the lease subsequently determines before the expiry of its term: see, for example, *Ellis v Rowbotham* [1900] 1 QB 740 and *Canas Property Co v KL Television Services* [1970] 2 QB 433. I do not consider that the case of termination of a lease by the lessee's exercise of a contractual option is properly to be treated differently; rights of restitution for failure of consideration do not depend on the absence of fault of the claimant: see, for example, *Dies v British and International Mining and Finance Corporation* [1939] 1 KB 724. The landlord's entitlement to recover as rent the full amount due in advance, notwithstanding the subsequent termination of the lease before the expiry of the term, is sufficiently explained by the fact that the contractual obligation to pay the rent had accrued before termination and that the law of unjust enrichment does not operate to circumvent the scheme of obligations and entitlements contained in a valid contract.

[64] A claim for recovery of the rent referable to the period between the termination of the lease and the end of the quarter must therefore rest on the terms of the lease itself. Clause 2.2 is set out in paragraph 9, above. [Counsel for the tenant] relies particularly on the words: 'and so in proportion for any period less than a year'. In my judgment the words will not bear that reliance.

[*The judge then referred to Dean Warburg and quoted from the judgment of Peter Gibson LJ.*]

Similarly in the present case, the term of the lease was from 18th December 2000 until 17th December 2015 and the rent was due on the usual quarter days. I consider that the words relied on by [Counsel for the tenant] do no more than deal with the fact that the commencement and expiry of the term did not coincide with the quarter days, so that proportionate payments would be required at either end of the lease. No such proportionate payment would be required in respect of the break clause, because the validity of the exercise of the option under that clause would not be capable of ascertainment at the preceding quarter day and because the lease makes no provision for a proportionate payment or for the pro rata recovery of any moneys attributable to the period after the expiry of the notice under the break clause.

10.56 In *PCE Investors Limited v Cancer Research UK*,[61] the tenant held premises pursuant to a lease granted for a term expiring on 27 September 2014, subject to a break clause exercisable on 11 October 2010 ('the Termination Date'). By clause 3 of the lease, the property was demised for a yearly rent of £190,000 payable as follows:

by equal quarterly payments in advance on the usual quarter day in every year the first such payment to be made on the rent Commencement Date and to be in respect of the period from and including the Rent Commencement Date until the next following quarter day.

10.57 The break clause provided as follows:

The Tenant may determine this Underlease on the expiration of the fifth year of the term ('the Termination Date') by satisfying the following conditions:

The Tenant must have served not less than 6 months prior written notice to determine on the Landlord; and

The Tenant must have paid the rents reserved and demanded by this Lease up to the Termination Date.

10.58 The tenant gave the necessary notice, but the landlord said it was not effective to break the lease because it (the tenant) had not (inter alia) paid a full quarter's rent on 29 September 2010, but had only paid rent apportioned up to the termination date.

[61] *PCE Investors Limited v Cancer Research UK* [2012] 2 P&CR 5.

**10.59** Peter Smith J held that the lease did require a full quarter's rent to be paid, even though, if the break was effective, the tenant would only have the right to use the premises for 13 days of the quarter beginning on 29 September 2010. He said (with emphasis in the original):[62]

> [29] It seems to me that the most important matter from a business point of view is certainty. The tenant will want to know precisely what obligations fall on him during the lease and upon its termination. The case for the Tenant is of course that once it has given the notice its [sic] only obligated to pay the rent for the period which ran from the usual September quarter day to the Termination Date.
>
> [35] On 29th September 2010 whilst the Underlease was still subsisting an obligation fell to pay the next quarter of the annual rent. Obviously that extended to the period ending on 25th December 2010 but the obligation subsisted at the time that the rent fell due on 29th September 2010. That is an obligation that is reserved under clause 11.2 and is due on that date. On that date of course it cannot be said with certainty that the Underlease will terminate on 11th October 2010. The Tenant might be in breach of some other provision. That can only be determined after the event and I cannot see that it is right as a matter of construction that the clear obligation on 29th September 2010 to pay a full quarter's rent can somehow be retrospectively reduced merely because an event after that date operates to terminate the Underlease *from that future date*. It is true that the obligation is to pay the rents up to the Termination Date but that does not in my view assist the Tenant. A quarter's rent fell due on 29th September 2010. I do not accept that those words make it unnecessary if the intention was that rents related to a period after the Termination Date needed to be paid.
>
> [36] Conversely it seems to me that the simple straightforward construction namely that all obligations under the lease subsist until an actual termination of it is anything other than a sensible business sense. A Tenant knows precisely what it has to do. If for example the Tenant tendered the short rent (as happened here) and for some reason the Underlease did not terminate it would become under an obligation to make up the shortfall and would on this analysis be retrospectively in breach of the obligation to pay the full quarter on 29th September 2010. That seems to me to be the type of uncertainty which a businessman would find unsatisfactory.

**10.60** The learned judge concluded as follows:[63]

> In my view the position on the construction of the Underlease is quite clear. A full quarter's rent fell due on the September Quarter Day. That was payable in advance and on that day it could not be certain that the lease would terminate on the Termination Date. There is a commercial and sensible certainty in requiring all obligations to operate until the very date of termination but not be retrospectively changed if an early termination occurs. For the Tenant to succeed it seems to me that the obligation to pay rent on the September Quarter Day as contended for by it requires the Underlease to be rewritten to include a variation of covenant 4.1 of the tenant's covenants to read 'to pay the yearly rent as reserved herein … unless this Underlease is subsequently terminated after the days when rent was payable in advance.' I can see no justification for any such rewriting of the Underlease. There is no ambiguity and no difficulty in my view.

**10.61** In *Canonical UK Ltd v TST Millbank LLC*,[64] the tenant served notice on the landlord to terminate a lease dated 15 February 2007 pursuant to a break clause on

[62] *PCE Investors Limited v Cancer Research UK* [2012] 2 P&CR 5, at [29], [35]–[36].
[63] *PCE Investors Limited v Cancer Research UK* [2012] 2 P&CR 5, at [54].
[64] *Canonical UK Ltd v TST Millbank LLC* [2013] L&TR 15.

22 August 2012 (ie part-way through the June quarter). One issue was whether the whole June quarter's rent was payable.

**10.62** The reddendum in the lease provided:

> The Landlord at the request of the Guarantor demises unto the Tenant all that the Premises ... To hold the Premises unto the Tenant ... for the Term ... Yielding and paying therefor:
>
> First yearly and proportionately for any part of a year the Yearly Rent specified in paragraph 8 of the Particulars (subject to review in accordance with Schedule 6) by equal quarterly payments to be made in advance on the usual quarter days in every year the first such payment or a proportionate part thereof (being a proportionate payment in respect of the period commencing on the Rent Commencement Date specified in paragraph 9 of the Particulars and ending on the day before the next succeeding quarter day) to be paid on the Rent Commencement Date.

**10.63** The break clause was worded as follows:

> 8.1 If the Tenant wishes to determine this lease at any time up to and including 15 February 2013 (the 'Break Period') and gives to the Landlord not less than 6 months' prior written notice to that effect (the date of expiry of the said notice during the Break Period being deemed the 'Break Date') and provided that the Tenant –
>
> 8.1.1 has paid the Yearly Rent and other monies reserved as rent under clause 3 of this Lease up to and including the Break Date.

**10.64** The tenant argued that, on a proper construction of the reddendum and the break clause, the words 'yearly and proportionately for any part of a year' were to be construed as meaning that the payment to be made up to the service of the break notice was only up to the date of termination. By contrast, the landlord argued that the, on a true construction, a full quarter's rent was due on 24 June 2012. The landlord said that, since Dean Warburg, the cases concerning similarly worded leases had been clear: rent was payable in full whether or not there had been a termination during the quarter.

**10.65** Vos J decided that the landlord's arguments were correct. After going through the authorities set out above, he said:[65]

> [27] ... Left to my own devices and free of any authority, I would hold that the words, 'yearly and proportionately for any part of a year' in the reddendum in this case refer to both the beginning and end of the lease, since in this case the lease was to expire by effluxion of time in the middle of a quarter. The question then is whether those words apply also to a quarter in which a break-date falls. There is no binding authority here because (1) *Capital & City* was a case about forfeiture and the termination was unknown as at the quarter-day, and (2) *PCE* is only persuasive authority, and the reddendum there had no similar words of apportionment. The break-clause was also not identical.
>
> [28] As it seems to me, however, the condition in the new break-clause cannot be used to alter the meaning of the reddendum because it is just that, a condition. It simply says that, 'Provided the tenant has paid the yearly rent up to and including the break-date' the lease shall terminate. It does not say, although it could have, that if a break notice is served, only an apportioned part of the rent payable for the quarter in which it expires is payable. The reddendum on the other hand is clear; it says that on each quarter-day a quarter's rent must be paid, the apportionment

[65] *Canonical UK Ltd v TST Millbank LLC* [2013] L&TR 15, at [27]–[28], [30].

wording allowing a reduction where the term starts or expires in the middle. I thought, when the argument commenced, that the service of a break notice might be regarded as representing the state of affairs established by the parties as prevailing as at the quarter-day, so that they could be taken to have assumed, a notice having been served, that the lease would end on 22nd August 2012. That seems now to me to be too simplistic. It is wrong to say that either state of affairs is prevailing. A notice has been served identifying the tenant's wish to terminate as at 22nd August 2012, but the tenant may if it wishes not comply with the conditions in the break-clause in which case the notice would have no effect. It would be as if it had been written in water. Neither can it be assumed that the conditions will not be complied with. It is simply unknown whether the lease will end in the middle of the quarter, just as it was in *Capital & City*. Thus the words must be given their natural meaning, assuming nothing. Assuming nothing, the reddendum requires a quarter's rent to be paid on the midsummer quarter-day. The words 'proportionately for any part of a year' even taken together with the provisions of the break clause cannot be taken as reducing the rent otherwise payable after a break notice has been served, just because the lease may end in the middle of that quarter ...

[30] The outcome seems harsh on the tenant, but in reality it should not be regarded as harsh, because the meaning of such clauses was reasonably well known even before the lease was entered into. Business certainty is, as Peter Smith J said [in *PCE Investors*], important. The effect of the break-clause is simply unknown as at the quarter-day and in my judgment the full quarter's rent must be paid leaving it to be later determined whether the excess rent is repayable. The alternative construction leads to uncertainty not only as to what will happen on 22nd August 2012 but also as to how the balance of the quarter's rent will be paid if the lease does not terminate.

**10.66** It may be noted that permission to appeal was given in both *PCE Investors* and *Canonical* (although both cases settled before the appeals were concluded).

**10.67** All of the above cases were reviewed by Morgan J in *Marks and Spencer Plc v BNP Paribas Securities Services Trust Co (Jersey) Ltd.*[66] In that case, the lease demised certain premises in Paddington for a term and at a rent, in the following terms:

To hold them to the Tenant for a term of years starting on 25 January 2006 and ending on 2 February 2018 paying during the Term by way of Rent:

(a) the basic rent ... paid yearly and proportionately for any part of a year by equal quarterly instalments in advance on the Quarter days the first payment to be made on 24 July 2007 in respect of the period from that date to the next Quarter day ...
(b) the Car park Licence Fee which shall be paid by equal quarterly instalments in advance on the Quarter days the first payment to be made on 25 January 2006 in respect of the period from that date to the day before the next Quarter Day.

**10.68** The tenant had the benefit of an option to determine the lease on 24 January 2012, conditional on certain matters. One of those matters was that, on or prior to the break date, the tenant paid to the landlord the sum of £919,800 plus VAT. On 7 July 2011, the tenant served on the landlord a notice pursuant to the break clause. The notice was expressed to determine the lease on 24 January 2012. The tenant paid the sum of £919,800 plus VAT on 18 January 2012. At trial, the tenant expressly accepted that it was obliged to pay a full quarter's rent on December 25, 2011. That was because 'on that date, it could

[66] *Marks and Spencer Plc v BNP Paribas Securities Services Trust Co (Jersey) Ltd* [2013] L&TR 31.

not be said with certainty that the lease would determine on January 24, 2012 as there were conditions that remained to be performed' (ie the payment of £919,800 plus VAT).[67] As to this, Morgan J said the following:[68]

> [27] I will begin by disregarding the existence of the break clause and by considering instead the amount of Basic Rent which would be payable on the last quarter day before the lease determines by effluxion of time on February 2, 2018. The last quarter day before that date would be December 25, 2017. I consider that the amount of Basic Rent payable on December 25, 2017 would be a proportionate part for the period from December 25, 2017 to February 2, 2018. I consider that this result would be clearly produced by the presence of the words 'proportionately for any part of a year' in the reservation of the rent. Indeed, even if these words had not appeared, the court would reach the same result following the common sense view expressed in *York v Casey* [1998] 2 EGLR 25 at 28A–B per Peter Gibson LJ. It follows from this that on the last quarter day before the term would expire by effluxion of time, the tenant does not have to pay a full quarter's rent and so there would not be a need for a tenant having paid a full quarter's rent to seek to recover an alleged overpayment in relation to the period after February 2, 2018.
>
> [28] I now turn to consider the position as to the Basic Rent payable at December 25, 2011. At that date, the claimant had served a notice to determine the lease pursuant to the break clause on January 24, 2012. If it had been certain as at December 25, 2011 that the term would end on January 24, 2012, then I consider that the tenant would have been in the same position as discussed above as at December 25, 2017, ie the tenant would have been obliged to pay only an apportioned part of a quarter's rent for the period from December 25, 2011 to January 24, 2012. However, the break clause in this case was conditional not only on there being no arrears of Basic Rent on the break date but was also conditional on the tenant paying [a break premium] on or prior to the break date. This sum had not been paid by December 25, 2011. Accordingly, it was not certain on December 25, 2011 that the term would end on January 24, 2012. Judged as at December 25, 2011 all one could say would be that the term might or might not end on January 24, 2012. Prima facie the amount of the Basic Rent payable on December 25, 2011 would be a full quarter's rent. The only possible alternatives to this would be either an apportioned part for the period to January 24, 2012 or no rent (on the ground that one did not know when the lease would end). If the first of those alternatives were right, it would be far from clear when the balance of the quarter's rent would be payable if the term did not end on January 24, 2012. The second alternative seems most improbable, allowing the tenant to defer payment of rent until it became clear what sum was in the end due. I consider that the true interpretation of the lease was that, in a case where one could not say on December 25, 2011 whether the term would end on January 24, 2012, that a full quarter's rent was payable on that date. This conclusion is consistent with the decisions at first instance in *PCE* and *Canonical* and indeed that conclusion is not challenged by the claimant in the present case.

**10.69** The central issue which Morgan J had to determine at trial was whether the tenant was entitled to be repaid by the landlord the part of the quarter's rent for the period from 24 January 2012–24 March 2012. On that issue, the learned judge's decision was overturned by the Court of Appeal.[69] However, the Court of Appeal did not

[67] *Marks and Spencer Plc v BNP Paribas Securities Services Trust Co (Jersey) Ltd* [2013] L&TR 31, at [16]. (The tenant went on to contend that it was entitled to be repaid by the landlord the part of the quarter's rent for the period from 24 January 2012–24 March 2012. This aspect of the case is considered in Chapter 11.)

[68] *Marks and Spencer Plc v BNP Paribas Securities Services Trust Co (Jersey) Ltd* [2013] L&TR 31, at [27]–[28].

[69] *Marks and Spencer Plc v BNP Paribas Securities Services Trust Co (Jersey) Ltd* [2014] L&TR 26.

disapprove of the above remarks regarding the liability of the tenant to pay the full quarter's rent on 25 December 2011. On the contrary, Arden LJ said:[70]

> The words 'proportionately for any part of a year' in the reddendum might at first sight be read as meaning that there should be an implied term for repayment of the rent for the broken period once the break premium has been paid and termination has taken place. But those words are in my judgment only applicable to a payment of rent for a broken period within the original term of the lease. So they do not apply in a case such as the present when on the last quarter day there was no certainty as to whether termination would take place on the break date.

10.70 The decision of the Court of Appeal was upheld by the Supreme Court.[71] In so doing, the Supreme Court nonetheless agreed with the approach taken by Morgan J as to the amount of rent which the tenant had to pay on 25 December 2011. The analysis of Lord Neuberger merits careful reading. He explained (with added emphasis):[72]

> A further point on which the claimant relies arises from the fact that the Basic Rent is stipulated in the Lease to be 'paid yearly *and proportionately for any part of a year* by equal quarterly instalments in advance' (emphasis added). It is common ground that the effect of the italicised words is that, if the Lease had run its full course to 2 February 2018, the tenant would only have had to pay an apportioned part of the Basic Rent due on 25 December 2017, because, as at that date, the parties would have known that the Lease would expire before the next quarter day, 25 March 2018. In the present case, it is common ground that, because the claimant had not paid the sum of £919,800 plus VAT due under clause 8.4 before 25 December 2011, it would not have been known as at that date whether the Lease would come to an end before 25 March 2012, and the tenant therefore had to pay the quarter's rent in full: it only became clear that the Lease would determine on 24 January 2012 when the claimant paid the £919,800 plus VAT on 18 January. *However, if the claimant had paid the £919,800 plus VAT before 25 December 2011, the claimant argues (rightly in my view) that it would have been clear on 25 December 2011 that the Lease would end on 24 January 2012, so that the claimant would only have had to pay an appropriate proportion of the Basic Rent on 25 December 2011.*

10.71 Lord Neuberger's comment in the second set of parentheses is important. It means that, if at the point that rent falls to be paid, it is 'clear' that the lease will determine on the break date (ie because there are no further conditions to be performed), then depending on the wording of the lease in question, the tenant may only be required to pay an appropriate proportion of rent for the period in question in order to exercise the break.

### (c) The Payment of Other Sums

10.72 Although the payment of rent is a commonplace precondition for the successful exercise of a break clause, it cannot be assumed that 'rent' means just the passing rent. The lease may give 'rent' an extended meaning (eg to include interest, insurance premiums or service charges). In addition the break clause may use a more general word

[70] *Marks and Spencer Plc v BNP Paribas Securities Services Trust Co (Jersey) Ltd* [2014] L&TR 26, at [40].
[71] *Marks and Spencer Plc v BNP Paribas Securities Services Trust Co (Jersey) Ltd* [2015] UKSC 72.
[72] *Marks and Spencer Plc v BNP Paribas Securities Services Trust Co (Jersey) Ltd* [2015] UKSC 72, at [53].

or phrase such as 'all monies due hereunder'. There is no substitute for a close scrutiny of the language used in the lease. Recent cases reveal that the language used may create a trap for the unwary tenant.

10.73 In *Quirkco*,[73] the tenant's break clause was subject to various conditions, including that, at the time of expiry of the break notice, there were 'no arrears of any rents reserved or any sums payable under this Lease'. On 8 March 2010, the tenant served a break notice on the landlord seeking to determine the lease on 18 December 2010. The landlord contended that the break notice was of no effect, because at the date of expiry of the notice, two of the conditions in the break clause were not satisfied: first, it was said that the tenant was in arrears of rent, in particular insurance rent; second, it was said that the tenant was in material breach of its repairing covenants under the lease.

10.74 Clause 2.3 of the lease provided for the tenant to pay the following by way of insurance rent:

> Within 14 days of written demand therefor and by way of further additional yearly rent without any deduction such yearly sum or sums ('the Insurance Charge') (and so in proportion for any part of a year) as the Lessor may from time to time expend in insuring and keeping insured the demised premises in accordance with Clause 5.1.

10.75 Further, clause 5.1.1 contained the following landlord's covenants in respect of insurance:

> That the Lessor will at all times during the term … insure and keep insured with reputable insurers the demised premises … against loss or damage by the Insured Risks in such amount as shall from time to time represent the full rebuilding or reinstatement value of the demised premises with provision for inflation to cover the period of rebuilding or reinstatement … and will whenever reasonably required produce to the Lessee the policy or policies of such insurance or other sufficient evidence of the nature extent ant terms thereof and the receipt for or other evidence of the payment of the last premium for the same.

10.76 The landlord arranged insurance cover for its commercial properties through insurance brokers and had for some years taken out a single policy of insurance with Zurich Insurance Plc in respect of all those properties. The relevant renewal date for that policy was 30 November 2010. On 9 November 2010, the broker sent to the claimant the schedule to the policy relating to the Property. On 23 November 2003 the claimant sent to the defendant an invoice for £3,609.72 in respect of 'Insurance Premium for the period 1st December 2010 to 30th November 2011'. The invoice was dated 1 December 2010. In fact, the renewal premium had not actually been paid by the landlord to the insurer on 1 December 2010. Rather, it was paid on 15 December 2010. The tenant did not pay the invoice. Holding that the tenant was not liable to do so, HHJ Keyser QC said as follows:[74]

> I hold that on its true construction cl.2.3 of the lease permits the landlord to serve a demand for payment of the insurance charge only in respect of such sums as it has already paid in insuring the Property in accordance with cl.5.1. As at the date of the demand, which I shall take to be December 1, 2010, the claimant had not paid any sums in insuring the Property.

[73] *Quirkco Investments Ltd v Aspray Transport Ltd* [2012] L&TR 19.
[74] *Quirkco Investments Ltd v Aspray Transport Ltd* [2012] L&TR 19, at [28].

In my judgment, therefore, the demand was invalidly served and did not give rise to a liability on the part of the defendant to pay the insurance charge before the expiry of the Notice under the break clause.

10.77 In *Avocet* (supra)[75] the lease was granted on 17 March 2005 for a term of 10 years. The tenant had an option to determine the lease on 17 March 2010 on giving to the landlord not less than three months' notice of its desire to exercise the break. The break clause was very detailed and laid down a number of particular requirements as to the validity of the break notice. In particular, clause 45.4.4 stated that the break notice should be of no effect if 'at the Break Date any payment under this lease due to have been paid on or before that date, has not been paid'.

10.78 Under clause 14.1 of the lease, the tenant had covenanted to pay default interest as follows:

> If any annual rent or any other money payable under this Lease has not been paid by the date it is due, whether it has been formally demanded or not, the Tenant shall pay the Landlord interest at the Default Interest Rate (both before and after any judgment) on that amount for the period from the due date to and including the date of payment.

10.79 The tenant duly served a break notice on 11 August 2009, intimating a desire to terminate the lease on the break date (ie 17 March 2010). The landlord challenged the validity of the break notice on numerous grounds, including that: (i) the tenant was liable to pay default interest on rental arrears under clause 14.1 even without the landlord having demanded payment of a sum by way of default interest; and (ii) the tenant's failure to pay such default interest was fatal to the exercise of the break clause. The sum due as default interest for late payments in the period from 12 August 2009 to 17 March 2010 was modest, calculated at about £130.

10.80 Morgan J decided this point in favour of the landlord, so that the break notice was invalid. He explained:[76]

> [94] … Default interest is payable under cl.14.1 when the conditions identified in cl.14.1 are satisfied. Default interest accrues and is payable from day to day. When the liability to pay has accrued, then default interest is due. When default interest is due in this way, it is a payment due to have been made for the purposes of cl.45.4.4 and the time for payment is from day to day as it accrues.
>
> [96] I fully recognise that the combined effect of cl.14.1, as I have construed it, and cl.45.4.4 represents something of a trap for a tenant. This is well illustrated by the way in which the landlord put its case. It searched through its records for the preceding five years of the term and identified every single late payment and then calculated default interest throughout that period. It then contended that the non payment of this default interest meant that the tenant had failed to operate the break clause. This was said to be so even where the landlord had not demanded payment of the default interest. I also recall the decision of the Court of Appeal in *Bass Holdings Ltd v Morton Music Ltd* [1988] Ch 493 where the court rejected a possible literal construction of a condition in an option agreement and distinguished between subsisting breaches of covenant and spent breaches of covenant because to do otherwise would have

[75] *Avocet Industrial Estates LLP v Merol Ltd* [2012] L&TR 13.
[76] *Avocet Industrial Estates LLP v Merol Ltd* [2012] L&TR 13, at [94], [96].

> produced a condition with which the grantee of the option would find it virtually impossible to comply: see per Kerr LJ at 518D–E. However, in this case, I have not felt able to construe either cl.14.1 or 45.4.4 in a way which would eliminate this trap.

10.81 Although Morgan J considered the result was 'harsh', it was one which, applying legal principle, he was 'obliged to reach'.[77]

## REPAIRING OBLIGATIONS

10.82 The successful exercise of a break clause may be dependent upon the tenant complying with its repairing obligations under the lease. Where such a pre-condition is unqualified, the tenant is likely to face serious if not insurmountable difficulties in ensuring compliance. For, as Nicholls LJ explained in *Bass Holdings Ltd v Morton Music Ltd*:[78]

> However diligent or even punctilious a tenant may be in carrying out his obligations under his lease, in such cases there will in practice inevitably be occasions when there will be outstanding some dilapidations which would, strictly, constitute breaches of the repairing or re-decorating covenants.

10.83 In practice, therefore, the relevant condition is usually qualified in some way, eg by requiring only 'material' or 'substantial' or 'reasonable' compliance by the tenant with its repairing obligations at the material time.[79] In this regard, it is also worth noting that the existence of physical defects at the material time will not necessarily be fatal to the exercise of the break. This is well-illustrated by the decision in *West Middlesex Golf Club Ltd v Ealing LBC*.[80] In that case, the tenant (represented by David Neuberger QC) claimed a declaration that it had validly exercised an option contained in a 21-year lease that entitled it to a further 21-year lease. The exercise of the option was subject to the fulfilment of various conditions, including compliance with the tenants' covenants. The landlord contended that the tenant was not entitled to exercise the option because, at the date of service of the notice exercising the option the tenant was in breach of its repairing obligations. On the facts, Roger Kaye QC (sitting as a Deputy Judge of the High Court) held that the tenant was not in breach of its obligations. Notably, he said:[81]

> the real question is whether the defendant, at the time of the exercise of the option, could have maintained an action against the plaintiff for breach, however trivial, of the repairing covenant in clause 4(g). There must however be an actionable breach. If the tenant has honestly performed and complied with his covenants as at that date he is not to be deprived of his right to renew if, for example, some damage has been caused by wind or weather, or by some vandal or trespasser at the last minute before the option is exercised by, for example, the breaking of

[77] *Avocet Industrial Estates LLP v Merol Ltd* [2012] L&TR 13, at [127]. (The tenant appealed to the Court of Appeal, before which the appeal was argued. However, the appeal was compromised before any decision was given by the court.)

[78] *Bass Holdings Ltd v Morton Music Ltd* [1988] 1 Ch 493, at 529A.

[79] See the commentary above at **9.51–9.67**.

[80] *West Middlesex Golf Club Ltd v Ealing LBC* (1994) 68 P&CR 461.

[81] *West Middlesex Golf Club Ltd v Ealing LBC* (1994) 68 P&CR 461, at 487. Given the wording of the repairing covenant in this case (ie '... at all times ... to repair ... and keep in good and substantial repair ...'), the correctness of the approach of the deputy judge may be open to some doubt: see *British Telecommunications Plc v Sun Life Assurance Society Plc* [1996] Ch 69.

> windows which the tenant has not had a reasonable time to repair. Glaziers and builders do not turn up instantly and miraculously the moment damage occurs. A covenant to keep in good repair is not, as both sides accept, an absolute warranty that the demised premises are at every moment in time in good repair. I cannot therefore conceive that a landlord would be entitled to sue for want of repair the instant some damage or disrepair occurred, but only if the tenant has failed to remedy that disrepair within a reasonable time of its occurrence.

**10.84** From a practical perspective, where the successful exercise of a break clause is dependent upon the tenant complying with its repairing obligations, the following steps might be taken:

(1) Engage a building surveyor well in advance of the break date, and follow his advice as to the work required to comply with the tenant's repairing obligations. As Mellish LJ said in *Finch v Underwood*:[82] 'The Court would be inclined to give credit to a survey thus honestly made, and would lean towards holding the condition precedent to have been complied with'.
(2) Attempt to agree a schedule of works with the landlord.
(3) Ensure that all remedial works are carried out in good time by a trustworthy contractor and under proper supervision.
(4) Invite the landlord's surveyor to inspect the completed works, and to state whether or not he is satisfied with them.

## REINSTATEMENT OBLIGATIONS

**10.85** Obligations to reinstate alterations are sometimes found in the lease but more usually in a subsequent licence to alter.[83] Sometimes the obligation may be absolute (ie the tenant must reinstate the premises by the time specified in the covenant); although more commonly a covenant to reinstate alterations will oblige the tenant to do so if the landlord shall so require by notice.

**10.86** Where the successful exercise of a break clause is dependent upon the tenant complying with an absolute reinstatement obligation, there are few conceptual difficulties, ie the tenant must simply reinstate the premises by the time specified in the covenant. However, problems can arise where a break clause inter-relates with the second type of reinstatement obligation. Specifically, the landlord might decide not to give the requisite notice to reinstate until it is too late for the tenant to carry out the reinstatement works in advance of the break date. The leading textbook on dilapidations suggests that such a reinstatement notice would be valid.[84] In those circumstances, the landlord will probably be treated as giving the tenant implied licence to remain on the premises after the term date for such reasonable time as may be necessary to effect the reinstatements. So,

[82] *Finch v Underwood* (1876) 2 Ch D 310, at 316.
[83] The fulfilment of an obligation contained in a separate licence to alter will not be a precondition to the successful exercise of a break clause dependent only upon the covenants of the lease having been performed at the material time.
[84] N Dowding and K Reynolds *Dilapidations: The Modern Law and Practice* (Sweet & Maxwell, 6th edn, 2018), §16.06.

for example, in *Matthey v Curling*,[85] a house let under the terms of a lease expiring on 25 March 1919 burnt to the ground only a short period of time before the term date (ie on 12 February 1919). The House of Lords considered the tenant's liability to reinstate. Lord Atkinson said:[86]

> The very fact that the lessor was in this case insisting on the performance by the lessee of the latter's covenant to reinstate, necessarily implied that, so far as he was concerned, he consented to the lessee and his authorized agents entering on the demised premises to commence and complete that work …
>
> We have not been referred to any authority establishing that in such a case as this reinstatement must take place within the term of the lease. Nor have I myself been able to find one. Until I have been referred to it, or discovered it, I fear I shall remain of opinion that in the case of an ordinary covenant to reinstate, a covenantor shall in the absence of words expressly or impliedly fixing a time for the performance of his covenant, have what is a reasonable time under all the circumstances of the case for its performance, whether, in the case of a leasehold, that time extends beyond the term or the contrary.

**10.87** The reasoning in the above passage may provide the solution to a scenario where there would otherwise arise a conflict between the tenant being required, on the one hand to deliver up vacant possession on the break date, and on the other hand complying with its reinstatement obligations.

[85] *Matthey v Curling* [1922] 2 AC 180; and see also *Scottish Mutual Assurance Society Ltd v British Telecommunications Plc* (unreported, 18 March 1994) and *Re Teathers Ltd* [2013] 1 P&CR 11.

[86] *Matthey v Curling* [1922] 2 AC 180, at 240. This analysis is consistent with the remarks of Rimer LJ in *NYK Logistics (UK) Ltd v Ibrend Estates BV* [2011] 4 All ER 539, at [46].

# 11

# *The Recovery of 'Overpaid' Rent and Other Sums*

## INTRODUCTION

**11.1** Chapter 10 considered the question whether, in circumstances where a break notice expires, or a break date falls, part-way through a rental period, the tenant nonetheless has to pay the full period's rent in order to make the break effective. As has been described, the current consensus of judicial decisions is that, normally, a tenant will have to pay the full period's rent in order to satisfy the relevant condition. Thus, the subsequent question arises: if the lease is successfully broken in such circumstances, how (if at all) can the tenant recover any apportioned 'overpayment'?

**11.2** In seeking an affirmative answer to the above question, tenants have deployed a number of arguments, albeit without a great deal of success. These arguments will be considered below under three broad headings: (i) implication of a term in the lease; (ii) implied agreement between the landlord and tenant; and (iii) restitution for unjust enrichment.

**11.3** It may be noted that, in the residential context, statute has now intervened so as to entitle a tenant under an assured shorthold tenancy of a dwelling-house in England to a repayment of rent from the landlord where:

> (a) as a result of the service of a notice under s 21 of the Housing Act 1988, the tenancy is brought to an end before the end of a period of the tenancy; (b) the tenant has paid rent in advance for that period; and (c) the tenant was not in occupation of the dwelling-house for one or more whole days of that period.[1]

## IMPLICATION OF A TERM IN THE LEASE

**11.4** It is often the case that a lease says nothing about what is to happen to any 'overpaid' rent following the exercise of a break clause. In this scenario, can the court imply a term into the lease which enables the tenant to get back the apportioned part of any advance payment of rent which relates to a period after the break date? This point was considered in detail in the *Marks and Spencer* litigation.[2]

[1] Section 21C(1) of the Housing Act 1988.

[2] *Marks and Spencer Plc v BNP Paribas Securities Services Trust Company (Jersey) Limited* [2013] L&TR 31; overturned on appeal at [2014] L&TR 26; with the appeal subsequently upheld at [2015] UKSC 72.

**11.5** In summary, the facts were as follows. There were four leases (strictly, sub-underleases) in materially the same terms, each for a separate floor of an office block in Paddington, London. Each lease contained a break clause, exercisable on 24 January 2012 (called the first break date) or 24 January 2016 (called the second break date) upon giving six months' advance notice. The break clause was subject to various conditions, including: (i) no arrears of 'basic rent' or VAT on rent on the break date; and (ii) payment of a 'break premium' of over £900,000. On 7 July 2011, the tenant served on the landlord break notices seeking to determine the leases on the first break date. The tenant duly complied with the conditions of the break clause to enable it to exercise the break. Thus, it paid the basic rent in full for the quarter starting on 25 December 2011 and the break premium. So, the leases came to an end on 24 January 2012. After that date, the tenant demanded repayment of the basic rent (and certain other sums) paid in advance for the period from 25 January to 24 March 2012, ie the broken period. The landlord refused to make repayment, and so the tenant commenced proceedings.

**11.6** At trial, the tenant put its claim on several bases: (i) the express terms of the leases; (ii) restitution for a total failure of consideration; and (iii) the existence of an implied term. At first instance, Morgan J rejected all these bases except the implied term.

**11.7** In arriving at this conclusion, Morgan J first cited from the decision of the Privy Council in *Attorney-General of Belize v Belize Telecom Limited*,[3] which identified the principles to be applied when considering whether a term can be implied into an agreement. In that case, Lord Hoffmann explained as follows:[4]

> [17] The question of implication arises when the instrument does not expressly provide for what is to happen when some event occurs. The most usual inference in such a case is that nothing is to happen. If the parties had intended something to happen, the instrument would have said so. Otherwise, the express provisions of the instrument are to continue to operate undisturbed. If the event has caused loss to one or other of the parties, the loss lies where it falls.
>
> [18] In some cases, however, the reasonable addressee would understand the instrument to mean something else. He would consider that the only meaning consistent with the other provisions of the instrument, read against the relevant background, is that something is to happen. The event in question is to affect the rights of the parties. The instrument may not have expressly said so, but this is what it must mean. In such a case, it is said that the court implies a term as to what will happen if the event in question occurs. But the implication of the term is not an addition to the instrument. It only spells out what the instrument means …
>
> [21] It follows that in every case in which it is said that some provision ought to be implied in an instrument, the question for the court is whether such a provision would spell out in express words what the instrument, read against the relevant background, would reasonably be understood to mean. It will be noticed from Lord Pearson's speech [in *Trollope & Colls Limited v North West Metropolitan Regional Hospital Board* [1973] 1 WLR 601] that this question can be reformulated in various ways which a court may find helpful in providing an answer – the implied term must 'go without saying', it must be 'necessary to give business efficacy to the

[3] *Attorney-General of Belize v Belize Telecom Limited* [2009] 1 WLR 1988 (which must now be read in light of *Marks and Spencer Plc v BNP Paribas Securities Services Trust Company (Jersey) Limited* [2015] UKSC 72).

[4] *Attorney-General of Belize v Belize Telecom Limited* [2009] 1 WLR 1988, at [17]–[21].

contract' and so on – but these are not in the Board's opinion to be treated as different or additional tests. There is only one question: is that what the instrument, read as a whole against the relevant background, would reasonably be understood to mean?

**11.8** Having referred to the *Belize Telecom* decision, Morgan J then said as follows:[5]

> Accordingly, I have to ask whether the implied term contended for by the Claimant would spell out in express words what the instrument, read against the relevant background, would reasonably be understood to mean. I have already held that the lease expressly provides that, in a case where the break clause is not operated, the rent is payable for the term to 2nd February 2018 and not for any period after that date. Further, I have held that if on the last quarter day before a break date it was certain that the term would end on the break date then the provisions as to the payment of rent by instalments do not require the lessee to pay a full quarter's rent but only an apportioned part of a quarter's rent. That leads a reasonable person reading the lease to expect that in a case where the break clause is operated to take effect on 24th January 2012, the rent is payable for the term to 24th January 2012 but not for any period after that date. I also consider it to be relevant that the break clause may only be effectively operated where the lessee pays to the lessor a sum equivalent to one year's rent. That provision shows that the parties applied their minds to the compensation which the lessor should receive for the fact that after the break date the lessor would have vacant possession rather than an income stream under a continuing lease. That fact makes it unlikely that the parties would have intended that, in addition, the lessor would be entitled to retain the full amount of the quarter's rent paid on the quarter day before the break date. It is also relevant that the provision as to the payment of rent on quarter days refers to the payment of 'instalments' of rent. The ordinary concept of an instalment is that the payer does not pay the full amount which is due in one go but pays the full amount by instalments. Conversely, the obligation to pay by instalments should not produce the result that the payer pays more than the full amount which is due. I consider that these matters point to the lease being reasonably understood to mean that if the lessee pays a full quarter's rent on the last quarter day before the break date and the lease then ends on the break date, in the middle of the quarter, then the lessor is obliged to pay back to the lessee the part of the instalment of rent which exceeds the full amount which is due.

**11.9** Morgan J reinforced this conclusion with a number of subsidiary reasons, namely that: (i) the implied term contended for by the tenant was eminently reasonable; (ii) what is obvious now (in light of the decisions in *Quirkco Investments Limited v Aspray Transport Limited*[6] and *PCE Investors Limited v Cancer Research UK*)[7] was less obvious when the leases were entered into; (iii) in view of the fact that rent was reserved 'proportionately for any part of the year' and that quarterly payments were 'instalments', it was fairly obvious what the parties thought should happen in such a case; (iv) the suggested implied term was necessary to give business efficacy to the leases and was obviously what the parties meant; and (v) the implied term could be easily and clearly expressed and did not contradict any express term of the leases. Thus, the judge concluded that the landlord should repay the sums demanded to the tenant.

[5] *Marks and Spencer Plc v BNP Paribas Securities Services Trust Company (Jersey) Limited* [2013] L&TR 31, at [35].

[6] *Quirkco Investments Limited v Aspray Transport Limited* [2012] L&TR 19.

[7] *PCE Investors Limited v Cancer Research UK* [2012] 2 P&CR 5.

**11.10** The landlord appealed to the Court of Appeal, challenging the judge's decision that there was an implied term as to repayment. The Court of Appeal unanimously allowed the appeal.[8] Arden LJ gave the only reasoned judgment. After setting out (i) the principal terms of the leases, (ii) some background about the exercise of the break clauses and the proceedings, and (iii) a summary of the judge's reasoning, she set out the appropriate legal principles as follows:[9]

> [25] … as Lord Hoffmann made clear in *Belize* … the starting point is that, if there is no express term, none should be implied because if the parties intended that a particular term should apply to their relationship they would have included a term to that effect, rather than left it to implication …
>
> [26] Furthermore, as this court made clear in *Mediterranean Salvage and Towage Ltd v Seamar Trading and Commerce Inc (The Reborn)* [2009] EWCA Civ 531 … the court will not imply a term as a matter of interpretation following the *Belize* approach unless it is necessary that the agreement should contain such a term to achieve the parties' express agreement, purposively construed against the admissible background.
>
> [27] Mr Fetherstonhaugh [Counsel for the tenant] accepts this but points out that the word 'necessary' is imprecise, and that courts have not always applied this test strictly (see per Lord Wilberforce in *Liverpool City Council v Irwin* [1977] AC 239). I agree that what is necessary must depend on the particular type of contract … In this case, however, there is little admissible evidence of communications between the parties beyond that contained in the lease, and so the exercise admits of less room for argument than might otherwise have been the case.
>
> [28] However, I would accept that a party does not show that a term is unnecessary simply by showing that the parties' agreement could work without the implied term. That approach overlooks the fact that as part of the process of interpretation the court seeks to find the parties' common aim in entering into the agreement. A term may be implied if it is necessary to achieve the parties' objective in entering into the agreement.

**11.11** Having directed herself as to the legal principles on implied terms, Arden LJ turned to the leases, which (it will be recalled) made no provision about the return of rent for the broken period. She then said as follows:[10]

> [35] What is the correct interpretation of the break clause so far as the right to repayment of the rent is concerned? … The first factor to bear in mind is that it would have been obvious to the parties before they signed up to the lease that there was a possibility that rent would have to be paid on the last quarter day in full for a period which went beyond the break date …
>
> [36] That position is reinforced by the state of the case law surrounding claims for repayment of rent for the broken period when a lease terminated before the end of the term of the lease, because the lessee operated a break clause or because the lease was forfeit. The judge set out the case law in full in his judgment and there is no need for me to go through it again [ie *Ellis v Rowbotham* [1900] 1 QB 740, *Capital & City Holdings Ltd v Dean Warburg* [1989] 1 EGLR 90 and *Re a Company* [2007] BPIR 1].

[8] *Marks and Spencer Plc v BNP Paribas Securities Services Trust Company (Jersey) Limited* [2014] L&TR 26.

[9] *Marks and Spencer Plc v BNP Paribas Securities Services Trust Company (Jersey) Limited* [2014] L&TR 26, at [25]–[28].

[10] *Marks and Spencer Plc v BNP Paribas Securities Services Trust Company (Jersey) Limited* [2014] L&TR 26, at [35]–[39].

[39] ... That case law forms part of the admissible background against which the lease is to be interpreted. It makes it all the more likely that a reasonable person, having knowledge of this background, would conclude that if the parties had really intended there to be an implied term for repayment they would have made express provision for it.

**11.12** To this, Arden LJ added the following:[11]

[41] That takes me to the judge's same position conclusion [ie where Morgan J held that a reasonable person would consider that a term was to be implied because the tenant should be in the same position as a lessee who paid the break premium on the last quarter day]. I am not persuaded that this entitles the court to read the agreement as subject to the implied term for repayment. I proceed on the basis (without deciding the point) that the lessee could make a proportionate payment of rent on the last quarter day if he had by then also paid the break premium: that would seem to be correct but the point was not fully argued before us. Nonetheless the force of the judge's point depends on saying that the situation where a proportionate payment of rent can be made on the last quarter day and the situation where termination does in fact take place on the break date because by then the lessee has paid the break premium are on all fours. I do not consider that that is so. In the latter case, the lessor remains uncertain about whether the lease will terminate on the break date until the break premium is paid. Why should not the parties have proceeded on the basis that the lessor was entitled to be compensated for that.

[42] Likewise the full compensation conclusion [ie where Morgan J held the break premium amounted to a year's rent (before any rent review) and so the parties should be taken to have agreed that this was the full amount of compensation for the lessor if the lessee exercised the right to break the leases and in those circumstances they were unlikely to have considered that the lessor should retain the rent for the broken period as well] assumes that the break premium constitutes the totality of the agreed compensation. However, the fact is that the lessor could be compensated in other ways ... If I am right in saying that there is a distinction between the cases where the break premium is paid on or before the last quarter day and cases where it is not paid until after that date, the assumption that the break premium should be full compensation is undermined.

**11.13** Accordingly, taking all the circumstances into consideration, Arden LJ concluded that:[12] 'the correct inference to draw is that the parties proceeded on the basis that the loss from a payment of rent for the broken period should lie where it fell. Thus no term for repayment is implied'.

**11.14** The tenant subsequently appealed to the Supreme Court. The Supreme Court unanimously dismissed the appeal, upholding the decision of the Court of Appeal.[13] Lord Neuberger observed that the decision in *Belize Telecom* had been 'interpreted by both academic lawyers and judges as having changed the law' in the sense of watering down the traditional tests for the implication of contractual terms.[14] However, he rejected

[11] *Marks and Spencer Plc v BNP Paribas Securities Services Trust Company (Jersey) Limited* [2014] L&TR 26, at [41]–[42].

[12] *Marks and Spencer Plc v BNP Paribas Securities Services Trust Company (Jersey) Limited* [2014] L&TR 26, at [43].

[13] *Marks and Spencer Plc v BNP Paribas Securities Services Trust Company (Jersey) Limited* [2015] UKSC 72.

[14] *Marks and Spencer Plc v BNP Paribas Securities Services Trust Company (Jersey) Limited* [2015] UKSC 72, at [24].

the suggestion that there had been any such dilution.[15] Having done so, Lord Neuberger succinctly concluded:[16]

> Save in a very clear case indeed, it would be wrong to attribute to a landlord and a tenant, particularly when they have entered into a full and professionally drafted lease, an intention that the tenant should receive an apportioned part of the rent payable and paid in advance, when the non-apportionability of such rent has been so long and clearly established [ie since at least the decision in *Ellis v Rowbotham* [1900] 1 QB 740]. Given that it is so clear that the effect of the case-law is that rent payable and paid in advance can be retained by the landlord, save in very exceptional circumstances (eg where the contract could not work or would lead to an absurdity) express words would be needed before it would be right to imply a term to the contrary.

**11.15** Thus, the tenant was not entitled to the repayment of an apportioned part of the quarter's rent which was paid on 25 December 2011.

**11.16** Notably, the principal area of dispute in the *Marks and Spencer* litigation concerned the repayment of an apportioned part of the 'overpaid' Basic Rent. However, it should be observed that the tenant also sought the repayment of other sums for the broken period, including the repayment of certain sums paid on account of service charge. In this regard, Morgan J at first instance said as follows:[17]

> [54] … Although this was originally in dispute, it was accepted at the trial that, following 24th January 2012, there were procedures as to the determination of the amount of the service charge which had not been completed and that those procedures could still be operated, notwithstanding the termination of the lease. The Defendants accepted that this was so adopting the approach in *Torminster Properties Ltd v Green* [1983] 1 WLR 676 in relation to the unfinished procedures for the determination of a reviewed rent. Thus when on 3rd September 2012, the lessor followed through the procedures for the 2011 service charge and awarded to the lessee a credit note for overpayments in that year, it is now accepted that the lessee is indeed entitled to the benefit of that credit …
>
> [55] However, merely having a credit against future service charge is of no use to the Claimant, as it will not be liable for future service charge. Accordingly, the Claimant wishes to be paid the amount of the credits when the final amount of the credits is known. The Claimant cited the decision of the Court of Appeal in *Brown's Operating System Services Ltd v Southwark Roman Catholic Diocesan Corporation* [2007] L&TR 375 in support of its argument that it was entitled to be paid the amount of the credits now that the lease has ended. The service charge provisions in that case are not the same as the provisions in the present. There was perhaps this similarity in that there was no express provision dealing with what was to happen in relation to a surplus which had been built up during the term of the lease which the landlord was allowed to expend on services during the term but, the Court of Appeal held, it was not entitled to expend on services provided after the end of the term. The Court of Appeal proceeded from that premise to hold that the tenant was entitled to be paid the surplus at the end of the term.

[15] *Marks and Spencer Plc v BNP Paribas Securities Services Trust Company (Jersey) Limited* [2015] UKSC 72, at [24]; and see also the remarks of Lord Clarke, at [77].

[16] *Marks and Spencer Plc v BNP Paribas Securities Services Trust Company (Jersey) Limited* [2015] UKSC 72, at [50].

[17] *Marks and Spencer Plc v BNP Paribas Securities Services Trust Company (Jersey) Limited* [2013] L&TR 31, at [54]–[56].

> The precise reasoning was not spelt out. It looks to me like a case of an implied term based on the principles in *Belize* giving effect to how the lease should reasonably be read and take effect. One feature of the *Brown's* case was that it was held that the situation which would pertain on the expiry of the term by effluxion of time also pertained where the lease was prematurely terminated pursuant to the operation of a tenant's break clause.
>
> [56] Following the citation of this decision, the Defendants accepted that they were 'in difficulty' in further resisting the Claimant's case to be paid the sum the subject of a credit note or credit notes calculated in the way described above. I am content to accept that concession by the Defendants. That disposes of the dispute in relation to the operation of the service charge provisions.

**11.17** In other words, the landlord conceded that the tenant was entitled to recover any service charges which it had paid that related to services which had not been provided by the break date, and to recover the amount of any credit which the tenant had earnt as a result of overpayments of service charges in the past, and which had not been used by the break date. This emphasises that, in respect of different types of sums (ie rent, service charge, insurance payments and so on), the principles for recoverability may vary.

**11.18** Since the conclusion of the *Marks and Spencer* litigation, it is common to find in a lease an express covenant entitling the tenant to recover 'overpaid' rent resulting from the successful exercise of a break. Particularly where the sum of money to be recovered may be substantial, it should be regarded as best practice for such an express covenant to be included.

## IMPLIED AGREEMENT

**11.19** A tenant may seek to demonstrate the existence of an agreement under which his landlord is liable to return any rental overpayment. Indeed, as Lord Goff said In *Woolwich Equitable Building Society v IRC*:[18]

> A payment may be made on such terms that it has been agreed, expressly or impliedly, by the recipient that, if it shall prove not to have been due, it will be repaid by him. In that event, of course, the money will be repayable … On the other hand, the mere fact that money is paid under protest will not give rise of itself to the inference of such an agreement; though it may form part of the evidence from which it may be inferred that the payee did not intend to close the transaction.

**11.20** An argument along these lines succeeded in *Nurdin & Peacock Plc v DB Ramsden & Co Ltd*.[19] In that case, the tenant held certain premises in Kingston upon Hull, Humberside, under the terms of a lease pursuant to which the rent with effect from 17 November 1995 was £207,683 per annum. However, by reason of uncertainty in the drafting of the lease, the rent was demanded by the landlord and paid by the tenant at the rate of £267,430 per annum. The tenant contended that certain overpayments were recoverable pursuant to an agreement by the landlord that they should be repaid

[18] *Woolwich Equitable Building Society v IRC* [1993] AC 70, at 165–66.
[19] *Nurdin & Peacock Plc v DB Ramsden & Co Ltd* [1999] 1 WLR 1249.

if it (the tenant) succeeded – as ultimately it did – on a claim for a declaration as to the true construction of the terms of the lease, alternatively for rectification of the lease. In this connection, the tenant relied on the fact that four overpayments were made to, and accepted by, the landlord following the issue of proceedings and the exchange of a number of letters at the end of July 1997, and in particular, a letter dated 25 July 1997 in which the tenant wrote that it would pay the higher rental sum 'without prejudice to [its] claim that the rent payable with effect from 17 November 1995 is £207,683. Obviously the overpayment will be refundable if [the tenant] is successful at trial'. In response, the landlord simply said: 'we note your comments with regard to payment of rent'.

11.21 Referring to this correspondence, Neuberger J said as follows:[20]

> On a fair reading of [the tenant's] letter of 25 July 1997, [the landlord] understood, or at least ought to have understood, that [the tenant] was indicating an intention to continue making the overpayments on the understanding that the overpayments would be repaid if [the tenant] was successful on the construction and rectification issues. Although it is true that [the landlord] merely 'noted' this, it appears to me that, by accepting rent at the higher rate, ie rent including the overpayments, without demur, [the landlord], by action rather than by words, effectively accepted the basis upon which [the tenant] was making it clear the rent had been paid at the higher rate. Whether there is a sufficient agreement that overpayments should be repaid in a particular case is to be judged by an objective assessment of the facts in the particular case. In my judgment, to use the words of Lord Goff in *Woolwich Equitable Building Society v Inland Revenue Commissioners* [1993] AC 70, 166 once the instant proceedings had been issued and served on [the landlord], and once [the landlord] had received and acknowledged [the tenant's] letter of 25 July 1997, [the landlord] could not realistically say that it is to be inferred that [the tenant] 'intend[ed] to close the transaction' when making the overpayments on and after 1 August 1997.

Thus, Neuberger J found that there was a concluded agreement the terms of which required the landlord to repay the 'overpaid' rent to the tenant.

11.22 Of course, whether the court is able to imply an agreement in any given case will be a fact-sensitive exercise. So, for example, in the *Woolwich* case (see above), the taxpayer had written as follows to the Inland Revenue:

> You should be aware that we are presently seeking leave to commence legal proceedings in connection with the Regulations' [*pursuant to which the Inland Revenue was claiming the payment of tax in that case*] 'and accordingly this payment is made without prejudice to any right to recover any payments made pursuant to the Regulations which may arise as a result of legal proceedings, or as a result of any future extinguishment or reduction of any liability under the said Regulations or otherwise.

11.23 It was argued that, following the taxpayer's successful challenge to the validity of the Regulations in question, the effect of payment and acceptance of the tax pursuant to that letter gave rise to a contract that the tax should be returned. In the House of Lords the majority held that, because the payment had been made by a taxpayer to a public authority, it was returnable. Lord Keith of Kinkel (who was admittedly in the minority) held that there was no agreement by the Inland Revenue to repay the taxpayer. He said that the taxpayer's letter did not state that the money was being offered on terms that it

[20] *Nurdin & Peacock Plc v DB Ramsden & Co Ltd* [1999] 1 WLR 1249, at 1267C–67E.

would be repaid if the taxpayer succeeded in overturning the Regulations but that the letter meant nothing more than that:[21]

> Woolwich were asserting a legal right to recover the payments in the event of the relevant Regulations being held to be ultra vires, and stating that the payments were made without prejudice to such right. In accepting the payments the revenue were doing no more than agreeing that they would not be treated as prejudicing any such right.

**11.24** Relying on *Nurdin*, it is possible that if there is doubt about whether a whole period's rent is payable in order to operate a break clause, the tenant may pay the full amount under sufferance, and attempt to recover it later: see *Dun & Bradstreet Software Service (England) Ltd v Provident Mutual Life Assurance Association* ('... a tenant can pay under protest and subsequently recover what he has overpaid ...').[22]

## RESTITUTION FOR UNJUST ENRICHMENT

### (a) Introduction

**11.25** A detailed discussion of the law of unjust enrichment is outside the scope of this work.[23] What is set out below is intended to be a summary of some of the points of potential relevance to the present issue.

**11.26** As English law stands, it does not recognise an action for the recovery of money simply on the grounds that it was not due when it was paid. This is clear from *Orakpo v Manson Investments*, where Lord Diplock said:[24]

> My lords, there is no general doctrine of unjust enrichment recognised in English law. What it does is to provide specific remedies in particular cases of what might be classified as unjust enrichment in a legal system which is based upon the civil law.

**11.27** To the same effect is the speech of Lord Brown-Wilkinson in *Woolwich Equitable Building Society v IRC*:[25]

> '... as yet there is in English law no general rule giving the plaintiff a right of recovery from a defendant who has been unjustly enriched at the plaintiff's expense ...'

**11.28** Rather, as Lord Clarke explained in *Menelaou v Bank of Cyprus UK Ltd*:[26]

> it is now well established that the court must ask itself four questions when faced with a claim for unjust enrichment. They are these: (1) Has the defendant been enriched? (2) Was the enrichment at the claimant's expense? (3) Was the enrichment unjust? (4) Are there any defences available to the defendant?

[21] *Woolwich Equitable Building Society v IRC* [1993] AC 70, at 150. Neuberger J accepted that the difference between the terms of the tenant's letter in *Nurdin* and the taxpayer's letter in *Woolwich* could be said to be a 'fairly fine one': see *Nurdin & Peacock Plc v DB Ramsden & Co Ltd* [1999] 1 WLR 1249, at 1269E.

[22] *Dun & Bradstreet Software Service (England) Ltd v Provident Mutual Life Assurance Association* [1998] 2 EGLR 175, at 180F.

[23] For a comprehensive review of the law, then the reader should refer to C Mitchell, P Mitchell and S Watterson Goff & Jones: *The Law of Unjust Enrichment* (9th edn, Sweet & Maxwell, 2016).

[24] *Orakpo v Manson Investments* [1978] AC 95, at 104C.

[25] *Woolwich Equitable Building Society v IRC* [1993] AC 70, at 196H.

[26] *Menelaou v Bank of Cyprus UK Ltd* [2016] AC 176, at [18].

11.29 Thus, in order to succeed on a claim in a restitution, a claimant must be able to point to a particular unjust element, such as: (i) payment under duress; (ii) payment under a mistake; or (iii) payment for consideration which has wholly failed. These will be considered in turn.

### (b) Payment under Duress

11.30 In the *Woolwich Equitable Building Society* case, Lord Goff said:[27]

> money paid as a result of actual or threatened duress to the person, or actual or threatened seizure of a person's goods, is recoverable. For an example of the latter, see *Maskell v Horner* [1915] 3 KB 106. Since these forms of compulsion are not directly relevant for present purposes, it is unnecessary to elaborate them; but I think it pertinent to observe that the concept of duress has in recent years been expanded to embrace economic duress.

11.31 Relying on this statement of principle, a tenant may argue that the fear of the break being ineffective should be treated as sufficient compulsion to enable it to recover money paid as a consequence of the same.

11.32 However, a similar argument (in the context of a purported threatened forfeiture) was advanced before, and rejected by, Neuberger J in the *Nurdin* case (see above), where he said:[28]

> Mr. Brock suggested that the fear of forfeiture or distress was enough, in light of observations in *Maskell v Horner* [1915] 3 KB 106, 118–20, and cases cited therein, as well as in more recent observations of the House of Lords in *Woolwich Equitable Building Society v Inland Revenue Commissioners* [1993] AC 70.
>
> I do not accept that. It appears to me that, if Mr. Brock is right, then any tenant who makes a payment under a lease which contains a forfeiture clause (ie virtually any lease), which payment would otherwise be irrecoverable in law, could recover it simply by saying that he was concerned that, if he did not pay, he would face distress or forfeiture. Indeed, as a matter of logic, it seems to go further than that: any individual or company who pays a debt because of a concern that failure to do so will result in bankruptcy or winding up proceedings could rely on that concern to justify recovery of the money which would otherwise be irrecoverable.
>
> So far as the authorities relied on by Mr. Brock are concerned, I do not consider that they assist him. It is true that in the Woolwich case, at p 164, Lord Goff of Chieveley cited *Maskell v Horner* [1915] 3 KB 106 with apparent approval, in support of the proposition that 'money paid as a result of actual or threatened duress to the person, or actual or threatened seizure of a person's goods, is recoverable', and that he went on to say, at p 165, that it would not be right 'to regard the categories of compulsion for present purposes as closed'. However, the very use of the words 'duress' and 'compulsion' indicates to me that something more than mere concern in the payer's mind is sufficient to bring himself within this category.

11.33 It is suggested that, by analogy with the position in *Nurdin*, it is unlikely that the fear of a break being ineffective can be regarded as duress sufficient to found a claim in unjust enrichment.

[27] *Woolwich Equitable Building Society v IRC* [1993] AC 70, at 164.
[28] *Nurdin & Peacock Plc v DB Ramsden & Co Ltd* [1999] 1 WLR 1249, at 1258–59.

### (c) Payment under Mistake

11.34 A payment made under a mistake, whether of fact or law, may be recovered by the payer (since the mistake renders the enrichment by the payee unjust). However, what suffices for a 'mistake' for these purposes? What if the tenant entertains doubts about whether the landlord is really entitled to a full quarter's rent, but pays that amount in any event just to ensure that the break is properly effective?

11.35 In *Kleinwort Benson Ltd v Lincoln City Council*,[29] Lord Hope said:

> Cases where the payer was aware that there was an issue of law which was relevant but, being in doubt as to what the law was, paid without waiting to resolve that doubt may be left on one side. A state of doubt is different from that of mistake. A person who pays when in doubt takes the risk that he may be wrong – and that is so whether the issue is one of fact or one of law.

11.36 In *Nurdin & Peacock (supra)*, the tenant made the following concession (which Neuberger J considered correct):[30]

> at least in the absence of any other factors, a payment is irrecoverable if it is made in circumstances where it is not due, and where the payer is aware that the payment may not be due, and, indeed, knows the basis upon which he may be able to defend his liability to make the payment.

11.37 More recently, in *Deutsche Morgan Grenfell Group Plc v IRC*,[31] Lord Hope elaborated on his observations in the *Kleinwort* case. He said:

> The difficult question is what degree of doubt is compatible with a mistake claim ... I see the issue as being essentially one of causation. What was the effect of the mistake on the payer? But the basic principle is, of course, that of unjust enrichment. At what point can it be said that the payee has been unjustly enriched? The answer to these questions will depend on the facts of the case ... [The] payer's reason for making the payment despite his doubt will have a part to play in resolving the issue as to whether the payer, who would not have made the payment had he known the true state of the facts or the law at the time of the payment, should bear the risk or can recover on the ground that he was mistaken.

11.38 In *Grenfell*, Lord Hoffmann also referred to the observations of Lord Hope in *Kleinwort*. Of these, he said:[32]

> I do not think that Lord Hope could have meant that a state of doubt was actually inconsistent with making a mistake. Contestants in quiz shows may have doubts about the answer ('it sounds like Haydn, but then it may be Mozart') but if they then give the wrong answer, they have made a mistake. The real point is whether the person who made the payment took the risk that he might be wrong. If he did, then he cannot recover the money.

11.39 Lord Hoffmann went on to say:[33]

> I would not regard the fact that the person making the payment had doubts about his liability as conclusive of the question of whether he took the risk, particularly if the existence of these

[29] *Kleinwort Benson Ltd v Lincoln City Council* [1999] 2 AC 349, at 410.
[30] *Nurdin & Peacock Plc v DB Ramsden & Co Ltd* [1999] 1 WLR 1249, at 1270.
[31] *Deutsche Morgan Grenfell Group Plc v IRC* [2007] 1 AC 558, at [65].
[32] *Deutsche Morgan Grenfell Group Plc v IRC* [2007] 1 AC 558, at [26].
[33] *Deutsche Morgan Grenfell Group Plc v IRC* [2007] 1 AC 558, at [27].

> doubts was unknown to the receiving party. It would be strange if a party whose lawyer had raised a doubt on the question but who decided nevertheless that he had better pay should be in a worse position than a party who had no doubts because he had never taken any advice, particularly if the receiving party had no idea that there was any difference in the circumstances in which the two payments had been made. It would be more rational if the question of whether a party should be treated as having taken the risk depended upon the objective circumstances surrounding the payment as they could reasonably have been known to both parties, including of course the extent to which the law was known to be in doubt.

**11.40** From the foregoing, it appears that the current state of the law is such that 'there may be cases in which a payer can still be said to be under a mistake, even if he has doubts, provided that he paid concluding that it was more likely than not that he was liable to pay'.[34] If a tenant can bring himself within such a category of payers, then it is arguable that he might be able to recover a rental 'overpayment'. However, to date, as far as the authors are aware, no tenant has successfully done so.

### (d) Total Failure of Consideration

**11.41** In *Giedo Van Der Garde BV v Force India Formula One Team Ltd*,[35] Stadlen J said as follows in relation to the doctrine of total failure of consideration:

> the starting point is the general principle formulated by the editors of Goff and Jones in these terms: 'The case law holds that a restitutionary claim, based on failure of consideration, will, therefore, succeed only if the failure is total' (ibid 19–009). Although the doctrine is commonly referred to as failure of consideration it is, as appears from the extract from Goff and Jones cited earlier in this judgment, based on a failure not of consideration but of performance: 'In English law, an enforceable contract may be formed by an exchange of a promise for a promise, or by the exchange of a promise for an act – I am excluding contracts under seal – and thus, in the law relating to the formation of contract, the promise to do a thing may often be the consideration, but when one is considering the law of failure of consideration and of the quasi-contractual right to recover money on that ground, it is generally speaking, not the promise which is referred to as the consideration, but the performance of the promise. The money was paid to secure performance and, if performance fails the inducement which brought about the payment is not fulfilled' (*Fibrosa Spolka Akeyjna v Fairbairn Lawson Combe Barbour Limited* [1943] AC 32 per Viscount Simon LC at page 48).

**11.42** Or, as it was put by Lord Goff in *Stoczina Gdanska v Latvian Shipping Company*:[36]

> 'The test is not whether the promisee has received a special benefit, but rather whether the promisor has performed any part of the contractual duties in respect of which the payment is due'.

[34] *Marine Trade SA v Pioneer Freight Futures Co Ltd BVI* [2010] Lloyd's Rep 631, at [76], per Flaux J (subsequently overruled on a point of contractual construction by the Court of Appeal in *Lomas v JFB Firth Rixson* [2012] 2 All ER (Comm) 1076).
[35] *Giedo Van Der Garde BV v Force India Formula One Team Ltd* [2010] EWHC 2373 (QB), at [261].
[36] *Stoczina Gdanska v Latvian Shipping Company* [1998] 1 WLR 574, at 588.

**11.43** Where a contract can be regarded as divisible, and some part of the consideration relating to a divisible part has wholly failed, that part can be recovered. This is well illustrated by *Ebrahim Dawood Limited v Heath (Est 1927) Limited*.[37] In that case, McNair J held that buyers of 50 tons of galvanised steel sheets at £73 10 shillings per ton were entitled to recover four-fifths of the purchase price as money paid on a consideration which had wholly failed because they had been entitled under s 30(3) of the Sale of Goods Act 1893 to reject four-fifths of the delivered sheets as not complying with the contractual specification. He said:[38]

> Now there are cases where the payment of the contract price has been made in advance for a total contracted number of articles, and there has then been failure by the seller to deliver the whole of those contracted quantities. In those circumstances, it is clear on the authority to which I shall refer in a moment, that the buyer's right of recovering so much of the purchase price as relates to the quantity short delivered, is a right to recover money paid to his use or money paid for a consideration which has wholly failed.

**11.44** Can such an apportionment approach be applied to rent payable under a lease? In *PCE Investors Limited v Cancer Research UK*,[39] Peter Smith J answered this question in the negative. He said:[40]

> It is not appropriate to separate out parts of the obligation in the Underlease and say that there is a total failure of consideration merely because the lease had been terminated in future as regards the rent that was payable in advance for that period. The Underlease contains a bundle of rights and obligations on both sides and as part of that in my view the Tenant agreed to pay rent in advance as part of the overall consideration for obtaining the Underlease from the Landlord. Merely because the provisions obligate him to pay rent in advance even after the Termination Date does not mean that there is a failure of consideration as regards that payment merely because beneficial use of the premises is not taken. One looks at the overall package in the Underlease and the Tenant obtained consideration in the form of the entirety of the Underlease.

**11.45** This accords with the decisions of HHJ Keyser (sitting as a judge of the High Court) in *QuirkCo Investments Limited v Asprey Transport Limited*[41] and of Morgan J in *Marks & Spencer Plc v BNP Paribas Securities Services Trust Co (Jersey) Limited*.[42] Therefore, at least at High Court level, it is not open for a tenant to rely on the doctrine of total failure of consideration as a means of recovering rental overpayments.[43]

[37] *Ebrahim Dawood Limited v Heath (Est 1927) Limited* [1961] 2 Lloyd's Rep 512.
[38] *Ebrahim Dawood Limited v Heath (Est 1927) Limited* [1961] 2 Lloyd's Rep 512, at 518–19.
[39] *PCE Investors Limited v Cancer Research UK* [2012] 2 P&CR 5.
[40] *PCE Investors Limited v Cancer Research UK* [2012] 2 P&CR 5, at [49].
[41] *QuirkCo Investments Limited v Aspray Transport Limited* [2012] L&TR 19, at [63].
[42] *Marks and Spencer Plc v BNP Paribas Securities Services Trust Co (Jersey) Limited* [2013] L&TR 31, at [41]–[46] (a point not challenged on appeal).
[43] See also *Bank of New York Mellon (International) Ltd v Cine-UK Ltd* [2021] EWHC 1013 (QB), at [221], where Master Dagnall rejected an argument to the effect that a 'partial failure of consideration' relieved a tenant of its rental liabilities under a lease. ('A partial failure of consideration can be a way of categorising a particular event which has meant that a party has not received an agreed benefit under a contract, but it is then a matter of contract law (eg that of construction of the contract including as to interdependent obligations, the law of breach of contract or the law of frustration) as to what is the consequence (if any) of that in terms of that party's rights and obligations.').

# 12

# *Redevelopment Break Clauses*

## CONDITIONS IN A LANDLORD'S BREAK CLAUSE

**12.1** In Chapter 10, the focus of discussion was on tenants' break clauses. However, leases commonly contain clauses entitling a landlord to break the lease. The content of these clauses is plainly a matter for negotiation between the parties. However, for obvious reasons, most tenants will be reluctant to agree an unconditional break in favour of the landlord. Thus, in practice, in the case of a landlord's break clause, the power to determine a lease is often expressed to be exercisable only when the landlord requires the demised premises for building or redevelopment.

**12.2** As with any break clause, the principle of strict compliance applies to the language used in a landlord's development break clause. Thus the landlord must satisfy whatever test the language of that break clause creates.

## INTENTION, DESIRE AND OTHER LINGUISTIC FORMULATIONS

### (a) 'Intends'

**12.3** Frequently, it is a condition to the exercise of a redevelopment break clause that the landlord 'intends' to develop the premises in question. Where this is the case, the court will probably construe the word 'intends' in the same way as the word is construed in the context of s 30(1)(f) of the Landlord and Tenant Act 1954 ('the 1954 Act') (ie opposition to a tenant's application for a new tenancy based on an intention to demolish or reconstruct the premises) or s 30(1)(g) (ie opposition to a tenant's application for a new tenancy based on an intention to occupy the premises for the purposes of a business or as a residence).

**12.4** Prior to the decision of the Supreme Court in *S Franses Ltd v Cavendish Hotels (London) Ltd* (the '*Franses*' case),[1] the law was well-settled as to the nature of the relevant intention to be established by the landlord for these purposes. As Asquith LJ said in *Cunliffe v Goodman*:[2]

> An 'intention' to my mind connotes a state of affairs which the party 'intending' – I will call him X – does more than merely contemplate. It connotes a state of affairs which, on the contrary, he decides, so far as in him lies, to bring about, and which, in point of possibility, he has a

[1] *S Franses Ltd v Cavendish Hotels (London) Ltd* [2019] AC 249.

[2] *Cunliffe v Goodman* [1950] KB 237, at 253; and see also *Fleet Electrics v Jacey Investments* [1956] 1 WLR 1027, at 1032–33, per Lord Evershed ('It is not now in doubt that the import of the word "intend" in

> reasonable prospect of being able to bring about, by his own act of volition … Not merely is the term 'intention' unsatisfied if the person professing it has too many hurdles to overcome, or too little control of events. It is equally inappropriate if at the material date that person is in effect not deciding to proceed but feeling his way and reserving his decision until he shall be in possession of financial data sufficient to enable him to determine whether the project will be commercially worth-while.

**12.5** The law has been 'significantly altered'[3] by the *Franses* case. There, the tenant was a textile dealership. It occupied the ground floor and basement of premises on Jermyn Street. The tenant served a notice requesting the grant of a new tenancy. The landlord served a counter-notice opposing the grant of a new tenancy under s 30(1)(f). A preliminary issue was directed whether that ground of opposition was made out. At trial, it was found that the landlord's proposed scheme of works was designed with the material intention of undertaking works that would have led to the eviction of the tenant, regardless of the works' commercial or practical utility and irrespective of expense. In other words, the proposed works were no more than a 'device' to obtain possession of the premises. The Supreme Court considered that, on the facts, the landlord did not 'intend' (within the meaning of s 30(1)(f) of the 1954 Act) to carry out the works specified in the scheme of works relied upon in opposition to the tenant's application for a new tenancy. Giving the lead judgment, Lord Sumption (with whom Baroness Hale, Lady Black and Lord Kitchen agreed) explained the relevant test as follows:[4]

> the landlord's intention to demolish or reconstruct the premises must exist independently of the tenant's statutory claim to a new tenancy, so that the tenant's right of occupation under a new lease would serve to obstruct it. The landlord's intention to carry out the works therefore cannot be conditional on whether the tenant chooses to assert his claim to a new tenancy and to persist in that claim. The acid test is whether the landlord would intend to do the same works if the tenant left voluntarily … In my judgment, a conditional intention of this kind is not the fixed and settled intention that ground (f) requires. The answer would be the same if what the landlord proposed was demolition, conditionally on its being necessary to obtain possession from the court.

**12.6** The *Franses* case was decided in the context of an opposed claim for a new tenancy under the 1954 Act. It is possible that Lord Sumption's 'acid test' might be applied by analogy in the case of a landlord's redevelopment break clause conditional upon the landlord having the requisite 'intention' at the material time, ie whether the landlord would

section 30(1)(f) of the Act is that at the appropriate date or dates … there must be a firm and settled intention not likely to be changed, or in other words that the proposal for doing the work has moved "out of the zone of contemplation into the valley of decision" …'); *Fisher v Taylors Furnishings Stores Ltd* [1956] 2 QB 78, at 84, per Denning LJ (the intention must be 'genuine and not colourable; that it is a firm and settled intention, not likely to be changed'); *Humber Oil Terminals Trustee Ltd v Associated British Ports* [2012] EWCA Civ 596, [2012] L&TR 27, at [16], per Rimer LJ ('The issue before the judge was whether ABP had established that intention. That was a question of fact for the judge which had to be answered by considering the two requisite elements making up the necessary intention: (a) did ABP have a fixed and settled desire to do that which it intended to do; and (b) did ABP have a reasonable prospect of being able to bring about its desired result … The first element of the test is a subjective one. The second is an objective one.'); *The Gulf Agencies Ltd v Ahmed* [2016] EWCA Civ 44, at [7]–[8], per David Richards LJ (citing from *Humber Oil and Taylors Furnishing*).

[3] *London Kendal Street No 3 Ltd v Daejan Investments Ltd* [2019] L&TR 22, at [41], per HHJ Saunders.

[4] *S Franses Ltd v Cavendish Hotels (London) Ltd* [2019] AC 249, at [19]. See, also, the concurring judgment of Lord Briggs (with whom Lady Black and Lord Kitchin agreed), at [32] ('… a tenant's statutory right to a new tenancy should not be circumvented by proposed works which, viewed as a whole, would not have been undertaken by the landlord if the tenant had left voluntarily …').

intend to do the same works if the tenant left voluntarily (regardless of the exercise of the break option). It follows that earlier decisions[5] suggesting that the motive behind a landlord's intention is irrelevant must be treated with some caution. As Lord Sumption said in *Franses*,[6] the landlord's motive may be material for testing the genuineness (or conditionality) of its intention.

**12.7** For the purposes of ss 30(1)(f) and 30(1)(g) of the 1954 Act, the landlord must demonstrate that he has the requisite 'intention' as at the date of the hearing of the application in court.[7] Importantly, it should be appreciated that the position might be different with a landlord's break clause, the wording of which may require the landlord to have formed his 'intention' to redevelop the premises at an earlier point in time, eg as at the date of service of the break notice itself.[8] In such a case, the break notice will be invalid if the requisite intention cannot be shown to have existed as at that earlier date.

### (b) 'Desires' or 'Wishes'

**12.8** In *Patel v Keles*[9] (which concerned opposition to the grant of a new lease under s 30(1)(g) of the 1954 Act), Arden LJ observed that the courts have 'set a high hurdle for establishing the necessary subjective intention' because, if the landlord succeeds in making out his ground of opposition to the tenant's application for a new tenancy, the tenant will have no right to renew his lease and will have to vacate the premises (thereby losing any goodwill attached to the business at those premises). In order to avoid such a 'high hurdle', a landlord may opt for different wording in the break clause. So, for example, in *Aberdeen Steak Houses Group Limited v Crown Estate Commissioners*,[10] the break clause in question provided:

> If the [Commissioners] shall desire to demolish or reconstruct the Building or a substantial part thereof or to carry out substantial work of construction on part thereof on or after the 10th day of October in the years 1995 or 2000 or 2005 and of such desire shall give to [Aberdeen] at least six months' previous notice in writing to expire on the relevant of the aforementioned dates then on the expiration of the said notice the term hereby granted shall cease

**12.9** Mr Anthony Grabiner QC (sitting as a Deputy Judge) held that the word 'desire' was an ordinary English word meaning 'simply to wish for something'; and that, as a

[5] *Commissioners of Inland Revenue v Southend-on-Sea Estates Co Ltd* [1915] AC 428, at 431, per Earl Loreburn; *Gregson v Cyril Lord Ltd* [1963] 1 WLR 41, at 45, per Upjohn LJ; *Turner v Wandsworth LBC* (1995) 69 P&CR 433, at 436, per Staughton LJ; *Zarvos v Pradhan* [2003] EWCA Civ 208, at [46], per Ward LJ.

[6] *S Franses Ltd v Cavendish Hotels (London) Ltd* [2019] AC 249, at [16] and [21].

[7] *Betty's Cafés Limited v Phillips Furniture Stores Limited* [1959] AC 20; *Somerfield Stores Limited v Spring (Sutton Coldfield) Limited* [2010] EWHC 2084 (Ch); *Crossco No 4 v Jolan Limited* [2011] EWHC 803 (Ch); *Hough v Greathall Limited* [2015] EWCA Civ 23.

[8] As is the case in other statutory contexts, eg the service of a counter-notice under s 151 of the Town and Country Planning Act 1990 objecting to a blight notice. The serving party is required to have formed the relevant intention as at the date of the counter-notice. See eg *Mancini v Coventry City Council* (1985) 49 P&CR 127, at 140, per Purchas LJ (decided under s 194(2)(b) of the Town and Country Planning Act 1971); *Charman v Dorset County Council* (1986) 52 P&CR 88, at 97–98, per JH Emlyn Jones FRICS; *Craddock v Secretary of State for Transport* [2021] UKUT 0002 (LC), at [82], per AJ Trott FRICS.

[9] *Patel v Keles* [2010] Ch 332, at 338H.

[10] *Aberdeen Steak Houses Limited v Crown Estate Commissioners* [1997] 2 EGLR 107.

matter of plain language, it was quite different from the word 'intention'. Indeed, such a distinction is helpfully pointed up in *Cunliffe v Goodman*,[11] where Asquith LJ explained:

> X cannot, with any due regard to the English language, be said to 'intend' a result which is wholly beyond the control of his will. He cannot 'intend' that it shall be a fine day tomorrow: at most he can hope or desire or pray that it will.

### (c) 'Proposes'

**12.10** Another variant is where the break clause is conditional on the landlord 'proposing' to undertake a development.[12] In *Trustees of the Magdalen and Lasher Charity v Shelower*,[13] it was suggested by Counsel for the tenant that the word 'proposes' puts a bigger burden on a landlord than the word 'intends' in s 30(1) of the 1954 Act. Rejecting this submission, Lord Denning MR said:

> The word "proposes" is different from the word "intends". A man may propose to do a thing without having formed a fixed and settled intention to do it.

### (d) 'Requires'

**12.11** One further variant is where the break clause is conditional on the landlord 'requiring' the demised premises for development purposes. Where this is the case, the court will probably construe the word 'requires' in the same way as it is construed in the context of Case B in Part I of Sch 3 to the Agricultural Holdings Act 1986 (ie one of the cases where the consent of the Tribunal to the operation of a notice to quit is not required). So, for example, in *Jones v Gates*,[14] the landlord served a notice to quit on the tenant contending that he required the demised premises (a field) for a use, other than for agriculture. As to its being so required the landlord said that he intended to sell the field as a sports ground and would have no difficulty in doing so. He had had inquiries from a business firm and a football club but had received no offers and was not in negotiations with anybody. Evershed MR expressly approved of the following observations of the trial judge:[15]

> On that evidence [Counsel for the landlord] says that a reasonable prospect of use is shown and that that satisfies the word 'required'. I do not think that in the absence of a definite person or persons willing to negotiate there could be said to be such a reasonable prospect and I am not, therefore, satisfied that the holding is 'required' for the purpose.

[11] *Cunliffe v Goodman* [1950] KB 237, at 253.

[12] This expression is used in s 17(1) of the Leasehold Reform Act 1967. So, where a tenancy of a house and premises has been extended under s 14, the landlord may, at any time not earlier than 12 months before the original term date of the tenancy, apply to the court for an order that he may resume possession of the property on the ground that 'for purposes of redevelopment he proposes to demolish or reconstruct the whole or a substantial part of the house and premises'.

[13] *Trustees of the Magdalen and Lasher Charity v Shelower* (1968) 19 P&CR 389, at 392 CA.

[14] *Jones v Gates* [1954] 1 WLR 222; *cf Paddock Investments Ltd v Lory* [1975] 2 EGLR 5 (part of farm had the benefit of a planning permission for the working of gravel; landlord in negotiations with a firm of gravel merchants at the date when notice to quit served; notice to quit valid).

[15] *Jones v Gates* [1954] 1 WLR 222, at 224.

**12.12** Whether the 'requirement' must be for development purposes on the break date or at a point in time thereafter will, of course, depend on the true construction of the provision in question.[16]

## THE SCOPE OF THE BREAK CLAUSE

**12.13** Whatever the wording of the break clause, it is important to consider whether it is apt to encompass the lessor's *actual* intended (or other) purpose. So, in *Coates v Diment*,[17] the landlord had reserved the right to re-enter at any time without notice upon such of the demised premises (an agricultural holding) as he required 'for building sites or planting or other purposes'. The landlord had obtained permission from the local planning authority to construct a sports stadium on part of the agricultural holding; and, as a consequence, he sent to the tenant a notice to quit in the following terms:

> I … hereby give you one months' notice from the date hereof … to quit [the land which was the subject of the planning permission] as I wish to … to enter upon the said lands for the purpose of effecting preparatory works for which permission has been granted.

**12.14** Streatfield J held[18] that the words 'or other purposes' in the break clause ought to be construed *eiusdem generis* with the preceding words. He said:

> In so far as a genus is to be found in the words, I think it is the normal user of land of the character concerned, and I cannot think that it was ever the intention for the parties to this contract that part of the land within a quarter of a mile of the farm-house should be used for building a sports stadium … I do not think that this was the kind of 'building site' contemplated, nor that the words 'or other purposes', construed eiusdem generis with the earlier words, cover such buildings as a sports stadium and other buildings purely ancillary to the main purpose of providing a sports ground.

**12.15** Similarly, in *City Offices (Regent Street) Limited v Europa Acceptance Group Plc*,[19] the landlord wished to exercise a break clause worded as follows:

> if the Landlord shall desire to determine the said term … for the purpose of the redevelopment or reconstruction of the demised premises … and shall give to the Tenant not less than six months previous notice in writing of such its desire then immediately upon the expiration of such notice the present demise and everything herein contained shall cease and be void

**12.16** The question was whether the works proposed to be carried out by the landlord constituted a 'redevelopment or reconstruction of the demised premises'. Holding that the works fell within the scope of the break clause, Nicholls LJ said:

> I am unable to accept the defendant's submissions on this matter. The word 'reconstruction' in clause 8 falls to be construed in its context. The context here is a lease of property which does not include any part of the structural framework of the building. The demise essentially is of an

[16] In *Rees v Windsor-Clive* [2021] 1 P&CR 12, it was common ground that for the purposes of 'Case B' the land in question had to be 'required' at the end of the period stated in the notice or within a relatively short time thereafter, rather than in the more distant future or at some as yet unascertained date.

[17] *Coates v Diment* [1951] 1 All ER 890.

[18] *Coates v Diment* [1951] 1 All ER 890, at 898–99.

[19] *City Offices (Regent Street) Limited v Europa Acceptance Group Plc* [1990] 05 EG 71.

air space with fixtures and fittings and a skin comprising, as I have already indicated, the plaster coverings of the party walls and of the structural walls and the coverings of the ceilings and the coverings of the floors, including a screed thereon. Clause 8 contemplates the possibility of the reconstruction or, I should add, the redevelopment of that particular unit – that 'eggshell' as it has been described. The works proposed to be done will involve the physical removal of most of that eggshell and its replacement, insofar as there will be a replacement, with something different. The floor coverings are to be removed and the replacement coverings will result in a slightly higher floor level. New and lower suspended ceilings will be installed. The wall surrounding the leased property … will be removed and not replaced, thus creating a single open floor space embracing in part the leased property and in part other property. The external walls which are not being replaced – for example, the Regent Street facade – will be dry-lined, thus reducing the useable lettable space of the leased property in those areas. Further, and importantly, the external brickwork walls fronting on to the two light wells will be demolished and taken away, leaving the leased property open and exposed to the elements for many months while the works proceed. New curtain walls will then be constructed and these will give the leased property an enlarged useable lettable area of about one square foot per foot of light well wall. … In short, as the works proceed, the demolition work will involve the physical demolition of most of the eggshell as part of the larger scheme and the rebuilding of something significantly different.

In my view, the judge was correct in deciding that works having this far reaching physical effect on the state of the leased property satisfied the requirement of 'reconstruction of the demised premises' in clause 8.

**12.17** Another example is *Parkinson v Barclays Bank Ltd*.[20] In that case, the bank let to a dental surgeon the upper floor of premises by a lease for 21 years. Clause 6 provided that if the bank was desirous of determining the lease at the expiration of the first 14 years of the term, they were entitled to do so 'but notwithstanding anything hereinbefore contained the lessors shall only be at liberty to determine the said term hereby created at the expiration of the first fourteen years thereof, if they shall require the premises hereby demised for the purposes of the business carried on by them'. The bank served a break notice pursuant to clause 6, making it clear that it did not want the premises immediately; but rather, they wanted the premises at sometime within seven years from the break date. The tenant issued proceedings claiming that the bank had no right to terminate the lease at the end of the 14 years, since it did not require the premises 'for the purposes of the business carried out by them'. Holding that the break clause was validly exercised, Somervell LJ said:[21]

In my view the natural meaning of those words is: if the landlord requires the premises for the purpose of the business carried on by him during the period referred to in the condition, that is, during the last seven years for which he will otherwise be deprived of possession of his property. That, I think, is the natural meaning in this context. The lessors are saying: 'We let you have these premises for fourteen years, because we do not foresee wanting them over that period, but with regard to the other seven years if we want them over that period then we reserve the right to give notice'. It would, I think, be rather absurd if the construction were that the bank had no right to terminate at the end of the fourteen years although it might be quite clear that they would want the premises for their own purposes in a year or so but could not say that they wanted to occupy them forthwith.

[20] *Parkinson v Barclays Bank Ltd* [1951] 1 KB 368.
[21] *Parkinson v Barclays Bank Ltd* [1951] 1 KB 368, at 378–79.

## REDEVELOPMENT BREAK CLAUSES UNDER THE 1954 ACT

**12.18** Reference should be made to Chapter 18 which considers the position under Part II of the Landlord and Tenant Act 1954.

## REDEVELOPMENT BREAK CLAUSES UNDER THE 1993 ACT

### (a) The Statutory Framework

**12.19** Chapter II of the Leasehold Reform, Housing and Urban Development Act 1993 ('the 1993 Act') gives a tenant of a flat who holds a lease granted for a term of more than 21 years the right to claim from the landlord a new lease of the flat for a term expiring 90 years after the expiry date of the current lease. The right is exercised by the service of a notice of claim under s 42 of the Act. Where a tenant has a right to a new lease, and has given a s 42 notice, the landlord is bound to grant him one in substitution for the existing lease: s 56(1).

**12.20** The rent[22] and term[23] of the new lease are fixed by the 1993 Act. All the other terms of the new lease are to be the 'same … as those of the existing lease' but with such modifications as may be required or appropriate to take account of the matters set out in s 57(1) and subject also to any agreement between the landlord and tenant under s 57(6).

**12.21** In addition, under s 57(7)(b), the terms of the new lease are required: '… to reserve to the person who is for the time being the tenant's immediate landlord the right to obtain possession of the flat in accordance with section 61'.

**12.22** In turn, s 61 confers on the landlord the right to terminate the new lease on grounds of redevelopment. So far as material, it provides:

> (1) Where a lease of a flat ('the new lease') has been granted under section 56 but the court is satisfied, on an application made by the landlord –
>
> (a) that for the purposes of redevelopment the landlord intends –
>
> (i) to demolish or reconstruct, or
>
> (ii) to carry out substantial works of construction on, the whole or a substantial part of any premises in which the flat is contained, and
>
> (b) that he could not reasonably do so without obtaining possession of the flat,
>
> the court shall by order declare that the landlord is entitled as against the tenant to obtain possession of the flat and the tenant is entitled to be paid compensation by the landlord for the loss of the flat.
>
> (2) An application for an order under this section may be made –
>
> (a) at any time during the period of 12 months ending with the term date of the lease in relation to which the right to acquire a new lease was exercised; and
>
> (b) at any time during the period of five years ending with the term date of the new lease.

[22] A peppercorn: s 56(1).

[23] A term expiring 90 years after the term date of the existing lease: s 56(1).

**12.23** The 1993 Act does not indicate what is the sanction (if any) for a failure to include such a provision in the new lease. Be that as it may, the leading textbook on the 1993 Act[24] suggests the following wording be inserted into a new lease for the purposes of complying with s 57(7)(b):

> The landlord may, (a) at any time during the period of 12 months ending on [insert the term date of the original lease], and (b) at any time during the period of five years ending on [insert the term date of the new lease] apply to the court under section 61 of the Leasehold Reform, Housing and Urban Development Act 1993 for an order for possession of the flat on the ground that for the purposes of redevelopment he intends to demolish or reconstruct, or to carry out substantial works of construction on the whole or a substantial part of any premises in which the flat is contained, and that he could not reasonably do so without obtaining possession of the flat, and the provisions of that section and Schedule 14 to the Act shall apply accordingly.

### (b) Conditions Governing the Exercise of the Break Clause

**12.24** The landlord's right to terminate a new lease on redevelopment grounds under the 1993 Act may be exercised on an application to the county court.[25] For these purposes, the 'landlord' means:[26] 'the party who granted the new lease under section 56 who, at that stage, would have been the competent landlord as defined in section 40'.

**12.25** As may be apparent from the wording of s 61(2) of the 1993 Act, the landlord has two periods of time within which he may make such an application. The first is 'at any time during the period of 12 months ending with the term date of the lease in relation to which the right to acquire a new lease was exercised' (ie the 12-month period ending with the term date of the original lease). The second is 'at any time during the period of five years ending with the term date of the new lease'.

**12.26** On an application under s 61, the landlord must satisfy the court that, for the purposes of redevelopment, he intends either 'to demolish or reconstruct' or 'to carry out substantial works of construction on' the 'whole or a substantial part of any premises in which the flat is contained'.[27] Further, he must also show that he could not 'reasonably do so without obtaining possession of the flat'.[28] The wording of s 61(1) mirrors that of s 31(1)(f) of the 1954 Act; and no doubt the reported authorities on the latter will be helpful in resolving any disputes under the former.

**12.27** If the court is satisfied that the landlord has the requisite intention, it has no discretion, but (as per s 61(1)) must declare that 'the landlord is entitled as against the tenant to obtain possession of the flat and the tenant is entitled to be paid compensation by the landlord for the loss of the flat'. Compensation is calculated under the complicated provisions of Sch 14, which are outside the scope of this work.

[24] A Radevsky, D Greenish *Hague on Leasehold Enfranchisement* (Sweet & Maxwell, 7th edn, 2021), §32–13.
[25] Section 90(1).
[26] *Kutchukian v Keepers and Governors of John Lyon School* [2013] 1 WLR 2842, at [48], per Lloyd LJ.
[27] Section 61(1).
[28] Section 61(2).

**12.28** In practice, there may be some argument as to whether the landlord's intended works fall within the scope of s 61(1). This is well-illustrated by *Majorstake v Curtis*[29] (which involved consideration of equivalent wording under s 47(2) of the 1993 Act). In that case, the tenant owned a flat (numbered 77) in a block of 50 flats in St John's Wood. He served a s 42 notice claiming a new lease of the flat. The landlord served a counter-notice under s 45 notifying the tenant that it intended to apply to the court for an order under s 47(1) for a declaration that the right to acquire a new lease was not exercisable by the tenant by reason of the landlord's intention to combine flat 77 with the flat beneath (numbered 74), so as to form a 'duplex' apartment. The only question for the House of Lords was whether the proposed works of construction would comprise works 'on the whole or a substantial part of the premises in which [flat 77] was contained'.

**12.29** The House of Lords was unanimous in holding the 'premises in which [flat 77] was contained' was the block of flats. Although, on the question whether the proposed works of construction were works on 'a substantial part' of the premises the House of Lords was not unanimous in its reasoning. Thus, Lord Scott said:[30]

> This is not a question which was addressed either in the county court or in the Court of Appeal. ... It is accepted, however, that the proposed works of construction are 'substantial works' for the purposes of section 47(2)(b). In the expression 'substantial works' the adjective 'substantial' denotes, in my opinion, works that are not trivial or, as one might say, insubstantial. There is no other yardstick than impression. The issue is one of fact and degree. The same approach should, in my opinion, be taken to the question whether Flats 74 and 77 constitute a 'substantial' part of Block B. They are two of the fifty flats in the Block. In percentage terms two out of fifty, four per cent, does not sound substantial. I doubt, however, whether that is the right approach. Each flat is a substantial item of property, an item of considerable value. Each flat, as part of the Block, could not, in my opinion, be regarded as a trivial or insignificant part. If this point had been the subject of proper examination and argument I would have taken a great deal of persuading that the proposed works of construction on Flats 74 and 77 were not works on a 'substantial part' of Block B for the purposes of section 47(2)(b).

**12.30** By contrast, Baroness Hale was of the following opinion:[31]

> It has hitherto been taken for granted that, if the premises are Block B, then two flats out of the fifty do not constitute 'a substantial part of' the premises. Were it otherwise there would have been no point in the appellant pursuing matters to this House. The respondent has not hitherto sought to argue otherwise. In my view, it was right not to do so. 'Substantial' is a word which has a wide range of meanings. Sometimes it can mean 'not little'. Sometimes it can mean 'almost complete', as in 'in substantial agreement'. Often it means 'big' or 'solid', as in a 'substantial house'. Sometimes it means 'weighty' or 'serious', as in a 'substantial reason'. It will take its meaning from its context. But in an expression such as a 'substantial part' there is clearly an element of comparison with the whole: it is something other than a small or insignificant or insubstantial part. There may be both a qualitative element of size, weight or importance in its own right; and a quantitative element, of size, weight or importance in relation to the whole. The works intended by this landlord are substantial in relation to each of the flats involved, but those flats do not in my view constitute a substantial part of the whole premises.

[29] *Majorstake v Curtis* [2008] 1 AC 787.
[30] *Majorstake v Curtis* [2008] 1 AC 787, at [18].
[31] *Majorstake v Curtis* [2008] 1 AC 787, at [40].

## THE ELECTRONIC COMMUNICATIONS CODE

### (a) Introduction

**12.31** The Electronic Communications Code ('the 2017 Code') was introduced by s 4 of and Schedule 1 to the Digital Economy Act 2017 ('the 2017 Act'). These provisions resulted in the insertion of a new Schedule 3A into the Communications Act 2003 ('the 2003 Act'), divided into 17 separate parts.[32] The 2017 Code contains a legal framework which 'deals with the acquisition, exercise and termination of "Code Rights"'.[33] The 2017 Code came into force on 28 December 2017.

**12.32** Prior to the enactment of the 2017 Code, an 'operator' of electronic communications apparatus was entitled to acquire rights to install and keep such apparatus on other people's land under the 'Telecommunications Code' ('the 2003 Code') found in Schedule 2 to the Telecommunications Act 1984 ('the 1984 Act'), to which effect was given s 106 of the 2003 Act. Curiously, s 106(1) of the 2003 Act referred to the 2003 Code under a different name, namely, the 'Electronic Communications Code'. Nonetheless, the title to Sch 2 to the 1984 Act remained as originally enacted.

**12.33** There was widespread dissatisfaction with the 2003 Code. This is because it was complex, outdated and made the rollout of electronic communications more difficult.[34]

**12.34** Although the 2003 Code has since been repealed,[35] the 2017 Code does not have retrospective effect. Therefore, it is inevitable that practitioners will need to be aware of the relevance of the 2003 Code to historic agreements.

### (b) The 2003 Code

**12.35** The 2003 Code has been famously labelled 'one of the least coherent and thought-through pieces of legislation on the statute book'.[36] As mentioned above, it enables an 'operator' of electronic communications apparatus to acquire rights to install

[32] A new Part 4A has since been inserted into the 2017 Code by s 1 of the Telecommunications Infrastructure (Leasehold Property) Act 2021.

[33] *Cornerstone Telecommunications Infrastructure Ltd v Compton Beauchamp Estates Ltd* [2020] 1 P&CR 15, at [10], per Lewison LJ.

[34] See the report of the Law Commission, 'The Electronic Communications Code' (Law Com 336), at §1.9–1.11 (referred to by Lewison LJ in *Cornerstone Telecommunications Infrastructure Ltd v Compton Beauchamp Estates Ltd* [2020] 1 P&CR 15, at [2]). It is worth noting that there has been widespread dissatisfaction with the 2017 Code also. Hence, on 27 January 2021, the Government published a Consultation Paper entitled 'Access to land: consultation on changes to the Electronic Communications Code' inviting views on whether changes to the 2017 Code were needed 'to ensure that the UK has sufficiently robust electronic communications networks to deliver the coverage and connectivity consumers and business need'. The closing date for comments was 24 March 2021.

[35] Subject to the transitional provisions specified in s 4(10) of and Schedule 2 to the 2017 Act and the Electronic Communications Code (Transitional Provisions) Regulations 2017/1008. For an important discussion of the effect of these provisions see *Cornerstone Telecommunications Infrastructure Ltd v Ashloch Ltd* [2021] EWCA Civ 90, at [86]–[105], per Lewison LJ.

[36] *The Bridgewater Canal Co Ltd v Geo Networks Ltd* [2010] 1 WLR 2576, at [7], per Lewison J (overturned on appeal at [2011] 1 WLR 1487).

and keep such apparatus on other people's land. The phrase 'operator' is defined as a person to whom the 2003 Code is applied 'by a direction given by OFCOM'.[37]

**12.36** The 2003 Code provides for what has been described[38] as a 'general regime' with a number of 'special regimes' running alongside. The 'special regimes' are expressly excluded from the 'general regime'.[39] The 'special regimes' only arise in comparatively rare circumstances (relating to street works, flying lines, tidal waters and linear obstacles). Therefore, this section will focus on the 'general regime'.

**12.37** The basic structure of the 'general regime' is to require the operator to acquire the rights it needs to install and keep electronic communications apparatus on land in the occupation and/or ownership of another 'by agreement in writing'.[40] However, if such agreement cannot be reached with the relevant person, then para 5 of the 2003 Code provides a mechanism by which the necessary rights are obtained through: (i) the operator giving a notice specifying the right he requires;[41] and, upon the expiry of that notice (ii) an application to the county court for an order conferring the proposed right.[42] In principle, it is seemingly possible to contract out of the provisions of the 2003 Code.[43]

**12.38** Importantly, paras 20–21 of the 2003 Code confer on an operator a particular form of security of tenure which, in practice, restricts the ability of a landlord to regain possession of land following the exercise a redevelopment break clause contained in a lease (or any other agreement in writing) to which the 2003 Code applies.

**12.39** Paragraph 20(1) of the 2003 Code states:

> Where any electronic communications apparatus is kept installed on, under or over any land for the purposes of the operator's network, any person with an interest in that land or adjacent land may (notwithstanding the terms of any agreement binding that person) by notice given to the operator require the alteration of the apparatus on the ground that the alteration is necessary to enable that person to carry out a proposed improvement of the land in which he has an interest.

**12.40** Paragraph 2(2) provides that references to the 'alteration of any apparatus' include references to the 'removal' of the apparatus. Thus, if a qualifying person requires electronic communications apparatus to be removed in order to carry out a proposed 'improvement' of a relevant piece of land, he is entitled to serve a notice on the operator requiring the removal. For these purposes, 'improvement' includes 'development and change of use'.[44] Where a notice is given under para 20(1) of the 2003 Code, the operator is entitled to give a counter-notice under para 20(2). Where a counter-notice is given, the

[37] Section 106(3)(a) of the 2003 Act; para 1(1) of the 2003 Code.
[38] *The Bridgewater Canal Co Ltd v Geo Networks Ltd* [2010] 1 WLR 2576, at [8], [14], per Lewison J.
[39] Para 2(9) of the 2003 Code.
[40] Para 2(1).
[41] Para 5(1).
[42] Para 5(3).
[43] Para 27(2).
[44] Para 20(9).

operator shall make the 'alteration' only if the county court on an application by the qualifying person makes an order requiring the alteration to be made.[45]

**12.41** Then there is para 21(1) of the 2003 Code. This entitles 'any person ... for the time being entitled to require the removal of any of the operator's electronic communications apparatus from any land (whether under any enactment or because that apparatus is kept on, under or over that land otherwise than in pursuance of a right binding that person or for any other reason)' to enforce the removal of the apparatus upon giving the requisite notice under para 21(2). Where a person gives notice under para 21(2), the operator is entitled to give a counter-notice under para 21(3). Where such a counter-notice is given to any person, that person can only enforce the removal of the apparatus in pursuance of an order of the court.[46]

**12.42** It follows from the above that, where there is a lease to which the 2003 Code applies and which contains a landlord's redevelopment break clause, the landlord will not be entitled to rely upon its break rights alone as a means of recovering possession of the land in question; but rather, the landlord will have to give the requisite notice pursuant to para 20(1) or 21(2) of the 2003 Code (presumably, following or contemporaneously with the service of the break notice pursuant to the terms of the lease). In such a scenario, serious complications arise if the lease is one which also has the protection of Part II of the Landlord and Tenant Act 1954 (since it is not altogether clear whether the existence of a statutorily protected 1954 Act tenancy might restrict the ability of the landlord to service the requisite notice under the 2003 Code).[47] Those complex issues are outside the scope of this work.

### (c) The 2017 Code

**12.43** As already mentioned, the 2017 Code contains a legal framework which deals with the acquisition, exercise and termination of 'code rights'. The expression 'code rights' carries an extended definition in the 2017 Code.[48]

**12.44** Part 2 of the 2017 Code is entitled 'Conferral of Code Rights and Their Exercise'. This makes clear that a 'code right in respect of land may only be conferred on an operator[49] by an agreement between the occupier[50] of the land and the operator'.[51]

[45] Para 20(3).
[46] Para 21(6).
[47] As the Upper Tribunal explained in *EE Ltd v Islington LBC* [2019] 2 P&CR 13, at [26]: 'Unless excluded by an agreement complying with section 38A, Landlord and Tenant Act 1954, a lease entered into for the purpose of conferring old code rights would create a tenancy to which Part II of the 1954 Act applied. Despite the statutes having existed side by side from 1984 until 2017 the relationship between old code rights and statutory security of tenure under the 1954 Act was largely *unexplored territory* as far as the courts were concerned ...' (emphasis in original). The previous uncomfortable relationship between the parallel statutory regimes under the 2003 Code and Part II of the 1954 Act has been avoided under the 2017 Code: see **12.47** below.
[48] Para 3 of the 2017 Code.
[49] Defined in para 2.
[50] Defined in para 105.
[51] Para 9.

**12.45** Part 4 of the 2017 Code is entitled 'Power of Court to Impose Agreement'.[52] The power to impose an agreement conferring code rights on an operator is found under para 20.[53] This can result in an 'order ... which imposes on the operator and the relevant person[54] an agreement between them which – (a) confers the code right on the operator, or (b) provides for the code right to bind the relevant person'.[55] The terms of such an order are governed by para 23.[56] An agreement imposed by an order under para 20 'takes effect for all purposes of [the 2017 Code] as an agreement under Part 2 ... between the operator and the relevant person'.[57]

**12.46** Part 5 of the 2017 Code is entitled 'Termination and Modification of Agreements'. An agreement to which Part 5 of the 2017 Code applies is referred to as a 'code agreement'.[58]

**12.47** Part 5 'applies to an agreement under Part 2'[59] with certain exceptions. The most important exception is 'a lease of land in England and Wales' if (a) 'its primary purpose is not to grant code rights' and (b) 'it is a lease to which Part 2 of the Landlord and Tenant Act 1954 ... applies'.[60] In determining whether a lease is one to which Part 2

[52] In the 2017 Code, 'the court' means, in relation to England and Wales, the county court: see para 94(1)(a). However, this is 'subject to provision made by regulations under paragraph 95' (para 94(2)). Those regulations include the Electronic Communications Code (Jurisdiction) Regulations 2017/1284, reg 3 of which provides that the functions conferred by the 2017 Code on the county court are also exercisable by the following tribunals: (a) in relation to England, the First-tier Tribunal (in a case where relevant proceedings are transferred to it by the Upper Tribunal); (b) in relation to England and Wales, the Upper Tribunal; and (c) in relation to Scotland, the Lands Tribunal for Scotland.

[53] This power is only exercisable if the two conditions in paras 21(2) and 21(3) are met: see para 21(1). The power is also subject to para 21(5), which provides that the Upper Tribunal may not make an order under para 20 'if it thinks that the relevant person intends to redevelop all or part of the land to which the code right would relate, or any neighbouring land, and could not reasonably do so if the order were made'. This wording is modelled on s 30(1)(f) of the 1954 Act: see *EE Ltd v Sir James H E Chichester* [2019] UKUT 164 (LC), at [39]. Therefore, the same approach to 'intention' applies as described at **12.3–12.7** above. This means that a 'redevelopment conceived purely to prevent the acquisition of Code rights, which the relevant person would not pursue if Code rights were not sought, will not satisfy the test in paragraph 21(5)': *Chichester*, at [39].

[54] Defined in para 20(1).

[55] Para 20(4). The Upper Tribunal has power to impose code rights by means of lease: *EE Ltd v Islington LBC* [2019] 2 P&CR 13.

[56] An order under para 20 'must require the agreement to contain such terms as the court thinks appropriate' (para 23(2)). This direction 'involves no presumption in favour of the operator's preferred terms': see *Cornerstone Telecommunications Infrastructure Ltd v London and Quadrant Housing Trust* [2021] L&TR 1, at [43]. Instead, the Upper Tribunal will exercise its discretion 'with the statutory purpose of the Code in mind' and 'will also have in mind the general structure of the Code, and the fact that Code rights are imposed on site providers at rates of consideration far below those which would be agreed in an open market': *London and Quadrant*, at [44]. The discretion conferred by para 23(2) is expressly subject to paras 23(3)–(8). Notably, para 23(8) provides: 'The court must determine whether the terms of the agreement should include a term – (a) permitting termination of the agreement (and, if so, in what circumstances) ...'

[57] Para 22.

[58] Para 29(5).

[59] Para 29(1). So, by virtue of para 22, this applies to agreements imposed under Part 4: see *Cornerstone Telecommunications Infrastructure Ltd v Ashloch Ltd* [2020] 1 P&CR 16, at [30], per Martin Rodger QC (upheld on appeal at [2021] EWCA Civ 90).

[60] Para 29(2). The position is also reflected in s 43(4) of the Landlord and Tenant Act 1954 (added by para 4 of Part 2 of Schedule 3 to the 2017 Act). However, as Lewison LJ observed in *Cornerstone Telecommunications Infrastructure Ltd v Ashloch Ltd* [2021] EWCA Civ 90, at [34]: '... It is to be noted that paragraph 29 excludes leases with protection under Part II of the 1954 Act (where the primary purpose was not to grant Code rights) only from Part 5 of the Code. It does not purport to exclude such leases from any other part of the Code (including Part 4) ...'

of the 1954 Act applies, 'any agreement under section 38A … of that Act is to be disregarded'. In other words, 'a tenant under a 1954 Act tenancy which was not contracted out and which had either not expired or was continuing under s 24 of the Act when the new Code commenced, cannot make use of Pt 5'.[61]

**12.48** Para 30(2) applies if (a) a code right is conferred by, or is otherwise binding on, a person (the 'site provider') as the result of a code agreement, and (b) under the terms of the agreement – (i) the right ceases to be exercisable or the site provider ceases to be bound by it, or (ii) the site provider may bring the code agreement to an end so far as it relates to that right.[62] Where para 30(2) applies, then the code agreement 'continues' so that – (a) the operator may continue to exercise that right, and (b) the site provider continues to be bound by the right.[63] Thus, subject to the following provisions of Part 5 of the 2017 Code, an operator is entitled to 'hold over' after the expiration or termination of a code agreement.

**12.49** Para 31 enables a site provider to give notice terminating a code agreement by giving notice on certain grounds.[64] These grounds include that 'the site provider intends to redevelop all or part of the land to which the code agreement relates, or any neighbouring land, and could not reasonably do so unless the code agreement comes to an end'.[65]

**12.50** Where a site provider gives a notice under para 31, the code agreement to which it relates 'comes to an end in accordance with the notice' unless (a) within the period of three months beginning with the day on which the notice is given, the operator gives the site provider a counter-notice,[66] and (b) within the period of three months beginning with the day on which the counter-notice is given, the operator applies (in practice) to the Upper Tribunal for an order under para 34.[67] On such an application, if the Upper Tribunal decides that the site provider has established any of the grounds for termination stated in the notice, it 'must order that the code agreement comes to an end in accordance with the order'.[68]

**12.51** Thus, in a similar fashion to the position under the 2003 Code, where a code agreement is comprised in a lease[69] which incorporates a landlord's redevelopment break clause, the landlord will not be entitled to rely upon its break rights alone as a means of recovering possession of the land in question; but rather, the landlord will have to give the requisite notice pursuant to para 31 of the 2017 Code (again, presumably, following or contemporaneously with the service of the break notice pursuant to the terms of the code agreement itself).

[61] *Cornerstone Telecommunications Infrastructure Ltd v Ashloch Ltd* [2020] 1 P&CR 16, at [50].
[62] Para 30(1).
[63] Para 30(2).
[64] Para 31(1). The requirements of such a notice are specified in para 31(2).
[65] Para 31(4)(c). This is the same wording as found in para 21(5). See footnote 52 above.
[66] Which must comply with the requirements of para 32(3).
[67] Para 32(1).
[68] Para 32(4). In this situation, a right to require the removal of electronic communications apparatus arises under para 37: para 37(3)(b).
[69] Subject to the exception in para 29(2). See **12.47** above.

# 13

# *Invalid Break Notices: Waiver, Estoppel and Withdrawal*

## INTRODUCTION

**13.1** Barring an operative waiver or estoppel, an invalid break notice will have no legal effect. In such circumstances, the lease will continue. However, depending upon the particular circumstances of the case, the server or recipient of an otherwise invalid notice might be precluded from challenging its invalidity.[1]

## WAIVER AND ESTOPPEL: GENERAL PRINCIPLES

### (a) Waiver

**13.2** 'Waiver' is a word which is sometimes used loosely to describe 'a number of different legal grounds on which a person may be debarred from asserting a substantive right which he once possessed or from raising a particular defence to a claim against him which would otherwise be available to him'.[2] The expression may refer to 'a forbearance from exercising a right or to an abandonment of a right'.[3] There are different categories of waiver, including: (i) waiver by election; and (ii) unilateral waiver.[4] The distinction between these two categories of waiver was usefully summarised by Potter LJ in *Glencore Grain Ltd v Flacker Shipping Ltd (The Happy Day)*,[5] as follows:

> Broadly speaking, there are two types of waiver strictly so-called: unilateral waiver and waiver by election. Unilateral waiver arises where X alone has the benefit of a particular clause in a

[1] For a detailed exploration of the law on waiver and estoppel see S Wilken and K Ghaly *The Law of Waiver, Variation, and Estoppel* (Oxford University Press, 3rd edn, 2012).

[2] *Kammins Ballrooms Co Ltd v Zenith Investments (Torquay) Ltd* [1971] AC 850, at 882H, per Lord Diplock.

[3] *Motor Oil Hellas (Corinth) Refineries SA v Shipping Corporation of India (The Kanchenjunga)* [1990] 1 Lloyd's Rep 391, at 397, per Lord Goff.

[4] Reference is sometimes made to another category of waiver, namely, 'waiver by estoppel.' See eg *Alfred Street Properties Ltd v National Asset Management Agency* [2020] EWHC 397 (Comm), at [93], per Phillips LJ. Strictly speaking, this type of 'waiver' (if it can be called such) is an application of the principle of equitable estoppel deriving from *Hughes v Metropolitan Railway Company* (1877) 2 App Cas 439. See, generally, the discussion in *Chitty on Contracts* (33rd Edition), §§24-007 and 24-008.

[5] *Glencore Grain Ltd v Flacker Shipping Ltd (The Happy Day)* [2003] 1 CLC 537, at [64]. In *TCG Pubs Ltd v The Master and Wardens or Governors of the Art or Mystery of the Girdlers of London* [2017] EWHC 772 (Ch), at [71]–[73], Mann J referred to the decision in *The Happy Day* but declined to consider whether the distinction identified by Potter LJ exists between the two kinds of waiver.

contract and decides unilaterally not to exercise the right or to forego the benefit conferred by that particular clause. It has been described as:

> 'The abandonment of a right in such a way that the other party is entitled to plead the abandonment by way of confession and avoidance if the right is thereafter asserted.'

See *Banning v Wright* [1972] 1 WLR 972 per Lord Hailsham LC at 97C–D. In such a case, X may expressly or by his conduct suggest that Y need not perform an obligation under the contract, no question of an election by X between two remedies or courses of action being involved. Waiver by election on the other hand is concerned with the reaction of X when faced with conduct by Y, or a particular factual situation which has arisen, which entitles X to exercise or refrain from exercising a particular right to the prejudice of Y. Both types of waiver may be distinguished from estoppel. The former looks principally to the position and conduct of the person who is said to have waived his rights. The latter looks chiefly at the position of the person relying on the estoppel. In waiver by election, unlike estoppel, it is not necessary to demonstrate that Y has acted in reliance upon X's representation: see per Lord Goff of Chieveley in *The Kanchenjunga* [1990] 1 Ll Rep 391 at 399 RHC.

**13.3** In either case, the waiver must be clear and unequivocal, made with full knowledge of all the facts relevant to the decision whether to waive or not.[6] This means actual, not constructive, knowledge.[7] Further, there must be 'some conscious decision' on the part of the person whom it is alleged has waived a particular right or obligation to do so.[8] Waiver is not to be lightly inferred. As Shaw LJ said in *Bremer Handels GmbH v C Mackprang Jr*:[9]

> What is beyond contention is that waiver of contractual rights is not to be facilely inferred or assumed. On the contrary, in human affairs and more especially in a commercial context the probabilities are against the voluntary sacrifice of vested rights which are or may be of material value. What is said to constitute a waiver must always be scrutinised with this in mind.

**13.4** The effect of a waiver was summarised by Lord Denning MR in *WJ Alan & Co Ltd v El Nasr Export & Import Co Ltd*,[10] as follows:

> the one who waives his strict rights cannot afterwards insist on them. His strict rights are at any rate suspended so long as the waiver lasts. He may on occasion be able to revert to his strict legal rights for the future by giving reasonable notice in that behalf, or otherwise making it plain by his conduct that he will thereafter insist upon them … But there are cases where no withdrawal is possible. It may be too late to withdraw: or it cannot be done without injustice to the other

[6] *Peyman v Lanjani* [1985] 1 Ch 457, at 500G, per Slade LJ; *Patel v Peel Investments (South) Ltd* [1992] 2 EGLR 116, at 118H, per Morritt J; *R (Bottomley) v The General Commissioners of Income Tax Pontefract Division* [2009] EWHC 1708 (Admin), at [21], per Kenneth Parker QC (sitting as a Deputy High Court Judge); *Hudson Bay Apparel Brands LLC v Umbro International Ltd* [2010] ETMR 62, at [60], per Lord Neuberger MR.

[7] *TCG Pubs Ltd v The Master and Wardens or Governors of the Art or Mystery of the Girdlers of London* [2017] EWHC 772 (Ch), at [76], per Mann J; *Leeds City Council v Barclays Bank Plc* [2021] EWHC 363 (Comm), at [173], per Cockerill J (who notes that knowledge 'to put the party onto enquiry of the extent of a breach' is 'likely' to be sufficient also).

[8] *BDW Trading Ltd v JM Rowe (Investments) Ltd* [2010] EWHC 1987 (Ch), at [45], per Peter Smith J (upheld on appeal at [2011] EWCA Civ 548); *Ropemaker Properties Ltd v Bella Italia Restaurants Ltd* [2018] L&TR 32, at [13], per Fancourt J.

[9] *Bremer Handels GmbH v C Mackprang Jr* [1979] 1 Lloyd's Rep 221, at 230.

[10] *W J Alan & Co Ltd v El Nasr Export & Import Co Ltd* [1972] 2 QB 189, at 213.

party. In that event he is bound by his waiver. He will not be allowed to revert to his strict legal rights. He can only enforce them subject to the waiver he has made.[11]

### (b) Estoppel

**13.5** An 'estoppel' is something which bars the object of it from 'asserting some fact or facts, or, sometimes, something that is a mixture of fact and law, that stands in the way of some right claimed by the person entitled to the benefit of the estoppel'.[12] However, it is to be noted that equitable estoppel is not 'a sort of joker or wild card to be used whenever the court disapproves of the conduct of a litigant who seems to have the law on his side. Flexible though it is, the doctrine must be formulated and applied in a disciplined and principled way. Certainty is important in property transactions'.[13]

**13.6** As with waiver, there are various species of estoppel. Those that are likely to be pertinent in the context of break clauses are promissory estoppel, estoppel by convention or estoppel by representation.

**13.7** The ingredients of promissory estoppel were succinctly explained by Oliver LJ in *James v Heim Gallery (London) Limited* (a case involving a rent review notice), as follows:[14]

> In order to found a promissory estoppel there has first to be found some clear and unequivocal representation either by words or conduct that the party claimed to be estopped will not rely upon his strict contractual rights. Secondly, the representation must be made with the intention, or at least the knowledge, that it is to be acted upon by the other party by altering his legal position; and thirdly, he must so alter his legal position in reliance upon the representation in such a way that it would be inequitable, or unfair, to permit the party claiming to be estopped from departing from the representation.

[11] This summary must be qualified by reference to the juristic nature of the waiver concerned. A waiver by election is final and has permanent effect. See *Kosmar Villa Holidays Plc v Trustees of Syndicate 1243* [2008] Bus LR 931, at [38], per Rix LJ. A 'waiver by estoppel' (as it is sometimes described) may have suspensory effect only, depending on whether it would be inequitable for the representing party to retract his waiver. See *Persimmon Homes (South Coast) Limited v Hall Aggregates (South Coast) Ltd* [2009] EWCA Civ 1108, at [52], per Patten LJ ('A party to a contract (A) may waive the obligation of the other party to the contract (B) to perform a stipulation in the contract that is for the benefit of A. A may waive the obligation without any request by B that A do so. But A will only be taken to have waived the obligation of B to perform that stipulation of the contract if (in the absence of a request to do so by B), A has made an unequivocal representation to B that A does waive the performance of the stipulation. That unequivocal representation can be by words or conduct, but does not have to be as blunt as 'I hereby waive' the other party's obligation to perform the stipulation. For the waiver to be effective, B must either act on the unequivocal representation of A to his detriment; or he must conduct his affairs on the basis of the waiver').

[12] *Cobbe v Yeoman's Row Management Limited* [2008] 1 WLR 1752, at [14], per Lord Scott; and see also *The Kanchenjunga* [1990] 1 Lloyd's Rep 391, at 399, per Lord Goff.

[13] *Cobbe v Yeoman's Row Management Limited* [2008] 1 WLR 1752, at [46], per Lord Walker.

[14] *James v Heim Gallery (London) Ltd* (1981) 41 P&CR 269, at 280; and see also, at 275, the comparable remarks of Buckley LJ ('… [Promissory estoppel] depends upon the party estopped having made to the other party to the estoppel a promise or an assurance or representation in the nature of a promise, that he will act or abstain from acting in some particular way in the future … it precludes him from acting inconsistently with his promise …').

**13.8** By contrast, estoppel by convention is founded, not on a representation of fact made by a representor and believed by a representee, but on an 'agreed statement of facts the truth of which has been assumed, by the convention of the parties' such that, when the parties have acted in their transaction upon the agreed assumption that a given state of facts is to be accepted between them as true, then as regards that transaction 'each will be estopped against the other from questioning the truth of the statement of facts so assumed'.[15]

**13.9** An estoppel by representation is said to arise where 'one by his words or conduct wilfully causes another to believe the existence of a certain state of things, and induces him to act on that belief, so as to alter his own previous position'.[16] In some circumstances,[17] silence of inaction can constitute a representation for the purpose of an estoppel. This is sometimes described as an estoppel by acquiescence. Of this, in *Willmott v Barber*, Fry J stated:[18]

> It has been said that the acquiescence which will deprive a man of his legal rights must amount to fraud, and in my view that is an abbreviated statement of a very true proposition. A man is not to be deprived of his legal rights unless he has acted in such a way as would make it fraudulent for him to set up those rights. What, then, are the elements or requisites necessary to constitute fraud of that description? In the first place the plaintiff must have made a mistake as to his legal rights. Secondly, the plaintiff must have expended some money or must have done some act (not necessarily upon the defendant's land) on the faith of his mistaken belief. Thirdly, the defendant, the possessor of the legal right, must know of the existence of his own right which is inconsistent with the right claimed by the plaintiff. If he does not know of it he is in the same position as the plaintiff, and the doctrine of acquiescence is founded upon conduct with a knowledge of your legal rights. Fourthly, the defendant, the possessor of the legal right, must know of the plaintiff's mistaken belief of his rights. If he does not, there is nothing which calls upon him to assert his own rights. Lastly, the defendant, the possessor of the legal right, must have encouraged the plaintiff in his expenditure of money or in the other acts which he has done, either directly or by abstaining from asserting his legal right. Where all these elements exist, there is fraud of such a nature as will entitle the Court to restrain the possessor of the legal right from exercising it, but, in my judgment, nothing short of this will do.

**13.10** In the well-known case of *Taylor Fashions Ltd v Liverpool Trustees Co Ltd*,[19] Oliver J referred to these observations and went on to say as follows:

[15] *Norwegian American Cruises A/S v Paul Mundy Ltd (the 'Vistafjord')* [1988] 2 Lloyd's Rep 343, at 349, per Bingham LJ (citing *Spencer-Bower and Turner on Estoppel by Representation*). See also the summary of the relevant principles found in *Republic of India v India Steamship Co Ltd (No 2)* [1998] AC 878, at 913E–G, per Lord Steyn; *Hiscox v Outhwaite* [1992] 1 AC 562, at 575, per Lord Donaldson; *Commissioners for Her Majesty's Revenue and Customs v Benchdollar Ltd* [2009] EWHC 1310 (Ch), at [52], per Briggs J; *Stena Line Ltd v Merchant Navy Ratings Pension Fund Trustees* [2010] EWHC 1805 (Ch), at [134]–[137], per Briggs J (upheld on appeal without discussing estoppel by convention at [2011] EWCA Civ 543); *Blindley Heath Investments Ltd v Bass* [2017] Ch 289, at [73], per Hildyard J (giving the judgment of the Court of Appeal); and *Tinkler v Commissioners for Her Majesty's Revenue and Customs* [2021] UKSC 39 (in particular, the judgment of Lord Burrows JSC).

[16] *Pickard v Sears* (1837) 6 Ad & El 439, at [474], per Lord Denman CJ.

[17] Discussed in more detail at **13.48–13.58** below.

[18] *Willmott v Barber* (1880) 15 Ch D 95, at 105. As to the current significance of Fry J's five probanda, see *Cobbe* (supra), at [56]–[59], per Lord Walker.

[19] *Taylor Fashions Ltd v Liverpool Trustees Co Ltd* [1982] 1 QB 133, at 147.

> It may well be (although I think that this must now be considered open to doubt) that the strict *Willmott v Barber* ... probanda are applicable as necessary requirements in those cases where all that has happened is that the party alleged to be estopped has stood by without protest while his rights have been infringed. It is suggested in *Spencer Bower and Turner, Estoppel by Representation*, 3rd ed (1977), para 290 that acquiescence, in its strict sense, is merely an instance of estoppel by representation and this derives some support from the judgment of the Court of Appeal in *De Bussche v Alt* (1878) 8 Ch D 286, 314. If that is a correct analysis then, in a case of mere passivity, it is readily intelligible that there must be shown a duty to speak, protest or interfere which cannot normally arise in the absence of knowledge or at least a suspicion of the true position. Thus for a landowner to stand by while a neighbour lays drains in land which the landowner does not believe that he owns (*Armstrong v Sheppard & Short Ltd* [1959] 2 QB 384) or for a remainderman not to protest at a lease by a tenant for life which he believes he has no right to challenge (*Svenson v Payne* (1945) 71 CLR 531) does not create an estoppel. Again, where what is relied on is a waiver by acquiescence, as in *Willmott v Barber* itself, the five probanda are no doubt appropriate. There is, however, no doubt that there are judicial pronouncements of high authority which appear to support as essential the application of all the five probanda over the broader field covering all cases generally classified as estoppel by 'encouragement' or 'acquiescence'.

## THE OPERATION OF WAIVER AND ESTOPPEL IN THE BREAK CLAUSE CONTEXT

**13.11** In the context of break clauses, the doctrines of waiver and estoppel might apply in a number of different scenarios. Indeed, given the rigours involved in the proper exercise of a break clause, it is not unusual to find tenants (in particular) resorting to these doctrines in an effort to save what would otherwise be an unsuccessful attempt to terminate the lease. It is important to emphasise that cases involving waiver and estoppel are 'highly fact sensitive'.[20] The authorities to which reference is made below are no more than illustrations of the applicability (or non-applicability, as the case may be) of the broader legal principles described above in the context of particular scenarios relevant to the exercise of a break clause.

### (a) Loss of the Right to Exercise the Break

**13.12** It is possible that the party with the benefit of a break clause (whether landlord or tenant) might so conduct himself as to waive the right to exercise, or be estopped from contending that he is entitled to exercise, the break. A contention to this effect arose in *Datnow v Jones*.[21] There, Mr Jones had been the tenant of a farm since 1934. He held the farm on a yearly tenancy, subject to 12 calendar months' notice, terminating on 29 September in any given year. In 1974, the landlords proposed, and Mr Jones agreed to, a scheme of amalgamation, the broad effect of which was to reorganise the physical configuration of Mr Jones' holding. During the course of the negotiations in connection

[20] *Avocet Industrial Estates LLP v Merol Ltd* [2012] L&TR 13, at [83], per Morgan J.
[21] *Datnow v Jones* [1985] 2 EGLR 1.

with the scheme of amalgamation, the landlords' agent gave Mr Jones assurances that, if he agreed to the amalgamation, the landlords would not thereafter seek any reduction in the parcels of his tenanted land during the continuation of his tenancy for the purposes of afforestation. These assurances were an 'abundant foundation'[22] for a finding that the landlords had estopped themselves from serving any notice to quit part of Mr Jones' holdings for the purposes of afforestation during his tenancy.

13.13 A similar result was arrived at in *John v George*.[23] In that case, Mr John was the tenant of a farm, including a farmhouse and a range of outbuildings. The tenancy agreement contained a repairing covenant on the part of the landlord. In January 1990, the outbuildings suffered storm damage to an estimated £65,000. The landlord (Mr George) had not insured the buildings and could not afford to repair them. Mr George therefore proposed that Mr John concur in a scheme whereby planning permission would be sought for conversion of the old farm buildings into a dwelling and for the construction of new buildings. The old buildings would then be sold with the benefit of planning permission. The sale would finance the new buildings, which Mr John would then use. Mr George applied for the requisite planning permission; and Mr John, at Mr George's request, wrote to the planning authority in support of the application. Planning permission was granted. Mr George then executed a deed of gift by which the old buildings and the land on which they stood were conveyed by him to two trustees to hold the land on trust for Mr George's daughter, thus severing the reversion. The new landlords served a notice to quit on Mr John in respect of the old buildings and the land. Mr John sought a declaration that the new landlords were estopped from relying upon the notice to quit. He was unsuccessful at trial, but appealed. The Court of Appeal unanimously allowed the appeal. Morritt LJ said:[24]

> Both Mr John and Mr George shared the assumption that Mr John would continue to carry on the business of a dairy farm with the use of the old buildings unless and until Mr George provided new buildings. The provision of the new buildings was the object of the single scheme proposed by Mr George and accepted by Mr John. One ingredient in the scheme was the grant of planning permission for the conversion of the old buildings; but that was for the purpose of implementing the scheme as a whole and was not an end in itself. Planning permission for the conversion of the old buildings was obtained unconditionally by means of the support both active and passive of Mr John rendered at the request of Mr George and on the basis of the assumption they shared that Mr John would continue to operate a dairy farm. In consequence the legal position of Mr John was altered and to his detriment.
>
> Mr John was not relying merely on his strict legal rights whatever they might be if the scheme was not implemented but on the assumption that they would not be altered in consequence of the scheme unless the scheme was implemented in full. This was the basis on which Mr George sought his support and this was the basis on which it was given. Thus both parties assumed that he would remain in possession of the old buildings unless and until he was provided with the new. The partial implementation of the scheme afforded to Mr George the means whereby to evict Mr John from the old buildings which he would not otherwise have had. By the service of the notice to quit the landlords seek to use the means so obtained for a purpose foreign to that

[22] *Datnow v Jones* [1985] 2 EGLR 1, at 2F, per Cumming-Bruce LJ.
[23] *John v George* (1996) 71 P&CR 375.
[24] *John v George* (1996) 71 P&CR 375, at 390.

for which they were obtained and contrary to the assumption on the basis on which the parties dealings had proceeded. In my judgment such a result would be unconscionable.

**13.14** This outcome may be contrasted with the result in *Crossco No 4 Unlimited v Jolan Ltd*.[25] That case concerned the lease of a building in Piccadilly, Manchester. The lease contained a landlord's break clause operable on three months' notice. Until 9 April 2009, the landlord was Crossco No 4 Unlimited ('Crossco'). On that day, it transferred the freehold reversion to Jolan Piccadilly Ltd ('Jolan'). Jolan wished to carry out an extensive development of the building; and so, on 26 October 2009, it served a notice on the tenant, Piccadilly, to operate the break clause. Inter alia, the tenant contended that the principle of estoppel could be relied upon with the overall result that Jolan was not entitled to rely upon the break clause in the way it sought to do.

**13.15** The dispute between the parties arose in the context of a complicated demerger of a group of family-owned companies (including Crossco, Jolan and Piccadilly). On one side of the transaction was Gill Noble and her respective family trusts and associated interests ('Gill's side'); and on the other side was Philip Noble and his respective family trusts and associated interests ('Philip's side'). The parties had negotiated on a commercial basis about the terms of the demerger, involving the division of the assets of the companies between the two sides. There was pressure to complete the demerger transaction by the end of February 2009. Not everything was agreed by that date, and each side had to trust the other side in respect of the outstanding issues. Crucially, there was a meeting on 18 February 2009 at which the parties discussed: (i) the proposal to transfer the freehold of the building from Crossco to Jolan; and (ii) thereafter, Piccadilly continuing to operate its business from the building. However, as Morgan J found at first instance:[26]

> The parties were content for the freehold to be transferred to Gill's side and for the question of the lease of the ground floor to be considered later, with neither party binding itself in relation to future negotiations as to the lease. Philip's side were content to proceed in that way because they believed they had a satisfactory lease of the whole building. They were mistaken about the lease because, in fact, it was subject to a three month break clause. That mistake was not attributable to any representation or assurance from Gill's side. Gill's side did not cause Philip's side to make this mistake. Gill's side did not even know that Philip's side was making this mistake. Gill's side did not commit itself by a promise or assurance about their future conduct as to any negotiations about a deed of variation or a new lease, nor as to the extent of any development. Philip's side did not rely on any such promise or assurance; they relied on their mistaken belief as to their rights under the existing lease. There is nothing there to raise an equity against Gill's side.

[25] *Crossco No 4 Unlimited v Jolan Ltd* [2011] EWHC 803 (Ch) (upheld on appeal at [2012] 1 P&CR 16). As a cautionary tale, Etherton LJ observed on appeal: '… it is a remarkable fact that a fifteen-minute discussion on February 18, 2009, followed by a modest number of communications passing between the parties from February 18, 2009 to March 10, 2009, has resulted in a trial of 35 days. I would add to that statement of wonder that those matters have also led to a judgment of the Judge running to 107 pages and 429 paragraphs, 178 pages of written submissions and five bundles of authorities on the present appeal, and an appeal hearing lasting two and a half days even though the appeal has been restricted to only some of the matters in dispute before the Judge'.

[26] *Crossco No 4 Unlimited v Jolan Ltd* [2011] EWHC 803 (Ch), at [361].

**13.16** In other words, Philip's side did not wake up to the fact that there was a break clause in the lease until after the demerger; whereas Gill's side did not know that Philip's side was labouring under a misapprehension as to the terms of the existing lease of the building. Thus, the mistake on Philip's side could not make the conduct of Gill's side in exercising the break clause unconscionable. Philip's side had no expectation of a certain interest in land (other than the lease itself, which was subject to the landlord's break clause).

**13.17** A similar argument based on waiver was rejected by the Privy Council in *Lancashire Insurance Co Ltd v MS Frontier Reinsurance Ltd*.[27] There, Lancashire Insurance Co Ltd ('the tenant') occupied certain premises at No 8 Par-la-Ville Road, Hamilton, under the terms of a lease due to expire at the end of 2008. The tenant wished, on the termination of its lease, to move to alternative premises at No 7 Par-la-Ville Road. MS Frontier Reinsurance Ltd ('the assignee') was willing to take a new lease of No 8 However, by June 2008, it was apparent that No 7 would not be ready for occupation before the expiry of the tenant's lease. In the circumstances, the tenant, the tenant's landlord and the assignee agreed that a new lease of No 8 would be granted to the tenant for a term commencing 1 January 2009; and that, when No 7 had become available for occupation by the Tenant, the Tenant would assign to the assignee the new lease of No 8. Under the terms of that agreement, completion of the assignment was to take place following service by the tenant of a notice that No 7 had become available for occupation. The assignment was to be completed by the execution of a deed on a date, defined in the agreement, as the 'condition date', ie no more than 15 working days after receipt by the assignee of the notice served by the tenant. Clause 6.6 of the agreement provided as follows:

> If for any reason the Condition Date has not occurred by the 31 December 2009 then the Tenant or the Assignee may serve written notice on the other to determine this Agreement and upon service of such this Agreement shall determine and cease to have effect and no party shall be under any further liability to any other party under this agreement without prejudice to any pre-existing right of action of any party in respect of any breach by any party of its obligations under this Agreement.

**13.18** In the events that occurred, the new lease of No 8 was granted to the tenant on 23 January 2009. The fit-out works to No 7 took longer to complete than anticipated. The tenant served the relevant notice on 18 December. The period of 15 working days after receipt of that notice expired on 13 January 2010. On that day, before completion had taken place, the assignee served notice of termination. The tenant raised a number of arguments, including one to the effect that the assignee had waived the right to give such a notice. On the material before the trial judge, it was impossible to contend that, in the period from 31 December 2009–13 January 2010, the assignee had acted in a manner which was consistent only with it having chosen not to exercise that right. Nor could it be said that, either during that period or at any earlier time, the assignee communicated to the tenant in clear and unequivocal terms an election not to exercise its right to serve a termination notice. Thus, the tenant's claim for specific performance of the agreement was refused.

[27] *Lancashire Insurance Co Ltd v MS Frontier Reinsurance Ltd* [2012] UKPC 42.

**13.19** The tenant in *Wigan Borough Council v Scullindale Global Ltd*[28] also failed in arguing that by waiver or estoppel the landlord was prevented from exercising a break option. That was a case in which the break option was exercisable by the landlord upon the occurrence of certain 'Events of Default' including 'the Lessee not achieving any or all of the Milestones defined in clause 4.6'. The 'Milestones' related to the commencement and completion of a development by 23 May 2018. The tenant did not achieve the Milestones by the stipulated date, but the landlord waited a further 16 months before serving a break notice. During that period, the landlord's representatives visited and inspected the property as the works were progressing. However, the landlord never made a clear and unequivocal communication that it would not in the future exercise the break clause. In any event, there was no detrimental reliance on anything said or done by the landlord, since the tenant would have undertaken the relevant works in any event.

### (b) Loss of the Right to Insist on a Break Notice Being Given at All

**13.20** Waiver or estoppel might operate so as to prevent the grantor of an option to determine a lease from insisting upon the grantee serving a break notice in order to exercise the break. This is illustrated by *Friary Holroyd and Healey's Breweries Ltd v Singleton*.[29] That case concerned an option, contained in a lease, to purchase certain freehold property (a beer house). The parties had entered into correspondence about the acquisition of that property, without giving any thought as to the requirement of a notice being given. The Court of Appeal (Lindley MR, Sir FH Jeune, and Rigby LJ) was of the opinion that:[30]

> the contracting parties had been negotiating on the assumption, which was in substance true, that the new company, the plaintiffs, were entitled to purchase the beerhouse for 450l., and that the defendant was bound to sell. When the abstract was sent, setting out the covenant giving the right of pre-emption or option of purchase, nothing was said about notice, and, in fact, no importance was attached to it. It was impossible, on the correspondence, to come to any other conclusion than that the defendant had waived her right to notice. It was not until some months after December, 1896, when the negotiations for the purchase commenced, that it occurred to anybody to raise the objection that the notice required by the lease had not been given. The learned judge below had addressed himself mainly to the legal question whether the new company was an 'assign', and he had attached too little weight to the correspondence, which appeared to be conclusive in favour of the new company, the plaintiffs.

**13.21** This may be contrasted with the outcome in *Ropemaker Properties Ltd v Bella Italia Restaurants Ltd*.[31] That case concerned, not a break option, but an agreement for lease which contained a provision (cl 14.2) entitling 'either the landlord or the

[28] *Wigan Borough Council v Scullindale Global Ltd* [2021] EWHC 779 (Ch).

[29] *Friary Holroyd and Healey's Breweries Ltd v Singleton* [1899] 2 Ch 261; and see also *Laine v Cadwallader* (2001) 33 HLR 36 (tenant dropping-in of keys treated by landlord as informal notice to quit).

[30] *Friary Holroyd and Healey's Breweries Ltd v Singleton* [1899] 2 Ch 261, at 263.

[31] *Ropemaker Properties Ltd v Bella Italia Restaurants Ltd* [2018] L&TR 32.

tenant ... at any time after the planning long stop date ... or the agreement long stop date ... to give written notice to the other and the guarantor to determine this agreement'. It was common ground that a tenant's notice under this provision had to be given both to the landlord and the guarantor, even though the guarantor was in the same group of companies as the tenant. On 16 May 2017, the tenant gave written notice to the landlord, but did not give equivalent notice to the guarantor. It was argued that the guarantor had waived the requirement for such notice. On the facts, this argument was rejected. Fancourt J explained:

> [31] ... in an earlier letter dated 5 June 2017, [the tenant's] solicitors ... had responded to the claimants' contentions that the cl.14.2 notice given on 16 May 2017 was invalid, by reason of non-service on the guarantor, by arguing that the point was entirely misconceived with nothing to commend it, and in particular: 'Our client did not serve a copy of its termination notice on the guarantor, but for the simple reason that it did not have to ...'
>
> [33] ... There is no suggestion that anything was said by the guarantor to waive its entitlement to notice. Waiver by conduct must therefore be relied upon. There is no evidence to suggest that the guarantor was aware that it had a right to waive its entitlement to notice. As the letter of 5 June 2017 makes clear, the guarantor's state of mind (if it had one at all, in relation to the [tenant's] notice) was that no such notice was necessary as a matter of interpretation of the agreement.

### (c) Loss of the Right to Insist on a Break Notice Being Given by the Correct Party

**13.22** In *Dun & Bradstreet Software Services (England) Limited v Provident Mutual Life Assurance Association*,[32] the named tenant under three leases (X) became the wholly-owned subsidiary of another company (Y). X transferred its assets to, and declared that it held the leases on bare trust for, Y. Thereupon, X ceased to trade or have any employees. Y took up occupation of the demised premises instead. In July 1991, the landlord was informed of the fact that X had become a subsidiary of Y; and that X wished to assign the leases to Y. The landlord granted a formal licence for the assignment, but in the event no assignment was ever executed.

**13.23** The leases granted to X contained break clauses entitling X upon giving not less than nine months' written notice served upon the landlord to determine the leases on 24 June 1995. In 1994, it was decided that notices under the break clauses would be served. In the event, however, the notices were served, not by X, but by Y. On 15 July 1994, a Miss McKune (the solicitor instructed by Dun & Bradstreet Corporation in the USA to serve the break notices) telephoned a Mr Wilkes (the landlord's property investment manager) and asked him to confirm that the notices were acceptable. This he did. She asked him to confirm this in writing, which he said he would do. The letter which Mr Wilkes subsequently wrote merely thanked the Dun & Bradstreet group for the notice of 'your company's intention to determine the ... lease'.

[32] *Dun & Bradstreet Software Services (England) Limited v Provident Mutual Life Assurance Association* [1998] 2 EGLR 175.

**13.24** At trial, the judge concluded that, based upon what Mr Wilkes said to Miss McKune during their telephone conversation, the landlord was estopped from challenging the validity of the break notices. This point was upheld on appeal. Peter Gibson LJ said:[33]

> To found an estoppel on this statement, it would have to be shown that it constituted a representation or promise which was intended to be acted upon and which was acted upon by the person to whom it was made.
>
> … To my mind, it is clear that the plaintiffs regarded it as important to obtain the assurance of Mr Wilkes … and the circumstance that no amended notice was served strongly suggests that the plaintiffs relied on that oral assurance. I can see no reason why that assurance should be construed as subject to the written confirmation sought.
>
> … If Mr Wilkes had wanted to leave it to the solicitors or otherwise qualify his assurance he could have done so, but he did not, nor in his letter did he retract anything he had said to Miss McKune.

**13.25** The opposite result was arrived at in *Prudential Assurance Co Ltd v Exel UK Ltd*.[34] In that case, a lease was vested in the joint names of Exel UK Ltd ('Exel') and its wholly-owned subsidiary, Tibbett & Britten Consumer Group Ltd ('Consumer'). A break notice was served in the name of Exel only, rather than in the names of both Exel and Consumer. Since the notice was not a valid exercise of the right to break the lease, an issue arose as to whether the landlord was estopped by representation or convention from disputing that there had been such a valid exercise. On the facts, Mr Jeremy Cousins QC (sitting as a Deputy Judge of the High Court) found no such estoppel. He recorded:[35]

> (i) The difficulty for the defendants is that the Notice was given in the name only of Exel when it should have been given in the name of Exel and Consumer. For any estoppel to be operative it is necessary that the assurance or convention went to this point. There would thus have had to have been an assurance or convention to the effect that Exel alone could exercise the break provision, and this despite the interests of any other tenant. It is only necessary to identify this requirement to recognise how improbable it is that any such estoppel would arise. No-one consciously acting for two joint tenants would be likely to seek any assurance to this effect, or seek to set up any such convention. It would be wholly unnecessary to do so, for the obvious reason that inserting the names of both tenants in a break notice would hardly be an onerous task. Equally, no-one acting for a landlord would be likely to give such an assurance.
>
> (v) In the circumstances there was no assurance or convention which led to the drafting of the Notice, nor was there any reliance upon communications from [the landlord's solicitors] or [the landlord] in such drafting. No detriment, unconscionability, or change of position can be established.

### (d) Loss of the Right to Insist on a Break Notice Being Given to the Correct Party

**13.26** There have been two relatively recent cases, in which conduct on the part of the landlord has had the effect of preventing the landlord from contending that service of a break notice upon the 'wrong' party rendered the notice invalid.

[33] *Dun & Bradstreet Software Services (England) Limited v Provident Mutual Life Assurance Association* [1998] 2 EGLR 175, 178M, at 179D–79E.

[34] *Prudential Assurance Co Ltd v Exel UK Ltd* [2010] 1 P&CR 7.

[35] *Prudential Assurance Co Ltd v Exel UK Ltd* [2010] 1 P&CR 7, at [203].

**13.27** In *Ben Cleuch Estates Ltd v Scottish Enterprise*,[36] the tenant occupied certain premises in Dundee under the terms of a lease which contained a tenant's break option. On 14 October 2002, the freehold reversion expectant upon the determination of the lease was acquired by Ben Cleuch Estates Ltd ('BCE'), a subsidiary of an entity called Bonnytoun Estates Ltd ('Bonnytoun'). The registered office of BCE was at the same address as that of Bonnytoun, and a Mr Cairns was a director and company secretary of both companies. From 21 October 2002 onwards the tenant received invoices from managing agents stating that they were 'Acting as agents for Bonnytoun Estates Ltd' in respect of quarterly rent under the lease. Subsequent correspondence from the managing agents and Mr Cairns also suggested that Bonnytoun was the landlord. On 6 January 2005 the tenant's solicitors sent copies of the break notice to Bonnytoun at its registered office, and sent a copy to the managing agents. On 1 March 2005 BCE's solicitors wrote to the tenant stating that, since the break notice had not been addressed to BCE (but to Bonnytoun), it was invalid and the lease would continue until 2016. BCE then raised an action for declarator that the tenant had not validly terminated the lease. The tenant averred that the break notice was not invalid, or alternatively that BCE was barred from denying that the break option had been validly exercised. The Court of Session, Outer House, held that the break notice was invalid. However, giving the opinion of the Court, Lord Macfadyen went on to say as follows:[37]

> [88] The question which arises in the present case, once it has been held as a matter of fact that Ben Cleuch represented, by means of the statements contained in the rent invoices, that Bonnytoun were the landlords, is therefore whether a reasonable person in the position of the defenders would have regarded those statements as intended to be accepted as a statement of the factual position and acted upon, and would have believed them. If that question is answered in the affirmative, the defenders were 'justified' in believing that Bonnytoun were the landlords. If they were justified in that belief, and acted upon it to their prejudice, Ben Cleuch are personally barred from denying that Bonnytoun were the landlord. That is so whatever the context may be in which the induced belief that Bonnytoun was the landlord was acted upon by the defenders.
>
> [92] There is nothing in the circumstances which would, in our view, lead to the conclusion that a reasonable man was not entitled to regard the representations in the invoice as seriously made and intended to be accepted. Applying the appropriate objective test, therefore, we are of opinion that the proper conclusion is that the defenders were justified in believing the representation that Bonnytoun were the landlords. Having induced that justified belief, Ben Cleuch is personally barred from maintaining that the facts were otherwise.
>
> [93] The [tenant] justifiedly believed that Bonnytoun was the landlord. One consequence of that justified belief was that they were entitled to think that the break notice should be given to Bonnytoun. It is beside the point that, if they had not been justified by the representations in believing that Bonnytoun was the landlord, various steps could appropriately have been taken to ascertain who the landlord was, and those steps would have disclosed that the landlord was Ben Cleuch. There was no occasion for them to take such steps so long as they were justified in their belief that the facts were as represented to them in the invoices. Nothing occurred to undermine their justified belief. Further inquiry was therefore not called for.

[36] *Ben Cleuch Estates Ltd v Scottish Enterprise* [2008] CSIH 1.
[37] *Ben Cleuch Estates Ltd v Scottish Enterprise* [2008] CSIH 1, [88], at [92]–[93].

**13.28** *MW Trustees Ltd v Telular Corporation*[38] concerned a lease dated 1 March 2005. The tenant had the benefit of an option to determine the lease on the fifth anniversary of the term upon giving to the landlord not less than six months' notice in writing to do so. On 10 August 2009, the tenant sent a break notice, not to the landlord, but to the landlord's predecessor in title. The recipient of the notice forwarded a copy to the landlord's managing agent. On 17 August 2009, the agent wrote to the tenant as follows: 'We accept the attached letter and can confirm we are happy for you to break the Lease, however, please could you re-address this letter to the following address ...' The tenant prepared a replacement notice, but it was not sent out (or was lost in the post). The latest date for service of the break notice was 1 September 2009. The landlord claimed that the notice served on 10 August 2009 was ineffective because it was neither addressed to, nor served on, the then landlord of the premises. The tenant argued that the email from the landlord's agent waived any defects in service. Peter Smith J resolved this issue in favour of the tenant. He said:[39]

> [46] ... Looked at objectively in my view [the agent] was accepting on behalf of the [landlords] that the documentation provided to them showed an intent on the part of the [tenant] to terminate the Lease and that they accepted that the documentation had the effect of terminating the Lease on March 1, 2010.
>
> [47] In sending the email in the form that he did in my view [the agent] represented that was the [landlords'] stance and accordingly they are estopped from subsequently challenging the validity of the Notice or alternatively they have waived the requirement for the Notice to be served in the way specified in the Lease. They could have withdrawn that concession at any time up until August 31, 2009. Withdrawing after that would be too late. The [tenant] has plainly in my view objectively acted on the basis that there was no issue but that it has served an effective Notice.
>
> [48] I do not see the further notice referred to in the email as affecting that. The [tenant] was entitled to conclude and did so conclude that the [landlords] accepted the earlier documents as being effective to terminate the Lease but required service of a further document for reasons for which were and are unexplained. Given the first sentence of [the agent's] email they cannot have formed the view that he was rejecting the earlier Notices and required further Notices to be served to terminate the Lease. They therefore acted on [the agent's] email by failing to serve a Notice in accordance with the Lease. Alternatively [the agent] by unequivocally accepting the earlier Notices thereby waived any requirement for the defendant to serve a fresh Notice compliant with the Lease.

### (e) Loss of the Right to Insist on a Break Notice Being Given within the Prescribed Time Limit

**13.29** In *Elsden v Pick*,[40] the defendant was the tenant of a farm under an agreement which was determinable on one year's notice in writing expiring on 6 April in any year. On 4 April 1977, the tenant discussed with the landlords' agent the possibility of his

[38] *MW Trustees Ltd v Telular Corporation* [2011] L&TR 19.

[39] *MW Trustees Ltd v Telular Corporation* [2011] L&TR 19, at [46]–[48].

[40] *Elsden v Pick* [1980] 1 WLR 898; and see also *Hackney LBC v Snowden* (2001) 33 HLR 49 (landlord waived the requirement under s 5(1) of the Protection from Eviction Act 1977 providing that no notice to quit shall be valid unless given not less than four weeks before the date on which it is to take effect).

having to give up the farm, and on 7 April he delivered to the agent a notice of his intention to quit the farm in April 1978 together with a letter requesting the agent to accept the notice. The agent agreed to treat the notice as valid notwithstanding that the length of the notice was short. When, later, the tenant contended that the notice was ineffective to determine his tenancy (ie seeking to resile from the mutually intended consequence of the defective notice to quit), the landlords brought an action for a declaration that they were entitled to possession of the farm in April 1978. The judge held that the tenant's notice was invalid as it contravened s 23(1) of the Agricultural Holdings Act 1948, and he dismissed the landlords' action. On appeal by the landlords, the Court of Appeal held that the landlords were entitled to waive the requirement for 12 months' notice and, having done so, the tenant was not entitled to insist upon compliance with the statute. Referring to the particular provision of the 1948 Act, Shaw LJ explained:[41]

> It is clear that it is designed principally to protect the tenant farmer from peremptory or unduly prejudicial ejectment on the part of the landlord. Nonetheless, it serves also to protect a landlord from the abandonment of a tenancy in circumstances which may cause discontinuity in cultivation ... Thus the time for the ending of a tenancy is a matter of common interest both to a landlord and to his tenant. It may suit them both to determine a tenancy without waiting for what may be as long as nearly two years to bring it to an end ... A contractual provision which enures for the benefit of a party can be waived by that party albeit that his right to that benefit is reinforced by statute.

13.30 *Patel v Peel Investments (South) Ltd* concerned a rent review.[42] On 7 July 1988, the landlords served notice on the tenant proposing a new rent of £19,500 per annum with effect from 29 September 1988. The tenant then had until 7 October 1988 by which to give a counter-notice requiring the rent to be determined by an independent surveyor. The time for giving the counter-notice was of the essence. In response to the initial notice, the tenant asked the landlords to 'quote new lettings' in support of the rental figure. On 15 September 1988, the landlords responded: 'We will shortly be going to inspect the premises and will contact you as soon as possible after this has taken place'.

13.31 Thereafter, little occurred for almost a year. However, on 15 August 1989, the landlords purported to give another notice (in apparent ignorance of the first notice), now proposing a rent of £23,000 per annum. On 8 September 1989, the tenant made a counter-proposal of £12,000 per annum. There then followed a period of negotiations. Finally, on 29 November 1989, the landlords wrote that the revised rent effective from 29 September 1988 is 'formally set in accordance with the notice'.

13.32 One issue for determination was whether the landlords' letter of 15 September 1988 constituted a waiver of their right to insist on the strict time limit for giving a counter-notice. Of this, Morritt J said:[43]

> The letter of September 15 1988 was in answer to a request for the comparables upon which they relied and merely stated that the plaintiffs' agent would be shortly going to inspect the premises and would contact the defendants' valuer as soon as possible after that date ... [It] is entirely

[41] *Elsden v Pick* [1980] 1 WLR 898, at 905–906.
[42] *Patel v Peel Investments (South) Ltd* [1992] 2 EGLR 116.
[43] *Patel v Peel Investments (South) Ltd* [1992] 2 EGLR 116, at 118J–18K.

> proper for a landlord not to point out to a tenant what he needs to do to protect his position. The onus … is on the tenant to ensure a counternotice is duly given. It seems to me that there is nothing in the letter of September 15 1988 in the context in which it was written to indicate that the plaintiffs were not going to rely on the time-limit of October 7 1988, by which date a counternotice had to be served. The fact that they were prepared to negotiate in the meantime did not, as it seems to me, give rise to any assurance, let alone one which is clear and unambiguous, to the effect that if the negotiations did not succeed, they would not rely on the time-limit expressed in the lease.

13.33 By contrast, waiver was established in *Fifield v W&R Jack Ltd*.[44] There, the Privy Council considered an appeal brought by Mr and Mrs Fifield (the landlords) against a decision allowing W&R Jack Ltd (the tenant) an extension of time within which to commence arbitration proceedings in relation to a rent review under a lease dated 4 November 1986. As in the Peel Investments case, the rent review machinery in the lease contemplated a number of sequential steps. The first was the service of a notice by the landlords specifying the proposed increase in rent. The second was the service of a counter-notice by the tenant within 28 days if it disputed the proposed new rent (then also requiring the new rent to be determined by arbitration). Time for service of the counter-notice was of the essence. Once the time had expired for service of the counter-notice, the proposed rent automatically became the contractual rent.

13.34 On 30 June 1989, the landlords served their notice. The 28-day period then expired on 2 August 1989. Following service of the notice, the parties entered into negotiations about the proposed new rent. On 6 September 1989, the landlords proposed to meet 'on mid ground and round the rental off at $69,000 pa'. On 15 September 1989, the tenant rejected the landlords' proposal and wrote: 'We wish to have this matter settled by arbitration'. Thus, the tenant gave a counter-notice, albeit out of time. Thereafter, the parties continued to negotiate.

13.35 The Privy Council considered that the conduct of the landlords was only consistent with their having agreed not to rely upon the lessee's non-compliance with the strict time requirement of the rent review provisions. As Lord Hobhouse explained:[45]

> When August 2 passed without any clause 3(b) notice from the lessee, the lessors chose not to stand on their rights under clause 3(c). They chose instead to discuss with the lessee the whole question of adjustment of the accounts between them, including the agreement of the new rents. They knew from shortly after August 23 that, failing a compromise agreement, the lessee wished to proceed to arbitration. Their response on September 6 was 'rather than getting into arbitration' to continue to try and reach a compromise and to get the settlement of the accounts.
>
> … The clause 3(b) letter of September 15 was not responded to with any rejection of its validity but with arguments on the merits and a request for the payment of the arrears. In the correspondence which subsequently passed between the parties the respondent repeatedly referred to the need to resort to arbitration if resolution of the differences could not be reached. It was not until May 1994 when the appellants through their solicitors contended that both rentals had been agreed to in 1992 that matters started to come to a head.

[44] *Fifield v W&R Jack Ltd* [2001] L&TR 4.
[45] *Fifield v W&R Jack Ltd* [2001] L&TR 4, at [17].

### (f) Loss of the Right to Insist on Compliance with Conditions

**13.36** Where the successful exercise of a break clause is dependent upon the satisfaction of certain conditions, and the party with the benefit of the break clause (typically, the tenant) has failed to comply with one or more of those conditions, it is commonplace for that party to seek to rely upon the doctrines of waiver or estoppel in an effort to render valid an otherwise invalid exercise of the break clause. In practice, however, it is rare for an argument based on waiver or estoppel to succeed in such circumstances. So, for example, in *West Country Cleaners (Falmouth) Limited v Saly*,[46] a lease dated 27 January 1951, granted for a term of 14 years, contained a covenant to renew which was conditional upon the tenant having 'duly observed and performed' their covenants. One of those covenants required the tenants in the last year of the term to paint the interior of the premises (which they failed to do). The landlord lived next door to, and was frequently in and out of, the premises. During her inspections, she did not complain about the state of repair of the premises. It was therefore suggested that there was a waiver or estoppel in respect of the breaches of covenant which would otherwise have precluded the successful exercise of the option. Danckwerts LJ rejected this suggestion. He said:[47]

> It seems to me that there cannot be either waiver or estoppel inferred from the landlord's visits ... [The] silence of the landlord here cannot amount to conduct which induced the tenants to change their position in any way.

**13.37** Another example in this context where an estoppel argument failed is to be found in *Capitol Park Leeds Plc v Global Radio Services Ltd*.[48] That case concerned a tenant's break option, the exercise of which was conditional upon the tenant giving vacant possession of 'the Premises' to the landlord on the break date. At first instance, the judge found that the tenant had not complied with this condition because it had given up considerably less than 'the Premises,' ie 'the Premises' minus various features of the property and/or landlord's fixtures. However, the tenant argued that the landlord was estopped from relying upon the failure to comply with the condition by reason of circumstances said to have arisen out of a meeting between the representatives of the parties on 9 June 2017. Essentially, the tenant maintained that, at the meeting, the parties came to an agreement to 'stop' the works then being undertaken by the tenant (which, if they had been completed, would have resulted in satisfaction of the relevant condition). On the facts, the judge found that there was no such agreement, which finding disposed of the estoppel argument.

### (g) Loss of the Right to Exercise a Landlord's Break Clause Following Acceptance of Rent

**13.38** It has sometimes been suggested that a landlord with the benefit of a break clause might lose the right to exercise the option by accepting rent from the tenant

[46] *West Country Cleaners (Falmouth) Ltd v Saly* [1966] 1 WLR 1485.
[47] *West Country Cleaners (Falmouth) Ltd v Saly* [1966] 1 WLR 1485, at 1489.
[48] *Capitol Park Leeds Plc v Global Radio Services Ltd* [2020] EWHC 2750 (Ch) (unaffected on this point on appeal at [2021] EWCA Civ 995).

(or otherwise acting or omitting to act in a manner consistent only with the lease continuing). This suggestion is erroneous. As Patten LJ said in *BDW Trading Ltd v JM Rowe (Investments) Ltd*:[49]

> The lease with a break clause entitling the landlord or tenant to terminate the lease after the end of part of the term does not have to be exercised immediately unless the lease so provides. In most cases it will remain exercisable at any time after the right has arisen. The continued acceptance of rent by the landlord will not, without more, operate as a waiver of his rights under the break clause because there is nothing inconsistent between the continuation of the landlord and tenant relationship and the reservation of the right to break. If it is exercisable at any time during the remainder of the term the landlord is not put to an election and does not make an election by continuing to perform the contract until he chooses to exercise his right to break.

**13.39** However, at least in the context of an option to renew a lease, the court may infer from the payment and acceptance of rent a renewal without an express notice. Indeed, an argument along these lines succeeded in *Moncure v Cahusac*.[50] That case concerned a house in Jamaica. In June 1982, a Mrs DeLisser let the house to Mr Moncure for a term of five years from 1 June 1982 to 31 May 1987. The lease contained a provision enabling Mr Moncure to obtain nine successive five-year renewals of the lease. Mr Moncure duly exercised his option to renew the lease on the first occasion (thereby obtaining a further five-year term from 1 June 1987–31 May 1992), but there was an issue as to whether he duly exercised the option on the second occasion (in order to obtain a 5 year term from 1 June 1992 to 31 May 1997). Nonetheless, Mr Moncure remained in possession of the house tendering the amount of rent that would have been payable if he had duly exercised the option and had obtained the further five-year term. On 4 April 1996, Mrs DeLisser served a notice to quit on Mr Moncure. The premise of the notice to quit was that Mr Moncure had failed to exercise his right to take a further term of the lease from 1 June 1992 to 31 May 1997. One of the issues before the Privy Council was whether Mrs DeLisser had become estopped from denying that he had done so. This issue was decided in favour of Mr Moncure. Delivering the opinion of the Board, Lord Scott explained:[51]

> In their Lordships' opinion it was not open to Mrs DeLisser, who must have known that Mr Moncure's payments were being made as rent calculated in accordance with the 2nd Schedule and due under the lease for the new term of five years from 1 June 1992, to retain the payments and subsequently, nearly five years after the payments had commenced to contend they had been retained on a different footing from that on which they had been paid. The retention by Mrs DeLisser of the payments made prior to the service of the Notice to Quit constituted a representation that Mr Moncure's status as lessee under the lease for that five year term was accepted. Her conduct in retaining the payments constituted, objectively viewed, an acceptance that Mr Moncure had renewed the lease for that term.

[49] *BDW Trading Ltd v JM Rowe (Investments) Ltd* [2011] EWCA Civ 548, at [78]; and see also *Bastin v Bidwell* (1880–1881) LR 18 Ch D 238, at 249, per Kay J.

[50] *Moncure v Cahusac* [2006] UKPC 54.

[51] *Moncure v Cahusac* [2007] UKPC 54, at [35].

## UNILATERAL WAIVER IN RESPECT OF PERFORMANCE OF CONDITIONS

**13.40** Where the performance of conditions upon which successful exercise of the break clause depends is solely for the benefit of one party, that party may unilaterally waive the right to insist on compliance with those conditions.[52] An early illustration of this proposition is to be found in *Bennett v Fowler*.[53] In that case a purchaser filed a bill, praying for specific performance 'if a good title could be made'. The master reported that the vendor could not make a good title. The purchaser was willing to accept the title, but the vendor insisted that the bill must be dismissed on the ground that conditional relief had been claimed and the condition had not been performed. Lord Langdale MR said:[54]

> I am of opinion that the obligation to which a vendor is subject to make out a title is intended for the benefit of the purchaser only, and that if he thinks fit to waive it, he has a right to do so.

**13.41** Thus, where (say) the exercise of a break clause is conditional upon the tenant observing and performing its covenants, if the tenant eg left premises in disrepair at the material time or otherwise failed to pay all sums due to the landlord, then the landlord would be entitled unilaterally to waive the requirement of compliance with the condition, thereby permitting the break to occur.

**13.42** In some cases, a lease may provide expressly that the landlord may waive compliance with conditions precedent to the successful exercise of a break clause by a tenant. Normally, this requires the waiver to be in writing. Where that is the position, it is thought that such a provision will be legally effective to prohibit an oral waiver.[55]

## THE SERVER OF A NOTICE CANNOT RELY UPON HIS OWN WRONG

**13.43** It is well-established by a long line of authority that a contracting party will not, in normal circumstances, be entitled to take advantage of his own breach as against the other party.[56] This may be of relevance if the lease permits a landlord or tenant to exercise

[52] See eg *Ropemaker Properties Ltd v Bella Italia Restaurants Ltd* [2018] L&TR 32, at [16], per Fancourt J ('... It is common ground that the guarantor was entitled to waive the requirement that the tenant give it written notice of termination, as being a provision of the agreement inserted solely for its benefit ...').

[53] *Bennett v Fowler* (1840) 2 Beav 302; and see also *Lloyd v Nowell* [1895] 2 Ch 744, at 746 (Kekewich J); *Heron Garage Properties Ltd v Moss* [1974] 1 WLR 148, at 153D–53F (Brightman J); *Ganton House Investments Ltd v Corbin* [1988] 2 EGLR 69 (HHJ Finlay QC).

[54] *Bennett v Fowler* (1840) 2 Beav 302, at 304.

[55] By analogy with *MWB Business Exchange Centres Ltd v Rock Advertising Ltd* [2019] AC 119 (concerning a 'no oral modification' clause in a contract). It is possible that estoppel may still have a role to play in preventing a party from relying on such a clause: see *MWB Business*, at [16], per Lord Sumption. Presumably, this would require some kind of double-assurance by a defendant both that the condition will be waived and that the required formalities for a waiver will not be required. See Martin Dixon, 'Estoppel, unconscionability and formalities in land law', CLJ 2000, 59(3), 453–55. *Cf Kinane v Mackie-Conteh* [2005] EWCA Civ 45 and *Dowding v Matchmove* [2017] 1 WLR 749 (concerning the relationship between proprietary estoppel and the requirements of s 2 of the Law of Property (Miscellaneous Provisions) Act 1989).

[56] *Rede v Farr* (1817) 6 M&S 121, at 124–25 (Lord Ellenborough CJ); *Doe d. Bryan v Bancks* (1821) 4 B&Ald 401, at 406–407 (Bayley J); *New Zealand Shipping Co Ltd v Societe des Ateliers et Chantiers de France* [1919] AC 1, at 9 (Lord Atkinson); *Quesnel Forks Gold Mining Co Ltd v Ward* [1920] AC 222, at 227 (Lord Buckmaster); *Cheall v Association of Professional Executive Clerical and Computer Staff* [1983] 2 AC 180,

a break clause in circumstances where that party has failed to satisfy a specified condition or set of conditions by a particular date.[57] If the specified condition(s) has (or have not) been satisfied because of the serving party's breach of contract, then the court will probably find that the server is not entitled to terminate the contract. This is well-illustrated by *Extra MSA Services Cobham Ltd v Accor UK Economy Holdings Ltd*.[58]

**13.44** In that case, planning permission was obtained for the development of a motorway services area into an 85-bedroom hotel. On 7 September 2007, the landlord entered into a conditional agreement for lease with the tenant. The lease was to be for a term of 15 years; and the hotel premises were to be constructed as a term of the arrangement. Clauses 3.6 and 4.2 of the agreement (respectively) provided as follows:

> 3.6 The Landlord will use all reasonable endeavours to satisfy the Conditions as soon as possible after the date of this Agreement …
>
> 4.2 If the Second Condition is not discharged in accordance with this Agreement by the Second Longstop Date, then either the Landlord or the Tenant may rescind this Agreement by giving to the other 10 working days' notice to that effect in which event this Agreement shall immediately cease to have effect and neither party shall have any further claim against the other save in respect of any antecedent breach of obligation.

**13.45** The landlord sought a declaration to the effect that the right to terminate the agreement under clause 4.2 was not conditional on it properly performing its obligations, ie clause 4.2 was entirely free-standing. Vos J rejected this contention. He said:[59]

> It seems to me therefore that clause 4.2 must be construed in such a way as not to permit the Claimant to rely on his own breaches as giving rise to a right to terminate clause 4.2. There are no express pointers in the Agreement, as there were in some of the other cases that I have cited, showing that the parties must have intended that the Claimants could simply sit on their hands and then terminate. Such a course was inconsistent with the detailed provisions of the Agreement elsewhere and the natural intention of the parties that the Agreement should result in the building of a hotel and the granting of a lease. In the end, therefore, the proper construction is simple. Clause 4.2 is conditional on the Claimant not having brought about his right to terminate by his own breaches of any clause in the Agreement and in particular clause 3.6. This can be achieved … by a process of construction or by a consideration of the implication of a term. Either way, I have formed the clear view that this is what the parties would reasonably be understood to have meant by the words they used in the Agreement.

at 188–89 (Lord Diplock); *Alghussein Establishment v Eton College* [1988] 1 WLR 587, at 592 (Lord Jauncey); *Richo International Ltd v Alfred C Toepfer International GmbH (The Bonde)* [1991] 1 Lloyd's Rep 136, at 144 (Potter J); *Petroplus Marketing AG v Shell Trading International Ltd* [2009] 2 Lloyd's Rep 611, at [17] (Andrew Smith J); *Extra MSA Services Cobham Ltd v Accor UK Economy Hotels Ltd* [2010] EWHC 775 (Ch), at [24]–[34] (Vos J); *BDW Trading Ltd v J M Rowe (Investments) Ltd* [2011] EWCA Civ 548, at [29]-[31] (Patten LJ).

[57] See, for example: *Sirhowy Investments Ltd v Henderson* [2014] EWHC 3562 (Ch) (break clause providing 'If the local Planning Authority shall object to the use of the Demised Premises for the use permitted in Clause 3.13 hereof the tenant shall use all reasonable endeavours to secure Planning Consent for such permitted use but if the Tenant shall fail to obtain such consent the tenant shall have the right to determine this Lease on giving not less than three months' notice and provided the Tenant shall have paid the rent and observed and performed the covenants contained in this Lease then on expiry of such notice the Term is to cease and determine immediately but without prejudice to any rights or remedies that may have accrued').

[58] *Extra MSA Services Cobham Ltd v Accor UK Economy Holdings Ltd* [2011] EWHC 775 (Ch).

[59] *Extra MSA Services Cobham Ltd v Accor UK Economy Holdings Ltd* [2011] EWHC 775 (Ch), at [46].

**13.46** To a similar effect is *Wigan Borough Council v Scullindale Global Ltd.*[60] That case concerned a lease containing a break clause entitling the landlord to serve a break notice following an 'Event of Default'. The specified 'Events of Default' included 'the Lessee not achieving any or all of the Milestones defined in clause 4.6'. The 'Milestones' were: (i) 'Within 6 months of the date of this Lease at the Lessee's own cost to commence the Works' and (ii) 'Prior to 23 May 2018 … to complete the Development in accordance with the Planning Permissions.' HHJ Hodge QC (sitting as a judge of the High Court) accepted that:

> [67] … the Lease is subject to an implied term which would prevent the Council [ie the landlord] from relying upon any delay in the completion of the Development that the Council itself may have caused … But I also hold that (by reason of clause 7.4 of the Lease),[61] that implied term cannot prejudice or abridge any of the Council's rights and powers as a local authority. Further, in order to rely upon this implied term, Scullindale [ie the tenant] must succeed in demonstrating a causal link between the conduct of the Council which it relies upon and the non-completion of the Development.

**13.47** On the facts, HHJ Hodge QC found that the delay in completing the Development was not caused by or contributed to by any conduct, still less any default, on the part of the Council landlord.[62]

## SILENCE

**13.48** Is the recipient of an invalid break notice under any obligation to point out defects in a notice, or can he remain silent and seek to take advantage of the serving party's error? What if a tenant mistakenly believes that it has properly complied with a condition on which the exercise of a break clause depends (when, in fact, it has not)? Is the landlord under any obligation to correct to mistake?

**13.49** Generally speaking, mere silence will not be sufficient to found an estoppel or waiver. As Rix LJ said in *ING Bank NV v Ros Roca SA*:[63]

> Outside the insurance context, there is no obligation in general to bring difficulties and defects to the attention of a contract partner or prospective contract partner. Caveat emptor reflects a basic facet of English commercial law … Nor is there any general notion, as there is in the civil law, of a duty of good faith in commercial affairs, however much individual concepts of English common law, such as that of the reasonable man, and of waiver and estoppel itself, may be said to reflect such a notion. In such circumstances, silence is golden, for where there is no obligation to speak, silence gives no hostages to fortune. If, however, the contractor speaks, then he may

[60] *Wigan Borough Council v Scullindale Global Ltd* [2021] EWHC 779 (Ch).

[61] Which provided: 'Nothing contained in this Lease shall prejudice or abridge any of the rights and powers for the time being vested in the local authority and the local planning authority for the Borough of Wigan and all such rights and powers shall in regard to the Premises or the tenant or occupier of them be enforceable and exercisable by the local authority and the local planning authority as fully and freely as if this Lease had not been executed.'

[62] *Wigan Borough Council v Scullindale Global Ltd* [2021] EWHC 779 (Ch), at [83].

[63] *ING Bank NV v Ros Roca SA* [2012] 1 WLR 472, at [92]; and see also *Taylor Fashions Ltd v Liverpool Victoria Trustees Co Ltd* [1982] QB 133, at 147C–47D, per Oliver J.

have to live up to what he says; so also where what is unsaid is sufficiently closely connected with what he has said to render what has been left unsaid misleading. In general, however, there is no duty of disclosure.

13.50 However, these general remarks should be read in light of *Avocet Industrial Estates LLP v Merol Ltd*.[64] There, the tenant had an option to determine its lease on 17 March 2010 on giving to the landlord not less than three months' notice of its desire to exercise the break. The break clause was very detailed and laid down a number of particular requirements as to the validity of the break notice. In particular, clause 45.4.4 stated that the break notice should be of no effect if 'at the Break Date any payment under this lease due to have been paid on or before that date, has not been paid'. Unfortunately, the tenant failed to pay about £130 of default interest which had accrued due under clause 14.1 of the lease in respect of late payments of rent over the period 12 August 2009–16 March 2010. The landlord claimed that the tenant's failure to do so was fatal to the exercise of the break clause. The tenant argued that the landlord was estopped so that it could not rely upon clause 45.4.4 in relation to such non-payment.

13.51 Morgan J found that the landlord had not made any kind of positive statement that the tenant was not liable to pay default in respect of late payments of rent over the relevant period.[65] However, the tenant went on to submit that the landlord had a duty to speak and to tell it that it owed default interest, and that the landlord's failure to inform the tenant of this amounted to a representation that it did not owe default interest. In this regard, the tenant pointed to the facts that: (i) by letters dated 11 August 2009 and 16 March 2010, the tenant relayed to the landlord its belief that it was up to date with all payments due under the lease; (ii) the landlord did not correct that belief; (iii) in particular, the landlord did not demand default interest; and (iv) if it had made such a demand, then the tenant would have paid the sum so demanded.

13.52 In considering this issue, Morgan J referred to the decision of Bingham J in *The Lutetian*.[66] In that case, the charterers of a ship believed that they had paid a sum of money which they were due to pay by a certain deadline. The owners of the ship *knew* that that was the belief of the charterers but the owners *also knew* that the charterers had underpaid and that that fact gave the owners the right to withdraw the ship. The owners did not correct the charterers' mistaken belief. However, Bingham J considered that the owners were under a duty, acting honestly and responsibly, to disclose their own view to the charterers. It was unjust for the owners to rely on the charterers' mistake which they had every opportunity to point out at an earlier stage.

13.53 Many of the ingredients which were found to exist in *The Lutetian* also existed in *Avocet*. Thus, the tenant believed it had paid all the sums due. The landlord knew of that belief (because the tenant had told the landlord of that belief). Further, if the landlord had told the tenant that it owed default interest in the sum of £130, then the

[64] *Avocet Industrial Estates LLP v Merol Ltd* [2012] L&TR 13.
[65] *Avocet Industrial Estates LLP v Merol Ltd* [2012] L&TR 13, at [109].
[66] *Tradax Export SA v Dorada Compania Naviera SA (The Lutetian)* [1982] 2 Lloyd's Rep 140; and see also *Pacol Ltd v Trade Lines Ltd (The Henrik Sif)* [1982] 1 Lloyd's Rep 456; *The Stolt Loyalty* [1993] 2 Lloyd's Rep 281; *Republic of India v India Steamship Co Ltd (The Indian Endurance)* [1996] 3 All ER 641.

tenant would have paid it. However, in the event, the tenant in *Avocet* failed because it was not able to establish that the landlord knew or even suspected, at any point prior to the end of 17 March 2010, that the tenant was mistaken when it stated in correspondence that it did not owe any sums under the lease.[67]

**13.54** The passage from *Ros Roca* referred to above was cited with approval by Peter Smith J in *PCE Investors Ltd v Cancer Research UK*.[68] In that case, clause 11.2 of the lease in question obliged the tenant to have 'paid rents reserved and demanded by this Underlease up to the Termination Date and by the Termination Date'. There was an issue as to whether this provision required the tenant to pay a full quarter's rent on 29 September 2010, notwithstanding that, following the exercise of a break clause, the lease was due to terminate part-way through the period, ie on 11 October 2010. This issue was resolved in favour of the landlord, with the consequence that the tenant (having paid only a proportionate part of the rent for the period) had failed properly to exercise the break clause.[69] In light of this ruling, the tenant sought permission to amend its statement of case, so as to plead that the landlord was estopped from contending that the exercise of the break notice was invalid.

**13.55** The relevant facts were as follows. On 25 September 2009, the tenant served a notice of its intention to determine the lease on 11 October 2010. On 21 September 2010, the landlord sent to the tenant an invoice for the full quarter's rent due on 25 September 2010. On 24 September 2010, the tenant sent an email to the landlord's agent informing that a rental payment had been made in the sum of £8,500 odd (being the apportioned rent in respect of the period 29 September–12 October 2010). The tenant asked for confirmation that this was 'the correct basis for calculating the liability for the short period'. A follow-up letter asked for the same confirmation. The landlord did not respond. In the circumstances, the tenant sought to contend that: (i) it believed it only had to pay apportioned rent up to the termination date; (ii) the landlord knew of that belief; (iii) the landlord thought the break would only be effective if a full quarter's rent was paid; and (iv) the landlord, acting honestly and reasonably, would have replied promptly to the email of 24 September or its follow-up letter.

**13.56** Refusing the tenant permission to amend its statement of case, Peter Smith J said:[70]

> It was up to the Tenant in my view to make the running. Absent a confirmation that the Landlord agreed with it, it should have taken stock before the break date. The only indication it had had from the Landlord was a demand for the full amount. It was therefore perfectly open to the Tenant to tender the full amount and seek to reclaim it by the subsequent proceedings.

[67] *Avocet Industrial Estates LLP v Merol Ltd* [2012] L&TR 13, at [121], [124] (although notably, at [114], Morgan J did say: '… If I were able to hold that the landlord did know that matter, then I would hold in the same way as was held in *The Lutetian* that the landlord cannot take advantage of the tenant's mistake which at the time the landlord knew that the tenant was making. Whether one calls it an estoppel by representation through silence or an estoppel by acquiescence may not matter. In such a case, I would hold that the landlord is estopped from taking advantage of the tenant's mistake …').

[68] *PCE Investors Ltd v Cancer Research UK* [2012] 2 P&CR 5, at [104].

[69] See **10.44–10.48** above.

[70] *PCE Investors Ltd v Cancer Research UK* [2012] 2 P&CR 5, at [89].

It chose to rest on the reduced payment. It therefore took the risk that the short payment would not be in compliance with the terms of the break clause as I have determined.

13.57 He added:[71]

[104] I gratefully adopt what Rix L.J. says in [92]. The general proposition is that in the common law (as opposed to the civil law) there is not generally a notion of good faith and as he says silence is golden for where there is no obligation to speak silence gives no hostages to fortune.

[105] Given that on the facts before me the Tenant cannot take advantage of the Landlord's failure to inform it that its assumption of this lesser rent only was due was a mistake. In any event when one looks at the circumstances summarised above if there was a duty I am satisfied that the Landlord sufficiently discharged that duty by demanding the full rent and not resiling from it. I do not believe the Tenant can draw any comfort from the silence and elevate that to a duty to tell it its assumption is wrong. As I have said earlier this does not seem to me to be the appropriate subject matter for an estoppel in any event because it is a legal question which was and probably remains a matter for debate.

[106] For that reason in any event I refuse the Tenant permission to amend because I find there is no basis for finding on such facts as put before me there was a duty on the part of the Landlord to tell the Tenant that the Landlord believed the full rent was due and consequently he believed that the Tenant was mistaken in its belief.

13.58 As Peter Smith J remarked in *PCE Investors*: silence is golden. Unless the circumstances of the case are such that it would be misleading not to speak, the recipient of an invalid break notice is under no obligation to point out any irregularity to the serving party.[72]

## WITHDRAWAL OF A BREAK NOTICE

13.59 In *May v Borup*, Lawrence J said:[73]

A tenant who has given a good notice to quit cannot subsequently cancel it without the consent of the landlord. If the tenant desires to continue his tenancy after giving notice it is a matter for negotiation with the landlord, who can accept or reject the tenant's proposals as he pleases.

13.60 To a similar effect, in *Tayleur v Wildin*[74] Kelly CB remarked:

whether [a] notice to quit is given by the landlord or the tenant, the party to whom it is given is entitled to insist upon it, and it cannot be withdrawn without the consent of both.

[71] *PCE Investors Ltd v Cancer Research UK* [2012] 2 P&CR 5, at [104]–[106].

[72] It is instructive to compare the position in the context of mistakes in litigation. As HHJ Hacon observed in *OOO Abbott v Econowall UK Ltd* [2016] EWHC 660 (IPEC), at [40]: '… parties to litigation are plainly not obliged to inform the opposing side of its mistakes – in the sense of steps taken or positions adopted which appear not to be in that other side's best interests. Each side must look after itself'. Thus, a solicitor acting for a defendant is not obliged to inform his or her opponent as to an error in service of a claim form: see *Higgins v ERC Accountants & Business* [2017] EWHC 2190 (Ch), at [41]–[42], per HHJ Pelling QC (sitting as a judge of the High Court).

[73] *May v Borup* [1915] 1 KB 830, at 832.

[74] *Tayleur v Wildin* (1868) LR 3 Exch 303, at 305.

**13.61** The Court of Appeal in *Freeman v Evans*[75] followed the decision in *Tayleur v Wildin* notwithstanding the fact that, as was acknowledged by Lord Sterndale MR,[76] *Tayleur v Wildin* had previously been very strongly criticised and, indeed, disapproved of entirely by the Court of Appeal in Ireland in *Lord Inchiquin v Lyons*.[77] It is thought that the observations here made in connection with notices to quit are equally applicable to the case of a break notice (unless the express terms of the lease provide otherwise).

**13.62** Where a notice to quit is treated by the parties as withdrawn, then a new tenancy may be created to take effect at the expiry of the old one. So much was said by Bramwell B in *Tayleur v Wildin*[78] ('If the notice is given, the tenancy is at an end; the parties may by a parol contract create a new tenancy, which is what is meant by the phrase withdrawing the notice, but the old tenancy no longer exists') and by Lord Sterndale MR in *Freeman v Evans*.[79] This does not present any real practical difficulties in the case of a periodic tenancy, but gives rise to a number of problematic implications in the case of a break notice withdrawn during the course of a fixed term tenancy. In the latter scenario, it is thought that the parties would be left with a new tenancy for a fixed term equal to the residue of the old tenancy. However, if this happens, then presumably:

(1) The landlord would lose the ability to claim against former tenants liable under privity of contract (for pre-1996 'old' leases) or under an authorised guarantee agreement (under post-1996 'new' leases).
(2) As regards liability to keep the demised premises in repair, any repairing obligation on the part of the tenant would be construed by reference to the condition of the premises at the time when the deemed new lease takes effect.[80]
(3) If the rent under the previous lease was payable, say, quarterly in advance on the usual quarter days, and the break notice is withdrawn half way through a quarter, the tenant could find himself liable to pay twice over for the remaining part of that quarter.
(4) The new lease (if for a term of longer than 7 years) would have to be registered at HM Land Registry. Failure to register the new lease will mean that the tenant has no legal title, and thus, only an equitable tenancy (which interest is vulnerable upon a transfer of the landlord's reversion).

**13.63** In *Lower v Sorrell*,[81] Donovan LJ felt compelled to follow *Freeman v Evans*, but advanced a more simple solution to these difficulties as follows:

> I take the ratio of the decision in *Freeman v Evans* to be this: that a notice to quit converts a tenancy from year to year into one which is to end on a fixed date, and that if thereafter the notice to quit is by agreement withdrawn, then another tenancy from year to year – which is a new tenancy altogether – replaces the tenancy ending on a fixed date.

[75] *Freeman v Evans* [1922] 1 Ch 36.
[76] *Freeman v Evans* [1922] 1 Ch 36, at 45.
[77] *Lord Inchiquin v Lyons* (1887) 20 LR Ir 474.
[78] *Tayleur v Wildin* (1868) LR 3 Exch 303, at 305–306.
[79] *Freeman v Evans* [1922] 1 Ch 36, 45; and see also *Lowenthal v Vanhoute* [1947] 1 KB 342, at 345, per Denning J ('... the law is now well settled that where a tenancy is determined by a notice to quit, it is not revived by anything short of a new tenancy ...').
[80] *Walker v Hatton* (1842) 10 M&W 249.
[81] *Lower v Sorrell* [1963] 1 QB 959, at 973–74.

> A different view, however, is, I think, open. Any tenancy from year to year possesses the inherent characteristic that by a valid notice to quit it may be determined at the end of some year of the tenancy; so that its full description is really a tenancy from year to year and until the date when it is validly determined. When the notice is given, the inherent characteristic becomes an actual feature of the tenancy. But no new tenancy comes into being. It is simply the old one with its ending fixed. If by agreement this date is cancelled, again no new tenancy is created. The life of the old one is simply prolonged, and it continues once more with its inherent quality of determination by a valid notice. I respectfully think that this more nearly represents the reality of the matter, and where it is what the parties intend shall happen, I can see no reason for imposing upon the parties the notion that they have agreed to a completely new tenancy.

**13.64** For SDLT purposes, HMRC takes the approach advocated by Donovan LJ in *Lower v Sorrell*. Thus, under HMRC's SDLT Manual 17030 ('Miscellaneous Provisions: Withdrawal of a Notice to Quit or Break Notice'), it is expressly stated that: 'In circumstances where a break notice or notice to quit is withdrawn, by agreement between the parties, before it takes effect the lease will be treated as continuing for SDLT purposes, notwithstanding any rule of law to the effect that a break notice or notice to quit may not be withdrawn and that any purported withdrawal creates a new lease'. Accordingly, a tenant will not have to file a land transaction return for the new tenancy.

## COUNTERMANDING A BREAK NOTICE

**13.65** It should be noted, however, that in any case, the server of a break notice may be able to countermand it (as opposed to withdrawing it), at least before the notice has been served. In *Kinch v Bullard*,[82] Neuberger J said:

> I am inclined to think that the position would be different if, before the notice was 'given', the sender had informed the addressee that he wished to revoke it. In such a case, it appears to me that the notice would have been withdrawn before it had been 'given'. After all, as is clear from the reasoning at first instance and in the Court of Appeal in *Holwell Securities Ltd v Hughes* [1973] 1 WLR 757, 761–62; [1974] 1 WLR 155, 158–59, 160–62, a notice sent by post is not 'served' in accordance with section 196(3) until it arrives at the premises to which it has been addressed. Accordingly, it seems to me that, while the notice is still in the post, it has not been given, and, until it is given, the sender has in effect a locus poenitentiae whereby he can withdraw the notice, but only provided his withdrawal is communicated to the addressee before the notice is given to, or served on, the addressee. I should emphasise, however, that this is no more than a tentative view.

## SEQUENTIAL BREAK NOTICES

**13.66** If, following service of a break notice, the serving party has any doubts as to its validity (either self-induced or because of something said by the recipient) then he might choose to serve a second notice.[83] If nothing is said about the first notice when serving

[82] *Kinch v Bullard* [1999] 1 WLR 423, at 429.

[83] See eg *Ropemaker Properties Ltd v Bella Italia Restaurants Ltd* [2018] L&TR 32, at [15], per Fancourt J ('… It is common ground that a prior invalid cl 13.2 notice does not prevent the service of a later valid cl 13.2 notice …').

the second notice (eg that the second notice is served without prejudice to the validity of the first notice) then there is a risk that the server might be estopped from relying upon the first notice.

**13.67** Where the first notice is in fact invalid, the position is clear: no estoppel will arise. As explained by Peterson J in *Bebington v Wildman*:[84]

> Assuming that regard can be had to the second notice, the question arises whether the tenant could when he received the first notice have acted upon it. It has been argued that the defendant after giving a bad notice could not have said that it was invalid at any time thereafter and accordingly that the tenant when he received the second notice was able to act with security on the two notices. If the opinion expressed by the Court on various occasions is correct – namely, that in order to be valid a notice to quit must be good when received, it follows that the notice by the defendant was bad when received by the plaintiff; and it seems to me to be established further by the authorities to which I have been referred – *Doe v Johnston*, *Johnstone v Hudlestone*, and *Doe v Milward* – that a man who gives a bad notice, that is, a notice which does not operate as a defeasance of the estate of the tenant, is not afterwards precluded or estopped from saying it is void.

**13.68** However, the position is more complicated where the first notice was a valid notice. This is well illustrated by *Cordon Bleu Freezer Food Centres Limited v Marbleace Limited*.[85] That case concerned the operation of a rent review. The rent review machinery contemplated the landlord first serving a trigger notice stating the amount which in its opinion was the market rent for the premises. The tenant then had two months within which to serve a counter-notice stating the amount which in its opinion was the market rent. If, on the expiration of one month from the date of service of the counter-notice, the parties had not agreed the rent, then the landlord was at liberty to apply for the appointment of an arbitrator to determine the rent. If, on the expiration of two months from the date of service of the counter-notice, the landlord had not done so, then the amount of rent was to be as stated in the counter-notice.

**13.69** On 21 March 1986, the landlord (through its solicitors) served a trigger notice. The tenant served a counter-notice on 15 April 1986. No agreement was reached on rent. On 24 June 1986, the landlord applied out of time for the appointment of a surveyor to determine the rent. Thus, the tenant sought a declaration that the rent was as stated in its counter-notice. However, it so happened that, on 21 March 1986, a second trigger notice had come to be served (this time, by managing agents appointed by the landlord's predecessor in title). On 17 April 1986, the tenant responded to the second notice by saying it was 'null and void'. Nonetheless, on 28 April 1986, the tenant sent a duplicate counter-notice to the managing agents. At trial, the judge concluded that it was 'a complete misapprehension to take the letter of April 28 as a counternotice to the solicitors' letter'.[86] However, on the assumption that the 28 April 1986 letter did constitute a second counter-notice, he went on to consider an argument based on estoppel. He said:[87]

> Mr Neuberger [Counsel for the landlord], who, as always, put his points attractively, put it this way in regard to these two notices: it does not matter which of the two notices was valid. If the

[84] *Bebington v Wildman* [1921] 1 Ch 559, at 565.
[85] *Cordon Bleu Freezer Food Centres Ltd v Marbleace Ltd* [1987] 2 EGLR 143.
[86] *Cordon Bleu Freezer Food Centres Ltd v Marbleace Ltd* [1987] 2 EGLR 143, at 146K.
[87] *Cordon Bleu Freezer Food Centres Ltd v Marbleace Ltd* [1987] 2 EGLR 143, at 146L–46M.

> party serving the notice, the tenant in this case, serves two notices, having served the second one you cannot go back to them with the first one unless the second one is served without prejudice to the others, and the second counter-notice refers to the two, and so one cannot then withdraw it.
>
> In the ordinary way I would accede to that. That perhaps would raise an estoppel. The notice itself is some sort of representation that the landlord is entitled to act on it. But when one reads them in their context, and especially having regard to the letter of April 17, when the actual validity of the landlord's [second] notice … was challenged, then I think the tenant cannot properly be said to be serving a notice to supersede the other. The notices of April 15 and April 28 are alternative notices, not cumulative notices, in the particular circumstances of this case.

13.70 Similarly, in *Patel v Peel Investments (South) Ltd*[88] (summarised at **13.30–13.32** above), the tenant contended that, having served the second notice on 15 August 1989, the landlord was estopped from relying upon the first notice served on 7 July 1988. On the facts, this submission was rejected by Morritt J, who said:[89]

> It would be perfectly possible to construe the letter of August 15 1989 as being a representation that the landlord was not relying on the earlier notice. That is a possible interpretation, but it does not seem, to me that it is necessarily the only one. When one turns to the reply from [the tenant's surveyor] of September 8 1989, it is plain from that that [he] did not read the second notice as amounting to a representation that the landlords were abandoning or forgoing any rights they had under the first … It seems to me, therefore, that the response of [the tenant's surveyor] demonstrates that the second notice was not sufficiently clear and unambiguous to amount to the requisite representation, or, alternatively, if it was, that he did not rely on it in that sense.

[88] *Patel v Peel Investments (South) Ltd* [1992] 2 EGLR 116.
[89] *Patel v Peel Investments (South) Ltd* [1992] 2 EGLR 116, at 119D–19E.

# 14

# *The Effect of Exercising a Break Clause*

## AS BETWEEN LANDLORD AND TENANT

### (a) The Extent to which the Parties are Relieved of the Need to Perform their Covenants

**14.1** As Lord Greene MR said in *Hankey v Clavering*,[1] break notices served in the proper manner and in the proper form 'have of their own force without any assent by the recipient the effect of bringing the demise to an end'.

**14.2** However, on the expiration of a valid break notice questions can sometimes arise as to the extent to which the parties are relieved of their need to perform the covenants which they would have been bound to perform if the length of the term had not been cut short. The answers to these questions will always depend upon the construction of the lease in each case. For example, a covenant to yield up the premises in a certain condition at the expiration 'or sooner' determination of the term will refer to the end of the demise, howsoever it terminates. By contrast, for example, in *Dickinson v St Aubyn*,[2] a tenant covenant (in clause 4) 'to paint in the last quarter of the term' was held to mean the last quarter of the original term of seven years; and, thus, the tenant was not obliged to paint the demised premises in the last quarter of the term shortened by the exercise of the break clause. As Goddard LJ explained:[3]

> When the lease is read, the first thing that appears is that the words used in cl. 3 are different from those in cl. 4. In cl. 3, the words are that the tenant is to deliver up the interior of the premises and certain fixtures and fittings in good condition 'at the end or sooner determination of the tenancy,' and there can be no doubt – it has not been argued to the contrary – that the tenant's obligation under this clause attaches when the tenancy is determined, whether that event occurs at the end of the seventh or of the fifth year. Different words, however, are found in cl. 4. It is a common thing in leases to provide for painting to be done at the end of particular periods, and frequently the period specified is one of seven years. In the present instance the tenant's obligation is 'to paint in the last quarter of the said term'. There is no question, to my mind, that 'the said term' there referred to is the term of seven years which has been previously granted under the lease.
>
> [Counsel for the landlord], however, argues that, as the proviso enables the tenant to give notice to determine the term at the end of five years, we must read 'the last quarter of the said term' as meaning the last quarter of the term which has in fact existed, whether it be five years or

[1] *Hankey v Clavering* [1942] 2 KB 326, at 329.
[2] *Dickinson v St Aubyn* [1944] KB 454.
[3] *Dickinson v St Aubyn* [1944] KB 454, at 457–58.

> whether it be seven. That would be reading the words as if they were 'to paint in the last quarter of the tenancy, be it five years or be it seven years'. That was the construction which Hilbery J put on the words, but, in my opinion, it is not the right one. If parties to a lease use in one covenant an expression which shows that they have in mind obligations to arise at the end of the tenancy, whether that be at the end of one period or at the end of another according to whether or not the tenant exercises an option which is given to him, and in the next covenant they use an expression which, prima facie, applies only to the full term which is created by the lease, the proper rule of construction to apply is that they mean something different in the two covenants. In my view, the covenant to paint 'in the last quarter of the said term' ought to be construed strictly against the landlords, and must mean that the tenant's obligation is to paint in the last quarter of the seventh year if he holds for the full period of seven years, but that he is under no obligation to paint in the last quarter of the term if he exercises his option and gives up the premises at the end of five years.

### (b) Liability for Existing Breaches of Covenant

**14.3** It has been argued that, where a break clause provides that, on the expiration of the term 'this demise and everything herein contained shall cease and be void', then, on termination of the lease, all rights of action for anything contained in the lease are brought to an end. This contention was rejected in *Blore v Giuliani*, where Wright J said:[4]

> As a matter of common sense, it is impossible to suppose that it was ever intended by the parties that the liability of the lessees to pay damages for the breaches of covenant already committed by them should be put an end to by mere determination of the lease. I think the point is sufficiently decided against such a contention by the decision in *Hartshorne v Watson*. There Tindal CJ said: 'The argument' (that the covenant to pay rent was gone) 'would equally apply to covenant for repairs, or other services to be rendered by the lessee, and is so unreasonable that it cannot be upheld.'

### (c) The Landlord's Entitlement to Claim Double Rent or Double Value

**14.4** Insofar as is relevant, s 1 of the Landlord and Tenant Act 1730 provides:

> In case any Tenant ... for any Term of Life, Lives or Years, or other Person or Persons who are or shall come into Possession of any Lands, Tenements or Hereditaments ... shall wilfully hold over any Lands, Tenements or Hereditaments after the termination of such Term or Terms, and after Demand made, and Notice in Writing given, for delivering the Possession thereof, by his ... Landlords or Lessors or the Person or Persons to whom the Remainder or Reversion of such Lands, Tenements or Hereditaments shall belong ... then and in such Case such Person or Persons so holding over, shall, for and during the Time he, she and they shall so hold over, or keep the Person or Persons intitled [sic], out of possession of the said Lands, Tenements, and Hereditaments, as aforesaid, pay to the Person or Persons so kept out of Possession ... at the Rate of double the yearly value of the Lands, Tenements and Hereditaments so detained, for so long as the same are detained, to be recovered in any of His Majesty's Courts of Record, by Action of Debt.

[4] *Blore v Giuliani* [1903] 1 KB 356, at 357–58.

**14.5** Section 1 of the Landlord and Tenant Act 1730 is to be read together with s 18 of the Distress for Rent Act 1737 which, insofar as is relevant, provides:

> And whereas great inconveniences have happened and may happen to landlords, whose tenants have power to determine their leases, by giving notice to quit the premises by them that hold them, and yet refusing to deliver up the possession, when the landlord has agreed with another tenant for the same; … in case any tenant or tenants shall give notice of his, her, or their intention to quit the premises by him, her, or them holden, at a time mentioned in such notice, and shall not accordingly deliver up the possession thereof at the time in such notice contained, that then the said tenant or tenants, his, her, or their executors or administrators, shall from thenceforward pay to the landlord or landlords, lessor or lessors, double the rent or sum which he, she, or they should otherwise have paid, to be levied, sued for, and recovered at the same times and in the same manner as the single rent or sum, before the giving such notice, could be levied, sued for, or recovered; and such double rent or sum shall continue to be paid during all the time such tenant or tenants shall continue in possession as aforesaid.

**14.6** Thus, if a tenant validly exercises an option to determine a lease, but then fails or refuses to deliver up possession on the break date, the landlord will be entitled to recover double rent. Similarly, if the landlord determines the lease, and the tenant wilfully holds over, then the landlord may recover double value.

**14.7** In *Oliver Ashworth (Holdings) Ltd v Ballard (Kent) Ltd*,[5] the Court of Appeal considered the question whether in circumstances where a landlord asserts that a tenant's break notice is invalid and treats the lease as continuing, and the tenant remains in occupation beyond the period specified in the break notice, the landlord is entitled to double rent under s 18 of the 1737 Act. Answering this question in the negative, the Court of Appeal held that, having regard to the 1737 Act as a whole, including the preamble and recitals, read with the related 1730 Act, a landlord's entitlement to double rent under s 18 arose only where the tenant held over as a trespasser after serving a valid notice to quit and the landlord treated him as a trespasser. As was said by Laws LJ:[6]

> Reading the Acts of 1730 and 1737 as a whole including the latter's preamble and recitals, it is to my mind entirely clear that the legislature was concerned only to compensate landlords for the potential loss of rent arising where a tenant holds over against the landlords' insistence that he should comply with his own notice to quit.

## AS REGARDS AN UNDERLESSEE

### (a) Where the Head Tenant Exercises the Break Clause

**14.8** As mentioned in 14.1 above, the effective exercise of a break clause has the effect of bringing the demise to an end. In *Pennell v Payne*,[7] Simon Brown LJ explained that,

[5] *Oliver Ashworth (Holdings) Ltd v Ballard (Kent) Ltd* [2000] Ch 12.
[6] *Oliver Ashworth (Holdings) Ltd v Ballard (Kent) Ltd* [2000] Ch 12, at 38–39.
[7] *Pennell v Payne* [1995] QB 192, at 197. (This is, of course, in contrast to the position with surrender and merger. See s 139 of the Law of Property Act 1925 and *St Marylebone Property Co Ltd v Fairweather* [1963] AC 510, at 546, per Lord Denning.)

at common law, 'the general rule is that, when the head tenancy comes to an end, any subtenancy derived out of it also automatically and simultaneously comes to an end'.

**14.9** In *Pennell*, Simon Brown LJ held,[8] at 202H–203A, that a tenant's upwards notice to quit had the effect of bringing to an end any sub-tenancy granted by the tenant. He also added[9] that:

> A tenant's exercise of his right to determine a lease under a break clause is precisely equivalent to his determining a periodic tenancy by notice to quit: in each case a term which would otherwise have continued by operation of law is being voluntarily determined.

**14.10** Thus, on termination of a head lease by a head tenant under a break clause, any sub-tenancy derived out of the head lease also ends. In *PW & Co v Milton Gate Investments Ltd*,[10] Neuberger J held that it is not possible to contract out of the rule in *Pennell* (viz a sub-tenancy cannot survive the determination of a head lease unless the head lease is determined by a consensual arrangement not provided for in the head lease).

**14.11** The rigour of the rule in *Pennell* may be mitigated by the fact that the subtenant can, in an appropriate case where its sub-tenancy has been determined in such circumstances, sue the tenant for breach of the express/implied covenant for quiet enjoyment and/or for derogation from grant.

### (b) Where the Head Landlord Exercises the Break Clause

**14.12** Subject to what is said in the following paragraph, in a similar fashion to the exercise of a tenant's break clause, on the termination of a head lease on the exercise of a landlord's break clause, any underlease created by the head tenant automatically falls with it.

**14.13** Importantly, in the residential context, statute intervenes to provide protection to Rent Act protected and statutory sub-tenants, and also to assured sub-tenants. Specifically:

(1) Under s 137(3) of the Rent Act 1977, where a dwelling-house (a) forms part of premises which have been let as a whole on a superior tenancy but do not constitute a dwelling-house let on a statutorily protected tenancy, and (b) is itself subject to a protected or statutory tenancy, then, from the coming to an end of the superior tenancy, the Rent Act 1977 shall apply in relation to the dwelling-house as if, in lieu of the superior tenancy, there had been separate tenancies of the dwelling-house and of the remainder of the premises, for the like purposes as under the superior tenancy, and at rents equal to the just proportion of the rent under the superior tenancy.

(2) Under s 18(1) of the Housing Act 1988, if at any time (a) a dwelling-house is for the time being lawfully let on an assured tenancy; and (b) the landlord under the

[8] *Pennell v Payne* [1995] QB 192, at 202H–203A.

[9] *Pennell v Payne* [1995] QB 192, at 199H–200A; and see also *Barrett v Morgan* [2000] 2 AC 264, at 270–72, per Lord Millett.

[10] *PW & Co v Milton Gate Investments Ltd* [2004] Ch 142, at [58]–[85].

assured tenancy is himself a tenant under a superior tenancy; and (c) the superior tenancy comes to an end, then, subject to s 18(2), the assured tenancy shall continue in existence as a tenancy held of the person whose interest would, apart from the continuance of the assured tenancy, entitle him to actual possession of the dwelling-house at that time.

**14.14** As a matter of practice, an intended sub-tenant should always inspect the head lease for the existence of a break clause because, where there is no break clause in the sub-lease, the superior landlord's termination of the head lease does not make the head tenant liable to the sub-tenant for breach of the express/implied covenant for quiet enjoyment. In this regard, see *Kelly v Rogers*[11] (in which a sub-tenant sued the head tenant for breach of his covenant for quiet enjoyment after the superior landlord forfeited the head lease for non-payment of rent), where Lopes LJ explained:

> In order to maintain an action on a covenant for quiet enjoyment in the present form, it is necessary to shew some act of interruption by the defendant or some person claiming by, through, or under him, against whose act he covenants. The plaintiff is unable to prove any such act here. The only act of interruption was by the superior landlord. I think it clear that this is not within the covenant.

[11] *Kelly v Rogers* [1892] 1 QB 910, at 912.

# 15

# *Break Clauses and Compulsory Purchase*

## INTRODUCTION

**15.1** The current law of compulsory purchase is a jigsaw of statute and case law developed over the past two centuries.[1] The statutes which now contain nearly all[2] of the statutory law on the subject of compulsory purchase are as follows:

(a) The Land Compensation Act 1961 (the '1961 Act'), which is the principal statute governing the assessment of compensation for compulsory purchase.[3]
(b) The Compulsory Purchase Act 1965 (the '1965 Act'), which is the principal statute governing the implementation of compulsory purchase orders.[4]
(c) The Land Compensation Act 1973 (the '1973 Act'), which introduced various major innovations to the law of compulsory purchase.[5]
(d) The Acquisition of Land Act 1981, which contains a uniform procedure for the making and confirmation of compulsory purchase orders.[6]
(e) The Compulsory Purchase (Vesting Declarations) Act 1981, which enables compulsory purchase orders to be implemented by a vesting declaration, as an alternative to the traditional notice to treat procedure.

**15.2** This chapter is concerned with the effect on compensation of a break clause in a lease.

[1] A detailed examination of the law of compulsory purchase is outside the scope of this work. Further reference can be made to the leading textbooks on the subject including the *Encyclopaedia of Compulsory Purchase and Compensation* (Looseleaf, Sweet & Maxwell), G Roots, *The Law of Compulsory Purchase* (3rd edn, Bloomsbury Professional 2018), B Denyer-Green, *Compulsory Purchase and Compensation* (11th ed, Routledge 2018) and M Barnes, *The Law of Compulsory Purchase and Compensation* (Hart Publishing, 2014).

[2] Less significant amendments to the law of compulsory purchase have been made by other Acts, including the Local Government (Miscellaneous Provisions) Act 1976, the Local Government, Planning and Land Act 1980 and the Planning and Compensation Act 1991. The Human Rights Act 1998 also requires existing compensation law to be interpreted and applied, as far as possible in conformity with the European Convention of Human Rights (s 3).

[3] The 1961 Act was a consolidation of parts of the Acquisition of Land Act 1919 and the Town and Country Planning Act 1959.

[4] The 1965 Act re-enacted, without material change, the extant provisions of the Land Clauses Consolidation Act 1845 (albeit without repealing that Act).

[5] For example, a new right to compensation for depreciation in the value of an interest in land by physical factors caused by the use of public works (s 1).

[6] This Act reproduced without substantive change the Acquisition of Land (Authorisation Procedure) Act 1946.

## COMPENSATION: GENERAL PRINCIPLES

**15.3** Where by or under any statute land is authorised to be acquired compulsorily, any question of disputed compensation and, where any part of the land to be acquired is subject to a lease which comprises land not acquired, any question as to the apportionment of the rent payable under the lease, shall be referred to the Upper Tribunal and shall be determined by the Tribunal in accordance with the provisions of the 1961 Act.[7] For these purposes, 'land' means 'any corporeal hereditament … and includes any interest or right in or over land and any right to water'.[8] This definition is apt to encompass freehold and leasehold estates.

**15.4** The underlying principle of statutory compensation for compulsory acquisition of land is sometimes referred to as the 'principle of equivalence'. That is:

> the right [of the owner] to be put, so far as money can do it, in the same position as if his land had not been taken from him. In other words, he gains the right to receive a money payment not less than the loss imposed on him in the public interest, but, on the other hand, no greater.[9]

**15.5** Or, as it has been put:

> The purpose of these provisions … is to provide fair compensation for a claimant whose land has been compulsorily taken from him. This is sometimes described as the principle of equivalence. No allowance is to be made because the resumption or acquisition was compulsory; and land is to be valued at the price it might be expected to realise if sold by a willing seller, not an unwilling seller. But subject to these qualifications, a claimant is entitled to be compensated fairly and fully for his loss. Conversely, and built into the concept of fair compensation, is the corollary that a claimant is not entitled to receive more than fair compensation: a person is entitled to compensation for losses fairly attributable to the taking of his land, but not to any greater amount. It is ultimately by this touchstone, with its two facets, that all claims for compensation succeed or fail.[10]

**15.6** Compensation for the compulsory acquisition of land is traditionally assessed under three distinct heads, namely: (i) the value of the land subject to acquisition;[11] (ii) other losses not based on the value of the land (eg removal expenses, business losses etc);[12] and (iii) injury to any retained land. This third head comprises two different elements, that is, 'severance' (ie "damage … sustained by the owner of the land by reason of the severing of the land purchased from the other land of the owner") and 'injurious affection' (ie 'damage … otherwise injuriously affecting that other land' by the construction and use of public works on the land compulsorily acquired).[13] Although compensation

[7] 1961 Act, s 1.

[8] 1961 Act, s 39(1). See also s 1(3) of the 1965 Act which defines 'land' as including 'anything falling within any definition of that expression in the enactment under which the purchase is authorised'.

[9] *Horn v Sunderland Corp* [1941] 2 KB 25, at 42, per Scott LJ.

[10] *Director of Buildings and Lands v Shun Fung Ironworks Ltd* [1995] 2 AC 111, at 125, per Lord Nicholls.

[11] 1961 Act, s 5(2).

[12] 1961 Act, s 5(6).

[13] 1965 Act, s 7. This provision applies where there is a 'purchase' of land. Section 10 of the 1965 Act contains separate rules for compensation for injurious affection where there is no 'purchase'.

may be assessed under these separate heads, the 'sum to be ascertained is in essence one sum, namely the proper price or compensation payable in all the circumstances of the case'.[14]

**15.7** Perhaps unsurprisingly, the primary head of compensation is normally the value of the land subject to acquisition. In the case of freehold estates and leasehold estates (save where the lessee has 'no greater interest in the land than as tenant for a year or from year to year'),[15] s 7 of the 1965 Act entitles the owner to the value of his interest. The value is determined in accordance with the statutory formula in s 5(2) of the 1961 Act, that is: '… the amount which the land if sold in the open market by a willing seller might be expected to realise'.[16]

**15.8** Although this provision refers only to a 'willing seller' it is implicit that there is a willing buyer also.[17]

**15.9** It is well-settled that compensation for the compulsory acquisition of land 'cannot include an increase in value which is entirely due to the scheme underlying the acquisition'.[18] This rule is often called the '*Pointe Gourde* rule' following the name of the case from which the quotation is taken. The rule requires that the value of the land to be acquired is assessed without increase or diminution entirely due to the scheme underlying the acquisition. So, the 'whole question must be approached upon a consideration of the state of affairs which would have existed if there had been no scheme'.[19] Although the *Point Gourde* rule has been developed judicially, its effect is reproduced or reflected in various provisions of the 1961 Act.[20] Indeed, since compulsory purchase is entirely a creation of statute, it may be more accurate to say that the principle which derives from *Point Gourde* 'involves an interpretation of the word "value" in those statutory provisions which require the compensation for compulsory acquisition to include the value of the lands taken'.[21]

**15.10** Another important principle of valuation is that things are to be taken as they actually are on the valuation date, except to the extent that the relevant statute postulates the hypothetical transaction requires a departure from reality. This is sometimes

[14] *Horn v Sunderland Corp* [1941] 2 KB 25, at 33, per Sir Wilfrid Greene MR.

[15] 1965 Act, s 20. This provision embodies a special procedure for dealing with a person 'having no greater interest than as tenant for a year or from year to year'. Such a person is not entitled to notice to treat. The authority may simply await the expiry of the contractual term, or serve notice to quit under the contract. See *Newham LBC v Benjamin* [1968] 1 WLR 964. In that case, there is no right to compensation under the 1965 Act, although there may be a right to a 'disturbance payment' under s 37 of the 1973 Act.

[16] This provision originates from the second of six 'rules' found in s 2 of the Acquisition of Land Act 1919.

[17] *Gajapatiraju v The Revenue District Officer, Vizagaptam* [1939] AC 302, at 312, per Lord Romer. *Cf* s 34 of the Landlord and Tenant Act 1954 which does not refer in terms to a willing lessee (though it refers to a 'willing lessor'). However, it is implicit in the concept of a letting 'in the open market' that both a willing lessor and a willing lessee are to be assumed for the purposes of assessing the rent to be set under this provision.

[18] *Pointe Gourde Quarrying and Transport Co Ltd v Sub-Intendent of Crown Lands* [1947] AC 565, at 572, per Lord Macdermott.

[19] *Fletcher Estates (Harlescott) Ltd v Secretary of State for the Environment* [2000] 2 AC 307, at 315, per Lord Hope.

[20] See, in particular, s 5(3) and s 6A.

[21] *Rugby Joint Water Board v Footitt* [1973] AC 202, at 214–15, per Lord Pearson.

described as the principle of reality. It requires that the 'world of make-believe should be kept as near as possible to reality'.[22] In other words, the valuer ought not to depart from the real world further than the hypothesis compels.[23]

**15.11** There are various other rules relating to the valuation exercise. So, for example, there are special assumptions as to planning permission;[24] increases in value due to unlawful uses must be disregarded;[25] enhancements carried out with a view to increased compensation are disregarded;[26] and compensation otherwise payable may be reduced by the amount of the increase in the value of other land which is contiguous or adjacent to the land being compulsorily acquired.[27]

**15.12** If the land is the subject of a notice to treat, the relevant valuation date is the earlier of the date when the acquiring authority enters on and takes possession of the land and the date when the assessment of compensation is made.[28] This is of particular relevance where the land being acquired is a leasehold estate. In a case where notice to treat is served, if the acquiring authority does not require possession of the land and there is no agreement on the level of compensation, a delay in the assessment of compensation will result in a corresponding adjustment to the valuation date. Since a lease is a wasting asset, a later valuation date may have a depressive effect on the value of the land being compulsorily acquired.

## COMPENSATION FOR AN INTEREST SUBJECT TO A BREAK CLAUSE

**15.13** As explained above (see **15.3**) compulsory acquisition of land may extend to a freehold subject to a lease or the lease itself. In either case, the lease may contain a break clause, exercisable by the landlord or the tenant or both. For the purposes of assessing compensation, both as to the value of the land being compulsorily acquired and other losses not based on the value of the land (such as loss of profits), the question may arise as to what assumption (if any) ought to be made regarding the possibility of the break clause being exercised.

**15.14** It is convenient first to consider the general rule as regards periodic tenancies. Here the position is that, subject to any statutory rights of protection which ought to be taken into account,[29] the landlord's or the tenant's interest is to be valued on the assumption that the tenancy is terminated at the earliest date on which it could be brought to an end by the service of a notice to quit after the valuation date.[30]

[22] *Trocette Property Co Ltd v Greater London Council* (1974) 28 P&CR 408, at 421, per Lawton LJ.

[23] *Hoare v National Trust* (1998) 77 P&CR 366, at 380, per Schiemann LJ.

[24] 1961 Act, s 14.

[25] 1961 Act, s 5(4).

[26] Acquisition of Land Act 1981, s 4(2).

[27] 1961 Act, s 6B.

[28] 1961 Act, s 5A(3). Section 5A(4) governs the position where the land is the subject of a general vesting declaration under the Compulsory Purchase (Vesting Declarations) Act 1981.

[29] See eg s 47 of the 1973 Act concerning the compensation of land subject to a business tenancy.

[30] *Minister of Transport v Pettitt* (1969) 20 P&CR 344; *Rugby Joint Water Board v Foottit* [1973] AC 202. In *Bishopsgate Space Management Ltd v London Underground Ltd* [2004] 2 EGLR 175, at [63], the Lands Tribunal

**15.15** This general rule appears to apply at least in a case where there is an unconditional landlord's break option in the lease. The point arose for consideration in *Bishopsgate Space Management Ltd v London Underground Ltd*,[31] in which the claimants sought the determination of certain preliminary issues arising from their claims for compensation under s 20 of the 1965 Act, made in response to the compulsory acquisition of their leasehold interests in a goods yard.

**15.16** The facts of *Bishopsgate* were relatively complicated. In short, in 1999, Railtrack granted to BSM a tenancy of part of the undercroft of an old railway structure for a term of 10 years. In 2000, Railtrack granted to Patto a tenancy of the upper level of the structure for a term to 31 January 2003. Both tenancies were determinable by either of the respective parties at any time upon six months' notice. Further, both tenancies were excluded from Part II of the Landlord and Tenant Act 1954. In January 2001, Patto granted a sub-tenancy of part of the upper level to Teamworks for a term from 25 September to 24 January 2003 on terms that either party could determine the sub-tenancy by giving five months and two weeks' notice. The interests of both BSM and Teamworks were the subject of compulsory purchase. However, there was a dispute as to the level of compensation payable, with the acquiring authority contending that the respective interests had to be valued on the assumption that each would terminate upon the earliest date of termination that could have resulted under a landlord's notice given on the date of entry. The Lands Tribunal agreed with the acquiring authority. It said as follows:

> In valuing an interest in land that has been compulsorily acquired, where there is a tenancy of such land, the interest is to be valued on the basis that the tenancy could have been terminated on the earliest date possible under the tenancy, and any prospect that there might have been in the no-scheme world of the tenancy continuing is to be disregarded. This rule applies equally to the valuation of the landlord's interest and to the valuation of the tenant's interest, and it applies also where possession has been taken under section 20. In our judgment, there is no reason in principle, when applying the rule, to distinguish between a periodic tenancy and a tenancy for a term of years subject to a break clause. As Lord Hodson put it in *Rugby Joint Water Board* in a passage we have quoted,[32] the ability on the part of the landlord to give an effective notice to quit is an element in the value of the land and cannot be disregarded. That consideration applies both to the landlord's interest and to the tenant's interest.

**15.17** The general rule, that a periodic tenancy and (it seems) a lease with a landlord's unconditional break option is to be assumed to be determined by notice as soon as it could be after the relevant valuation date, has been the subject of academic criticism.[33] Suppose, for example, that the freehold reversion of a lease containing an unconditional landlord's break option is actually sold on the open market. The actual purchaser

observed with reference to these cases that there was 'good authority' for the proposition that 'it is necessary as a matter of law, when assessing compensation under section 20 [of the 1965 Act], to assume that a periodic tenancy, or a tenancy with less than a year unexpired, or a tenancy for a term of years subject to a break clause, would determine on the earliest date of termination that could have resulted under a landlord's notice given on the date of entry'.

[31] *Bishopsgate Space Management Ltd v London Underground Ltd* [2004] 2 EGLR 175.

[32] *Rugby Joint Water Board v Foottit* [1973] AC 202, at 220A ('... The ability to give an effective notice to quit is an element in the value of the land and cannot be disregarded. When the precise nature of the interest has been ascertained then the land can be valued ...').

[33] See eg Denyer-Green, op cit, p 289 and Barnes, op cit, para 4.97.

will then be the person who decides whether and (if so) when to exercise the option. Depending on the circumstances (where, say, the lease was over-rented or there was no or only limited tenant demand for the premises) the purchaser might be unlikely to do so. Thus, the assumption of the lease terminating as soon as possible could result in an artificially low valuation: it presupposes that the hypothetical purchaser will act as the actual purchaser might not. This appears contrary to the principle of equivalence, the presumption of reality and the *Pointe Gourde* rule, which – it might be thought – should require compensation to be assessed having regard to the likelihood (in the absence of the relevant project) of the break option being exercised.[34]

**15.18** As already mentioned, the decision in *Bishopsgate* specifically concerned the effect on compensation of an unconditional landlord's break option. It is unclear whether the approach in *Bishopsgate* applies also in the case of a landlord's conditional break option or a tenant's break option (whether conditional or unconditional).[35] In the absence of authority, it is submitted that the better approach is not to make any automatic assumption that the relevant break right can and will be exercised. Rather, the interest should be valued taking into account the possibility of the right being successfully exercised. Where the interest being acquired is a freehold reversion, and the lease contains either (i) a landlord's unconditional or (ii) a tenant's conditional or unconditional break option, it seems unprincipled to assume that the lease will be terminated upon the occurrence of events which are outside of the purchaser's control. By contrast, where the interest being acquired is a lease which contains a tenant's break option (whether conditional or unconditional), there is no – or not necessarily any – reason to assume that the purchaser of the leasehold interest would bring the lease to an end as soon as possible after the purchase, particularly if to do so would be contrary to the purchaser's own interests.

[34] There is a further anomaly arising out of the *Bishopsgate* case, as identified in *Bishopsgate Parking (No 2) Ltd v The Welsh Ministers* [2012] UKUT 22 (LC). In the latter case, at [125], the Upper Tribunal observed that, in a contradistinction to a licensee claiming compensation under s 37 of the 1973 Act, 'a short leaseholder is not … able to have disturbance compensation assessed having regard to the period for which the land occupied by him may reasonably have been expected to be available for the purpose of his business'. There does not appear to be any reason why, following *Pettit*, *Foottit* and *Bishopsgate*, a tenant should be treated less favourably than a licensee.

[35] In *Klein v London Underground Ltd* [1996] 1 EGLR 249, the Lands Tribunal (AP Musto FRICS) assessed loss of goodwill on the total extinguishment of the claimant's business on the basis that, in the absence of evidence, there was no reason to conclude that a landlord's redevelopment break clause would have been exercised. However, no authorities are referred to in the report and it contains no discussion as to why this was considered the correct approach.

# 16

# *Break Clauses and Rent Review*

## INTRODUCTION

**16.1** Break clauses are relevant in the context of rent review provisions in at least two respects, considered separately below:

(i) Procedural – the presence of a break clause may have the effect of rendering time of the essence for the operation of rent review provisions.
(ii) Substantive – the presence of a break clause may impact upon the assumed terms of, and the quantum of rent for, the hypothetical tenancy under the rent review provisions.

## PROCEDURAL RELEVANCE

### (a) Introduction

**16.2** In *United Scientific Holdings Ltd v Burnley Borough Council*,[1] the majority of the House of Lords held that there was a general presumption that, in the case of rent review provisions, time is not to be treated as being of the essence. This is because the detriment to the landlord of losing his review altogether by failure to adhere strictly to the stipulated time limit will be wholly disproportionate to the disadvantage of the tenant of a delay in the assessment of the rent.

**16.3** However, this 'general presumption' may be rebutted where the lease contains indications to the contrary. As Lord Simon said:[2]

> Where a rent review clause is associated with a true option (a 'break' clause, for example), it is a strong indication that time is intended to be of the essence of the rent review clause – if not absolutely, at least to the extent that the tenant will reasonably expect to know what new rent he will have to pay before the time comes for him to elect whether to terminate or renew the tenancy (*cf Samuel Properties (Developments) Ltd v Hayek* [1972] 1 WLR 1296).

**16.4** Similarly, Lord Fraser remarked:[3]

> The rule [viz. that time is not be treated as being of the essence] would of course be excluded if the review clause expressly stated that time was to be of the essence. It would also be excluded if

[1] *United Scientific Holdings Ltd v Burnley Borough Council* [1978] AC 904.
[2] *United Scientific Holdings Ltd v Burnley Borough Council* [1978] AC 904, at 946C–46D.
[3] *United Scientific Holdings Ltd v Burnley Borough Council* [1978] AC 904, at 962F–62G.

the context clearly indicated that that was the intention of the parties as for instance where the tenant had a right to break the lease by notice given by a specified date which was later than the last date for serving the landlord's trigger notice. The tenant's notice to terminate the contract will be one where the time limit was mandatory, and the necessary implication is that the time limit for giving the landlord's notice of review must also be mandatory.

### (b) Where the Inter-relationship between a Break Clause and the Rent Review Machinery has Made Time of the Essence of the Review

**16.5** There is a significant number of cases in which the inter-relationship between a break clause and the rent review machinery has sufficed to make time of the essence of the landlord's notice of review. The rationale which underpins these cases is that, because time limits for the exercise of a break option are strict, the parties are taken to have intended that the tenant should be in a position to know what reviewed rent he will be liable to pay before deciding whether or not to exercise the break option. These cases are set out in chronological order below.

**16.6** In *C Richards & Son Ltd v Karenita Ltd*[4] the rent review clause provided:

> If the landlords shall by giving notice in writing to the tenants at any time during the first three months of the seventh year of the term hereby created require a review of the rent payable hereunder, such rent shall be revised with effect from the expiration of the seventh year.

The time for the landlord to give the review notice was followed by a period in which the tenant, to whom alone the right was given, was entitled to serve a notice to determine the term. Goulding J rejected the argument that time was not of the essence of the rent review provision.

**16.7** *Rahman v Kenshire*[5] concerned a lease for a period of 21 years from 24 June 1965. The lease contained a rent review provision entitling the landlord to give a notice in writing to the tenant 'not less than nor more than twelve months before any and every seventh anniversary of the 24th day of June 1965 requiring the rent from such anniversary … to be reviewed'. In addition, the lease contained a tenant's break clause worded as follows:

> If the lessee shall be desirous of determining the present lease at the expiration of the seventh or fourteenth year of the term hereby granted and of such his desire shall give six calendar months' previous notice in writing to the lessors … then and in such case immediately after the expiration of such seventh or fourteenth years of the said term as the case may be this present lease and everything herein contained shall cease and be void.

**16.8** The latest date on which the tenant could have given notice to determine the lease on 24 June 1979 (ie the fourteenth anniversary of the term) was 24 December 1978. No such notice was given. On 15 January 1979, the landlord gave notice to the tenant

[4] *C Richards & Son Ltd v Karenita Ltd* (1972) 221 EG 25 (Described as the 'paradigm of rent review clause in which time is of the essence': see *Central Estates Ltd v Secretary of State for the Environment* [1996] 72 P&CR 482, at 494, per Glidewell LJ).

[5] *Rahman v Kenshire* [1981] 2 EGLR 102.

requiring the rent of the premises to be reviewed as from 24 June 1979. The tenant contended that the notice was invalid because it was given out of time, ie less than 12 months before the relevant review date. Cantley J accepted this submission. After referring to the decision in *United Scientific Holdings*, he said:[6]

> Is there a contra-indication in the interrelationship of the rent review clause and other clauses or in the surrounding circumstances? In this lease there are only two occasions in fact when the landlord may require the rent under this lease to be reviewed. The first is the seventh anniversary and the second is the 14th. On the 21st anniversary the lease ends by effluxion of time. Correspondingly, there are only two occasions when the lessee may terminate the lease by notice: the first is at the seventh anniversary and the second is at the 14th. It will terminate itself at the 21st. If the landlord gives notice as specified 12 months before the relevant anniversary, the lessee then has six months in which to consider whether to respond by terminating the tenancy by six months' notice.
>
> In my view the two clauses are interrelated, and the implication is that time is of the essence in the review clause, as it certainly is in the break clause.

**16.9** In *Al Saloom v Shirley James Travel Service Ltd*,[7] there was a clause which provided that the lessee should have the right to give not less than six months' notice in writing prior to the expiration of the third year of the term to determine the lease; and a further provision that, subject to the lessee's right of determination, the lessor should have the right, on giving to the lessee not more than 12 months' nor less than six months' notice in writing prior to the expiration of the third year of the term, to review the yearly rent for the time being payable thereunder. In other words, the timetable laid down in the lease required the review notice to be served not later than the last date on which a break notice might be served. Of this, Waller LJ said:[8]

> both provisions about break and rent review in this case were in the same clause and closely allied to each other. The words 'not less than six months' notice in writing prior to the expiration of the third year of the term' were used for both break and rent review. Whether the word 'interrelated', 'correlated' or 'associated' is used, the implication of the use of the same phrase in the same clause is overwhelming ... I have no doubt that in both cases here time was of the essence.

**16.10** In *Coventry City Council v J Hepworth & Sons*,[9] a 42-year lease of business premises granted in 1953 contained a rent review clause, with a provision that the landlord should give notice in writing on or before 31 December 1974, together with a provision entitling the tenant to break the lease on 31 March 1975 should he so wish. The landlord failed to give the required notice before 31 December 1974, and took no further action over the rent review in the belief that they were out of time. Following the decision in *United Scientific Holdings*, they sought to implement the rent review clause, arguing that time was not after all of the essence. The Court of Appeal held that the combined effect of the requirement for a landlord's trigger notice and the corresponding right for the tenant to break the lease, did amount to contra indications in the lease such as to

[6] *Rahman v Kenshire* [1981] 2 EGLR 102, at 104B–104C.
[7] *Al Saloom v Shirley James Travel Service Ltd* (1981) 42 P&CR 181.
[8] *Al Saloom v Shirley James Travel Service Ltd* (1981) 42 P&CR 181, at 185.
[9] *Coventry City Council v J Hepworth & Sons* [1983] 46 P&CR 170.

displace the presumption that time was not of the essence. The landlord was accordingly debarred from operating the clause.

**16.11** *Legal & General Assurance (Pension Management) Ltd v Cheshire County Council*[10] concerned a 21-year lease. Clause 3 had two sub-clauses; one containing a rent review provision and the other a tenant's break option. The rent review provision was in these terms:

> At the expiration of the seventh and fourteenth years of the term hereby granted ... the landlord shall have the right to review the yearly rent hereinbefore reserved on giving to the tenant not less than six months' notice in writing prior to the date of his intention to do so.

**16.12** The break option was in these terms:

> If the tenant shall desire to determine the present demise at the expiration of the seventh or fourteenth years of the said term and shall give not less than six months' previous notice in writing, then immediately upon the expiration of such notice the present demise and everything herein contained shall cease.

**16.13** A notice requiring a rent review was served by the landlord out of time. Dillon LJ, with whose judgment Sir John Donaldson MR and May LJ agreed, referred to *United Scientific Holdings* and to *Al Saloom*, and said:

> As it seems to me the decision of the court in the Al Saloom case is indistinguishable from the present case and binding on us, and that is enough to dispose of the appeal.

**16.14** However, he went on to consider the implications of the break option on the question whether time was of the essence of the rent review procedure. He said:

> The learned judge in the present case was fully entitled, in my view, to say, as he did in his judgment: 'I think the tenant could reasonably expect that the notice would be given in sufficient time for him to decide whether he wanted to break or not'. The reason for having coincident dates is obviously that the tenant should have in mind, when he decides whether he is going to break or not, whether or not the landlord is going to invoke rent review procedure, and the reasoning which has led the courts to hold that time is of the essence of a rent review clause where the tenant's break clause is in the same lease is geared to a date later than the date prescribed for the service of the landlord's rent review notice leads equally, I think, to the conclusion which this court reached in the *Al Saloom* case and I would reach in this case, that time was of the essence of the rent review clause in this lease.

**16.15** In *William Hill (Southern) Ltd v Govier*,[11] a 40-year lease of office premises contained a rent review clause and a tenant's break clause. The relevant review date was 25 December 1982 and the relevant part of the review clause provided that, if the landlord and the tenant failed to agree the reviewed rent nine months before the review date, then either party could within a further period of one month refer the question of the amount of rent to a chartered surveyor. The tenant's break clause was operable by at least three months' previous written notice to expire on 25 December 1982. No steps to agree a reviewed rent or to refer the matter for determination were taken prior to the review date. The tenant argued that time was of the essence for the reference to the chartered surveyor

[10] *Legal & General Assurance (Pension Management) v Cheshire County Council* [1984] 269 EG 40.
[11] *William Hill (Southern) Ltd v Govier* [1984] 1 EGLR 121.

and that the right to review was lost. Mr Edward Evans-Lombe QC, sitting as a Deputy High Court Judge, held that on the true construction of the lease, the rent review clause and the break clause were linked in a way which indicated an intention by the parties that the tenant should know whether the landlord was seeking an increase in rent, and, accordingly, time was of the essence of the provision requiring a reference to a chartered surveyor within the month succeeding the commencement of the ninth month before the review date, and the right to review had been lost.

**16.16** *Stephenson & Son v Orca Properties Ltd*[12] concerned office premises in York. The premises were demised by a lease dated 29 August 1979, for a term of 21 years from 1 January 1979. Clause 4(b) contained a rent review provision, which was worded as follows:

> Either party shall be at liberty to give to the other six months' notice in writing to expire at the end of the seventh or fourteenth year of the term hereby created requiring a revision of the rent hereby reserved in accordance with the rents prevailing at the date of the expiration of such notice.

**16.17** Clause 4(d) conferred a break option on the tenant. It was in these terms:

> If the tenant shall desire to terminate the term hereby granted at the expiration of the seventh or fourteenth year thereof and shall give to the landlord six months previous notice in writing of such their desire ... Then immediately on the expiration of the seventh and fourteenth year, as the case may be, the present demise and everything herein contained shall cease and be void.

**16.18** Thus, the last date by which the review notice and the break notice could be served was the same. On 1 July 1979, the landlord gave notice to the tenant requiring the rent of the premises to be reviewed as from 1 January 1986 (ie the seventh anniversary of the term). However, it was common ground at trial that the latest date on which the landlord was able to give the notice was 30 June 1979. Scott J considered that he was bound by the decisions of the Court of Appeal in *Al Saloom* and *Legal & General Assurance*. He said:[13]

> These two Court of Appeal decisions are binding on me. [Counsel for the landlord] has naturally sought to distinguish them. He has pointed to three differences between the lease in the present case and the leases in the two Court of Appeal cases. First, the rent review machinery in the lease with which I am concerned can be triggered off either by the landlord or the tenant. In the other two leases only the landlord could do so. Second, the rent review under the lease in the present case may lead to a reduction as well as to an increase in the rent. In the other two leases a reduction in the rent was not a possible consequence of the rent review. Third, the juxtaposition of the rent review provision and the break option is different in the present case from the corresponding juxtaposition in the other two leases.
>
> In my judgment, however, none of these points is a basis of legitimate distinction of the two Court of Appeal authorities.
>
> The third point is, I think, of no weight whatsoever. The first two points do not, in my view, incline against the conclusion reached by the Court of Appeal in the two cases I have mentioned

[12] *Stephenson & Son v Orca Properties Ltd* [1989] 2 EGLR 129.
[13] *Stephenson & Son v Orca Properties Ltd* [1989] 2 EGLR 129, at 132H–32K.

> that time should be of the essence of the rent review provision. The decisions in the two Court of Appeal cases require me, in my view, to hold that time is of the essence of the rent review provision in the present case. The construction and effect of leases, and in particular leases of commercial premises, ought not, in my view, to be subjected to variation caused by minor and apparently unimportant differences in language. Certainty is highly important. It would be a disservice to the law if I were, in reliance on such points of distinction as have been relied on in the present case, to give to the rent review clause in the present case a different effect to that given to the rent review clauses in the two Court of Appeal cases in question.

**16.19** All of the above cases concerned leases which contained break options conferred on the tenant alone. By contrast, in *Central Estates Ltd v Secretary of State for the Environment*,[14] the lease provided that either party might determine the lease at the end of the 21st year by 6 months' previous written notice; further, that either party might require a rent review in the 14th, 21st, 28th and 35th year by serving a notice in writing 12 months in advance of the following period. There was therefore an interrelation of the break clause and the rent review procedure in respect of the 21st year, with 29 September 1991 being the latest date for service of notice requiring rent review and 29 March 1992 for service of notice determining the lease. The landlord wrote to the tenant on 14 April 1992 giving notice of a rent review to take effect on 29 September 1992. The tenant refused to accept the notice as being out of time. The landlord issued proceedings for a declaration that time was not of the essence and that the letter of 14 April 1992 was valid and effective. The landlord was successful at trial. The tenant appealed.

**16.20** On appeal, the Court of Appeal held that the presumption that time was not of the essence of the rent review clause was displaced. After considering the various authorities referred to above, Morritt LJ said as follows:[15]

> In my view the clear trend of all these cases supports the proposition for which the [the tenant] contends, namely that the presumption is displaced and time is of the essence if the timetable laid down by the lease allows a period after the service of the review notice in which to consider whether or not to serve a break notice for if time is not of the essence the period allowed for the service of the break notice as to which time is of the essence is eliminated or eroded.
>
> The essential question is whether the terms of this lease give rise to any meaningful distinction. A number of points were relied on which I will seek to deal with in turn.
>
> First it was emphasised that this lease provides for four rent reviews but only one break. This certainly distinguishes this case from all the others to which I have referred …
>
> I do not accept that this point of distinction justifies the conclusion that time was not of the essence for service of the notice to trigger a review of the rent payable during the third period. The principle described in the speech of Lord Diplock [in United Scientific Holdings] is whether the interrelation between the rent review clause and the other provisions of the lease displaces the presumption that time is not of the essence. The relevant interrelation only exists in respect of the third period. I see no reason why in relation to that period for which the context is different the same words should not bear a different meaning to that which they bear in respect of the other periods. The question is therefore whether in respect of the third period the interrelation is sufficient.

[14] *Central Estates Ltd v Secretary of State for the Environment* [1996] 72 P&CR 482.
[15] *Central Estates Ltd v Secretary of State for the Environment* [1996] 72 P&CR 482, at 490–91.

> This raises the second point of distinction. In this case unlike the others to which I have referred both the rent review, which may be upwards or downwards, and the break clause may be activated by either the landlord or the tenant. It is submitted that as either party considering whether to determine the lease could require a rent review if knowledge of the future rent was required there was no reason why he should not initiate the review …
>
> I do not accept this as a distinction which points to a different result either. A tenant will seek a rent review if he thinks that the rent should be reduced; likewise the lessor will seek a review if he thinks it should be increased. Neither will seek a review just for the sake of it. In each case the other party is entitled to give notice to determine the lease. Thus as the rent review may be both up and down and either party may trigger its operation and give notice to determine the term the effect of the timetable contained in the lease is to confer on both parties that which in the first category of case to which I have referred was conferred on one of them only namely, the tenant. In my judgment this mutuality requires that time should be of the essence for the service of the rent review notice by whichever party it is served in the same way and for the same reasons as in the cases in the first category time is of the essence of the landlord's notice triggering the rent review because of its relation to the tenant's right to determine the term.
>
> The remaining point is the same as that which failed to impress Scott J in *Stephenson & Son v Orca Properties Ltd* namely, juxtaposition. In my view to conclude that this was a valid distinction would be to put form before substance. The point was not pressed and it is unnecessary to say any more about it.

### (c) Where the Inter-relationship between a Break Clause and the Rent Review Machinery has not Made Time of the Essence of the Review

**16.21** Notwithstanding the above authorities, it does not necessarily follow that, where a rent review clause is associated with an option to determine, time is of the essence of the rent review clause. Rather, there is a rebuttable presumption that time is to be of the essence. So, in the *Coventry City Council* case,[16] Lawton LJ said:

> where you have a triggering off of a rent review provision started by the landlord, followed by an option given to the tenant to break the lease if he so wishes, then time is to be presumed to be of the essence of the agreement, unless there are contra-indications.

**16.22** Likewise in *Metrolands Investments Ltd v Dewhurst Ltd*,[17] Slade LJ observed:

> in a case where a lease contains a break clause as well as a rent review clause and the timetables of the two clauses are closely interlocked, the interrelation of the two causes is *likely* to suffice as a contra-indication sufficient to rebut the ordinary presumption – though everything must depend on the wording of the particular lease. (Emphasis in original.)

**16.23** In *Metrolands* itself, the lease under consideration had an unusual feature. The event in the rent review clause as to which the tenant contended that time was of the essence was the *actual obtaining* of an arbitrator's decision in relation to the new rent. It was readily conceivable, therefore, that the landlord might have acted with irreproachable

[16] *Coventry City Council v J Hepworth & Sons* [1983] 46 P&CR 170, at 176.
[17] *Metrolands Investments Ltd v Dewhurst Ltd* [1986] 52 P&CR 232, at 244.

promptness and diligence in setting in motion the rent review arbitration machinery provided for by the lease, but that, without any fault whatever on the landlord's part, the arbitrator's decision might not have been obtained until after the specified date. Further, any potential hardship to the tenant which might otherwise have arisen through tardy action by the landlord in initiating the rent review could be eliminated or, at least, substantially mitigated by the tenant initiating such action itself. For these reasons, the ordinary presumption that, where a rent review clause is associated with a break clause, time is of the essence of the rent review clause, was rebutted. In giving the judgment of the Court, Slade LJ said:[18]

> Throughout this debate, we think it must be borne in mind that the ultimate object of the court in construing a rent review clause, like any other contractual provision, must be to ascertain the parties' intention from the particular words which they have used to express those intentions, read, of course, in the light of any admissible evidence as to surrounding circumstances; albeit with the assistance of the guidelines as to construction afforded by earlier authorities. In many, perhaps most, cases, of which the present is one, the rent review (if any) can result only in an increase, and thus is only for the landlord's benefit. Essentially, therefore, the question to which the court has to direct its mind is this: is the proper intention to impute to the parties, from the words which they have used, the intention that the landlord shall lose his right to a review if the stipulated timetable is not strictly adhered to in the relevant respects.

**16.24** As mentioned above, a particular and distinguishing feature of the rent-fixing machinery in *Metrolands* was that the timing of the procedure was under the control, not of the landlord, but of the arbitrator. This feature was the reason why, in the end, in Slade LJ's view, time should not be treated as of the essence. As he explained:[19]

> If time was to be treated as being of the essence in respect of this date, this would have meant that … a delay in the obtaining of the arbitrator's decision by only one day beyond August 19, 1981 would have entirely deprived the lessor of its right to a review in respect of the last seven years of this 21 year term and would have left it saddled with a continuing annual rental as low as £1,800, which had been the rental payable for the preceding eleven years. In these circumstances, we think that the following observations of Lord Dilhorne in the *United Scientific* case are apposite, spoken as they were in relation to a lease which, apart from the absence of a break clause, bore a marked similarity to that under consideration in the present case:
>
> > 'It is most unlikely in these circumstances that the lessors, if they had been asked at the time the leases had been entered into to agree that time should be of the essence, would ever have agreed to that, and I see no reason for imputing to them an intention which no reasonable landlord would have had.'

**16.25** A similar result was arrived at in *Edwin Woodhouse Trustee Co Ltd v Sheffield Brick Co Plc*.[20] In that case, a lease provided for a rent review on 25 December 1982. There was no express provision for a landlord's 'trigger notice'. Rather, the reviewed rent was to be:

> such sum or amount as the parties shall agree as being or (failing agreement at least six months next before [the rent review date]) as a Valuer appointed by the parties or (failing appointment

[18] *Metrolands Investments Ltd v Dewhurst Ltd* [1986] 52 P&CR 232, at 243.
[19] *Metrolands Investments Ltd v Dewhurst Ltd* [1986] 52 P&CR 232, at 245–246.
[20] *Edwin Woodhouse Trustee Co Ltd v Sheffield Brick Co Plc* [1984] 1 EGLR 130.

> at least two months next before [the rent review date]) nominated at the request of either party by the President ... shall determine as being the yearly rental value of the demised premises.

**16.26** The lease further gave the tenant an option to determine the tenancy at 7 or 14 years, by notice given at least 6 months before the last day of the period in question. When the landlord sought to review the rent out of time, the tenant argued that terms were implied in the lease to the effect that the landlord must serve a notice either at least six months before the appropriate review date, or alternatively a reasonable time before the six months' deadline for operating the break clause; and that the review provisions and the break provisions were accordingly interrelated so as to displace the presumption that time was not of the essence in respect of the review clause.

**16.27** His Honour Judge Finlay QC (sitting as a Deputy Judge of the High Court) held that, on a true construction of the lease, there were no clear terms which indicated that the landlord was under a duty to serve anything in the nature of a trigger notice in order to set the rent review in motion. Nor was it possible to find within the lease anything which imposed on the landlord any such duty. The consequence of this was that time was not of the essence in relation to any implied obligation upon the landlord to serve a notice to bring into operation the rent review provisions of the lease.

## SUBSTANTIVE RELEVANCE

### (a) Introduction

**16.28** Where a lease contains a break option, various issues may arise when considering: (i) whether the break option should be included in the hypothetical lease; and (ii) if so, what the valuation consequences might be.

### (b) The Inclusion of the Break Option in the Hypothetical Lease

**16.29** Typically, a rent review clause will direct the parties to value the rent payable under a hypothetical lease on the same terms as the actual lease, subject to various express assumptions and disregards. If the actual lease contains a break clause, this may result in the break clause being included in the hypothetical lease. Whether that is the case will depend upon a close analysis of the language used in the rent review provisions.

**16.30** In this context, there is an important distinction to be drawn between (i) a break clause in the actual lease which is expressed to operate by reference to anniversaries of the term (which may be capable of easy incorporation into the hypothetical lease) and (ii) a break clause in the actual lease which is expressed to operate on a specific date or specific dates (in which case it may not be so easy, at least not without re-writing the wording of the break option). This distinction is well-illustrated by *R & A Millett (Shops) Ltd v Legal & General Assurance Society Ltd*.[21]

[21] *R & A Millett (Shops) Ltd v Legal & General Assurance Society Ltd* [1985] 1 EGLR 103.

**16.31** That case concerned a lease for a term of just under 35 years commencing on 27 February 1972, subject to a landlord's break option worded as follows (with added emphasis):

> Notwithstanding anything herein contained, if the landlord shall, *after the expiration of the first 12 years of the term hereby granted* desire to demolish or reconstruct or rebuild the whole or part of the demised premises or the building or if the landlord is called upon by the local or other authority to rebuild, support or reconstruct the whole or any part of the demised premises or the building, the landlord shall be entitled, on giving to the tenant not less than six months previous notice in writing or such other shorter notice that the landlord may himself receive from such local or other authority, *to determine the term hereby granted.*

**16.32** The lease also contained a rent-review clause providing for the reviewed yearly rent to be (again, with added emphasis):

> sum as shall be agreed between the landlord and the tenant as representing the fair rack rental market value of the demised premises for a term of years equivalent to the then unexpired residue of the term hereby granted commencing on the relevant date of review as between a willing landlord and a willing tenant with vacant possession ... But upon the supposition, if not a fact, that the tenant has complied with all the obligations as to repair and decoration herein imposed on the tenant and *in all other respects on the terms and conditions of this lease, including the provisions of this clause.*

**16.33** The principal issues between the parties concerned the meaning which was to be given to the emphasised words above. The tenant argued that the break option, when referring to the landlord's right to 'determine the term hereby granted' was a reference to the term granted by the actual lease; so that, after the expiration of the first 12 years of the term the break option was a spent force, save to the extent that it remained terminable on six months' notice in the circumstances contemplated therein. Once the 12-year period had expired, there was nothing in the rent review provision which required or directed the valuer ascertaining the rent to substitute some new 12-year period.

**16.34** By contrast, the landlord argued that the rent review provision required the valuer to assume a notional lease to be for the residue of the original term on the identical terms of the actual lease (apart from rent). Therefore, the landlord contended, the hypothetical lease contained the break clause verbatim, with the result that (on this construction) the 12-year period referred to in the break clause commenced again for the purpose of the rent review every time there was a review.

**16.35** Mr Michael Wheeler QC (sitting as a Deputy Judge of the Chancery Division) preferred the tenant's formulation. He said:[22]

> In construing the effect of the rent-review clause and the impact on it of [the break clause], it is in my view fair to bear in mind that the object of the exercise expressed between the parties on that rent review is to find out what rent will represent the fair rack rental value of the premises for a term of years equivalent to the unexpired residue of the term hereby granted as between a willing landlord and a willing tenant with vacant possession, and so on. That, as it seems to me, shows quite clearly that what the parties are seeking to attain by the implementation of

[22] *R & A Millett (Shops) Ltd v Legal & General Assurance Society Ltd* [1985] 1 EGLR 103, at 104.

the provisions which they are agreeing is a sensible and businesslike commercial result, and the revised rent is to be a fair rent.

These considerations, coupled with what seem to me to be the unambiguous and clear words of [the break option], lead me to the conclusion that the tenant's construction of the lease is to be preferred. [The landlord's] construction, on the other hand, appears to require the expert to fix the revised rent on the basis of a notional lease which differs quite materially from the legal position which he accepts still continues to bind the parties under the original lease and, of course, the assignment.

**16.36** Subject always to the wording of the rent review provisions, it is unlikely that a purely personal break clause will appear in the hypothetical lease. For example, *St Martin's Property Investments Limited v CIB Properties Limited*[23] concerned a rent review in respect of two leases granted to Citicorp International Plc ('Citicorp'), one of which had since been assigned to an associated company, CIB Properties Limited ('CIB'). The leases each contained a personal break clause worded as follows:

6.3.1 If [Citicorp] wishes to determine the Term on the 23rd June 2001 or on the 23rd June 2011 [Citicorp] shall give to the Landlord not less than 12 months and not more than 18 months prior written notice of such wish specifying such date and the date so specified shall be the 'Termination Date'.

6.4 The rights in this Clause 6 are personal to [Citicorp] (and to any company to which [Citicorp] may lawfully assign this Underlease …).

**16.37** The reviewed rent was to be the open market rent, which was defined as the full yearly open market rent for which the demised premises might reasonably be expected to be let as a whole on the relevant review date in the open market by a willing landlord to a willing tenant with vacant possession without taking a premium, for a term equal in duration to the original term hereby granted and (importantly) otherwise 'upon the terms and conditions' of the leases in question.

**16.38** During negotiations between the parties as to the reviewed rent to be set in 1996 it became apparent that they could not agree how the necessary valuation should be carried out. To resolve those differences the landlord issued proceedings seeking various declarations including that the hypothetical lease granted to the hypothetical tenant the personal right to break the hypothetical lease at the end of the 15th and 25th years of the term on the terms (mutatis mutandis) of clause 6 of each actual lease. At trial, the judge decided that the landlord was not entitled to such a declaration. The landlord appealed.

**16.39** The Court of Appeal unanimously dismissed the appeal. Giving the lead judgment, Aldous LJ said the following:[24]

a right to break in clause 6 was a personal right of Citibank and associated companies. The declaration sought envisaged the right to break would be exercisable by somebody who was not Citibank. He submitted that that conflicted with the presumption of reality and clause 1.5.3. The hypothetical lease could, without stultifying the rent review provisions, contain a break

[23] *St Martin's Property Investments Limited v CIB Properties Limited* [1999] L&TR 1.
[24] *St Martin's Property Investments Limited v CIB Properties Limited* [1999] L&TR 1, at 13–14.

> clause exercisable by Citibank and associated companies in the terms of clause 6. Whether a lease with such a break clause would command any additional value is a matter of valuation not of law.
>
> The judge came to the right conclusion. [The landlord's] submission requires the insertion of the name of a hypothetical tenant. Will it be more likely to want to break the clause than Citibank? If so, how would that affect the valuation? Such questions show the difficulty of rewriting clause 6 in the way that she suggested. There is, in my view, no need to do so and it would be wrong to do so having regard to the provisions of clause 1.5.3. The lease is as stated to be on the same terms and conditions as the underlease. That points to the review being conducted upon the assumption of reality, namely that the hypothetical lease will include clause 6 with Citibank having a personal right to terminate. The introduction of the name of a hypothetical tenant would not coincide with the reality as it is Citibank that have the personal right to terminate. If they assign the lease that right expires, but that could not happen if the name of a hypothetical tenant were to be substituted for Citibank in clause 6.

**16.40** Buxton LJ agreed, saying:[25]

> [The declaration sought] falls on the basis that clause 6 of this lease on a true construction confers a personal right, as my Lord has demonstrated, and thus if it is included in the hypothetical lease it would simply be otiose. It would certainly not attach for the benefit of the hypothetical tenant. It may to some extent demonstrate the difficulty that the appellant has in this respect that the declaration sought, which the judge refused, was in terms that the review should proceed on the basis that the hypothetical lease grants to the hypothetical tenant the personal right to break the hypothetical lease at certain times. If the right is declared to be a personal one, as in my judgment it is, it cannot be granted to the hypothetical tenant.

### (c) Valuation Consequences

**16.41** The presence of a break clause in the hypothetical lease may have an effect on the rental valuation for the subject premises. The effect on rent will almost inevitably depend on a mixture of fact and valuation evidence. For example, in the case of a landlord's redevelopment break option, it will be necessary for the valuer to form a view (based upon evidence of fact) as to the likelihood of the relevant redevelopment occurring. If (say) any redevelopment is impracticable because of planning or other logistical or financial difficulties, then the prospects of this happening may be remote.

**16.42** Conversely, in the case of a tenant's break clause, the effect on rent will be informed by the conditions upon which the successful exercise of the break clause depends. Naturally, the more onerous the conditions, the less likely it is that they will be fulfilled by the hypothetical tenant. This consideration will affect the value to be attached to the inclusion of such a break option.

[25] *St Martin's Property Investments Limited v CIB Properties Limited* [1999] L&TR 1, at 19.

# 17

# *Professional Liability*

## INTRODUCTION

17.1 The number of traps and pitfalls attendant upon both the drafting and the exercise of a break clause provides fertile ground for professional liability claims, not only against solicitors, but also against managing agents and surveyors.

17.2 Naturally, the existence of a claim for professional liability will depend heavily on what the professional was retained to do in the first place. As was famously said by Oliver J in *Midland Bank Trust Co Ltd v Hett, Stubbs & Kemp*,[1] in a passage specifically referring to solicitors, but applicable to professionals generally:

> The extent of his duties depends upon the terms and limits of [the] retainer and any duty of care to be implied must be related to what he is instructed to do.
>
> Now no doubt the duties owed by a solicitor to his client are high, in the sense that he holds himself out as practising a highly skilled and exacting profession, but I think that the court must beware of imposing upon solicitors – or upon professional men in other spheres – duties which go beyond the scope of what they are requested or undertake to do. It may be that a particularly meticulous and conscientious practitioner would, in his client's general interests, take it upon himself to pursue a line of inquiry beyond the strict limits comprehended by his instructions. But that is not the test. The test is what the reasonably competent practitioner would do having regard to the standards normally adopted in his profession, and cases such as *Duchess of Argyll v Beuselinck* [1972] 2 Lloyd's Rep 172, *Griffiths v Evans* [1953] 1 WLR 1424 and *Hall v Meyrick* [1957] 2 QB 455 demonstrate that the duty is directly related to the confines of the retainer.

17.3 Although, in *Mortgage Express Ltd v Bowerman & Partners*,[2] Bingham LJ observed:

> A client cannot expect a solicitor to undertake work he has not asked him to do, and will not wish to pay him for such work. But if in the course of doing the work he is instructed to do the solicitor comes into possession of information which is not confidential and which is clearly of potential significance to the client, I think that the client would reasonably expect the solicitor to pass it on and feel understandably aggrieved if he did not.

[1] *Midland Bank Trust Co Ltd v Hett, Stubbs & Kemp* [1979] Ch 384, at 402H–403C.

[2] *Mortgage Express Ltd v Bowerman & Partners* [1996] 1 All ER 836, at 842; and see also *Boyce v Rendalls* (1983) 268 EG 268, at 272, per Lawton LJ ('... if, in the course of taking instructions, a professional man like a land agent or a solicitor learns of facts which reveal to him as a professional man the existence of obvious risks, then he should do more than merely advise within the strict limits of his retainer. He should call attention to and advise upon the risks ...').

**17.4** A detailed discussion of the law of professional liability is outside the scope of this work.[3] However, set out below are some common examples of circumstances in which professionals have found themselves liable in the context of drafting and exercising of break clauses.

## FAILURE TO ADVISE DURING A TRANSACTION

**17.5** The extent of a solicitor's duty to advise a client when negotiating the terms of a lease, including a break clause, is a very fact-sensitive one. As Lord Scott of Foscote said in *Pickersgill v Riley*:[4]

> It is plain that when a solicitor is instructed by a client to act in a transaction, a duty of care arises. But it is also plain that the scope of that duty of care is variable. It will depend, first and foremost, upon the content of the instructions given to the solicitor by the client. It will depend also on the particular circumstances of the case. It is a duty that it is not helpful to try to describe in the abstract. The scope of the duty may vary depending on the characteristics of the client, in so far as they are apparent to the solicitor. A youthful client, unversed in business affairs, might need explanation and advice from his solicitor before entering into a commercial transaction that it would be pointless, or even sometimes an impertinence, for the solicitor to offer to an obviously experienced businessman.

**17.6** This is consistent with the well-known remarks of Donaldson LJ in *Carradine Properties Ltd v D J Freeman & Co*,[5] where he said:

> An inexperienced client will need and will be entitled to expect the solicitor to take a much broader view of the scope of his retainer and of his duties than will be the case with an experienced client.

**17.7** So, depending on the particular circumstances, a solicitor may be under an obligation to point out to a client proposing to take a lease the effect of a clause 'in an unusual form' which might constitute a 'trap' for a layman;[6] or to advise on risks which is or ought to be alerted to but which 'might elude even an intelligent layman';[7] or to draw a client's attention to any 'hidden pitfall' a contract might contain;[8] or to give a warning that the solicitor's 'preferred interpretation' as to the meaning and effect of a break option may be wrong.[9]

[3] For a comprehensive review of the subject, then the reader should refer to the leading text books, including J Powell, R Stewart and R Jackson *Jackson & Powell on Professional Liability* (Sweet & Maxwell, 8th edn, 2017) and W Flenley and T Leech *Solicitors' Negligence and Liability* (Bloomsbury Professional, 4th edn, 2020).

[4] *Pickersgill v Riley* [2004] PNLR 31, at [7].

[5] *Carradine Properties Ltd v D J Freeman & Co* [1955–95] PNLR 219, at 226; and see also *Minkin v Landsberg* [2015] EWCA Civ 1152, at [38], per Jackson LJ ('An experienced businessman will not wish to pay for being told that which he/she already knows. An impoverished client will not wish to pay for advice which he/she cannot afford. An inexperienced client will expect to be warned of risks which are (or should be) apparent to the solicitor but not to the client.').

[6] *Sykes v Midland Bank Executor Co* [1971] 1 QB 113, at 123G–24C, per Harman J.

[7] *Country Personnel Ltd v Alan Pulver & Co* [1987] 1 WLR 916, at 922E, per Bingham LJ.

[8] *Reeves v Thrings & Long* [1996] PNLR 265, at 275, per Sir Thomas Bingham MR.

[9] *Baker v Baxendale Walker Solicitors* [2016] EWHC 664 (Ch), at [147], per Roth J. See also *Queen Elizabeth's Grammar School Blackburn Ltd v Banks Wilson* [2002] PNLR 14, at [47], per Sedley LJ and *Herrmann v Withers LLP* [2012] PNLR 28, at [73]–[74], per Newey J.

**17.8** For example, in *Donmez v Barnes & Partners*,[10] the plaintiff tenant had instructed the defendant solicitors to act on her behalf in connection with the grant of a lease of premises in Islington. The lease contained an option to purchase the freehold at £150,000 to be exercised before the expiry of the first two years of the term (with time being of the essence). The two-year anniversary fell due on 29 May 1994, but the tenant did not manage to get in touch with the landlords with a view to exercising the option. On 1 June 1994, she received a communication stating that the option had expired. The tenant then brought a claim against the solicitors alleging breach of contract and negligence in failing to explain to her the terms of the lease and the need to take the necessary steps for the exercise of the option. Giving judgment for the plaintiff, Judge Prosser QC (sitting as a judge of the High Court) held that the lease contained 'difficult terms for anyone to handle' and the solicitor 'did not appreciate how much [the tenant] needed careful advice'. Instead, in breach of retainer and/or negligently, he treated the transaction as 'a straightforward matter with no major pitfalls'.

**17.9** An obvious example of a 'trap' or 'hidden pitfall' is where a lease contains a break clause expressed to be purely personal to the original named tenant. Indeed, as Etherton LJ warned in *Linpac Mouldings Ltd & Ors v Aviva Life and Pensions UK Ltd*:[11]

> it would be reasonable to expect, both before and after the cases just mentioned, that competent property advisers would take particular care to make unambiguously clear, if intended, that a person will be entitled to break a lease not only when they are the tenant, but even after they have assigned the lease.[12]

**17.10** The failure to give just such advice formed the basis of a claim in *3M United Kingdom Plc v Linklaters & Paines*.[13] In that case, the tenant, 3M United Kingdom Plc, entered into three leases on 4 December 1987. Each lease contained a tenant's break clause exercisable at the end of the tenth year. The break clauses were personal to the original tenant, ie they contained the introductory wording: 'If the Tenant (here meaning only 3M United Kingdom Plc) shall desire to determine the term …' In 1989, the 3M group of companies carried out a corporate restructuring. The effect was that the trading activities of 3M United Kingdom Plc was transferred to a subsidiary, 3M Manufacturing Limited. The former then changed its name to 3M UK Holdings Plc; whilst the latter then changed its name (confusingly) to 3M United Kingdom Plc.

**17.11** Linklaters & Paines were retained to act as solicitors in the restructuring. As part of the restructuring, the three leases were assigned, by transfers dated 3 May 1989, from the old 3M United Kingdom Plc to the new 3M United Kingdom Plc. However,

[10] *Donmez v Barnes & Partners* [1996] EGCS 129.

[11] *Linpac Mouldings Ltd & Ors v Aviva Life and Pensions UK Ltd* [2010] L&TR 10, at [47].

[12] The professional adviser may also be expected to draw attention to the fact that a purely personal break clause will not be taken into account on a rent review, unless the lease specifically provides for it: see *St Martin's Property Investments Limited v CIB Properties Limited* [1999] L&TR 1 (which is more particularly considered in Chapter 16 above).

[13] *3M United Kingdom Plc v Linklaters & Paines* [2006] PNLR 30.

in accordance with *Max Factor Ltd v Wesleyan Assurance Society*,[14] the effect of the assignments was that the break clauses ceased to be exercisable. As Chadwick LJ explained:[15]

> That was because the new tenant – although known as 3M United Kingdom Plc – was not the company of that name to which, alone, the options had been granted in 1987. That was not appreciated at the time; or, if it were appreciated by Linklaters, they did not advise that the 3M companies that the assignments would have – or had had – that effect. It is accepted that failure to give that advice was in breach of the duties which Linklaters owed under their retainer.

**17.12** Another 'trap' or 'hidden pitfall' is where a tenant's option to determine the lease falls part way through a rental period. In such a scenario, a competent advisor should (when acting for the tenant) usually insist upon the inclusion of, or (whether acting for the landlord or tenant) at least draw the client's attention to the consequences of not including, an express apportionment clause providing for the tenant to be reimbursed for a portion of the rent in respect of the period after the break date. Indeed, in *Canonical UK Ltd v TST Millbank LLC*[16] and *Marks & Spencer Plc v BNP Paribas Securities Services Trust Co (Jersey) Ltd*,[17] it has been made clear that, in light of authorities stretching back to *Ellis v Rowbotham*,[18] absent such an apportionment clause, the tenant will be liable to pay the full period's rent irrespective whether the break occurs part-way through the period.[19]

**17.13** The cases above concern the position of a solicitor advising a client who intends to take a lease. Similar considerations may arise where a solicitor advises a client who intends to purchase the reversion expectant upon the determination of a lease. So, for example, in *Manotarn Ltd v Rose & Birn (a firm)*,[20] the claimant company purchased commercial premises as a long-term investment. The first and second floors of the premises were let to tenants on 25-year leases, in each case, subject to break options entitling the tenants to determine their leases on 12 months' notice at the end of the 5th, 10th, 15th and 20th anniversaries of the terms. The defendant solicitor acted for the claimant in connection with the purchase, but failed to advise as to the existence of the break options. The defendant admitted that the failure to do so was negligent. The claimant was awarded damages equivalent to the value of the premises as at the transaction date had there been no break clauses and the actual value of the premises at that time.

[14] *Max Factor Ltd v Wesleyan Assurance Society* (1997) 74 P&CR 8.

[15] *3M United Kingdom Plc v Linklaters & Paines* [2006] PNLR 30, at [5].

[16] *Canonical UK Ltd v TST Millbank LLC* [2013] L&TR 15, at [30], per Vos J.

[17] *Marks & Spencer Plc v BNP Paribas Securities Services Trust Co (Jersey) Ltd* [2014] L&TR 36, at [37], per Arden LJ; upheld on appeal at [2015] UKSC 72.

[18] *Ellis v Rowbotham* [1900] 1 QB 740.

[19] However, see the discussion in **10.67–71**. In light of the observations of Lord Neuberger in *Marks and Spencer Plc v BNP Paribas Securities Services Trust Co (Jersey) Ltd* [2015] UKSC 72, at [53], it is apparent that if, at the point that rent falls to be paid, it is 'clear' that the lease will determine on the break date (ie because there are no further conditions to be performed), then depending on the wording of the lease in question, the tenant may only be required to pay an appropriate proportion of rent for the period in question in order to exercise the break.

[20] *Manotarn Ltd v Rose & Birn (a firm)* (unreported, 20 July 1995).

## FAILURE TO REMIND OF AN APPROACHING BREAK DATE

**17.14** Absent express instructions to carry out the steps required to bring about the termination of a lease by the exercise of a break clause, it is doubtful whether a solicitor would be under a duty to remind the person wishing to exercise the break clause that the time for service of the break notice was approaching. This is illustrated by the decision of the Court of Appeal in *Yager v Fishman & Co and Anr*.[21]

**17.15** In that case, Mr Yager, an experienced businessman, was the guarantor under a lease which contained a break clause entitling the lessee (a company which he owned and controlled) to determine the lease by six months' previous notice at the end of the third, seventh and fourteenth years of the term. Mr Yager had, from time to time, retained the services of a firm of solicitors to advise him about certain legal difficulties he had in connection with the lease. On the facts, the solicitors were justified in assuming that Mr Yager was alive to the terms of the break clause in the lease. Further, Mr Yager was found never to have expressly raised the question of how the break clause should be exercised. In the circumstances, the solicitors could not be criticised for failing to advise Mr Yager as to when the break clause should have been exercised, and how.

**17.16** However, in *Yager*, Goddard LJ warned:[22]

> The nature and amount of advice which, in a matter of this sort, a solicitor would be expected to give to a person wholly unacquainted with business may differ very materially from what he would offer to an experienced business man, who would naturally decide for himself the course he thought it in his interest to take [viz. to exercise the break clause or not].

**17.17** By contrast with *Yager*, an example of a solicitor negligently failing to warn an inexperienced client of an impending time limit is to be found in *RP Howard Ltd & Anr v Woodman Matthews & Co*.[23] That case concerned a lease renewal under Part II of the Landlord and Tenant Act 1954, as to which, Staughton J explained:[24]

> Part II of the Landlord and Tenant Act 1954 provides a measure of security for business tenants. If the landlord gives the tenant notice to terminate the tenancy, the tenant must do two things: first, he must notify the landlord within two months that he will not be willing to give up possession of the property comprised in the tenancy; secondly, he must apply to the court for a new tenancy not less than two nor more than four months after the giving of the landlord's notice.

**17.18** On 30 September 1975, the landlord of certain premises in Chelmsford gave notice to the tenant under the Act to terminate its tenancy. The tenant consulted solicitors in connection with the receipt of the notice. However, the solicitors failed to take the second of the two steps required by the Act, ie 30 January 1976 came and went without any application by the tenant to the county court for a new tenancy. Although a new lease was eventually agreed and executed, it was on terms significantly less favourable than the tenant would have obtained from the county court.

[21] *Yager v Fishman & Co and Anr* [1944] 1 All ER 552.
[22] *Yager v Fishman & Co and Anr* [1944] 1 All ER 552, at 556.
[23] *RP Howard Ltd & Anr v Woodman Matthews & Co* [1983] BCLC 117.
[24] *RP Howard Ltd & Anr v Woodman Matthews & Co* [1983] BCLC 117, at 118F–18G.

**17.19** On the facts, the solicitors were held liable to the tenant in negligence. Staughton J said the follows:[25]

> In general the duty of a solicitor, when his client as tenant is served with a notice under Part II of the Landlord and Tenant Act 1954, is clear. He must tell his client of the two time limits. He must also take such steps as are sufficient, in all the circumstances of the case, to ensure that if either time limit is allowed to expire without the appropriate step being taken, that it is the fault of the client. By 'fault' I mean, either that the client shall have consciously allowed time to expire, or that the client shall have failed to exercise that degree of attention to his affairs which any person of his education and background could be expected to show.

**17.20** Then, after referring to the *Carradine* case (see **17.6** above), Staughton J went on to say:[26]

> [the tenant] was, as [the solicitor] must have known, an engineer. He was not a lawyer or man of any formal business training. He did not, I imagine, have a fully trained company secretary or a legal department. In short, he was precisely the sort of man who could be expected to rely on his solicitor to remind him when legal steps ought to be taken. It was [the solicitor's] duty to do so.

## FAILURE TO DRAW ATTENTION TO PRECONDITIONS

**17.21** Professional liability may arise in connection with a failure to advise of the need to comply with certain conditions precedent to the successful exercise a break notice. Such liability was established against a managing agent and a firm of solicitors in *The Secretary of State for the Environment, Transport and Regions v Unicorn Consultancy Services Ltd & Anr.*[27]

**17.22** In that case, the Secretary of State for the Environment, Transport and Regions ('SoS') was the lessee of premises in Bristol. The lease contained a break clause in the following terms:

> If the Tenant ... shall be desirous of determining this Lease on the 25th day of December 1995 and of such his desire shall serve on the Landlord not less than six months' notice in writing ... and shall also pay to the Landlord a sum equal to one half of the annual rent payable as at the date of such notice such sum to be payable not later than the 18th day of December 1995 ... then and in such case this Lease shall cease and be void at midnight on the 24th December 1995.

**17.23** In 1993, Unicorn Consultancy Services Ltd ('Unicorn') was appointed as managing agent in respect of a large portfolio of properties held by the SoS, including the premises in Bristol. In March 1994, SoS appointed Veale Wasbrough ('VW') to provide various legal services. By March 1995, the SoS had decided to exercise the break option in the lease and, to that end, instructed Unicorn and VW to serve the break notice. The break

[25] *RP Howard Ltd & Anr v Woodman Matthews & Co* [1983] BCLC 117, at 121E–21F.

[26] *RP Howard Ltd & Anr v Woodman Matthews & Co* [1983] BCLC 117, at 122B.

[27] *Secretary of State for the Environment, Transport and Regions v Unicorn Consultancy Services Ltd & Anr* [2000] NPC 108.

notice was properly served, but both Unicorn and VW forgot about the requirement to pay to the landlord a sum equal to one half of the annual rent payable as at the date of the notice (being £100,000.00). Because this sum had not been paid in full and on time, the break clause was not properly exercised and the SoS had to negotiate an expensive surrender of the lease.

**17.24** On the facts, Rimer J found that Unicorn owed a contractual duty to advise the SoS of the impending need to make the one-off payment of £100,000.00 due no later than 18 December 1995 (notwithstanding the fact that there was no specific provision in Unicorn's contract of engagement showing that it clearly had a duty to advise about the need to make such a payment). Similarly, VW was found to have owed to the SoS a duty to arrange for the making of the payment of £100,000.00 in the correct manner and in time to comply with the conditions of the break option. Unicorn and VW failed to discharge these obligations and was liable in damages to the SoS.

**17.25** Another example is to be found in *Credit Lyonnais SA v Russell Jones & Walker*.[28] That dispute concerned the termination of a lease dated 30 August 1991, entered into by Credit Lyonnais SA ('CL') in respect of certain premises in Kent. The lease was for a term of 25 years. By 1994, CL decided that it wanted to close down those premises. To do that, it needed to exercise a break option contained in clause 12 of the lease, which was worded as follows:

> It is hereby agreed by the parties that the Lessee (here meaning Credit Lyonnais Bank) may terminate this Lease on the third anniversary of the Term ('the Termination Date') by giving to the Lessor not less than six calendar months previous written notice ('the Termination Notice') and upon payment by the Lessee to the Lessor of the sum of £11,500 such payment to be made not later than the Termination Date then upon the Termination Date this demise and all that is contained in this Lease shall determine absolutely.

**17.26** Thus, the exercise of the break option was dependent upon compliance with a number of conditions, including the service of six months' prior written notice and payment of £11,500. In the event, CL failed to make the termination payment on time with the consequence that it was unable to exercise the break. After CL had managed to buy its way out of the lease, it brought proceedings against Russell Jones & Walker ('RJ&W'), the solicitors appointed to act on its behalf in relation to the exercise of the break clause. CL alleged that, in breach of retainer and/or negligently, RJ&W had failed to warn CL of the risk created by the terms of clause 12 of the lease, in particular, the need to make the termination payment on time.

**17.27** Notably, the employee at CL who was responsible for the transaction (Mr Evans) was not a lawyer although he had a reasonable amount of knowledge and experience of property management and related matters. The solicitor at RJ&W who looked after CL's interests (Mr Stanton-Reid) was a corporate lawyer, ie he was not and had never claimed to be a property lawyer. Giving judgment for CL, Laddie J said the following:[29]

> the effect of paragraphs 3 and 6 [of the letter of instruction] is to require Mr Stanton-Reid to read at least Clause 12 of the lease. If Mr Stanton-Reid had been an experienced property

[28] *Credit Lyonnais SA v Russell Jones & Walker* [2003] PNLR 2.
[29] *Credit Lyonnais SA v Russell Jones & Walker* [2003] PNLR 2, at [33], [36].

> lawyer, on reading that Clause he would have been aware of the considerable risk to which the client was exposed. As I have said already, there is no reason why Mr Stanton-Reid should have been confident that CL needed no warning on this issue. It follows that RJ&W should have warned their client. Their failure to do so was a breach of duty …
>
> … Since Mr Stanton-Reid was required to read the lease, it appears to me that, at the very least, it was necessary to consider the terms of clause 8 and 12. For reasons already given, that should have alerted him to the risk facing CL under the latter clause and they should have been warned. The failure to do so is a further breach of duty to the client.

## FAILURE TO GIVE PROPER NOTICE

**17.28** It is self-evident that, if a professional is instructed to exercise a break clause on behalf of a landlord or tenant, he will be liable for breach of retainer and/or negligence if (depending on the scope of his instructions) he fails to draft the notice in accordance with the terms of the lease, or fails to serve the notice by a contractually prescribed method, or fails to give the notice to the correct recipient, or otherwise fails to serve the notice in time. So, for example, in *Roberts v JW Ward & Son*,[30] the plaintiff had entered into an option agreement as purchaser with two others as vendors. The plaintiff's solicitors had approved the agreement, in which the option was expressed to be exercisable 'at a price to be agreed, by notice to the intending vendors'. The solicitors served a notice, which failed to mention a price, on only one of the two vendors. The option had not been validly exercised and the defendant solicitors were held to have been negligent in failing to specify the purchase price on the face of the notice.

## CONTRIBUTORY NEGLIGENCE

**17.29** An award of damages for professional liability may be reduced or even extinguished by virtue of contributory negligence on the part of the client. This was the case in *Unicorn Consultancy* (mentioned at **17.21** above). There, the SoS was found to be guilty of contributory negligence in that it had failed to take care of its interests in the way in which it reasonably ought to have done. Given the importance of the payment of £100,000.00, Rimer J found it astonishing that the SoS was so passive about the matter. He remarked:[31] 'I can see no reason at all why [the SoS] could not and should not at least have put in hand its own internal reminder of the need to make the payment on time'.

**17.30** This might be contrasted with the result in the *Manotarn* case (mentioned at **17.13** above). In that case, the solicitor sent a letter to the director of the claimant company advising as to the terms of the leases, enclosing copies of the same. The letter did not refer to the break clauses in the leases, but concluded with the words: 'No doubt you will discuss the matter further with me when you have perused the

[30] *Roberts v JW Ward & Son* (1981) 125 SJ 120.

[31] *Secretary of State for the Environment, Transport and Regions v Unicorn Consultancy Services Ltd & Anr* [2000] NPC 108, at [128].

documents'. The defendant solicitor argued that this should have put the claimant's director on inquiry and should have led him to read the leases. This argument was rejected by the judge, Gower J, who said:

> I am wholly satisfied that it would be totally unreasonable to expect somebody in the position of Mr Schneiderman to trawl through those leases in order to satisfy himself that there was no snag which for one reason or another his solicitor had failed to draw to his attention. I am satisfied that he acted entirely reasonably in relying upon the advice which Mr Birn gave him, and nothing more was to be expected of Mr Schneiderman.

# 18

# *Business Tenancies*

## INTRODUCTION

**18.1** This chapter is concerned with those tenancies to which Part II of the Landlord and Tenant Act 1954 (the '1954 Act') applies. Various questions arise, both in relation to existing business tenancies which incorporate break clauses; and on lease renewal, where the landlord or the tenant seeks the inclusion of a break clause in the new lease. These questions are considered below.

## TERMINATION OF BUSINESS TENANCIES BY THE LANDLORD

**18.2** Under the common law, apart from surrender or forfeiture, a tenancy may come to an end: (i) by effluxion of time, if for a term of years certain; or (ii) by notice given by the tenant to the landlord or vice versa, if a periodic tenancy or a tenancy for a term of years certain subject to a break clause. The latter kind of notice given under a break clause, as well as the former given under a periodic tenancy, is in the 1954 Act called a 'notice to quit': see the definition in s 69(1). For the purposes of this chapter, that phrase shall be used in its extended statutory meaning.

**18.3** However, the 1954 Act modifies terms of tenancies relating to their coming to an end by effluxion of time or by notice to quit given by the landlord to the tenant. Thus, s 24(1) of the 1954 Act begins:

> 'A tenancy to which this part of this Act applies shall not come to an end unless terminated in accordance with the provisions of this part of this Act …'

**18.4** As a consequence, if the landlord serves a break notice, which successfully determines the contractual term of a lease, the tenant will remain entitled to occupy the demised premises, subject to the tenancy being one to which Part II of the 1954 Act applies. In other words, if the landlord wishes to determine the tenant's continuation of the tenancy then it will need to serve a notice pursuant to s 25 of the 1954 Act. This is clear from *Weinbergs Weatherproofs Ltd v Radcliffe Paper Mills Co Ltd*,[1] in which the landlords served a notice to quit to operate a break clause, albeit not in accordance with the form prescribed by s 25 of the 1954 Act. Harman J held that the notice was good to curtail the term under the break clause, although having regard to s 24 of the 1954 Act it did not bring the lease to an end.

[1] *Weinbergs Weatherproofs Ltd v Radcliffe Paper Mills Co Ltd* [1958] Ch 437.

**18.5** In *Scholl Manufacturing Limited v Clifton (Slim-Line) Limited*,[2] the Court of Appeal considered whether a single notice could operate as both a break notice and a notice under s 25 of the 1954 Act.

**18.6** In that case, the lease in question contained a break clause which provided:

> If either party shall desire to determine this demise on [25 March 1966] and shall give to the other six months' previous notice in writing of such desire then immediately on the expiration of such notice this present demise … shall cease.

**18.7** On 11 May 1965, the landlord sent to the tenant by registered post a notice under s 25 of the 1954 Act giving notice to terminate the tenant's tenancy on 25 March 1966. A letter accompanying the notice said: 'We enclose herewith a landlord's notice to terminate the business tenancy …'. The tenant denied that the contractual tenancy had been determined by the notice given by the landlord. Therefore, the landlord issued proceedings seeking a declaration that the lease had been duly determined. The landlord succeeded at first instance, and the tenant appealed.

**18.8** Dismissing the appeal, Harman LJ said as follows:[3]

> the question is whether, having regard to section 25 of the Act, the landlords may determine a lease having a break clause such as the present one under that section provided only that the termination date is not earlier than the date on which the break clause could operate. The judge held that the landlords could do this without first going through the formality of serving a notice to bring the break clause into operation. In my opinion the judge was right and, in fact, I think that section 25 so provides in express terms.

**18.9** Diplock LJ agreed, saying:[4]

> As regards a tenancy which would, apart from the Act, come to an end by notice to quit given by the landlord in accordance with the terms of the lease or tenancy agreement, the provision substituted by the Act is that such tenancies may be terminated by the landlord by giving notice to quit in the prescribed form. The statutory provisions to which I have referred are not in addition to but in substitution for those terms contained in the lease or tenancy agreement which relate to tenancies coming to an end by effluxion of time or by notice to quit given by the landlord to the tenant.

**18.10** In other words, *Scholl* decided that, where a lease contains a landlord's break clause, the landlord does not have to serve a contractual break notice provided that the statutory notice complies with the contractual requirements of the lease, as well as the statutory requirements of s 25 of the 1954 Act. *Scholl* has since been cited with approval by Robert Walker LJ in *Blunden v Frogmore Investments Limited*[5] and by Lewison LJ in *Siemens Hearing Instruments Limited v Friends Life Limited*.[6]

[2] *Scholl Manufacturing Limited v Clifton (Slim-Line) Limited* [1967] Ch 41.
[3] *Scholl Manufacturing Limited v Clifton (Slim-Line) Limited* [1967] Ch 41, at 48.
[4] *Scholl Manufacturing Limited v Clifton (Slim-Line) Limited* [1967] Ch 41, at 50. Diplock LJ made it clear that he was using the expression 'notice to quit' in the extended sense which it bears in the 1954 Act.
[5] *Blunden v Frogmore Investments Limited* [2003] 2 P&CR 6, at [23]–[24].
[6] *Siemens Hearing Instruments Limited v Friends Life Limited* [2014] 2 P&CR 5, at [14].

## TERMINATION OF BUSINESS TENANCIES BY THE TENANT

**18.11** If a lease incorporates a tenant's break clause and is within the protection of the 1954 Act a tenant might be tempted to break the lease and then apply (per a s 26 request) for a new lease. The temptation could be strong if the passing rent was higher than the market rent, and the tenant wished to achieve a rent reduction. However strong the temptation, the tenant should resist it. The Court of Appeal decided in *Garston v Scottish Widows' Fund and Life Assurance Society*[7] that if a tenant broke a lease then it could not serve a s 26 request seeking a new lease. As Nourse LJ said:[8]

> One of the main purposes of Part II of the Act of 1954 is to enable business tenants, where there is no good reason for their eviction, to continue in occupation after the expiration of their contractual tenancies. It is not a purpose of the Act to enable a business tenant who has chosen to determine his contractual tenancy to continue in occupation on terms different from those of that tenancy.

## THE POSITION OF SUB-TENANTS

**18.12** At common law, the basic rule is that, where a head-tenancy comes to an end by operation of a break clause, any derivative interest, such as a sub-tenancy, falls away with it.[9] However, if the sub-tenancy is one to which Part II of the 1954 Act applies, then it will continue by operation of s 24(1). In this scenario, the head-landlord will become the 'competent landlord' of the sub-tenant entitled to give a notice under s 25.[10]

**18.13** In *Keith Bayley Rogers & Co v Cubes Ltd*,[11] the defendant head-landlord had demised the third floor of a building in EC2 to the head-tenant under the terms of a lease containing a landlord's break clause exercisable at the expiration of the first 14 years of the term. In turn, the head-tenant granted a sub-lease of the premises to the plaintiff sub-tenant. On 16 August 1973, the head-landlord served a plethora of notices, one of which was sufficient to exercise the break clause in the head-lease and to be a s 25 notice to the sub-tenant. The sub-tenant contended that the head-landlord could not, on one and the same day, determine the head-lease and serve a s 25 notice on the occupying business tenant. The sub-tenant relied upon s 44 of the 1954 Act which identified the 'landlord' entitled to give a s 25 notice as the owner of the fee simple or a tenancy which will not come to an end within 14 months of effluxion of time or by virtue of a notice to quit already given by the landlord and is not in itself in reversion expectant on an interest which fulfils those conditions. The sub-tenant went on to contend that, until the head-landlord exercised the break clause and that exercise reached the person for whom it was intended, the head-landlord could not say for

[7] *Garston v Scottish Widows' Fund and Life Assurance Society* [1998] 1 WLR 1583.
[8] *Garston v Scottish Widows' Fund and Life Assurance Society* [1998] 1 WLR 1583, at 1589.
[9] *Pennell v Payne* [1995] QB 192; *Barrett v Morgan* [2000] 2 AC 264.
[10] Section 44(1); Sch 6, para 1.
[11] *Keith Bayley Rogers & Co v Cubes Ltd* (1976) 31 P&CR 412.

certain that their interest was not in reversion expectant on an interest which exceeds 14 months. These submissions were rejected by Templeman J, who said:

> in my judgment, when section 44 talks of a notice to quit already given it means a notice launched before the section 25 notice arrives, or alternatively effective before the section 25 notice expires. Alternatively, when a landlord has power to serve two notices in sequence, notice exercising the break clause followed by notice under section 25, and he launches both notices on the same day, it is to be assumed that the notices were delivered in the correct sequence and it is not necessary to pester the postman to see which notice was delivered first.

**18.14** In other words, where a head-landlord has power to serve, one after the other, a notice exercising a break clause in a head-lease, followed by a s 25 notice against an occupying sub-tenant, and he serves both on the same day, it is to be assumed that the notices were served in the correct order (ie so that both are valid).

## THE EXTENT OF THE 'BROKEN' DEMISE

**18.15** It should also be observed that, under the 1954 Act, a s 25 notice must relate to the entire premises that are demised by a lease.[12] However, a break clause need not be so limited. This inconsistency produced an injustice in the case of *Southport Old Links Limited v Naylor*.[13] In that case, the lease of a golf course contained a break clause in relation to the course itself, but not to the club house. The landlord served a valid break notice, relating to the course. However its s 25 notice, which similarly related to the course but not to the club house, was found by the Court of Appeal to be invalid. As Oliver LJ said:[14]

> There is simply no machinery in the [1954] Act for determining a business tenant's tenancy for part, or separate parts of a holding, leaving the tenancy of the remainder to continue and putting the tenant in the position of seeking a new lease – or, I suppose, new leases – of the parts of the holding in respect of which his tenancy has been determined.

**18.16** Notably, Oliver LJ added that the 1954 Act may be 'defective' in not providing for this situation.[15] However, the Law Commission, after reviewing the position, decided not to recommend a change in the law. Presently, therefore, if a landlord is desirous of achieving what the landlord in *Southport Old Links* was not able to achieve, then great care must be taken to ensure that the lease is drafted appropriately, eg by drafting a lease containing two separate demises,[16] or by including a provision to the effect that the exercise of a break clause in relation to part of the demise creates a separate and distinct tenancy of that part for a term of years expiring on the date specified in the break notice (which tenancy can then properly be determined by a notice under s 25 of the 1954 Act).

[12] *Dodson Bull Carpet Co Ltd v City of London Corporation* [1975] 1 WLR 781, at 786, per Goff J.
[13] *Southport Old Links Limited v Naylor* [1985] 1 EGLR 66.
[14] *Southport Old Links Limited v Naylor* [1985] 1 EGLR 66, at 67.
[15] *Southport Old Links Limited v Naylor* [1985] 1 EGLR 66, at 69.
[16] As in eg *Moss v Mobil Oil Co Ltd* [1988] 1 EGLR 71.

## THE INSERTION OF BREAK CLAUSES INTO NEW LEASES UNDER THE 1954 ACT

### (a) The Jurisdiction

**18.17** The terms of a new tenancy under the 1954 Act are governed by ss 32–35. Section 32 deals with the property to be comprised in the new tenancy; and s 34 deals with rent. Neither is relevant to the present matter.

**18.18** Section 33 concerns the duration of the new tenancy. It says:

> Where on an application under this Part of this Act the court makes an order for the grant of a new tenancy, the new tenancy shall be such tenancy as may be agreed between the landlord and the tenant, or, in default of such an agreement, shall be such a tenancy as may be determined by the court to be reasonable in all the circumstances, being, if it is a tenancy for a term of years certain, a tenancy for a term not exceeding fifteen years, and shall begin on the coming to an end of the current tenancy.

**18.19** By contrast, s 35(1) concerns the other terms of the new tenancy (apart from duration and rent). It says:

> The terms of a tenancy granted by order of the court under this Part of this Act (other than terms as to the duration thereof and as to the rent payable thereunder) ... shall be such as may be agreed between the landlord and the tenant or as, in default of such agreement, may be determined by the court; and in determining those terms the court shall have regard to the terms of the current tenancy and to all relevant circumstances.

**18.20** When considering whether to insert a break clause into a new lease under the 1954 Act, it is not altogether clear whether the court should make a determination under s 33 or under s 35. In *O'May v City of London Real Property Co Ltd*,[17] Lord Wilberforce appears to have taken it that the introduction of a break clause was a matter to be determined under s 35. In so holding, Lord Wilberforce referred to *Adams v Green*; but in that case, Stamp LJ (with whom Roskill and Cumming-Bruce LJJ agreed) declined to express a view as to which of s 33 or s 35 was applicable.[18] This might justify the observation of Lewison J in *Davy's of London (Wine Merchants) Limited v City of London Corporation*:[19] 'it is fair to say that the cases do not speak to one voice'.

**18.21** The point is not necessarily an academic one because s 35 requires the court, in reaching its decision, to have regard to the terms of the current tenancy. Section 33 does

[17] *O'May v City of London Real Property Co Limited* [1983] 2 AC 726, at 747H. In *Vodafone Ltd v Hanover Capital Ltd* [2020] EW Misc 18 (CC), at [26], Mr Martin Rodger QC (sitting as a judge of the county court) referred to this passage from *O'May* and said (with added emphasis): '*The form* of any break clause to be included in the new tenancy is a question to be determined under section 35 of the 1954 Act ...' See also *Leslie & Godwin Investments Ltd v Prudential Assurance Co Ltd* [1987] 2 EGLR 95, at 96 (per Hoffmann J) and *Eason & Son (NI) Ltd v Central Craigavon Ltd* (Lands Tribunal of Northern Ireland, Case No BT/80/2001), at [8], per Mr MR Curry FRICS.

[18] *Adams v Green* [1978] 2 EGLR 46, at 47 ('Whichever section is applicable, the court plainly has a wide discretion to direct the inclusion of such clauses as are fair and proper in all the circumstances ...').

[19] *Davy's of London (Wine Merchants) Limited v City of London Corporation* [2004] 3 EGLR 39, at 42L.

not, and it leaves the question of reasonableness at large. Furthermore, as Lord Hailsham explained in *O'May*,[20] under Section 35:

> the burden of persuading the court to impose a change [in the terms of the current tenancy] against the will of either party must rest on the party proposing the change, and that the change proposed must, in the circumstances of the case, be fair and reasonable.

**18.22** Therefore, in an appropriate case, it may be more advantageous for a landlord seeking to insert a redevelopment break clause in the new lease to rely upon the jurisdiction conferred by s 33, as opposed to the jurisdiction under s 35.

## (b) Insertion of Landlord's Break Clauses

**18.23** For various reasons, including harmonising lease expiry, where site assembly for future development is concerned, landlords quite often seek to include a break clause in a new lease that is granted pursuant to the 1954 Act. Such a clause is often referred to as a 'redevelopment break clause', although it may not be conditional upon the landlord establishing a future intent or desire to redevelop. Instead it may be unfettered in scope, eg operable at any time on, say, six months' prior notice.

**18.24** The courts have considered whether, and (if so) in what terms, such a landlord's break clause should be included in a new lease on several occasions. The relevant authorities are set out in chronological order below.

**18.25** *Adams v Green*[21] concerned an application for a new lease of a shop occupied by the tenant, Mr Adams, for the purposes of carrying on business as a confectioner and tobacconist. The shop was within a parade of 12 units owned by the landlords, Mr and Mrs Green. By the time the matter came before the judge, all the terms of the new tenancy had been agreed between the parties except the length of the term and provisions as to a rent review. The landlords were content with a 14-year lease provided that there was a break clause giving them the right to determine the tenancy at any time by giving not less than two years' notice in writing determining on one of the usual quarter days should they wish to demolish or reconstruct the premises. This was on the basis that the row of shops was '*rather elderly*', and that it was likely that the landlords in the future would want to redevelop the premises. Seven other shops had already been let with similarly worded break clauses. At first instance, the judge refused the landlord's request for a break clause (and ordered that the term of the new lease should be seven years with no break clause). This was principally on the basis that the premises were not ripe for redevelopment. The landlords appealed.

**18.26** The Court of Appeal allowed the appeal. Giving the main judgment, Stamp LJ said:[22]

> There are in my judgment, several considerations to which the learned judge in the court below did not refer which persuaded me that he was wrong to conclude that because the property was not, in his view, ripe for redevelopment there should be no rebuilding clause.

[20] *O'May v City of London Real Property Co Limited* [1983] 2 AC 726, at 740F.
[21] *Adams v Green* [1978] 2 EGLR 46.
[22] *Adams v Green* [1978] 2 EGLR 46, at 47F.

**18.27** To this, he then added as follows:[23]

> In the first place, there can be no certainty regarding the future. There can be dramatic changes in market conditions and no certainties today as to what may be profitable redevelopment in four or five years' time ...
>
> The second thing which I think falls to be taken into consideration is that it was no part of the policy – and I underline the word 'policy' – of the 1954 Act to give security of tenure to a business tenant at the expense of preventing redevelopment ...
>
> It is no doubt correct that if the break clause is inserted the property comprised in the tenancy will be of less value on the market than it would otherwise be, but as Denning LJ, as he then was, said in *Gold v Brighton Corporation* [1956] 1 WLR 1291 at 1294, it was no part of the 1954 Act to confer on a tenant a saleable asset: it was primarily to protect him in the enjoyment of his business ...
>
> Another matter ... is this, namely, that the unfairness to the tenant of including the proposed break clause can well be exaggerated. If the tenant's submission that the property will not be ripe for development within the next seven years is well founded, he will not be disturbed by the existence of the break clause during the continuance of his seven-year tenancy, because the right to break will, of course, not be exercisable.
>
> Furthermore ... if the break clause is included the tenant will nevertheless be protected by the terms of the Act itself from the effect of any notice not given bona fide for the purpose for which it is intended, but if the tenancy is determined by a notice it will be open to the tenant to apply for a new tenancy, and the then landlords, in order to sustain an objection to granting a new tenancy, would have to prove the intention to redevelop.

**18.28** It is worth emphasising the word 'preventing' in the second paragraph quoted above. This is not the same as 'delaying'. Indeed, in *Adams*, the landlord had no plans for redevelopment but wished to have the flexibility to sell to a developer. The Court of Appeal, reversing the decision of the trial judge, ordered the inclusion in the new tenancy of a break clause operable on two years' notice. To that extent, the tenant had guaranteed security of tenure.

**18.29** *Amika Motors Limited v Colebrook Holdings Limited*[24] concerned two units on Tooting High Street, which were occupied by a company carrying on business there as a motor dealer. The units comprised showrooms fronted by a forecourt area. The tenant company had also invested heavily in an adjoining unit (used as service facilities), just at about the time when the landlord had served its s 25 notice not opposing the grant of a new lease. In due course, the tenant applied to court for a new tenancy. However, by the time the matter came to trial, the landlord was in a position to redevelop a building adjoining the tenant's premises, which redevelopment included the erection of a one-storey building on the forecourt area. The judge found that the landlord did intend to carry out the development; and that it could not reasonably be carried out until the tenant's rights in the existing holding came to an end. Equally, however, the effect of redevelopment would cause the tenant to suffer a significant loss of recently invested capital. In the circumstances, the judge ordered a new lease with a five-year contractual term,

[23] *Adams v Green* [1978] 2 EGLR 46, at 47F–47L.
[24] *Amika Motors Limited v Colebrook Holdings Limited* [1981] 2 EGLR 62.

with an option for the landlord to terminate the lease for the purpose of reconstruction by giving not less than six months' notice, such notice not to expire before three years from the date of the commencement of the lease. The tenant appealed.

**18.30** The Court of Appeal dismissed the appeal, thereby (in effect) compelling the landlord to wait for three years to carry out its redevelopment plans. Notably, in arriving at the decision, Dunn LJ said as follows:[25]

> Once the judge had accepted that the landlords had a bona fide intention of reconstructing the whole of the ground floor of the premises in Tooting High Street ... then I cannot say that the Judge was wrong in principle in refusing to grant a long lease ... [Where] a landlord has a bona fide intention of developing his land, even if that intention is not capable of immediate realisation, the terms of a new tenancy should not impede it.

**18.31** *JH Edwards & Sons Limited v Central London Commercial Estates Limited*[26] concerned two shops in Tottenham Court Road, London. The shops formed part of a parade which stood on both sides of the main entrance to a large building then trading as a hotel. At trial it was found as a fact that the possibility existed that the landlords for the time being would wish to acquire the two units in order to improve the hotel. However, the judge refused the landlord's request to insert redevelopment break clauses into the new leases (instead ordering the grant of new leases of terms of 10 and 12 years respectively). The landlord appealed.

**18.32** The Court of Appeal allowed the appeal and made new orders for tenancies, in each case including a redevelopment break clause. Giving the only reasoned judgment, Fox LJ said:[27]

> It is clear, as a matter of law, that the 1954 Act is not to be used to inhibit development
>
> If it is likely that the superior landlord for the time being may wish to develop the property, then (since it is not the policy of the 1954 Act to inhibit development) he should not be saddled with a lease which may prevent such development. In that connection a present intention to redevelop immediately is not necessary: (see *Adams v Green* 247 EG 49; *Amika Motors v Colebrook Holdings Limited* 259 EG 243). Accordingly it seems to me that it must be wrong in principle, in the present case, to order the grant of new leases for such substantial periods of 12 and 10 years respectively without development 'break' clauses. That has the effect of preventing development without the consent of the tenants during the period of the leases. I conclude, therefore, that the judge's decision was wrong and that the matter is at large before us.
>
> In considering what would be proper leases in the circumstances of this case I think that the predominant considerations are two. First, that so far as reasonable the lease should not prevent the superior landlord from using the premises for the purposes of development. Secondly, that a reasonable degree of security of tenure should be provided for the tenant. Those considerations are to some degree in conflict. The function of the Court is to strike a reasonable balance between them in all the circumstances of the case.

[25] *Amika Motors Limited v Colebrook Holdings Limited* [1981] 2 EGLR 62, at 64M–65A.

[26] *JH Edwards & Sons Limited v Central London Commercial Estates Limited* [1984] 2 EGLR 103.

[27] *JH Edwards & Sons Limited v Central London Commercial Estates Limited* [1984] 2 EGLR 103, at 103K, 104L–105A.

> I also bear in mind that it is not the purpose of the Act to give a tenant saleable assets but rather to protect him in the conduct of his business ...
>
> Having regard to the fact that the hotel has at present no firm proposals for incorporating [the two units], I think that a fair solution would be that the tenants should each be granted a new lease for 7 years with ... a redevelopment 'break' clause ... so that the notice in writing therein referred to shall not expire earlier than the expiration of five years from the commencement of the term.

**18.33** Thus, even though the landlord had no formulated redevelopment plans, the Court of Appeal held that the break clause should be exercisable after the first five years of the new tenancy. In allowing the appeal, Fox LJ expressly said that the function of the court is to strike a fair balance between two competing aspirations, viz the landlord's desire to use the premises for redevelopment, and the tenant's wish for security of tenure. This may require the landlord to wait for some time before being able to regain possession of the premises.

**18.34** In *National Car Parks Limited v The Paternoster Consortium Limited*,[28] the tenant occupied a multistorey car park beneath Paternoster Square. The car park was at the centre of an island site amounting to some seven acres. The landlords wished to redevelop the site, although planning permission had not been obtained and there was the serious problem of securing vacant possession of the mixed batch of properties occupying the site on tenancies for varying terms and with different expiry dates. Sir Nicolas Browne-Wilkinson V-C had to determine a preliminary issue as to whether a break clause should be inserted in that new lease, and if so what its provisions should be.

**18.35** The Vice Chancellor decided that the new lease should include a break clause giving the landlord a general right to terminate the new contractual term on giving six months' notice of its desire to reconstruct the property. Giving reasons, the Vice Chancellor said as follows:[29]

> It is quite clear that there has been a major effort – and efforts are still being made – to bring about what is on any footing a difficult development facing major problems, which may or may not be capable of being overcome.
>
> The first question which I have to decide is, whether in those circumstances (where it is far from certain that a development requiring the possession of the car park under Paternoster Square will or will not take place, let alone the date on which it will take place) it is right that there should be a break clause in the new lease which it is now common ground the tenant should obtain.
>
> There is no dispute as to relevant law applicable. In cases where a landlord is unable to show that he is immediately in a position to effect a desired reconstruction of the land comprised in the tenancy, if there is a real possibility (as opposed to a probability) that the premises in question will be required for reconstruction during the continuance of the proposed new tenancy, it is right to include in the terms of the new tenancy a break clause which will enable such reconstruction to take place. It is not the policy lying behind Part II of the 1954 Act to permit the rights of the tenant under the new tenancy to stand in the way of reconstruction and redevelopment of commercial property.

[28] *National Car Parks Limited v The Paternoster Consortium Limited* [1990] 1 EGLR 99.

[29] *National Car Parks Limited v The Paternoster Consortium Limited* [1990] 1 EGLR 99, at 101G–101H.

**18.36** The judge evaluated the evidence and said: 'I am left in no doubt that there is here a real possibility that this development will be practicable within the next 10 years' with the consequence that 'a break clause ought to be included, unless there is some major factor pointing the other way'.[30] On the facts, he found that 'the disturbance element in this case [was] ... very small compared with the majority of cases', so that there was no matter of substance against the inclusion of a break clause; and all the more so given that, even after the break clause was operated, the tenant would still 'have his rights under the' 1954 Act, ie even after the landlord has served a notice terminating the contractual tenancy under the break clause, it would not be entitled to possession unless it could prove that the case fell within s 30(1)(f) of the 1954 Act.[31]

**18.37** *Leonard Becker v Hill Street Properties Limited*[32] concerned a dental surgeon who applied for a new lease of his surgery that occupied part of a building in Upper Wimpole Street, London. The landlords had acquired the whole of the building at an auction, with the potential for a profitable residential conversion. On 4 July 1989, the judge ordered a new lease for a term which expired on 24 December 1993, without a break clause. The judge's order also provided for rent review three years from the date of his order, ie 4 July 1992. The landlord appealed, asking the Court of Appeal to grant a lease term expiring on an earlier date than 24 December 1993, alternatively, that there should be in the new tenancy a break clause enabling the landlords to determine the tenancy for redevelopment on six months' notice in writing (operable either at any stage during the term of the tenancy, or only after the elapse of a certain period of time).

**18.38** Although the Court of Appeal held that the judge had misdirected himself, it nevertheless upheld his decision. Referring to the 'balancing exercise' described by Fox LJ in *Edwards* (see **18.31** above), Dillon LJ said as follows:[33]

> I have very much in mind the fact that the term which the judge has granted is not a very long term. It is merely until 24th December 1993, that is to say, at the time of the judge's decision, just under four-and-a-half years. One of the factors to be borne in mind in the balancing exercise to which Fox LJ referred is that there should be a reasonable degree of security of tenure provided for the tenants. Mr Becker has been the tenant of these premises since Christmas 1979 ... His business is a specialised dentistry practice, such as is obviously most conveniently located in the Harley Street/Wimpole Street neighbourhood. He has been in that neighbourhood since about 1962 ... At the time of the hearing before the learned judge he was, as he said in evidence, 66 years old. He is self-employed and he contemplated retirement at Christmas 1993. That is obviously a factor which the judge took into account in fixing that date as the date to which the new tenancy should run.
>
> There were plainly a number of other factors to be sorted out by the present landlords before they proceeded to carry out redevelopment of the property. I have read the passage in the judgment where the evidence was given that it would take them twelve months to get on site. That, again, is something to be taken into account. One suspects that they would not be over-surprised if it took a little longer. But they obviously purchased this property with a view to redeveloping it as residential flats. They have prepared various schemes, though they have not

[30] *National Car Parks Limited v The Paternoster Consortium Limited* [1990] 1 EGLR 99, at 102D–101E.
[31] *National Car Parks Limited v The Paternoster Consortium Limited* [1990] 1 EGLR 99, at 102E–102K.
[32] *Leonard Becker v Hill Street Properties Limited* [1990] 2 EGLR 78.
[33] *Leonard Becker v Hill Street Properties Limited* [1990] 2 EGLR 78, at 81G–81J.

yet alighted on the one preferred version and they have not made any necessary applications for planning permission – should that be required – or for bye-law consent, or anything of that nature, or superior landlords' consent.

I would for my part have thought it unthinkable to include in the lease a break clause under which the lease could be brought to an end at a date earlier than the rent review date three years from the date of the judge's decision, 4th July 1989.

**18.39** Thus, the effect of the Court of Appeal decision was that the landlords were compelled to wait some three-and-a-half years after becoming ready to develop before being entitled to re-take possession of the premises.

**18.40** In *Davy's of London (Wine Merchants) Limited v City of London Corporation*,[34] the tenant held the lease of a wine bar for a term of 25 years expiring in March 2002. The landlord did not oppose the tenant's request for a new tenancy under Part II of the 1954 Act. At the hearing of the tenant's application, the judge found that: (i) the building containing the premises required extensive refurbishment, and that this could not take place while the tenant was in occupation; (ii) at the date of the hearing, the landlord did not intend to carry out the works but was committed to selling the building to a developer who intended to redevelop it; (iii) the assembly of a site for redevelopment would take in excess of three years; (iv) no planning permission had been submitted for the redevelopment; and (v) the proposed redevelopment was not viable. However, the judge ordered the grant of a new 14-year tenancy with a rolling redevelopment break clause exercisable on 11 months' notice after the first five years of the term. Both parties appealed. Prior to the hearing of the appeal, the landlord sold the building to a third party, Saxon Land BV, which stated that it intended to redevelop the building as a stand-alone development (rather than as part of a larger site). Saxon Land was added as a defendant to the proceedings. In the event, the tenant abandoned its appeal. However, the (then ex) landlord and Saxon Land continued an appeal against the terms of the break clause inserted into the new lease.

**18.41** The hearing of the appeal came before Lewison J, who allowed the appeal to the extent of varying the terms of the break clause so that it was exercisable on 11 months' notice not to be served earlier than 1 July 2007. Giving reasons for his decision, he said:[35]

I must of course balance the redevelopment aspirations of the landlords against the business interests of the tenant; not allowing the latter to frustrate the former. Any tenant running a serious business needs to plan ahead. It is not much consolation to a businessman to be told that if the landlord is not ready to redevelop, the break clause will not be exercised. The uncertainty paralyses business planning. Of course, when the break clause comes to be exercised, Davys will be entitled to put the landlords to proof of their intentions. The changes both to the substantive provisions of the 1954 Act and to the procedure of the Court should mean that proceedings for the grant of a new tenancy (or for termination of a tenancy without renewal) will be less protracted than in the past … [The decision] gives Davy's three-and-a-half years' guaranteed security. Such a period is about the same as that ordered in *Becker* (where the landlord was ready to redevelop) and less than that ordered in *Edwards* (where it was not).

[34] *Davy's of London (Wine Merchants) Limited v City of London Corporation* [2004] 3 EGLR 39.
[35] *Davy's of London (Wine Merchants) Limited v City of London Corporation* [2004] 3 EGLR 39, at 48C–48D.

**18.42** From the above authorities, the following propositions emerge:

(1) It is no part of the policy behind the 1954 Act to give security of tenure to a business tenant at the expense of preventing (as opposed to delaying) redevelopment. In other words, the 1954 Act is not to be used to inhibit development.[36]
(2) Similarly, it is not the policy of the 1954 Act to confer upon the tenant a saleable asset.[37]
(3) In considering whether or not to include a landlord's break clause in a new lease and (if so) the terms of such a clause, the function of the Court is to strike a reasonable balance between the following competing considerations: (i) that so far as reasonable the lease should not prevent the landlord from using the premises for the purposes of development; and (ii) that a reasonable degree of security of tenure should be provided for the tenant.[38]
(4) In striking this reasonable balance, the landlord may have to wait some time before being able to exercise the redevelopment break clause.[39]
(5) A redevelopment break clause may be included even if the landlord's intention to redevelop it not capable of immediate realisation[40] or the landlord has no firm proposals for redevelopment[41] or the landlord itself does not intend to carry out the redevelopment.[42]
(6) It should be sufficient for the landlord to show that there is a real possibility (as opposed to a probability) that the premises in question will be required for reconstruction during the continuance of the proposed new tenancy.[43]
(7) A redevelopment break clause should not be refused merely because the premises are not 'ripe for redevelopment'.[44]
(8) A redevelopment break clause may be included even if it causes financial hardship to the tenant.[45]

### (c) Insertion of Tenant's Break Clauses

**18.43** Perhaps surprisingly, there is no reported authoritative decision which addresses the situation where a tenant is desirous of having a break clause inserted into

[36] *Adams v Green* [1978] 2 EGLR 46; *JH Edwards & Sons Limited v Central London Commercial Estates Limited* [1984] 2 EGLR 103.
[37] *Adams v Green* [1978] 2 EGLR 46; *JH Edwards & Sons Limited v Central London Commercial Estates Limited* [1984] 2 EGLR 103.
[38] *JH Edwards & Sons Limited v Central London Commercial Estates Limited* [1984] 2 EGLR 103.
[39] *Leonard Becker v Hill Street Properties Limited* [1990] 2 EGLR 78; *Davy's of London (Wine Merchants) Limited v City of London Corporation* [2004] 3 EGLR 39.
[40] *Amika Motors Limited v Colebrook Holdings Limited* [1981] 2 EGLR 62; *National Car Parks Limited v The Paternoster Consortium Limited* [1990] 1 EGLR 99.
[41] *JH Edwards & Sons Limited v Central London Commercial Estates Limited* [1984] 2 EGLR 103.
[42] *Adams v Green* [1978] 2 EGLR 46.
[43] *National Car Parks Limited v The Paternoster Consortium Limited* [1990] 1 EGLR 99.
[44] *Adams v Green* [1978] 2 EGLR 46.
[45] *Amika Motors Limited v Colebrook Holdings Limited* [1981] 2 EGLR 62.

a renewal lease.[46] The cases decided at county court level display an inconsistency of approach. These are reviewed below.

**18.44** It has been suggested that, when it comes to the incorporation of a tenant's break option, 'the test for incorporation of a landlord's redevelopment break clause may apply by analogy, ie is there a realistic prospect of the event happening (usually affecting the tenant's relocation of its business), for which the break is sought during the duration of the term to be granted'.[47] This approach has been adopted in at least two county court decisions.

**18.45** First, in *Dukeminster Ltd v West End Investments (Cowell Group) Ltd*,[48] the tenant sought to insert in the new lease a break clause exercisable in the event that a neighbouring development became intolerable and the tenant was not able to have quiet enjoyment of the premises. Proceeding by analogy with cases involving the insertion of a landlord's break option, HHJ Saggerson asked whether there was a 'real possibility' of the event occurring. He thought not. He held:

> [45] I do not doubt that the redevelopment of the former embassy into a hotel ... is a radical project that will have a short-term negative impact on properties in the immediate vicinity, including the building, in some of the ways anticipated by the claimant; albeit in my judgment to a much lesser extent than is feared ... However, I reject the contention that there is any realistic likelihood of the building being rendered uninhabitable or its occupation intolerable as a result of the redevelopment.

**18.46** The second is *MPS2 Ltd v The Department for Housing, Communities and Local Government*.[49] That case concerned a renewal lease of the county court at Huddersfield. The tenant (acting via HMCTS) sought the insertion of a tenant-only break option on the third anniversary of the term. The tenant did not seek to justify a tenant-only break option by reference to HMCTS' known or anticipated future requirements for the premises in particular. Rather, the tenant relied upon its general reform programme, which would 'likely result in a future need to review the court accommodation requirement

[46] *Cf* the authorities where a tenant has sought a tenancy with a short duration (under s 33), eg (i) *Charles Follett Ltd v Cabtell Investment Ltd* [1986] 2 EGLR 76 (unaffected on this issue by the appeal at (1988) 55 P&CR 36) (tenant wanted a one-year term to 'keep its options open so it can make another application for a new tenancy in a year's time, and in the interim it can look around in case it can find its ideal premises at a more acceptable rent'; 10-year term ordered); (ii) *CBS United Kingdom Ltd v London Scottish Properties Ltd* [1985] 2 EGLR 125 (tenant sought a comparatively short term until 31 August 1986; landlord said that the tenant ought to have a 14-year term; tenant requested a short term because it was in the process of moving out of the premises to other factory premises in Aylesbury; short term ordered); (iii) *Ganton House Investments v Crossman Investments* [1995] 1 EGLR 1995 (tenant wanted a one-year term on the basis that 'we are looking for somewhere else to go; we would like to move premises; we would like to find somewhere a bit more desirable in which to locate our business'; 14-year term ordered); (iv) *Dukeminster Ltd v West End Investments (Cowell Group) Ltd* [2019] L&TR 4 (tenant sought a five-year term; landlord sought as 12-year term; the court decided that a 10-year term was appropriate, placing little (if any) weight on the fact that the tenant wished 'to keep its options as open as possible': see the judgment, at [35]).

[47] K Reynolds & W Clark, *Renewal of Business Tenancies* (Sweet & Maxwell, 5th edn 2016), at §8-87.

[48] *Dukeminster Ltd v West End Investments (Cowell Group) Ltd* [2019] L&TR 4.

[49] *MPS2 Ltd v The Department for Housing, Communities and Local Government* (unreported, 11 June 2019).

in Huddersfield' (judgment, at [73]). In other words, it was HMCTS' policy to have the ability to terminate its leases early. In these circumstances, HHJ Klein said:

> [72] [Counsel for the tenant] accepted, rightly in my view, that, if the Defendant makes its request for a tenant-only break option only because it has a policy reason for doing so, then it has not made out a sufficient case for the addition of that option in the new lease.
>
> [74] … I am satisfied that the tenor of Mr Prince's evidence [Mr Prince was HMCTS' principal asset manager for the North East region], HMCTS, as a matter of policy, wishes to have the ability to terminate its leases early. In these circumstances, I am not satisfied that the new lease should contain a tenant-only break option.

**18.47** However, in other cases, the court has declined to apply by analogy the test for the incorporation of a landlord's break option, instead treating the matter as one to be decided by reference to the *O'May* test of 'essential fairness'.[50]

**18.48** For example, in *Vodafone Ltd v Hanover Capital Ltd*,[51] the tenant (Vodafone) sought a short term and an unconditional break clause because of its concern that the landlord might be awarded a tenancy at a rent which was much higher than the tenant considered it would achieve under the Electronic Communications Code. As Martin Rodger QC explained the position:

> [36] … If the operators' view of how the Code applies to such tenancies prevails in the Court of Appeal or Supreme Court, Vodafone wishes to be able to take advantage of the rights Parliament intended it to have by terminating the tenancy it will have obtained under the 1954 Act and negotiating a new one exclusively within the framework of the Code. It is prevented from doing that for this renewal by the current understanding of the law. A short term or an unconditional break clause would enable Vodafone to free itself of the new tenancy and secure a new agreement at a lower rent on the basis of the favourable assumptions in paragraph 24 of the Code, free of the overlay of the different assumptions in section 34 of the 1954 Act. If the meaning of the Code is eventually settled in the operators' favour, Vodafone will therefore wish to determine the new tenancy it obtains in these proceedings as soon as possible by giving 6 months' notice and simultaneously claim a new agreement under Part 5 of the Code, paying a rent determined by reference to paragraph 24.

**18.49** Martin Rodger QC had no hesitation in concluding that the duration of the new tenancy should be as contended for by the landlord, albeit with a break clause exercisable on six months' notice expiring on the fifth or subsequent anniversary of the term. He said:

> [40] In reaching that conclusion I have given weight to the needs of Vodafone's business, and to the rights which Parliament intended operators to enjoy under the Code. I also take into account the burden of these proceedings on both parties in terms of costs and commitment … In the circumstances of this case I consider that the operator's wish for flexibility must be balanced against the landlord's understandable desire for a respite from uncertainty and expense. That balance is satisfied by a minimum commitment of 5 years, with the operator being entitled to greater flexibility at fixed intervals after that period has expired.

[50] *O'May v City of London Real Property Co Limited* [1983] 2 AC 726, at 741C (an approach also followed in *Eason & Son (NI) Ltd v Central Craigavon Ltd* (Lands Tribunal of Northern Ireland, Case No BT/80/2001), at [12]).

[51] *Vodafone Ltd v Hanover Capital Ltd* [2020] EW Misc 18 (CC).

> [41] The tenancy will be terminable during the first 5 years for the limited operational reasons the parties have agreed to carry forward from the 2008 lease. I do not think Vodafone's reasons for seeking greater flexibility, by either a very short term or a rolling 6-month break clause, justify the resulting uncertainty and I consider they would be unfair to the landlord after the expense and disruption of these proceedings.

**18.50** Another, more recent, example is *HPUT Trustee No 1 Ltd v Boots UK Ltd*.[52] In that case, the landlord (HPUT) sought a ten-year term, with no tenant's break option. The tenant (Boots) sought a five-year term, with a tenant's break option exercisable on the third anniversary of the term. The tenant sought a break clause because of its requirement to have flexibility, given the uncertainty in the retail market. HHJ Dight CBE considered that, in order to give the tenant the degree of flexibility which it really required, it would be appropriate to afford them a break clause in the manner requested.

**18.51** As may be apparent from the discussion above, the authorities (such as they are) do not speak with one voice and articulate different tests which are applicable when it comes to the insertion of a tenant's break option. Absent authoritative guidance, the uncertainty as to the legal position will remain.

[52] *HPUT Trustee No 1 Ltd v Boots UK Ltd* (unreported, 24 May 2021).

# 19

# *Residential Tenancies*

## INTRODUCTION

**19.1** This chapter will consider the position under:

(1) Rent Act tenancies;
(2) assured tenancies;
(3) assured shorthold tenancies;
(4) contractual tenancies without any statutory security of tenure.[1]

**19.2** In most cases now encountered in practice, the letting of a dwelling-house by a private sector landlord will be an assured tenancy or, more likely, an assured shorthold tenancy (a sub-species of assured tenancy), both of which are governed by the provisions of the Housing Act 1988. However, there still remains a large number of residential tenancies protected by the Rent Act 1977 or with no statutory protection at all (save to the limited extent provided for by the Protection from Eviction Act 1977).

## TERMINATION OF RENT ACT TENANCIES

**19.3** A 'protected tenancy' is a contractual tenancy satisfying the definition contained in s 1 of the Rent Act 1977 (the '1977 Act'), namely that it is a tenancy under which a dwelling-house (which may be a house or part of a house) is let as a separate dwelling. Such a tenancy is a protected tenancy unless it is prevented from being so by one of the exceptions contained in ss 4–16 and 24(3) of the 1977 Act. A 'statutory tenancy' arises after the termination of the protected tenancy if the protected tenant occupies the dwelling-house previously subject to the protected tenancy as his residence.[2] Since 15 January 1989, it has not been possible to create a Rent Act protected tenancy.

**19.4** The effect of these provisions is to make a distinction between: (i) a protected tenant who is in possession of a dwelling-house under a contractual tenancy (but still enjoys the protection of the 1977 Act); and (ii) a statutory tenant whose only right to

[1] Section 81 of, and Sch 29 to, the Coronavirus Act 2020 made provision about notice periods in relation to possession proceedings in respect of certain residential tenancies, including Rent Act protected and statutory tenancies, assured tenancies and assured shorthold tenancies. This was a temporary provision in force for 'the relevant period', meaning the period (a) beginning with the day on which the Coronavirus Act 2020 was passed, and (b) ending with (i) in relation to England, 31 May 2021, and (ii) in relation to Wales, 30 June 2021 (para 1(1) of Sch 29). Given the temporary nature of the provision, no more will be said about it.

[2] Section 2(1).

occupy the dwelling-house is given to him by the 1977 Act. The statutory tenancy will arise immediately upon the determination of the protected tenancy (provided, of course, that the tenant continues to occupy the dwelling-house as his residence). Thus, termination of a protected tenancy by operation of a break clause will not, of itself, give the landlord a right to go to court for an order for possession. The landlord of a Rent Act tenant is not entitled, even after termination of the protected tenancy, to recover possession against the will of the tenant in the exercise of his common law rights.

**19.5** Here, two points may be observed:

(1) It is not possible to contract out of the 1977 Act, whether in respect of rent, the recovery of possession or any other matter. See, for example, *Foster v Robinson*[3] (a decision under the Increase of Rent and Mortgage Interest (Restrictions) Act 1920). Moreover, under the Rent Acts, 'the court was required to consider whether those Acts applied, in any case in which they might apply, regardless of whether the tenant took the point at all, and even if the point was first taken on appeal'.[4]

(2) Section 3(1) of the 1977 Act provides that a person who retains possession of a dwelling-house as a statutory tenant must observe and is entitled to the benefit of all the terms and conditions of the original contract of tenancy so far as they are consistent with the provisions of the 1977 Act. In other words, in general, the terms of the statutory tenancy are the same as the terms of the protected tenancy. However, terms of the original contractual tenancy which are inconsistent with the provisions of the 1977 Act (eg a term of the original tenancy that it is terminable on notice) are not carried over into the statutory tenancy. So, in *Shuter v Hersh*[5] (another case concerning the Increase of Rent and Mortgage Interest (Restrictions) Act 1920), Scrutton LJ observed[6] that the statutory tenancy continues 'whether or not a notice to quit is given'.

**19.6** If a landlord is desirous of determining a protected tenancy by operation of a break clause, he must ensure that he complies with: (i) any stipulated contractual requirements contained in the tenancy agreement; and (ii) the obligations laid down by the relevant provisions of the Protection from Eviction Act 1977, including that the notice contains the material prescribed by the Notices to Quit (Prescribed Information) Regulations 1988. As to these requirements, see **19.43–19.44** below.

**19.7** Once the protected tenancy has been terminated, the landlord can only recover possession of the dwelling-house by obtaining an order for possession from the court. Section 98(1) of the 1977 provides that:

> a court shall not make an order for possession of a dwelling-house which is for the time being … subject to a statutory tenancy unless the court considers it reasonable to make such an order and either –
>
> (a) the court is satisfied that suitable alternative accommodation is available for the tenant or will be available for him when the order in question takes effect, or
>
> (b) the circumstances are as specified in any of the Cases in Part I of Schedule 15 to this Act.

[3] *Foster v Robinson* [1951] 1 KB 149.
[4] *Broadway Investments Hackney Ltd v Grant* [2007] HLR 23, at [16], per Lloyd LJ.
[5] *Shuter v Hersh* [1922] 1 KB 438.
[6] *Shuter v Hersh* [1922] 1 KB 438, at 450.

**19.8** Section 98(2) adds:

> If, apart from subsection (1) above, the landlord would be entitled to recover possession of a dwelling-house which is for the time being let on or subject to a regulated tenancy, the court shall make an order for possession if the circumstances of the cases are as specified in any of the Cases in Part II of Schedule 15.

**19.9** It follows that, in order to obtain an order for possession against a statutory tenant, the landlord will have to satisfy the court that:

(1) it is reasonable for it to make such an order and there is suitable alternative accommodation available for the tenant or will be available for him when the order in question takes effect; or
(2) it is reasonable for it to make such an order and the circumstances in any of the Cases in Part I of Sch 15 to the 1977 Act are made out; or
(3) the circumstances of the case are as specified in any of the Cases in Part II of Sch 15 to the 1977 Act.

## TERMINATION OF ASSURED TENANCIES

**19.10** Part I of the Housing Act 1988 (the '1988 Act') came into force on 15 January 1989 and introduced two new types of tenancy, namely, the assured tenancy and the assured shorthold tenancy. Subject to certain exceptions in Sch 1 of the 1988 Act (eg tenancies where the rent is over £100,000.00 per annum),[7] an assured tenancy is a tenancy under which a dwelling-house is let as a separate dwelling if and so long as: (a) the tenant or, in the case of joint tenants, each of the joint tenants is an individual; and (b) the tenant or, in the case of joint tenants, at least one of the tenants occupies the dwelling-house as his only or principal home; and (c) the tenancy is not one which, by virtue of s 1(2) or 1(6) cannot be an assured tenancy.[8]

**19.11** An assured tenancy cannot be brought to an end by the landlord except by: (a) obtaining an order of the court for possession of the dwelling-house under s 7 or s 21, and the execution of the order; (b) obtaining an order of the court under s 6A (a demotion order); or (c) in the case of a fixed-term tenancy, which contains power for the landlord to determine the tenancy in certain circumstances, by the exercise of that power.[9] Under s 45(1) of the 1988 Act, a fixed-term tenancy is any tenancy other than a periodic tenancy. It follows, therefore, that a landlord may terminate a fixed-term assured tenancy by operating a break clause.

**19.12** However, under s 5(2) of the 1988 Act, if an assured tenancy which is a fixed-term tenancy comes to an end otherwise than by virtue of (i) an order of the court of the

[7] Para 2(1)(b) of Sch 1 to the 1988 Act (as amended by art 3 of the Assured Tenancies (Amendment) (England) Order 2010 (SI 2010/908)).
[8] Section 1(1).
[9] Section 5(1).

kind mentioned in s 5(1)(a) or (b) or any other order of the court, or (ii) a surrender or other action on the part of the tenant, then, subject to s 7, the tenant shall be entitled to remain in possession of the dwelling-house let under that tenancy and, subject to s 5(4), his right to possession shall depend upon a periodic tenancy arising by virtue of s 5(2). Thus, a statutory periodic tenancy will arise where a fixed-term tenancy is terminated under a break clause.

**19.13** Under s 5(3) of the 1988 Act, the statutory periodic tenancy:

(1) takes effect in possession immediately on the coming to an end of the fixed-term tenancy;
(2) is deemed to have been granted by the person who was the landlord under the fixed-term tenancy immediately before it came to an end to the person who was then the tenant under that tenancy;
(3) comprises the same dwelling-house as was let under the fixed-term tenancy;
(4) is one under which the periods of the tenancy are the same as those for which rent was last payable under the fixed-term tenancy;
(5) is otherwise on the same terms as the fixed-term tenancy immediately before it came to an end, except that any term which makes provision for determination by the landlord or the tenant shall not have effect while the tenancy remains an assured tenancy. So, for example, a break clause contained in the original fixed-term contractual tenancy will not be carried over into the statutory periodic tenancy.

**19.14** The court cannot make an order for possession of a dwelling-house let on an assured tenancy except on one or more of the 16 statutory grounds in Sch 2 to the 1988 Act.[10] Of these, Grounds 1 to 8 are mandatory grounds for possession (ie if the court is satisfied that any of these grounds is established, it must make an order for possession);[11] and Grounds 9 to 16 are discretionary grounds for possession (ie if the court is satisfied that any of these grounds is established, it may make an order for possession if it considers it reasonable to do so).[12] Subject to ss 7(1)–7(6A) of the 1988 Act, the court may make an order for possession of a dwelling-house on grounds relating to a fixed-term tenancy which has come to an end; and where an order is made in such circumstances, any statutory periodic tenancy which has arisen on the ending of the fixed-term tenancy shall end (without any notice and regardless of the period) in accordance with s 5(1A) (ie when the order of the court for possession is executed).[13]

**19.15** It should be observed that the 1988 Act does not place restrictions on the tenant's right to terminate the tenancy in any manner which would be valid at common law. Thus, a tenant's break clause will be effective to determine a fixed-term assured tenancy.

[10] Section 7(1).
[11] Section 7(3).
[12] Section 7(4).
[13] Section 7(7).

## TERMINATION OF ASSURED SHORTHOLD TENANCIES

### (a) The General Position

**19.16** By operation of s 19A of the 1988 Act, any assured tenancy which: (a) is entered into on or after the day on which that section came into force (ie 28 February 1997) otherwise than pursuant to a contract made before that date; or (b) comes into being by virtue of s 5 of the 1988 Act on the coming to an end of an assured tenancy which was itself entered into on or after 28 February 1997 (otherwise than pursuant to a contract made before that date), is an assured shorthold tenancy unless it falls within one of the exceptions found in Sch 2A to the 1988 Act.

**19.17** Apart from the general statutory grounds for possession applicable to assured tenancies referred to in **19.14** above, in the case of assured shorthold tenancies, s 21 of the 1988 Act provides further mandatory grounds for possession. So, on or after the coming to an end of an assured shorthold tenancy which was a *fixed-term* tenancy, a court shall make an order for possession of the dwelling-house if it is satisfied: (a) that the shorthold tenancy has come to an end and no further assured tenancy (whether shorthold or not) is for the time being in existence, other than an assured shorthold periodic tenancy (whether statutory or not); and (b) the landlord or, in the case of joint landlords, at least one of them has given to the tenant not less than two months' notice in writing stating that he requires possession of the dwelling-house.[14] A notice under s 21(1)(b) may be given before or on the day on which the tenancy comes to an end; and that subsection shall have effect notwithstanding that on the coming to an end of the fixed-term tenancy a statutory periodic tenancy arises.[15]

**19.18** In addition, the court must make an order for possession of a dwelling-house let on an assured shorthold tenancy which is a *periodic* tenancy if it is satisfied: (a) that the landlord or, in the case of joint landlords, at least one of them has given to the tenant a notice in writing stating that, after a date specified in the notice, being the last day of a period of the tenancy and not earlier than two months after the date the notice was given, possession of the dwelling-house is required by virtue of this section; and (b) that the date specified in the notice is not earlier than the earliest day on which, apart from s 5(1), the tenancy could be brought to an end by a notice to quit given by the landlord on the same date as the notice under s 21(4)(a).[16] In the case of a dwelling-house in England, s 21(4)(a) has effect with the omission of the requirement for the date specified in the notice to be the last day of a period of the tenancy.[17]

[14] Section 21(1). There are separate requirements in the case of an assured shorthold tenancy of a dwelling-house in England if it is a fixed-term tenancy for a term certain of not less than two years and the landlord is a private registered proprietor of social housing: see ss 21(1A) and 21(1B) and the decision in *Livewest Homes Ltd v Bamber* [2019] 1 WLR 6389.

[15] Section 21(2).

[16] Section 21(4).

[17] Section 21(4ZA). This provision was inserted by s 35 of the Deregulation Act 2015 and has been in force since 1 October 2015. In England, prior to the insertion of this provision, a notice served pursuant to s 21(4) was – and as remains the case in Wales, is – required to specify a date which was (or is) the last day of a period the tenancy. A notice that failed (or fails) to specify a date that was the last day of a period of the tenancy was (or is) invalid: see *Fernandez v McDonald* [2004] 1 WLR 1027 (although the reasoning in that case has

**19.19** Section 21(8) provides that the Secretary of State may by regulations made by statutory instrument prescribe the form of a notice under s 21(1) or (4) given in relation to an assured shorthold tenancy of a dwelling-house in England. In exercise of this power, the Secretary of State made the Assured Tenancies and Agricultural Occupancies (Forms) (England) Regulations 2015 (SI 2015/620), reg 3(fa) of which provides that, for a notice under s 21(1) or (4) informing a tenant that the landlord intends to seek recovery of possession of a dwelling-house let on an assured shorthold tenancy, Form No 6A should be used.

**19.20** A notice under s 21(1) or 21(4) may not be given in relation to an assured shorthold tenancy of a dwelling-house in England: (a) in the case of a tenancy which is not a replacement tenancy, within the period of four months beginning with the day on which the tenancy began; and (b) in the case of a replacement tenancy, within the period of four months beginning with the day on which the original tenancy began.[18] Importantly, however, this restriction does not apply where the tenancy has arisen due to s 5(2) (ie if the fixed-term tenancy comes to an end otherwise than by virtue of an order of the court or a surrender or other action on the part of the tenant).[19]

**19.21** Proceedings for an order for possession under this section in relation to a dwelling-house in England (but not in Wales) may not be begun after the end of the period of six months beginning with the date on which the notice was given under s 21(1) or 21(4).[20] However, where: (a) a notice under s 21(4) has been given in relation to a dwelling-house in England; and (b) s 21(4)(b) requires the date specified in the notice to be more than two months after the date the notice was given, proceedings for an order for possession under this section may not be begun after the end of the period of four months beginning with the date specified in the notice.[21]

**19.22** Where an order for possession under s 21(1) or 21(4) is made in relation to a dwelling-house let on a tenancy to which s 19A applies (ie an assured shorthold tenancy),

been doubted in *Spencer v Taylor* [2014] HLR 9). Instead of specifying a termination date, a s 21(4) notice may legitimately contain a saving formula referring to the last day of a period of a tenancy, thereby enabling the tenant to work out when it expires. See *Lower Street Properties Ltd v Jones* (1996) 28 HLR 877, at 882, per Kennedy LJ ('... Because of the wording of section 21(4), if an actual date is to be given in the notice it must be the last day of the period of the tenancy and there is an obvious risk of a minor arithmetical error giving rise to the argument that the notice is invalid which no doubt is why the printed form suggests as a possible form of wording that the notice will expire at the end of the period of your tenancy which will end after the expiry of two months from the service upon you of this notice. In my judgment this is a form of words which does meet the requirements of section 21(4) because the tenant knows or can easily ascertain the date referred to ...'); *Notting Hill Housing Trust v Roomus* [2006] 1 WLR 1375; and *Hussain v Bradford Community Housing Trust Ltd* [2010] HLR 16.

[18] Section 21(4B). Section 21(6) provides that the reference to the 'original tenancy' is: (a) where the replacement tenancy came into being on the coming to an end of a tenancy which was not a replacement tenancy, to the immediately preceding tenancy; and (b) where there have been successive replacement tenancies, to the tenancy immediately preceding the first in the succession of replacement tenancies. A 'replacement tenancy' is defined in s 21(7) as a tenancy: (a)which comes into being on the coming to an end of an assured shorthold tenancy; and (b) under which, on its coming into being, (i) the landlord and tenant are the same as under the earlier tenancy as at its coming to an end, and (ii) the premises let are the same or substantially the same as those let under the earlier tenancy as at that time.

[19] Section 21(4C).

[20] Section 21(4D).

[21] Section 21(4E).

the order may not be made so as to take effect earlier than: (a) in the case of a tenancy which is not a replacement tenancy, six months after the beginning of the tenancy; and (b) in the case of a replacement tenancy, six months after the beginning of the original tenancy.[22]

**19.23** It is thought that, during the fixed-term of an assured shorthold tenancy, a landlord can successfully claim possession relying on s 21 of the 1988 Act if there is a contractual break clause in the tenancy allowing the landlord to recover possession before the expiry of the term. Further, if there is a break clause allowing the landlord to terminate the tenancy on giving notice within the fixed term, then, depending on the wording used in the tenancy agreement itself, service of a notice pursuant to s 21(1) of the 1988 Act may be sufficient to activate the break. This view is based on *Fawaz v Aylward*.[23]

**19.24** In that case, the plaintiff landlords granted the defendant tenant an assured shorthold tenancy of a property for a term of one year. Clause 7 of the tenancy agreement provided that:

> The landlord or the tenant may determine the tenancy hereby created at or at any time after the end of the first 6 months of the tenancy provided one months' prior notice in writing of such desire is given to the other party.

**19.25** On 13 February 1996, the landlords served on the tenant a notice pursuant to s 21(1) of the 1988 Act requiring possession of the dwelling after 14 April 1996. Upon expiry of the notice, the landlords brought proceedings for possession of the property. The tenant defended the claim on the basis that the notice served on him had not validly determined the term of the tenancy in accordance with clause 7 of the tenancy agreement. The judge held at first instance that the notice was sufficient both to determine the tenancy and to comply with s 21(1), and made an order for possession. The tenant appealed to the Court of Appeal.

**19.26** Dismissing the appeal, Cazalet J said:[24]

> Here the notice specified a specific date within the time span of clause 7, the break clause of the tenancy agreement. The notice states itself to be an exercise of the right to obtain possession. On the face of the notice possession is required: it is not a possible exercise of such a right. Further the document is clearly a notice to determine the tenancy.
>
> I consider that the notice served by the [landlords] was clear and unambiguous. It indicated in terms that possession of the premises was required. In my view the judge was right to hold, as he did, that it was a valid notice both under clause 7 of the tenancy agreement and under section 21(1)(b). The requirement of possession was only consistent with the determination of the fixed term of the tenancy agreement, with due notice being given under clause 7 – one month – and in respect of section 21(1)(b) – not less than two months.

**19.27** Given that a s 21 notice may be used to exercise a break clause during the fixed term of an assured shorthold tenancy,[25] it is important to consider the existence of

[22] Section 21(5).
[23] *Fawaz v Aylward* (1997) 29 HLR 408 (approved in *Livewest Homes Ltd v Bamber* [2019] 1 WLR 6389, at [22], per Patten LJ).
[24] *Fawaz v Aylward* (1997) 29 HLR 408, at 412.
[25] See **17.23** above.

various sets of statutory restrictions on the ability of the landlord to serve such a notice. The provisions of these restrictions are convoluted and have traps for the unwary landlord. It is suggested that resort be had to a specialist text. What follows is only intended as a summary of the restrictions, which are in connection with: (i) the payment of tenancy deposits; (ii) the prevention of retaliatory evictions; and (iii) certain other prescribed requirements. Each will be considered in turn below.

### (b) Tenancy Deposits

**19.28** Under s 213(1) of the Housing Act 2004 (the '2004 Act'), any 'tenancy deposit'[26] paid to a person in connection with a 'shorthold tenancy'[27] must, as from the time when it is received, be dealt with in accordance with an 'authorised'[28] scheme. Specifically, where a landlord receives a tenancy deposit in connection with a shorthold tenancy, the initial requirements of an authorised scheme must be complied with by the landlord in relation to the deposit within the period of 30 days beginning with the date on which it is received.[29] For these purposes, 'the initial requirements' of an authorised scheme are such requirements imposed by the scheme as fall to be complied with by a landlord on receiving such a tenancy deposit.[30] In addition, a landlord who has received such a tenancy deposit must give the tenant and any 'relevant person'[31] such information relating to (a) the authorised scheme applying to the deposit, (b) compliance by the landlord with the initial requirements of the scheme in relation to the deposit, and (c) the operation of provisions of Chapter 4 of Part VI of the 2004 Act in relation to the deposit, as may be prescribed.[32] This information must be given to the tenant and any relevant person (a) in the prescribed form or in a form substantially to the same effect, and (b) within the period of 30 days beginning with the date on which the deposit is received by the landlord.[33] The 2004 Act also makes clear that no person may, in connection with a shorthold tenancy, require a deposit which consists of property other than money.[34]

[26] Defined as 'in relation to a shorthold tenancy … any money intended to be held (by the landlord or otherwise) as security for – (a) the performance of any obligations of the tenant, or (b) the discharge of any liability of his, arising under or in connection with the tenancy' (s 212(8)).

[27] Defined as 'an assured shorthold tenancy within the meaning of Chapter 2 of Part 1 of the Housing Act 1988' (s 212(8)).

[28] Defined as 'in relation to a tenancy deposit scheme … that the scheme is in force in accordance with arrangements under subsection (1)' (s 212(8)). A 'tenancy deposit scheme' is a scheme which '(a) is made for the purpose of safeguarding tenancy deposits paid in connection with shorthold tenancies and facilitating the resolution of disputes arising in connection with such deposits, and (b) complies with the requirements of Schedule 10' (s 212(2)).

[29] Section 213(3).

[30] Section 213(4).

[31] Defined as 'any person who, in accordance with arrangements made with the tenant, paid the deposit on behalf of the tenant' (s 213(10)).

[32] Section 213(5). The prescribed information for the purposes of s 213(5) is contained in art 2 of the Housing (Tenancy Deposits) (Prescribed Information) Order 2007 (SI 2007/797).

[33] Section 213(6).

[34] Section 213(7).

**19.29** Section 215 of the 2004 Act contains certain sanctions for non-compliance with the foregoing provisions. Thus, subject to s 215(2A):

(1) If (whether before, on or after 6 April 2007) a tenancy deposit has been paid in connection with a shorthold tenancy, no 'section 21 notice'[35] may be given in relation to the tenancy at a time when the deposit is not being held in accordance with an authorised scheme.[36]
(2) If a tenancy deposit has been paid in connection with a shorthold tenancy on or after 6 April 2007, no section 21 notice may be given in relation to the tenancy at a time when s 213(3) has not been complied with in relation to the deposit.[37]
(3) If section 213(6) is not complied with in relation to a deposit given in connection with a shorthold tenancy, no section 21 notice may be given in relation to the tenancy until such time as s 213(6)(a) is complied with.[38]

However, these provisions do not apply in a case where (a) the deposit has been returned to the tenant in full or with such deductions as are agreed between the landlord and tenant, or (b) an application to the county court has been made under s 214(1) (ie an application to the county court on the grounds of non-compliance with s 213) and has been determined by the court, withdrawn or settled by agreement between the parties.[39]

**19.30** Additionally to the above, if any deposit given in connection with a shorthold tenancy could not be lawfully required as a result of s 213(7), no s 21 notice may be given in relation to the tenancy until such time as the property in question is returned to the person by whom it was given as a deposit.[40]

**19.31** It is worthwhile noting that s 32 of the Deregulation Act 2015 (the '2015 Act') inserted new ss 215A–15C into the 2004 Act. The effect of these long and complicated provisions may be summarised as follows:

(1) Section 215A mitigates the effect of an earlier decision of the Court of Appeal in *Superstrike v Rodrigues*.[41] Thus, if on 26 March 2015, a periodic shorthold tenancy was in existence and all or part of the deposit paid in connection with the fixed-term tenancy continued to be held in connection with the period tenancy, the time for compliance with s 213(3) and (5) was extended. If a periodic tenancy did once exist but no longer existed on 26 March 2015 (or a deposit was held in connection with the periodic tenancy), s 213(3), (5) and (6) are treated as if they had been complied with by the landlord in relation to any deposit that was held in connection with the periodic tenancy.
(2) Section 215B reverses the effect of a widely-publicised (but unreported) decision from the county court at Birmingham: *Gardner v McCusker*. This section applies where (a) on or after 6 April 2007, a tenancy deposit has been received by a landlord

[35] Defined as 'a notice under section 21(1)(b) or (4)(a) of the Housing Act 1988) …' (s 215(5)).
[36] Section 215(1).
[37] Section 215(1A).
[38] Section 215(2).
[39] Section 215(2A).
[40] Section 215(3).
[41] *Superstrike v Rodrigues* [2013] 1 WLR 3848.

in connection with a shorthold tenancy ('the original tenancy') (b) the initial requirements of an authorised scheme have been complied with by the landlord in relation to the deposit (ignoring any requirement to take particular steps within any specified period), (c) the requirements of s 213(5) and (6)(a) have been complied with by the landlord in relation to the deposit when it is held in connection with the original tenancy (ignoring any deemed compliance under s 215A(4)), (d) a new shorthold tenancy comes into being on the coming to an end of the original tenancy or a tenancy that replaces the original tenancy (directly or indirectly), (e) the new tenancy replaces the original tenancy (directly or indirectly), and (f) when the new tenancy comes into being, the deposit continues to be held in connection with the new tenancy, in accordance with the same authorised scheme as when the requirements of s 213(5) and (6)(a) were last complied with by the landlord in relation to the deposit. In such circumstances, in their application to the new tenancy, the requirements of s 213(3), (5) and (6) are treated as if they had been complied with by the landlord in relation to the deposit.

(3) Section 215C deems ss 215A and 215B as having had effect since 6 April 2007, subject to various exceptions. The principal exception is that ss 215A and 215B do not have effect in relation to a claim under s 214 of this Act or section 21 of the Housing Act 1988 in respect of a tenancy which is settled before 26 March 2015 (whether or not proceedings in relation to the claim have been instituted), or proceedings under either of those sections in respect of a tenancy which have been finally determined before that date.

### (c) Prevention of Retaliatory Evictions

**19.32** The second set of restrictions arises out of ss 33 and 34 of the 2015 Act, which came into force on 1 October 2015. In effect, these provisions afford protection to assured shorthold tenants of dwelling-houses in England (but not in Wales) from the risk of punitive or retaliatory eviction in response to, amongst other things, a complaint by a tenant concerning the condition of the dwelling subject to the tenancy. In broad terms, the protection operates to prohibit the service of a notice pursuant to s 21 of the 1988 Act requiring possession of a dwelling-house if certain conditions are met; and, additionally, to render a notice which has already been served invalid in prescribed circumstances. Subject to certain exceptions,[42] the protection regime applies only to assured shorthold tenancies granted on or after 1 October 2015.[43]

**19.33** Where a 'relevant notice' is served in relation to a dwelling-house in England, a s 21 notice may not be given in relation to an assured shorthold tenancy of the dwelling-house: (a) within six months beginning with the day of service of the relevant notice; or (b) where the operation of the relevant notice has been suspended, within six months beginning with the day on which the suspension ends.[44] The phrase

[42] Section 41(2), (3).
[43] Section 41(1).
[44] Section 33(1).

'relevant notice' is defined[45] as a notice served under s 11 of the Housing Act 2004 (improvement notices relating to category 1 hazards), a notice served under s 12 of that Act (improvement notices relating to category two hazards), or a notice served under s 40(7) of that Act (emergency remedial action).

**19.34** A s 21 notice will also be invalid where:

(a) before the s 21 notice was given, the tenant made a complaint in writing to the landlord regarding the condition of the dwelling-house at the time of the complaint;
(b) the landlord:
    (i) did not provide a response to the complaint within 14 days beginning with the day on which the complaint was given;
    (ii) provided a response to the complaint that was not an adequate response;[46] or
    (iii) gave a s 21 notice in relation to the dwelling-house following the complaint;
(c) the tenant then made a complaint to the relevant local housing authority about the same, or substantially the same, subject matter as the complaint to the landlord:
(d) the relevant local housing authority served a relevant notice in relation to the dwelling-house in response to the complaint; and
(e) if the s 21 notice was not given before the tenant's complaint to the local housing authority, it was given before the service of the relevant notice.[47]

**19.35** Notably, references to a relevant notice served, or complaint made, in relation to a dwelling-house include a relevant notice served, or complaint made, in relation to any common parts of the building of which the dwelling-house forms a part.[48] However, this applies only if: (a) the landlord has a controlling interest in the common parts in question; and (b) the condition of those common parts is such as to affect the tenant's enjoyment of the dwelling-house or of any common parts which the tenant is entitled to use.[49]

**19.36** A s 21 notice will be invalid despite the requirement in s 33(2)(a) for a complaint to be in writing not having been met where the tenant does not know the landlord's postal or e-mail address;[50] and despite the requirements in s 33(2)(a) and (b) not having been met where the tenant made reasonable efforts to contact the landlord to complain about the condition of the dwelling-house but was unable to do so.[51]

**19.37** The court must strike out proceedings for an order for possession under s 21 of the 1988 Act in relation to a dwelling-house in England if, before the order is made,

[45] Section 33(13).
[46] The phrase 'adequate response' is a response in writing which: (a) provides a description of the action that the landlord proposes to take to address the complaint; and (b) sets out a reasonable timescale within which that action will be taken (s 33(3)).
[47] Section 33(2).
[48] Section 33(10).
[49] Section 33(11). A 'controlling interest' means an interest which is such as to entitle the landlord to decide whether action is taken in relation to a complaint within this section or a relevant notice (s 33(13)).
[50] Section 33(4).
[51] Section 33(5).

the s 21 notice that would otherwise require the court to make an order for possession in relation to the dwelling-house has become invalid under s 33(2).[52]

**19.38** There are various exemptions from the protection regime contained in s 33 of the 2015 Act. Thus, ss 33(1) and 33(2) do not apply where:

(1) The condition of the dwelling-house or common parts that gave rise to the service of the relevant notice is due to a breach by the tenant of: (a) the duty to use the dwelling-house in a tenant-like manner, or (b) an express term of the tenancy to the same effect.[53]
(2) At the time the s 21 notice is given the dwelling-house is genuinely on the market for sale.[54]
(3) The landlord is a private registered provider of social housing.[55]
(4) The dwelling-house is subject to a mortgage granted before the beginning of the tenancy; the mortgagee is entitled to exercise a power of sale conferred on the mortgagee by the mortgage or by s 101 of the Law of Property Act 1925; and at the time the s 21 notice is given the mortgagee requires possession of the dwelling-house for the purpose of disposing of it with vacant possession in exercise of that power.[56]

### (d) Other Restrictions

**19.39** Thirdly, ss 38 and 39 of the 2015 Act inserted into the 1988 Act new ss 21A and 21B, both of which restrict the ability of a landlord of a dwelling-house in England to serve a notice pursuant to s 21(1) or 21(4). As above, subject to certain exceptions,[57] these provisions apply only to assured shorthold tenancies granted on or after 1 October 2015.[58] Thus, a notice s 21(1) or 21(4) may not be given in relation to an assured shorthold tenancy of a dwelling-house in England at a time when the landlord is in breach of:

(1) a prescribed requirement;[59]
(2) a requirement imposed by regulations under s 21B(1).[60]

[52] Section 33(6).
[53] Section 34(1).
[54] Section 34(2). For these purposes, a dwelling-house is not genuinely on the market for sale if, in particular, the landlord intends to sell the landlord's interest in the dwelling-house to: (a) a person associated with the landlord; (b) a business partner of the landlord; (c) a person associated with a business partner of the landlord; or (d) a business partner of a person associated with the landlord (s 34(3)). References to a person who is associated with another person are to be read in accordance with s 178 of the Housing Act 1996 (s 34(4)). A business partner of a person ('P') is a person who is: (a) a director, secretary or other officer of a company of which P is also a director, secretary or other officer; (b) a director, secretary or other officer of a company in which P has a shareholding or other financial interest; (c) a person who has a shareholding or other financial interest in a company of which P is a director, secretary or other officer; (d) an employee of P; (e) a person by whom P is employed; or (f) a partner of a partnership of which P is also a partner (s 34(5)).
[55] Section 34(6).
[56] Section 34(7). For these purposes 'mortgagee' includes a receiver appointed by the mortgagee under the terms of the mortgage or in accordance with the Law of Property Act 1925 (s 34(8)).
[57] Section 41(2), (3).
[58] Section 41(1).
[59] Section 21A(1). The requirements that may be prescribed are requirements imposed on landlords by any enactment and which relate to: (a) the condition of dwelling-houses or their common parts; (b) the health and safety of occupiers of dwelling-houses; or (c) the energy performance of dwelling-houses (s 21A(2)).
[60] Section 21B(3), ie regulations requiring information about the rights and responsibilities of a landlord and a tenant under an assured shorthold tenancy of a dwelling-house in England (or any related matters) to be given

**19.40** The requirements prescribed for the purposes of s 21A of the 1988 Act are the requirements contained in: (a) reg 6(5) of the Energy Performance of Buildings (England and Wales) Regulations 2012 (requirement to provide an energy performance certificate to a tenant or buyer free of charge); and (b) para (6) or (as the case may be) para (7) of reg 36 of the Gas Safety (Installation and Use) Regulations 1998 (requirement to provide tenant with a gas safety certificate).[61] For the purposes of s 21A of the Act, the requirement prescribed by reg (1)(b) is limited to the requirement on a landlord to give a copy of the relevant record to the tenant and the 28 day period for compliance with that requirement does not apply.[62]

**19.41** For the purposes of s 21B of the 1988 Act, a landlord under an assured shorthold tenancy of a dwelling-house in England, or a person acting on behalf of such a landlord, must give the tenant under that tenancy the version of the document entitled 'How to rent: the checklist for renting in England', as published by the Department for Communities and Local Government, that has effect for the time being.[63] The information may be provided to the tenant: (a) in hard copy; or (b) where the tenant has notified the landlord, or a person acting on behalf of the landlord, of an e-mail address at which the tenant is content to accept service of notices and other documents given under or in connection with the tenancy, by e-mail.[64] However, this does not require a landlord, or person acting on behalf of the landlord, who has provided the tenant with the document to supply a further copy of the document each time a different version of that document is published during the tenancy.[65] In addition, this requirement does not apply: (a) where the landlord is a private registered provider of social housing; or (b) where (i) the tenancy ('the new tenancy') is a replacement tenancy, (ii) the landlord, or a person acting on behalf of the landlord, provided the tenant with the document under an earlier tenancy, and (iii) the version of the document provided to the tenant under the earlier tenancy is the same version as the version which is in effect on the first day of the new tenancy.[66]

## TERMINATION OF CONTRACTUAL TENANCIES WITHOUT ANY SECURITY OF TENURE

**19.42** Before a landlord can succeed in obtaining a possession order against an unprotected tenant who lacks any security of tenure (eg where the annual passing rent exceeds the assured shorthold tenancy threshold of £100,000.00), he must ensure that the contractual fixed term has come to an end. Here, consideration should be given to the effect of s 5 of the Protection from Eviction Act 1977 (the '1977 Act').

by a landlord under such a tenancy, or a person acting on behalf of such a landlord, to the tenant under such a tenancy (s 21B(1)).

[61] Reg 2(1) of the Assured Shorthold Tenancy Notices and Prescribed Requirements (England) Regulations 2015 (SI 2015/1646).

[62] Reg 2(2).

[63] Reg 3(2).

[64] Reg 3(3).

[65] Reg 3(4).

[66] Reg 3(5). For these purposes, 'replacement tenancy' has the same meaning as s 21(7) of the 1988 Act (reg 3(6)).

**19.43** Section 5(1) of the 1977 Act provides that no notice by a landlord or a tenant to quit any premises let (whether before or after the commencement of this Act) as a dwelling shall be valid unless: (a) it is in writing and contains such information as may be prescribed; and (b) it is given not less than four weeks before the date on which it is to take effect. The 'prescribed information' to be included in such a notice to quit is contained in the Schedule to the Notices to Quit etc (Prescribed Information) Regulations 1988 (SI 1988/2201).

**19.44** Whether this provision applies in the case of a fixed-term tenancy containing a break clause exercisable by the service of a break notice depends on what is meant by the phrase 'notice to quit'. If 'notice to quit' is apt to cover a break notice then, in the case of any tenancy to which s 5 of the 1977 Act applies, a break notice must comply with the requirements of s 5(1)(a) and (b) (as well as any other contractual and common law requirements). There is no authority on this point of which the authors are aware, although it is thought that this construction of s 5 of the 1977 Act is the correct one, by analogy with *Edell v Dulieu*[67] and *Gladstone v Bower*[68] (on the meaning of 'notice to quit' in Section 28 of the Agriculture Act 1920 and s 25(1) of the Agricultural Holdings Act 1923). See **20.3** below. The prudent course will be to draft the break notice to comply with s 5 of the 1977 Act.

[67] *Edell v Dulieu* [1924] AC 38.
[68] *Gladstone v Bower* [1960] 1 QB 170.

# 20

# *Agricultural Tenancies*

## INTRODUCTION

**20.1** As regards lettings of agricultural land, the common law relating to the relationship of landlord and tenant is modified by statute, in particular, by the Agricultural Holdings Act 1986 (the '1986 Act') and the Agricultural Tenancies Act 1995 (the '1995 Act'). The 1986 Act applies in relation to tenancies of 'agricultural holdings' entered into before 1 September 1995. Save for limited exceptions, any agricultural tenancy created on or after 1 September 1995 will be a 'farm business tenancy' governed by the 1995 Act. As may be expected, these statutes restrict the manner in which a contract for an agricultural tenancy of an agricultural holding or a farm business tenancy (as the case may be) can be determined.[1]

## TERMINATION OF TENANCIES OF AGRICULTURAL HOLDINGS

**20.2** Subject to certain exceptions, the 1986 Act applies in relation to tenancies of 'agricultural holdings'[2] whenever created.[3] Probably the most important exception is that the 1986 Act shall not apply in relation to any tenancy beginning on or after 1 September 1995.[4] One of the principal features of the 1986 Act is the security of tenure it offers agricultural tenants. So, for example, a letting of agricultural land shall take effect, with the necessary modifications, as if it were an agreement for the letting of land for a tenancy from year to year (thus restricting a landlord's ability to let agricultural land for less than a period of a year).[5] Furthermore, a tenancy of an agricultural holding

[1] For a more detailed exposition of the 1986 Act and the 1995 Act readers should refer to P Williams *Scammell, Densham & Williams Law of Agricultural Holdings* (LexisNexis, Butterworths, 10th edn, 2015) and J Muir Watt and J Moss *Agricultural Holdings* (Sweet & Maxwell, 15th edn, 2018).

[2] Defined as 'the aggregate of the land (whether agricultural land or not) comprised in a contract of tenancy which is a contract for an agricultural tenancy, not being a contract under which the land is let to the tenant during his continuance in any office, appointment or employment held under the landlord' (s 1(1) of the 1986 Act). A contract of tenancy relating to any land is a 'contract for an agricultural tenancy' if, having regard to (a) the terms of the tenancy, (b) the actual or contemplated use of the land at the time of the conclusion of the contract and subsequently, and (c) any other relevant circumstances, the whole of the land comprised in the contract, subject to such exceptions only as do not substantially affect the character of the tenancy, is let for use as agricultural land (s 1(2) of the 1986 Act). The phrase 'agricultural land' means (a) land used for agriculture which is so used for the purposes of a trade or business, and (b) any other land which, by virtue of a designation under s 109(1) of the Agriculture Act 1947, is agricultural land within the meaning of that Act (s 1(4) of the 1986 Act).

[3] Section 98(1) of the 1986 Act.

[4] Section 4(1) of the 1995 Act (this exception is itself subject to a variety of exceptions).

[5] Section 2(1) of the 1986 Act.

for a term of two years or more shall, instead of terminating on the term date, continue (as from that date) as a tenancy from year to year, but otherwise on the terms of the original tenancy so far as applicable, unless (a) not less than one year nor more than two years before the term date a written notice has been given by either party to the other of his intention to terminate the tenancy, or (b) s 4 of the 1986 Act applies (death of the tenant prior to the term date).[6]

### (a) Part III of the 1986 Act: 'Notices to Quit'

**20.3** Part III of the 1986 Act contains a number of provisions which regulate the minimum length and otherwise impose restrictions on the operation of a 'notice to quit' an agricultural holding or part of an agricultural holding. Unlike in Part II of the Landlord and Tenant Act 1954,[7] the 1986 Act contains no definition of the phrase 'notice to quit'. However, in *Gladstone v Bower*,[8] Diplock J said that s 25(1) of the Agricultural Holdings Act 1923 (in materially identical terms to s 25(1) of the 1986 Act) 'applies to any tenancy where the tenant's leasehold interest is determinable by notice, such as determination under a 'break' clause in a lease for a fixed term'. Thus, for the purposes of Part III of the 1986 Act, it is thought that the phrase 'notice to quit' is apt to encompass a break notice. Consequently, it is necessary to consider in more detail the provisions of that Part.

### (b) Restrictions on Length of a 'Notice to Quit'

**20.4** A notice to quit an agricultural holding or part of an agricultural holding shall (notwithstanding any provision to the contrary in the contract of tenancy of the holding) be invalid if it purports to terminate the tenancy before the expiry of 12 months from the end of the then current year of tenancy.[9] This provision applies equally to notices by tenants as well as to notices by landlords.[10] The effect of this provision is 'merely a fetter' on the right of the landlord or the tenant to give a valid notice to quit in all cases except those specified in the proviso.[11] Thus, if a party to a contract for an agricultural tenancy wishes to exercise a break clause then, subject to certain statutory exceptions (on which see below), and notwithstanding any provision to the contrary in the contract of tenancy of the holding, a break notice will be invalid if it purports to terminate the tenancy before the expiry of 12 months from the end of the then current year of tenancy.

[6] Section 3(1) of the 1986 Act.

[7] Section 69(1) of which provides that a 'notice to quit' means 'a notice to terminate a tenancy (whether a periodical tenancy or a tenancy for a term of years certain) given in accordance with the provisions (whether express or implied) of that tenancy'. This extended statutory definition is apt to encompass a break notice.

[8] *Gladstone v Bower* [1960] 1 QB 170, at 177.

[9] Section 25(1) of the 1986 Act.

[10] *Flather v Hood* (1928) 44 TLR 698 (a decision on s 25(1) of the Agricultural Holdings Act 1923).

[11] *Gladstone v Bower* [1960] 12 QB 384, at 394, per Pearce LJ.

**20.5** There are a limited number of statutory exceptions from s 25(1). These are as follows:

(1) where the tenant is insolvent;[12]
(2) to a notice given in pursuance of a provision in the contract of tenancy authorising the resumption of possession of the holding or some part of it for some specified purpose other than the use of land for agriculture;[13]
(3) to a notice given by a tenant to a sub tenant;[14]
(4) where the tenancy is one which by virtue of s 149(6) Law of Property Act 1925[15] has taken effect at a term of 90 years determinable by one month's notice expiring on a quarter day, following a relevant death or marriage;[16]
(5) where on a reference under s 12 of the 1986 Act[17] with respect to an agricultural holding, the arbitrator or third party determines that the rent payable in respect of the holding shall be increased, a notice to quit the holding by the tenant at least six months before it purports to take effect shall not be invalid by virtue of s 25(1) if it purports to terminate the tenancy at the end of the year of the tenancy beginning with the date as from which the increase of rent is effective;[18]
(6) where the Tribunal[19] has, on an application with respect to an agricultural holding under para 9 of Part II of Sch 3 to the 1986 Act,[20] granted a certificate specifying a minimum period of notice for termination of the tenancy (not being a period of less than two months) and directed that the period shall apply instead of the period of notice required in accordance with s 25(1);[21]
(7) in relation to a tenancy entered into before 25 March 1947, to a notice to quit given by the Secretary of State under the provisions of the tenancy where possession is required for naval, military or air force purposes or to a notice given by a corporation

[12] Section 25(2)(a) of the 1986 Act. For the purposes of the 1986 Act, a tenant is 'insolvent' if (a) he has been adjudged bankrupt or has made a composition or arrangement with his creditors, or (b) where the tenant is a body corporate, a winding-up order has been made with respect to it or a resolution for voluntary winding-up has been passed with respect to it (other than a resolution passed solely for the purposes of its reconstruction or of its amalgamation with another body corporate) (s 96(2)).

[13] Section 25(2)(b) of the 1986 Act. It should be observed that the reference to 'some specified purpose' is distinct from a 'specific purpose'. A general (ie unspecific) provision allowing the landlord to break the contract for agricultural tenancy and to resume possession 'for any non-agricultural purpose' is common and falls within the exception. See, for example, *Paddock Investments Ltd v Lory* [1975] 2 EGLR 5, where a lease of agricultural land contained a power for the landlord to resume possession of any portion of the land 'for the purpose of development only under the Agricultural Holdings Act 1948' upon giving the tenant at least two months' notice.

[14] Section 25(2)(c) of the 1986 Act.

[15] Which relates to '… any lease or underlease, at a rent, or in consideration of a fine, for life or lives or for any term of years determinable with life or lives, or on the marriage of the lessee, or on the formation of a civil partnership between the lessee and another person …'.

[16] Section 25(2)(d) of the 1986 Act.

[17] Under which the landlord or tenant of an agricultural holding may by notice in writing served on the other demand that the rent to be payable in respect of the holding as from the next termination date shall be referred to arbitration or third-party determination under the 1986 Act. Section 84A contains detailed provisions regarding third-party determinations under the 1986 Act.

[18] Section 25(3) of the 1986 Act.

[19] Meaning: (a) where the agricultural holding (or the greater part of the holding) is in England, the First-tier Tribunal; and (b) where the agricultural holding (or the greater part of the holding) is in Wales, the Agricultural Land Tribunal (s 96(1) of the 1986 Act).

[20] Ie where the landlord applies to the Tribunal for a certificate that the tenant is not fulfilling his responsibilities to farm in accordance with the rules of good husbandry.

[21] Section 25(4) of the 1986 Act.

carrying on a railway, dock, canal, water or other undertaking, or by a government department or local authority, for certain specified purposes;[22]

(8) where an arbitrator has specified a date for the termination of the tenancy by notice to quit under art 7, or where there has been an extension of time under art 14, of the Agricultural Holdings (Arbitration on Notices) Order 1987.[23]

**20.6** The requirement for 12 months' notice can be waived by the recipient of the notice. In *Elsden v Pick*,[24] the landlord accepted the tenant's notice to quit which gave less than 12 months' notice. The landlord was allowed to obtain an order for possession when the tenant later attempted to rely on the invalidity of his own notice. As Shaw LJ explained:[25]

> I have read section 23 (1) [of the Agricultural Holdings Act 1948, which is in materially the same terms as Section 25(1) of the 1986 Act]; the first matter to observe is that the subsection uses the word 'invalid' and not 'unlawful'. Thus there is no penal prohibition; it is simply that provision in the tenancy agreement for a shorter notice than 12 months is nugatory. So also any variation of a tenancy agreement in relation to an agricultural holding which purports to make a shorter period of notice than 12 months effective will fail of its purpose. This produces the situation that there can be no operative provision whereby notice can in prospect be made effective if it is less than 12 months; but a notice is of course a unilateral act available to one party or the other without the ad hoc consent of the party to whom the notice is given. There seems to me to be no impediment created by section 23 (1) to the party in receipt of a notice to quit to waive his strict right that the notice should expire on a particular day or that it should be of particular duration. A contractual provision which enures for the benefit of a party can be waived by that party albeit that his right to that benefit is reinforced by statute. There may be circumstances which might qualify this situation, as where an element of public interest is involved, but in such a case one would expect the statutory provision to speak in terms of illegality (thus: 'it shall be unlawful') rather than of mere invalidity.

### (c) Method of Service of a 'Notice to Quit'

**20.7** Section 93 of the 1986 Act contains a number of provisions relating to the service of any 'notice, request, demand or other instrument under this Act'[26] (including a notice to quit). Thus, a notice to quit shall be duly given to or served on the person to or on whom it is to be given or served if:

(1) it is delivered to him;[27] or
(2) left at his proper address;[28] or
(3) sent to him by post in a registered letter or by the recorded delivery service.[29]

[22] Section 98(2) and para 4 of Sch 12 to the 1986 Act.
[23] SI 1987/710.
[24] *Elsden v Pick* [1980] 1 WLR 898.
[25] *Elsden v Pick* [1980] 1 WLR 898, at 906C.
[26] Section 93(1) of the 1986 Act.
[27] It does not matter how the notice is 'delivered'. As Megaw J explained in *Re Poyser and Mills' Arbitration* [1964] 2 QB 467, at 479 (concerning s 92(1) of the Agricultural Holdings Act 1948): 'If the letter is delivered to the tenant, it matters not whether it is personally handed to him by the landlord or handed to him by some

**20.8** A notice to quit shall be duly given to or served on an incorporated company or body if it is given or served on the secretary or clerk of the company or body.[30] In addition, a notice to quit to be given to or served on a landlord or tenant shall, where an agent or servant is responsible for the control of the management or farming, as the case may be, of the agricultural holding, be duly given or served if given to or served on that agent or servant.[31]

**20.9** Notably, where there has been a change of landlord, unless or until the tenant of an agricultural holding has received (a) notice that the person who before that time was entitled to receive the rents and profits of the holding ('the original landlord') has ceased to be so entitled, and (b) notice of the name and address of the person who has become entitled to receive the rents and profits, any notice or other document served upon or delivered to the original landlord by the tenant shall be deemed for the purposes of this Act to have been served upon or delivered to the landlord of the holding.[32] In such circumstances, a tenant's break notice may be validly served on the original landlord (as defined).

## (d) **Restrictions on Operation of a 'Notice to Quit'**

**20.10** S 26(1) of the 1986 Act contains an important restriction on the ability of a landlord to break a contract for an agricultural tenancy. Thus, where (a) notice to quit an agricultural holding or part of an agricultural holding is given to the tenant, and (b) not later than one month from the giving of the notice to quit the tenant serves on the landlord a counter-notice in writing requiring that s 26(1) shall apply to the notice to quit, then, subject to s 26(2),[33] the notice to quit shall not have effect unless, on an

servant or agent of the landlord, and if the landlord chooses to entrust it to the post otherwise than by registered post, then the post office is the agent of the landlord for that purpose. It still remains necessary in that case for the landlord to prove that the letter has actually been received by the tenant, but if he does so, then due service has been effected, because it has been proved that the letter has been delivered by one of the methods making due service under the Act'.

[28] For the purposes of s 93 of the 1986 Act and s 7 of the Interpretation Act 1978 the proper address of any person to or on whom any such instrument is to be given or served shall, in the case of the secretary or clerk of an incorporated company or body, be that of the registered or principal office of the company or body, and in any other case be the last known address of the person in question (s 93(4) of the 1986 Act). As to meaning of 'leaving' a notice, see the discussion at **7.53–7.67** above.

[29] Given the wording of s 93(4) of the 1986 Act, it is thought that s 7 of the Interpretation Act 1978 applies to a notice to quit served by post in a registered letter or by the recorded delivery service pursuant to s 93(1). In consequence, the service is deemed to be effected by properly addressing, pre-paying and posting a letter containing the document and, 'unless the contrary is proved', to have been effected at the time at which the letter would be delivered in the ordinary course of post. In other words, it is open to the recipient or intended recipient to prove that the notice was not received in time, or was not received at all. See eg *Gidden v Chief Constable of Humberside* [2010] RTR 9, at [10], per Elias LJ ('The effect is that there is a rebuttable presumption that service has been effected in the ordinary course of post …').

[30] Section 93(2) of the 1986 Act.

[31] Section 93(3) of the 1986 Act (ie even if the agent or servant is not in fact authorised to accept service of the notice).

[32] Section 93(5) of the 1986 Act.

[33] Which provides that s 26(1) shall not apply in any of the Cases set out in Part I of Sch 3 to the 1986 Act. Thus, the Tribunal has no jurisdiction in relation to a notice to quit which expressly specifies that it is given for one of the reasons set out in any of those Cases. The Cases where a tenant's right to serve a counter-notice is expressly excluded comprise: (i) Case A – retirement: statutory smallholdings; (ii) Case B – planning consent: non-agricultural use; (iii) Case C – certificate of bad husbandry; (iv) Case D – non-compliance with a notice to pay rent or notice to remedy; (v) Case E – irremediable breach; (vi) Case F – insolvency; (vii) Case G – death of tenant; and (viii) Case H – Ministry amalgamations.

application by the landlord, the Tribunal[34] consent to its operation. Thus, a landlord who has received a counter-notice must apply to the Tribunal for consent to the operation of the notice to quit; and, if he does not, his notice to quit is rendered of no effect.

**20.11** An application by the landlord for the Tribunal's consent to the operation of a notice to quit, made by a landlord after service on the landlord by the tenant of a counter-notice, the notice of application must be made within two months after the date of service of the counter-notice.[35]

**20.12** The Tribunal shall consent under s 26 to the operation of a notice to quit an agricultural holding or part of an agricultural holding if, but only if, they are satisfied as to one or more of the matters mentioned in s 27(3), being a matter or matters specified by the landlord in his application for their consent.[36] The matters mentioned in s 27(3) are:

(1) That the carrying out of the purpose for which the landlord proposes to terminate the tenancy is desirable in the interests of good husbandry as respects the land to which the notice relates, treated as a separate unit.[37]
(2) That the carrying out of the purpose for which the landlord proposes to terminate the tenancy is desirable in the interests of sound management of the estate of which the land to which the notice relates forms part or which that land constitutes.[38]
(3) That the carrying out of the purpose for which the landlord proposes to terminate the tenancy is desirable for the purposes of agricultural research, education, experiment or demonstration, or for the purposes of the enactments relating to smallholdings.[39]
(4) That the carrying out of the purpose for which the landlord proposes to terminate the tenancy is desirable for the purposes of the enactments relating to allotments.[40]
(5) That greater hardship would be caused by withholding than by giving consent to the operation of the notice.[41]
(6) That the landlord proposes to terminate the tenancy for the purpose of the land being used for a use, other than for agriculture, not falling within Case B.[42]

**20.13** Further, even if it is satisfied as mentioned in s 27(1) of the 1986 Act, the Tribunal shall withhold consent under s 26 to the operation of the notice to quit if in all the circumstances it appears to them that a fair and reasonable landlord would not insist on possession.[43] The Tribunal may also impose conditions on any consent under s 26 to

[34] See footnote 19 above.
[35] Rule 27(4)(b) of the Tribunal Procedure (First-tier Tribunal) (Property Chamber) Rules 2013 (SI 2013/1169). The Tribunal has the jurisdiction to extend the time for compliance with this rule, even if the application for an extension is not made until after the time limit has expired (r 6(3)(a)).
[36] Section 27(1) of the 1986 Act.
[37] Section 27(3)(a).
[38] Section 27(3)(b).
[39] Section 27(3)(c).
[40] Section 27(3)(d).
[41] Section 27(3)(e).
[42] Section 27(3)(f).
[43] Section 27(2).

ensure that the land to which the notice to quit relates will be used for the purpose for which the landlord proposes to terminate the tenancy.[44]

**20.14** Where a landlord seeks to exercise a break clause in a contract for an agricultural tenancy, and none of the Cases in Part I of Sch 3 to the 1986 Act applies, then he should make it clear and unambiguous on the face of the break notice that he intends to terminate the tenancy subject to s 26(1) of the 1986 Act.[45]

### (e) Compensation Following a 'Notice to Quit'

**20.15** It should be noted that an agricultural tenant possesses certain statutory rights to claim compensation on termination of his lease under Part V of the 1986 Act. Compensation is payable to a tenant of an agricultural holding under the 1986 Act when, inter alia, his tenancy is 'terminated' by reason of a notice to quit the holding given by the landlord.[46] For these purposes, 'termination' means the cesser of the contract of tenancy by reason of effluxion of time or from any other cause.[47] It is clear that this covers the situation where either the landlord or the tenant has given notice to quit or a break notice. There is only very limited scope for the parties to contract out of the statutory entitlement to compensation. Indeed, save as expressly provided in the 1986 Act, a tenant or landlord shall be entitled to compensation in accordance with the provisions therein and not otherwise, and shall be so entitled notwithstanding any agreement to the contrary.[48]

[44] Section 27(4). Where, on an application by the landlord, the Tribunal are satisfied that, by reason of any change of circumstances or otherwise, any condition ought to be varied or revoked, they shall vary or revoke the condition accordingly (s 27(5)). The statutory sanction for breach of a condition is found in s 27(6), which empowers the Tribunal by order to impose on the landlord a penalty of an amount not exceeding two years' rent of the holding at the rate at which rent was payable immediately before the termination of the tenancy, or, where the notice to quit related to a part only of the holding, of an amount not exceeding the proportion of the said two years' rent which it appears to the Tribunal is attributable to that part.

[45] *Cowan v Wrayford* [1953] 1 WLR 1340 (concerning a notice purportedly given under s 24(1) of the Agricultural Holdings Act 1948), at 1343, per Somervell LJ ('The first point, therefore as it seems to me is whether this document brought home to the tenant in clear and unambiguous language that the landlord was intending to terminate the tenancy subject to section 24(1), irrespective of any breaches by the tenant. I do not think it did. We were invited, and I think rightly, to consider this document and the meaning it would convey to a reasonable mind in the light of the Act'); at 1346, per Denning LJ ('In the present case the notice purported to be given under subsection (2); but considered as such, it was a bad notice because it said the tenant had failed to remedy certain breaches, whereas in fact the period allowed for remedy had not then expired. It being a bad notice under subsection (2), it is not, in my judgment, now permissible for the landlord to pray it in aid as a notice under subsection (1). It certainly was not a clear and unambiguous notice for that purpose. If the landlord had intended to go under subsection (1), he should have made it quite clear').

[46] Section 60(1)(a) of the 1986 Act.

[47] Section 96(1) of the 1986 Act.

[48] See s 78(1) of the 1986 Act. Interestingly, the 1986 Act does not contain an equivalent to s 50 of the Agricultural Holdings Act 1923. The latter provided that 'any contract (whether under seal or not) made by a tenant of a holding, by virtue of which his right to claim compensation thereunder was taken away or limited, shall to that extent be void'. In *Re Disraeli Agreement* [1939] 1 Ch 382 (decided under the 1923 Act) a contract for an agricultural tenancy contained a proviso that the landlord could resume possession of any portion of the land so leased in case it was required for building purposes without compensation, but with a proportionate reduction in the rent attributable to the area so taken by the landlord. Cross J held that this proviso deprived the tenant of its right to compensation for disturbance and, thus, was rendered invalid. See also *Coates v Diment* [1951] 1 All ER 890 and *Parry v Million Pigs Ltd* [1980] 260 EG 281.

## TERMINATION OF FARM BUSINESS TENANCIES

**20.16** The 1995 Act introduced a new code applicable to 'farm business tenancies.' One of the principal features of the 1995 Act is that the tenant has virtually no security of tenure other than that bargained for with the landlord. Unlike the position under the 1986 Act, there is little interference with the parties' common law rights to bring their tenancy to an end or with the general law on notices to quit/break notices. Save for limited exceptions, a tenancy beginning before 1 September 1995 cannot be a farm business tenancy because the statute is not retrospective.

**20.17** For the purposes of the 1995 Act, a tenancy is a 'farm business tenancy' if (a) it meets the 'business conditions'[49] together with either the 'agriculture condition'[50] or the 'notice conditions',[51] and (b) it is not a tenancy which, by virtue of s 2 of the 1995 Act[52] cannot be a farm business tenancy.[53]

### (a) Farm Business Tenancies for a Term of More than Two Years

**20.18** A farm business tenancy for a term of more than two years shall, instead of terminating on the term date,[54] continue (as from that date) as a tenancy from year to year, but otherwise on the terms of the original tenancy so far as applicable, unless at least 12 months before the term date a written notice has been given by either party to the other of his intention to terminate the tenancy.[55] This provision has effect notwithstanding any agreement to the contrary.[56] In other words, in the absence of written notice at least 12 months before the term date, once the term date has passed, the farm business tenancy becomes an annual periodic tenancy.[57]

[49] The business conditions are (a) that all or part of the land comprised in the tenancy is farmed for the purposes of a trade or business, and (b) that, since the beginning of the tenancy, all or part of the land so comprised has been so farmed (s 1(2) of the 1995 Act).

[50] The agriculture condition is that, having regard to (a) the terms of the tenancy, (b) the use of the land comprised in the tenancy, (c) the nature of any commercial activities carried on on that land, and (d) any other relevant circumstances, the character of the tenancy is primarily or wholly agricultural (s 1(3) of the 1995 Act).

[51] The notice conditions are (a) that, on or before 'the relevant day', the landlord and the tenant each gave the other a written notice (i) identifying (by name or otherwise) the land to be comprised in the tenancy or proposed tenancy, and (ii) containing a statement to the effect that the person giving the notice intends that the tenancy or proposed tenancy is to be, and remain, a farm business tenancy, and (b) that, at the beginning of the tenancy, having regard to the terms of the tenancy and any other relevant circumstances, the character of the tenancy was primarily or wholly agricultural (s 1(4) of the 1995 Act). 'The relevant day' means whichever is the earlier of the following (a) the day on which the parties enter into any instrument creating the tenancy, other than an agreement to enter into a tenancy on a future date, or (b) the beginning of the tenancy (s 1(5) of the 1995 Act). The written notice referred to in s 1(4) must not be included in any instrument creating the tenancy (s 1(6) of the 1995 Act).

[52] That is, if (a) the tenancy begins before 1 September 1995, or (b) it is a tenancy of an agricultural holding beginning on or after that date with respect to which, by virtue of s 4 of 1995 Act of the 1986 Act applies.

[53] Section 1(1) of the 1995 Act.

[54] 'The term date', in relation to a fixed-term tenancy, means the date fixed for the expiry of the term (s 5(2) of the 1995 Act).

[55] Section 5(1).

[56] Section 5(4).

[57] Section 5(4).

**20.19** Importantly, the requirement of 12 months' previous written notice to terminate does not apply to a tenancy for a term of two years exactly or to a tenancy of less than two years (both of which will expire by effluxion of time under the common law).

**20.20** Section 7 of the 1995 Act is of particular relevance where a farm business tenancy of more than two years contains a break clause. Specifically, where a farm business tenancy is a tenancy for a term of more than two years, any notice to quit the holding or part of the holding given in pursuance of any provision of the tenancy shall (notwithstanding any provision to the contrary in the tenancy) be invalid unless it is in writing and is given at least 12 months before the date on which it is to take effect.[58] Thus, for all break clauses contained in fixed-term tenancies of more than two years' duration, at least 12 months' notice is required to exercise the break.

**20.21** This provision does not apply in relation to a counter-notice given by the tenant under s 140(2) of the Law of Property Act 1925 (apportionment of conditions on severance of reversion);[59] and does not apply to a tenancy which, by virtue of s 149(6) of the Law of Property Act 1925 (lease for life or lives or for a term determinable with life or lives or on the marriage of, or formation of a civil partnership by, the lessee), takes effect as such a term of years as is mentioned in that provision.[60]

**20.22** From a practical perspective, a landlord can avoid the restrictions imposed by ss 5 and 7 of the 1995 Act: (i) by entering into a farm business tenancy for a fixed term of two years or less; alternatively (ii) by not allowing a fixed-term tenancy of more than two years to lapse and, thereby, to become a tenancy from year to year.

### (b) Periodic Farm Business Tenancies

**20.23** S 6 of the 1995 Act applies to farm business tenancies which are annual periodic tenancies, whether from inception or as a result of the operation of s 5(1).[61]

**20.24** At common law, subject to any express provision to the contrary, an annual periodic tenancy can be determined only upon six months' notice expiring at the end of the first or any subsequent year of the term.[62] However, where a farm business tenancy is a tenancy from year to year, a notice to quit the holding or part of the holding shall (notwithstanding any provision to the contrary in the tenancy) be invalid unless (a) it is in writing, (b) it is to take effect at the end of a year of the tenancy, and (c) it is given at least 12 months before the date on which it is to take effect.[63] Section 6(1) does not apply in relation to a counter-notice given under s 140(2) of the Law of Property Act 1925.[64]

[58] Section 7(1).
[59] See **3.47–3.53** above.
[60] Section 7(3) of the 1995 Act.
[61] See **20.18** above.
[62] *Doe d. Clarke v Smaridge* (1845) 7 QB 957.
[63] Section 6(1).
[64] Section 6(3).

**20.25** Where a farm business tenancy for a term of more than 2 fixed term years is to continue (as from the term date)[65] as a tenancy from year to year, a notice to quit which complies with s 6(1) and which is to take effect on the first anniversary of the term date shall not be invalid merely because it is given before the term date.[66]

**20.26** The above requirements apply equally to notices given by landlords and by tenants. Importantly, however, these provisions do **not** apply when the farm business tenancy is for a period of less than a year, for example, where the tenancy is month to month or quarter to quarter.[67]

### (c) Method of Service of a 'Notice to Quit'

**20.27** Section 36 of the 1995 Act contains its own provisions as to the service of 'any notice or other document which is required or authorised to be given' thereunder.[68] This provision broadly replicates s 93 of the 1986 Act,[69] with three principal differences:

(1) A notice to quit is no longer duly given to a person if sent to him by post in a registered letter or by the recorded delivery service.[70]
(2) However, a notice to quit is duly given to a person if it is given to him in a manner authorised by a written agreement made, at any time before the giving of the notice, between him and the person giving the notice.[71]
(3) A notice or other document to which this section applies is not duly given to a person if its text is transmitted to him by facsimile or other electronic means otherwise than by virtue of s 36(2)(c).[72]

### (d) Compensation Following a 'Notice to Quit'

**20.28** It is worth noting that, in a similar manner to the position under the 1986 Act, the tenant under a farm business tenancy is entitled, on the termination[73] of the tenancy, to obtain from his landlord compensation in respect of certain matters.[74] This is apt to include the termination of a farm business tenancy upon exercise of a break clause.

[65] See footnote 54 above.
[66] Section 6(2).
[67] See eg *Land Settlement Association v Carr* [1944] KB 657 (a case concerning the Agricultural Holdings Act 1923 in which the contract of tenancy was for a period of 364 days).
[68] Section 36(1).
[69] See **20.7–20.9** above.
[70] Section 93(1) of the 1986 Act.
[71] Section 36(2)(c) of the 1995 Act.
[72] Section 36(3) of the 1995 Act.
[73] Meaning 'the cesser of the tenancy by reason of effluxion of time or from any other cause' (s 38(1) of the 1995 Act).
[74] Section 16(1) of the 1995 Act.

ALLOTMENTS

**20.29** The Allotments Act 1922 (as amended by the Allotments Act 1950) (the '1922 Act') contains special provisions regarding the determination of 'allotment gardens'.[75]

**20.30** Where land is let on a tenancy for use by the tenant as an allotment garden or is let to any local authority or association for the purpose of being sub-let for such use the tenancy of the land or any part shall not (except as hereinafter provided) be terminable by the landlord by 'notice to quit' except by 'a twelve months' or longer notice to quit expiring on or before the sixth day of April or on or after the twenty-ninth day of September in any year'.[76]

**20.31** The expression 'notice to quit' is not defined in the 1922 Act. It is considered that, by analogy with the position under the 1986 Act,[77] it is apt to encompass a break notice.

**20.32** As described, the 1922 Act contains express provision that the statutory notice should apply to the terms of the tenancy, notwithstanding any agreement to the contrary. Thus, there is no need to specify the contractual date of determination in the statutory notice because of the express words used in the 1922 Act.[78]

[75] Defined in s 22(1) as 'an allotment not exceeding forty poles in extent which is wholly or mainly cultivated by the occupier for the production of vegetable or fruit crops for consumption by himself or his family'.

[76] Section 1(1)(a).

[77] See **20.3** above.

[78] *Wombwell Urban District Council v Burke* [1966] 2 QB 149 (albeit Danckwerts and Salmon LJJ felt difficulty about the matter).

# 21

# *Drafting Break Clauses*

## GENERAL REMARKS

**21.1** A significant proportion of leases incorporate break clauses. They are included at the behest of landlords, of tenants, or both of them. They are included for many reasons. For tenants, break clauses introduce flexibility. For landlords, they can assist with site assembly, particularly where a major development might be in prospect.

**21.2** Whatever the immediate or long-term estate management benefit that is sought to be gained from the inclusion of a break clause it is important to remember that the presence of a break clause in a lease can have economic influences. Thus the presence of such a clause is likely to affect the value of a landlord's reversion.[1] In addition, with any lease that incorporates provisions for rent review, the presence of a break clause is likely to affect the rent payable on review. This means that if a break clause is incorporated in a lease then the rent review provisions should be examined to consider the valuation consequences that the break clause may have on the reviewed rent. A key point will be whether or not the break clause is incorporated in the hypothetical lease. This point should be addressed by the inclusion of express wording in the clause of the lease that deals with the rent reviews.

**21.3** Part 3 of the RICS Code for Leasing Business Premises (1st edition, February 2020) (the 'Lease Code') gives the following guidance:

> [2.3] Any break rights or options for renewal for either party should be clearly specified, including the dates (or range of dates) when a party can end the lease, the length of prior notice to be given and any pre-conditions for the break being effective.
>
> [2.4] Unless the parties have agreed stricter conditions in the heads of terms, a tenant's break should be conditional only on the tenant payable all basic rent payable on any date before the break date, giving up occupation and leaving no subtenants or other occupiers. Disputes about the state of the premises, or what has been left behind or removed, should be settled later as at normal lease expiry.
>
> [2.5] Leases should require landlords to repay any rent, service charge or insurance paid by the tenant for any period after a break takes effect. Repayment of service charges may be deferred until the service charge accounts are finalised.

[1] Which explains why, particularly in a recessionary environment, it is common to see lease transactions by which the tenant becomes entitled to a reverse premium if it does not exercise the break. Where the economic conditions are different, the break clause may provide for the tenant to pay a premium or 'penalty'. Compliance with such provisions is often the source of disputes.

**21.4** The above paragraph is expressed to indicate 'good practice'.[2] While not mandatory, it remains important because members' non-compliance may be used as evidence in support of a professional liability claim against the professional responsible for negotiating and/or drafting the lease. Of course, since the Lease Code has no statutory force the parties to a lease are legally free to draft break clauses in any way they wish, and there is plenty of scope for parties and their advisers to use their negotiating and drafting skills to gain an advantage. Quite often this advantage is not obvious until the break clause falls to be operated.

**21.5** Broadly speaking those acting for parties seeking the benefit of break clauses should strive to achieve clauses that are as simple as possible, whereas those who will be the recipient of break notices should strive to make break clauses as complicated and as qualified as possible.

## MATTERS TO BE ADDRESSED WHEN DRAFTING A BREAK CLAUSE

**21.6** The specific matters to be considered in the course of drafting a break clause include the following:

(1) Who is to have the benefit of the clause? If the benefit of a tenant's break clause is to be personal to a particular named tenant, then: (i) can the named tenant re-acquire the benefit by an assignment from an assignee; (ii) is the right to break to attach for the benefit of the hypothetical tenant upon a rent review?
(2) If the benefit of the break clause is given to joint landlords or joint tenants, then each will need to authorise the operation of the clause, unless the clause gives one party express authority to operate the clause on behalf of the others.
(3) When is the break clause to be exercisable? Is it to be at any time (a 'rolling break'), at any time after a specified date, or operative on one or more specified dates?
(4) If the break notice is to expire in the middle of a rental period, the legal adviser will want to consider whether or not to include an apportionment provision regulating the repayment of sums paid in advance of, and relating to the period after, the break date.
(5) What pre-conditions are to be specified as necessary before the break clause can be exercised? The party with the benefit of the break clause will want to cut down the number of pre-conditions and/or introduce words of qualification in respect of the required standard of performance of pre-conditions.
(6) When are the pre-conditions to be satisfied? (At the time of service of the break notice, when it expires, or both?)
(7) How is the break notice to be served? Are there any particular persons that have to be served, eg someone who is not the landlord or the tenant?
(8) Should the break notice be in any particular form (eg on paper of a particular colour)? And, should the break notice contain any particular words?

[2] See p 5 of the Lease Code.

(9) If the lease contains a rent-review provision, how will this inter-relate with the operation of the break clause, both in terms of: (i) making time of the essence of the rent review; and (ii) whether the break clause will be incorporated into the hypothetical lease?

(10) When a lease is granted to a tenant who is given an option to determine, and the tenant sublets to a third party, it is essential for the tenant to reserve a right to terminate the sub-lease otherwise he cannot effectively terminate the head lease without possibly incurring liability in damages to the superior landlord (for breach of the covenant to yield up vacant possession) and/or to the third party (for breach of the covenant for quiet enjoyment). A head tenant's right to terminate the sublease can be made conditional upon the head tenant's desire to end the head lease by means of the following type of wording: 'The power of the landlord [ie the headlessor] to terminate this lease is exercisable only if the landlord desires to terminate the superior lease under which he holds'.

(11) In the case of business tenancies, the draftsman should be aware of the incidence of compensation under s 37 of the Landlord and Tenant Act 1954. If, for example, the landlord has the right to break the lease at the expiry of the fourteenth year of the term, rather than at the expiry of, say, the twelfth year of the term, the tenant's right to compensation on quitting may be halved.

(12) Also in the case of business tenancies, the draftsman may want to consider whether the lease should contain an express provision to the effect that service of a notice under s 25 of the Landlord and Tenant Act 1954 shall be sufficient notice for the purposes of exercising a landlord's break clause.

# 22

# *Practical Advice when Exercising a Break Clause*

## ADVICE FOR THE PARTY SEEKING TO EXERCISE THE BREAK CLAUSE

### (a) Three Warnings

**22.1** First, and most obviously, the party seeking to exercise the break clause should comply strictly with all the requirements of a break clause. As Lewison LJ succinctly explained in *Siemens Hearing Instruments Ltd v Friends Life Ltd*:[1]

> The clear moral is: if you want to avoid expensive litigation, and the possible loss of a valuable right to break, you must pay close attention to all the requirements of the clause, including the formal requirements, and follow them precisely.

**22.2** Secondly, the party seeking to exercise the break clause should not anticipate goodwill from the intended recipient of the break notice.[2] In *Orchard (Developments) Holdings Plc v Reuters Ltd*,[3] Rix LJ said of a tenant's break clause:

> The provisions regarding a break clause option are there for the tenant to operate, and he fails to operate them correctly and timeously at his peril. He has no reason to think that, if he fails to do so, he can rely on the landlord's goodwill to save him.

**22.3** Thirdly, the party seeking to exercise the break clause might expect the court to rebuff pleas of hardship in the event of non-compliance with the requirements of a break clause. As Lewison J said in *Standard Life Investments Property Holdings Limited v W & J Linney Limited*:[4]

> '… one part of fairness is that contractual stipulations are complied with. The exercise of a break clause has important consequences for both landlord and tenant and there are powerful policy considerations for certainty in this area of the law'.

[1] *Siemens Hearing Instruments Ltd v Friends Life Ltd* [2014] EWCA Civ 382, [2014] 2 P&CR 5, at [66].

[2] Indeed, the intended recipient of a break notice will want to avoid making any representations which, if relied upon by the serving party, could give rise to an estoppel.

[3] *Orchard (Developments) Holdings Plc v Reuters Ltd* [2009] EWCA Civ 6, at [52].

[4] *Standard Life Investments Property Holdings Limited v W & J Linney Limited* [2011] L&TR 9, at [25]; and see also *Ageas (UK) Ltd v Kwik-Fit (GB) Ltd* [2013] EWHC 3261 (QB), at [38], per Green J ('… In the context of commercial transactions certainty is undeniably important. It enables the parties to know where they stand and to take commercial decisions in the light of such knowledge …').

### (b) Preconditions

22.4 The party seeking to exercise the break clause should, well in advance of the break date, draw up a list of all the pre-conditions that need to be satisfied. If (for example) a tenant's break clause is conditional upon the tenant complying with its repairing obligations under the lease, then efforts should be made to engage with the landlord as to the extent of any remedial work which might be necessary. If the landlord declines to engage with the tenant on any work that is needed, then the tenant will need to obtain its own professional advice (eg from a reputable surveyor) as to the work that may be required. Any such work should be carried out well before the deadline prescribed by the break clause. Once the work has been carried out the landlord should be invited to confirm that it is satisfied with the state of repair of the premises.

22.5 The break clause may be conditional upon the payment of rent or other sums. If there is a dispute between landlord and tenant as to the amount that is payable (eg a dispute over the quantum of service charges) or a dispute over the period for which payment is due (eg because it is not clear whether the tenant should pay a full quarters rent, or only a proportion) then the prudent course is to pay the maximum amount alleged by the landlord to be payable. However, that payment should be made under protest and with a reservation of the right to claim back any overpayment.[5]

### (c) Drafting the Break Notice

22.6 A copy of the break notice should be prepared in draft, ensuring it complies with any requirements, and mirrors the language of the lease. Creative drafting should be avoided. The notice should be checked (and re-checked by an independent colleague) to ensure that it is worded correctly and identifies the correct recipient(s). If there is any conceivable doubt as to the identity of the correct intended recipient of the break notice, then a search of HM Land Registry should be undertaken and/or recent rent demand notices examined. A significant number of negligence cases have resulted from service of a notice on the 'wrong' landlord, either because there has been a simple change of landlord or because that landlord has granted a concurrent or overriding lease, inserting an intermediate landlord between the original landlord and the tenant. If the break notice is served under cover of letter, then care should be taken to ensure that the wording of the letter does not give rise to any confusion or inconsistency with the notice.

### (d) Service of the Break Notice

22.7 Any provisions in the lease regulating the method of service of a break notice should be checked and complied with. If in doubt copies of the break notice may be sent

[5] Although, as discussed in Chapter 11, the legal basis upon which the tenant might seek to recover any 'overpayment' is replete with difficulty.

by various means to various possible addresses, each without prejudice to the validity of the others. Evidence as to service should be preserved until it is no longer relevant. If possible, an acknowledgement as to receipt of the break notice should be obtained from the recipient.

## ADVICE FOR THE RECIPIENT OF A BREAK NOTICE

### (a) Compliance with Preconditions

**22.8** Until the decision of the Court of Appeal in *Fitzroy House Epworth Street (No 1) Limited v Financial Times Limited*,[6] a belief had been engendered amongst some professional advisers that the recipient (or intended recipient) of a break notice had a duty to act reasonably and to co-operate with the serving party. It was believed that this assistance extended to giving advice as to eg what money was owed by the tenant, or what work was needed to ensure compliance with a condition in the break clause. However, the advice now to be given to the recipient (or intended recipient) of a break notice is not to render any assistance to the serving party whatsoever (unless to maintain silence would be misleading). This is reflective of the remarks of Rix LJ in *ING Bank NV v Ros Roca SA* (referred to at **13.49** above).[7]

### (b) The Break Notice

**22.9** The recipient of a break notice should check the following:

(1) that the notice has been served by the proper party;
(2) that the notice has been served on the proper party;
(3) that the notice has been served by the prescribed method;
(4) that the notice has been served within the prescribed time limit; and
(5) that the contents of the notice fully comply with the requirements of the break clause.

**22.10** There is no obligation upon the recipient of a break notice to point out to the serving party any flaws in the notice or other defect in the purported exercise of the break clause. Indeed, particularly in those cases where only one opportunity is afforded to the tenant to break the lease, and the landlord wishes to retain the tenant, then it would be commercial folly for the landlord to say anything at all.[8]

## LITIGATION TACTICS FOR THE TENANT

**22.11** If a tenant has sought to exercise an option to determine, but there is a dispute as to whether that exercise has been successful, then failing a negotiated settlement

[6] *Fitzroy House Epworth Street (No 1) Ltd v Financial Times Ltd* [2006] 1 WLR 2207.
[7] *ING Bank NV v Ros Roca SA* [2012] 1 WLR 472, at [92]; and see also *Taylor Fashions Ltd v Liverpool Victoria Trustees Co Ltd* [1982] QB 133, at 147C–47D, per Oliver J.
[8] Although see the discussion in **13.49–13.57** above.

between the parties, litigation is needed to break the deadlock. For practical reasons the claimant is often the landlord. This is because, by the time a claim form is issued, the tenant will have vacated the premises and stopped paying rent. There will normally be no reason for the tenant to incur the costs of litigation. In contrast, the landlord will still be demanding rent, which the tenant will not be paying. In addition there may be pressure from third parties to cause the landlord to break the impasse. A common situation is where the rating authority pursues the landlord for payment of rates, on the basis that the tenant has informed the authority that its lease has come to an end. Litigating against the tenant may be a necessary step in order to prove to the rating authority that the landlord is contending that the lease is still alive, and that it is the tenant that remains liable for rates. Production of the claim form in the relevant magistrates court is normally successful in persuading magistrates to adjourn proceedings.

22.12 If the landlord issues a claim then it has a choice as to how it formulates the proceedings. The claim can be limited to the recovery of unpaid rent, and other monies that are due pursuant to the lease. This has the advantage of simplicity, since the Particulars of Claim need only recite the lease, the obligations to pay and the failure to effect payment. The drawback however is that the tenant's defence will then allege that the lease is broken, perhaps merely referring to the break notice. The landlord will then need to serve a Reply, which explains why the break was ineffective, giving reasons. In turn the tenant will no doubt wish to serve a Rejoinder,[9] explaining why (contrary to the landlord's case) the break is effective. This elongates the pleadings stage of the proceedings. In order to speed up the pace of the litigation, the landlord may also claim a declaration that the lease remains unbroken. The Particulars of Claim served by the landlord will then refer to the details of the dispute regarding the break and contain averments explaining why the tenant's contentions (which have presumably already been identified in correspondence) are wrong. An example of a landlord's Particulars of Claim that embodies claims both for unpaid monies and declaratory relief appears as a precedent in Appendix 5. An example of a Defence and Counterclaim, to be used by the tenant, appears in Appendix 6.

## LITIGATION TACTICS FOR THE LANDLORD

22.13 If the landlord has sought to exercise a break clause, whether it be pursuant to an unconditional break or a redevelopment clause, and the tenant disputes the validity of that break, either the landlord or the tenant could initiate litigation. As mentioned above, in practice, the landlord is normally the claimant, because the tenant is content to remain in occupation. Furthermore, the maximum commercial advantage for the tenant is often gained by inactivity. This forces the landlord not only to issue proceedings but also to try to have these expedited.[10] If the landlord does initiate proceedings then the

[9] For which the court's permission will be required: see CPR, r 15.9.
[10] In accordance with the principles in eg *JW Spear & Sons Ltd v Zynga Inc* [2012] EWHC 1374 (Ch).

Particulars of Claim will normally seek declaratory relief (that the lease has been broken) plus possession of the premises.

**22.14** The tenant may decide to initiate proceedings, seeking a declaration that its lease remains effective, where it is to the tenant's advantage to seek to achieve clarity as to its position. Plainly if there remains a doubt as to whether a lease has been successfully broken then the tenant may be unable to make any long-term plans for its business in the relevant premises.

# Appendix 1

## *Break Clause for the Landlord – On One or More Specified Dates*

1.1 The following definitions apply:
**Break Date(s)** – [Either insert a specific date or dates, or cross refer to other date(s) in the Lease, eg the day before a rent review date(s)]
**Break Notice** – Notice in the form set out in the Schedule hereto.

1.2 The Landlord may terminate this Lease by serving a Break Notice on the Tenant at least [Insert Period] months before the specified Break Date.

1.3 [A Break Notice shall only be effective if, at the Break Date the Landlord desires/intends]

1.4 [Subject to Clause 1.3], following service of a Break Notice, this Lease shall terminate on the Break Date.

1.5 Termination of this Lease on the Break Date shall not affect any other right or remedy that either party may have in relation to any earlier breach of this Lease.

**The Schedule – The Form of the Landlord's Break Notice**

To [Insert Name and Address of Tenant].

Re: A lease date [Insert Date] of premises at [Insert address of Premises] ('the Lease').

We refer to Clause [Insert Clause Number] of the Lease. By this notice the Landlord hereby exercises its right to terminate the Lease pursuant to the above Clause on [Insert the Break Date]

..................................

[On behalf of, and with the authority of] the Landlord.

# Appendix 2

## *Break Clause for the Landlord – Incorporating a Rolling Break*

1.1 In this Clause, the following definitions apply:
**Break Date** – the date stated in the Break Notice on which this Lease shall terminate.
**Break Notice** – notice in the form set out in the Schedule hereto.

1.2 Subject to the provisions in the remainder of this Clause, the Landlord may terminate this Lease at any time by serving a Break Notice on the Tenant at least [Insert Period] before the Break Date.

1.3 The Break Notice must specify the Break Date, but shall not specify as the break date any date which is earlier than date [Insert the earliest Break Date].

1.4 [The Break Notice shall only be effective if, at the Break Date, the Landlord desires/intends to demolish/develop/refurbish/ all (or a part) of the Premises]

1.5 Subject to Clause 1.4, following service of a Break Notice, this Lease shall terminate on the Break Date.

1.6 Termination of this Lease on the Break Date shall not affect any other right or remedy that either party may have in relation to any earlier breach of this Lease.

**The Schedule – Form of Landlord's Break Notice**

To [Insert Name and Address of Tenant].

Re: Lease dated [Insert Date] of premises at [Insert address of Premises] ('the Lease').

We refer to Clause [Insert Clause Number] of the Lease. By this notice the Landlord exercises its right to terminate the Lease pursuant to the above Clause on [Insert the Break Date].

.................................

[On behalf of, and with the authority of] the Landlord.

# Appendix 3

## *Break Clause for the Tenant – On One or More Specified Dates*

1.1 The following definitions apply:
**Break Date(s)** – [Either insert a specific date or dates, or cross refer to other date(s) in the Lease eg the day before a rent review date(s)]
**Break Notice** – Notice in the form set out in the Schedule hereto.

1.2 The Tenant may terminate this Lease by serving a Break Notice on the Landlord at least [Insert Period] months before the specified Break Date.

1.3 [The right to serve a Break Notice is personal to the original Tenant, provided the term of this Lease has never been assigned].

1.4 A Break Notice shall only be effective if, at the Break Date:

- (i) The Tenant has paid all rent and other monies due under the Lease.
- (ii) Vacant possession of the whole of the Premises is given.
- (iii) There is no [material] [substantial] breach of any of the Tenant covenants in the Lease [relating to the state of repair and condition of the premises] [relating, and say what particular covenant(s) must be complied with].
- (iv) The Tenant pays, on or before the Break Date, the sum of [insert the sum]

1.5 Subject to Clause 1.4, following service of a Break Notice, this Lease shall terminate on the Break Date.

1.6 Termination of this Lease on the Break Date shall not affect any other right or remedy that either party may have in relation to any earlier breach of this Lease.

**The Schedule – The Form of the Tenant's Break Notice**

To [Insert Name and Address of Landlord].

Re: A lease dated [Insert Date] of premises at [Insert address of Premises] ('the Lease').

We refer to Clause [Insert Clause Number] of the Lease. By this notice the Tenant hereby exercises its right to terminate the Lease pursuant to the above Clause on [Insert the Break Date]

...................................

[On behalf of, and with the authority of] the Tenant.

# Appendix 4

## *Break Clause for the Tenant – Incorporating a Rolling Break*

1.1 In this Clause, the following definitions apply:
**Break Date** – the date stated in the Break Notice on which this Lease shall terminate.
**Break Notice** – notice in the form set out in the Schedule hereto.

1.2 Subject to the provisions in the remainder of this Clause, the Tenant may terminate this Lease at any time by serving a Break Notice on the Landlord at least [Insert Period] before the Break Date.

1.3 [The right to serve the Break Notice is personal to the original Tenant, provided that the term of this Lease has never been assigned].

1.4 The Break Notice must specify the Break Date, but shall not specify as the Break Date any date which is earlier than [Insert the earliest Break Date].

1.5 The Break Notice shall only be effective if:

(i) The Tenant has paid all rent and other monies due under the Lease.
(ii) Vacant possession of the whole of the Premises is given.
(iii) There is no [material] [substantial] breach of any of the Tenant covenants in the Lease [relating to the state of repair and condition of the premises] [relating, and say what particular covenant(s) must be complied with]
(iv) The Tenant pays, on or before the Break Date, the sum of [Insert the sum].

1.6 Subject to Clause 1.5, following service of a Break Notice, this Lease shall terminate on the Break Date.

1.7 Termination of this Lease on the Break Date shall not affect any other right or remedy that either party may have in relation to any earlier breach of this Lease.

### The Schedule – Form of Tenant's Break Notice

To [Insert Name and Address of Landlord].

Re: Lease dated [Insert Date] of premises at [Insert address of the Premises] ('the Lease').

We refer to Clause [Insert Clause Number] of the Lease. By this notice the Tenant exercises its right to terminate the Lease pursuant to the above Clause on [Insert the Break Date].

..................................

[On behalf of, and with the authority of] the Tenant.

# Appendix 5

## *Particulars of Claim – Landlord's Claim for Declaration etc*

**IN THE HIGH COURT OF JUSTICE    Claim No:**

**BUSINESS AND PROPERTY COURTS OF ENGLAND AND WALES**

**PROPERTY TRUSTS AND PROBATE LIST (ChD)**

**BETWEEN**

ABC LIMITED

**Claimant**

And

XYZ LIMITED

**Defendant**

PARTICULARS OF CLAIM

1 By a lease dated [date] ('**the Lease**'), made between the Claimant of the first part, and the Defendant of the second part, the Claimant demised to the Defendant the premises known as and situate at [insert name of premises] ('**the Demised Premises**') for a term commencing from [date] and expiring on [date], subject to earlier determination pursuant to [clause number], and otherwise subject to the covenants on the part of the Defendant therein contained.

2 By the Lease, the Defendant covenanted to pay to the Claimant:

(i) The yearly rent of [amount] per annum by equal quarterly payments in advance on the usual quarter days ([clause number]).

(ii) Interest, payable and calculated pursuant to [clause number].

3 Further, by the Lease, the Defendant covenanted with the Claimant as follows:

(i) At all times during the term to keep in good and substantial repair and condition the Demised Premises ([clause number]).

(ii) In [date] and every fifth year thereafter and also in the last six months of the term (howsoever determined) in a good and workmanlike manner to prepare and decorate or otherwise treat as appropriate all interior and exterior parts of the Demised Premises required to be so treated ([clause number]).

4 At clause [number] of the Lease there was a tenant's break clause ('the Break Clause') in the following terms:

> 'If the Tenant (here meaning XYZ Limited) wishes to terminate this Lease on [date] and shall give to the Landlord not less than 12 months' notice in writing of that wish and shall up to the time of such determination pay the rents reserved by and materially perform and observe the covenants contained in this Lease then upon the expiry of such notice the Term shall immediately cease and determine.'

5 On or about [date] a company called DEF Limited served a notice (**'the Notice'**) upon the Claimant, as Landlord, purportedly pursuant to the Break Clause.

6 In order for the Lease to terminate on [date], pursuant to the Notice, it was not only necessary for the Defendant (as opposed to DEF Limited) to serve the Notice, but it was also necessary for the Defendant, up to [date], to pay the rents reserved by, and materially perform and observe the covenants contained in, the Lease.

7 As mentioned in paragraph 5 above, the Defendant did not serve the Notice.

8 Further, the Defendant failed to pay to the Claimant the rents reserved by the Lease up to [date]:

<u>PARTICULARS OF SUMS UNPAID</u>

[Insert particulars]

9 Further, the Defendant did not materially perform and observe the covenants contained in the Lease up to [date]:

<u>PARTICULARS OF MATERIAL NON-PERFORMANCE & OBSERVANCE</u>

[Insert particulars]

10 By reason of the foregoing matters, the Break Clause was not validly exercised and the Lease continues.

11 Further, pursuant to clause [number] of the Lease, the Defendant is liable to pay to the Claimant the sums set out in paragraph 8 above.

12 Further, the Claimant is entitled to interest upon the aforegoing monies, pursuant to clause [number] of the Lease or, alternatively, pursuant to Section 35A of the Senior Courts Act 1981.

AND the Claimant claims:

(1) A declaration that the Lease has not been determined by the operation of the Break Clause and that the said Lease remains in full force and effect.

(2) [The sums set out in paragraph 8 above.]

(3) Interest as aforesaid.

(4) Costs, pursuant to clause [number] of the Lease.

(5) Further or other relief.

<u>STATEMENT OF TRUTH</u>

Etc.

# Appendix 6

## *Defence and Counterclaim – In Response to Landlord's Claim for Declaration etc*

**IN THE HIGH COURT OF JUSTICE Claim No:**

**BUSINESS AND PROPERTY COURTS OF ENGLAND AND WALES**

**PROPERTY TRUSTS AND PROBATE LIST (ChD)**

BETWEEN

ABC LIMITED

**Claimant**

And

XYZ LIMITED

**Defendant**

DEFENCE AND COUNTERCLAIM

**DEFENCE**

1 The Defendant joins issue with the Claimant's claim and, save as is expressly admitted or not admitted herein, every allegation in the Claim Form and the Particulars of Claim is denied as if separately set out and traversed.

2 Save where is otherwise stated to the contrary:

(i) References herein to paragraph numbers are references to the corresponding numbered paragraphs in the Particulars of Claim.

(ii) Definitions used in the Particulars of Claim are adopted herein.

3 Paragraphs 1–3 are admitted.

4 As to paragraph 4, whereas it is admitted that the Notice was served by DEF Limited, it is averred that, at all material times:

(i) DEF Limited had general authority to act on the Defendant's behalf in connection with all matters concerning the Lease, including the service of the Notice.

(ii) The Claimant knew that DEF Limited was so authorised.

5 Paragraph 5 is admitted.

6 Paragraph 6 is denied for the reasons set out above. The Notice was served by DEF Limited for and on behalf of the Defendant.

7 Paragraph 7 is denied. The Defendant has paid the rent in full up to [date].

<u>PARTICULARS OF SUMS PAID</u>

[Insert particulars]

8 Paragraph 8 is denied. It is averred that:

(i) On [date], Mr [name], of DEF Limited, acting on behalf of the Defendant, had a meeting at the Demised Premises with Mr [name], acting on behalf of the Claimant. At the meeting, the parties agreed what works needed to be carried out in and upon the Demised Premises in order for the Break Clause validly to be exercised ('**the Agreed Works**').

(ii) Over the course of [dates], in reliance upon the forgoing agreement, the Agreed Works were carried out in and upon the Demised Premises by the Defendant.

(iii) On [date], DEF Limited, on behalf of the Defendant, wrote to the Claimant, inviting it to inspect the Demised Premises and to confirm that it was satisfied that the works had been carried out.

(iv) Thereafter, despite receiving the said letter, the Claimant said nothing to indicate to the Defendant that it required any further work to be carried out to the Demised Premises.

9 Paragraph 9 is denied. For the reasons aforesaid, the Break Clause was validly exercised and the Lease terminated on [date].

10 For the reasons given in paragraph 7 above, paragraph 10 is denied. It is further denied that the Claimant is entitled to the interest claimed or any interest.

<u>COUNTERCLAIM</u>

Paragraphs 3–10 herein are repeated.

AND the Defendant counterclaims:

(1) A declaration that the Lease was determined by the operation of the Break Clause on [date].

(2) Costs.

(3) Further or other relief.

STATEMENT OF TRUTH

Etc.

# Index


**administration:**
companies in administration:
exercising break clauses, 8.23
**administrators:**
exercising break clauses, 4.62
intestacy, 4.67–4.69
**agency:**
exercising break clauses, 4.42
general agency, 4.43–4.52
ratification, 4.54
unidentified/undisclosed principles, 4.53
service of notice, 8.20
**agricultural holdings,** 1.19
notice to quit, 20.3
compensation, 20.15
length of, 20.4–20.6
method of service, 20.7–20.8
operational restrictions, 20.10–20.14
termination, 20.2–20.15
*see also* farm business tenancies
**allotments,** 20.29–20.32
**alterations:**
reinstatement obligations, 10.85–10.87
**assignment:**
"all estate" clauses, 3.27
common law, 3.1
effect on lease, 3.2
equitable assignees, 3.56–3.62
right to end tenancy, 3.3
"touch and concern" test, 3.4
equitable assignees, 3.46
common law, 3.56–3.62
Land Registration Act, 3.72–3.76
Landlord and Tenant (Covenants) Act, 3.70–3.71
Law of Property Act, 3.63–3.69
*see also* equitable assignees
formalities:
*Griffith v Pelton*, 3.30–3.33
Landlord and Tenant (Covenants) Act 1995, 3.16–3.21
Law of Property Act 1925, 3.1, 3.7–3.15, 3.26–3.29
legal history, 3.1–3.4
landlord assigning reversion:
old tenancies, 3.7–3.14
severance of reversion, 3.47–3.53
new tenancies, 3.17–3.21
old tenancies:
assignment by landlord, 3.7–3.14
assignment by tenant, 3.15
partial assignment, 3.54–3.55
restrictions, 3.34
hybrid break clauses, 3.40–3.44
purely personal break clauses, 3.35–3.39
reversion:
severance of reversion, 3.47–3.53
split reversion, 3.48–3.53
transfer of reversion by landlord, 3.7–3.14
side letters, 3.77–3.80
statutory provisions:
Landlord and Tenant (Covenants) Act 1995, 3.16–3.21
Law of Property Act 1925, 3.1, 3.7–3.15, 3.26–3.29
**assured shorthold tenancies,** 19.16–19.41
termination:
landlord in breach, 19.39–19.41
retaliatory evictions, 19.32–19.38
tenancy deposits, 19.28–19.31
**assured tenancies:**
termination, 19.10–19.15

***Braganza*** **restrictions,** 1.16–1.18
**breach of covenant,** 1.9
forfeiture, 1.9–1.10
repudiation, 1.9–1.10
server's own breach, 13.43–13.47
spent breaches, 9.46–9.50
strict compliance principle, 9.15–9.35
*see also* compliance
**'break date',** 1.1
mistake, 5.33
invalidating a notice, 5.34
not invalidation a notice, 5.35–5.40
professional liability:
failure to remind, 17.14–17.20
vacant possession, 10.20–10.29
**business tenancies,** 1.19
broken demise, extent of, 18.15–18.16
farm business tenancies:
notice to quit, 20.27–20.28
periodic farm business tenancies, 20.23–20.26
termination, 20.16–20.28

new leases, 18.17–18.22
landlord's break clauses, 18.23–18.42
tenant's break clauses, 18.43–18.51
subtenancies, 18.12–18.14
termination:
farm business tenancies, 20.16–20.28
landlord, 18.2–18.10
tenant, 18.11

**collateral contracts,** 2.2
**companies in administration:**
service of notice, 8.23
**companies in liquidation:**
service of notice, 8.24
**compensation:**
compulsory purchase:
general principles, 15.3–15.12
interest subject to break clauses, 15.13–15.18
termination:
agricultural holdings, 20.15
farm business tenancies, 20.28
**compliance:**
compliance periods, 9.28–9.45
de minimis failure to comply, 9.26–9.27
indispensable conditions, 5.2–5.7
party seeking to exercise break clause:
drafting, 22.6
preconditions, 22.4–22.5
service of notice, 22.7
warnings, 22.1–22.3
recipients of break notices, 22.9–22.10
preconditions, 22.8
service of notice, 7.2–7.20, 9.84
settlement, 9.68–9.83
side agreements, 9.68–9.83
spent breaches, 9.46–9.50
strict compliance, 9.15–9.26
qualification of, 9.51–9.67
*see also* strict compliance
**compulsory purchase:**
statutory law, 15.1
compensation:
general principles, 15.3–15.12
interest subject to break clauses, 15.13–15.18
**concurrent lessees:**
parties able to exercise break clauses, 4.19–4.20
service of notice, 8.5–8.10
**conditions:**
de minimis failure to comply, 9.26–9.27
identifying preconditions, 9.2–9.14
negotiated settlements, 9.68–9.83
server's own breach, 13.43–13.47
service without fulfilling conditions, 9.84
side agreements, 9.68–9.83
strict compliance, 9.15–9.26
qualification of strict compliance, 9.51–9.66
unilateral waiver, 13.40–13.42
validity of break clauses:
payment of rent, 10.38–10.81
reinstatement obligations, 10.85–10.87
repairing obligations, 10.82–10.84
spent breaches, 9.46–9.50
strict compliance principle, 9.15–9.35
vacant possession, 10.2–10.37
*see also* compliance; estoppel; waiver
**construction of notice,** 5.20–5.30
covering letters, 5.31–5.32
notice period, 6.44–6.55
redevelopment break clauses, 12.3–12.12
service:
Interpretation Act, 7.73–7.74
strict compliance, 9.52–9.66
**contractual discretion,** 1.17–1.18
**contributory negligence:**
professional liability, 17.29–17.30
**countermanding break notices,** 13.65
**Crown:**
service of notice on, 8.24

**drafting:**
generally, 21.1–21.5, 22.6
specific matters:
beneficiaries, 21.6
business tenancies, 21.6
form, 21.6
joint landlords, 21.6
joint tenants, 21.6
options to determine, 21.6
pre-conditions, 21.6
rent review provisions, 21.6
repayment, 21.6
service, 21.6
subtenancies, 21.6
**duress:**
overpayment, recovery of, 11.30–11.33

**Electronic Communications Code,** 12.31–12.34
2003 Code, 12.35–12.42
2017 Code, 12.43–12.51
**equitable assignees,** 3.46
common law position, 3.56–3.62
exercising break clauses, 4.24
Land Registration Act 2002:
owners' powers, 3.72–3.76
Landlord and Tenant (Covenants) Act 1995, 3.70–3.71
Law of Property Act 1925, 3.63–3.69
service of notice, 8.12

**equity:**
leases taking effect in equity:
parties able to exercise break clauses, 4.21–4.23
service of notice, 8.11
**estoppel:**
general principles, 13.5–13.10
*see also* validity; waiver
**executors:**
exercising break clauses, 4.66–4.67
service of notice on, 8.27
**exercise of break clauses,** 6.1
commencement of term, 6.6–6.11
effect:
entitlement to double rent, 14.4–14.7
landlord and tenant, between, 14.1–14.7
liability for breach of covenant, 14.3
parties relieved of need to fulfil covenant, 14.1–14.2
subtenancies, 14.8–14.14
maximum period for, 6.2
minimum period of notice, 6.2
notice periods, *see* notice periods
pre-conditions, 22.4–22.5
specified period commencing on a specified date, 6.40–6.42
specified period from/after a specified date, 6.28–6.39
specified point before a specified date, 6.18–6.27
strict approach, 6.3
warnings, 22.1–22.3
"within a specified period", 6.12–6.17

**farm business tenancies:**
notice to quit:
compensation, 20.28
method of service, 20.27
termination, 20.16–20.22
periodic tenancies, 20.23–20.26
notice to quit, 20.27–20.28
*see also* agricultural holdings
**fixed-term leases:**
termination, 1.1, 19.44
assured tenancies, 19.11–19.15
assured shorthold tenancies, 19.17, 19.20, 19.23
farm business tenancies, 20.20–20.22
**forfeiture:**
breach of covenant, 1.9–1.10
**formalities,** 2.1–2.3
**former landlords/tenants:**
parties able to exercise break clauses, 4.40–4.41
service of notice, 8.13–8.19

**hybrid break clauses:**
assignment, 3.40–3.44

**implied terms,** 1.16–1.17
recovery of overpaid rent, 11.4–11.18
server's own breach, 13.46
**inflexibility rule,** 1.14
**Interpretation Act 1978**
service, 7.73–7.74
**intestacy,** 4.67–4.69

**joint landlords:**
assured shorthold tenancies:
termination, 19.17–19.18
drafting break clauses, 21.6
parties able to exercise break clauses, 4.11
service of notice, 8.2
successors of, 4.12
**joint tenants:**
assured tenancies:
termination, 19.10
drafting break clauses, 21.6
notice to quit, 1.2
parties able to exercise break clauses, 4.6–4.10
service of notice, 8.2
severance, 7.60, 7.69
successors of, 4.12

**Land Registry,** 2.5
**Land Registration Act 2002:**
equitable assignees:
owners' powers, 3.72–3.76
requirement for registration:
failure to comply, 4.22
**Landlord and Tenant Act 1954:**
form of notice, 5.31–5.32
redevelopment break clauses, 12.3, 12.18
**Landlord and Tenant (Covenants) Act 1995,** 3.5, 3.16–3.21
assignment, 3.70–3.71
*see also* new tenancies (post-1995)
**landlords:**
assignment:
old tenancies, 3.7–3.14
severance of reversion, 3.47–3.53
assured shorthold tenancies:
termination, 19.39–19.41
business tenancies:
termination of, 18.2–18.10
defined, 3.45–3.46
effect of exercise of break clause, 4.1
entitlement to double rent, 14.4–14.7
liability for breach of covenant, 14.3
parties relieved of need to fulfil covenant, 14.1–14.2
subtenancies, 14.8–14.14
joint landlords
parties able to exercise break clauses, 4.11
successors of, 4.12

landlord as tenant, 4.13–4.18
litigation tactics, 22.13–22.14
old tenancies:
assignment by landlord, 3.7–3.14
transfer of reversion by landlord, 3.7–3.14
parties able to exercise break clauses, 4.1
former landlords/tenants, 4.40–4.41
joint landlords, 4.11
landlord and/or tenant, 4.1
landlord as tenant, 4.13–4.18
non-landlords/tenants, 4.40–4.41
termination of business tenancies, 18.2–18.10
transfer of reversion, 3.7
advantages of break clauses, 3.8–3.9
case law, 3.11–3.14
disadvantages of break clauses, 3.10
**Law of Property Act 1925:**
assignment:
equitable assignees, 3.63–3.69
old tenancies, 3.7–3.15
service of notice:
applicability, 7.43–7.48
effect, 7.49–7.52
"left at", 7.53–7.67
sending notice, 7.68–7.72
transfer of reversion, 3.7–3.14
**Leasehold Reform, Housing and Urban Development Act 1993:**
redevelopment break clauses, 12.19–12.23
right to terminate a new lease, 12.24–12.30
**limited liability partnerships,** 4.60
administration, 4.62
service of notice, 8.21
**limited partnerships,** 4.57–4.59
service of notice, 8.21
**liquidation:**
companies in liquidation:
exercising break clauses, 8.24
**liquidators:**
exercising break clauses, 4.63
**litigation:**
tenants' tactics, 22.11–22.12
landlords' tactics, 22.13–22.14

**managers:**
exercising break clauses, 4.64–4.65
service of notice, 8.3–8.4, 8.25
**mistakes,** 5.8–5.19
break date, 5.33
invalidating notice, 5.34
not invalidating notice, 5.35–5.40
identity of demised premises, 5.60–5.61
identity of recipient, 5.54
invalidating notice, 5.55–5.56
not invalidating notice, 5.57–5.58
identity of serving party, 5.41–5.42
invalidating notice, 5.43–5.49
not invalidating notice, 5.50–5.53
overpayment, recovery of, 11.34–11.40
**multiple parties:**
service of notice, 8.3–8.4

**new tenancies (post-1995):**
assignment, 3.17–3.21
Landlord and Tenant (Covenants) Act 1995, 3.5, 3.16–3.21
effect, 3.19
old tenancies (pre-1995) compared, 3.5–3.6
**notice periods:**
"at least", 6.50–6.55
corresponding date rule, 6.56–6.63
fractions of time, 6.64–6.73
"not less than", 6.44–6.49
unspecified, 6.43
**notice to quit,** 3.48–3.53
agricultural holdings, 20.3
compensation, 20.15
length of, 20.4–20.6
method of service, 20.7–20.8
operational restrictions, 20.10–20.14
farm business tenancies:
compensation, 20.28
method of service, 20.27
break clause distinguished, 1.2–1.4

**old tenancies (pre-1996):**
assignment by tenant, 3.15
new tenancies (post-1995) compared, 3.5–3.6
transfer of reversion by landlord, 3.7
advantages of break clauses, 3.8–3.9
case law, 3.11–3.14
disadvantages of break clauses, 3.10
**option, break clauses as,** 1.11–1.15

**partial assignment,** 3.54–3.55
**parties able to exercise break clauses:**
administrators, 4.62
agents, 4.42
general agency, 4.43–4.52
ratification, 4.54
unidentified/undisclosed principles, 4.53
concurrent lessees, 4.19–4.20
equitable assignees, 4.24
former landlords/tenants, 4.40–4.41
joint lessees, 4.6–4.10
successors of, 4.12
joint lessors, 4.11
successors of, 4.12
landlord and/or tenant, 4.1
landlord as tenant, 4.13–4.18

landlord only, 4.1
leases containing personal break clauses, 4.25–4.39
leases taking effect in equity, 4.21–4.23
liquidators, 4.63
managers, 4.64–4.65
non-landlords/tenants, 4.40–4.41
partnerships:
limited liability partnerships, 4.60
limited partnerships, 4.57–4.59
private partnerships, 4.55–4.56
personal representatives, 4.66–4.69
receivers, 4.64–4.65
tenant only, 4.1
silent/unclear leases, 4.2–4.5
trustees in bankruptcy, 4.61

**partnerships:**
exercising break clauses:
limited liability partnerships, 4.60
limited partnerships, 4.57–4.59
private partnerships, 4.55–4.56
service of notice, 8.21

**periodic tenancies,** 1.2
assured shorthold tenancies, 19.17–19.18
assured tenancies, 19.11–19.14
business tenancies, 18.2
farm business tenancies, 20.18, 20.23–20.24
notice to quit, 3.3
joint tenants, 4.10
validity, 3.67
withdrawal, 13.62

**personal break clauses:**
assignment, 3.35–3.38, 4.25–4.39
rent review provisions, 16.36

**personal representatives:**
exercising break clauses:
executors, 4.66–4.67
service of notice, 8.27–8.30

**private partnerships,** 4.55–4.56
service of notice, 8.21

**professional liability,** 17.1–17.4
contributory negligence, 17.29–17.30
failure to advice on lease terms, 17.5–17.13
failure to draw attention to pre-conditions, 17.21–17.28
failure to give proper notice, 17.28
failure to remind on approaching break date, 17.14–17.20

**Public Trustee:**
exercise of break clause, 4.67
service of notice, 8.28–8.30

**receivers:**
exercising break clauses, 4.64–4.65
service of notice, 8.25

**redevelopment break clauses:**
condition in landlord break clause, 12.1
Electronic Communications Code, 12.31–12.34
2003 Code, 12.35–12.42
2017 Code, 12.43–12.51
interpretation:
"desires", 12.8–12.9
"intention", 12.3–12.7
"proposes", 12.10
"requires", 12.11–12.12
Landlord and Tenant Act, 12.18
Leasehold Reform Housing and Urban Development Act, 12.19–12.23
right to terminate a new lease, 12.24–12.30
scope, 12.13–12.17

**registration,** 2.4–2.6
requirement for registration:
failure to comply, 4.22
transfers of unregistered leases, 2.5

**reinstatement:**
obligations in break clause, 10.85–10.87

**rent:**
overpayment, recovery of:
generally, 11.1–11.3
implied agreement, 11.19–11.24
implied terms, 11.4–11.18
payment condition in break clause, 10.38–10.81

**Rent Act 1977:**
termination of tenancies, 19.3–19.9

**rent reviews,** 16.1
procedural relevance of break clauses, 16.2–16.4
time is not of the essence, 16.21–16.27
time is of the essence, 16.5–16.20
substantive relevance of break clauses, 16.28
break options in a hypothetical lease, 16.29–16.40
valuation consequences, 16.41–16.42

**repairs**
obligation in break clause, 10.82–10.84

**repudiatory breach,** 1.9–1.10

**residential tenancies,** 1.19
termination:
assured shorthold tenancies, 19.16–19.41
assured tenancies, 19.10–19.15
Rent Act tenancies, 19.3–19.9
unprotected tenancies, 19.42–19.44

**restitution:**
unjust enrichment, 11.25–11.29
duress, 11.30–11.33
failure of consideration, 11.41–11.45
mistake, 11.34–11.40

**reversion:**
assignment:
equitable assignees, 3.56–3.61
service of break notice, 3.47
severance of reversion, 3.47–3.49

**right of re-entry:**
severed reversion, 3.47–3.49
**right of recovery,** 11.27, 11.43
**right to terminate:**
unilateral nature, 1.5–1.8

**separate documents,** 2.1
side letters, 3.77–3.80
**sequential break notices,** 13.66–13.70
**service of break notice,** 1.3, 22.7
common law, 7.75–7.79
failure to serve, 6.4
indirect service, 7.36–7.42
late service, 6.74–6.78
Law of Property Act 1925, s.196
applicability, 7.43–7.48
effect, 7.49–7.52
"left at", 7.53–7.67
sending notice, 7.68–7.72
method of service:
prescribed contractual method, 7.2–7.20
personal service, 7.21–7.26
service by post/fax/email, 7.27–7.28
place of service, 7.29–7.35
notice to quit compared, 1.2
service without fulfilling conditions, 9.84
short service, acceptance of, 6.79
statutory provisions:
Law of Property Act 1925, 7.43–7.72
Interpretation Act, 7.73–7.74
**service of notice to quit:**
agricultural tenancies:
agricultural holdings, 20.7–20.8
farm business tenancies, 20.27
break notices compared, 1.2
**settlement,** 9.68–9.83
**severance of reversion,** 3.47–3.53
**side agreement:**
formalities, 2.1
negotiation, 9.68–9.83
validity, 2.1
**side letter:**
assignment, 3.77–3.80
formalities, 2.1
validity, 2.1
**split reversion,** 3.48–3.53
**standard clauses,** 1.20
**strict compliance rule,** 1.14, 9.15–9.26
de minimis failure to comply, 9.26–9.27
indispensable conditions, 5.2–5.7
party exercising break clause, 22.1
qualification of strict compliance:
"material", 9.61–9.66
"reasonable", 9.52–9.60
"substantial", 9.66
time for compliance, 9.28–9.45
**"subject to contract",** 5.65–5.66
**subtenancies:**
business tenancies, 18.12–18.14
effect of exercising break clauses:
head landlord exercising clause, 14.12–14.14
head tenant exercising clause, 14.8–14.11
**successors in title,** 2.4, 3.45–3.46
**surrender,** 1.6–1.7

**tenancy deposit schemes,** 19.28–19.32
**tenant defined,** 3.45–3.46
**tenants:**
business tenancies, 1.19
new leases, 18.43–18.51
termination, 18.11
definition, 3.45–3.46
joint tenants, 21.6
notice to quit, 1.2
parties able to exercise break clauses, 4.6–4.10
successors of, 4.12
landlord as tenant, 4.13–4.18
old tenancies:
assignment by tenant, 3.15
parties able to exercise break clauses, 4.1
former landlords/tenants, 4.40–4.41
joint tenants, 4.6–3.10
landlord and/or tenant, 4.1
landlord as tenant, 4.13–4.18
non-landlords/tenants, 4.40–4.41
silent/unclear leases, 4.2–4.5
subtenancies:
business tenancies, 18.12–18.14
effect of exercising break clauses, 14.8–14.14
**termination:**
agricultural holdings, 20.2–20.15
assured shorthold tenancies:
landlord in breach, 19.39–19.41
retaliatory evictions, 19.32–19.38
tenancy deposits, 19.28–19.31
assured tenancies, 19.10–19.15
business tenancies, 1.19
farm business tenancies, 20.16–20.28
landlord, 18.2–18.10
tenant, 18.11
effluxion of time, 1.1
farm business tenancies, 20.16–20.28
fixed-term leases, 1.1, 19.44
assured tenancies, 19.11–19.15
assured shorthold tenancies, 19.17, 19.20, 19.23
farm business tenancies, 20.20–20.22
Leasehold Reform, Housing and Urban Development Act:
right to terminate a new lease, 12.24–12.30
Rent Act, 19.3–19.9

right to terminate, 1.5–1.8
redevelopment break clauses, 12.24–12.30
unprotected tenancies, 19.42–19.44
**total failure of consideration doctrine,** 11.41–11.45
**transfer of reversion:**
landlord, 3.7
advantages of break clauses, 3.8–3.9
case law, 3.11–3.14
disadvantages of break clauses, 3.10
*see also* assignment
**trustees in bankruptcy:**
exercising break clauses, 4.61
service of notice on, 8.22

**unjust enrichment,** 11.25–11.29
duress, 11.30–11.33
failure of consideration, 11.41–11.45
mistake, 11.34–11.40
**unprotected tenancies:**
termination, 19.42–19.44

**vacant possession:**
condition in break clause, 10.2–10.37
**validity:**
mistake, 5.33–5.40
payment of rent, 10.38–10.81
reinstatement obligations, 10.85–10.87
repairing obligations, 10.82–10.84
sequential break notices, 13.66–13.70
side letters, 2.1
spent breaches, 9.46–9.50
strict compliance principle, 9.15–9.35
vacant possession, 10.2–10.37
variation of leases, 2.1
withdrawal of break notices, 13.59–13.64
**valuation:**
break clauses in hypothetical leases, 16.41–16.42
**variation of leases,** 2.1

**waiver:**
breach of contract, 13.43–13.47
break clauses, relationship to, 13.11
loss of right to exercise break, 13.12–13.19
loss of right to insist on break notice, 13.20–13.35
loss of right to insist on compliance, 13.36–13.37
loss of right to exercise landlord's break clause, 13.38
defects in notice
recipient's silence, 13.48–13.49
general principles, 13.2–13.4
unilateral waiver, 13.40–13.42
*see also* validity
**wills:**
executors:
exercising break clauses, 4.66–4.67
service of notice on, 8.27
**withdrawal of break notices,** 13.59–13.64
**without prejudice communications:**
validity, 5.62–5.64